DARK QUADRANT

Organized Crime, Big Business, and the Corruption of American Democracy

From Truman to Trump

Jonathan Marshall

ROWMAN & LITTLEFIELD
Lanham • Boulder • New York • London

Published by Rowman & Littlefield
An imprint of The Rowman & Littlefield Publishing Group, Inc.
4501 Forbes Boulevard, Suite 200, Lanham, Maryland 20706
www.rowman.com

6 Tinworth Street, London SE11 5AL, United Kingdom

Distributed by NATIONAL BOOK NETWORK

British Library Cataloguing in Publication Information Available

Library of Congress Cataloging-in-Publication Data

Names: Marshall, Jonathan, 1955– author.
Title: Dark quadrant : organized crime, big business, and the corruption of American
    democracy / Jonathan Marshall.
Description: Lanham : Rowman & Littlefield, [2021] | Includes bibliographical references
    and index.
Identifiers: LCCN 2020047801 (print) | LCCN 2020047802 (ebook) | ISBN
    9781538142493 (cloth) | ISBN 9781538142509 (epub)
Subjects: LCSH: Political corruption—United States—History. | Organized crime—
    Political aspects—United States—History. | Big business—Political aspects—United
    States—History. | Business and politics—United States—History. | Democracy—
    United States—History. | United States—Politics and government—1945-1989. |
    United States—Politics and government—1989-
Classification: LCC JK2249 .M374 2021 (print) | LCC JK2249 (ebook) | DDC
    364.1060973—dc23
LC record available at https://lccn.loc.gov/2020047801
LC ebook record available at https://lccn.loc.gov/2020047802

♾️™ The paper used in this publication meets the minimum requirements of
American National Standard for Information Sciences—Permanence of Paper
for Printed Library Materials, ANSI/NISO Z39.48-1992.

Contents

Acknowledgments

I AM GRATEFUL TO SEVERAL FRIENDS who provided encouragement or commented on portions of this book, including crime reporters Gus Russo and Dan Moldea; Louis Trager and Mark Paul, independent historians and former reporters; Peter Dale Scott, professor emeritus at the University of California, Berkeley; Ryan Gingeras, professor of history at the Naval Postgraduate School in Monterey; and independent writer Ray Welch. Former *Wall Street Journal* reporter Jim Drinkhall provided documents from his voluminous files on the Teamsters Union. Special thanks to Phyllis Schultze at Rutgers University's Center for Law and Justice, who made available papers that she rescued from the files of the late criminologist Alan Block. I also appreciate the many helpful staffers at the National Archives in Maryland (especially Robert Reed of the Special Access and FOIA Branch), Library of Congress manuscript division, George Washington University's National Security Archive, and several presidential libraries. The overworked staff at the FBI's Freedom of Information office also provided useful documents, though some requested files remained inaccessible due to inordinately long processing times. Finally, I am grateful for permission to reuse material that previously appeared in *The Lobster* ("Blackmail in the Deep State," Summer 2017) and the *Journal of Global South Studies* ("The Dictator and the Mafia: How Rafael Trujillo Partnered with U.S. Criminals to Extend His Power," v. 35, no. 1, Spring 2018 by the University of Florida Press).

1

Introduction

AS CITIZENS OF A GLOBAL SUPERPOWER in the waning stages of its supremacy, Americans today are experiencing a crisis of confidence over their nation's slipping military, economic, and technological leadership. At the core of that crisis is their rapidly declining faith in the fairness of its governing institutions and even its democratic model. The disruptive GOP candidate Donald Trump owed his surprise victory in the 2016 presidential race in no small part to his promise to "drain the swamp." Upon taking office, however, he deepened the bog in unprecedented ways, flagrantly turning the White House into a virtual subsidiary of his family enterprise. After a year of his presidency, 44 percent of Americans in a national poll said that corruption was pervasive in the White House, a jump from 36 percent in 2016.[1] Shortly before the midterm elections in 2018, nearly a third of voters said corruption in Washington was the "most important" subject for political candidates to address, ahead even of health care and the economy.[2] In December 2019, the House of Representatives approved two articles of impeachment against President Trump, both concerning corrupt actions related to Ukraine.

These popular concerns are grounded in reality. In 2018 the United States slipped to #22 on Transparency International's corruption index, below most other developed nations and only just ahead of the United Arab Emirates.[3] The organization observed:

> The US faces a wide range of domestic challenges related to the abuse of entrusted power for private gain, which is Transparency International's definition of corruption.

Key issues include the influence of wealthy individuals over government; "pay to play" politics and the revolving doors between elected government office, for-profit companies, and professional associations; and the abuse of the US financial system by corrupt foreign kleptocrats and local elites.

The current US president was elected on a promise of cleaning up American politics and making government work better for those who feel their interests have been neglected by political elites. Yet, rather than feeling better about progress in the fight against corruption over the past year, a clear majority of people in America now say that things have become worse.[4]

Corruption—and widespread perceptions of corruption—entail a host of public and private costs. One of the most serious and lasting is the erosion of confidence in the very legitimacy of public governance. Observes Patricia Moreira, Transparency International's managing director, "Corruption chips away at democracy to produce a vicious cycle, where corruption undermines democratic institutions and, in turn, weak institutions are less able to control corruption."[5]

Serious students of American government are every bit as alarmed as ordinary members of the public. Harvard University political scientist Stephen Walt titled one 2019 article, "America's Corruption Is a National Security Threat."[6] Numerous social scientists who might once have recited the virtues of democratic pluralism in the United States today warn of rapidly growing concentrations of wealth and economic power, which in turn foster immense and corrupting disparities in political power, aggravated by minimal regulation of campaign spending and lobbying.[7]

Popular and scholarly discussions of the frightening erosion of American political and legal norms sometimes contrast the Trump era with an age of robust democracy in the latter half of the twentieth century, when the United States was governed by statesmen rather than grifters. "From the end of World War II until about 1980, democracy worked reasonably well because we were less complacent and more interested in institution building," commented Brookings Institution Senior Fellow Isabel Sawhill. "[T]he period from the end of World War II until the end of the Cold War was unique; it required U.S. leadership and a willingness to use our resources and power to check tyrants and encourage democracy around the world. Without a commitment to provide that kind of 'indispensable' leadership going forward, a liberal world order and democracy itself are at risk."[8]

Without denying the novelty and vigor of President Trump's recent assault on traditional ethical and legal norms, this book challenges the myth of a golden age of American democracy. It tells a largely neglected story of how well-protected criminals systematically organized the corruption of American politics and business at a national level in the post–World War II era.

Instead of offering a general survey, I have chosen to dive more deeply but selectively into several largely forgotten (or unknown) cases from the first quarter century of the Cold War, when the "greatest generation" governed the nation. National dismay over political corruption in the Truman administration was an important driver of the Republicans' landslide victory in the 1952 elections. It seriously threatened Lyndon Johnson's political career in 1963 and 1964. It also brought down Richard Nixon after his historic reelection in 1972 and his celebrated foreign policy triumphs with China and the Soviet Union. These cases exposed ongoing and systemic failings of the US political system, not simply isolated examples of personal wrongdoing. Those failings had—and today still have—serious consequences. As garment workers' union official Gus Tyler observed decades ago,

> Crime-in-politics is a direct challenge to the *moral* basis of American liberalism. . . . The growth of the welfare state, as an economic phenomenon, is no proof that the people will be free or unoppressed. . . . Crime-in-politics shakes faith in government, any government, as a creator of commodities or a dispenser of services. . . . Crime-in-politics is a direct challenge to the *political* basis of liberalism.[9]

That assessment, published in 1962, is even more relevant today in the wake of the Trump presidency. American historians have yet to fully acknowledge those challenges, however. Historians today address a host of national shortcomings but appear to regard corruption as a barely detectable eddy in the larger current of events, with no lasting political significance. Some scholars even question its moral significance.[10] Biographer Alonzo Hamby belittled widespread corruption in Truman's administration as "piddling" and a mere problem of "public relations." Historian Robert Ferrell claimed that the "mess in Washington" during the Truman years was "basically about minor or irrelevant matters." The only scholarly volume on those scandals, by Andrew J. Dunar, calls them "tempests from teapots" resulting from "minor flaws in Truman's makeup."[11] As chapter 2 explores in detail, such assessments hardly seem valid ways to characterize revelations that rocked the Internal Revenue Bureau, Reconstruction Finance Corporation, Democratic National Committee, and the White House itself, leading to dozens of resignations, indictments, and convictions and contributing to Truman's humiliating defeat in a 1952 presidential primary race.

The corrupt behavior and associations of Lyndon Johnson's close friend and political aide Robert "Bobby" Baker provides grist for four chapters in this book. Baker's misdeeds, which implicated several national politicians as well as powerful mobsters, ignited one of the biggest US political scandals of the 1960s. That controversy created serious rifts between the Kennedy brothers and the vice president in 1963 and even raised doubts about whether LBJ would remain on the ticket in 1964 (chapter 5). At the same time, Washington was gripped by another major scandal, also linked to Baker, over the Pentagon's suspect decision to procure the TFX fighter jet at a record projected cost of $7 billion, from a contractor accused of influence peddling and bribery (chapter 7). A congressional investigation of this huge procurement award rocked the Kennedy administration, prompted the resignation of the navy secretary and threatened both Defense Secretary Robert McNamara and Vice President Johnson. Yet Arthur Schlesinger Jr.'s classic account of the Kennedy White House, *A Thousand Days*, makes no mention of Baker or the TFX. Robert Caro's massive volume on LBJ's vice presidency offers a detailed chapter on the Baker affair, calling it a "scandal on a grand scale," but ignores the TFX controversy. Historian Robert Dallek's 750-page history of Johnson's career after the 1960 election similarly finds no room for the TFX and relegates Baker to just two paragraphs, while getting some of the details wrong.[12] Major historical works also ignore the alliance between Baker and the powerful Murchison brothers of Dallas, whose corrupt dealings with Johnson and other leading politicians, as well as nationally prominent mobsters, are the subject of chapter 6.

If most general chroniclers of modern US history slight the issue of corruption, their works render virtually invisible one of its causes, organized crime.[13] There is no legitimate reason for this aversion, which borders on abdication. Mobsters had their claws deep into Hollywood studios; a wide range of professional sports; major unions (Teamsters, Laborers, Hotel and Restaurant workers, Longshoremen); industries including real estate, oil, autos, hotels, defense, and banking; and big-city political machines. Robert Kennedy came to national prominence through his service as chief counsel to a Senate committee investigating labor racketeering. Televised congressional hearings into the nationwide threats posed by mobsters to unions, businesses, and clean government attracted more viewers than even the 1951 World Series. *The Untouchables* television series won as devoted an audience in its heyday (1959–1963) as *The Sopranos* did forty years later (1999–2007). Lee Bernstein had to remind fellow scholars that "The dominant political and popular culture of the 1950s perceived organized crime as a conspiratorial threat to national security as serious as that posed by communism."[14] As we will see, those two threats were connected: Organized crime figures directly encouraged the nation's post–World War II mobilization against Communism. Yet James Patterson, in his award-winning survey of US history in the thirty years after World War II, barely mentions organized crime in more than eight hundred pages. The same glaring gap afflicts many other period surveys and edited volumes.[15] Even books that focus on political corruption shy away from discussing its close cousin, organized crime. Dunar's monograph on the Truman scandals nowhere mentions the persistent favoritism shown by senior administration officials toward leading racketeers—including the suspicious early parole of several leaders of the Chicago Outfit—which was the subject of outraged journalistic and congressional investigations at the time (chapter 2). Ferrell's biography of Truman altogether ignores the Kefauver Committee's historic fourteen-city investigation of organized crime in 1950–1951; in a brief mention, Hamby unjustifiably dismisses it as having "little substantive purpose beyond self-promotion."[16] Moving on to the Kennedy–Johnson years, Caro's otherwise excellent treatment of Bobby Baker overlooks his highly publicized business partnerships with organized crime figures, which posed a particularly grave political threat to LBJ (chapters 5–7). Similarly, major accounts of the TFX scandal show no awareness of the fact that the fighter plane's prime contractor was controlled by a powerful business partner of the Chicago Outfit (chapter 7). Most Nixon biographies and accounts of Watergate leave the topic untouched as well, even though Nixon's decision to put his political career in the hands of one of Southern California's leading mob lawyers, and his choice of seedy friends and business partners in Florida, set an ethical standard he carried all the way to his presidency (chapters 2, 3, 8, 9).[17] The secret involvement of top mobsters in CIA efforts to assassinate Fidel Castro, and the complex web of political intrigues that followed, even had a material impact on President Nixon's downfall in the Watergate scandal (chapter 9). One can only hope that future historians will not shy away from examining Donald Trump's remarkable ties to both American and foreign mobsters. His complex relations with Russian and Ukrainian oligarchs in particular appear relevant to the events leading to the historic impeachment vote by the House of Representatives in 2019 (chapter 10).

No reader should conclude from the long catalog of misdeeds described in this book that they reflect a full picture of post–World War II US politics. The "man from Missouri," who led the Senate's oversight of government contracting in World War II, advocated for civil rights, and instituted the Marshall Plan, was far more than a mere appendage of the corrupt Pendergast machine in Kansas City. Lyndon Johnson will long be remembered as the father of the Civil Rights Act, Voting Rights Act, and Medicare despite his unscrupulous business and political methods and his egregious record of military escalation and deception in Vietnam. Even Richard Nixon broke free of his past to renew relations with China, sign two landmark arms control treaties with the Soviet Union, and support creation of the Environmental Protection Agency. Throughout this period, Congress sometimes played an important role in investigating corruption and passing significant legislation to fight organized crime, influence peddling, and campaign abuses. There are reasons why much of the world has long admired American democracy. As the crisis of the Trump presidency reminds us, however, we cannot take such progress for granted. History does not follow a linear path toward greater enlightenment, in politics or any other human endeavor. Americans must arm themselves with greater knowledge of the long-neglected "dark quadrant" of our national politics in order to shrink its power and strengthen our democracy.

The Legacy of Prohibition

Organized crime in America was a natural outgrowth of the country's increasingly organized economic and political power. In the nation's leading commercial center, New York City, gangs and politicians developed close alliances as early as the first half of the nineteenth century.[18] Marxist criminologist William Chambliss asserted that similar alliances emerged after the Civil War between gangs and business leaders:

> In the face of massive worker unrest and demands for the right to organize trade unions, big business hired thugs as strikebreakers. Rather than rely on the uncertain supply of local talent to control recalcitrant workers, large corporations imported gangs from other cities. This required a degree of organization and cooperation that ended in the creation of companies specializing in "strike breakers." Many of these same groups later became involved in organized crime networks.[19]

Criminal networks proliferated in the years 1920 to 1933, when Prohibition created a nationwide illicit market for bootleg alcohol. The enormous profits generated from this underground market not only attracted tens of thousands of enterprising and ruthless criminals, but established entrepreneurs. Many of the new criminals were urban immigrants, eager to avoid a bleak future of low-wage manual labor and discrimination. The New York crime lord Arnold Rothstein, who organized and bankrolled transatlantic liquor imports, international narcotics shipments, high-end bookmaking, and citywide political protection from the Democratic Party machine known as Tammany Hall, mentored an entire generation of multiethnic gangsters. They included the Russian-Jewish Meyer Lansky, the Sicilian Charles "Lucky" Luciano, the Calabrian Frank Costello, and the Swedish-Irish Frank Erickson. Chicago's great gang leader, Al Capone, married an Irish girl and recruited colleagues of Jewish, Greek, Welsh, and Italian descent, among others.

The size and complexity of organizations required to manufacture spirits, smuggle them across borders, and run far-flung sales networks under the eyes of law enforcement officials drove them to form highly sophisticated criminal gangs. Through a Darwinian process, surviving gangsters grew adept at organizing efficient logistics, violent protection of their markets, and the corruption of public officials. Their job was made easier by a high degree of public tolerance, especially in bigger cities, for the continued consumption of alcohol and popular admiration for the daring gangsters who supplied it. The potential profits were well worth the risk of fines or other modest criminal penalties. One Ohio bootlegger cleared an estimated $40 million (about $500 million today) in just three years of selling illegal liquor, while his protector, President Harding's attorney general Harry Daugherty, pocketed a million dollars over the same period.[20] As organized crime prospered, the primary victims of Prohibition were the civic norms upon which the rule of law and democratic government depend.

The repeal of the Eighteenth Amendment in 1933 ended the superprofits from the liquor trade, but the criminal organizations spawned by Prohibition, and their systemic corruption of politicians and police, lived on. Gangsters enriched by the black market in liquor applied their skills and market power to expand other illicit ventures, including gambling, narcotics, loan sharking, extortion, and labor racketeering. They also took advantage of advancing technology to extend their reach geographically. Long-distance communications pioneered by Western Union and AT&T allowed bookies to manage risks by laying off bets across the country. In order to maximize their profits from such national operations, criminal organizations in major cities learned to cooperate, building on market-sharing agreements that arose during Prohibition.[21]

Greatly extending the regional and national power of farsighted organized crime leaders was the post-Prohibition surge in labor organizing made possible by the Wagner Act (1935) and other New Deal reforms. Successful unions amassed huge pension and welfare funds, as well as political clout, making them prime targets of criminal extortionists and racketeers. Once in charge of unions, underworld gangs could pad payrolls, loot union funds, extort employers, and deliver votes to favored politicians. As one lifelong New York mobster told a Senate committee in 1988, "We got our money from gambling, but our real power, our real strength came from the unions."[22]

Among the most prominent unions infiltrated by the mob was the International Brotherhood of Teamsters (IBT). Founded in Chicago in 1903, it was plagued from the start by the corruption of some officers.[23] By 1949, the Teamsters had more than a million members, immense financial resources, and close alliances with mobsters in Chicago, Detroit, Cleveland, and New York. A major force behind the union's dramatic rise was the burly and relentless Midwest organizer Jimmy Hoffa. Today he is best remembered for his untimely and still-unexplained disappearance from a suburban Detroit parking lot in 1975, as memorialized in the 2019 movie *The Irishman*. Hoffa rose to leadership ranks after enlisting friends in the Detroit underworld to help win a series of violent strikes against recalcitrant employers and crush rivals in the militant Congress of Industrial Organizations. ("Twenty years ago, the employers had all the hoodlums working for them as strike-breakers," Hoffa told one interviewer. "Now we've got a few and everybody's screaming.")[24] In the process he befriended Moe Dalitz, a former bootlegger and leader of the Cleveland Syndicate who became a major force in illegal Midwest gambling and later an owner of Las Vegas and Havana casinos. Hoffa also made common cause with the Chicago Outfit, which controlled unions from the Midwest to California. In 1949, Hoffa began handing over Teamster insurance business to Paul Dorfman, president of the mob-controlled Chicago Scrap Handlers Union, and his stepson Allen. Under their tutelage, Hoffa turned Teamster pension, health, and welfare funds into giant banks for shady investments in casinos, real estate developments, and banks.[25] A Teamster local in Miami established by Hoffa actually served as an office for South Florida Mafia boss Santo Trafficante Jr.[26] Hoffa took over as president of the Teamsters in 1957, a few months before the outgoing president, Dave Beck, was convicted of embezzlement and tax evasion.[27] The same year, Hoffa and a host of mob associates, including Trafficante, became targets of a relentless investigation by the chief counsel for the Senate rackets committee, young Robert F. Kennedy. He would haunt Hoffa as attorney general in the Kennedy and early Johnson administrations, finally winning convictions against the union leader in two major cases.

For many other unions, fear was more important than institution-building as a factor in their takeover by racketeers. By 1930, through a systematic campaign of kidnapping and murder, Al Capone's brainy lieutenant, Murray "The Camel" Humphreys, was taking violent control of Chicago union locals, from theater janitors to teamsters, while shaking down employers.[28] New York criminals were doing the same, in industries ranging from water-front commerce to garment manufacturing. In the process, mobsters found allies among corporate leaders who viewed organized labor as a much greater menace than the underworld. Some businesses (notably in the auto and coal industries) recruited and paid gangsters to attack union organizers and run them out of town.[29] Where unions could not be stopped, employers seeking labor peace frequently signed with mob-controlled locals, as in the case of movie industry craft workers, hotel and restaurant employees, longshoremen, and teamsters. Based on his investigations for the Senate rackets committee, Robert Kennedy observed that

> with the present-day emphasis on money and material goods many business-men were willing to make corrupt "deals" with dishonest union officials in order to gain competitive advantage or to make a few extra dollars. . . . Furthermore

we found that we could expect very little assistance from management groups. Disturbing as it may sound, more often the business people with whom we came in contact—and this includes some representatives of our largest corporations—were uncooperative. . . . Labor-management corruption is a crooked two-way street.[30]

Postwar America and the Rise of the "Supermob"

The quarter century after World War II was, paradoxically, both a golden age and one of the darkest eras in American history. The US economy enjoyed remarkably strong growth that left the Great Depression only a bad memory and bestowed once-unthinkable consumer abundance on America's new middle class. These Cold War years also launched what Time-Life publisher Henry Luce called the "American Century," a global military, economic, and political empire unequalled in human history.[31] Through these times, however, Americans were always reminded of what their political leaders called "the price of freedom": worldwide competition with Communism, the terrifying prospect of nuclear holocaust, major armed conflicts in Korea and Vietnam, and the ceaseless diversion of resources to what President Eisenhower termed the "military-industrial complex."

This period was also a troubled time for American democracy and law. Power was being centralized as never before in federal government bureaucracies, including secretive branches of the mushrooming national security state. As the nation's financial and industrial sectors grew in size and sophistication, big business challenged popular government by exercising great economic and political power. Many unions went national, too, becoming a secondary but significant political and economic force with a mixed record of protecting worker interests.

The fast-growing economy and federal government created a fertile environment for corruption in national politics, as the pool of potential spoils expanded in tandem with the centralized power to distribute them to special-interest groups.[32] Federal spending as a share of gross domestic product doubled from the decade of the 1930s to the first normal ten-year period after World War II (1947–1956).[33] Enlarged bureaucracies such as the Reconstruction Finance Corporation, Maritime Commission, Federal Power Commission, Civil Aeronautics Board, Internal Revenue Bureau, and Alien Property Custodian provided opportunities for graft. "More often than not, rapid economic and political development lies behind political corruption," observes political scientist Doron Navot.[34]

These conditions particularly favored one entrenched group with special expertise in exploiting weak individuals and institutions: organized crime.

Strongly represented in the "underworlds" of many cities were Italian-born and second-generation Italian American criminals who came to be popularly known as members of an American "Mafia." (The FBI referred to them simply as "hoodlums" and later as members of "La Cosa Nostra.") Sensational journalistic exposés portrayed them as exotic, foreign figures outside the mainstream of American life and commerce.[35] Much less visible were some of their close allies (and competitors), sophisticated entrepreneurs of various ethnic backgrounds who recycled vast profits from crime into large real estate developments, movie and entertainment conglomerates, legalized gambling companies, sports teams, and even defense companies, many of them listed on national stock exchanges. Like growing national corporations in the postwar period, they expanded their market focus from big East Coast and Midwest cities to fast-growing Sunbelt regions like Florida and the Caribbean, Southern California, and Las Vegas. In the process, they also expanded their political focus from local "machines" to national offices and even the White House. How they did so, in alliance with other business interests and political institutions, is a prime focus of this book.

Such criminals have resisted study precisely because of their success in buying legitimacy and avoiding media and law enforcement scrutiny. "Penetration of the cloak of legitimacy created by their efforts is sometimes almost impossible," the Justice Department's Special Group on Organized Crime reported in 1959. "The profits of criminal operations are being more and more channeled into legitimate investments in business and industry. The result is that some of the most important syndicate leaders are men of outstanding public reputation with no criminal records or, at least, none for two or more decades."[36] Significant examples, explored in chapters 6 and 7, include the Murchisons of Dallas, owners of a huge and diverse business empire based on oil, and Henry Crown, whose vast holdings included hotels, real estate, railroads, and a controlling share of defense giant General Dynamics. Their rough, predatory, and sometimes illegal tactics, though far from unique in the business world, were facilitated by strong ties to organized crime and national political leaders.[37]

Reporting in 1962, a special agent in the FBI's Los Angeles office observed that organized crime was evolving into an almost untouchable, quasi-legal milieu of financiers, casino owners, and real estate investors:

All seem plentifully supplied with investment money. Today they exist in an environment of smart attorneys, accountants, and tax experts. . . . They have wisdom, experience, "connections," the Fifth Amendment, personal philanthropy, and apathy to help them and to lend them respectability. These men are neither ashamed nor reformed. . . . On the contrary, they are arrogantly proud and socially acceptable, because of money if for no other reason. They are mysterious and powerful. . . . They've waved their money wands over industry, invading legitimate businesses to an undefinable degree. Who indeed can now separate their illicitly gained money from their legitimate profits?[38]

Much more recently, organized crime historian Gus Russo has written extensively about a group of these shape-shifting criminals, many hailing from Chicago, which he calls the "Supermob." Documenting their enormous impact on the political economy of the United States in the mid-twentieth century, Russo observed:

> They became quintessential capitalists, exerting such far-flung influence that the repercussions were felt by practically every American of their era, with an economic impact that could only be measured in the trillions of dollars. Through deniable, often arm's-length associations with the roughneck Italian and Irish mobsters imprinted in the popular imagination, the Supermob and the hoods shared a sense of entitlement regarding tax-free income. [They] stressed brains over brawn and evolved into a real estate powerhouse, an organized-labor autocracy, and a media empire.[39]

Organized Crime, Organized Corruption, Anti-Communism, and the FBI

As the power and reach of such criminals grew after World War II, so did their ability—and need—to find and cultivate corrupt allies in political and law enforcement institutions at the national and even international level. (With a focus on the growing transnational reach of organized crime, chapter 4 examines alliances between US mobsters and rulers of the Dominican Republic in the 1950s and 1960s.) They took advantage of an existing ecosystem of corruption in Washington created by other businesses and special interests and used their own resources to encourage its growth. Sophisticated mobsters also found and motivated partners in major "legitimate" businesses to act as fronts for their ill-gotten investments.

Students of organized crime have long understood its intimate connection with the state, both as a corrupter of political institutions and as an unacknowledged instrument of state power. As criminologists Alan Block and William Chambliss emphasized years ago, "corruption of political-legal organizations is a critical part of the lifeblood of the crime network. The study of organized crime is thus a misnomer; the study should consider corruption, bureaucracy, and power."[40]

A special Senate committee established in 1950 to investigate the growing power of organized crime, led by Sen. Estes Kefauver of Tennessee, emphasized these issues. "Organized crime and political corruption go hand in hand," Kefauver declared. "[There can] be no big-time organized crime without a firm and profitable alliance between those who run the rackets and those in political control."[41] Alarmed by the "quasi-immunity of top-level mobsters," his committee pointed to forces more subtle—and ultimately more sinister—than simple bribery of local police and sheriffs: "The fix may also come about through the acquisition of political power by contributions to political organizations or otherwise, by creating economic ties with apparently respectable and reputable businessmen and lawyers, and by buying public good will through charitable contributions and press relations," the Kefauver Committee reported.[42] A decade later, Attorney General Robert Kennedy would say, "The racketeer is at his most dangerous not with a machine gun in his hands but with public officials in his pocket."[43]

Political corruption, of course, long preceded the 1950s and was not invented by organized crime.[44] The Cold War years, however, were especially conducive to building alliances between organized crime, big business, and national politicians. Although the specter of gangland crime drew widespread indignation from reformers and the media, the apparently existential threat of domestic and worldwide Communism loomed larger for most leaders of business, politics, and law enforcement. They were inclined to tolerate organized crime as a distorted but recognizable form of capitalism and free enterprise. Unlike Communism, it did not threaten the American way of life.[45] Leaders of crime syndicates worshipped money and sometimes even God, not the class struggle. Mobsters shared with Wall Street investors, the heads of the FBI and CIA, members of Congress, and presidents an intensely anti-Communist, patriotic ideology. The famous mobster Meyer Lansky was proud to send his younger son to West Point. Chicago crime boss Al Capone spoke for many gangsters when he warned in 1931: "Bolshevism is knocking at our gates. We can't afford to let it in. We have got to organize ourselves against it and get our shoulders together and hold fast. . . . We must keep [the American worker] away from red literature and red ruses; we must see that his mind remains healthy."[46] By endorsing and promoting anti-Communism as a state ideology, sophisticated criminals could win some degree of official forbearance, if not acceptance. Chapter 3 looks closely at the de facto political alliance between members of organized crime, the FBI, business groups, and Congress in promoting the growth of militant anti-Communism in the United States after World War II. By collaborating with intelligence agencies against Communists at home and abroad, which some mobsters did in part out of genuine patriotism, they could even invoke "national security" as a shield against prosecution. As a case study, chapter 9 examines the sordid political and criminal legacy of the CIA-Mafia alliance to assassinate Fidel Castro, from its inception in 1960 to the downfall of Richard Nixon in 1974.

For many years, until Robert Kennedy took charge of the Justice Department in 1961, federal authorities gave low priority to fighting the mob.[47] A major reason was bureaucratic opposition from FBI director J. Edgar Hoover. Hoover built his popular reputation by fighting unorganized gangsters like John Dillinger, while avoiding more entrenched crime syndicates like the multiethnic Chicago Outfit, heir to the Capone organization. (The reasons are still debated, but may have included his fear that organized criminals would corrupt bureau agents and that investigations of the mob would cost the FBI support among corrupt national politicians.) He also targeted domestic radicals, often at the expense of honest unions and other institutions. The FBI's obsession with political policing, for example, contributed significantly to the growing domination of the Teamsters Union by organized crime before World War II. According to the late criminologist James Jacobs:

> In the 1930s, the most powerful Teamster leader in Minnesota was Farrell Dobbs, a socialist and brilliant labor organizer. He organized over-the-road freight drivers, dock workers and warehousemen throughout the Midwest. His Teamster protégé and eventual rival was Jimmy Hoffa, who recruited thugs linked to organized crime to help him battle employers. The FBI attacked Dobbs, while leaving Hoffa to prosper. In the late 1930s and early 1940s, Dobbs and more than two dozen militant socialist trade unionists were indicted under the anti-Communist Smith Act. Dobbs himself was imprisoned until the end of World War II. Jimmy Hoffa became the undisputed leader of the Teamsters in Minnesota and soon in the entire Midwest. Hoffa's connections with organized crime were instrumental in vaulting him to the IBT presidency and figured prominently in his administration of the union.[48]

After World War II, with equal fanfare, Hoover turned his attention to unmasking Soviet spies and fighting political subversion. At the same time, he pointedly refused to cooperate with the Kefauver Committee's landmark investigation of organized crime in 1950–1951 and resisted subsequent Justice Department prosecution drives. Hoover insisted that fighting crime syndicates was a matter for local law enforcement, not the FBI.[49] William Hundley, who became chief of the Justice Department's skeletal organized crime section in 1958, recalled his frustrations with Hoover:

> Very frankly, at that time the Director of the FBI had no interest in the program; had no program of his own; and quite frankly did little, if anything, at that time in the field of organized crime. Organized crime drives had always been sort of a sporadic thing with the Department of Justice. . . . The FBI just wouldn't get involved at that time at all. . . . We really could have done a lot more had we been able to get the type of push from the President on down.[50]

In late 1957, Hoover was embarrassed when state police in rural Apalachin, New York, made national headlines by disrupting a convention of dozens of mob leaders from all over the country. Caught by surprise, Hoover temporarily tasked dozens of agents to begin surveilling and compiling files on suspected "top hoodlums." Even so, as of 1959, the bureau's New York office still assigned more than four hundred agents to Communism, but only four to organized crime.[51] In his 1958 book *Masters of Deceit*, Hoover maintained that "Communism is the major menace of our time. Today, it threatens the very existence of our Western civilization."[52] The FBI director specifically called out the feeble and thoroughly infiltrated America Communist Party as "a greater menace to the internal security of our Nation today than it ever has [been]" in a memo to Robert Kennedy just two weeks before President Kennedy's inauguration in 1961.[53]

Hoover's ideological zealotry served the needs of an expanding national security state to mobilize public opinion against a common foreign and domestic enemy. But Hoover's focus on the Red Menace also meshed perfectly with the interests of many employers and mobsters. By driving Communists from the labor movement, "this retreat left their natural enemies, the gangsters, in yet stronger positions," observed crime historian Stephen Fox.[54] Among his allies in the fight against Communism, Hoover cultivated not only unscrupulous and corrupt politicians like Senators Joseph McCarthy and Pat McCarran (chairman of the Judiciary Committee), but major mob-connected businessmen such as liquor magnate Lewis Rosenstiel, attorney Roy Cohn, hotelier J. Myer Schine, and Texas oil millionaire Clint Murchison, names that will recur throughout this book. As veteran crime reporter Hank Messick observed, the legendary FBI chief was at the center of a "continuing alliance of crime, business and politics" during the heyday of the Cold War.[55] Or as one leader of the Chicago Outfit declared after Jack Kennedy's victory in the 1960 presidential election, "Kennedy and those guys . . . they better not fool with that FBI. That's a good department. . . . Hoover is a good boy."[56]

Unfortunately for major US racketeers, RFK did "fool with that FBI" when he became attorney general. Armed with new legislation extending federal authority over organized crime, he relentlessly pushed a reluctant Hoover to expand the surveillance of suspects on the bureau's list of "top hoodlums." In early 1962, one Las Vegas sports bookmaker complained to the head of the Chicago mob, "You told me when they put his brother in there we were gonna see some fireworks but I never knew it would be like this. This is murder. The way that kid keeps running back and forth I don't know how he keeps going."[57] As we will see in chapter 5, Kennedy's drive against organized crime also threatened several national politicians, including Vice President Lyndon Johnson. The FBI uncovered evidence that Johnson's close friend and former top aide Bobby Baker was doing business with associates of some of the nation's biggest mobsters. As president, Johnson had to wield all of his political muscle to prevent the Baker investigation from delving into those associations at the expense of his election chances in 1964.

The "Protectors," the "Deep State," and "Deep Politics"

The symbiotic relationship between organized crime and state actors is typically mediated by trusted agents who operate outside the glare of publicity or the scrutiny of law enforcement. In 1933, two scholars identified a type of criminal lawyer responsible for ensuring the success of organized criminals: "[H]e guides and protects the racketeers in the matter of counsel, before the courts, in the realm of politics, and often is to be found exercising the powers of an actual officer in the racket structure. . . . [T]he lawyer, or a certain type of him, is probably the most important cog in the machinery of crime."[58] A half century later, the President's Commission on Organized Crime highlighted the importance of a broader group of criminal facilitators it called "the protectors." It described these agents of influence as "corrupt public officials, attorneys and businessmen" who protect criminal syndicates from investigation and prosecution "through abuses of status and/or privilege and violation of the law."[59] What makes such protectors so successful is the trust they command in both the underworld and the upperworld, giving them an ability to move seamlessly between the realms of politics, business, intelligence, and crime.

Such individuals appear repeatedly throughout this book. Few are household names, precisely because their roles required discretion. One of the best known was Edward Bennett Williams, a brilliant defense attorney who represented Teamster president Jimmy Hoffa, New York mob bosses Frank Costello and Vito Genovese, and Chicago Outfit leader Sam Giancana. He also defended key political figures, including Joseph McCarthy, Bobby Baker, and Baker's mobbed-up investment partner, Las Vegas casino owner Edward Levinson. Reflecting his position of trust within established institutions at the center of power, Williams lent his great talents to the *Washington Post* and the Democratic National Committee during Watergate, then represented former CIA director Richard Helms on a perjury charge. Williams was even offered the job of CIA director by President Reagan. He figures in chapters 5 and 9.

Another operator who got around in Washington less visibly was lawyer-lobbyist Thomas Corcoran, an early New Dealer who became a masterful political insider. Described by Robert Caro as "[Lyndon] Johnson's bluntest weapon," Corcoran was a prodigious fundraiser and valued adviser to the up-and-coming Texas congressman. In 1952, *Fortune* magazine called him "a master and purveyor of concentrated influence" with "the finest intelligence service in Washington."[60] Only a handful of cognoscenti knew at the time that many of his clients—including United Fruit Co., Civil Air Transport, and American International Underwriters Corp.—worked closely with the CIA in Asia and Latin America. He appears in chapter 3, lobbying behind the scenes to promote US aid to the Nationalist Chinese, the authoritarian Franco regime in Spain, drug-smuggling generals in Thailand, and Guatemalan military officers who served the interests of United Fruit by overthrowing their country's elected government.

Unlike Williams and Corcoran, the career of Washington attorney Edward P. Morgan has never been explored by a biographer. A former aide to J. Edgar Hoover who helped direct the FBI's war on Communism, Morgan was the secret glue who bound together major casino owners and mobsters in Las Vegas (Moe Dalitz, Cliff Jones, John Rosselli); billionaire Howard Hughes; crusading journalists Jack Anderson, Drew Pearson, and Hank Greenspun; Teamster boss Jimmy Hoffa; and several of Bobby Baker's close associates. His wealth of criminal, political, and intelligence connections made him an ideal conduit for blackmail and influence operations that grew out of the CIA-Mafia assassination plots of the early 1960s (chapter 9).

The giant of them all was a Washington lobbyist, promoter, and public relations man named I. Irving Davidson. The affable but ambitious son of a Pittsburgh meat market owner, Davidson once described himself to an FBI agent as a "five percenter [influence peddler] out to make a fast buck," who "hated Communists." A biographer of one of Davidson's many powerful friends, Louisiana Mafia boss Carlos Marcello, described this wheeler-dealer as "the representative of all that Jack and Bobby [Kennedy] fought against— [Dominican dictator Rafael] Trujillo, Hoffa's Teamsters, the Somozas' Nicaragua, the Texas rich, the CIA, Castro, Nixon, the mob."[61] For good measure, he was friends with J. Edgar Hoover, Nixon's campaign adviser and mob lawyer Murray Chotiner, nationally syndicated columnists Drew Pearson and Jack Anderson, and at least two senior Israeli intelligence officers. Davidson was an arms broker for the Nicaraguan, Israeli, and Indonesian militaries; a lobbyist for Haitian dictator "Papa Doc" Duvalier; a key interlocutor with the State Department during the Dominican Republic crisis in 1965; a business associate of Bobby Baker; a publicist and business scout for the uber-wealthy Murchison brothers in Dallas; a backer of both Lyndon Johnson and Richard Nixon in 1960; a recipient of Teamster pension fund loans; and a schemer who plotted to spring Hoffa from the clutches of federal prosecutors. Investigative reporter Jack Anderson said, "when you get to know him you find he's got better contacts than Clark Clifford. . . . In fact, he's got *unbelievable* contacts. . . . I've investigated a lot of five percenters and promoters but I've never run across anybody like him."[62]

In 1958, the US attorney for the southern district of New York referred to organized criminals and their powerful protectors as "The Invisible Government." He told an audience of attorneys, "In this country today, we have a second government . . . eating at the democratic and moral foundations of our society. This invisible government has millions of dollars at its disposal. It issues its own edicts. It enforces its own decrees. It carries out its own executions. It collects its own revenues. It includes the major criminals of the country, and it has as its allies some public officials tempted by the lure of money and power, as well as short-sighted business and labor leaders."[63]

Such discussions of "invisible" or "shadow" governments sound familiar today, as avid conspiracy theorists, including President Trump and many of his defenders, condemn the alleged machinations of a hostile "deep state."[64] As addressed by more serious students of government, the concept refers not to a centralized conspiracy, but to a variety of intelligence and national security institutions that exert power without democratic accountability and oversight, often in league with powerful corporate and other private interests. Former congressional staffer Michael Lofgren called the deep state "an outgrowth of illiberal tendencies in liberal democracy, tendencies that have given disproportionate influence to a militarized foreign policy, secrecy and surveillance at home, and entrenched disparities of wealth."[65]

Often forgotten in contemporary discussions of the "deep state" is the important role of organized crime. The term was originally applied to Turkish politics during the violent 1980s, when the Special Operations Department of the Turkish national police hired gangsters to assassinate political enemies of the state, including Armenian militants and members of the Marxist Kurdish Workers Party. This secret alliance was partially exposed in 1996, after a car crash whose victims included a prominent conservative member of Turkey's parliament, a top police official from Istanbul, and a notorious Turkish terrorist and international heroin trafficker on Interpol's most wanted list.[66] An American parallel might be the meeting in December 1942 in the New York apartment of mob leader Frank Costello (dubbed the "Prime Minister of the Underworld") with former New York district attorney William O'Dwyer, influence peddler Irving Sherman, Judge Anthony Savarese, and Tammany Hall boss Michael Kennedy to approve O'Dwyer's run for mayor in the next election.[67] Nearly two decades later, the CIA-Mafia alliance to assassinate Fidel Castro raised many obvious parallels to the criminal model of the deep state in Turkey.

Although it is undeniable that secretive institutions do wield undemocratic power in the United States—the history of the FBI under Director Hoover is replete with examples—"deep state" is problematic as an analytic term for at least two reasons. First, whatever its original merits, the phrase has become hopelessly fraught with partisan and conspiratorial meaning. Second, and perhaps more important, it implies that secretive groups operating outside the normal channels of government have sufficient stability and common interests to be considered a shadow state. Both assumptions are highly questionable.

I prefer a more fluid term coined by retired University of California professor Peter Dale Scott—"deep politics"—which he broadly defined as "the ongoing, unacknowledged processes linking so-called legitimate political and economic activities to their criminal underpinnings." Deep political acts and processes, he wrote, are characterized by "collusive secrecy and law-breaking." They typically occur "outside general awareness as well as outside acknowledged political processes." A familiar example of deep politics at the local level, Scott stated, was "the way Tammany Hall, in alliance with ethnic gangsters, refined patronage and corruption into a working system for dividing the spoils in an ethnically divided New York City." An example of deep politics on a transnational scale was the much more secretive way in which "U.S. occupying forces in Italy, using Tammany politicians, imported U.S. mafia figures to oppose left-wing Italian and Sicilian movements," with lasting repercussions for Italian political and social development. Scott was careful to emphasize that his focus on such secretive areas "does not mean that I believe them to be the determinant areas or facts of our political life; only that fuller understanding of our politics, toward the goal of public control of political life, requires a fuller understanding of these areas as of others."[68]

In this book, I examine deep politics as a form of *organized and systematic corruption,* or *covert influencing of policy and administration, on a scale that subverts national democratic norms.* Using a wide range of original archival materials, declassified intelligence files, and other sources, I describe ways in which political and business actors, all the way up to presidents and major corporate chieftains, developed alliances with sophisticated criminals during the Cold War. To illustrate the nature of these alliances, I focus selectively on the criminal associations of three presidents—Harry Truman, Lyndon Johnson, and Richard Nixon—and their administrations. The Eisenhower years figure heavily in chapter 4's discussion of transnational alliances between US mobsters and political figures in the Caribbean, especially Dominican dictator Rafael Trujillo. Chapter 9 addresses the "blowback" from some of those Caribbean intrigues, particularly the CIA-Mafia plots to assassinate Fidel Castro, on politics in the Kennedy through Nixon years, culminating in Watergate. The concluding chapter sketches some of the continuities and changes in organized crime and national politics over the past four decades.

It explores Donald Trump's unique role as a bridge between traditional US Mafia families, which have taken severe blows from law enforcement, and newer transnational criminal actors including East European oligarchs and gangsters. His long-standing association with such criminals helps explain the rampant corruption and lawlessness that characterized his administration, and some of his otherwise mysterious relations with Russia and Ukraine.

Just as I part company from the many scholars who ignore the nexus of organized crime and national politics, so I depart from the many writers of popular crime literature who focus on "the activities of street-level actors who physically perpetrate crimes . . . while the affairs of the most important players ('legitimate' businessmen/public officials/power brokers) are relegated to the periphery."[69] My work certainly does not stand alone, however. I owe a great debt to many previous researchers, journalists, and scholars. Among those who most bravely and productively explored the subterranean intersection of politics and organized crime were reporters Drew Pearson, Clark Mollenhoff, Hank Messick, Ed Reid, Ovid Demaris, Jeff Gerth, Dan Moldea, and Gus Russo; criminologist Alan Block; historian Alfred McCoy; and the unconventional scholar Peter Dale Scott. Despite my admiration, I have tried to assess their works and claims as carefully and critically as any others.[70] In so doing, I have chosen not to relate a number of colorful stories for lack of adequate substantiation. To check and supplement their published works, and explore many new angles, I draw extensively on under- or never-before-utilized documentation from presidential libraries and other archives. My sources include hundreds of thousands of pages of files released by the Federal Bureau of Investigation (some at my request); documents from the Federal Bureau of Narcotics and Central Intelligence Agency; numerous congressional hearings; and long-forgotten news stories from dozens of newspapers. Files of the Watergate special prosecutor, opened to me through the Freedom of Information Act, proved valuable in assessing claims about Nixon's organized crime connections. Inevitably, given the tremendous secrecy surrounding these matters, available records still leave numerous gaps in our knowledge of events. Through careful and discriminating use of these varied materials, however, historians can use proven scholarly methods to illuminate the impact of criminal entrepreneurs on America's political economy. Indeed, I hope this book will persuade other scholars to acknowledge that the history of Cold War America can be told in full only by taking into account this dark quadrant of our nation's politics.

Part I
THE TRUMAN YEARS

2

Organized Crime and Corruption Scandals in the Truman Era

HARRY S. TRUMAN WAS THE FIRST American president to emerge, albeit accidentally, as the handpicked candidate of political bosses allied with modern organized crime. Franklin Roosevelt may have accepted underworld support to win the Democratic nomination in 1932, but as governor and president he backed reformers in New York who battled the mob.[1] Unlike the patrician Roosevelt, Truman was a true product of his native state's political machine. The failed businessman and law school student began his political career in 1922 with his appointment as county court judge. He owed the job to Kansas City's Democratic kingmaker, the burly liquor wholesaler and public works contractor Thomas Pendergast. "Under the Pendergast regime," the *New York Times* recalled, "Kansas City was one of the most wide-open and corrupt cities in America, a center of vice, crooked gambling and crime. Racketeers from all over the country congregated there."[2] One friendly Truman biographer concedes that Pendergast was the "ruling spirit" behind the "roaring business" of "gambling, prostitution, bootlegging, the sale of narcotics, and racketeering" in Kansas City.[3] He did so in partnership with Ninth Ward political boss John Lazia, an ally of Al Capone's Chicago Outfit who was gunned down in 1934 after threatening to "blow the lid" on corruption at his upcoming federal trial for tax evasion.[4]

Judge Truman took full political advantage of the boss system without enriching himself. He salved his conscience by keeping a notebook where he carefully recorded the virtue underlying his political compromises. "I had to let a former saloon keeper and murderer, a friend of the Big Boss, steal about $10,000 . . . from the general revenues of the County," Truman wrote in one entry, but that was worthwhile to "keep the crooks from getting a million or more" from a public bond issue.[5] With Pendergast's help, Truman won election to the Senate in 1934 just days after a federal grand jury indicted senior police officials in Kansas City for perjury. The grand jury's scathing report condemned "men holding places of high authority" for protecting "criminal mobs and racketeers." Their alleged crimes ranged from "unbridled gambling" to permitting a gangland massacre that resulted in the deaths of an FBI agent, a police chief from Oklahoma, and two Kansas City police officers. Truman's Republican incumbent opponent declared prematurely that the indictment had "wrecked the hopes of the Kansas City political machine to send its handpicked candidate to the United States Senate."[6] Truman won by a landslide. Within a few years, he was doing everything in his power to block a threatened federal investigation of rampant vote fraud in the 1936 election.[7]

Senator Truman was reelected in 1940, despite Pendergast's conviction in 1939 for tax evasion. Truman went on to earn deserved credit during World War II for his investigations of military contracts. Still, his selection as President Roosevelt's running mate during the 1944 Democratic convention shocked many reformers. It followed FDR's decision to dump Vice President Henry Wallace from the ticket. After prolonged negotiations, Truman won critical support from Bronx Democratic boss Edward J. Flynn, Jersey City boss Frank Hague, and Chicago mayor Edward Kelly, host of the convention. Another key Truman supporter was Democratic National Chairman Bob Hannegan, himself a former ally of Pendergast and co-leader of the St. Louis political machine, who would become Truman's postmaster general. Also playing a critical role in the selection of Truman as a running mate was New York labor leader Sidney Hillman, who paid Louis Buchalter, head of the notorious "Murder, Inc." gang, to terrorize manufacturers and rival labor activists. Interior Secretary Harold Ickes, a former Chicago journalist, privately decried "the method of [Truman's] nomination and the seeming dominating position that the corrupt city bosses now have in the Democratic National organization."[8]

The ailing Roosevelt died just five months after being elected to his historic fourth term. This fluke of history elevated Truman to the White House. Instead of asserting his independence from the political machines that helped elect him, as Roosevelt had or as Jack Kennedy did after the 1960 election, President Truman loyally began paying back their favors. He began by issuing pardons to fifteen members of the Pendergast machine who had been convicted of vote fraud in the 1936 elections.[9] Three weeks into his term as president, Truman fired the US attorney in Missouri who had prosecuted vote fraud in Kansas City and sent Pendergast to prison along with more than 250 members of his organization.[10] Although many historians brush off these acts as mere demonstrations of excessive loyalty to friends, biographer Richard Lawrence Miller forthrightly condemned Truman's "fanatic, unthinking, and eternal devotion" to the Pendergast machine and his role in "protecting the power of thieves and murderers."[11]

The Truman Administration's Record of Crime and Corruption

Those were just the first of many acts of political favoritism, influence peddling, and outright corruption that plagued the Truman administration until voters repudiated the Democratic Party in the 1952 election. His administration's cavalier behavior provided endless grist for congressional investigations and journalistic exposés, by Democrats and liberals as well as partisan Republicans. In a major roundup of Truman's record published in 1951, two veteran national political reporters at *Look* magazine condemned the "friendships, favoritism and frauds" that had fostered "immorality" and "corruption" under Truman's auspices. "Political morality in Washington has sunk to the lowest depth in a quarter of a century," they charged, citing "four members of the White House staff," and "fourteen high Federal officials" among the nearly "900 federal employees" who had been "caught trying to improve their private fortunes through their positions on the public payroll."[12] Investigations of corruption in the federal tax system alone led to the conviction, indictment, or firing of the president's appointments secretary, head of the tax division at the Justice Department, and more than 160 employees of the Internal Revenue Bureau—including the commissioner of Internal Revenue, the assistant commissioner, the bureau's chief counsel, and six regional directors—for bribery, extortion, embezzlement, tax evasion, and fixing tax cases.[13] A lengthy investigation by *Life* magazine in late 1951 concluded presciently that "Tax racketeering may even become the biggest single political issue of 1952 and a direct cause of Harry Truman's departure from the White House." A respected national reporter declared indignantly in 1952, "Today we have government of the people, by corruption, for the privileged. The misuse of the federal government in our era exceeds anything known in those two outstanding past epochs of political sin, the Grant and Harding Administrations."[14]

As noted in chapter 1, historians have not only downplayed those scandals, but ignored almost entirely the contributions of organized crime. Successful efforts by mobsters to win protection or profit through national political influence were no secret at the time, however. One major vehicle for such influence was New York City's Democratic machine, Tammany Hall, which for many years was dominated by Luciano's successor in New York's underworld, Frank Costello. In early 1949, Costello attended a dinner held in

Washington, D.C., by New York Democratic leaders to celebrate Truman's inauguration.[15] Truman in turn protected Costello and Tammany Hall in 1950 when their chief protégé, Mayor William O'Dwyer, resigned in the midst of a giant police corruption scandal. Truman appointed O'Dwyer ambassador to Mexico, even though the mayor had been condemned by a grand jury for protecting the murderous boss of New York's waterfront from prosecution.[16] Testimony in the police corruption case established that O'Dwyer's former chief aide, who later went to prison for extortion and tax evasion, had arranged a meeting between the mayor and several leading bookmakers during the 1949 campaign.[17] The Kefauver Committee condemned O'Dwyer for appointing friends of two New York Mafia bosses to high public office and for promoting "the growth of organized crime, racketeering, and gangsterism in New York City."[18] Soon after retiring as ambassador in 1953, O'Dwyer was dogged by reports that he and Mexico's corrupt President Miguel Alemán were seeking rights to open a gambling casino in Acapulco.[19]

Closer to home, President Truman's attorney general, Tom Clark, protected Pendergast's successor, the racketeer and former bootlegger Charles Binaggio, by restricting an FBI investigation into the blatant theft of ballots during the 1946 Kansas City Democratic congressional primary on behalf of Truman's favored candidate.[20] The president had been thrilled by the local political machine's work, writing his wife, Bess, "Everybody is elated."[21] But when someone had the audacity to murder several key witnesses and break into the Kansas City courthouse to steal ballot boxes containing evidence of the fraud, the local scandal became a national embarrassment. A subsequent congressional report called it "the gravest crisis that challenged the Department of Justice under the administration of Tom Clark" and called his interference in the matter "a gross departure from the usual channels of authority, which has not yet been adequately explained or defended by any of the officials involved."[22] Binaggio avoided prosecution and helped Truman raise $150,000 during his hard-fought 1948 presidential campaign. He didn't celebrate for long, however; the gangster and party boss was shot to death along with his chief enforcer at the Truman Road Democratic Club in 1950. The *Kansas City Star* called the assassination "a major development in a national threat from organized crime." The crusading Republican newspaper attacked the Truman administration for its inattention to the menace and railed against senior Justice Department officials for maintaining that the FBI had no jurisdiction in the case.[23]

One of those officials was Assistant Attorney General Theron Lamar Caudle, who compliantly did Clark's bidding as head of the Justice Department's criminal division and later its tax division. Over the years he settled cases while enjoying gifts of mink coats, new cars, and a trip to Europe. President Truman finally had enough and fired him. "Caudle got into real trouble when he took five thousand dollars from Larry 'the Fixer' Knohl, a syndicate money man, later Meyer Lansky's partner in a plush resort on the Florida keys," wrote crime reporter Hank Messick. "Knohl was convicted of attempting to fix a grand jury investigating the disappearance of Mafia boss Joe 'Bananas' Bonanno, and still later he was convicted of illegal possession of three hundred thousand dollars in stolen Treasury notes." Caudle was finally convicted with Truman's former appointments secretary in a St. Louis tax case in 1956.[24]

Look magazine also reported that the Truman administration's Alcohol Tax Unit "granted scores of liquor licenses to known hoodlums and mobsters." For example, the head of the tax unit from 1946 through 1949 arranged a federal liquor license for New York businessman Louis Pokrass, in return for a new Pontiac, a fur coat, and a $5,000 contribution to the New York State Democratic Committee. Pokrass had previously been denied a license for concealing his criminal record, which included four arrests for violations of the National Prohibition Act. There was much more to the story. As summarized by Truman critic Jules Abels:

> Pokrass was closely linked to the underworld. He built the Flamingo Hotel in Nevada with Bugsy Siegel. His firm, Tele-King Television, was owned in part by [New York crime bosses] Frank Costello and Meyer Lansky. Tele-King got defense contracts during the Korean War period for $2,000,000 and at prices twenty-five per cent higher than bids of competitors. . . . His vice-chairman of Tele-King . . . was given a job on Defense Mobilizer [Charles] Wilson's staff without an FBI check, on recommendation of [President Truman's friend] General [Harry] Vaughan.[25]

The criminal underworld exercised much of its influence over the Truman administration through entirely legal political channels. In 1948, for example, Abe Allenberg, the attorney for prominent New York bookmaker Frank Erickson, became the Miami treasurer of the Truman-Barkley campaign committee. Allenberg organized a lavish $250-a-plate fundraising dinner at Miami Beach's Roney Plaza hotel, where Erickson ran a secret gambling concession. Erickson himself bought ten tickets to the affair. Democratic National Committee treasurer George Killion later thanked Allenberg for providing "material help to the Democratic party in preparing for its 1948 Presidential campaign."[26]

"Material help" of this kind was often repaid by the Truman administration through its bottomless well of patronage, the Reconstruction Finance Corporation (RFC).[27] Congress established this entity in 1932 to jump-start the economy during the Depression by financing businesses as well as state and local governments. Long after the Depression ended, however, the RFC continued making loans, many to influential political borrowers and some to "syndicate interests" in Miami Beach, Cleveland, Detroit, and other cities.[28] One such loan went to a jukebox maker whose vice president was the above-mentioned Larry Knohl, despite his prison record for criminal violation of the bankruptcy laws.[29] In another case, the RFC approved a $1.5 million loan to the Saxony hotel in Miami Beach in 1949. The loan examiner spent ten days at the "ultra swank" hotel, with all expenses paid by the owner, George Sax, before recommending that hotelier be permitted to use $200,000 of the loan to pay his personal income taxes. Presidential assistant Donald S. Dawson, whose wife worked at the RFC, also frequented the hotel, once with his entire family, at Sax's expense.[30] Sax's family, based in Chicago, was the nation's largest manufacturer of primitive gambling devices called punchboards, in partnership with the head of the Chicago Outfit's slot machine operations.[31] In 1949, his hotel granted an illegal gambling concession to New York bookmaker Charles Brudner, who would resurface as cashier of a Lansky-directed casino in the Bahamas in the early 1960s.[32] The Saxony Hotel was later sold to Lansky's business partner Sam Cohen.[33] In 1962, the FBI's Chicago office reported that "George Sax has been known to associate with numerous of Chicago top hoodlums who have in the past utilized the facilities of the [Sax family-owned] Exchange National Bank in carrying out their banking transactions."[34]

In 1949 the RFC also made a highly speculative loan of more than $300,000 to Florida-based Ribbonwriter Corporation of America to manufacture an invention for making multiple typewriter copies without use of carbon paper. It approved the loan despite unfavorable reports by technical experts. Just two months later, the firm went bankrupt and the money disappeared. One of Ribbonwriter's chief stockholders was Broward County (Florida) sheriff Walter Clark, who had informed the RFC in the loan application that he was "a very close personal friend of the President."[35] Clark's twenty-year run as sheriff came to an end in 1950 when the Kefauver Committee exposed his record of operating illegal slot machines throughout his county and permitting nationally prominent East Coast gangsters—Meyer Lansky, Frank Costello, Joe Adonis, and others—to run posh gambling casinos under his watchful eye.[36]

Then there was the case of Flo Bratten, the redheaded confidential secretary to Vice President Alben Barkley. She teamed up with the general counsel to the Small Business Administration to steer RFC loans to mob-owned businesses in Florida and the Midwest. One of the many recipients they favored was Mercury Record Corp. of Chicago, which reputedly "used the channels of organized crime to market its product and force its records on jukebox operators." In recognition of her friendship with Newport, Kentucky, hoodlum Red "The Enforcer" Masterson, she was named an honorary deputy sheriff of Campbell County, Newport's home.[37] Newport, which made no secret of its major industry, was a notorious center of illegal gambling controlled by members of the "Cleveland Syndicate," who went on to pioneer legal gambling in Havana and Las Vegas (chapter 5).[38]

At least one mob-linked scandal reached all the way into the White House. The culprits were President Truman's poker partner and military aide, Gen. Harry Vaughan, and Vaughan's friend John Maragon, an ex-bootlegger from Kansas City who peddled influence in Washington until he was finally convicted of perjury.[39] In 1947, Maragon began representing the owners of Tanforan racetrack near San Francisco. The track had gone into disrepair when it was used to hold Japanese Americans forced to relocate during World War II. When the owners attempted to refurbish the facility, they were blocked by the Civilian Production Administration, which allocated scarce building materials to essential housing after the war. Contacted by his friend Maragon, Vaughan intervened with the office of the federal housing expediter to complain about mistreatment of the track owners. Yielding to pressure, the office granted the track a permit for $150,000 worth of building materials.[40] Congressional investigators discovered there was more to the story. The track had been owned by Joseph Reinfeld, one of New Jersey's biggest bootleggers. In 1946, William Helis, a New Orleans oilman, almost bought the track; though he passed on the opportunity, his son put in a call to their old friend Vaughan to help sort out its permit problems.[41] Helis was a business partner of New York mobsters Frank Costello and Phil Kastel.[42] Worse yet, though unremarked at the time, Helis was a partner in the oil business with Sicilian Mafia boss Santo Sorge, while at the same time being a friend of FBI director Hoover.[43] Vaughan admitted under questioning that Helis had sent him contributions totaling $7,000 for the controversial Democratic congressional primary race in Missouri in 1946 and another $5,000 for the 1948 national campaign.[44] Columnist Drew Pearson testified that he was in the office of Assistant Attorney General James P. McGranery in 1946 when Vaughan called to question an income tax prosecution against W. T. Burton, a "New Orleans oil man" and "very good friend of William Helis."[45] Years later, in a strange twist of fate, the CIA granted Helis "covert security approval" for two undisclosed intelligence operations, though the agency was well aware that he had "business dealings with the notorious Frank Costello" and corrupt Louisiana governor Huey Long.[46]

The Chicago Parole Scandal

One of the most egregious scandals of the Truman era involved the suspicious parole of half a dozen leaders of the Chicago crime syndicate barely a third of the way into their ten-year sentences for conspiring to extort more than a million dollars from several major Hollywood studios. One breathless reporter called it "the almost incredible story of an invisible government in the United States, which draws its sinews from underworld gutters, yet finds familiar footing in high places, including the White House." A Chicago crime historian branded the outcome "one of the most shameful episodes in the entire history of American penology and jurisprudence." It was one of the few cases where the editorial views of the Republican *Chicago Tribune* and the Communist *Daily Worker* were fully aligned.[47] Yet one year after the *Tribune* called for impeaching Attorney General Clark, President Truman elevated him to the Supreme Court.[48] The case produced extended investigations by Congress and the FBI, stonewalling by Clark, and protracted litigation before the Supreme Court. The Eisenhower administration finally closed the books on the unsolved mystery. Only years later did secretly recorded conversations by a leader of the Chicago Outfit come to light, suggesting that Clark may indeed have used his influence to free the gangsters as a favor to Chicago's Democratic machine.[49]

Chapter 3 will revisit the criminal extortion plot that sent the mobsters to prison, but here are the facts in brief. When the bootlegging business dried up with the repeal of Prohibition, Al Capone's successors in the Chicago Outfit stepped up their use of violent "protection" tactics, including kidnappings, to control unions in Chicago and milk their treasuries. On the side, a petty criminal named Willie Bioff, working with George Browne, who headed the stage hands' union in Chicago, extorted movie theater owner Barney Balaban to support a soup kitchen for unemployed union members. (Balaban would soon become head of Paramount Pictures.) With their first $20,000 from Balaban, Browne and Bioff interested the Outfit in expanding the scope of their extortion racket. Frank Nitti, Capone's successor as head of the city's crime syndicate, demanded half their take. In return, he mobilized underworld support from across the country to elect Browne president of the International Alliance of Theater and Stage Employees (IATSE) at its 1934 convention. Using strong-arm methods, including assassinations, these mobsters took over IATSE locals and threatened strikes to extort the studio bosses. They also began taking a small cut from the paychecks of every member of the international union. The Chicago mob then moved in on unions representing bartenders and hotel and restaurant employees, as well as performers represented by the American Guild of Variety Artists.

The whole scheme began unraveling when Bioff was arrested in 1939 on old pandering charges in Chicago. The Justice Department indicted Bioff and Browne in 1941 for extorting more than a million dollars from Loew's, Paramount Pictures, Twentieth Century-Fox, and Warner Bros. Faced with a possible ten-year sentence and $20,000 fine, Bioff agreed to testify against several top Chicago mobsters, including Nitti, Louis Campagna, Paul Ricca, Philip D'Andrea, Charles Gioe, and John Rosselli. When the indictment came down in March 1943, Nitti committed suicide. The others were found guilty that December. Most received terms of ten years and fines of $10,000 and began serving their sentences in 1944. Both defense and prosecution attorneys agreed that the convicted men would never have any serious chance of parole.

But two brilliant leaders of the Outfit, Murray Humphreys and Anthony Accardo, set in motion a complex scheme that worked miracles. Through a former Missouri legislator and saloon owner, they recruited Paul Dillon, a St. Louis attorney and former Senate campaign manager for Truman. His first job was to move Ricca and Campagna from prison in Atlanta to Leavenworth, where they would be housed with Gioe and Rosselli much closer to home. Dillon was no stranger to the Outfit, having previously represented John Nick, a vice president of IATSE who went to prison for extortion. Dillon had also been attorney to Kansas City racketeer John Lazia and to Boss Pendergast himself. He remained on good terms with Truman, often dropping in on the president when visiting Washington.[50]

In 1945, the warden in Atlanta complained to the Bureau of Prisons, "It is quite evident that money is being paid to obtain the transfer of these men to Leavenworth and I do not believe they should be transferred at this time for this reason."[51] Crime historian Gus Russo noted, "It may never be known exactly whom Dillon leaned on, but buried in documents discovered years later among the Bureau of Prison files is a memo noting that '[Attorney General] Tom Clark would like the subjects transferred to Leavenworth.'"[52] Once the convicts were relocated in July 1945, Outfit leaders Accardo and Humphreys met with them frequently, entering the prison with false credentials.[53]

The next hurdle was lifting a federal tax lien of about $680,000 against the two gang leaders, Campagna and Ricca. Remarkably, the Internal Revenue Bureau agreed to settle for only $128,000, about twenty cents on the dollar, six days before the 1946 election. At the same time, some eight or nine people anonymously dropped off bundles of cash with the mobsters' tax attorney, a disreputable Chicago Democratic political operative named Eugene Bernstein. Bernstein testified he had no idea who these generous donors were. As he told a House panel, "There [was] a tremendous amount of money brought in, Congressman. I was more disturbed about it than you. . . . These people I don't ask any questions of."[54]

Last but not least, the Justice Department paved the way for the paroles by dropping pending mail fraud charges against the convicted men in May 1947. Clark offered a reasonable explanation: The charges covered the same basic crimes as the original indictment, and likely would have resulted in concurrent sentences, if sustained. Critics nonetheless found it suspicious that an attorney hired by a friend of the gangsters, who was a former Texas state Democratic chairman and a lifelong friend of Clark, spoke with three top Justice Department officials shortly before the attorney general decided to drop the remaining charges.[55] Suddenly no legal issues stood in the way of the parole board considering their cases, as soon as the men completed one-third of their sentences.[56]

On August 6, 1947, in the words of one reporter, attorney "Dillon dropped in to see his old friend, T. Webbe Wilson, chairman of the federal parole board, in Washington. Seven days later, almost to the very day they became eligible for parole, the four gangsters walked out of prison." The board kept no record of its deliberations. It disregarded the recommendations of the original judge, and of the prosecutor who had previously reported to the attorney general that "The convicted defendants are notorious as successors to the underworld power of Al Capone. They are vicious criminals who would stop at nothing to achieve their ends. The investigation and prosecution were attended by murder, gunplay, threatening of witnesses, perjury, etc." The parole board's chairman retired to his home in Mississippi just days after he joined Clark's two appointees on the board to grant the unthinkable paroles.[57] The FBI heard weeks later from another prison inmate that Charles Gioe had boasted of paying $300,000 to parole officials for their rulings.[58]

A *Chicago Tribune* reporter who followed the case closely concluded that the paroles were granted in return for the Outfit's efforts to elect Democratic candidates in Chicago in November 1946. According to his sources, the mobsters prevailed on several Republican ward committeemen, who oversaw mostly Italian American districts, to quietly support the Democrats against their own party. The Outfit raised money to pay off the tax liens and attorney fees by arranging for friendly sheriffs to look the other way while slot machines were installed in towns around Chicago, such as Cicero.[59] In the 1948 election—just a year after the parole decision—the Cook County Democratic political machine helped deliver Illinois to President Truman by a margin of less than 34,000 votes.[60]

The House committee investigating the parole scandal declared, "The syndicate has given the most striking demonstration of political clout in the history of the republic."[61] Although it found no evidence that President Truman personally intervened in the case, the report condemned the FBI and Justice Department for refusing to assist its probe. It also noted that the Chicago gangsters improperly failed to disclose their full criminal records when they applied for parole. Embarrassed by this revelation, the parole board ordered the rearrest of three of the former inmates. Several years of legal battles ensued as the case went all the way to the Supreme Court. The tide began to turn against the government when a federal judge in Chicago ruled in September 1952 that it had no right to revoke Ricca's parole. Given two months to appeal, the department failed to act—losing by default. The criminal division explained this remarkable dereliction as the result of overwork.[62]

Dismayed by his own office's performance, Attorney General James McGranery—by all accounts an honest public servant—ordered a new FBI investigation into the parole scandal.[63] As with an earlier investigation ordered by Clark, it was inconclusive. Months later, the Eisenhower administration's new assistant attorney general in charge of the criminal division, Warren Olney III, was startled to find two lawyers handling the case, surrounded by four-foot-high stacks of FBI reports. Olney quickly concluded that the matter was a hopeless "mare's nest" and closed the investigation.[64] The Justice Department eventually convicted Truman's friend Dillon of income tax evasion, for which he was sentenced to fifteen months in prison and a $2,500 fine.[65]

The parole case soon became moot for the free but nearly broke Chicago gangster Philip D'Andrea. He died of an illness in 1952.[66] In 1954, Charles Gioe was riddled with bullets while reaching for the ignition in his car.[67] The bank robber, murderer, and labor racketeer Louis Campagna died of a heart attack in 1955.[68] Paul Ricca, branded the nation's "most important criminal" by a Senate investigating committee, continued supervising operations of the Outfit with Anthony Accardo until a tax conviction sent him to prison in 1959.[69] As we will see in chapter 9, a secondary member of the extortion plot, John Rosselli, went on to a long career in crime, secret intelligence, and political intrigue until he was assassinated in 1975.[70] Meanwhile, the man whose testimony sent them all to jail in the first place, Willie Bioff, was blown to bits in 1955 by a car bomb while living in Arizona under a new name.[71]

Years after the FBI dropped its investigation of the mysterious parole, its well-placed bugs picked up conversations by Outfit boss Murray Humphreys boasting of how he had arranged to free his colleagues. It was he who paid the two attorneys, friends of President Truman and Attorney General Clark, to swing the deal. "The trick was to get to Tom Clark," he told a trusted friend. "He had the power to see that that [pending] indictment in New York could be vacated. But he had a lot of problems with that. What a cry would go up if the 'Capone guys' were dismissed. Finally a deal was made: if he had the thick skin to do it, he'd get the next appointment to the Supreme Court."[72] In another conversation, Humphreys explained that once the scandal broke, the formerly compliant attorney general panicked. "He became a mean [obscenity]," the Outfit boss said. "Before that, he was a hundred percent! A hundred percent!" After Congress began investigating, however, "he was through, he quit. You couldn't get a favor off of him. Nothing. . . . You see, he did this [parole] as a favor."[73]

Such tales are not proof of Clark's guilt, but they can hardly be dismissed. Clark likely suspected that the FBI had plenty of such scuttlebutt in its files. As he did with other public officials, J. Edgar Hoover came to an unspoken accommodation:

> [Supreme Court Justice] Clark reaffirmed his antiradical and pro-law-and-order credentials in his steady correspondence with Hoover. Clark even aided the FBI's public relations and propaganda programs by working directly with Hoover to educate other judges about the bureau's position on criminal law and national security matters. And Clark kept Hoover apprised of how best to stay in the good graces of the largest organization of attorneys, the American Bar Association. . . . In his letters, Clark praised Hoover's public critiques of the justice system and wrote to Hoover with some of his own criticism about the "foggy" area of search-and-seizure law that the Supreme Court had created.[74]

Organized Crime, Corruption, and Republicans

Contrary to Republican charges, Truman and the Democrats had no monopoly on corruption. Truman's dismal record of cronyism was a political gift to Republican politicians, but much of their ammunition was supplied by reform-minded Democrats, including Sen. Estes Kefauver of Tennessee and Arkansas senators J. William Fulbright and John McClellan. It was McClellan's Committee on Expenditures in the Executive Departments, for example, whose probe of influence peddling in defense procurement helped force the resignation of Democratic National Committee chairman William Boyle—an architect of Truman's 1948 election victory—in October 1951.[75] A junior member of that committee was California's opportunistic young Republican senator, Richard Nixon. Joining General Eisenhower on the GOP ticket in 1952, Nixon took the lead in hammering away at the issues of "Korea, crime, Communism, and corruption," a winning political formula that came to be known as K1C3.

Nixon's attacks on the ethics of the Truman administration were more than a little hypocritical given his own record. To finance his first race for Congress in 1946, against liberal Democratic incumbent Jerry Voorhis, Nixon amassed tens of thousands of dollars in unreported contributions from Southern California oil companies, banks, and movie moguls. Nixon would soon begin repaying his benefactors by supporting legislation to curb unions, exempt key industries from antitrust action, promote oil drilling, and cut funding for public housing and education. As one biographer observed, "Most of the lavish 1946 financing was never acknowledged. Richard Nixon's furtive, mincing attitude toward political money, the gradual atrophy of ethics that ended so painfully thirty years later, began in the first campaign."[76]

Nixon's 1946 campaign was also critical because it began his career-long partnership with his ruthless political consultant, Murray Chotiner.[77] Chotiner had one word of advice: attack. Nixon's successful House and Senate campaigns in 1946 and 1950 were notoriously ugly, full of insinuations that his opponents were soft on Communism and crime. Between campaigns, Chotiner was a rumpled, cigar-chomping Beverly Hills lawyer whose clients were mostly bookmakers and gamblers. These criminals flourished in a fast-growing metropolis that embraced vices of every kind. Chotiner and his brother reportedly handled 221 bookmaking cases in a single four-year period—nearly always arranging suspended sentences or minor fines.[78]

In 1946, Chotiner allegedly introduced Nixon to the biggest and brashest gambler in all of Southern California: Mickey Cohen. Cohen had been raised by an Orthodox Jewish family in Brooklyn before setting out to become a professional boxer. He developed connections with leaders of the Jewish mob in Cleveland, a group that later pioneered the development of modern Las Vegas as a gambler's mecca. Next he became an enforcer for Al Capone's outfit in Chicago. In the late 1930s Cohen moved to Los Angeles to build his own gang while representing the interests of the Cleveland, Chicago, and New York syndicates. When Cohen's thugs got into trouble, they turned to Murray Chotiner and his brother for legal help. Implicated in murder, gambling, narcotics trafficking, and wholesale bribery of police and other public officials, Cohen was convicted of tax evasion in 1951 and again in 1961, ending up in Alcatraz prison.[79]

In 1946, Chotiner arranged for Nixon to meet Cohen for lunch at a fish house in Los Angeles, according to the mobster. Cohen said he donated $5,000 to the fledgling Republican's first congressional campaign—about $50,000 in today's dollars.[80] For Cohen, it was just the usual cost of doing business. "It was politically necessary for me to give the money," he explained years later. "It was explained to me that it was very important for the Orange County operation to run. . . . Chotiner had a lot of strength with some local politicians. Chotiner was very instrumental in adding to some contact in Sacramento that I had that I needed strengthened."[81]

Cohen claimed that in 1950, while Chotiner was managing Nixon's expensive statewide campaign for Senate, he dramatically upped his support for the candidate on orders from East Coast crime syndicate leaders.[82] According to an affidavit Cohen signed in 1962, he invited 250 fellow gangsters, including leaders of the underworld in Los Angeles and Las Vegas, to dine with Nixon at a Hollywood hotel. After the candidate and Chotiner spoke, Cohen put the squeeze on his colleagues for contributions: He wouldn't let them out of the banquet room until they met Chotiner's quota of $25,000, equal to a quarter million dollars today.[83]

Cohen's story had some inaccuracies and changed in some details over the years, which may simply reflect failures of memory. One might suspect that Cohen invented the account in his 1962 affidavit to win leniency from a Democratic administration, but his story actually began circulating in the mid-1950s, when it put Cohen at some political risk. When his story later surfaced in a broadcast by Drew Pearson, Chotiner flatly denied enlisting Cohen's support in any of Nixon's campaigns, or that Cohen had raised any money for Nixon's 1950 Senate race. However, the often litigious Chotiner never sued Pearson, who ran the story several times, as late as 1968.[84]

Henry Grunewald: Bipartisan Fixer

Following his successful race, the Nixon campaign reported 1950 expenditures of only $62,899. Some political observers doubted that number, and it evidently did not include any generous contributions from Mickey Cohen's friends.[85] Nixon also received a secret $5,000 contribution to his 1950 primary race—one of the largest he received—from Republican campaign paymaster Owen Brewster, a right-wing, McCarthyite senator from Maine.[86] When discovered and made public, Brewster's contribution to Nixon caused a stir because it violated an unwritten GOP rule not to interfere in primary races.

Brewster disguised the payment by passing it to Nixon through his friend Henry "the Dutchman" Grunewald. Born in South Africa to German parents, Grunewald had a colorful career including collaring German spies in World War I as an agent for the Bureau of Investigation and chasing bootleggers as a corrupt agent of the Treasury Department's alcohol tax unit.[87] For many years thereafter, he worked as a private investigator and hatchet man for New York insurance executive Henry Marsh, who admiringly described Grunewald as "utterly amoral. He doesn't know right from wrong. Just tell him what to do and he'll do it." Marsh himself was "a mover, a shaker, and a manipulator," in the words of political insider Thomas Corcoran. He used Grunewald to deliver cash to members of Congress. In 1940, Marsh offered Grunewald's services to the Roosevelt administration, through FDR's confidant Corcoran. The New Deal lawyer and wheeler-dealer made extensive use of Grunewald's unique and highly confidential "investigative" services to aid Roosevelt's reelection campaign in 1940, and to a lesser extent in 1944. But Corcoran's attempt to exploit Grunewald's talents in 1942, on behalf of pro-FDR senator George Norris, a Nebraska Independent, failed spectacularly. Corcoran found him an easy job with the Alien Property Custodian in Omaha. That gave Grunewald plenty of time to promote Marsh's insurance interests and build support for Norris among Nebraska's large German population, but to Corcoran's regret he didn't last long:

No sooner had Gruenwald [sic] reached Omaha than he checked into a fine hotel and hosted an extraordinary party. Almost every prostitute in town was there and he had a bottle of gin for each. The party was loud, but the hotel manager was even louder when he called the police to throw Gruenwald out. The scandal was loudest of all and Gruenwald had to be fired. Senator Norris was not reelected. Such were the unpredictable problems that could arise when campaign finance, domestic politics, and international affairs became entangled.[88]

With the benefit of a large bequest from Marsh, Grunewald soon bounced back. He had a remarkable ability to cultivate friends in both major parties and at all levels, "from Senators to doormen, Representatives to pages."[89] In time, the Dutchman earned a reputation as "Washington's best connected wirepuller." Awed reporters noted that Grunewald installed a telephone trunk line directly from his home to the Bureau of Internal Revenue, so he could fix tax cases more efficiently. He was thanked by President Truman for making a hefty $1,600 contribution in 1948, praised by Vice President Alben Barkley, and lauded by Senator Brewster as a man who "seemed simply interested in doing good and never asking for anything." Brewster told congressional investigators that he had "complete confidence" in Grunewald: "If I wanted a man who had a capacity to keep his mouth shut, I think he was one."[90]

When the young Republican attorney William Rogers arrived in Washington in 1947, Brewster introduced him to Grunewald, who found Rogers an apartment and then got him hired as chief counsel to the Senate Subcommittee on Investigations. Rogers soon was on "intimate" terms with the Dutchman, and allegedly even more intimate terms with Grunewald's daughter, Erna.[91] Rogers would later become attorney general under President Eisenhower and secretary of state under President Nixon.

Even as he was passing cash to Nixon, Grunewald was leaving his fingerprints as a bipartisan "fixer" on many of the most egregious misdeeds of the Truman administration, including tax scandals that led to dozens of official resignations and convictions:

> Grunewald knew Commissioner of Internal Revenue Schoeneman well enough that Schoeneman's office record shows forty-five personal visits from him. Schoeneman's house was built on a lot that Grunewald acquired and sold to the commissioner at cost as a service to him. Grunewald also arranged financing for the home. Grunewald was a friend of [scandal-tainted War Assets Administration head] Jess Larson and gave him a television set. Harry Woodring, the former Secretary of War, shared Grunewald's Washington hotel suite, went to Germany on a deal for Grunewald and was paid by him. Louis Johnson, Truman's Secretary for Defense, was familiar enough that Grunewald could ask him to intervene with the White House for a pay raise for [IRB chief counsel Charles] Oliphant.

> Grunewald knew some senators well enough that "he could walk into their offices without taking his hat off." . . . By his own account, he could get J. Edgar Hoover on the phone to discuss a personal problem. . . . [Alien Property Custodian Leo] Crowley said that he didn't know him . . . but there was a letter from Crowley that Grunewald should act as director in his absence.[92]

Grunewald also had serious underworld connections, some dating from his work as a corrupt Prohibition agent. He drew a contempt citation from a House subcommittee for refusing to explain his part in a half-million-dollar extortion plot involving senior Internal Revenue Bureau officials and a former attorney for Al Capone, Abraham Teitelbaum. Grunewald was caught working on a huge black market liquor operation with American Distilling Company, headed by Samuel Rothberg, a partner of Meyer Lansky in the Flamingo hotel-casino in Las Vegas. Grunewald also handled cash payoffs for the S&G Syndicate, which had a lock on bookmaking in Miami Beach throughout much of the 1940s. To hide the source of his huge cash fees, Grunewald claimed to have won $220,000 over a five-year period at racetracks.[93] For the better part of a decade, Grunewald was investigated for illegal wiretapping and extortion, held in contempt of Congress, indicted twice for perjury, and convicted of bribery to fix federal tax prosecutions, but he remained evasive and tight-lipped to his death in 1958.[94]

Joe McCarthy, the "Pepsi Cola Kid"

Campaigning for Nixon in the 1950 California Senate race was an emerging star of the Republican Party and fellow anti-Communist crusader, Wisconsin senator Joseph McCarthy. Well before his name became synonymous with red-baiting, McCarthy used his platform on the Senate Investigations Subcommittee to warn that President Truman's coddling of influence peddlers would "lead to unlimited graft and corruption in the government."[95] After Nixon's election to the Senate, McCarthy arranged to put him on the Investigations Subcommittee, giving him a platform to attack the Democratic administration.

But McCarthy was at least as dirty as Nixon. Like many other right-wing anti-Communists, his record reeked of favoritism toward special interests. During World War II, he failed to file taxes on stock market windfalls.[96] In 1947, the newly elected Wisconsin senator met and befriended John Maragon, the five-percenter with White House and mob connections. Maragon introduced McCarthy to the seamy world of lobbyists working for sugar producers, importers, and consumers (chapter 4). At the time of their meeting, Pepsi Cola was exploring how it could evade continued federal rationing of sugar. One of its free-spending lobbyists, Long Island Pepsi bottling plant owner Russell Arundel, introduced the senator to Pepsi president Walter Mack. Before long, McCarthy was giving impassioned speeches on the Senate floor for decontrolling sugar, winning him the moniker, "Pepsi Cola Kid." McCarthy managed to push through a bill lifting federal controls on October 31, 1947, six months ahead of schedule. When the senator suffered a heavy loss on the stock market, he knew where to turn for help: Russell Arundel. The Pepsi man guaranteed a $20,000 note to stop foreclosure on a $53,000 bank loan to McCarthy.[97] One day later, McCarthy followed the soft drink company's lead in attacking the army for purchasing Cuban sugar at the expense of commercial users.[98] Building on this success story, Pepsi-Cola Co. emerged a few years later as the financial savior of Richard Nixon.

In 1953, bucking furious assaults by McCarthy, the Senate Privileges and Elections Committee issued a little-noticed report reprimanding the Communist hunter from Wisconsin for numerous improprieties, including his dealings with Pepsi:

> McCarthy's acceptance of the $20,000 favor from the Washington representative of the Pepsi-Cola Company at the very time he was attacking the government for its manner of handling sugar control makes it difficult to determine whether Senator McCarthy was working for the best interests of the government as he saw it or for the Pepsi-Cola Company.

McCarthy's only comment was, "I don't answer charges, I make them."[99] Largely forgotten today is the fact that the Senate's belated censure of McCarthy in 1954, which brought his demagogic career to an end, was based not only on his anti-Communist smear campaign, but also on his attempts to obstruct the subcommittee's investigation of his finances.[100]

McCarthy also got caught up in a scandal involving the Reconstruction Finance Corporation and Lustron, a Columbus, Ohio, manufacturer of prefabricated steel houses. Lustron came under congressional investigation for receiving more than $37 million in loans from the patronage-ridden RFC. McCarthy, a member of the Senate Banking and Currency Committee, was instrumental in drafting a provision of the Housing Act of 1948 that gave the RFC authority to extend $50 million in loans to makers of prefabricated homes like Lustron. McCarthy also happened to be a member of the Senate Investigating Subcommittee, which was probing RFC loans to Lustron. In 1948, McCarthy received $10,000 (about $100,000 in today's dollars) to write an article for Lustron on home building. He solicited the fee—which was later deemed "highly improper" by the Subcommittee on Privileges and Elections—from the company's CEO while the two men were at a racetrack. McCarthy then contacted the head of the federal Housing and Home Finance

Administration—whose salary McCarthy had helped increase—for help in writing the article. Lustron paid McCarthy just in time to save him from defaulting on overdue bank debts. With his finances temporarily spared, McCarthy then invested in a railroad company financed by the RFC, possibly on insider information. He sold half his shares in 1951 for a profit of more than $35,000 (equal to more than $350,000 today).[101]

Epilogue

Although corruption in Washington was truly bipartisan, and President Truman did take belated steps to fire some crooked officials and reform some federal bureaucracies, his party took great heat over the issue. By February 1952, Truman's popularity hit a low of only 22 percent, owing to popular discontent with corruption along with the Korean War and fears of Communist infiltration into the federal government. After the anti-crime crusader Estes Kefauver beat him in the New Hampshire primary, Truman withdrew his name from the race. Although he had not been seriously running for another term, the defeat stung. Announcing his decision on March 29, a deeply wounded Truman defended his record. "I stand for honest government," he insisted. "I have worked for it. I have probably done more for it than any other President."[102]

Republicans would have none of it. In its 1952 platform, the GOP emphasized its promise "to put an end to corruption, to oust the crooks and grafters, to administer tax laws fairly and impartially, and to restore honest government to the people." In his speech accepting the Republican nomination on July 11, 1952, General Eisenhower pledged to "sweep from office an Administration which has fastened on every one of us the wastefulness, the arrogance, and corruption in high places . . . which are the bitter fruit of a party too long in power." During a campaign stop in Iowa on September 18, the World War II hero declared, "We are going to cast out the crooks and their cronies. . . . And when we are through, the experts in shady and shoddy government operations will be on their way back to the shadowy haunts, the sub-cellars of American politics from whence they came. . . . The first thing we have to do is get a government that is honest."[103]

The Republicans' message that too many years of Democratic rule had thoroughly tainted the federal government echoed in respected, mainstream media. In a full-page editorial shortly before the election, titled "Hoodlum Politics," *Life* magazine laid out a devastating case against the Democrats by tying corruption to the threat posed by organized crime to American democracy:

That expert on ethics, the retiring President of the United States, has declared that General Eisenhower suffers from moral blindness and is therefore unfit to succeed him in office. . . . Look who's talking.

Harry Truman began his political career as a doorbell ringer for the Tom Pendergast machine in the wide-open town of Kansas City. Kansas City was then both sanctuary and resort for bigtime gangsters on the lam from all parts of the country. One in every 10 of its cops had a criminal record. . . . In addition to his flesh-and-blood minions [Pendergast] had a block of 60,000 "ghost votes" he would throw into action as reserves. . . .

Unfortunately for Uncle Tom, the Kansas City *Star* and the U.S. District [sic] Attorney, Maurice M. Milligan, obtained overwhelming evidence of election fraud that led to convictions. They were sustained all the way to the U.S. Supreme Court.

What has all this to do with Harry Truman? Everything. All that he knows about politics he learned at Tom Pendergast's knee. . . . Every elective office he ever held until 1944 was given him by the Pendergast machine. . . . In 1938, while the vote fraud trials were still in court, Harry Truman denounced the trials and their prosecutor on the floor of the U.S. Senate. On becoming President one of Harry Truman's first acts was to pardon 15 of the Pendergast mob who had been convicted of ballot-stuffing. Milligan he fired. When old Tom died early in 1945 after a prison term, Vice President Truman flew to his funeral in an Army bomber.

In 1946 Harry Truman sent orders to Jim Pendergast—old Tom's nephew who inherited the machine—for the defeat of Representative Roger Slaughter in the Democratic primaries. Once again the alert *Star* obtained evidence of election fraud. The evidence disappeared when the vault in the Pendergast-controlled courthouse was blown open and the impounded ballots were stolen. . . .

At present the most nauseous center of gutter politics is probably Chicago. . . . Wrote Estes Kefauver,

"There was no doubt in the minds of any of us, after the sort of testimony we heard in Chicago, that *organized crime and political corruption go hand in hand*, and that in fact there could be no bigtime organized crime without *a firm and profitable alliance between those who run the rackets and those in political control*." (our italics). . . .

And this brings us to our second thought about the coming election. Adlai Stevenson was a good governor of Illinois. His personal relations with the Cook County machine, while not exactly innocent, are not to be compared with Truman's kinship with Kansas City crookedness. Nevertheless, just as Truman owed his vice presidential nomination in '44 to the big-city bosses, so Stevenson could not have been nominated this year—and probably cannot be elected—without their backing.

The "politics-for-profit" morality of these bosses has permeated and corrupted our Federal government. . . . If Stevenson is elected, the cultural elite of New York, Hollywood and the campuses may take some of the credit. But

Stevenson will owe much, much more to the vice-and-racket machines that turn out the marginal votes in the three strategic states of New York, Missouri, and Illinois. These machines are American politics at their sleaziest and ugliest.[104]

Such warnings, repeated in speeches and publications across the country, powerfully swayed public opinion. "The crusade against secrecy and corruption stayed at the forefront of the campaign and swept Eisenhower and Nixon into office on November 4," wrote prize-winning investigative reporter Clark Mollenhoff. "When the electoral vote was tallied, it stood 422 Republicans to 89 Democrats—a genuine mandate to clean up 'the mess in Washington.'"[105]

3

Anti-Communism

Mobsters, the FBI, and the China Lobby

More than any great power's that I can think of, America's political system
is wide open to foreign interference in a variety of legitimate and illegiti-
mate ways. . . . If you can win over a respected and well-placed representative or senator . . . there's a good chance a lot of the other lawmakers will
follow their lead. Back in the 1950s, for example, Sen. William Knowland
(R-Calif.) was often derided as the "Senator from Formosa" because of his
consistent opposition to communist China and ardent support for Taiwan.
. . . The influence of self-interested foreigners increases even more when
they can partner with domestic groups that share their objectives, and that
will use their testimony to sell whatever course of action they are trying to
promote.

—Stephen M. Walt, Harvard University, 2019[1]

THE EXPANSION OF ORGANIZED CRIME's political influence on the national
level after World War II went hand in hand with efforts by some syndicate entrepreneurs to bury their criminal records to achieve social standing
and political legitimacy. To that end, more than a few mobsters and their
political allies helped promote the growth of anti-Communism in the early
Cold War years as a shield to protect themselves against serious investigation by Hoover's FBI, political rivals, and journalists. Anti-Communism
was naturally embraced by millions of Americans who feared Soviet power
and brutality. At the same time, however, it became a powerful weapon,
easily manipulated for corrupt purposes, in the hands of cynical politicians,

employers, and special-interest groups. Criminals joined in that ideological racket, starting with their indirect influence on investigations of Communism by the House Un-American Activities Committee (HUAC), and extending to the subsequent rise of McCarthyism and the "China lobby." Along the way, they enjoyed unstinting support from Hoover's FBI and mob-backed politicians such as Richard Nixon and Nevada senator Pat McCarran. The weaponization of virulent anti-Communism poisoned American democracy for decades to come.

Hollywood, HUAC, the Mob, and the Rise of Anti-Communism

Anti-Communism had deep roots in American politics. The Red Scare following the 1917 Bolshevik Revolution saw the federal government, along with private organizations like the American Protective League and American Legion, target Communist sympathizers as well as anarchists, aliens, labor organizers, and hyphenated Americans. As chief of the General Intelligence Division of the Justice Department's Bureau of Investigation, a young J. Edgar Hoover began amassing centralized files on suspected radicals. The harsh public crackdown on dissent helped trigger the rise of a domestic surveillance state, often deployed in the service of big business against organized labor.[2] Anti-Communism reemerged as a powerful force in American politics toward the end of World War II, when the Allies could afford to act on their profound political differences. The Soviet occupation of Eastern Europe alarmed millions of Americans with family roots in the region. Less than a year after Nazi Germany's surrender, former British prime minister Winston Churchill was warning in Fulton, Missouri, that "an iron curtain has descended across the continent" and that "communist fifth columns" were subverting much of Europe.[3] One year after that chilling speech, President Truman fed the growing scare by introducing a Loyalty Program for all federal civil service employees. Soon his administration published the Attorney General's List of Subversive Organizations, which became an unofficial blacklist for many employers. It also greatly expanded the FBI's political mandate.[4] Revelations of Soviet atomic espionage further aroused popular alarm.

Greatly contributing to the postwar rebirth of anti-Communism were narratives promoted over the years by the House Un-American Activities Committee, which raised the specter that well-concealed Communists were secretly influencing American society and government. "It may fairly be asserted that McCarthyism would never have been possible had not the Un-American Activities Committee, and its predecessor, the Dies committee, paved the way from 1938 on," declared political scientist Robert Carr.[5]

The notoriously anti-Semitic Texas representative Martin Dies began probing connections between Jews and Communists in the movie industry in 1939. Following the Republican victory in the 1946 election, chairmanship of HUAC passed to J. Parnell Thomas (R.-NJ), a vulgar opportunist who used the committee to target unions in several industries, especially Hollywood, before being convicted of salary fraud in 1949. His chief investigator, Robert Stripling, was described by one historian as "a southern white supremacist who had previously assisted . . . a former publicist for the [pro-Nazi] Bund."[6] Joining that unsavory committee in 1947 was a freshly minted Republican congressman from Southern California, Richard Nixon.

Hollywood has often been portrayed as a victim of HUAC's right-wing purges, but the truth is more complex. Through the late 1930s and into the war years, mob-controlled Hollywood union leaders joined powerful studio owners such as Louis Mayer (a former Republican state chairman) and Jack Warner to brand as Communist independent unions that fought plunging wages and longer working hours during the Great Depression.[7] In 1933, the Association of Motion Pictures Producers hired the handsome racketeer and former bootlegger John Rosselli as a "labor consultant" to help break a strike called by one of the movie industry's most powerful unions, the International Alliance of Theatrical Stage Employees (IATSE). Rosselli was a West Coast representative of the Chicago Outfit and "man about town" in Hollywood. His close friends included Columbia Pictures owner Harry Cohn, screen star Jean Harlow, and William Wilkerson, publisher of the influential *Hollywood Reporter*. Promising to "fight fire with fire," Rosselli hired local bruisers to take on the strikers and ensure safe passage for strikebreakers through picket lines. In 1934, Rosselli—still on the producers' payroll—helped spearhead the Chicago Outfit's wholesale takeover of IATSE, described in chapter 2.[8] By offering producers guarantees of labor peace and low wages in an era of worker militancy, union president George Browne and convicted pimp William Bioff took hundreds of thousands of dollars from cooperative motion-picture studios and theater companies. Meanwhile, Rosselli and labor attorney Sidney Korshak served as the Chicago Outfit's ambassadors to the studio bosses, ensuring that the industry paid up while its needs were met.[9] Over the course of several years, the studios reportedly saved $15 million in employee salaries and benefits, a huge return on their coerced investment.[10]

Movie producers also encouraged the Los Angeles Police Department's notorious Red Squad as it beat up strikers and union leaders while protecting racketeers from Chicago and New York. During a Hollywood strike in 1937, provoked by widespread wage cuts, the Red Squad actually handed out pistol permits to gangsters imported by the studios and IATSE to crush labor militants.[11] The LAPD finally provoked a political backlash that year when an agent in its intelligence division bombed the home of a civic reformer who had exposed payoffs to the mayor's office from hundreds of brothels, book-makers, and whorehouses.[12]

Meanwhile, the studios engaged friendly reporters and columnists to smear labor militants as Communists. (Hollywood certainly had its share of Communists, but they were never a dominant force.)[13] Among the loudest anti-Communist voices in journalism was Rosselli's friend Billy Wilkerson, who pioneered the infamous Hollywood Blacklist at about the same time he partnered with New York gangsters Bugsy Siegel and Meyer Lansky in the mid-1940s to build the Flamingo hotel-casino in Las Vegas.[14]

IATSE's mob-backed leaders also wielded verbal smears against their union rivals. In 1938, Browne declared his enemies "Communists" and "parlor pinks" after one craft union leader rejected a $56,000 bribe. In 1940, Browne's position became more precarious as Bioff faced investigations for tax evasion and beating a prostitute. At IATSE's convention that year, Browne lambasted labor progressives and cited findings by HUAC to support his claim that Communism was "the most imminent and dangerous force standing in the path of our continued success." Senior executives from Louis Mayer's M-G-M and other studios huddled with Browne and Bioff to help them maintain control of the union.[15]

Their efforts failed. Caught evading taxes related to his payoffs to Browne and Bioff, Twentieth Century-Fox chairman Joseph Schenck agreed to testify. So did Bioff himself, after convictions for tax evasion and extortion in 1941. In a subsequent trial, as we saw in chapter 2, six leaders of the Chicago under-world went to prison, including Rosselli. Attorney Korshak escaped prosecu-tion, despite Bioff's testimony that he had been introduced to the lawyer by an Outfit leader who declared, "he is our man. . . . Any message he might deliver to you is a message from us."[16] In the wake of the extortion trials, Hollywood studios and unions continued to take direction from Korshak. Chicago crime bosses called the shots through Browne's many remaining allies in IATSE, and through the Teamsters union, which controlled deliveries to the studios.[17]

According to crime historian Gus Russo, soon after the extortion trial ended, the Chicago Outfit's Murray Humphreys "utilized his Hollywood con-nections to organize a wartime bond rally at Chicago's Soldier Field. Pressed into service were such luminaries as Bob Hope, George Raft, Jimmy Durante, and a young up-and-comer named Frank Sinatra." After the war, as we have seen, Rosselli and others convicted in the extortion case won early parole, apparently through the Outfit's political influence with Attorney General Tom Clark. Within a few months of his release, Rosselli found a job in Hol-lywood as a minor but successful movie producer (*Canon City, He Walked by Night*). Russo notes that Rosselli "was sponsored right back into the motion picture business by, of all people, Joe Schenck, who had also been imprisoned during the Hollywood shakedown and had supposedly been extorted by Rosselli's Chicago bosses."[18] (President Truman had quietly pardoned Schenck in 1945.[19]) Chapter 9 examines how this patriotic mobster was recruited years later by the CIA to help assassinate Cuban revolutionary Fidel Castro.

With the end of World War II, Hollywood, like many industries, faced renewed labor militancy as workers demanded compensation for their wartime sacrifices. In 1945, IATSE dispatched a tough new operator to run its Hollywood operations, Roy Brewer. One of Brewer's key tasks was to fight the upstart Conference of Studio Unions (CSU), which had been founded in 1941 in part to "fight against the gangster interests" in the movie business.[20] Each of the rival unions had about ten thousand members serving the film industry, but only IATSE had the silent backing of the studios, the mob, and the FBI. With their support, Brewer exploited jurisdictional disputes to trigger CSU labor actions and deplete its resources. One such debilitating dispute led to a pitched battle in front of Warner Bros. studio in 1945. Wilkerson's *Hollywood Reporter* depicted the CSU as Red, even though the Communist Party had denounced its strike.[21]

In September 1946, another jurisdictional battle prompted the CSU to strike once again. The studios then locked out its members and hired IATSE members as scabs. The strikebreakers were protected by the head of the Teamster local, against the wishes of his own members. The orders came all the way from the international Teamster president Daniel Tobin, a tough anti-Communist with a mixed record of addressing corruption and organized crime infiltration. Meanwhile, like Rosselli, the Teamster local's business manager was hired by Joseph Schenck to become Twentieth Century-Fox's labor relations director.[22] The bitter labor struggle between the studios and CSU lasted thirteen months. Time and again the CSU accepted a mediator's proposals for settling the action, only to be ignored by IATSE. Brewer confessed to one mediator that he was "engaged in a war—a war to the finish" with the CSU. In early 1947, kidnappers dressed as policemen—almost certainly gunmen from Chicago—grabbed the CSU's leader, beat him severely, and dropped him in the desert.[23]

Brewer continued to blame all the troubles on Communists, claiming the Soviet Union had plotted since 1934 to take over the motion picture industry.[24] Reading from the same script was the new president of the Screen Actors Guild, Ronald Reagan. (Reagan owed his union leadership to Lew Wasserman of MCA, a talent agency founded in Chicago with Outfit help.) The future president of the United States warned of a "Soviet effort to gain control over Hollywood and the content of its films." While Reagan informed the FBI of suspected Communists in Hollywood, members of the Motion

Picture Alliance for the Preservation of American Ideals (MPA) provided names to HUAC. Founded in 1944 to fight alleged Communist infiltration of Hollywood unions, MPA was chaired in 1947 by the former head of the Hollywood Teamster local. Its executive board included IATSE's Brewer.[25]

By the end of 1947, the CSU was crushed. Some of its members never again found work in Hollywood. With attorney Korshak holding court, the studios enjoyed decades of labor peace with IATSE and the Teamsters. And—of more significance to national politics—"the Hollywood strikes set the context for HUAC coming to town in 1947," noted historian Donald Critchlow.[26] Appearing before the committee in October 1947, studio boss Jack Warner declared, "Ideological termites have burrowed into many American industries, organizations, and societies. Wherever they may be, I say let us dig them out and get rid of them. My brothers and I will be happy to subscribe generously to a pest-removal fund."[27] Warner and other studio heads were protected against charges of being soft on Communism by junior HUAC member Richard Nixon—said by one historian to have been the only person whose career actually benefited from the raucous hearings.[28] There were plenty of victims, however. In the ensuing political maelstrom, entertainers testified against fellow entertainers, ten uncooperative witnesses were jailed for contempt, blacklists were created, and careers were blighted. The anti-Communist scare was gaining momentum.

Hollywood studio bosses and at least one of their underworld partners also played a hitherto unrecognized role in stoking public fears through the Committee on the Present Danger (CPD). CPD was a private organization founded by several dozen eminent Americans in late 1950 literally to scare the public into supporting a vast military buildup, including universal conscription for a huge standing army. The organization emerged as the key enabler of the Truman administration's National Security Memorandum 68 (NSC 68), prepared in April 1950 after a major review of US foreign and military policy led by the Departments of State and Defense. The document proposed *tripling* US military spending to contain the Soviet Union.

Government planners understood that such a drastic program would require a hard sell to win support in Congress. Robert Lovett, a Wall Street investment banker and foreign policy adviser, declared during an interagency review of NSC 68, "We must have a much vaster propaganda machine to tell our story at home and abroad." Assistant Secretary of State for Public Affairs Edward Barrett advised that the ambitious initiative must be accompanied by a "scare campaign" to create "full public awareness of the problem."[29]

Undertaking to organize that "scare campaign" were the CPD's two cofounders, former undersecretary of the army Tracy Voorhees and Harvard University president James Conant. Voorhees had been a member of the administration's ad hoc committee in charge of planning how to implement NSC 68's recommendations. Conant, who became CPD's chairman, had consulted on the drafting of the document. Members of their committee used speeches, broadcasts, pamphlets, and other communications vehicles to warn the public, in the words of Conant, that "the United States is in danger. . . . We have no time to lose."[30]

The CPD included many prominent internationalist Republicans, who helped deflect attacks against the Truman administration by right-wing, Asia-first conservatives. Much of the committee's financial support came from California-based business leaders. They included former Studebaker president Paul Hoffman, drugstore king Justin Dart, Crown Zellerbach chairman James Zellerbach, rubber czar Leonard Firestone, and oil millionaire Edwin Pauley, a leading Democratic fundraiser and Truman ally. But the key movers behind the California committee were the powerful Hollywood producer Samuel Goldwyn and Floyd Odlum, a vastly wealthy investor and owner of RKO Pictures, which released many of Goldwyn's pictures. (On Odlum, see below and chapter 7.) Other film industry members included Walt Disney, Jack L. Warner, Paramount Pictures president Y. Frank Freeman, Twentieth Century-Fox cofounder William Goetz, former RKO president N. Peter Rathvon, and Ronald Reagan. Goldwyn pledged that the California group would contribute half of CPD's start-up costs during its first six months.[31]

The California committee included another more obscure figure: Sam Genis. Known to police as an associate of such infamous East Coast mobsters as Meyer Lansky, Frank Costello, Abner Zwillman, and Joseph Stacher, Genis had an arrest record (but no convictions) for embezzlement, mail and securities fraud, and passing bad checks. He was also owner of record of a Los Angeles real estate holding company called Store Properties, Inc. Despite its unassuming name, the company eventually acquired more than $200 million worth of property in California, Arizona, Florida, and other states. Genis's public partner was Chicago-born attorney Paul Ziffren. In the 1950s, Ziffren became California's delegate to the Democratic National Committee and one of the party's top fundraisers, until a 1960 article in *Reader's Digest* exposed him as a front man for the Chicago Outfit. The Kefauver Committee established as early as 1951 that a silent partner in Store Properties was Alex Greenberg, a former partner of Al Capone who became the "key to the [Outfit's] massive, hidden investments in, and control over, the Golden State," in the words of Gus Russo. Russo adds that Greenberg "may have learned the ropes from his brother-in-law, Izzy Zevlin," a mob investment whiz who served as personal secretary to IATSE's corrupt president, George Browne.[32] Genis's membership in the committee may have owed something to the fact that Goldwyn was a good friend of John Rosselli, the Chicago Outfit's ambassador to Hollywood.[33]

The FBI, Nixon, and Anti-Communism

Even before the Hollywood probe began, Nixon took part in HUAC's hearings on Communist influence in several affiliates of the militant Congress of Industrial Organization. The first of those hearings, in February 1947, concerned a strike by a United Auto Workers local in Wisconsin.[34] The investigation brought him to the attention of Wisconsin representative Charles Kersten, a fellow Republican, devout Catholic, and fierce critic of Communist tactics. Pleased to indoctrinate an eager new student of anti-Communism, Kersten introduced Nixon to his mentor, Father John Cronin of the National Catholic Welfare Conference. More than a moralist, Cronin was a dogged investigator with a secret pipeline to the FBI.

Cronin had begun probing the infiltration of the Baltimore dockworkers' unions by Communists in the early 1940s. He later recalled:

> About that time the FBI approached me to find out what I knew about this. . . . I got to know many agents intimately. Cardinal—then Archbishop—Mooney heard of my knowledge in this area, so he asked me to prepare a secret report on communism for the American bishops, and I was able to use classified material that had come my way. . . . By this time I was known, in Catholic circles, as something of an expert on communism. Charlie Kersten heard this, and came to see me. Later he brought Nixon, and I told them about certain Communists in atomic espionage rings and in the State Department.[35]

Appreciative of its strong anti-union message, the US Chamber of Commerce distributed four hundred thousand copies of Cronin's report on "Communist Infiltration in the United States" in 1946. The next year, the chamber distributed another pamphlet by Cronin, "Communists within the Government." The FBI, having fed Cronin much of his material, cited his screeds in its requests to Congress for funding to fight subversion.[36]

In addition to advising Nixon on Communist tactics, Cronin helped Nixon break through onto the national political stage with the Alger Hiss case. Hiss was a former State Department official—a US delegate to the Yalta conference in 1944, executive secretary to the Dumbarton Oaks conference the same year, and secretary-general of the United Nations Charter conference in 1945—accused in 1948 HUAC hearings of having secretly been a Communist in the 1930s. In 1950, a jury convicted him of perjury for testifying that he had never passed government documents to a spy for the Soviets. Nixon's theatrical performance in the hearings, followed by Hiss's conviction, rocketed the junior congressman into national prominence.

Nixon first heard of Hiss from Father Cronin in February 1947. Cronin leaked to him confidential FBI reports, based on wartime interviews with two confessed spies, which the Roosevelt administration had never acted on. Cronin recalled that a friendly FBI agent "would call me every day, and tell me what they had turned up, and I told Dick, who then knew just where to look for things, and what he would find."[37] Characteristically, Nixon later lied rather than reveal his secret relationship with Cronin and the FBI; in his political memoir *Six Crises*, Nixon wrote that Chambers's HUAC testimony in August 1948 "was the first time I had ever heard of either Alger or [his brother] Donald Hiss."[38] Nixon's deception reflected HUAC's official stance that the "success of the FBI" required it to "conceal its operations from the public view."[39]

The FBI's support for Cronin's campaign and for Nixon's grilling of Hiss were part of a secret, multiyear program launched by J. Edgar Hoover and senior bureau officials in February 1946 "to publicize the dangers of Communist subversion and to undermine traditional liberal tolerance of radical dissent," in the words of historian Kenneth O'Reilly. The operation was led by Assistant FBI Director Louis Nichols, who worked closely with Nixon on the Hiss case.[40] Well-placed leaks of bureau files allowed the FBI to manipulate public opinion without leaving any fingerprints. As Hoover explained, "Committees of Congress have served a very useful purpose in exposing these [subversive] activities which no Federal agency is in a position to do." During HUAC's 1947 investigation of Hollywood, Hoover ordered his agents to "extend *every* assistance to this Committee," with the proviso that their secret disclosures "not in any way embarrass the Bureau." O'Reilly observed, "With or without the FBI, the Cold War would have developed. Its domestic fallout, however, would have been far different if FBI officials had not worked to nurture an anticommunist consensus by underwriting . . . McCarthyites . . . and HUAC."[41]

HUAC provided the perfect meeting ground for Republican opponents of the Truman administration and the FBI's Communist hunters. HUAC's Chairman Thomas later admitted that he agreed "to set up the spy hearings" under pressure from the chairman of the Republican National Committee "in order to keep the heat on Truman" and help elect Thomas Dewey president in 1948.[42] Nixon was quick to see the political opportunities. "The record of the administration is completely vulnerable and should be attacked," he told Dewey's foreign policy adviser, John Foster Dulles, just a few weeks after the Hiss hearings began. Truman, he added, "should be charged with placing politics above national security."[43] HUAC's chief counsel called attention to the claim that Hiss "sat with Roosevelt at Yalta when Poland and the rest of Eastern Europe were abandoned by the West, and the Far East was laid open to Communist aggression."[44]

Nixon practiced such campaign themes in his ugly 1950 race for the Senate against liberal incumbent Helen Gahagan Douglas. "If [Douglas] had had her way, the Communist conspiracy in the United States would never have been exposed," Nixon charged.[45] The chief architect of Nixon's infamous "pink lady" campaign was his veteran political adviser, mob attorney Murray Chotiner.

McCarthy, the FBI, and the Mob

Nixon's labors with HUAC also provided an opening for more demagogic members of his party, most notably Senator McCarthy, to upend American politics with unfounded accusations of treason. "The full import of this tragedy may be greater than has even now been realized," remarked columnist Marquis Childs, no friend of Hiss, shortly before the 1950 election. "For it is against the background of the Hiss case that the evil of McCarthyism has been worked. From conspiracy to Communism to homosexuality, the cloud of suspicion has broadened and darkened."[46]

McCarthy's record of wheeling and dealing had done his reputation back home no good. By 1950, he was searching for an issue to polish his tarnished image ahead of the 1952 election. On January 7, 1950, McCarthy raised this problem while dining with Father Edmund Walsh, vice president of Georgetown University and dean of its Foreign Service school. Walsh, author of the fiery anti-Communist tract *Total Power* and a member of the Committee on the Present Danger, urged him to focus on the Truman administration's failure to confront the Red menace.[47]

McCarthy needed little persuasion. On February 9, 1950, only two weeks after the sensational conviction of Alger Hiss, the senator began testing his message with a speech in Wheeling, West Virginia. He told astonished members of the local Republican Women's Club that 205 "known" Communists were "still working and shaping the policy of the State Department."[48] As McCarthy soared to national prominence with his sensational charges, the FBI supplied grist for his fiery speeches. Ralph de Toledano, an avid champion of both Nixon and the FBI, wrote, "Hoover spent many hours with Joe McCarthy talking 'business'—lecturing him on Communist strategy and tactics, giving him leads and insights into the Communist apparatus in the United States, and pointing him in the direction of suspect individuals."[49]

De Toledano was a member of the small but influential American Jewish League Against Communism, which offered vital support to the Catholic senator from Wisconsin.[50] Its leaders included the right-wing Hearst columnist George Sokolsky, Schenley Industries CEO Lewis Rosenstiel, and, later, the scrappy New York lawyer Roy Cohn, who was infamous as chief counsel to Senator McCarthy's investigating committee.[51] John Rosselli's close friend Harry Cohn of Columbia Pictures was the first studio executive to join the organization.[52]

Some of the league's movers and shakers may have wrapped themselves in anti-Communism to avoid scrutiny of their own personal behavior. Rosenstiel, a former bootlegger turned liquor magnate, first ingratiated himself with Hoover in 1939 by arranging with underworld associates to hand over to the FBI New York labor racketeer and "Murder, Inc." boss Louis "Lepke" Buchalter. Years later, Rosenstiel kept in the director's good graces by purchasing and distributing to schools twenty-five thousand copies of Hoover's book, *Masters of Deceit*.[53] Rosenstiel also donated $1 million to the J. Edgar Hoover Foundation, incorporated in 1965 "to safeguard the heritage and freedoms of the United States of America . . . and to perpetuate the ideas and purposes to which the Honorable J. Edgar Hoover has dedicated his life."[54] In 1957, with recommendations from Roy Cohn and George Sokolsky, both of whom were on Rosenstiel's payroll, Hoover's assistant Louis B. Nichols joined Schenley as vice president to lobby for passage of a controversial tax law that saved the liquor company millions of dollars. As noted above, Nichols had been Nixon's key FBI contact during the Hiss investigation. He later became a member of Nixon's six-man senior advisory committee during the 1968 presidential campaign.[55]

With his FBI background, Nichols proved particularly helpful in disputing allegations that Rosenstiel led a secret life in the mob. In hearings before New York's Joint Legislative Committee on Crime in 1970, Rosenstiel's bitterly estranged fourth wife, Susan, linked her former husband to some of the biggest names in the underworld: Meyer Lansky, Frank Costello, and Frank Erickson of New York; Cleveland Syndicate bosses Moe Dalitz and Sam Tucker; and Angelo Bruno of Philadelphia. She recalled being welcomed in 1957 to a huge suite at Havana's Hotel Nacional with flowers and a personal card from Meyer and Jake Lansky. She testified that her husband discussed liquor sales with New Jersey mobster Joseph Zicarelli (chapter 4), who allegedly had a secret interest in Schenley's New Jersey warehouses. In the late 1950s, she said, Rosenstiel invited Lansky, Zicarelli, and New Jersey crime boss Gerardo Catena (chapter 6), to his cabana at the Fontainebleau Hotel in Miami Beach.[56]

Nichols went before the committee in 1971 to insist that his employer had been "unjustly maligned" by Susan Rosenstiel's "vituperation, falsehoods, half-truths and innuendoes." Nichols noted that his boss was never prosecuted, although he was indicted in 1929 for illegal liquor trading. The Schenley CEO, Nichols declared, "shunned any connection with the underworld like the plague," even though former bootleggers Joseph Linsey (Boston) and Joseph Fusco (Chicago), and convicted black marketer Robert Gould (Miami), were Schenley distributors and social friends of Rosenstiel. There are certainly reasonable grounds to question Susan Rosenstiel's credibility, but the committee's chair, New York State senator John Hughes, stated that her testimony had been "checked and the committee has every reason to believe she is telling the truth."[57]

Rosenstiel's lawyer Roy Cohn epitomized the marriage of anti-Communism and organized crime. As a young prosecutor, he won national fame for winning the conviction of Julius and Ethel Rosenberg as Soviet atomic spies. Senator McCarthy asked Cohn to become chief counsel to his investigations subcommittee, thus starting their notorious partnership.[58] Cohn in turn recruited another aide: David Schine, son of hotelier J. Myer Schine, a friend of both Nixon and Hoover. The elder Schine leased an illegal betting concession at his Roney Plaza hotel in Miami Beach first to prominent New York bookmaker and Lansky partner Frank Erickson, and then to a group of local Jewish criminals known as the S&G syndicate. As president and general manager of his father's hotels, David wrote and distributed to all their rooms a historically illiterate, six-page screed against Soviet Communism. After Schine joined McCarthy's team, Cohn pressured the US Army to exempt him from the draft, and then to grant him special privileges. The resulting scandal became such an embarrassment that McCarthy lost his political leverage to hold off a Senate resolution of censure.[59] Schine nonetheless remained on close personal terms with Hoover for many years.[60]

After Cohn was forced to resign from McCarthy's committee in 1954, he became chief counsel to American News Co., a mob-linked distributor of newspapers and magazines financed by William Molasky of St. Louis, who made a fortune supplying racing news to bookies before going to prison for tax fraud.[61] Later, when Cohn wasn't busy defending himself against federal indictments for fraud, bribery, and conspiracy, he represented the notorious New York gangsters Anthony "Fat Tony" Salerno and Carmine Galante, as well as casino developer Donald Trump. Cohn also represented Rosenstiel, but took advantage of the ailing millionaire to fraudulently alter his will.[62] In 1986, the appellate division of the New York State Supreme Court disbarred Cohn for "dishonesty, fraud, deceit, and misrepresentation." It termed Cohn's conduct toward Rosenstiel "highly unethical" and called his testimony "untruthful" and "misleading."[63] Cohn died two months later, facing a federal suit demanding more than $7 million in unpaid income taxes, interest, and penalties.[64]

The China Lobby

One of founders of the American Jewish League Against Communism, and a chief supporter of McCarthy, was New York textile importer Albert Kohlberg.[65] He and league cofounder George Sokolsky, the Hearst columnist, were also among the most visible members of the "China lobby." This informal collection of pundits, paid lobbyists, legislators, and Nationalist Chinese officials prevailed on Congress and the White House to grant extraordinary financial and political support to the Nationalist Chinese regime led by Generalissimo Chiang Kai-shek (Jiang Jieshi), first on China's mainland, and then on Taiwan (also known as Formosa). The China lobby later leveraged US power to prevent the United Nations from seating the People's Republic of China. Its cause won overwhelming support in Washington partly because it aligned so squarely with the nation's growing anti-Communism—but also, as we will see, because of deeply corrupt pressure campaigns. In May 1950, as its influence was still waxing, Washington columnist Marquis Childs wrote,

> No one who knows anything about the way things work here doubts that a powerful China lobby has brought extraordinary influence to bear on Congress and the Executive. It would be hard to find any parallel in diplomatic history for the agents and diplomatic representatives of a foreign power exerting such pressures—Nationalist China has used the techniques of direct intervention on a scale rarely, if ever, seen.[66]

The lobby began coalescing informally in the late 1930s when friends and associates of Chiang's cosmopolitan brother-in-law, banker T. V. Soong, started pressuring the Roosevelt administration to aid China in its life-and-death struggle against the invading Japanese army. Soong, who served as China's foreign minister and finance minister, cultivated friends like Sokolsky and President Roosevelt's White House assistant Lauchlin Currie to acquire almost miraculous intelligence and influence in Washington. Soong's wiliest American ally was Thomas Corcoran. The young, Harvard-trained lawyer made his first great mark in Washington during the New Deal by drafting legislation to establish the Securities and Exchange Commission. By 1937, "White House Tommy" was already reputed to be more powerful than most cabinet members, known as a man who could "get things done."[67] Corcoran and his future law partner William Youngman sat on the board of China Defense Supplies, which managed China's wartime purchases, funded with hundreds of millions of dollars of US aid. Corcoran and Youngman also helped Republican businessman William Pawley (who briefly headed Pan Am's China subsidiary) and US Air Force Maj. Gen. Claire Chennault recruit American pilots for the Flying Tigers to fight for Nationalist China. Some of these brave but unconventional American aviators supplemented their pay by smuggling opium, gold, sulfa drugs, prostitutes, gems, and other valuables, with Chennault's knowledge.[68] In return for his wartime services, Chinese officials rewarded him with a secret cash payment of $250,000.[69]

After World War II, under the new banner of anti-Communism, the rein-vigorated China lobby fought for renewed American aid to Nationalist China, this time against the Reds. Chennault became one of the regime's most tire-less advocates. In the late 1940s, Corcoran helped Chennault and his partner Whiting Willauer, the former executive secretary of China Defense Supplies, set up a cargo carrier called Civil Air Transport (CAT) to make "some real big money" by flying United Nations relief goods into China's inland cities.[70] Soon, however, their growing air fleet took on intelligence missions for the CIA and began evacuating beleaguered Nationalist troops in the face of advancing Com-munist armies.[71] An American diplomat reported hearing that Chennault's airline was also colluding with senior Chinese officials to smuggle commercial goods for profit, which he took as evidence that "under the guise of militant anti-Communism, lie the real motives of self-interest and self-enrichment."[72] In 1950, Corcoran and former Office of Strategic Services (OSS) chief Wil-liam Donovan masterminded Civil Air Transport's successful legal battle to win title to Pan Am's former Chinese air fleet, which the international carrier moved to Hong Kong just ahead of the Red Army.[73] Corcoran also handled negotiations that led to the secret sale of Civil Air Transport to the CIA. Kept busy by wars in Korea and Indochina, the airline became one of the CIA's big-gest "proprietary" (front) companies in Asia, in partnership with Nationalist China.[74] After General Chennault died in 1958, Corcoran became the intimate consort of his Chinese-born widow, Anna, a dynamic businesswoman and pro-digious Republican fundraiser who served as Nixon's secret emissary to South Vietnam's president Nguyen Van Thieu during the 1968 election campaign.[75]

Members of the US intelligence community also assisted Nationalist China through more questionable forms of domestic lobbying and propaganda, especially after the Republican sweep of the 1952 elections. Pro-Taiwan orga-nizations like the Committee to Defend America by Aiding Anti-Communist China and the Committee on National Affairs included among their offi-cers or directors several notable front men for CIA propaganda operations, including William Donovan; Jay Lovestone, a CIA-funded foreign labor orga-nizer; and Cord Meyer, who took charge of the agency's International Orga-nizations Division in 1954. The CIA also covertly funded anti-Communist organizations such as the Free Asia Committee and Aid Refugee Chinese Intellectuals, which reinforced the China lobby's messages.[76]

Some China lobbyists were just that—official, registered foreign lobby-ists on the payroll of Nationalist China. William Goodwin—described by reporter Benjamin Bradlee as having "a stormy background of Wall Street finance, [far-right] Christian Front activity, Tammany Hall politics, and big-time public relations"—received $25,000 a year plus expenses from Chiang's government. Goodwin boasted of entertaining a hundred congressmen a year to promote the Nationalist cause.[77] He also took credit for helping to inspire Senator McCarthy's crusade against the State Department for "losing" China to the Communists.[78]

Equally important was David Charnay's Allied Syndicates, a public relations firm retained by the Soong family's Bank of China in the summer of 1949 for $60,000 a year. A White House investigator learned that Charnay's key contact was Louis Kung, a nephew of Chiang and son of former finance minister H. H. Kung, one of the wealthiest Chinese living in the United States. He also learned that Charnay's employees wrote inflammatory attacks on the State Department's China policy for Sen. Styles Bridges, a New Hampshire Republican and chair of the powerful Appropriations Committee. The White House staffer concluded that "this Kung-Charnay-Styles Bridges axis is probably the backbone of the so-called China Lobby."[79]

Charnay exemplified the nonideological sleaziness of many Washington lobbyists. He got his start in public relations working for New York's Copacabana nightclub, flacking for Frank Costello, the powerful New York mobster and Tammany Hall backer. He also dabbled in the mob-infested world of boxing promotion. Charnay went on to represent Eversharp, owned by a leading financial supporter of ultra-right-wing causes, Patrick Frawley. Besides Senator Bridges, Charnay counted among his allies Truman's adviser Clark Clifford, who became counsel to the Allied Syndicates after he left the White House in January 1950. Charnay hired Truman's former assistant secretary of defense Paul Griffith as his firm's vice president. Former navy secretary John L. Sullivan became chairman of Allied Syndicates before joining a law firm retained by Charnay to advise the Bank of China.[80] In the mid-1950s Charnay represented Louis Wolfson (chapter 5), a controversial investor whose illegal campaign contributions to Florida's pro-gambling governor in 1948 were the subject of hearings by Senator Kefauver's crime committee in 1950. Charnay promoted Wolfson's attempts to take over retail giant Montgomery Ward, allegedly in partnership with syndicate investors from Las Vegas and Detroit. Charnay later advised Dave Beck's corrupt Teamsters union, whose relations with Richard Nixon are noted in chapter 8.[81]

Many other China lobbyists were partisan Republicans like Bridges who attacked the Truman administration for allowing the "fall of China." Commenting on their demagogic tactics, including demands to purge professional China experts from government, *Reporter* magazine called these advocates

the nearest thing to an effective Communist Party our country has ever had. There is no other outfit to which the China Lobby can be compared, with its hard core of fanatical, full-time operators, its underground, its legion of naïve, misled fellow travelers, its front organizations, and its foreign officials, in Washington with diplomatic immunity, who dutifully report to central headquarters.[82]

The "Gamblers' Senator" and the China Lobby

One of the more unlikely leaders of the drive for more aid to Nationalist China was Sen. Pat McCarran, D-Nev. He epitomized the close alliance between right-wing politicians and "patriotic" mobsters. Historians of the McCarthy era largely ignore the fact that as chairman of the Judiciary Committee, he earned a reputation as "the gamblers' senator."[83] McCarran arbitrated underworld disputes in Las Vegas. He interceded with Henry Grunewald's ally, Internal Revenue Bureau chief counsel Charles Oliphant, to drop tax charges against two prominent syndicate gamblers, Moe Sedway and Gus Greenbaum.[84] In 1946, FBI agents investigated his support for New York gangster and Lansky partner "Bugsy" Siegel, who was circumventing federal controls on scarce construction materials to build the opulent Flamingo hotel-casino on the Las Vegas Strip. In 1949, McCarran apparently intervened with Nevada state officials to award a casino license at the Desert Inn to former Midwest bootlegger and racketeer Moe Dalitz.[85] Over the next couple of years, the Judiciary Committee chairman did his best to block contempt citations against prominent racketeers who refused to testify before the Kefauver Committee's investigation into interstate crime; he also succeeded in derailing nearly all of its legislative recommendations. McCarran reputedly also made a deal with Democratic kingmaker Jacob Arvey, the political boss of Chicago and a power broker of the 1952 Democratic convention, to grease the way for investments by the Chicago Outfit in Las Vegas casinos.[86] Pat McCarran was surely the model for the corrupt Nevada senator Pat Geary depicted in the film *Godfather II*.[87]

McCarran was also a cranky but crafty and effective right-winger. He sponsored the McCarran Internal Security Act of 1950, which required all Communist and Communist-front organizations to register with the Justice Department (opening their members to prosecution under the Smith Act); created the Subversive Activities Control Board to investigate individuals suspected of radical activities; and gave the president the power to detain people deemed disloyal in times of emergency. Although nominally a Democrat, McCarran sought to discredit the Truman administration's policies on employee loyalty and China as enthusiastically as the most partisan Republicans. When Senator McCarthy ran into trouble for making the reckless and absurd charge that China expert Owen Lattimore was the Soviet Union's top espionage agent, McCarran launched his newly created Internal Security Subcommittee on a massive investigation of the Institute of Pacific Relations, a research and public affairs organization to which Lattimore belonged. With tortuous logic and minimal evidence, McCarran accused the respected organization of contributing to "the advance of the red hordes into the Far

East."[88] The FBI's Hoover was only too happy to support McCarren's political agenda despite the senator's shady dealings with organized crime figures; on the director's orders, the bureau passed secret information from its "loyalty" investigations to the Internal Security Subcommittee. McCarran's top aide, in turn, assured Hoover that his boss "would do just about anything the Director asked him to do."[89]

McCarran could always be counted on to favor more aid to Nationalist China. In February 1949, he introduced a bill to provide $1.5 billion in loans to Chiang's faltering government. A key provision suggested McCarran's deeper motive: The bill provided half a billion dollars to fund purchases of silver in the United States to prop up China's rapidly depreciating currency. As a representative of the nation's chief silver mining state, McCarran was delighted to support one of the few countries that had used silver as the standard for its currency.[90]

McCarran's little-noticed bill at first did not even make it onto a committee calendar for consideration. Before long, however, it triggered a frenzy of China lobby activity. The controversy began that April, when Secretary of State Dean Acheson wrote the chairman of the Senate Foreign Relations Committee to insist that generous loans and grants would not save China, given the failure of $2 billion in previous US aid to make any difference. Senator Bridges quickly accused Acheson of "sabotage" against Nationalist China and demanded a congressional investigation into Truman's failed China policy.[91] As chairman of the Appropriations Committee, Bridges was "about the most powerful member of the Senate, though also the most crooked" in the estimation of Drew Pearson.[92] As we have seen, he was also one of Capitol Hill's earliest and most strident China lobbyists.[93] Around his offices were often seen members of a Chinese "technical mission" sent to Washington in early 1948 by the Bank of China. In September 1948, Bridges approached former senator D. Worth Clark, a client of Henry Grunewald and a law partner of Thomas Corcoran, to lead a mission to report on China's financial, economic, and military conditions. Not surprisingly, Clark's report advocated providing an additional $125 million in aid to the regime.[94] To reward Bridges for his faithful services, a Nationalist agent allegedly delivered to him $500,000 in cash "for the campaign expenses of various Republican senators."[95] Bridges also made money on the side with Chinese partners in an illegal aviation gasoline deal.[96]

For politicians like Bridges, corruption was a way of life, not limited to a single cause. Like McCarran, Brewster, and Corcoran, Bridges was inevitably drawn to the ubiquitous influence peddler Henry Grunewald, who somehow found time to arrange the sale of one hundred fighter planes from North American Aviation to the Nationalist Chinese for a $75,000 fee.[97] On

September 29, 1949, Bridges rose in the Senate to propose a 40 percent salary increase for that "outstanding" public servant Charles Oliphant, chief counsel of the Bureau of Internal Revenue and a friend of Grunewald's. At about the same time, Grunewald called up another friend, Secretary of Defense Louis Johnson, to help persuade President Truman to back a raise for Oliphant. The sudden interest of Bridges and Grunewald in the size of Oliphant's salary came just as the Internal Revenue Bureau (IRB) was considering a major tax case against Hyman Harvey Klein, a wealthy Baltimore liquor dealer. Klein had parlayed a $4,000 investment into a $5 million profit between 1944 and 1947, by importing Canadian whiskey into the United States using Cuban dummy corporations to evade federal price regulations. Senator Bridges made numerous calls to the IRB to support Klein's case, while Grunewald lavished expensive gifts on Oliphant. A few months later, the IRB dropped its charges against Klein. After a change of administrations, however, Klein and two associates were convicted of income tax evasion and sentenced to long prison terms.[98]

Governed by no higher principles, McCarran, Bridges, and other opportunists weaponized the China issue, deriding the loyalty of Asia experts and senior administration officials. Calling the State Department's Far Eastern Affairs Division "definitely soft to Communist Russia," McCarran said it was "impossible to understand how our State Department can go all out for aid to Europe in its fight against Communism and at the same time vigorously oppose even the suggestion of any aid to fight the rising tide of Communism in Asia."[99] The debate unleashed by McCarran's aid bill was soon joined by General Chennault, who told a closed, but leaky, congressional panel that US inaction could allow all of Asia to go Communist, including Japan and the Philippines. Facing resistance from Secretary of State Acheson, however, Congress appropriated only $75 million in new aid for the Nationalists in the summer of 1949.[100]

Louis Johnson: The China Lobby's Inside Man

Most of Secretary Acheson's foes were Republicans on Capitol Hill. One, however, held a top post in the Truman administration: Secretary of Defense Louis Johnson. The imposing, bald-headed attorney first achieved national prominence in 1930 as national commander of the American Legion, itself a potent lobbying organization and a major anti-Communist force in the United States. From 1937 to 1940, he served as assistant secretary of war. Two years later, Leo Crowley, the head of the Alien Property Custodian—which administered enemy assets seized by the federal government during World

Wars I and II—appointed Johnson president of General Aniline and Film (GAF), a company associated with the notorious German chemical combine I. G. Farben. Johnson's biographer rightly called the job "a political plum and a financial windfall." In addition to his large salary, Johnson profited from the huge retainers earned by his law firm from work for GAF. Johnson maintained close relations with the Washington fixer Grunewald, an intimate of Crowley, in connection with this work. Through Crowley, Johnson also befriended Victor Emanuel, who controlled one of America's biggest wartime aircraft manufacturers, Convair. Before long, Emanuel invited Johnson to join Convair's board.[101]

Johnson cemented his power within the Democratic Party in 1948 by taking on the thankless job of chairing the party's finance committee, just two months before the November election. (Fellow China lobbyist William Pawley had been offered the job but turned it down.)[102] The party's coffers were empty. Truman's chances of beating Republican governor Thomas Dewey looked hopeless. But Johnson pulled off a miracle by raising almost $2 million to send Truman across the country by train on a 30,000-mile "whistlestop tour." Johnson took money from representatives of his law client Pan American Airways; Convair investor Floyd Odlum, who donated or raised $23,000; William Helis, the mob-connected oilman from New Orleans (chapter 2); and wealthy American Jews who secured Truman's support for the new state of Israel.[103] Right after the election, Johnson collected a large contribution from his friend and former client, Schenley's Lewis Rosenstiel.[104] Two scandalmongering but well-informed reporters further asserted that he raised funds from the Chicago Outfit through Cook County Democratic Party boss Jacob Arvey, whose machine helped put Truman just barely over the top in Illinois.[105]

President Truman repaid his huge political debt by appointing Johnson to run the Pentagon in March 1949.[106] Soon Defense Secretary Johnson approved a big air force award to Convair for the B-36 bomber, despite its outmoded design and mediocre performance. His budget cuts to the navy and marines prompted a "revolt of the admirals," who spread word that the B-36 award reflected Johnson's close personal and business ties to Convair owners Victor Emanuel and Floyd Odlum. However, an investigation by the House Armed Services Committee cleared Johnson of wrongdoing.[107]

Johnson was also an outspoken advocate for unstinting assistance to Nationalist China. *Time* called him "the Administration's most severe critic of State's lethargy in China." In June 1949, Johnson sent a tough memo to colleagues on the National Security Council, calling for a more "comprehensive plan" to contain Communism in Asia.[108] In later testimony before Congress, Johnson recalled that "the Defense Department battled day in and day out to keep Formosa out of enemy hands." It waged that battle particularly with Chiang's critics in Dean Acheson's State Department. Johnson's policy war with Acheson grew so vicious that "the feud was threatening all the nation's international policies," *Time* reported. Truman finally fired Johnson when he was "reported to be hobnobbing with Maine's Republican Senator Owen Brewster and feeding him with ammunition to be fired against Acheson."[109]

Scholars have since determined that Johnson was running a back channel to the Nationalist Chinese, passing documents and reporting to their ambassador, Wellington Koo, on top secret National Security Council debates.[110] Johnson's biographers reported,

> Koo's papers reveal that Tommy Corcoran, former Roosevelt aide and Washington lobbyist who was representing the military procurement arm of the Nationalist government, arranged a private dinner between Madame Chiang and Secretary Johnson which took place on October 22, 1949, at Madame's residence in Riverdale, New York. Through conversations at this dinner and messages relayed . . . , there is little doubt that Johnson provided assurances to the Nationalist government that he would fight to change Acheson's opposition to military assistance for Formosa.[111]

Why was Johnson such a die-hard supporter of Chiang? His convictions may have been sincere, but Drew Pearson reported in 1951 that senior Nationalist Chinese financier H. H. Kung had influenced Johnson by hiring him as his private attorney. Pearson also recorded in his diary that Johnson once offered him $10,000 to make favorable reference to Kung in his nationally syndicated column.[112] Johnson angrily denied working for Kung, but a Truman administration official noted in 1951, after the former defense secretary had stepped down, that

> Johnson has informed me that he was the personal attorney of Dr. H. H. Kung, brother-in-law of Chiang Kai-Shek. He has been most active in working for Kung, and . . . urged the State Department to transfer Myron Cowen from Australia to be Ambassador to the Philippines. Cowen is a law associate of Johnson who has helped in regard to Kung. Many of Kung's and the Soong's holdings are in the Philippines.[113]

Johnson was also closely attuned to the interests of Pan American Airways, which lost one of its biggest Pacific markets to the Chinese Communists.[114] His biographers write, "It was common knowledge that Pan Am had been paying huge fees to [Johnson's law firm] Steptoe & Johnson for years for legal and lobbying work aimed at . . . having Pan Am designated as the 'chosen instrument' of U.S. policy on foreign aviation."[115] Johnson picked an assistant vice president of Pan Am to serve as his deputy fundraiser during Truman's

1948 campaign.[116] As secretary of defense, Johnson continued to promote the airline's financial interests.[117] Upon leaving the government in September 1950, Johnson became counsel to Pan Am.[118] Former Senate aide Bobby Baker recalled that Johnson "gave cash and envelopes to quite a few people" in his role as a corporate attorney and lobbyist.[119]

Whatever his motives, Johnson helped deliver a subtle but key change of administration policy toward Nationalist China. His biographers wrote:

> Johnson acted on his strongly held views about the need to defend Formosa. As the first step in his attempt to change U.S. policy toward Formosa, Johnson, adopting an idea advocated by Tommy Corcoran, urged the [Joint Chiefs of Staff] in September 1949 to send a military mission to Formosa to determine the true situation "because our information and the State Department information did not agree." . . . The Joint Chiefs were still in the process of finalizing their latest recommendations when the Nationalist government and its exhausted army fled to Formosa on December 10. . . .
>
> Spurred on by events in China and Johnson's admonitions, the Joint Chiefs recommended . . . sending a military mission to determine what assistance would be required to defend Formosa against an attack. Armed with the backing of the Joint Chiefs, Johnson began actively lobbying for the military mission. However, Acheson bitterly resisted his proposal on the grounds that such action would constitute a reversal of the U.S. policy of disengagement from Chiang and that even if the aid were sent it offered virtually no chance of saving the regime.
>
> As Acheson pushed for maintenance of the current policy, Johnson pushed even harder for its reversal and he went to the president on at least three occasions in December to urge that the mission to Formosa be sent. . . . All his appeals were for naught, however, as Truman told him that he would not support military assistance to help defend Formosa. . . . The hands-off policy lasted until June 25, 1950, when the North Koreans attacked South Korea.[120]

The State Department's policy was actually more nuanced than this account suggests. Acheson opposed direct US military intervention on Chiang's behalf, but the State Department did not abandon Taiwan. It quietly opened an embassy in Taipei, headed by a chargé d'affaires.[121] It also approved the export of three hundred tanks to Taiwan under the 1948 China Aid Act and agreed to permit unofficial aid missions.[122] Secretary Acheson told reporters on January 6, 1950, that the administration had no objection to the Nationalist government hiring retired or reserve US officers as advisers.[123]

Seizing that opening, and drawing on a secret fund in the United States, Nationalist Chinese officials offered to pay US military officers to organize a volunteer foreign legion to defend Taiwan, much as they had employed Chennault to round up fliers to combat Japan. They succeeded in hiring retired admiral Charles M. Cooke, who had commanded the US Seventh

Fleet until February 1948. In April 1950, just two months before the onset
of the Korea War, Cooke led a group of retired American military officers
to Taiwan to provide technical and military assistance—and to raise awareness of Nationalist China's plight. "The primary purpose of this unit, apart
from some financial transactions conducted for the KMT [Kuomintang, the
Nationalist Chinese ruling party] which were alleged to have been unortho-
dox, apparently was to use its former U.S. Armed Forces knowledge and connections to press the Truman Administration to increase aid to China," wrote
historian Nancy Tucker.[124]

Cooke's mission remains shrouded in a good deal of mystery. As Communist forces swept across mainland China, he became convinced that the
United States must preserve a KMT military bastion in order to rally large
communities of ethnic Chinese in Southeast Asia and prevent Japan from
entering the "Communist orbit." To direct US aid efficiently, he told the
Detroit Economic Club in September 1949, "We must do it primarily with
advisors."[125] After consulting with Madame Chiang Kai-shek in New York,
Cooke coordinated his advisory efforts with Chennault's former partner in
the Flying Tigers, ultra-conservative businessman and ambassador William
D. Pawley.[126] On November 7, 1949, Pawley requested State Department
approval for a small number of American ex-military officers to help save the
Chinese Nationalists. Ambassador Koo sent a virtually identical request to
Secretary Acheson in late December.[127] Acheson did not object. In the mean-
time, friends of the Nationalist regime leaked to Cooke secret US intelligence
reports painting a dire picture of Chiang's chances of survival. Determined to
see for himself, Cooke arranged for William Randolph Hearst's International
News Service to send him to Taiwan in early February as an accredited journalist. Soon, along with General Chennault, he began privately lobbying US
intelligence officials and members of Congress to support a vast program of
aid to Chiang's forces. He also pressed the office of the Chief of Naval Operations to send surplus US naval vessels to the island.[128]

By March 1950, Cooke had recruited another retired admiral and three
retired marine generals to join his band of more than two dozen advisers.
They worked under the auspices of a small US military contractor called
Commerce International Corp. Its Delaware subsidiary, Commerce International (China), or CIC, had sold surplus US tanks and obsolete British
arms to the Nationalists in late 1948.[129] With State Department approval, the
company negotiated a $750,000 contract to provide technical and military
assistance to Chiang's forces.[130] A senior CIC official assured Chiang Kai-shek
that the company was "making strong efforts to influence more US senators
to support U.S. military aid to your government" and had set up a "special
fund" to that end.[131] One Chinese historian credits Cooke's "covert military

training and reform projects" with playing "a crucial role in strengthening the tottering Nationalist government in Taiwan before the tide turned in Washington" with the outbreak of the Korean War.[132]

The entire mission eventually collapsed in scandal. In 1951, two dismissed Chinese Nationalist procurement officers claimed that CIC president Satiris Galahad Fassoulis, a former American pilot in China, had tried to defraud their government by offering bribes of more than $150,000 to sell twenty-five surplus P-51 fighter planes. Most of the planes were either junk or nonexistent. Further revelations implicated the company in phony sales of millions of gallons of aviation gasoline, smuggling, bribery, forgery, and other crimes. The activities of CIC drew investigations by the FBI, army, air force, and navy into allegations of influence peddling, graft, and the diversion of US aid funds, but political pressure apparently blocked the probe. A *New York Times* reporter called details of the story "so weird, intricate, and contradictory that they were confounding all factions that have taken part in the bitter post-war controversy in Washington over support for the Chiang regime."[133]

The twenty-eight-year-old Fassoulis went on to a long and distinguished career as a swindler. In 1955, FBI agents arrested him for providing counterfeit AT&T bonds, possibly from underworld sources, as collateral to an Ohio bank for a $350,000 loan.[134] In 1959, the Securities and Exchange Commission halted trading in shares of Bon Ami Company, which had been controlled by Fassoulis and two other notorious swindlers.[135] In 1970, he was convicted of defrauding banks in six states of $713,000 using phony loan collateral; a lawyer for other defendants in that case called Fassoulis "a very undesirable and greasy character with a long record as a con man."[136] In 1971, Fassoulis was named in Senate testimony as a major dealer in stolen securities with organized crime figures.[137]

Allegations of Bribery

As we have seen, the Nationalist Chinese had full faith in the power of money to help forge an effective political lobby. Typically, the Bank of China disbursed funds to the Chinese embassy in Washington, which then doled out cash to friendly propaganda organs (such as the KMT press in America), public relations agencies, law firms, lobbyists, and outright bribes. "President Chiang Kai-shek probably sent more cash to senators than anybody in history," remarked former Senate aide Robert "Bobby" Baker. "It's just unbelievable."[138]

An investigation sponsored by *Reporter* magazine turned up evidence—too explosive and unconfirmed to publish—that "the Nationalist government pumped more than $2,000,000 into the Republican campaign in 1948."[139] In 1949, Rep. Mike Mansfield, a Montana Democrat and future Senate majority leader, demanded an official probe into whether some US aid "illicitly diverted to private use . . . is actually being used to promote new legislation for aid to China by which more money would be made available." He also wanted to know "whether American money provided to help China, but siphoned off for private use, is being used to finance attacks on our Secretary of State and other officials charged with conducting our relations with China." A timely dispensation of $800,000 from Nationalist Chinese officials to their New York office financed a successful campaign to squelch that proposed investigation.[140]

Mansfield had good reason to worry about the illegal diversion of US aid. From 1945 to 1949, Chiang's regime received about $2.8 billion in foreign and military aid, much of which was never accounted for. Of "special interest" to US officials was $500 million granted to China to stabilize its currency, including $200 million in gold. "Some members of Congress and some Government officials estimate that as much as the full amount of this credit has found its way back into this country into the private accounts of wealthy Chinese, former officials as well as private citizens," the *New York Times* reported.[141] Some unknown fraction of that aid was also used to line the pockets of Nationalist China's supporters in the United States, who lobbied for yet more aid.

One such supporter was Richard Nixon. As a congressman, Nixon voted to kill an administration-backed military and economic foreign aid program until it was amended to include funds for Taiwan. His loyalty to the Nationalist cause was well rewarded. Drew Pearson found a witness who saw Chiang Kai-shek's nephew Louis Kung meeting with Nixon at the Ambassador Hotel in Los Angeles in the fall of 1950 and contributing large sums to Nixon's campaign from his "bankroll of $100 bills." Days after that meeting, Nixon went on statewide radio to condemn the Truman administration for its "failure to aid free China." Nixon won his 1950 race for Senate, according to one biographer, "by making the Administration's failures in Asia his major issue."[142] Nixon was introduced to his future running mate General Eisenhower in 1951 by China lobbyist Alfred Kohlberg.[143]

China lobby paymaster Louis Kung drew operational funds from a bank in Tangier via Irving Trust Co., a bank prominently involved in illicit trafficking in Indochinese piasters with Chinese and French Corsican racketeers. He enjoyed diplomatic status, so he could pass through customs without a check.[144] He was also the largest shareholder in Yangtze Trading, incorporated in 1943 by Louis Johnson's law firm to serve as a front for the financial operations of Chiang's brothers-in-law, T. V. Soong and H. H.

Kung. Johnson's law firm owned roughly a fifth of its stock and several of its partners served as executives or board members of the trading company. In 1951 the Department of Commerce imposed stiff sanctions on Yangtze Trading and three of Johnson's law partners for illegally selling scarce tin to the Chinese Communists.[145]

Another suspected source of funding for the China lobby was a windfall profit of $30 million earned by Chinese officials who cornered the US market for soybeans shortly before the start of the Korean War. The fighting cut off the supply of soybeans from China, one of the world's largest producers. Prices of the legume on the Chicago Board of Trade soared nearly 50 percent.[146] "The excessive interest of the Chinese . . . aroused official suspicions here that they had advance knowledge of a war that caught this country wholly unprepared," the *New York Times* reported.[147] One of the speculators—who bought half a million bushels of soybeans—was T. V. Soong's brother, T. L. Soong, whose son Eugene was manager of Yangtze Trading Corp.[148] Also notably active in speculative but profitable trading in soybeans, with help from Louis Kung, was Wisconsin senator Joseph McCarthy.[149]

Deeply disturbed by the specter of political corruption undermining his foreign policy, President Truman ordered an extraordinary secret investigation of the China lobby by the departments of Commerce, Justice, State, and Treasury, as well as the CIA. On June 11, 1951, the president wrote the commissioner of Internal Revenue, "I am very much perturbed at the operations of the Lobbies here in Washington, particularly the China Lobby and the Real Estate Lobby. I want a complete investigation made of the operations of the men who run these Lobbies, particularly as it affects their use of money without reporting it on their income tax returns." Truman sent similar notes to several cabinet members.[150]

A review of executive branch files by White House investigators turned up numerous intriguing leads, but no smoking guns. The CIA reported, for example, that in January 1949 "Chiang Kai Shek withdrew approximately 40 million dollars from the Bank of China for purposes of propaganda work and bribery in the U.S." The agency declined to offer further details about Chinese fund transfers, however, "for fear of compromising valuable intelligence sources."[151]

The White House official assigned to coordinate this broad review of executive branch files reached cautious but disturbing conclusions:

1. It is apparent that a substantial amount of money, largely from unascertained sources, has been devoted in this country to a wide-spread publicity and propaganda campaign on behalf of Chiang Kai-shek and the Nationalist Government.

2. It is also apparent that there is a very close connection between many of the people prominently associated with this propaganda campaign and certain American politicians and public figures who are most active in the support of the Nationalist Government of China.

3. There are indications that this close relationship is not strictly limited to philosophic agreement. . . . It is apparent that some political influence is sought through the employment of prominent attorneys in Washington and New York by Nationalist Chinese agencies and affiliated organizations. There are some *indications* but no clear proof that direct financial transactions have taken place, outside the relationship of lawyer and client, between Chinese Nationalist sympathizers and officials and American political personalities.

4. From the information made available to us out of the files of the Executive agency, we do not have satisfactory legal evidence sufficient to substantiate the details concerning any such financial transactions.

5. There is available evidence of large-scale corruption and profiteering on the part of certain officials of the Chinese Nationalist Government during and immediately following the end of the war. . . . There seems to be no question but that it would be possible to establish the identity of the Chinese officials involved and that it would probably be possible, upon thorough investigation, to trace the transfer of funds from China and Formosa to the United States into accounts controlled by Chinese officials now located both in Formosa and in this country.

. . .

7. Since the passing of money, if any, between Chinese persons and American politicians has been skillfully conducted in very devious manners, it is felt that such transactions cannot be successfully exposed without a more comple[te] investigation by skilled investigators and even then probably could not be adequately revealed unless credible informers can be found.[152]

Follow the Money: Drugs and Organized Crime

The White House failed to consult the files of the Federal Bureau of Narcotics for its investigation of "unascertained sources" of China lobby funds. In 1960, political scientist Ross Koen declared, "There is . . . considerable evidence that a number of [Nationalist] Chinese officials engaged in the illegal smuggling of narcotics into the United States with the full knowledge and connivance of the Nationalist Chinese Government. The evidence indicates that several prominent Americans have participated in and profited from these transactions. It indicates further that the narcotics business has been an important factor in the activities and permutations of the China Lobby."[153]

There are good reasons to believe his claim. Ever since the late 1920s, Chiang, his finance minister T. V. Soong, and the KMT had relied on funds from the government's sale of opium, and on political alliances with drug-smuggling gangs, to consolidate power in China. Evidence strongly suggests that they even used drug revenues from Chinese American gangs to purchase US aircraft for China's fledgling air force in the 1930s. In World War II, with US knowledge and connivance, Chiang's feared secret police chief Tai Li financed his far-flung operations with revenue from opium sales. According to a former French intelligence officer with extensive experience in the Far East, Tai Li's chief agent in China's Washington embassy "contributed to the creation of what has since been called 'the China Lobby.'"[154] US officials reported that another major beneficiary of China's wartime narcotics trade was Vice Premier H. H. Kung, Chiang's brother-in-law and a linchpin of the China lobby.[155]

After the Communist victory in mainland China, KMT troops fled not only to Taiwan, but also to Burma. Thousands of Nationalist Chinese soldiers settled down in the hills of northern Burma to cultivate poppies and traffic opium while ostensibly awaiting orders to liberate Red China. Their smuggling was fully sanctioned by the government in Taiwan, which sent supplies and directed their operations through its military attaché in Bangkok. In the mid-1950s, a Bangkok-based official of the Soong family's Bank of Canton was identified by the Federal Bureau of Narcotics for his role in a major international heroin-smuggling ring. A senior US narcotics official also learned that the "top KMT agent" in Bangkok "finances all of her intelligence operations with opium." That agent's sister married a senior aide to a leader of Thailand's ruling military junta, Gen. Phao Sriyanonda. General Phao, widely known as "Mr. Opium," headed Thailand's heavily armed national police force. His forces guarded enormous caravans of opium brought south by KMT soldiers from tribal regions in Burma for export through Bangkok. Until 1957, when he was ousted in a military coup, Phao was indisputably one of the world's biggest narcotics traffickers.[156] His banker was an ethnic Chinese tycoon who established a Chinese-language newspaper in Bangkok to promote closer ties with the KMT.[157]

Washington was thoroughly implicated in the KMT's activities. The Truman administration tasked the CIA with bolstering anti-Communist military forces on China's border and winning allies among Southeast Asia's ethnic Chinese communities. Civil Air Transport, operated for the CIA by Chennault with financing from Chiang's government, flew arms and other supplies to the KMT's opium-smuggling forces in Burma. The CIA also created a front company in Bangkok, called Sea Supply, to provide arms to the KMT and General Phao's Border Patrol Police. An American diplomat in Bangkok actually told a British reporter in 1952, "It cannot be denied that we are in the opium trade."[158] Years later, historian Alfred McCoy observed,

> CIA support for Phao and the KMT seems to have sparked . . . a "takeoff" in the Burma-Thailand opium trade during the 1950s: modern aircraft replaced mules, naval vessels replaced sampans, and well-trained military organizations expropriated the traffic from bands of illiterate mountain traders.
>
> Never before had [Burma's] Shan States encountered smugglers with the discipline, technology, and ruthlessness of the KMT. Under General Phao's leadership Thailand had changed from an opium-consuming nation to the world's most important opium distribution center.[159]

The tens of millions of dollars in aid provided by the CIA's covert aid program also had an enormous impact on the politics of the region. It turned Phao "into the most powerful man in the country," states Bertil Lintner in his history of Burma's opium-financed insurgencies.[160] By the mid-1950s, confirms historian Daniel Fineman, "CIA arms and training . . . allowed him to monopolize the opium trade from the Thai end," which in turn "financed many of Phao's political activities."[161] Taking advantage of his lavishly funded military police force, Phao cemented his position as Thailand's most ruthless strongman in 1951. Later, US Ambassador to Bangkok William Donovan—the former head of OSS and a resourceful ally of the CIA—lauded Thailand under Phao's rule as "the free world's strongest bastion in Southeast Asia." U.S. Army Secretary Robert Stevens recognized the general's "exceptionally meritorious service" with the Legion of Merit in 1954.[162] Members of the US embassy in Bangkok were less sanguine, viewing Phao's blatant corruption as "a threat to the internal political and economic security of the country."[163]

Back in the United States, Mr. Opium had important allies as well. One was the superbly well-connected Thomas Corcoran, whose Washington law firm lobbied on behalf of Phao's regime as well as Taiwan. In the early 1950s, Corcoran used his influence with the Thai general to try to win a multibillion-dollar highway contract for Brown & Root, a Texas construction company whose huge cash contributions fueled the political career of Corcoran's protégé Lyndon Johnson. (The road-building project fell through, but Brown and Root returned in 1958 to build Thailand's tallest dam.)[164]

One of Corcoran's partners on the highway deal was the ambitious and worldly Miami attorney Paul Helliwell. After graduating from University of Miami's law school, Helliwell served during the early years of World War II in army intelligence in the Middle East. He then transferred to the China theater, where he headed all strategic intelligence for the Office of Strategic Services. There he learned to appreciate the value of narcotics as a means of exchange. Running guerrilla operations against Japan in China and Southeast Asia, he sometimes paid friendly guerrilla forces with bars of opium; he also liaised with the head of Chiang's secret police, Tai Li, who made no secret of funding his operations through narcotics trafficking. After the war, Helliwell returned to South Florida, where he engaged in law, banking, real estate, and statewide Republican politics. He and his wartime colleagues also kept a hidden hand in intelligence matters, focused on fighting Communism in the Far East. In 1949, Helliwell and Corcoran introduced Chennault to CIA officials who agreed to take CAT covertly under the government's wings. In 1950 he incorporated Sea Supply, the CIA proprietary that aided General Phao's police and the KMT in Burma. By 1951, he had become Thailand's consul in Miami.[165]

In 1954 and 1955, Helliwell joined his old OSS boss Donovan, who had just stepped down as ambassador to Thailand, to lobby Congress for more US aid to Phao's regime in the wake of France's defeat in Indochina. (Donovan was reportedly paid $100,000, no small sum.) Their influence campaign was capped with a visit to Washington in late 1954 by the brutal but persuasive General Phao himself. The Thai lobby's efforts paid off with administration promises of an additional $28 million in economic and military aid in December 1954, followed by another $12.2 million in July 1955.[166] Peter Dale Scott notes that in 1955 and 1956, Helliwell's consular office in Miami "passed over $30,000 to its registered foreign lobbyist in Washington, Tommy Corcoran's law partner James Rowe," funds that may well have originated from opium sales.[167]

In 1957, a rival general seized power, forcing General Phao to flee to Switzerland. Washington shifted its loyalties to his successor, but Helliwell (and apparently Corcoran) remained loyal to their patron. Helliwell traveled to Switzerland to confer with Phao, who was scheming to retake power. In a letter to Corcoran, Helliwell complained that the "Boys in Blue"—the CIA—were not paying sufficient attention to Thailand's instability or Phao's political aspirations. The Miami attorney confided that if and when Phao did return, "I am confident we have the inside track which, apart from questions of personal economics and business opportunities, could and should be of value both to the boys in blue and [Civil Air Transport] should they want to utilize it."[168] Helliwell's bet on Phao never did pay off. The Miami attorney resurfaced in the 1960s and 1970s as one of the founders of Castle Bank and Trust, a Bahamian bank that secretly handled money for the CIA, wealthy ex-mobsters, and American business moguls. (See "Nixon's Caribbean Milieu" online at rowman.com.)

Impact of the China Lobby

The China lobby was more than a historical curiosity. The Committee of One Million Against the Admission of Communist China to the United Nations, formed in 1953, helped block official US recognition of the most populous nation on earth until 1979. The lobby's intimidation tactics decimated the ranks of independent Asia experts in government during the McCarthy era.[169] Historian Ellen Schrecker observed,

> The purges had so thoroughly weeded out the government's China hands that by the mid-fifties no one who knew anything about that part of the world remained in the State Department's Far Eastern division. As a result, a combination of ignorance, fear, and their own conservatism led American policymakers to embrace a hard-line, Manichaean view of East Asia that bore little relation to what was happening there. Federal officials were afraid to take any initiative that might let congressional right-wingers accuse them of condoning the communist regime. . . . There was no trade, no diplomatic contact, and so much willful blindness about the regime that for years the CIA hesitated to report on the existence of the Sino-Soviet dispute.[170]

China lobbyists also helped create the political infrastructure for many other right-wing lobbies. Among the leading advocates of postwar support for the Spanish dictatorship of General Franco, for example, were the now-familiar Senators Owen Brewster, Styles Bridges, and Pat McCarran, as well as influence peddlers Thomas Corcoran and William Pawley. Together, with the help of a free-spending Washington lobbyist for Madrid, they overcame President Truman's loathing of Franco and unlocked $1.7 billion in US aid to Spain from 1950 to 1962.[171] Corcoran and Pawley were also key movers and shakers behind the overthrow of Guatemala's democratic government by a CIA-backed military coup in 1954. Corcoran was a highly paid lawyer and political strategist for United Fruit Co., the largest foreign investor in Guatemala and a fierce critic of the government's labor and land reforms. Joining in this covert action was Ambassador to Honduras Whiting Willauer, Corcoran's friend and Chennault's former partner in Civil Air Transport, which supplied pilots for the operation.[172] In the mid-1950s, key China lobbyists also organized the American Friends of Vietnam, which promoted South Vietnam's anti-Communist leader Ngo Dinh Diem. The founder of the organization employed Marvin Liebman, who ran the Committee of One Million Against the Admission of Communist China to the United Nations for nearly sixteen years. Among his many conservative causes, Liebman assumed leadership of the American Jewish League Against Communism at the request of Roy Cohn.[173]

The direct impact of the so-called Vietnam lobby paled in comparison to the indirect impact of the China lobby on decision makers who launched the United States on its disastrous war in Vietnam. The legacy of McCarthyism conditioned a generation of American politicians to fear appearing soft on Communism, no matter how irrational the results. As David Halberstam remarked, "The Democrats, in the wake of the relentless sustained attacks on Truman and Acheson over their policies in Asia, came to believe that they had lost the White House when they lost China. . . . The fear generated in those days lasted a long time, and Vietnam was to be something of an instant replay after China."[174]

For no president was that more true than Lyndon Johnson. He knew full well that Vietnam was a hopeless cause and a likely quagmire. As he told his national security adviser in 1964, "it looks like to me that we're getting into another Korea. It just worries the hell out of me. I don't see what we can ever hope to get out of there with once we're committed. . . . I don't think it's worth fighting for and I don't think we can get out. And it's just the biggest damn mess that I ever saw."[175] But he had also vowed just two days after taking office, "I am not going to be the president who saw Southeast Asia go the way China went." In February 1964, he confided to publisher John Knight that if he pulled US forces out of Vietnam, then "God Almighty, what they said about us leaving China would just be warming up compared to what they'd say now." Looking back several years later, Johnson confirmed the power of his conviction:

> I knew Harry Truman and Dean Acheson had lost their effectiveness from the day that the Communists took over in China. I believed that the loss of China had played a large role in the rise of Joe McCarthy. And I knew that all these problems, taken together, were chickenshit compared with what might happen if we lost Vietnam.[176]

The most demagogic anti-Communists during the early Cold War—men such as Bridges, Brewster, Chennault, Cohn, McCarran, McCarthy, Nixon, and Pawley—had much in common besides ideology: connections with the Catholic and Jewish Right; the FBI; the China lobby and other pressure groups; and organized crime. Their zealotry went hand in hand with organized corruption in Washington. Right-wingers, syndicate criminals, lobbyists, and Hoover's FBI found common ground in their shared opportunism, hostility to political reform, and cynical attraction to power. Through their secretive promotion of private interests at the expense of open democratic processes, they created fertile ground for the growth of organized crime in America into the 1970s.

The failure of many journalists and scholars to grapple with this deep political history has had lasting consequences. "In the 1950s the widening scandals of the China Lobby and its links to organized crime were contained and focused on a single scapegoat—the late Senator Joe McCarthy," remarked Peter Dale Scott. "[T]his continuous process of catharsis through scapegoating has led . . . to national schizophrenia. The American people are unable to understand their own history . . . and this lack of national self-knowledge has seriously aggravated the corruption at the center and the inability of democratic controls to restrain it."[177]

The next chapter examines yet another foreign source of corrupting influence—the Dominican sugar lobby—and the American mobsters who served its master, Generalissimo Rafael Trujillo.

Part II

FROM IKE TO LBJ

4

The Dominican Connection

Dictators, Mobsters, and Caribbean Intrigues

U S CRIMINALS BEGAN TARGETING Caribbean nations for exploitation as early as the mid-nineteenth century. As New York and Boston investors plowed money into the region to develop sugarcane and fruit plantations, US organized crime interests followed closely behind. In Guatemala and Honduras, originally through control of the New Orleans docks, they established ties to the big banana companies, the drug trade, and gambling.[1] In Mexico, they established footholds through gambling and narcotics, particularly in the 1940s.[2] In Cuba, under the protection of Gen. Fulgencio Batista, North American mobsters such as Meyer Lansky and Santo Trafficante grew rich from casino gambling, luxury hotels, and nightclubs until Fidel Castro booted them out of the country.[3] These criminal activities long predated the surge of interest in "transnational crime" that began in the 1990s as globalization unleashed vast flows of criminal funds and personnel across national borders.[4]

This history also demonstrates how popular depictions of global criminals preying on victim states and peoples ignore the reciprocity between state institutions, public officials, and foreign criminals. North American mobsters who delivered suitcases of cash to President Batista in return for gambling licenses were simply following a lesson they had learned at home: Smart criminals buy protection from politicians and law enforcement to grow their business and undercut their competition. But relations between states and foreign criminals sometimes take darker forms than mere corruption. For example, intelligence agencies often recruit such criminals for their expertise in the ways of violence, bribery, and seduction; their savviness about the workings of local institutions; and their deniability if caught. Thus, the CIA enlisted the Corsican Mafia to break the hold of Communist unions on the Marseilles docks after World War II.[5] It also armed opium traffickers in Southeast Asia and Afghanistan over several decades to battle Communist armies. The CIA indirectly fostered Latin drug "cartels" as a consequence of supporting the Nicaraguan Contras in the 1980s.[6] Foreign governments have used similar tactics on US soil. In 1976, the Chilean military junta enlisted a gang of drug-trafficking neofascists to carry out the sensational car bombing of a leading political exile in Washington, D.C. In 1984, Taiwan's military intelligence service sent members of the United Bamboo Gang, a leading triad organization, to murder a Chinese American journalist in San Francisco.[7] This chapter will examine similar cases involving Dominican Republic dictator Rafael Trujillo and the US mob.

Over his thirty-one-year reign, the notoriously cruel Trujillo demonstrated how a poor and weak client, with enough savvy and determination, can manipulate a much more powerful patron. By systematically corrupting US politicians and media with money and sex, Trujillo gained a cadre of loyal followers in Congress who championed his interests and helped build his fortune, even in the face of White House opposition. Nationally syndicated columnist Jack Anderson remarked with some amazement in 1960, "Such things as free junkets and gold medals apparently can override American foreign policy. For President Eisenhower is powerless to carry out the agreement of the Western Hemisphere foreign ministers to apply economic sanctions against the bloodiest dictator in the Caribbean."[8]

Trujillo also made tactical alliances with powerful US mobsters—experts in gambling, money laundering, and arms trafficking—to extend his power in the United States and other neighbors such as Cuba. US organized crime figures were drawn to the Dominican Republic as a playground that could host the kind of lucrative gambling, prostitution, and drug franchises they enjoyed in Cuba before the revolution. They served Trujillo loyally, but they continued operating in the country long after he was "rubbed out" by political opponents in a gangland-style shootout in 1961. They paved the way for a new wave of US corporate and criminal investment in the Dominican Republic under Trujillo's successor, President Joaquín Balaguer.

Rafael Trujillo: Gangster and Generalissimo

The Dominican Republic, Haiti's eastern neighbor on the island of Hispaniola, had all the makings of a banana republic, without the bananas. US capital deeply penetrated the country through loans and sugar investments in the late nineteenth century. In response to political unrest and instability, President Theodore Roosevelt claimed a right to exercise "international police power" under the Monroe Doctrine and sent warships to seize the country's customs houses in 1904–1905. Following continued turmoil, President Woodrow Wilson dispatched the US Marines to impose military rule over the unruly nation in 1916. Creating a new class of local clients, the marines established a national guard to help crush rural insurgents. The marines finally returned home in 1922, but not before elevating their young protégé Rafael Trujillo to a senior role in the national guard. By the late 1920s, he had become chief of staff of its successor, the new national army.[9]

After Trujillo seized power in 1930, he unleashed a reign of terror across the country. A senior US diplomat described him as "the head of a band of gangsters."[10] The Dominican strongman repurposed a gang of underworld thugs with whom he had run as a young man into one of Latin America's most formidable death squads. Named *La 42*, after a rapacious company of US Marines, these thugs roamed the country, killing former cabinet ministers, senators, journalists, businessmen, labor leaders, and students suspected of opposing the new dictator.[11]

Trujillo was a natural ally of mobsters. He ran his totalitarian state like a Mafia fiefdom, as the unquestioned boss of bosses. He used public displays of brutality to cow potential rivals in politics, business, and personal affairs. Trujillo's ubiquitous secret police hired informers throughout the country and in Dominican communities abroad to monitor his subjects' loyalty. Trujillo encouraged acolytes to call him "El Benefactor," but others privately called him "the beast of the Caribbean." They had good reason. "Torture and assassination awaited those who resisted," wrote Fred Goff and Michael Locker. "Political opposition was erased or manipulated by co-option, imprisonment, exile, or murder. . . . Every official, high or low, was subjected to constant notice by orders from 'El Jefe.'"[12]

Like a Mafia boss, Trujillo ran his regime as a family business. He made his firstborn son, Ramfis, a brigadier general at the age of nine. He also put two brothers in charge of criminal rackets to augment their collective fortune. One of them, Amable Romeo Trujillo ("Pipí"), trafficked in prostitutes across the Caribbean and sold protection for illicit gambling and prostitution in the capital. Another brother, Lt. Gen. José Arismendi Trujillo ("Petán"), engaged in counterfeiting and oversaw most of the country's slot machines, gambling casinos, loan-sharking, and numbers rackets.[13] Petán also controlled the regime's main radio propaganda organ, La Voz Dominicana. In 1958, journalist and former Dominican congressman Germán Ornes described that radio station as the vehicle of one of the most lucrative international numbers rackets, which operated by a mobsters' syndicate spread out through the length of the Caribbean. The "hoods" in Havana, Panama, and Caracas sell numbers in combination with a seemingly harmless *Voz Dominicana*'s raffle supposedly intended as a giveaway of small prizes to its Dominican audience. The syndicate rigs the daily winning numbers in their own favor and then cables them to Arismendy who dutifully announces them over his radio station. This peculiar racket . . . produces a weekly income to Petan figured in five ciphers. This, however, is by no means all profit for Petan. Part of the proceeds have to be turned over to the Benefactor himself, who has a pronounced allergy to the sight of other people getting too wealthy, even his own brothers. The latter appear as a front in many businesses and rackets ultimately owned by the Generalissimo.[14]

As the boss of bosses, Trujillo appropriated most of the spoils of office for himself. He took personal control of the country's major means of production, including large shares of its sugar, rice, milk, and shipping industries. By the late 1950s, his fortune was plausibly estimated at more than half a billion dollars, making him one of the richest men in the Americas.[15]

Trujillo's Image: Sweetened by Sugar

Smart Mafia leaders cultivate friendly judges, sheriffs, and legislators for protection. Trujillo bought political support where he needed it most—in Washington. In 1933, Trujillo hired Joseph E. Davies—a famous Washington attorney, confidant of President Roosevelt, and future ambassador—to lobby the new Democratic administration for loans. Davies, who called the dictator "one of the greatest men in the world, a man who would be great in any age," served as general counsel to Trujillo's regime until 1945. Another hire was Oliver P. Newman, former director of publicity for the Democratic National Committee, who fed glowing stories about the dictator to the Associated Press. In 1939, a timely payment of $25,000 transformed Rep. Hamilton Fish of New York, the ranking Republican on the House Foreign Affairs Committee, from a harsh critic into an admirer who lauded Trujillo as the "creator of a golden age."[16]

Washington's goodwill waned temporarily with the appointment of Spruille Braden, a champion of democracy, as assistant secretary of state for Inter-American Affairs in September 1945. In a decisive change of policy, he vetoed a major arms sale to the Dominican government on grounds that Trujillo could have only two enemies in mind: neighboring Haiti or his own people. President Truman's new secretary of state, James Byrnes, called Trujillo the "most merciless" dictator of the Western Hemisphere and advised the president that "we ought scrupulously [to] avoid even the appearance of giving him any support."

To counter such critics, Trujillo hired FDR's two-term attorney general, Homer Cummings, as his general counsel to replace Davies. Cummings tried to convince skeptics that Trujillo was a boon to "material progress, education, agricultural development, the well-being of the masses, and the maintenance of law and order." Trujillo also put on his payroll Manuel A. de Moya, a poker-playing friend of President Truman and a future Dominican ambassador who lavished cash on the regime's friends in the United States.[17]

As the Cold War began to heat up, Washington saw new value in pliable client states. Trujillo's fortunes improved accordingly. In 1947, the State Department lifted the embargo on US arms sales to the Dominican Republic. The dictator worked his way back into the good graces of the world's leading democracy by voting slavishly with the United States in the United Nations and other international organizations, welcoming an air force missile testing facility on his territory, and signing a bilateral military assistance pact with Washington in 1953. The Eisenhower administration set a low bar for Trujillo's behavior; Secretary of State John Foster Dulles once warned, "Wherever a dictator is replaced in Latin America, communism will triumph."[18] Singing Trujillo's praises were anti-Communists ranging from the commander of the US Caribbean fleet to Francis Cardinal Spellman of New York.[19] The CIA, rarely averse to supporting dictators, "delivered suitcases full of cash to Trujillo when he visited New York City to attend sessions of the United Nations," according to one historian.[20]

To further strengthen his hand, Trujillo systematically cultivated corrupt allies in Congress. Legislators on Capitol Hill could make or break the Dominican economy—and Trujillo's personal fortune—by their treatment of the country's all-important sugar exports. Sugar accounted for more than half of the nation's government revenue, and Trujillo personally controlled more than 60 percent of its sugar production. In 1934, Congress began favoring certain foreign sugar exporters with an import quota system that also protected domestic sugar producers. Offering a net benefit of two cents per pound, the sugar quota was worth more than $200 million a year to certain foreign producers, mostly in the Caribbean, by the early 1960s. That kind of money bought a great degree of political loyalty from client states like the Dominican Republic. Perversely, however, it also gave them the means and incentive to corrupt Congress to their advantage.[21] As Senate Foreign Relations Committee chairman J. William Fulbright remarked during an investigation of foreign lobbyists in the early 1960s, "Where the sugar is, there you will find the flies!"[22]

Payoffs and Prostitutes

Trujillo spent lavishly on Capitol Hill to buy support for a large sugar quota and to blunt criticism of his dictatorship. A memo prepared by one of his American agents commented, "There is no mystery when it comes to relations with Congress. All that has to be known is who the important people are, to be able to establish contact with them and to have the money to pay them. At times too much can be spent but it is better to spend too much and to win than to spend too little and to lose."[23] For members of Congress who preferred exotic sex to money, Trujillo's agents were happy to oblige with attractive prostitutes and a "love nest" located just outside the Dominican capital.[24]

In an exposé published after the dictator's death, Trujillo's former intelligence chief, Gen. Arturo Espaillat, wrote of the "banquets of greenbacks" served up to Washington officials in the late 1950s:

> Trujillo acted like he was trying to buy up the whole U.S. government. I would estimate that he showered at least $5,000,000 on those officials—not to mention the cost of providing many of them with beauticious and capable bed partners. Influential Americans who flourished on Trujillo's various forms of bounty numbered literally in the hundreds. . . .
>
> Some of the Congressmen formed lasting attachments with Trujillo's courtesans. One prominent Southern Senator fell in love with one of the Palace girls. She was quickly shipped off to our Washington embassy where she was made readily available. Another semi-señorita was sent to Washington to become the permanent mistress of a New York Congressman. . . .
>
> Through a middleman, Trujillo turned over $75,000 to a powerful Atlantic seaboard senator. So the senator suddenly became intensely alarmed about Red infiltration in the Caribbean. Forthwith, his committee embarked on an "investigation." . . . Altogether, payoffs to that one senator totaled about $225,000.
>
> Trujillo had . . . price lists for the purchase of some U.S. Congressmen. An ordinary, run-of-the-mill Representative would cost about $5,000 or less. A few House committee chairmen could be had for about three times that much, depending on the committee. Senators came higher, of course. A chairman of a key committee could run from $50,000 to $75,000.[25]

One of Trujillo's beneficiaries was almost certainly Sen. James Eastland, a Mississippi Democrat and chair of the Judiciary Committee, who took to the Senate floor in 1960 to praise the dictator's many fine qualities.[26] The Southern senator who enjoyed the charms of a Trujillo-supplied prostitute was Louisiana Democrat Allen Ellender, chairman of the Senate Agriculture Committee and a prime guarantor of the Dominican Republic's sugar quota. Ellender once asserted that the United States would benefit from "a Trujillo in all of the South and Central American countries." After returning from a visit to Ciudad Trujillo in 1959, Ellender called Trujillo "a human dynamo" who was "beloved by the people of the Dominican Republic because of vast improvements he has made in order to benefit the people of that Republic as a whole."[27]

Another "key committee" member who held out his hand for $75,000 was Sen. Olin Johnston of South Carolina. He ranked just behind Ellender on the Agriculture Committee and chaired the Judiciary Subcommittee on Internal Security.[28] Johnston declared that Trujillo's regime had "rendered a greater force in deterring the spread of communism in Latin America than any other country in the Caribbean area."[29] One of Trujillo's agents in Washington said of Johnston,

> He has courage, is implacable, completely controls the Justice Committee and the Internal Security Sub-Committee and will do anything for money. We need a strong man in the Senate to speak up in favor of the Dominican Republic, not only in the upper chamber itself, but also in his dealings with and negotiations with other Senators, as is being done by McCarran for Spain and Knowland for Nationalist China. Whatever Johnston's faults may be, whenever he was paid sufficiently he has worked.[30]

Drew Pearson and Jack Anderson called Trujillo "probably the champion foreign influence-seeker of all time."[31] The journalists pointed accusing fingers at House Agriculture Committee chairman Harold Cooley, D-NC, who more than anyone determined winners and losers under the annual sugar quota. Cooley's close relatives vacationed in the Dominican Republic at Trujillo's expense, they noted. Pearson and Anderson also pointed out that House Speaker John McCormack, D-MA, was decorated by Trujillo.[32] They would not have been surprised to learn that he accepted $75,000 from the dictator as well.[33]

Trujillo attempted to influence the executive branch by giving a lucrative sugar deal to President Eisenhower's brother-in-law, Col. Gordon Moore. El Benefactor gave mining concessions to Eisenhower's foreign policy consultant William Pawley (see chapter 3) and to Henry Holland, former assistant secretary of state for Latin American affairs. The dictator also provided thousands of dollars' worth of vacation perks to Secretary of State John Foster Dulles's son-in-law.[34]

The highest-ranking recipient of Trujillo's largess was Vice President Nixon, who allegedly pocketed $25,000 in cash in September 1956 for his reelection campaign. The payoff came from freelance detective John Frank, who pleaded guilty several years later to being an unregistered agent for the Dominican Republic.[35] A year earlier, Vice President Nixon had stopped off in the Dominican Republic while touring Central America and the Caribbean. There, observes Stephen Ambrose, "he was effusive in expressing his thanks to Generalissimo Rafael Trujillo for his support of the United States in the United Nations." In his trip report to the cabinet and National Security Council, Nixon criticized Trujillo's "moral flexibility" but praised him for keeping the country "clean" with "drinkable water." Nixon did not particularly admire "one-man rule," but asserted, "We must deal with these governments as they are and work over a period of time towards more democracy."[36]

Lobbyists and Media Acolytes

Trujillo also bankrolled a small army of lobbyists to boost the Dominican Republic's sugar quota. One of the biggest names was former representative Franklin D. Roosevelt Jr., who reportedly "got a $60,000 fee for a year's service as special counsel to the Dominican Republic in partnership with the flamboyant Charles Patrick Clark . . . chief lobbyist for Franco of Spain." Espaillat reported that the late president's son did little work for the Dominican regime, "but retaining Roosevelt had one positive result: as long as he was legal adviser, Mrs. Eleanor Roosevelt refrained from knocking the Old Man through the host of liberal organizations to which she belonged."[37]

One of Trujillo's most colorful agents was publicist and Hearst society columnist Igor Cassini. This purveyor of gossip about the rich and famous boasted twenty million readers. He was a close friend of international playboy Porfirio Rubirosa, Trujillo's son-in-law and ambassador to Batista's Cuba. After Castro took power, Cassini "instantly envisioned the Dominican Republic's capital . . . as the reborn Havana, the ultimate Jet Set playground, and one that would be totally pro-American," writes popular historian William Stadiem. Cassini used his Bahamian public relations subsidiary and his column to bolster Trujillo's image as a modernizer, anti-Communist ally, and "friend of Israel." Just as important, Cassini was an intimate of the Kennedy family; his brother Oleg was Jaqueline Kennedy's favorite dress designer. After the *Saturday Evening Post* exposed his activities, the Justice Department prosecuted Cassini for violating the Foreign Agents Registration Act, which requires representatives of foreign governments to register with the Justice Department. Cassini pleaded no contest in 1963 to accepting $200,000 in fees from the Dominican government to disseminate political propaganda.[38]

Trujillo also bought favorable media in the United States. He reportedly controlled two of Puerto Rico's leading newspapers.[39] International News Service, which merged with United Press in 1958 to become UPI, took Trujillo's money to distribute an anti-Communist newsletter.[40] He twisted the arms of

US sugar mill owners to buy full-page ads praising him in the *New York Times* and other papers.[41] He paid a *Miami Herald* columnist to write magazine and newspaper stories lauding his leadership. Most notably, he paid $750,000 in cash to Alexander Guterma, president of the Mutual Broadcasting System, in return for a promise of more than seven hours of favorable news and commentary on the Dominican Republic each month. Guterma needed the cash after getting into dire legal and financial trouble over multiple stock frauds he committed with major organized crime associates. The arrangement was brokered by Cassini and Rubirosa. The broadcast network filed for bankruptcy after its corrupt deal was exposed, and Guterma was convicted in 1960 of acting as an unregistered Trujillo agent.[42]

Trujillo's Business Allies

Trujillo also cultivated American business allies with political influence in both parties. They included right-wing diplomat-businessman William Pawley, a close friend of Vice President Nixon; prominent Democratic Party fundraisers (and molasses dealers) A. I. and J. M. Kaplan; senior diplomat (and sugar executive) Adolf A. Berle Jr.; and Gen. George Olmsted, an international banker and law client of Nixon's known for his "assertive networking through members of Congress." Many of these prominent men were also enmeshed with the highest levels of the US intelligence community.[43]

Ambassador Pawley, as noted in chapter 3, helped to execute the Eisenhower administration's covert operation to overthrow the democratic government of Guatemala (with support from Trujillo). He was tasked by President Eisenhower the same year to help prepare a top secret report on how to make the CIA more effective in its mission to "subvert, sabotage, and destroy our enemies." Later he advised senior CIA officers on affairs in Cuba, where he owned major investments that were nationalized by Castro.[44]

Pawley became deeply involved with Trujillo in 1955, while visiting the Dominican capital for a business conference. The generalissimo, learning of Pawley's extensive mining and oil interests in Mexico, asked him to draft legislation to encourage foreign extractive investments in the Dominican Republic. In return for a share of any profits, Trujillo granted Pawley mineral rights over a million acres. For political clout, Pawley brought on board former assistant secretary of state Henry Holland. Pawley's survey team soon discovered the largest nickel deposit in the Western Hemisphere, multiplying his (and Trujillo's) fortune. Pawley also acted as an unregistered public relations agent for Trujillo; among other projects, he arranged the production of a four-part series in the *Miami Herald* on the "innovations and benefits" that Trujillo had fostered in his country.[45] By the late 1950s, Pawley's mining interests were the only significant private US holdings left in the Dominican Republic besides the extensive plantations of South Puerto Rico Sugar Company.[46]

Pawley grew even closer to the Dominican dictator by successfully mediating a nasty dispute that nearly led to war between Trujillo and Batista in 1956. Pawley finally convinced the two rivals to stop slandering each other in their radio broadcasts. Trujillo canceled a planned invasion of Cuba and reestablished diplomatic relations with Havana. Trujillo showed his gratitude to Pawley by giving him sole rights to foreign sales of new Dominican postage stamps.[47]

All of these friends in Congress, the media, and business bolstered Trujillo's influence in Washington. Equally important to Trujillo's success, however, was the fact that until the mid-1950s, he faced little organized opposition. As one US diplomat put it, "The situation over many years had been that the United States didn't exactly approve of him, but he kept law and order, cleaned the place up, made it sanitary, built public works and he didn't bother the United States. So that was fine with us."[48] Then, suddenly, Trujillo made a major nuisance of himself, and Washington was no longer fine with him. At that point, Trujillo began looking increasingly to North American mobsters for support.

The Galíndez Kidnap-Murder Case

US relations with Trujillo started their downhill slide in March 1956 after the mysterious disappearance from New York City of Spanish Basque exile and anti-Trujillo activist Dr. Jesús de Galíndez, a lecturer at Columbia University. Journalists and human rights activists quickly blamed Trujillo, noting that Galíndez was about to publish a lengthy doctoral dissertation critical of the regime. The dictator was likewise accused of murdering the American pilot who flew Galíndez to meet his presumed death in the Dominican Republic.

In time, evidence would implicate several Trujillo agents. One of them was former FBI agent and CIA legal adviser John Frank, who served as Trujillo's bodyguard, surveillance expert, and bagman for the payoff to Vice President Nixon.[49] New Jersey mobster Joseph Zicarelli, who reportedly chartered the getaway plane that flew Galíndez to the Dominican Republic, was an even more exotic agent.[50] "Bayonne Joe" belonged to the New York crime family of Joseph Bonanno. He dominated underworld gambling in two New Jersey counties, grossing $50,000 per week. FBI informants also identified him as a primary US distributor of heroin smuggled from Europe by the Cotroni crime family based in Montreal.[51] His senior partner in the narcotics trade and many other rackets was New York Mafia underboss Carmine Galante. Galante was himself a political assassin, responsible for the 1943 murder of anti-fascist Italian American editor Carlo Tresca.[52] Unlike many of his more parochial peers, Zicarelli was drawn to international intrigues, particularly in the Caribbean. In 1959, he joined several other anti-Communist mobsters in urging the US government to oust Fidel Castro, who had seized their Havana hotels and casinos.[53] The same year, an FBI agent reported that Zicarelli had "been active in" running guns to Cuba, gambling in Mexico and Venezuela, and paying kickbacks for contracts in Venezuela during the brutal reign of his friend, President Marcos Pérez Jiménez (1952–1958). The report also linked the mobster to the murder of Galíndez and an attempted assassination against a Venezuelan political leader (undoubtedly Rómulo Betancourt, a bitter enemy of both Pérez Jiménez and Trujillo, who spent several years in exile in New York City). Highlighting the Trujillo connection, the FBI report added that "another government agency has furnished information that Zicarelli has been authorized to purchase $1,000,000 of rockets and machine guns for the Dominican Republic." In 1961, the CIA's deputy director confirmed that Zicarelli was believed to be "a key man in the Galíndez case."[54] Later, FBI wiretaps revealed that Zicarelli was also "on the best of terms with" Rep. Cornelius Gallagher, a New Jersey Democrat and a member of the House Foreign Affairs Committee—a valuable connection indeed for Trujillo.[55]

Galíndez was not Trujillo's first victim on US soil. In 1935, an agent of El Benefactor murdered a Dominican exile in Manhattan, mistaking him for a prominent member of the opposition. In 1952, on orders of the Dominican consul in New York, Zicarelli allegedly arranged the murder of an anti-Trujillo editor in Manhattan.[56] Galíndez was the first victim to enjoy a wide circle of friends and supporters who rallied to demand a serious investigation into his disappearance. Several outspoken members of Congress made his kidnapping a *cause célèbre* and demanded that US aid to the Trujillo regime be suspended. President Eisenhower, Attorney General Herbert Brownell, and FBI director J. Edgar Hoover were dragged against their will into the Galíndez case to address questions raised by critics.[57] The administration was reluctant to discipline Trujillo lest he stop supporting the United States in the UN or terminate guided missile facilities that the air force deemed "vital" to US defense interests.[58] Nonetheless, when President Eisenhower sent a new ambassador to the Dominican Republic in August 1957, he selected a former FBI special agent who was skilled in covert operations, with instructions to help ease Trujillo out of power.[59]

To counter growing opposition to his regime in Washington, Trujillo redoubled his spending on lobbying and public relations. He hired two notorious influence peddlers, the brothers Joseph H. and Francis N. Rosenbaum, to draft replies to all diplomatic inquiries from the United States concerning the Galíndez case.[60] To reinforce their team, the Rosenbaums persuaded Trujillo to hire Sydney Baron, the public relations agent for Frank Costello's ally, Tammany Hall boss Carmine DeSapio. Baron billed Trujillo more than half a million dollars for his services.[61] That total allegedly included payments arranged by the Rosenbaums to friendly members of Congress, including five members of the House Foreign Affairs Committee.[62]

The FBI's investigation of the kidnap-killing was inconclusive. In the end, the only significant judicial sanction for the murder of Galíndez was the conviction of John Frank as an unregistered foreign agent.[63] Frank escaped more serious charges thanks to his long-standing ties to the CIA, which prevailed on the Justice Department to leave the case officially unsolved.[64] Zicarelli also managed to avoid serious prosecution for quite some time, despite his involvement in heroin trafficking, gambling, arms dealing, and political assassination. Years later the FBI would note that his criminal network "had been afforded a high degree of immunization from law enforcement interference through the selective utilization of political corruption."[65] (See online appendix at rowman.com for additional background on Zicarelli, Irving Davidson, and Israel.)

Trujillo and US Organized Crime

Kidnapping Galíndez on US soil was only one of several reckless plots undertaken by Trujillo and his henchmen in the latter half of the 1950s against foreign leaders and regimes in the region.[66] Trujillo's mob allies in the United States helped execute these plots and provide political protection. Zicarelli, as we have seen, helped him target Venezuela's Betancourt. To undertake the murder of Costa Rica's democratically elected president in 1956, Trujillo recruited the head of security for a Cuban casino owned by Santo Trafficante.[67] Once Castro took power in Cuba, Trujillo would enlist other US mobsters close to Trafficante to wage war against the former guerrilla leader. Such secret alliances helped make Trujillo's otherwise small and poor regime a feared power in the Caribbean. They also strengthened his hand in Washington. Among El Benefactor's strongest supporters were four members of Congress with notable East Coast Mafia connections.[68]

To attract their support, Trujillo encouraged investments by North American gamblers and gangsters.[69] Gambling was legal in fancy tourist hotels, such as the Embajador and Jaragua, and in Trujillo-owned nightclubs. Catering to American cruise-ship passengers, they minted money.[70] During at least some of the Trujillo years, the Jaragua was operated by Miami hotelier Morris Lansburgh, a front man for Meyer Lansky.[71] Concessionaires paid Trujillo or members of his family for the operating privileges.[72]

In May 1957, Francis Rosenbaum, Trujillo's Washington, D.C., lawyer, brought a group of prominent Las Vegas and Havana gamblers, along with a former lobbyist for Howard Hughes, to investigate buying operating concessions at government-owned hotels and casinos in the Dominican Republic.[73] The same year, a senior member of the Chicago Outfit visited Ciudad Trujillo and told Trujillo's secret police chief, Gen. Arturo Espaillat, "The place has real potential. I'd like to bring in 3,000 slot machines, set up special gambling flights from Miami, build a new casino. We'd make this town a second Havana."[74]

Despite these forays, the Dominican Republic couldn't compete with Cuba or the Bahamas as a destination for American tourists. The country was a longer hop from the United States, and the menacing reputation of Trujillo's police state discouraged visitors.[75] Nonetheless, Philadelphia Mafia boss Angelo Bruno made headway in tapping the country's potential for gambling. Bruno had climbed up the gangster hierarchy in the City of Brotherly Love by working the numbers racket. The pudgy, eyeglasses-wearing don built a "vast" criminal empire and became a member of the informal national Mafia "commission" that settled business disputes between major urban crime families.[76] He made Cuba his first foreign target, investing in the Monte Carlo casino at Havana's Plaza Hotel. A lenient parole officer permitted Bruno, following a gambling conviction at home, to visit Florida and Cuba in 1957 to manage his investments. On the same trip, he stopped off at the Dominican Republic.[77] Bruno and two associates reportedly considered buying the Hotel Presidente in Ciudad Trujillo to open a casino.[78]

Bruno's interest in the Dominican Republic grew out of a huge World Fair erected by Trujillo for the Year of the Benefactor from 1955 to 1956. The Dominican dictator spent $40 million to create and lavishly promote the "International Fair of Peace and Brotherhood of the Free World" on the western edge of Ciudad Trujillo. Among the distinguished guests at its grand opening was Vice President Richard Nixon. One of the fair's major tourist attractions was Independencia Park, an amusement center modeled on New York's Coney Island.[79] There tourists could play slot machines, provided by a Philadelphia racketeer who fronted for Bruno. The fair's manager, Bernard Allen of Miami, continued to lease Independencia Park for several years after the fair closed, with Bruno as a hidden partner. In 1960, Allen and his partners won approval from the regime to install at least two hundred slot machines across the country, in return for sharing profits with the government and paying kickbacks to Trujillo's uncle, Interior Secretary Virgilio Álvarez Piña.[80]

Following Trujillo's murder in May 1961, influential Dominicans demanded the closure of Allen's many gambling parlors. That June, the caretaker government of President Joaquín Balaguer received a letter from South Carolina senator Olin Johnston, one of Trujillo's well-paid allies on the Agriculture Committee, seeking to protect Allen's $200,000 investment. The senator pointed out that "the operation of this business was through the personal orders of your beloved late chief, Generalissimo Rafael Leonidas Trujillo Molina." Balaguer wrote an obsequious reply, and Johnston thanked him for "all the courtesies shown to my friend," noting that Allen had told him "just how you had bent over backwards in trying to assist him."[81] Left unsaid was the fact that Angelo Bruno was a partner in Allen's enterprise.[82] That was not the first time Senator Johnston carried water for mobsters. Six years earlier, he had (unsuccessfully) introduced a private bill to block the deportation to Italy of a notorious Kansas City racketeer and convicted narcotics trafficker.[83]

Trujillo v. Castro: The Morgan Plot and the Mafia

US mobsters became important allies of Trujillo against his mortal enemy: Fidel Castro. Showing up in Caracas just three weeks after his triumph in Havana, the new Cuban leader rallied support for the overthrow of his Dominican rival, saying "Everywhere I hear the chant, 'Trujillo next, Trujillo next!'" Castro put guns and troops behind his rhetoric. In June 1959, a Cuban-led team of two hundred Dominican exiles invaded Trujillo's domain but was quickly annihilated.

Trujillo, meanwhile, cranked up his own anti-Castro propaganda machine in early 1959. Spending heavily on national defense, he assembled a mercenary foreign legion from the ranks of ultra-rightists in Spain, Germany, and Yugoslavia.[84] Trujillo also stepped up his intelligence gathering around the Caribbean to detect potential plots against his regime. In Florida, he recruited at least three Miami police officers, including two in the department's intelligence unit who tracked anti-Trujillo activists and one who supplied prostitutes for officials in Ciudad Trujillo.[85]

Trujillo and his ruthless chief of military intelligence, Johnny Abbes García, took their fight to Castro's home base. In early 1959 they secretly enlisted William Morgan, a renowned young American soldier of fortune who had led a band of several thousand Cuban guerrillas in the Escambray Mountains against Batista. Following Castro's victory, Morgan was at loose ends. Apparently disenchanted with the new regime's socialist ideology, he restlessly began looking for new adventures, and income to supplement his government stipend of $125 a month. A US intelligence report pegged the size of Morgan's partially demobilized force at between five hundred and one thousand men, but said it could be "quickly augmented by several thousand other seasoned Cuban veterans who served under Morgan."[86] The CIA looked into recruiting Morgan for its own psychological and paramilitary operations but decided he was an "extreme . . . psychopath" and unfit for service.[87]

In February 1959, Morgan wrote Trujillo offering to "bounce Fidel Castro from power."[88] The Dominican dictator jumped at the opportunity, ordering Johnny Abbes to oversee the operation. Trujillo and Abbes promised Morgan a million dollars and the backing of hundreds of fighters in their foreign legion as well as armed Cuban exiles in the Dominican Republic.[89] Those Cuban soldiers were led by Gen. José Eleutorio Pedraza, Batista's former army chief of staff.[90] Pedraza had arrived in the Dominican Republic shortly after Batista and quickly began training a "Cuban Liberation Army" to topple Castro.[91]

Their plan was to sail or fly from the Dominican Republic to connect up with Morgan's forces in Cuba, sabotage the Cuban air force, assassinate the Castro brothers, and establish a provisional government.[92] Trujillo's business friend Pawley established a $1 million line of credit for the conspirators at a New York bank. He also reported enthusiastically to the CIA that "Generalissimo Trujillo was in a position more than willing to cooperate in all ways possible to him so that the Cuban opposition would be organized to overthrow the present communist regime."[93]

Not everyone was so enthusiastic, however. Batista himself characterized Trujillo's Cuban mercenaries as a group of "murderers, vermin and riffraff," dominated by "criminal elements." He predicted they would provoke a "tragic bloodbath" if they succeeded in toppling Castro. Through the ubiquitous wheeler-dealer Irving Davidson, Batista made certain that US intelligence services were informed of Trujillo's plans, in the vain hope that Washington would nip them in the bud.[94]

The locus of Dominican plotting with Morgan was Miami, a melting pot of Latin millionaires, mercenaries, gangsters, and exiles. General Espaillat called the city's underworld a "teeming anthill" of "policemen and deputy sheriffs, jewel thieves, gunrunners, mobsters, gambling syndicates, homosexuals, *bolita* operators, killers, [and] Cuban rebels." He added that "catering to Latin violence is a major Miami industry."[95]

Among the Miami-based supporters of Trujillo's plot were wealthy Cuban exiles. One had been a co-owner of Santo Trafficante's casino at the Havana Hilton, who reportedly raised millions of dollars to fight Castro.[96] Another was the former chief of detectives for the Cuban National Police, who was said by FBI informants to have pocketed $3 million from Cuban gambling interests and to have explored distributing counterfeit US twenty-dollar bills with a top associate of Trafficante in Havana.[97] Former Venezuelan dictator Marcos Pérez Jiménez, ousted from power in 1958 and exiled to the Dominican Republic and then Miami, allegedly donated $200,000 to overthrow the new regime.[98] Reflecting political direction from their masters, the FBI and CIA monitored these anti-Castro conspirators without getting in the way.[99]

Meyer Lansky and other American racketeers also began supporting a counterrevolution in Cuba to restore their enormously lucrative gambling concessions. Some of them now became deeply enmeshed in Trujillo's anti-Castro plots. Morgan himself came from the lowest ranks of their milieu. Hailing from Ohio, he was dishonorably discharged from the army, arrested for armed robbery in 1946, and then arrested for robbery and escape in both 1948 and 1949. A captain of the Toledo Police Department reported that Morgan was an "associate of the hoodlum element in the city of Toledo."[100]

A key American supporter of the Trujillo-Morgan plot emerged from that criminal milieu in Toledo: Dominick Bartone. Bartone had employed Morgan years earlier, possibly as a driver.[101] By early 1959 they had reconnected, and Bartone began financing a public relations campaign to boost his image as a dashing guerrilla leader.[102] Bartone saw Morgan not only as a valuable business contact in Cuba, but as an important counterweight to growing Communist influence in Castro's regime.

Described by one business associate as "a very large robust type individual, [of] typical hoodlum appearance," who "would resort to physical force as a means of persuasion," Bartone ran a sand and gravel company in Cleveland. He had been arrested in 1956 for check fraud, was wanted by police for larceny, and was implicated in the fraudulent sale of stock in a worthless uranium mine. He was also tight with Nunzio Louis "Babe" Triscaro, a member of the Cleveland Mafia who presided over the city's Teamster local. On Bartone's behalf, Triscaro obtained Teamster president Jimmy Hoffa's blessing for a $300,000 loan from the union's pension fund to finance an arms deal connected to the Morgan plot.[103] A trusted aide to the union leader said, "The whole . . . thing was purely and simply Hoffa's way of helping some of his mob buddies who were afraid of losing their business in Cuba. So they were trying to score points with Castro right after he moved in."[104]

The arms deal originated in early 1959 as a scheme to sell military surplus C-74 Globemaster cargo planes to the new Castro government, which had not yet shown its Communist colors. Acting as agent for the planes' owner, Bartone flew to Havana half a dozen times in February and March 1959 to meet his friend Morgan and a senior Cuban Air Force official to manage the sale. Bartone actually delivered one plane from Arizona (where it had been stored by former Detroit mobster Pete Licavoli) for inspection by the Cubans, but the deal fell through.[105]

Working with his old pal Morgan, Bartone lined up a new buyer: the Trujillo regime, which wanted the planes for its anti-Castro plot. Bartone met in Miami with Morgan and Trujillo's consul general, Augusto Ferrando, in mid-May to close the deal. Morgan said he would provide between 1,000 and 1,500 fighters to overthrow the Cuban regime. A Cuban gambling associate of Santo Trafficante, who attended the meeting as a representative of General Pedraza, then handed $50,000 to Morgan as a down payment.[106]

As Bartone was arranging to send a planeload of arms and ammunition to Ciudad Trujillo, disaster struck. On May 22, customs agents arrested Bartone at Miami International Airport. He was indicted the next month with Ferrando for conspiring to export arms illegally and to bribe US Customs officials. Several months later, in a private meeting with associates, Bartone revealed that his criminal case had been "fixed" and would never come to trial. That December, Bartone and Consul General Ferrando pleaded guilty. A federal district judge in Miami placed Bartone on probation and fined him $10,000. The fine was later reduced to $7,500.[107]

The arrests set back the Dominican plotters only temporarily. On June 18, in Bartone's Miami hotel room, Ferrando handed Morgan another $10,000 as a show of Trujillo's good faith. A few weeks later, Bartone confided to an anti-Castro activist that he was still moving arms and expected to share a $1 million reward with Morgan for aiding an invasion of Cuba. Bartone said he and his friend from Toledo planned to use their reward to open an import-export business in the Caribbean.[108]

Meanwhile, Morgan was conferring closely with Trujillo's agents about their plans to assassinate Castro and overthrow his regime. Abbes, the secret police chief, visited Morgan twice in Miami.[109] On July 30, as the uprising became imminent, Ferrando gave Morgan $200,000 and directions to a boat full of arms anchored off the coast of Florida.[110]

All this time, Morgan was moving freely in and out of the United States, unhindered by federal agents. The FBI's attaché in Havana reported on July 29 that Morgan planned to start his revolt by killing Cuban leaders in coordination with a landing of Cuban exile fighters commanded by General Pedraza.[111] The CIA asserted prematurely that "the group headed by Morgan planned to assassinate Castro sometime between 31 July and 3 August and immediately thereafter touch off an uprising by 5,000 members of the Cuban Army."[112] A couple of days later, the FBI's man in Havana cautioned, "Most sources believe [Morgan] has no chance of success and that his invasion will merely unite anti-Batista and pro-Castro groups."[113] By then, the plot was an open secret. Concerned that its exposure by other parties would rupture relations with Cuba, the US ambassador in Havana tipped off the regime that Morgan was planning to kill Premier Castro.[114]

Cuba remained quiet for several days. Morgan finally left Miami for Cuba on the evening of August 5, aboard the large, arms-laden yacht provided by Ferrando. On August 11, Abbes arranged to airdrop military supplies to a beach near the city of Trinidad on the south coast. Morgan declared that the revolt against Castro had begun. "Trinidad is ours!" Morgan radioed the Dominican dictator. "Don't let us down! We need men, guns, supplies!" Thrilled by the news, Trujillo began broadcasting about the Cuban uprising, crying, "Fire, fire, fire to that demon Fidel Castro and his brother Raúl!" Abbes dispatched a planeload of arms to Morgan's army, then another cargo plane with soldiers.

The emerging fighters joined Morgan in chants of "death to Castro." But their joy was short-lived. Stepping out from the shadows around the plane were Castro and several thousand of his loyal troops. Within days, the Cuban regime was celebrating its victory over the humiliated Trujillo. "Everyone played his assigned parts," Castro crowed. "It was better than a movie." As the CIA had learned several days before the climax, Morgan was a Cuban double agent, luring Trujillo and Abbes into Castro's trap.[115]

Morgan's betrayal led to the arrest of thousands of suspects in Cuba.[116] The CIA reported that Castro tightened his hold on power by acting as a "savior of Cuba in the face of aggressive action by 'capitalist imperialists.'"[117] Powerful foes of Castro in Congress, including Senators James Eastland of Mississippi and George Smathers of Florida, got the State Department to revoke Morgan's US citizenship. He in turn denounced them for being "bribed by Trujillo gold."[118]

Bartone didn't get to split the million-dollar reward promised to Morgan, but he still came out ahead. In October, Bartone showed an FBI informant two $50,000 cashiers' checks, drawn from a foreign bank, which apparently were Dominican payments for his help in supplying arms to Morgan.[119] He began plowing money into a sand and gravel venture, while pursuing other business ventures with Teamster goons and underworld figures.[120]

Trujillo Courts the Mafia to Take Revenge

Trujillo, not surprisingly, was furious over Morgan's betrayal, which cost the dictator a small fortune along with his pride. In late August 1959, he dispatched a wealthy Cuban exile to Miami with word that anti-Castro activists could count on him for "weapons and money" if they formed a united revolutionary front against the regime in Havana. Trujillo also put a price of $500,000 on Morgan's head.[121] Morgan took the threat against his life seriously. He surrounded his house with heavily armed bodyguards. Asked by an American reporter, "How does it feel to have a half-million-dollar price on your head?" Morgan answered, "Well, it isn't too bad. They are going to have to collect it. And that's going to be hard."[122] But Morgan was guarding against the wrong enemy. Eventually he would die at the hands of Castro, not Trujillo, as punishment for counterrevolutionary activities.

Word of Trujillo's bounty soon reached Norman Rothman, one of Trafficante's former casino managers in Havana. He met on August 23 with a leading Cuban exile in Miami to discuss "having an American crime syndicate sign a contract" to kill Morgan on behalf of Trujillo. Rothman "added that he personally expected to receive a hundred thousand dollars for a share in the contract to assassinate Morgan."[123] His confidence may have been inspired by his friendship with Trujillo's secret police chief, Johnny Abbes.[124]

Rothman was at the same time financing sabotage missions and offering Cuban exile leaders millions of dollars from US gambling interests to finance the Mafia's return to Cuba.[125] His offer may have been bluster, but his underworld connections were real enough. After his expulsion from Cuba, Rothman became manager of the Biltmore Terrace Hotel in Miami Beach, a noted meeting place for top Batista supporters. Its principal owner was Alberto Ardura Moya, a wealthy Cuban gambling czar and close friend of Batista's brother-in-law. Ardura purchased the hotel from Miami Beach investor Sam Kay, a friend and business partner of Trafficante and other mobsters.[126]

In 1962, federal prosecutors put Rothman and his Western Pennsylvania mob patron Sam Mannarino on trial for using bonds stolen from a Canadian bank in May 1958 to raise funds for both Batista and Castro, hoping to win their favor.[127] The mastermind of that $13.5 million theft was "Bayonne Joe" Zicarelli's Canadian heroin supplier, Giuseppe Cotroni. A CIA report called the robbery "one of the biggest . . . of modern criminal history." It went on,

> Rothman was suspected of having been a key man in disposing of the loot, which included gems, securities and cash, in a labyrinthine conspiracy which was investigated by the FBI, by the Canadian National Police and by detectives in Switzerland and Interpol. . . . [T]he robbery was touched off when the Canadian branch of the Mafia received a hurry-up order from the Caribbean for arms, destination undisclosed. . . . It reportedly called on the U.S. Mafia for assistance, and it was at that point that Rothman entered the picture.[128]

Federal investigators strongly suspected Zicarelli of involvement with Cotroni in the stolen bond conspiracy but did not have enough proof to indict him.[129]

Rothman and Mannarino were eventually acquitted in the stolen bond case.[130] Rothman was instead convicted of helping to steal machine guns from a national guard armory in Ohio in October 1958—a job financed by the stolen bonds and organized by the Mannarino brothers. The arms were apparently intended to buy goodwill for mobsters still operating in Cuba. While he appealed that conviction, Rothman tried but failed to get the charges dropped in return for helping the CIA undertake violent missions against the Castro regime.[131]

Such legal complications did little to dampen the enthusiasm of mobsters working with Trujillo. Dominick Bartone was still on probation for his 1959 gunrunning conviction when he spoke with Manuel de Moya, former Dominican ambassador to the United States, at the office of Trujillo confidant William Pawley on April 8, 1960. Bartone said he could get his hands on a small force of B-25 bombers and P-51 planes for bombing raids against sugar mills in Cuba's Camaguey Province. All he needed from Trujillo was $300,000.[132] De Moya claimed he turned down the offer, but he continued meeting with mobsters and schemers who claimed they could help Trujillo punish Castro.

Mobsters dispossessed by Castro got a boost in the fall of 1960 when the CIA secretly approved plans to murder the new Cuban dictator. The CIA's plotters intersected repeatedly with those of Trujillo. To recruit mobsters to carry out the hit on its behalf, the CIA enlisted Robert Maheu, a former employer of John Frank, who was a leading suspect in the abduction of Galíndez in 1956. The CIA's first Mafia recruit was John Rosselli, the Chicago syndicate representative based in Hollywood and Las Vegas (chapters 2, 3, and 9). Rosselli then recruited his own boss, Outfit leader Sam Giancana, and Florida's Santo Trafficante.[133] Both gangster chiefs had investments in Dominican gambling, so the CIA was effectively, if inadvertently, backing some of Trujillo's closest allies in the US underworld.

Trujillo had one last fling with the US gangster elite before his own demise. Carlos Marcello, the Mafia boss of Louisiana, was a close ally of Trafficante, an investor in Guatemalan casinos, and allegedly a partner with Rothman, Mannarino, and a senior Guatemalan official in the heroin trade.[134] He was also one of Attorney General Robert Kennedy's top targets (chapter 5). Threatened with deportation to Italy or Tunisia, Marcello met with a former registered lobbyist for Trujillo in January 1961 to discuss paying him $200,000 for safe refuge in the Dominican Republic. Before they could work out a deal, federal immigration agents deported the gangster to Guatemala, where Marcello had previously obtained a forged birth certificate. With the help of friendly local officials, and reportedly Trujillo as well, the Mafia boss finally made his way back to the United States, where his lawyers blocked further deportation attempts.[135] Trujillo's ending was not so happy. On May 30, 1961, just two days after Marcello's return, eight Dominican conspirators stopped Trujillo's car and, in gangland style, riddled his body with bullets.

The Tide Shifts against Trujillo

Trujillo's secret alliance with the mob against Castro was motivated as much by self-preservation as ideology. A Special National Intelligence Estimate prepared by the Eisenhower administration in March 1959 noted that "the Generalissimo has become increasingly concerned with threats from abroad to his government's existence, a fear increased by Castro's encouragement of exile efforts to overthrow Trujillo and other dictators in Latin America."[136] Three months later, a Dominican-marked transport plane departed from Cuba for the hills outside Ciudad Trujillo with fifty-six Dominican exiles and crates of machine guns and bazookas supplied by the government of Venezuela. Their goal was to spark an insurrection against Trujillo's police state. Within a few days they had all been captured or slaughtered. The Dominican navy also sank several boats sent from Cuba with about 150 to 200 armed men to support the mini-invasion.[137]

Although it failed, the invasion inspired hundreds of Dominican dissidents to organize. Trujillo responded by savagely escalating his repression. Increasingly he targeted members of the country's elite, whom he suspected—often correctly—of disloyalty. Economic hard times, including falling sugar prices, fed popular discontent. A US National Intelligence Estimate issued at the end of December reported that "the entrenched position [Trujillo] has built up for 30 years is showing the first signs of deteriorating." Learning of a possible plot against his life, Trujillo ordered the arrest of thousands of businessmen, professionals, students, society women, and other victims.[138]

Trujillo's ruthless crackdown dismayed even the conservative Catholic Church. On January 31, 1960, the country's archbishop issued a Pastoral Letter denouncing the regime's suppression of human rights.[139] The situation seemed potentially ripe for a revolution. Senior officials in the Eisenhower administration began discussing how to rid the country of its dictator while preventing the rise of another Castro.[140] To encourage a peaceful exit by Trujillo, President Eisenhower enlisted the help of several of Vice President Nixon's most trusted allies. One was Florida senator George Smathers, chairman of the Senate Subcommittee on Latin American Trade. Smathers, whom Trujillo considered "a very good friend of our country," had invested with Pawley in Dominican bauxite mines; his Miami law firm also represented the Dominican steamship line.[141] On February 9, 1960, the administration sent Smathers, Pawley, and Nixon's close friend, Charles "Bebe" Rebozo, on a secret mission to persuade the dictator to resign and hold free elections. Smathers lavished praise on the generalissimo for his fight against Communism but suggested he create a succession path to avoid another Cuba. The fiercely right-wing Pawley took Trujillo's side and declared that the "outside world did not understand government by parties was not possible here under (the) circumstances because Dominicans desired one party." Needless to say, this delegation failed to arouse any latent democratic instincts in the country's absolute ruler. At the close of the meeting, Smathers let himself be photographed with Trujillo at a mass baptism ceremony for newborn Dominican babies. On his return, Smathers publicly praised the Dominican dictator's willingness to hold elections.[142] The powerful Florida senator also met with top State Department officials to vent his displeasure with the administration's "exceptionally tough policy toward the Dominican Republic." Although Smathers claimed to have "no brief" for the Trujillo dictatorship, he asserted that it was "clearly anti-communist and had always been friendly toward the United States."[143] Smathers even urged the administration to name Pawley to a powerful new post, undersecretary of state for Latin American affairs. The State Department refused, citing Pawley's business interests in the Dominican Republic and Cuba and friendship with the dictators of those two countries.[144]

By now, key members of the State Department—starting with Ambassador Joseph S. Farland—were ready to look at every option for getting rid of Trujillo, lest his misrule breed another Castroite rebellion. Farland called Trujillo's record "appalling" and warned his superiors that "we . . . will eventually lose for us the friendship of the really substantial people of this country unless we do something" to force Trujillo out. He continued, "I think the time has come for certain agencies of our Government, without attribution, to establish and implement a definite, constructive program to influence the course of events in the Dominican Republic. My conversations with the Secretary [of State] and with [CIA director] Allen Dulles emphasized the problem and the possibilities of this type of approach. . . . A new phase of operation is a virtual necessity."[145] By the spring of 1960, President Eisenhower was largely sold on replacing Trujillo with a military junta that would hold elections.[146] As he told a meeting of the National Security Council in July, "Until Trujillo is eliminated, we cannot get our Latin American friends to reach a proper level of indignation dealing with Castro."[147]

The Assassination of Trujillo

Far from making plans to retire, Trujillo was secretly plotting the assassination of one of his perennial critics, Venezuelan president Rómulo Betancourt. On June 24, 1960, an agent hired by Johnny Abbes planted sixty-five kilos of TNT in the trunk of a car parked along a presidential parade route in Caracas. The detonation hurled Betancourt's Cadillac across the street and set it on fire, killing a passenger and at least one bystander but only wounding the president. An investigation by the Organization of American States (OAS) soon fingered Trujillo. That August, the OAS foreign ministers voted to condemn the Dominican Republic and to impose an arms embargo and other economic sanctions. In quick succession, the member states broke diplomatic relations. The United States downgraded its embassy to a consulate.[148]

President Eisenhower also sought to reduce the Dominican Republic's sugar quota, which had soared that summer after Castro's Cuba lost its own large quota. Eisenhower called Trujillo's big sugar bonus "seriously embarrassing to the U.S. in the conduct of its foreign relations throughout the hemisphere." However, Trujillo rallied his friends in Congress to keep his windfall. Trujillo also overcame attempted boycotts and pickets against his regime in the United States. To ensure that Dominican ships could unload their sugar, his military intelligence service bought support from a ruthless Teamster boss and close ally of union president Jimmy Hoffa in Puerto Rico.[149]

Meanwhile, dissident Dominican leaders approached Ambassador Farland, asking for high-powered rifles to take out Trujillo. Farland returned to the United States in May 1960, leaving the matter with Deputy Chief of Mission Henry Dearborn. Assistant Secretary of State Richard Rubottom informed the CIA's chief of Western Hemisphere operations that "the Government of the United States was prepared to provide the Dominican dissidents with a small number of sniper rifles or other devices for the removal of key Trujillo people from the scene."[150] The CIA put on hold its delivery of a dozen rifles when the dissidents got cold feet.[151] But Dearborn had no illusions. He told Washington in October 1960 that Trujillo would depart only in a casket: "If you recall Dracula, you will remember it was necessary to drive a stake through the heart to prevent a continuation of his crimes."[152]

On January 12, 1961, the Eisenhower administration's senior covert action policy group formally approved the transfer of weapons to anti-Trujillo forces. Dearborn responded that his Dominican "friends" were "of course delighted" by the promised delivery of what he euphemistically called "the exotic equipment." That spring the CIA handed over several Smith & Wesson pistols and three M-1 carbines. It also sent four M3 machine guns, which were never delivered to the opposition.[153]

The incoming Kennedy administration inherited without qualms the policy of ousting Trujillo but was in no hurry to take action. It focused instead on the impending Bay of Pigs invasion of Cuba by CIA-trained Cuban exiles. In March 1961, Dearborn warned impatiently that "the longer Trujillo continues to dominate the D.R. the more susceptible the country is becoming to leftist extremists, and that, therefore, Trujillo's overthrow in the near future would be in the interest of the U.S."[154] A memo from former secretary of state Herter advised rallying civilian and military dissidents with promises of US military support "to forestall a pro-Castro takeover by seeking actively to bring about the early overthrow of Trujillo." President Kennedy approved that general policy in April 1961.[155]

To give the new president more political room for action against the Dominican regime, administration officials quietly took on the country's well-funded influence peddlers.[156] In mid-February, Secretary of State Dean Rusk forcefully told House Agriculture Committee chairman Harold Cooley that buying more Dominican sugar would forfeit "the support and sympathy which we need" from other Latin countries, which viewed Trujillo "as a threat equally as serious as Castro." Rusk added, pointedly, that "Trujillo's propaganda machine" was "well financed" and "a cause of concern to our intelligence agencies."[157] Meanwhile, Attorney General Robert Kennedy authorized secret FBI wiretaps and bugs to keep tabs on Trujillo's allies.[158] The targets included his Washington lawyers, his embassy and consulates, and Cooley himself. "As far as can be determined by existing records," writes FBI historian Tim Weiner, "it was the first time since the Harding administration that an attorney general had ordered a member of Congress wiretapped." Bobby Kennedy eventually lost his nerve and cut the investigation short, as it threatened to expose too many powerful Democrats in Congress.[159]

Indeed, too thorough an investigation of Trujillo's US supporters would have hit uncomfortably close to home. In the spring of 1961, Joseph Kennedy raised with his son Jack the specter of Communists taking over after Trujillo. The family patriarch had been alerted to that danger by his friend, the unregistered Trujillo lobbyist Igor Cassini.[160] To assuage his father, the president dispatched Cassini and veteran diplomat Robert Murphy, an archconservative member of the President's Foreign Intelligence Advisory Board, to Ciudad Trujillo. Murphy, whose admiration for right-wing regimes extended back to Vichy France, "was a poor choice of emissary for a new administration bent on promoting democracy in the Caribbean," notes historian Michael Hall. "Before leaving, he conferred secretly with Trujillo's eldest son, Ramfis, in New York, where he advised that Trujillo could get Washington to back off by creating the appearance—an aide to Ramfis called it 'an elaborate smoke-screen'—of a move toward democracy."[161]

Murphy returned to Washington on April 16, a day after meeting with Trujillo and a day before the disastrous Bay of Pigs invasion. The emissary described the Dominican Republic as "stable and calm." He reported that Trujillo was committed to providing "better opportunities for the average man." Murphy said the Dominican leader had "no plans to perpetuate a Trujillo dynasty" and pointed to upcoming presidential elections in May 1961 as evidence of his commitment to constitutional government. Murphy counseled offering "friendly guidance" to help the regime "institute democratic reforms." He recommended lifting sanctions and restoring the country's full sugar quota.[162]

Aghast at this whitewash, Kennedy's national security advisor, McGeorge Bundy, warned the president that any such policy reversal would cast doubt on "the whole concept of the Alliance for Progress." He added that "if the public were to know that Igor Cassini is providing public relations help to Trujillo, your own personal position as a liberal leader might be compromised."[163] JFK no doubt agreed but asked his father to tell Cassini that he was "very impressed with the magnificent report prepared by Robert Murphy."[164]

Still smarting from the Bay of Pigs fiasco, the president decreed in early May that "the United States should not initiate the overthrow of Trujillo before we knew what government would succeed him."[165] Adolf Berle, a senior adviser on Dominican policy and former chairman of SuCrest Corp., let the CIA know that "we did not wish to have anything to do with any assassination plot anywhere, any time."[166] President Kennedy himself soon declared, "We must not run the risk of US association with political assassination since the US as matter of general policy cannot condone assassinations."[167] The White House instructed Consul Dearborn not to pass any machine guns to the opposition.[168]

It was too late; the CIA had already handed over three M1 carbines to the anti-Trujillo conspirators.[169] After months of nervous dithering the opposition finally acted. On May 30, 1961, a small band of assassins put an end to Trujillo's cruel reign. But their coup plans died stillborn. Johnny Abbes quickly began rounding up and torturing suspects. Dearborn and all CIA personnel in the country destroyed records of their contacts with the opposition and hustled back to Washington.[170] Fearing possible retribution from the Trujillo family, the US Secret Service reinforced its protective detail around President Kennedy.[171]

Trujillo's puppet president, Joaquín Balaguer, stayed on as head of state. The Kennedy administration backed him, fearful that disorder could favor Castro. The White House directed three aircraft carriers, three dozen support ships, and five thousand marines to float conspicuously off the coast of Ciudad Trujillo. Meanwhile, however, Trujillo's eldest son, Ramfis, and secret police chief Abbes retained significant power.[172] Ramfis was described by Dearborn as the "most unstable, ruthless, US-hating, untrustworthy and cynical occupant of whole Trujillo nest and we should avoid him like bubonic plague." Even President Balaguer privately called him "the worst of the lot."[173] The North American public, however, was steadily fed reassuring news of the regime's democratic intentions, courtesy of Igor Cassini.

Ramfis surprised his worst detractors by forcing Abbes into exile. He curbed some police excesses, allowed the formation of opposition political parties, turned some of the family's huge sugar plantations over to the state, and gave Balaguer political space to enact some reforms. He passed word to Washington, through William Pawley and Robert Murphy, that he wanted to move the country toward democracy.[174] Pawley reported that Ramfis was acting with "statesmanship, courage, and ability."[175] However, the State Department warned that "if the Trujillos try to hang on, a revolutionary movement will develop."[176] In November 1961, faced with another intimidating display of US naval power, Ramfis decamped first to France and then to Spain, where he took charge of the enormous fortune plundered by his father from the Dominican Republic. He was soon followed into exile by his uncles Arismendi and Héctor. With the Trujillos gone, tens of thousands of Dominicans took to the streets to celebrate their "libertad."[177]

Ramfis's exile brought no stability to the Dominican Republic, however. Thousands of Dominicans staged a general strike to demand the resignation of Trujillo's former puppet, Balaguer. On January 16, 1962, just ten days after the United States restored full diplomatic relations, right-wing military officers overthrew Balaguer, forcing him into exile. Before long, a civil-military Council of State took charge. Although official graft was endemic, the Kennedy administration sent $25 million to keep the economy afloat, along with military and police aid to suppress popular demonstrations. The new US ambassador, John Bartlow Martin, twisted arms to arrange new elections in December 1962.[178] The overwhelming (and unexpected) victor was Juan Bosch, a prominent liberal exile who had opposed Trujillo for decades.

The Mob in the Dominican Republic under Bosch

As leader of the reformist Partido Revolucionario Dominicano (PRD), Bosch was elected on "a platform advocating distribution of Trujillo land to landless *campesinos*, formation of cooperatives, an increase in agricultural wages, construction of small-town communal eating halls, public works, and development of new industry around untapped mineral resources to reduce unemployment."[179] He took office on February 27, 1963. Bosch appreciated the support, but not the heavy-handed micromanagement, of Ambassador Martin.[180] His hold on office was precarious, however. Conservatives slandered him as a Communist; business leaders snubbed him; senior military officers regularly hatched plots to overthrow him; and many of his supporters resented the glacial pace of his reforms.[181] Ambassador Martin called Bosch's government "one of the most dollar-honest governments in the Republic's history," but noted that "slot machines spread to remote areas of the Republic, as they had under Trujillo. . . . At one point known racketeers from

Chicago and Las Vegas tried to move in."[182] A Justice Department memo later commented on the "singularly large contingent of known gambling figures and Mafia types" who descended on Santo Domingo during Bosch's brief administration in hope of winning "the rich gambling concessions of the Dominican Republic."[183]

That invasion began well before Bosch took office, however. Soon after the Cuban revolution, powerful North American criminals began scoping out opportunities for turning the country into a sinful playground for affluent tourists. One such mobster was George Levine, a "trusted friend" of Batista and acquaintance of gambling bosses Meyer Lansky and Santo Trafficante. In Cuba, Levine had owned the Oriental Park racetrack and its gambling casino in partnership with three prominent East Coast mobsters. In late 1961, while the Trujillo family was still clinging to power in the Dominican Republic, an FBI informant said Levine was working "on securing the gambling concession at the Jaragua Hotel," the largest luxury accommodation in the country. Apparently, Levine had been promised gambling rights at the hotel after he saved Trujillo's favorite son-in-law, Porfirio Rubirosa, from being assassinated in Cuba. Levine's plans were crimped, however, by his 1962 conviction in Miami for transporting counterfeit securities with Midwest Teamster official Gene San Souci (chapter 5).[184] In January 1963, two associates of Levine's group began negotiating to lease the Jaragua's casino. The Dominican Republic's political instability soon discouraged them, however. One of these gamblers told the FBI in May 1963 that "the threat of possible war involving that country would discourage most people from investing a substantial amount of money necessary to finance a gambling proposition in Santo Domingo."[185]

When Bosch assumed office, other US mobsters tried to deal directly with him to promote rackets in the Dominican Republic. One was Sam Giancana, who took charge of the Chicago Outfit after Paul Ricca's semiretirement in the late 1950s (chapter 2). The FBI's Chicago office reported in the summer of 1963 that Giancana was "negotiating with persons in Dominican Republic for purpose of establishing gambling interests and operations in that country under his control." That May, Giancana reportedly made two trips to the country in the company of various gamblers and hotel investors; he was also said to be planning a trip to Paris to meet with Porfirio Rubirosa. Financial backers of his planned gambling venture reportedly included Meyer Lansky, two cousins of Al Capone, and Detroit mobster Pete Licavoli, a hidden investor with Giancana in the Desert Inn casino in Las Vegas.[186] Harassed by constant FBI surveillance, however, Giancana gave up on Dominican gambling, which he belittled as "a losing proposition."[187]

South Florida's Santo Trafficante Jr. was more persistent. He established a gambling outpost in Santo Domingo at the Hispaniola Hotel. One of his local associates, Rafael "Macho" Gener, oversaw gambling operations at the Union Club in the capital. (Gener had arranged Trafficante's release from jail in Cuba in 1959 and later smuggled poison pills into Cuba for a CIA-backed plot to assassinate Castro.) By early 1963, Trafficante was pursuing several new projects in the Dominican Republic: installing slot machines all over the country, turning the Trujillo family's yacht into a floating gambling casino, operating the casino at the Hotel Embajador, and buying another nightclub to operate as a casino. His schemes went nowhere. The Bosch government turned down his request for slot machine concessions, priced the yacht too high, and said the Ambassador Hotel was already leased to a subsidiary of Pan American Airlines. Trafficante took the news badly. The Florida crime boss had recently lost $400,000 on a coffee deal in Brazil and more than $2 million when Castro nationalized the Havana Hilton. He could not afford to lose more.[188]

Trafficante soon had a change of heart, however. In the summer of 1963, he and Philadelphia Mafia boss Angelo Bruno recruited a well-connected intermediary to help them reopen talks with the Bosch government: the prominent Cuban exile José Alemán. A Miami hotel operator and baseball stadium owner, Alemán was the son of a former Cuban education minister who had been ousted in 1947 for conspiring with Bosch, then a young revolutionary, to overthrow Trujillo.[189] The younger Alemán was reluctant initially to get involved with Trafficante, having testified in 1960 against two of his associates, Sam Mannarino and Norman Rothman, in the stolen arms case. But he came around once Trafficante dangled the prospect of arranging Teamster pension fund loans to bail out Alemán's troubled real estate ventures.[190] Alemán traveled to the Dominican Republic as a representative of Inter-Continental Homes in Philadelphia, a venture backed by Bruno and Trafficante. Alemán and Bruno met with President Bosch and other government leaders about building low-cost housing in the country in exchange for payoffs to Dominican officials. They also discussed plans to build a dairy plant and concrete plant, to import mules from Sicily, and to import surplus slot machines from one of Bruno's warehouses. None of these plans went anywhere in the few months that Bosch clung to power.[191]

Enter Bobby Baker and the Las Vegas Mob

The FBI learned that one of Bruno's key political contacts in the Dominican Republic in the summer of 1963 was an American—Robert "Bobby" Baker, secretary to the Senate Majority Leader, Mike Mansfield, D-Mont.[192] The next three chapters will have much more to say about Baker, whose far-flung political and business dealings rocked Washington in 1963 and 1964 and threatened to derail Lyndon Johnson's political career. In addition to his remarkable collection of friends in the US government, Baker had a history of contacts with Dominican officials dating back to the Trujillo era.[193] Baker had met with Bosch himself in New York City in December 1962. Baker then joined his former boss, Vice President Johnson, at Bosch's presidential inauguration two months later. (Also on hand for the festivities was Angelo Bruno.)[194] One of Baker's well-placed contacts in the new Bosch government was the secretary of state for Industry and Commerce, Diego Bordas, a wealthy shipping executive who oversaw hotel gambling concessions and had a reputation as an "opportunist" and a "buccaneer."[195]

Baker's interest in the Dominican Republic unexpectedly came to the FBI's attention in early 1961, after the new attorney general tasked Hoover with investigating Dominican influence peddling. The bureau learned in May 1961 that Baker had befriended the Dominican consul general in Washington, D.C.—the point man for the country's lobbying effort. At the same time, Baker was exploring business deals in the Dominican Republic with Diego Bordas, then an expatriate living in Puerto Rico. Also involved in their dealings was Senator Smathers, a close friend of Baker's (chapter 5). Baker ingratiated himself with the Dominican diplomat by passing along political gossip, often describing his conversations with Smathers and Vice President Johnson. In one case, Baker reported on an "urgent meeting" that Johnson held with Sen. William Fulbright, chairman of the Foreign Relations Committee and a critic of sugar lobbyists; days later, Baker arranged the first of several meetings between the consul and Johnson himself. A registered lobbyist for the Dominican Republic described Baker accurately as a man who "has his hand out for money." Baker leaned on the consul for help in getting a business proposal, apparently involving cement, approved by the Dominican government.[196]

Before long, the Senate aide had become a business partner with two major US casino owners with ambitions to enter the Dominican Republic, Edward Levinson and Clifford Jones. Levinson, then president of the mob-controlled Fremont Hotel-Casino in Las Vegas, joined Baker in the Dominican Republic to celebrate Bosch's inauguration. He was apparently seeking opportunities for his less successful brother, Louis "Sleep Out" Levinson, a veteran of illegal gambling casinos in Kentucky who had been barred from doing business in Nevada.

Levinson and Baker had another partner with political pull in the Dominican Republic, a sleazy Miami entrepreneur named Jack Cooper. Cooper, Levinson, and Meyer Lansky were all investors in the Miami International Airport Hotel.[197] As a partner in the Dominican banana export business with one of Trujillo's brothers, Cooper once persuaded a newspaper columnist to describe him grandiosely as the "undisputed banana king of Miami" and "the power behind the throne of . . . Trujillo." Cooper was convicted in 1961 of income tax evasion stemming from a scam with Ramfis Trujillo involving a fraudulent sale of forty-two P-51 fighter planes to the Dominican Republic.[198] Cooper joined mobster George Levine in scoping out Dominican gambling opportunities in 1961, after Trujillo's murder. Perhaps acting in his role as "a front man for the investment of crime syndicate funds" (the FBI's words), Cooper joined Baker and Levinson on at least one of their visits to the Dominican Republic in 1963.[199]

Also sniffing around the newly democratic Caribbean nation was Levinson's Las Vegas casino partner, Albert Parvin. The Chicago-born interior decorator had furnished the mob's first great hotel-casino on the Las Vegas Strip, the Flamingo. Parvin later took control of the property before selling it to a front group for Meyer Lansky in 1960 and paying the mobster a $200,000 finder's fee. His lawyer on that deal was Ed Levinson. Parvin set up a private foundation later that year with some of the proceeds of the Flamingo sale.[200] Just a month before Bosch's inauguration, the Parvin Foundation decided to earmark all of its resources to developing "leadership" in the Dominican Republic. Its main beneficiary was one of Bosch's closest political allies, Sacha Volman, a Romanian-born CIA agent and director of the Inter-American School for Political Training in the Dominican Republic.[201]

Following Bosch's inauguration, Baker made four trips to Santo Domingo to investigate gambling opportunities on Levinson's behalf.[202] In June 1963, while still serving as secretary to the Senate Majority, Baker approached a vice president of Pan American World Airways for an introduction to the head of its subsidiary, Intercontinental Hotels. Intercontinental operated hotels throughout the Caribbean, including the Embajador in Santo Domingo. (Prior to Castro's victory, it also managed the celebrated Hotel Nacional in Havana, whose casino was operated by Lansky and members of the Cleveland Syndicate.)[203] On June 20, Baker brought Levinson to see the chairman of the hotel chain in New York. The seasoned Las Vegas pro made a pitch to operate Intercontinental's casinos in Santo Domingo and Curaçao.[204] However, Levinson was barred by Nevada law from running gambling operations outside the state so long as he held casino licenses there. Intercontinental Hotels would not accept Levinson's brother Louis as a substitute.[205]

Baker next introduced the hotel executive to Clifford "Big Juice" Jones, a former lieutenant governor of Nevada who once fronted for the Lansky brothers in a Las Vegas casino. By 1963, he was operating three small casinos in the Caribbean and one in Quito, Ecuador. Jones was also a friend of Levinson. The two men were co-investors in the Bank of World Commerce, a Bahamian money laundromat for American mobsters. Jones was also an investor with Levinson and Baker in a Tulsa bank and a Honolulu savings and loan association.[206] Jones had no casino licenses in Nevada, and Intercontinental approved his bid. That August, President Bosch approved Jones's casino lease at the Embajador. A few months later, Jones took charge of the Pan Am subsidiary's casino in Curaçao as well. Jones gave Baker $10,000 for his help getting the valuable concessions.[207] Levinson's hapless brother had to settle for running the third-rate "Coney Island" casino at the old World's Fair site in Santo Domingo, part-owned by Angelo Bruno.[208] Chapter 5 has much more to say about Baker, Levinson, and Jones.

On to Balaguer

Bosch's failure to ally himself with powerful US mobsters was noble, but it reflected his general failure to acquire influential political allies. The Dominican Republic's first elected leader lasted fewer than ten months in power. In September 1963, just a week after rejecting a corrupt proposal by the head of his air force to purchase British war planes, Bosch was ousted by a military coup and exiled to Puerto Rico.[209] Dominican military leaders defended their takeover on the basis of Bosch's alleged ineptitude, corruption, and laxity toward Communism. ("It was strange to hear Bosch, who dismissed the one adviser suspected of corruption, being accused of corruption by people who clearly have no general objection to it," commented one US academic expert at the time.)[210] In short order, the military installed a civilian figurehead from one of the country's oligarchic families, Donald Reid Cabral, to lead a ruling triumvirate. Although favored by the US ambassador, Reid proved highly unpopular with his countrymen, thanks in part to his tolerance of "flagrant corruption by high military and police officials." His government also revived Trujillo-era death squads to engage in vicious political repression against union leaders and opposition newspapers.[211]

The triumvirate, like Trujillo, was also friendly toward North American criminals. An FBI informant reported in April 1964 that Angelo Bruno was "now ready to go ahead in the Dominican Republic" with his plans for gambling casinos.[212] Bruno was reported to have hired Lansky's former Havana lieutenant Dino Cellini to run a casino at the Jaragua Hotel in 1964. (Dino's brother Eddie had been working there on and off at least since 1962.)[213] However, one of Bruno's agents reported back from a trip to Santo Domingo in May 1964 that conditions for expansion of casinos in the Dominican capital were disappointing. Gambling operations at the Hotel Embajador, run by "friends of Santo" Trafficante, were making little money because of a ban on slot machines. Competition was looming at another major hotel from "the people from Chicago." Two rival government ministers and the chief of police were demanding payoffs. Bruno told his representative that the key to their future on the island was getting better political leadership: "Balaguer is all right, you know . . . I rather see Balaguer. [He] can make a connection in the right place. The other way you got to go through this guy, that guy, that guy."[214]

The country's political volatility discouraged foreign investment by both criminal and legitimate interests.[215] When Reid repeated Bosch's mistake of trying to eliminate "a contracts racket operated by top military men," the generals forced him to resign in April 1965. Younger, more reformist officers then revolted, triggering a popular political uprising. Widespread support for Bosch's return alarmed Johnson administration officials. On White House orders, the CIA and even FBI sprang into action, planting false stories alleging that Bosch was collaborating with the Communist Party.[216] Citing that bogus menace, along with the threat to American lives, President Johnson sent 23,000 US soldiers to the Dominican Republic to reinstall the military junta and prevent the former elected president from regaining power.[217]

The intervention implicated corporate interests almost as much as the overthrow of Guatemalan president Arbenz did in 1954. President Johnson's secret delegate to Bosch during the occupation was his close personal adviser Abe Fortas, Bobby Baker's former attorney and a longtime director of Sucrest Corp., one of the country's largest sugar refiners. The State Department's chief adviser on the Dominican Republic was Adolf Berle Jr., who served as board chairman of Sucrest until 1964. A leading partner in Sucrest's Wall Street law firm and business partner of Ed Levinson and Jack Cooper, Maxwell Rabb, was named vice chairman of National Citizens for Johnson and Humphrey just months before the US invasion. Johnson's ambassador to the Organization of American States and special envoy to the Dominican Republic, Ellsworth Bunker, was the former chairman, president, and director of National Sugar Refining Co. Ambassador Averell Harriman, appointed by LBJ to defend the intervention to governments throughout Latin America, came from a New York investment bank that owned 5 percent of National Sugar Refining Co.[218]

Balaguer Takes Charge

In the chaotic months that followed, Trujillo's former front man, Balaguer, maneuvered to win Washington's favor as the country's future leader. He was more conservative and pro-business than Bosch, and his civilian status made him more acceptable than any military leader for president. Balaguer latched on to his friend, the veteran Washington lobbyist Irving Davidson, to become his intermediary with Washington. Davidson was a registered agent for

Caribbean dictators Anastasio and Luis Somoza and François Duvalier. He also peddled influence for Louisiana Mafia boss Carlos Marcello and corrupt Teamsters president Jimmy Hoffa, both of whom had their hooks into Trujillo.[219] During the Dominican crisis in 1965, Balaguer made Abe Fortas and State Department officials schedule meetings through Davidson.[220] Davidson intimated to Dominican officials that he had the ear of the White House, and of President Johnson himself.[221]

In 1966, Balaguer won a thoroughly rigged election to become president. He had ample financial and logistical help from the CIA.[222] Balaguer also enjoyed political support lined up in Washington by New Jersey mobster Joseph Zicarelli. Zicarelli's point man in Congress, New Jersey representative and Foreign Affairs Committee member Cornelius Gallagher, lobbied the State Department on Balaguer's behalf and joined Vice President Hubert Humphrey's official delegation to celebrate Balaguer's inauguration.[223] Balaguer chose Zicarelli's attorney, Stephen Hoffman, and Irving Davidson to act as his government's political agents in the United States.[224] Unlike Bosch, this long-lived Dominican leader understood the importance of cultivating powerful allies in the United States, including members of the underworld.

Like Trujillo, Balaguer ruled at times with the ruthlessness of a Mafia boss. He appointed as head of the Dominican National Police a police captain who was implicated in killing the American pilot in the Galíndez case, and who oversaw the assassination of more than three thousand leftists from 1966 to 1974.[225] Unlike Trujillo, however, Balaguer opened the country wide to US capital. His greatest beneficiary was the high-flying US conglomerate, Gulf and Western (G&W). That was a savvy choice. G&W's Wall Street attorney, Ed Weisl Sr., was New York's state delegate to the Democratic National Committee. He had been one of Lyndon Johnson's closest political confidants since the late 1930s, and one of his main conduits to Hollywood and Wall Street money.[226] In 1965, Johnson sent Weisl's law partner and protégé Cyrus Vance to the Dominican Republic with Fortas to establish a provisional government after the US invasion.[227] As conditions in the country stabilized with the election of Balaguer in 1966, G&W began buying shares and taking control of South Puerto Rico Sugar, the largest private landholder in the Dominican Republic. It soon broke the back of the sugar mill workers' union. Meanwhile, the Balaguer regime showered financial benefits on the firm, including a twenty-year tax holiday. Washington rewarded Balaguer (and G&W) with a major increase in the Dominican Republic's sugar quota.[228] Former senator Smathers, the longtime political ally of Trujillo and Balaguer, joined G&W's board around this time.

G&W also invested millions of dollars in exclusive coastal resorts and luxury hotels—including the lucrative, mob-run casino at the Hotel Hispaniola in Santo Domingo.[229] G&W's record in the country was controversial to say the least.[230] After a multiyear investigation into numerous fraud allegations, the Securities and Exchange Commission sued G&W in 1979 for conspiring with Dominican officials to speculate in sugar while withholding millions of dollars due the government. The SEC settled with the company in 1981.[231]

G&W was not just another big multinational corporation. It represented the sophisticated new face of money and personnel once associated with the mob. Before expanding into the Dominican Republic, the company had developed high-level connections to the Chicago Outfit. G&W's CEO Charles Bludhorn was a friend and client of attorney Sidney Korshak, the Chicago mob's trusted legal representative in the entertainment and hospitality industries. G&W's attorney, Weisl, was a close friend of Chicago businessman Julius Stein, who built MCA, another Korshak client, into an entertainment powerhouse with help from the Capone organization. Stein was also the largest shareholder in Paramount Pictures, whose executive committee was headed by Weisl. When G&W CEO Charles Bludhorn began thinking about acquiring a big-name studio in 1966, Korshak and Weisl introduced him to Stein, and then arranged G&W's purchase of Paramount that October.[232] Soon after that deal, according to crime historian Gus Russo, G&W also became deeply embroiled with representatives of the New Jersey and Italian Mafia.[233]

In the years to come, traditional organized crime would lose its foothold in the Dominican Republic. Angelo Bruno maintained hidden interests in Dominican gambling until 1970, when he was indicted with two members of the Gambino crime family in New York for criminal contempt and perjury stemming from an investigation into his attempts to buy into the casino at G&W's Hispaniola Hotel in Santo Domingo. Bruno spent three years in prison in the early 1970s. He was finally put to rest by a gangland hit in 1980.[234] Within a decade, North American gangsters like Bruno would be shunted aside by enormously wealthy Latin cartels, which used the Dominican Republic as a way station for serving the North American drug market.[235]

Chapter 9 returns to the Caribbean to examine how the deep political intrigues of influence peddlers, mobsters, and intelligence operatives there "blew back" to poison US national politics in the 1960s and early 1970s, setting the stage for the Watergate crisis in President Nixon's second term.

5

The Friends of LBJ—I

Bobby Baker and the Mob

IF MOST HISTORIANS HAVE SUFFERED collective amnesia about the bipartisan scandals and corruption of the Truman years, the same cannot be said
of Lyndon Johnson's career. Even friendly biographers confirm Johnson's
ruthless drive to gain power and wealth by any means: advancing to the
Senate via a stolen primary election in 1948, raising vast sums of campaign
cash from government contractors and oil millionaires, and wielding influence over federal agencies to build his family's fortune. Yet they have almost
completely ignored the deep ties of one of his closest associates to some of the
most sophisticated mobsters of their time.

The venal record of Johnson's close circle is of more than passing historical
interest. LBJ's long-standing friendship with his former Senate aide, Robert
"Bobby" Baker, helped bring the vice president to the brink of political ruin
in 1963 and 1964. It jeopardized his career before he had put his giant stamp
on American society with passage of the Civil Rights Act, Medicare, and, far
less nobly, the Vietnam War. His ambitions were rescued by one of the most
dramatic turning points of modern American history, the assassination of
President John F. Kennedy. Out of the nation's tragedy came Johnson's unex-
pected opportunity. As biographer Robert Caro relates,

> A pair of scandals on [a grand] scale had been looming over the vice president
> for months and were both coming to a head on the morning of November 22
> [1963]. One, involving Johnson's protégé Bobby Baker (known in Washington
> as "Little Lyndon"), had during the weeks before the assassination become a
> sensational cover story in national magazines. Baker was later to say that if he
> had talked, Johnson "might have incurred a mortal wound by these revelations.

. . . They could have driven him from office," but he hadn't talked yet. Nor had any of his associates, and as a result the vice president had not been directly implicated. But on the morning of November 22, at the very time that the motorcade was carrying Kennedy and Johnson through Dallas, back in Washington, that had been about to change. And at the same time, the other scandal . . . was escalating to a new stage in New York, in a conference at the offices of *Life* magazine, where a team of nine reporters had been working for weeks on a series of articles, with the working title of "Lyndon Johnson's Money." Editors were dividing up areas for final investigation and trying to decide whether to run the first article in the next week's issue, which would shortly go to press, when suddenly, all over *Life*'s newsroom, phones began ringing frantically, and a secretary ran into the office shouting the news [of JFK's assassination].[1]

Even as president, LBJ had to employ all of his famous political skills to blunt multiple investigations related to Baker. One of his first calls upon returning to Washington after the tragedy in Dallas was to Abe Fortas, his crisis adviser and Baker's attorney, to get an update on a burgeoning congressional investigation into Baker's influence peddling, sweetheart business deals, and Washington sex. Johnson spoke with great anxiety about the case on dozens of subsequent recorded calls from the Oval Office and on an unknown number of unrecorded calls and in-person conversations. LBJ was haunted by his memory of the scandals that drove President Truman out of the race in 1952. "My judgment is that they're going to holler corruption on us to death," he moaned to Larry O'Brien, his 1964 campaign director. "Between now, it's going to be Korea and corruption and something else. And they're going to do everything they can. . . . I'm afraid of this corruption issue."[2] Several years later, Fortas would declare, "The political implications and political potentialities at the time were enormous."[3]

Serious political commentators at the time considered the Baker scandals, and the larger culture of political rot they exposed, to be of major national significance. Harkening like Johnson back to the Truman scandals, national columnist Robert Donovan observed in November 1963, "Not in a dozen years has Washington been so much preoccupied with talk of sex hijinks, conflict-of-interest, tax evasion, favoritism and congressional junkets. . . . Scarcely a week passes without some new disclosure of deals by Baker with businessmen, politicians or Las Vegas gamblers."[4]

In a long investigative article published in *Life* magazine's fateful November 22, 1963, issue, Keith Wheeler reported that

the Baker scandal, gathering both bulk and momentum, has been enough to embarrass severely some members of the Senate and to outrage the rest. It has scared numerous other individuals into funk holes from which they may never emerge. . . . Its influence has set off subsidiary scandals of its own and, in the mood of general uproar, other cases of official hanky-panky are breaking out for the first time or are being dragged out for another look. Altogether this proliferation of scandal reveals a dumfounding atmosphere of personal, political and business amorality in today's official Washington and the satellites which orbit around it.[5]

As the investigation gained steam, *New York Times* reporter Cabell Phillips declared, with reference to a political scandal that stained President Eisenhower's chief of staff,

> The Bobby Baker case is rapidly developing into the political scandal of the middle sixties. . . . For the Baker case is strongly symptomatic of a chronic amorality that has been eroding the public conscience, within government principally but in other spheres of national life as well, for a long time. . . . [T]he Baker affair has an ominous potentiality for the Democratic cause and for some individual Democrats in and out of Congress. . . . [I]t is a dead certainty that the Bobby Baker case, whatever its ultimate resolution, will haunt the Democrats' table in 1964 like the ghost of [President Eisenhower's chief of staff] Sherman "Banquo" Adams.[6]

Two months later, congressional Democrats finally managed to contain the investigation and cut off dangerous new avenues of inquiry. They succeeded in protecting President Johnson and other senior politicians, but at a cost to American democracy. *New York Times* Washington bureau chief and columnist James Reston observed that the case was "now coming to a close but not an end," leaving behind many unresolved questions, especially about favoritism in government contracting and the corrupting role of money in political campaigns. In the process, Reston lamented, "the Baker case has damaged not only Baker but the confidence of the public in the integrity of the legislative process."[7] That loss of confidence in government, compounded by growing public distrust in the Warren Commission's findings regarding the JFK assassination and the "credibility gap" that widened as the Vietnam War dragged on, became a lasting blight on American politics.

Among Johnson's major biographers, Caro tells by far the most detailed and compelling story of the Baker scandal. Yet even this careful chronicler, otherwise unshrinking in his examination of Johnson's dark side, completely ignores the leading role played by organized crime. Through Baker's influence, businessmen with ties to the underworld infiltrated Washington political circles and made lucrative investments with powerful insiders, much as they did in the Dominican Republic. The political significance of this alliance was profound. It represented a blatant challenge to the Kennedy administration's war on organized crime, with the potential to drive a deeper wedge between two determined rivals: Bobby Kennedy and Lyndon Johnson.[8] The failure of most historians to address this important facet of the scandal is inexplicable, given that Baker's mob ties made national headlines and put Johnson at special political risk. Years later, Baker himself acknowledged, "the reason they all went crazy over me was that Meyer Lansky was in on it."[9] The Baker story is so rich that I return to it in chapter 6 on the Murchison family and chapter 7 on Henry Crown and the TFX scandal. These interconnected stories demonstrate the critical but underappreciated importance of political influence and endemic corruption to advancing the ambitions of organized criminals and their business partners in the United States during the 1950s and 1960s.

The Bobby Baker Scandal Unfolds

Baker began his career as a lowly Senate page at the age of fourteen. The job, which he landed as a political favor to his family, was his ticket out of Pickens, South Carolina. Through unstinting hard work and efforts to please, he rose to become secretary to the Senate Democratic majority—right-hand man to Majority leader Lyndon Johnson—while his wife worked the other side of the aisle for Vice President Nixon. No less important, Baker became secretary-treasurer of the Senate Democratic Campaign Committee, in charge of raising and distributing campaign funds. Baker's superb political skills and connections set him apart from many other quick-buck operators of his time. Johnson and other senators regarded him as indispensable for his uncanny ability to count votes.[10] Some Washington insiders called Baker the "101st Senator." *Life* magazine described him as Johnson's "legman, mouthpiece and satrap of power."[11] Although never elected to any post, Baker wielded enough clout to help swing the appointment of Sen. Edward Long, a Missouri Democrat and thirty-year friend of mob attorney Morris Shenker, to the powerful Judiciary Committee in 1961.[12] (For more on Long, see chapter 9.) Baker himself boasted imprudently, "On any issue I have at least ten Senators in the palm of my hand."[13]

Succumbing to temptation, Baker began in the mid-1950s leveraging his political friendships and influence for personal gain. By his own account, he entered into business deals with "senators, lobbyists, a JFK cabinet member, and other public officials or former politicians." On a comfortable but modest Senate salary of less than $20,000 a year, he reported a personal net worth of more than $2.1 million in 1963, including bank deposits of more than $1.5 million.[14]

Baker's far-flung business dealings first came to the attention of the media and Congress when a business rival filed a $300,000 lawsuit against him on September 9, 1963. The suit charged Baker with influencing a defense contractor to hire a vending machine company, Serv-U, in which Baker held a hidden interest, at the expense of the plaintiff, who had paid Baker to steer the deal to his own company. Baker's main partner in Serv-U was a $200,000-a-year "management consultant" (lobbyist) for North American Aviation Corp. named Fred Black Jr. Reporting on the lawsuit, *Newsweek* described Baker as "so much the protégé of Lyndon Johnson . . . that he is known as 'Lyndon's Boy.'" Such stories threw the vice president into a panic while traveling in Europe on official business. Johnson canceled appointments for an entire day while he conferred with various aides, and his political adviser Abe Fortas, about how to contain the potential scandal. He then cut short the rest of his trip to rush home. Johnson sent his most trusted assistant, Walter Jenkins, to impress upon Baker the need to contain the matter, lest Bobby Kennedy use it to embarrass the vice president. On October 7, Baker resigned his Senate post, hired Fortas as his attorney, and turned for advice to Johnson's supremely able fixer, Thomas Corcoran.[15] That October, Vice President Johnson met or spoke over the phone with Baker's lawyer on at least twelve occasions, three times more than in all the previous six months.[16] Clearly, LBJ was deeply concerned not only about Baker's fate, but also his own.

He had reason to worry. The stories about Baker had caught the attention of Sen. John J. Williams, a Delaware Republican known as the "conscience of the Senate." A tenacious investigator, Williams had spent two years uncovering corruption in the Internal Revenue Bureau before blowing the whistle on dozens of Truman administration officials in 1951. He was well aware of the malign political power of organized crime, having exposed a "remarkably chummy relationship . . . between the revenuers and Frank Costello, the New York gambler," as one newspaper profile recalled in 1964. Unlike some of his more conservative colleagues, moreover, Williams won widespread respect for joining in the Senate's censure of Joseph McCarthy, supporting civil rights legislation, and voting to cut the oil-depletion tax break.[17]

On October 10, 1963, the Senate adopted a resolution sponsored by Williams to task the Rules and Administration Committee with investigating conflicts of interest and other improprieties by current or former Senate employees. Baker was the main target of hearings that began October 29. The core of the investigation lasted only through March 1964, but troublesome issues kept it alive through May 1965. In the end, the Senate's Democratic majority sharply curtailed the scope of the probe to limit unwelcome political damage. Even so, the investigation garnered headlines, fertilized public distrust of Washington, and aroused great political angst from the White House to the Capitol.

Sex was one acute cause of that angst. On November 8, Drew Pearson learned from a reliable source that "Bobby [Baker] was the pimp, apparently, for President Kennedy, Lyndon Johnson, George Smathers, and various others in procuring girls. . . . Bobby Baker apparently realized that the way to get ahead in Washington was through sex and thereby gained a lot of influence. How much of this is going to come out at the Senate hearings remains to be seen. . . . Lyndon is worried over the developments. This, of course, could knock Lyndon off the ticket for 1964."[18]

Pearson's source was well informed. Baker introduced members of Congress to beautiful women at the plush Carousel resort motel he owned in Maryland and at the intimate Quorum Club he helped establish across from the New Senate Office Building. The "Q" Club was a cozy place for top military brass, senators, lobbyists, and rich businessmen to relax in the company of "party girls." The club's president and Baker's business partner was Scott Peek, administrative assistant to Florida senator George Smathers, one of Johnson's closest political allies and one of Baker's business benefactors.[19] One particularly memorable waitress at the "Q" Club, said to resemble Elizabeth Taylor wearing a "scanty black skin-tight uniform," was a suspected East Germany spy named Ellen Rometsch. She was also a regular at the Carousel motel and reportedly attended one particularly debauched party with senior US military officers. A railroad lobbyist friendly with Baker and Smathers introduced Rometsch to President Kennedy; later, as reporters began to get wind of their fling, JFK's brother ordered her flown back to West Germany. The attorney general begged Hoover to deflect congressional investigations into her sexual relations with "high White House officials." That was easy to accomplish, since prominent members of both parties had indiscretions of their own to hide. In private briefings, RFK and Hoover persuaded Senate Minority leader Everett Dirksen, R-Ill., that a full probe "would disclose such a large percentage of the Senate as being of such low morals it could undermine the confidence of the people in the integrity of our government and may even prove disastrous to our country."[20]

Johnson later confided to a few trusted reporters that his close friend and gossip partner, FBI director Hoover, had "Jack Kennedy by the balls" because of the president's many sexual indiscretions.[21] But Johnson himself did not feel immune. In January 1964, he asked Smathers about a tape recording involving Ellen Rometsch and her alleged connections to many powerful politicians, including "the attorney general and me and you and everybody." Neither man admitted knowing her. Smathers responded, "Thank God, they've got [Republican Rules Committee member] Hugh Scott in [the tape]. He's the guy that was asking for it. But she's also mentioned him, (laughs) which is sort of a lifesaver. So I don't think that'll get too far now."[22]

The public hearings into Baker delved into more traditional issues of political influence and avarice: alleged contributions to the 1960 Democratic presidential campaign disguised as payments for construction of the D.C. stadium; improper payments to Baker's law partner to influence legislation affecting freight forwarders; a payoff to influence the granting of a federal bank charter; insider stock deals to win government favors for a private mortgage insurance company; suspicious commissions to Baker on a Haitian meat-importing contract that won federal approval; and various unsecured bank loans to Baker for lucrative stock purchases.

Most immediately damaging to Johnson was testimony by Maryland insurance broker Don Reynolds, a friend and business partner of Baker's. He told the committee that Johnson had demanded illegal kickbacks in exchange for letting Reynolds write $200,000 in life insurance policies between 1957 and 1961. Reynolds's gift of an expensive hi-fi set to the Johnson family triggered memories of gifts (a deep freezer and mink coat) that had aroused fierce public condemnation of senior officials in the Truman administration. The premiums had been paid by the LBJ Company, owned by Johnson's wife, Lady Bird. The link to her company stoked a major investigation by *Life* magazine into the means by which Johnson, on a government salary, had acquired radio and TV stations, thousands of acres of ranchland, and shares in nine Texas banks. As noted by Caro, the magazine's multipart exposé was called off at the last minute by the assassination of President Kennedy.[23]

In public, Johnson minimized not only his dealings with Reynolds, but even those with Baker. In earlier, better days, Johnson had described Baker as being like a son to him, "my strong right arm, the last man I see at night, the first I see in the morning." (Johnson had also praised Baker for serving "without regard to what he will get in return.")[24] Although the vice president claimed to have no knowledge of Baker's business affairs, Alfred Steinberg noted,

Johnson voiced no objection in 1959 when Baker combined his Senate work with a restaurant project in partnership with Governor Luther Hodges of North Carolina, who later became Kennedy's Secretary of Commerce. Nor did Johnson object when Baker went into partnership with two builders to construct the Carousel, a million-dollar motel at Ocean City, Maryland. In fact, on opening day, Vice President and Mrs. Johnson were the guests of honor among dozens of Senate freeloaders at the "high-style hideaway for the advise and consent set," as Baker described his motel. . . . Many times Baker was in need of sudden cash, and he told a jury of one experience in July 1962 when he needed $300,000. He said he told Johnson of this, and the Vice President called [Oklahoma senator Robert] Kerr, who arranged a loan for $250,000.[25]

Moreover, Johnson must have figured something was up with Baker's finances when his former aide moved into a posh neighborhood in Northwest

Washington, "only a hop and a skip from LBJ's home as vice president," as Baker put it. Baker's partner in Serv-U, the defense lobbyist Fred Black, owned a mansion that shared a back fence with Johnson's home.[26]

Johnson was quick to remind people that he stopped being Baker's boss when he left the Senate. From 1961 to 1963, however, the vice president saw or spoke with Baker more than fifty times, according to his official calendar. Sometimes they met for business during the day and then regrouped for dinner or a boat cruise with their wives.[27] Not shown in Johnson's official calendar is the fact that Baker also accompanied the vice president on a trip to the Dominican Republic in late February 1963 to celebrate the inauguration of the country's first freely elected president, Juan Bosch. Also on hand for the festivities, as noted in chapter 4, were Philadelphia Mafia boss Angelo Bruno and Lansky associate Ed Levinson.[28]

Last but not least, Johnson never disclosed the embarrassing detail that on August 21, 1963, just a few weeks before Baker resigned in disgrace, the Senate aide joined Fred Black and an executive from their Serv-U client North American Aviation, a California aerospace company, to meet with Johnson in the Executive Office Building.[29] Johnson chaired the Kennedy administration's National Aeronautics and Space Council, which oversaw NASA, one of North American Aviation's biggest customers. Bobby Baker's main mentor and benefactor in the Senate after Johnson's departure, Oklahoma Democrat Robert Kerr, succeeded LBJ as chair of the Senate Committee on Aeronautical and Space Sciences and helped swing the appointment of James Webb as NASA Administrator. (Webb had worked for one of Senator Kerr's oil companies in the 1950s.) In early 1963, the FBI installed a bug in Black's luxury suite at the Sheraton-Carlton, where Baker and other friends of the lobbyist "repaired to conduct business, drink, play cards, or entertain ladies."[30] As related by reporter Clark Mollenhoff,

> [T]heir monitored conversations disclosed an arrangement between the late Senator Kerr and North American officials in the awarding of the Apollo [space] contract.
>
> The first phase of the multi-billion-dollar contract was let to North American in the late fall of 1961 instead of to Martin Marietta which was at first judged the best qualified. At the same time, North American Aviation switched its vending-machine dealer. Baker's Serv-U Vending Corporation was substituted for a firm which had handled NAA's vending machine business for years. This change was made despite the fact that Serv-U had no employees, vending machines, or experience when the multimillion-dollar contract was awarded. . . .
>
> The financing of Serv-U Vending was arranged through the Kerr-controlled Fidelity National Bank in Oklahoma City, one of whose major stockholders was [NASA administrator] James E. Webb. . . . The wiretap on Black raised

questions about Senator Kerr's influence in the awarding of the Apollo contract to North American. Following his death, an inventory of Kerr's estate showed that he had owned an interest in lands which had benefited from North American's decisions to construct new plants in Oklahoma.[31]

Baker, Las Vegas, Lansky, and International Money Launderers

Johnson had a special reason to distance himself from Baker: His close friend had chosen to make his fortune in consort with organized criminals, including some of the Kennedy Justice Department's top targets for prosecution. This disturbing fact emerged from illegal FBI bugs hidden in the offices of Las Vegas gamblers tied to Lansky and other notorious mobsters. Even before the Baker scandal broke, President Kennedy privately warned Johnson that Baker's mob associations could haunt the vice president. Kennedy also put the onus on Johnson to fix the problem. As LBJ recalled the conversation a few years later, Kennedy told him, "I'm very distressed that Bobby Baker has been having conversations with some bad people out at Las Vegas and some bad people over at the Dominican embassy, some bad people down at . . . Miami, and I think you ought to get him to resign." Johnson disclaimed responsibility, pointing out that Baker was "employed by all the Senate," but asked what he had done. Kennedy then filled Johnson in on what the FBI bugs and wiretaps indicated about Baker's choice of business partners. Even as Johnson recounted this episode to one of his political advisers in December 1966, he expressed continuing anxiety over possible wiretapping by RFK's investigators.[32] LBJ was certain throughout the Baker investigation that his political rival, the attorney general, was leaking damaging information against him. Hoover fed the president's deep insecurity by sending Johnson reports that Bobby Kennedy's assistants in the Justice Department were conspiring to keep the Baker case alive at his expense.[33]

Johnson also received a personal warning about Baker's underworld connections straight from Hoover himself. In his retirement, LBJ finally explained to Baker why he never publicly defended him: "All that was within me wanted to come to your aid, but Bobby Kennedy would have crucified me, the Republicans would have crucified me, the press would have crucified me. . . . J. Edgar Hoover came to me shortly after I became president and said he had electronic evidence that you were mixed up with a bunch of Las Vegas gamblers. He warned me against lifting a finger to help you. I felt helpless."[34] Hoover also warned Senate Majority leader Mike Mansfield that his employee was associating with "known gamblers."[35]

Johnson knew that any talk of Las Vegas connections would put him directly in the sights of the attorney general. Bobby Kennedy had made no secret of his belief that "the underworld syndicate lords of Chicago, New York, Detroit, Cleveland, and Los Angeles have a secret vested interest in Las Vegas gambling." Despite efforts by Nevada senators Howard Cannon and Alan Bible to stop his investigation, the *Boston Globe* reported, "Kennedy has had FBI agents roosting in [Las Vegas] for more than a year. There are so many federal cops on this investigation that they seem to be part of the growth pattern of Las Vegas."[36] As word of their findings leaked out to reporters, Johnson would have learned that RFK had grand juries investigating nearly $19 million in Teamster pension fund loans to casinos and other properties in Las Vegas alone. One of Kennedy's targets was Edward Levinson, president of the Fremont Hotel, which owned the largest casino in downtown Las Vegas. It received a $4 million loan from the Teamster pension fund in 1961 to finance a fourteen-story addition. Levinson's partner in applying for the loan was the Los Angeles attorney and property manager for Joseph "Doc" Stacher, a wealthy former bootlegger and gambling partner of Meyer Lansky and New Jersey gangster Abner Zwillman.[37] In July 1963, Levinson and his Fremont partner Edward Torres refused to testify before a grand jury investigating tax evasion by Stacher on grounds of potential self-incrimination.[38] (Stacher avoided prison by emigrating to Israel in 1965, invoking its Law of Return.) As the Baker hearings got under way in the fall of 1963, a new book, subtitled "The Truth about Las Vegas—Where Organized Crime Controls Gambling— And Everything Else"—identified Levinson as a former "Florida and Kentucky bookmaker" and casino partner of "Stacher, a New Jersey gangster."[39]

Fragmentary but juicy details of Baker's involvement with such underworld figures and front men began emerging in press reports within weeks of the scandal breaking. On November 7, 1963, Wallace Turner reported on the front page of the *New York Times* that Baker had "acted as an intermediary in behalf of a prominent Las Vegas gambler who has extensive associations with notorious underworld figures." Turner's story quoted the head of Pan Am's Intercontinental Hotels subsidiary about efforts by Baker and Levinson to operate casinos at the company's hotels in the Dominican Republic and Netherlands West Indies (chapter 4). The story added, "For weeks officials not directly connected with the Baker investigation have said privately that he had been involved in the entry of Las Vegas gamblers into other business activities" across the country. Turner noted that Levinson refused to discuss whether he had any financial stake in Baker's Serv-U Corp. (He did.) The *Times* soon opined that Baker's actions as "the middleman between gambling interests and legitimate business" should be investigated "fully and fearlessly."[40] When he heard all the bad publicity about Baker's ties to gangsters, Philadelphia Mafia boss Angelo Bruno told an associate that Baker had unwisely underestimated Bobby Kennedy's interest in finding ways to push Johnson out of office.[41]

Turner's well-informed report was no fluke. He had spent months talking with federal and state law enforcement officials for a five-part series on the mob's takeover of Las Vegas and its implications for the American society. His front-page exposé, which began running on November 18, 1963, declared that Nevada's huge gambling industry was "a new force in American life—a force with a hidden impact so great that it is of deep concern to top law enforcement officials throughout the nation." Turner warned that the casino bosses, almost all drawn from the ranks of the underworld, brought with them "the ways of the gang and the racket. Powerful through great wealth, these men serve as a transmission belt through which the tactics of the underworld are introduced into legitimate businesses and economic and socio-political structures." Turner called out the industry's malign association with "the complex affairs of Robert G. Baker," as well as the Teamster Union's pension fund, various Wall Street scandals, and "the criminal conspiracy known as Cosa Nostra."[42]

Linking Baker's name to that "criminal conspiracy" was a big deal. "La Cosa Nostra" ("Our Thing") had just entered national parlance as a term used by the FBI to describe Italian American crime organizations. It was introduced to the American public just weeks earlier in nationally televised hearings before the Senate Investigations Subcommittee. The show was exploited by Attorney General Kennedy to highlight the national threat of organized crime and to pressure Congress into passing comprehensive anti-crime legislation. As the lead witness on September 25, Kennedy told the subcommittee that the Justice Department was fighting "a private government of organized crime, a government with an annual income of billions, resting on a base of human suffering and moral corrosion" and protected by corrupt public officials. RFK called for new federal wiretapping laws to address "the legitimate needs of law enforcement for authority, closely circumscribed, to use this means of gathering evidence."

The subcommittee's star witness was turncoat New York mobster Joseph Valachi. He was serving a life sentence in Atlanta, Georgia, for crimes including murder and narcotics trafficking. Valachi's agreement to break his oath of silence represented, in the words of FBI director Hoover, "the biggest intelligence breakthrough yet in combating organized crime and racketeering in the United States."[43] His testimony was also the biggest public relations coup for that effort in many years. As the squat, swarthy hoodlum described the sinister workings of "Cosa Nostra" families, from their blood initiation rituals to their merciless use of violence to terrorize opponents, millions of Americans watched with rapt attention. "Under television floodlights, Joseph Valachi has been telling the Senate Investigations Committee spine-chilling stories of the New York underworld," the *New York Times* observed. "An army of reporters sent thousands of words to newspapers across the land yesterday. . . . Not since Frank Costello's fingers drummed the table during the Kefauver hearings 10 years ago has there been so fascinating a show."[44]

Unfortunately for Johnson, these hearings indirectly highlighted the significance of Baker's ties to front men for the syndicate. FBI bugs revealed that several secret partners of Baker and Black in Serv-U—Levinson, his Miami business partner Benjamin Sigelbaum, and Miami investor Jack Cooper—were senior associates of Meyer Lansky and other "hoodlums" (Hoover's favorite term). Their partner Fred Black also had underworld associations, as confirmed by the FBI bug in his hotel suite.[45]

Black grew up in the shadow of the Pendergast machine in Missouri. At age nineteen he became a driver for Senate candidate Harry Truman. Soon he befriended Clifford Jones, who would become lieutenant governor of Nevada and a leader of the state's Democratic Party—known as "Big Juice" for his political connections.[46] Jones was a former attorney for the estate of New York mobster and Lansky partner Bugsy Siegel. He once owned 11 percent of the Thunderbird casino in Las Vegas and smaller interests in several other local casinos, even though Nevada gaming authorities charged that he was fronting for associates of the Lansky brothers.[47] In prerevolutionary Cuba Jones operated the casino at the Hotel Havana Hilton, whose silent partners included Florida crime boss Santo Trafficante. By the early 1960s, Black owned a small share in several Caribbean casinos owned by Jones.[48] As noted in chapter 4, Baker, Jones, and Levinson crossed paths again in 1963 while pursuing a major casino concession in the Dominican Republic. In 1966, Jones was indicted on perjury charges by a federal grand jury investigating Baker's business deals, but he was finally acquitted in 1972.[49]

An avid gambler, Black apparently settled his debts by giving stock in Serv-U Corp. to Edward Levinson.[50] He also befriended several powerful casino owners, including Moe Dalitz, a former bootlegger, Lansky business partner, and head of the Cleveland Syndicate. After running bookmaking and numbers rackets in Cleveland and illegal casinos in Kentucky, Dalitz moved to Las Vegas in the late 1940s to manage the Desert Inn hotel-casino.[51] In Turner's front-page *New York Times* series in November 1963 on Las Vegas gambling, the reporter highlighted the importance of Dalitz's mob, beginning with a quote from the public safety director of Cleveland:

"At the top of Cleveland's bootleggers were Morris Kleinman, Lou Rothkopf, Moe Dalitz, Sam Tucker, and Maxie Diamond. They were at the helm of the board of directors. They had the suppliers of Canadian whiskey, and their salesmen and thugs to distribute the contraband and to reap the harvest of money. . . . Ruthless beatings, unsolved murders and shakedowns, threats and bribery came to this community as a result of the gangsters' rise to power."

These were also capable businessmen, trained in the rackets' hard school of business. Dalitz has also always operated laundries; during World War II he even did business for the Army. Moreover, Dalitz was once highly successful in helping an acquaintance gain control of two companies that were merged as Detroit Steel Corporation. . . . [T]his may have given the Cleveland organization a taste for the profits to be had from successful deals in corporate finance, and other non-gambling business ventures. . . .

Today [the group] has branches in hospital construction and operation, golf course construction, apartment development, building management, and home development.

The Desert Inn group moved into Havana when Fulgencio Batista, who was running Cuba at the time, opened the city to gambling casinos. . . . They left a lot of their money in Havana. Those from the Desert Inn who had to rid themselves of interest in the Hotel Nacional de Cuba Casino in Havana included M. B. Dalitz, Thomas Jefferson McGinty, Morris Kleinman and Wilbur Clark.[52]

Dalitz and his Cleveland partners had secret partners at the Desert Inn. One was Chicago Outfit boss Sam Giancana, who was officially banned from the business by Nevada gaming authorities. One of Giancana's leading representatives in Las Vegas was Fred Black's close friend John Rosselli, who ran a talent booking agency at the hotel's casino. As noted in chapter 2, Rosselli went to prison for his role in the 1930s Hollywood extortion scandal, until he was paroled with some of Chicago's leading gangsters during the Truman administration. By the late 1950s, according to his biographers, Rosselli had become "instrumental in arranging financing" for Las Vegas casinos, "often through the offices of the Teamsters Central States Pension Fund, which was controlled by Chicago mob figure Paul Dorfman and his son Allen."[53] Years later, when Rosselli was back in prison on other charges, Black used his political influence to get the dethroned gangster transferred from his chilly misery at McNeil Island to a minimum-security facility in Arizona. In 1975, while testifying before Congress on his secret role in CIA-led plots to assassinate Fidel Castro—the subject of chapter 9—Rosselli stayed in Black's Watergate apartment.[54] Black's connection to Rosselli and the Chicago Outfit may explain why Serv-U sourced its vending machines from a company secretly owned by Giancana.[55]

Black was introduced to Levinson by his casino partner Clifford Jones in 1961. Baker also met Levinson in January 1961, at a pre-inauguration party for the Kennedy-Johnson ticket thrown by both Nevada senators.[56] Baker already knew his way around the city of sin. Three years earlier, he and Senator Johnson had been guests of honor at the grand opening of the Stardust

Casino, owned by a front man for the Chicago Outfit and operated by Dalitz and his Cleveland partners.[57] In the same year, Nevada senator Alan Bible, Pat McCarran's successor, praised Baker as "a man who gets things done with the minimum amount of time and a maximum of efficiency." Bible paid Baker the ultimate compliment, calling him "Lyndon, Jr."[58]

Baker and Levinson quickly hit it off. In an interview with an FBI agent in February 1963, just before traveling to the Dominican Republic with Baker, Levinson described him as "one of his closest" associates, "a young, energetic, politically minded young man, and one that has done many favors for many people." Levinson said that whenever he visited Washington, D.C., he made sure to spend most of his time with Baker. Levinson was unaware that an FBI bug had recently overheard him arranging with Baker to fix the award of a federal architectural contract on behalf of a Las Vegas firm, in return for its owners purchasing eight $1,000 tickets to a Democratic fundraising dinner hosted by President Kennedy and Vice President Johnson in January 1963. Much worse, as we will see, the bug exposed Levinson's conspiracy with mobsters across the country to hide their secret casino profits from the IRS.[59]

Hailing from Detroit, Levinson freely admitted to the FBI having worked there a leading bookmaker and numbers operator. He had also been a bookmaker in Miami and managed illegal casinos in Covington and Newport, Kentucky. In the mid-1950s he took charge of casino operations at the luxurious Havana Riviera, owned by Meyer Lansky, leaders of the old Cleveland Syndicate, New York's Frank Costello, and Chicago's Sam Giancana.[60] Following the mob's ouster from Cuba, Levinson invested in the Sands hotel and casino in Las Vegas with Frank Sinatra and several notorious gamblers from around the country who held hidden shares. They included Lansky, his New Jersey gambling and bootlegging partner Joseph Stacher, New Jersey Mafia boss Jerry Catena, Frank Costello, and Chicago Outfit representative Louis Lederer.[61] Levinson soon joined many of these investors in the Teamster-funded Fremont hotel-casino, where he became president.

Levinson was respectable enough to rub shoulders with J. Edgar Hoover, Vice President Nixon, Lyndon Johnson, and Senator Smathers at the exclusive Del Charro Hotel in La Jolla, California, owned by Dallas oil millionaire Clint Murchison (chapter 6).[62] People in high places must have experienced heartburn, therefore, in November 1963 when *Times* reporter Wallace Turner connected a $10 million stock fraud through Levinson to Bobby Baker. Turner stated that the tie-in was "now coming under scrutiny" as part of the Kennedy Justice Department's fraud prosecution. Much of the story concerned members of the Cleveland group at the Desert Inn and their friend Sam Garfield, a Michigan oil investor who helped orchestrate the swindle. "Officials have said that Garfield has had relationships with Meyer Lansky, the gambler; Gerardo V. Catena, who is described as holding things together in New Jersey for the jailed [New York Mafia boss] Vito Genovese, and with Edward Levinson, the leading figure in the Fremont Hotel in downtown Las Vegas," Turner reported. What the FBI knew, but Turner did not report, was that Levinson had made $48,000 in profits in a single year from his oil-drilling investments with Garfield; that Garfield had acquired the key shell company used in the fraud from the Murchisons, who were also partners in the oil business with Catena; that Catena was a secret owner in many Las Vegas casinos; and that Catena and Lansky were leading recipients of unreported cash "skimmed" by Levinson and his associates from the casinos' winnings to evade taxes.[63] In the next chapter we will revisit Catena's business relationship with Baker's close associates, the Murchison brothers of Dallas.

Behind his legitimate facade, Levinson was the mob's main casino skim master in Las Vegas. His couriers carried millions of dollars of untaxed cash from Las Vegas gambling halls to their secret underworld owners across the United States, and into their numbered bank accounts abroad.[64] Deeply implicated in the same racket was his partner Edward Torres, vice president for business operations at the Fremont. FBI agents also observed Torres having lunch with Meyer Lansky in Cleveland in 1964, after visiting oil-drilling sites with Sam Garfield.[65] On Levinson's advice, Torres invested $25,000 in Serv-U, which he cashed out for $75,000—"a pretty fair profit," he told the Rules Committee. Torres said he recalled seeing Baker at the Fremont Hotel, at "approximately the time that they had a dinner or some kind of fundraising thing for Senator Cannon—just about that time."[66] That off-the-cuff comment was an embarrassing reminder that Baker had attended, and possibly helped organize, a $100-a-plate fundraising dinner for Nevada Democrat Howard Cannon, a member of the Rules Committee, at the Flamingo hotel on April 19, 1963.[67] In 1964, according to an FBI report, Cannon missed "several important votes in the Senate" in order to attend the funeral of Levinson's wife.[68] During Rules Committee deliberations on Baker, Cannon was notable for his frequent complaints that calling more witnesses to testify would just be a "fishing expedition."[69]

Life magazine, which publicly exposed the mob's money-laundering operation in 1967, explained what Levinson and Torres were up to:

> The true bonanza the Mob has struck in legitimate business is "skimming"— diverting a portion of cash receipts off the top to avoid taxes. . . . It follows that the money derived from the skim is ideal for greasing the wheels of organized crime. It pays off politicians, crooked cops and killers. . . .
>
> The biggest skim yet discovered took place in the legalized gambling casinos of Las Vegas from 1960 to 1965. . . . Some $12 million a year was skimmed for gangsters in just six Las Vegas casinos: the Fremont, the Sands, the Flamingo, the Horseshoe, the Desert Inn and the Stardust. . . .

Skimming in Las Vegas, from casino counting room to Swiss bank, has always been overseen by Lansky. . . . Each month, when the skim was running smoothly, the bagmen shuttled between Las Vegas and Miami with satchels of cash. The couriers also brought the skim from Bahamian casinos to Miami. There Lansky counted it all, took his own cut and then parceled out the rest to the couriers who were to carry it to the designated Cosa Nostra hoods, or to the Swiss banks where they have their accounts.[70]

The article went on to name one of the couriers as "Benjamin Sigelbaum, 64, business partner of Robert G. (Bobby) Baker" (in Serv-U and other ventures) and "a man with general affinity for political connections." In 1958, he received a full and unconditional pardon by President Dwight D. Eisenhower for his 1936 guilty plea to bankruptcy fraud.[71] Sigelbaum, said to be "a short and scrappy wheeler-dealer who had made his money in the electrical supply business,"[72] invested with Levinson in at least two leading mob money laundromats: the Bahamas-based Bank of World Commerce (BWC) and the Geneva-based Exchange and Investment Bank.[73] On each of his trips from Las Vegas to Miami, Sigelbaum toted an estimated $100,000 in cash. The FBI's physical surveillance showed Sigelbaum frequently in the company of Meyer Lansky.[74] Much of this intelligence bounty dried up, however, when a syndicate mole in the Justice Department leaked a highly confidential report on money laundering to the targets of these investigations in August 1963, shortly before the Baker scandal became public.[75]

Joining Sigelbaum as a courier for all this cash in the early 1960s was Miami businessman and Dominican investor Jack Cooper (chapter 4). Cooper was a business partner of Lansky and point holder in the Flamingo hotel-casino in Las Vegas, with a 1961 conviction for income tax evasion.[76] The FBI's hidden microphones revealed that Levinson and Sigelbaum—likely fronting for Lansky—also joined Cooper in a venture to build airport hotels across the country.[77] The chairman of the company was Maxwell Rabb, former secretary to President Eisenhower's cabinet but a prominent backer of Johnson in 1964.[78] (After another cofounder of the hotel company attended a special White House evening for friends of President Nixon in 1970, the *Washington Post* reported on a federal strike force investigation into the "Mafia ties" of his "companions and representatives.")[79] Among his other political connections, Cooper boasted that he spent $100,000 a year to "own George Smathers" through campaign contributions, fees to his Miami law firm, and "women for the Florida Senator's considerable appetite."[80] Last but not least, Cooper was one of the earliest investors in Serv-U, until Fred Black bought him out to avoid unwelcome law enforcement scrutiny.[81]

Levinson and Sigelbaum invested with Baker in several other enterprises that leveraged his political clout. One of them was District of Columbia

National Bank, which gave Baker a home loan for $125,000 without even checking his financial statements. (In the words of one bank officer, "he is a gentleman with innumerable friendships and connections whose good offices on behalf of our bank could be very valuable to our group.")[82] This institution, whose investors and officers included political insiders on both sides of the aisle and several prominent journalists, was the first new bank in Washington, D.C., to open in twenty-nine years. Comptroller of the Currency James J. Saxon authorized it to do business in 1962, less than a month after he was confirmed by the Senate.[83]

One of the bank's other investors was the wife of Rep. Abe Multer of New York, a senior Democrat on the House Banking and District of Columbia Committees. Years later, a polite obituary would recall Multer's "insistence on supporting in vigorous House debate the interests of his close friends in private business."[84] The congressman was an ardent defender of Jimmy Hoffa, Rafael Trujillo, Spanish dictator Francisco Franco, and the American Jewish League Against Communism.[85]

The Kennedy Justice Department was most interested in the fact that Multer chartered and then became president of Guarantee Trust Company in Nassau, the Bahamas. It advertised to select clients the benefits of its secret, Swiss-style accounts, "with the additional advantage of freedom from taxation which the Swiss banks do not enjoy."[86] The bank's vice chairman, Leonard Bursten, had previously been a director of the Miami National Bank, another notorious repository of syndicate cash.[87] (Following indictments of five of its past presidents, the Miami National Bank was named in 1971 in a federal indictment of Meyer Lansky and several associates for laundering millions of dollars from the Flamingo hotel-casino in Las Vegas to evade taxes.)[88] Multer's involvement with such banks received almost no media coverage and was never investigated by the Rules Committee.

Guaranty Trust Company typified a cluster of offshore financial institutions described in a secret 1965 Justice Department memo on the "Banking of 'Hot' Money." They were "shell" banks "established in the Bahamas by individuals closely connected with gambling interests, international underworld couriers, James Hoffa and the Teamsters Union" to conceal "skimmed gambling money from the United States."[89] Another such institution was the above-mentioned Bank of World Commerce, chartered in Nassau in March 1961. An IRS investigator concluded that BWC "was established by well-organized American underworld interests for the purpose of maintaining a liquid supply of funds to be used for setting up new gambling casinos in the Caribbean area wherever and whenever the opportunity presents itself."[90] Presiding over that bank was Meyer Lansky's financial adviser John Pullman, a former bootlegger who resided in Toronto. Jimmy Hoffa was represented on the bank's board by Indianapolis Teamster boss Gene San Souci. Pullman arranged for funds moved through the bank—including much of Lansky's skim from Las Vegas—to be deposited in numbered accounts at the International Credit Bank in Geneva, run by Tibor Rosenbaum. The ultra-orthodox Rosenbaum, a Hungarian Holocaust refugee and treasurer of the World Jewish Congress, served in his spare time as an agent of Israel's military and intelligence services.[91]

An Israeli connection also surfaced in Multer's Guarantee Trust Company, possibly reflecting the ardent support for Israel shown by many Jewish racketeers, as well as Jimmy Hoffa.[92] In March 1960, Hoffa's confidant Irving Davidson—who among his myriad roles was a registered US agent for the Israeli military and friend of two future Israeli military intelligence chiefs—wrote Yehuda Assia, managing director of the Swiss-Israel Trade Bank in Geneva, asking him to help Multer and his new Bahamian bank profit from "the many connections which I know the group has." Davidson added that Multer "has been and is a staunch fighter for and supporter of Israel, as you well know. . . . The Congressman has been to Israel many times and is known to Prime Minister Ben Gurion. I am sure that when you and he meet you will find you have many mutual friends." Assia responded by promising his full cooperation, saying he would look for qualified bankers in Switzerland to work at the new bank.[93] Years later, the Israeli media revealed that Assia and his Geneva bank "helped raise funds for the Mossad in its early days"—and even collected money to build Israel's nuclear reactor in Dimona, the centerpiece of its covert nuclear bomb program.[94] According to one informed account, the "clandestine aspects" of Assia's bank "were eventually assumed by Tibor Rosenbaum's infamous [International Credit Bank]."[95]

Despite his efforts on its behalf, even Davidson came to regard Multer's Bahamian bank as "cancerous."[96] Guarantee Trust landed in the Justice Department's crosshairs in the early days of the new Kennedy administration. Drew Pearson reported in June 1961:

> On the eve of the Teamster convention in Miami Beach, Attorney General Robert Kennedy has sent a secret task force to Florida to dig into Teamster scandals which might upset the expected re-election of Jimmy Hoffa as union president.
>
> The biggest case Kennedy hopes to crack is a counterfeit bond mystery, involving 256 phony $1,000 Ohio turnpike bonds which a high Teamster official deposited in a Bahamas bank, in the British West Indies. . . . The bogus bonds have been traced to the late [Teamster pension fund trustee and Bank of World Commerce director] Gene San Soucie [sic], a Hoffa confidant, who headed the Indiana Teamsters Conference. Shortly after the counterfeit scandal was uncovered, San Soucie died in the mysterious crash of his private plane. . . .

> The bonds were delivered to the Guarantee Trust Company in Nassau. . . .
> The Justice Department's task force . . . has been digging into the Guarantee
> Trust, apparently to see if it may be a secret repository of Teamster payoffs. . . .
> The Justice Department task force tried to grab the bank's records by issuing a
> subpoena. . . . But Federal Judge Emmett Choate ruled that the United States has
> no right to examine the records of a British bank in the Bahamas.[97]

Multer was not indicted, although witnesses were said to have implicated him in grand jury testimony.[98] However, a *New York Times* reporter
did briefly cite the congressman's involvement with Guarantee Trust in a
November 1963 article on the "large questions" raised by the Bobby Baker
case about conflicts of interest on Capitol Hill.[99] From what we know now
of the international criminal operations of Baker's partners, those questions
appear larger than ever.

President Johnson: Back from the Brink

The mob's deep involvement with Bobby Baker, the Teamsters, a major
defense lobbyist, and several powerful members of Congress had huge implications for Johnson. Baker's friends and business partners included several
top targets of the Kennedy Justice Department. LBJ could easily be tainted
by these associations. Baker himself said years later that if he had testified
about his knowledge of "loose campaign money, outright bribes, conflict-
of-interest investments, sex habits," and other misdeeds, Johnson "might
have incurred a mortal wound" and been driven from office. That was not
simply an idle boast. As the Baker investigation burst open, concerns in the
White House fueled rumors that LBJ might be dropped from the ticket in
1964. Many historians doubt whether the Kennedy brothers ever seriously
contemplated such a drastic move. However, JFK's trusted personal secretary, Evelyn Lincoln, recalled that on November 19, 1963, just three days
before the president's fateful trip to Texas, she asked about his plans for a
running mate. "At this time I am thinking about Governor Terry Sanford of
North Carolina. But it will not be Lyndon," the president told her. Lincoln
told Robert Caro, "the ammunition to get him off [the ticket] was Bobby
Baker."[100]

Johnson's political troubles did not end with JFK's death. As LBJ looked
forward to the 1964 election, biographer Alfred Steinberg observed, "The largest incendiary bomb was the Baker Case."[101] Johnson caught an early break
upon becoming president, however, when Baker hired a brilliant new defense
counsel, Edward Bennett Williams. Baker's choice of attorney said much
about the strength of his connections to organized crime. Despite potential

conflicts of interest, Williams also defended Ed Levinson and Fred Black. He had become famous representing celebrity criminal defendants such as Frank Costello, Sam Giancana, and Jimmy Hoffa. Drawing on his experience with such clients, Williams advised Baker and Levinson to refuse to answer any questions from the Rules Committee on constitutional grounds. On February 19, 1964, Williams turned the tables on the government by showing reporters an FBI bug discovered in Levinson's Las Vegas office. At the same time, Williams filed a $500,000 suit against Central Telephone Company of Las Vegas for invading Levinson's privacy.[102] Levinson had discovered the bug after a senior official in the Justice Department or FBI leaked him a summary of the FBI's transcripts of his conversations.[103]

Meanwhile, the new president assiduously worked his friends in the media to launch attacks on Senator Williams, the prime mover behind the Baker investigation, and his star witness, Don Reynolds.[104] Johnson also rallied his supporters in Congress to curtail the Baker investigation. One of his most important allies was North Carolina Democrat B. Everett Jordan, who chaired the Rules Committee probe. Just two weeks after taking office, Johnson spoke with Jordan, listening sympathetically to the senator's plea for help with cotton subsidy legislation. Then Johnson handed the phone over to his special assistant Walter Jenkins, who managed the White House's day-to-day response to the Baker investigation. Jordan filled Jenkins in on the day's hearings and reassured Johnson's aide that he was doing everything in his power to contain the investigation: "I'm trying to keep the Bobby [Baker] thing from spreading too. . . . Because, Hell, I don't want it to spread, either. It might spread a place where we don't want it spread. I don't want it to spread at all, but it may be a place we can't stop it from spreading. Mighty hard to put a fire out when it's out of control."[105]

Johnson repaid Jordan by backing legislation to benefit cotton farmers but despaired over the committee chairman's inability to rein in partisan Republican members. On January 10, after damaging new allegations surfaced about his alleged receipt of a kickback from Reynolds, the president complained to his longtime ally Senator Smathers. Smathers tried to reassure him, but the mob issue remained a sticking point. "I think we can handle everybody on our side," the Florida senator told LBJ. "Howard Cannon is the smartest fellow over there, but he's a little afraid to do anything because he himself figures he was involved out in Las Vegas."[106]

Days later, Smathers was himself caught up in the scandal. Reports surfaced that in 1957 he had cut Baker in on a lucrative Florida land deal near the future site of NASA's Cape Canaveral launch facility.[107] Speaking with Johnson at the end of January, Smathers could not contain his panic: "This whole thing is going to come down on all of our heads. We might as well forget about the election."[108] Fortunately for him, the Rules Committee chairman showed some backbone and declared, "We're not investigating senators."[109]

Within weeks, panic gave way to relative calm as committee Democrats finally began to contain the investigation. On March 12, 1964, FBI deputy director Cartha "Deke" DeLoach, the bureau's liaison to Congress, reassured President Johnson that the committee's probe was "going to close up" and that no one was paying attention to the insurance kickback charges.[110] The same day, Sen. Hugh Scott, R-PA, blasted Democrats for trying to end the investigation "as soon as they thought they could do so without incurring the wrath of the American public." Calling the case "one of the most sordid scandals in Washington in recent memory," he accused them of "watching the calendar" rather than the facts: "The November elections are approaching and they are determined to put this skeleton back into the closet." Scott's Democratic counterpart from Pennsylvania, Joseph Clark, assured the White House a few days later, "I remain in a position of seeking one major goal: the end of the investigation."[111] Sure enough, on March 23, the Senate Rules Committee took a series of party-line votes to bring the probe to a virtual close. "Meeting throughout the day in executive session, the nine-man body voted down, one after another, Republican proposals to take additional testimony in the highly controversial case," the *New York Times* reported.[112]

Even so, Johnson could not let his guard down. In early May, Senate Republicans proposed yet again expanding the investigation to explore new issues, including campaign contributions. With his eye on November, Johnson told Vice President Humphrey that shutting down the Baker investigation—even by threatening to authorize FBI investigations into Republican misdeeds—was "more important than anything." LBJ cautioned, however, that his fingerprints could not be on any intervention, and that their conversation was "between you and me and God."[113] A day later, the Senate voted down the Republican-sponsored resolution.[114] That September, as new charges bubbled up sporadically, Johnson complained that Baker had "damned near destroyed us" and attributed the entire affair to Bobby Kennedy's rivalry.[115]

Fortunately for LBJ, Sen. Barry Goldwater's extremist politics nullified the appeal of Republican complaints about presidential ethics. 1964 campaign historian Robert David Johnson observed that "while Watergate and the Lewinsky affair produced resignation or impeachment, Johnson got away with obstructing administrative and legislative inquiries. He lived in an era with a less suspicious press, and the media's almost unrelenting hostility to Goldwater caused journalists to overlook what seemed like minor indiscretions by the president."[116]

Baker and the Marcello Connection

The Rules Committee's refusal to dig deeper had profound consequences that have never been addressed. In particular, it prevented disturbing new facts about Baker's mob connections from coming to light—facts that might have linked the former Senate Majority secretary to Carlos Marcello, the mob boss of Louisiana.

Only in December 1964, after Johnson's election as president, did the Senate Rules Committee publish its members' behind-closed-doors discussion of a staff investigator's interview with Paul Aguirre, a wealthy Puerto Rican mortgage banker, real estate developer, and friend of Baker. The interview aroused a brief flurry of media interest for its titillating revelation that Baker had brought his secretary and mistress, Carole Tyler, along with the stunning German call girl Elli Rometsch, with him on a trip to New Orleans in May 1963 for several days of partying and business. Aguirre refused to testify before the committee about these events, saying, "I will deny it even if they have photographs. My wife is expecting a denial and she will get it. I'll take the First through the Twenty-Eighth [Amendments]." His attorney added a novel twist on Aguirre's constitutional rights: "Certainly a married man who admitted meeting women for a party in New Orleans would tend to incriminate himself with his wife."[117] The substance of their business dealings went largely unexplored, either by the committee or the media.

Aguirre had met Baker in 1959 after seeking funding from Jimmy Hoffa for some housing developments. The committee learned that the purpose of their visit to New Orleans was to meet with two local businessmen: Nick Popich, owner of Popich Marine Construction Co., and Wilson Abraham, a builder and developer. Baker and Aguirre were interested in purchasing a trailer park site and a housing subdivision project. The committee's counsel said that little was known about Popich except that "he met Baker during the Kennedy campaign for President; he owns a restaurant in New Orleans, and he became friendly with Baker. He was constructing a pipeline in Washington, D.C. for the Washington Gas Light Co., privately owned, and saw Baker on several occasions socially." Popich told a committee investigator that he had previously seen Baker in San Juan, where he went to try to drum up some construction business through Aguirre.[118] Popich also accompanied Baker, Aguirre, and Abraham in July 1963 to attend Floyd Patterson's boxing rematch with the mob-controlled heavyweight fighter Sonny Liston in Las Vegas. Las Vegas casino owner Ed Levinson refused to say whether he attended the prizefight with them. Baker declined to answer whether he made telephone calls to Popich as part of his official duties, or whether he was involved in a NASA construction project near New Orleans with Popich's company.[119]

Without questioning Popich, Abraham, and other witnesses, the committee reached a dead end. Sen. Claiborne Pell, D.-R.I., said it "would be a fishing trip" to call them. Republican members, however, suspected there was much more to the story. Sen. Carl Curtis speculated, "Baker might have been getting some money from some very unworthy sources in order to invest in legitimate enterprises for them as well as for himself." Sen. John Sherman Cooper of Kentucky said he believed one of the men Baker met in New Orleans "was connected in some way with the underworld." Sen. Hugh Scott chimed in,

> One thing that underlies the investigation and has never surfaced, . . . is this: We haven't gotten on it, but I think the production of some of these witnesses might lead to the alleged running of "hot" money from gamblers and underworld characters into some of these hands around Washington, including Bobby Baker. Several people have called me up to say that Fred Black was the man who ran the "hot" money, and the man who worked not only with Baker but many other people to try to find a supposedly legitimate outlet for the "hot" money. . . . I think it is one of the reasons for calling people like Popich. It may be some of the reasons why some of these gamblers have taken the Fifth Amendment.[120]

The committee was unaware of what the FBI knew about Baker's New Orleans associates. In February 1963, under intense pressure from the attorney general, Hoover directed his field office there to aggressively develop new informants and initiate electronic surveillance of suspected underworld members. Had Hoover been authorized to share information, the Rules Committee would have learned that Louisiana mob boss Carlos Marcello was reputedly a hidden partner in Popich's Vieux Carré restaurant on Bourbon Street in New Orleans. (Testifying before Congress in executive session years later, Marcello confirmed that he and Popich had been close friends since childhood and did business together.) It would have learned that Popich was involved with a 1961 shipment of two thousand machine guns and a number of M-1 rifles to a "big wheel" allied with a group of disaffected Honduran military officers. It would have discovered that Popich received at least two calls in 1964 from Charles "The Blade" Tourine, a senior Lansky associate and former Havana casino operator living in Miami Beach.[121]

The FBI may not have known at the time an even more explosive bit of information about Nick Popich: He owned land near Lake Pontchartrain on which militant anti-Castro exiles were training in 1963 to undertake illegal raids into Cuba. Their activities violated the Neutrality Act and the Kennedy administration's firm policy of preventing such raids from US soil in the wake of the Cuban Missile Crisis.[122] Without naming Baker's New Orleans contact, the guerrilla training camp became the subject of testimony before the Warren Commission in 1964, while the Rules Committee was still investigating

Baker. The commission learned that President Kennedy's presumed assassin, Lee Harvey Oswald, may have attempted to infiltrate the camp in the summer of 1963 while living in New Orleans.[123] The camp disbanded that August only after the FBI raided a nearby arms cache maintained by anti-Castro activists, seizing more than a ton of dynamite, twenty bomb casings, fuses, and fixings for napalm. The militants acquired these explosives for a planned bombing raid against oil refineries near Havana.[124] Their stockpile was allegedly financed by a dispossessed Havana casino owner and his partner, who was described years later in Senate testimony as "a dealer in counterfeit money . . . [who] has been involved in dealing with stolen securities and other securities closely associated with . . . gamblers in Miami." Authors Warren Hinckle and William Turner observed, "the Lake Pontchartrain raid was evidence that circles existed within circles. The most violent and rabidly rightist of exile elements, feeling that JFK had betrayed them, were turning to the mob and the radical paramilitary right wing for help in a war that was to turn against the government itself."[125] To say the least, members of the Rules Committee apprised of such facts would have been duty bound to dig further into the background of Baker's associates.

Marcello, the Kennedys, and LBJ

The fact that the secretary to the Senate Majority was attempting to do business with a close associate of Marcello would have given the Baker scandal entirely new force in 1964. Marcello was one of the nation's most powerful mobsters, with a small army of Louisiana politicians and law enforcement officers on his payroll. ("He knows everybody in the state," said his lobbyist friend Irving Davidson.)[126] Shortly after his birth in French Tunisia in 1910, Marcello's Italian parents moved to New Orleans but failed to naturalize him. By the 1940s Marcello had gravitated from run-of-the-mill crimes such as robbery, to wholesale narcotics trafficking and the distribution of thousands of slot and pinball machines. He operated in Texas as well as Louisiana, in partnership with New York mobsters Frank Costello and Phil Kastel. Marcello, along with Lansky, Costello, and Kastel, owned the Beverly Club, a posh supper club and gambling casino in Jefferson Parish that attracted nationally known entertainers such as Jimmy Durante and Zsa Zsa Gabor. In 1947, when New Orleans Mafia boss "Silver Dollar" Sam Carolla was deported to Italy, Marcello became the state's unchallenged rackets leader.[127]

Marcello's importance in crime circles was publicly established in 1951, when he refused to testify before the Kefauver Committee and was named in its final report as a corrupter of state politicians and law enforcement officers.

"In every line of inquiry, the committee found the trail of Carlos Marcello," the report declared. Calling him "one of the leading criminals in the United States," it added, "the question was raised as to why he had not been deported."[128] In late 1957, Marcello's brother Joseph attended the infamous national convention of mobsters in Apalachin, New York. In February 1964, while the Baker hearings were at their height, a major story in the *Saturday Evening Post* identified Marcello as one of the nation's most powerful Mafia leaders. The report estimated that his organization earned more than a billion dollars a year from both legal and illegal enterprises.[129]

Marcello was also a particular enemy of the Kennedy family. Robert Kennedy began putting the mob boss in his investigative sights by 1959. As chief counsel to the Senate Select Committee on Improper Activities in Labor and Management, RFK took testimony on Marcello's powerful criminal reach and political influence in Louisiana and neighboring states. Kennedy hauled Marcello himself before the committee, forcing the gangster to invoke his constitutional rights to avoid answering dozens of embarrassing questions. Even before President Kennedy took office, news of his brother's intention to deport Marcello leaked to the New Orleans media. To prevent that fate, Marcello sought help from at least one congressman and from his close ally Santo Trafficante. The Florida Mafia boss even enlisted Frank Sinatra to intervene on Marcello's behalf with the Kennedy family, but to no avail.[130]

A briefing memo by congressional staff investigators in 1978 provides a chilling addendum:

> When Robert Kennedy became Attorney General in 1961 under his brother's administration, Marcello was targeted as one of the organized crime figures against which the Justice Department was to launch an unprecedented onslaught. On April 4, 1961, Marcello was deported to Guatemala in a manner which he allegedly described to associates as a "kidnapping." Approximately 2 to 3 months later, he clandestinely re-entered the United States. The crackdown of the Kennedy Justice Department allegedly infuriated Marcello. At his retreat at Churchill Farms in September of 1962, Marcello is alleged to have complained to a meeting of his associates that Bobby Kennedy was a "stone" in his shoe and to have assured the group that both Kennedys would be killed.[131]

Baker's connection to Marcello's world carried especially great political significance because the Kennedys had reason to suspect that his patron, Lyndon Johnson, had been on the take for years from the mobster. Jack Halfen was a Texas slot machine racketeer and partner of Marcello who claimed to have delivered hundreds of thousands of dollars to Johnson from his syndicate-backed businesses over the span of a decade, until Halfen's 1954 conviction for tax evasion. Halfen's claims are uncorroborated and necessarily suspect, but evidence introduced at his trial showed that his payoffs to politicians and law enforcement officials amounted to $50,000 per *week*. His prosecutor later told a reporter, "We knew, and proved, that Jack Halfen was a payoff man of unbelievably large proportions. But we never knew the identities of all those he paid. Jack wouldn't tell us. But Jack never told us any lies." Halfen's files reportedly contained a letter from Johnson on Halfen's behalf to the Texas Board of Pardons and Paroles, which granted his release in 1966 after another conviction, and "800 feet of movie film showing three couples—Lyndon and Lady Bird Johnson, Halfen and his wife, and former Harris County (Houston) Sheriff Neal Polk and his wife—together on a hunting trip."[132] Michael Dorman, a former *Houston Post* reporter who first broke the Halfen story in 1968, asserted that as a senator, Johnson provided valuable services in exchange for Halfen's payoffs:

> Halfen's syndicate had helped elect Johnson to Congress, and to reelect him over a ten-year period. They had given Johnson $500,000 in cash and campaign contributions—payments averaging $50,000 a year.
>
> In return Johnson had aided racketeering interests on the floor of Congress and, more important, in its back rooms. He had not been alone. There were other congressmen on Halfen's payroll and on the payrolls of other Mob leaders.
>
> Johnson helped to kill in committee all anti-rackets legislation that concerned Halfen. Whenever a crusading congressman or a hotshot lawyer in the Justice Department would come up with a bill to ban the interstate transportation of slot machines, or to regulate racing wires, or to rewrite the tax laws to make it tougher on gamblers, Johnson was expected to see that the legislation died a quiet death. . . .
>
> When a law finally was enacted to ban interstate transportation of slot machines . . . it came out full of loopholes. . . .
>
> While Halfen was still making his astronomical payoffs, Kefauver had launched his celebrated investigation of organized crime. His committee toured racket-infested cities, but never made it to Houston—in fact, it never even entered Texas. This singular exception was due in no small part to Halfen's pressuring Johnson to pressure Kefauver to keep the committee away from Houston. Johnson later wrote Halfen—in language intended to veil the details—about his efforts on Halfen's behalf. This letter, on government stationery, remains among Halfen's carefully preserved files.[133]

In 1961, Attorney General Robert Kennedy reportedly took Halfen's claims seriously enough to open a criminal investigation.[134] Marcello's biographer, John Davis, learned from a former Justice Department official that "at the time of President Kennedy's assassination, there was a thick investigative file on Robert Kennedy's desk in the Justice Department detailing the Marcello-Halfen-Johnson connection that Kennedy was debating whether to pursue."[135]

Marcello was one of Hoffa's closest mob allies. Their ties were illustrated most notably by Baker's other contact in New Orleans, Baton Rouge developer and hotel owner Wilson P. Abraham. The Rules Committee was apparently unaware that he was indicted by a federal grand jury in early 1964 on sixteen counts of violating Federal Housing Administration regulations relating to homes he sold in the Baton Rouge area. In 1968, Abraham and his companies pleaded no contest to four of the counts. More important, the committee might have learned with further investigation that Abraham was, in the words of one FBI report, "a longtime associate and friend of New Orleans [La Cosa Nostra] 'Boss' Carlos Marcello."[136]

Several years after his meetings with Baker, Abraham became a key partner with Marcello in attempts to overturn one of Attorney General Kennedy's proudest achievements: the 1964 conviction of Teamster president Jimmy Hoffa for jury tampering. A former congressional aide declared in a sworn affidavit that Hoffa had delivered $100,000 in cash to President Johnson's campaign in 1964 to influence his prosecution, to no avail.[137] Then, in 1967, *Life* magazine declared that it had

> found conclusive evidence that Hoffa's pals—some in the union, some in the Mob, some in both—dropped $2 million into a spring-Hoffa fund late last year. The money was placed at the disposal of Cosa Nostra mobsters, and it was to be made payable to anyone who could wreck the government's jury-tampering case on which Hoffa had been convicted. In due course the money was made available to Marcello to do the job.

A week later, in a story titled "Carlos Marcello: King Thug of Louisiana," the magazine suggested that Marcello's agents had enlisted New Orleans district attorney Jim Garrison in their free-Hoffa campaign. Garrison had recently grabbed national headlines by opening a new investigation into JFK's assassination. The DA was, among other things, putting unwelcome political pressure on the federal government, and the CIA in particular, by investigating reports linking Oswald to the anti-Castro training camp located on Nick Popich's land. As part of his JFK probe, moreover, Garrison also began investigating a Louisiana Teamster official, Edward Partin, who had been the government's main witness against Hoffa in the witness-tampering case. In June 1967, Abraham and Santo Trafficante's lawyer Frank Ragano, who was representing Hoffa's appeal of the jury-tampering conviction, met with Partin. They urged him to sign a sworn affidavit accusing the Justice Department of using illegal wiretapping to gather evidence against Hoffa. Ragano promised that Hoffa would call off rival Teamsters who were muscling in on Partin's territory. Abraham indicated that he needed the affidavit to get approval from the Teamster pension fund for a $32 million loan to build a hotel in Las Vegas. Days later, Abraham called Partin to warn that President Johnson's close friend, Louisiana senator Russell Long, and various federal judges appointed to the bench at Long's direction, would destroy Partin if he did not cooperate with Hoffa. The Department of Justice fought back, convening a grand jury in New Orleans "to investigate the continuing efforts to bribe and intimidate Partin." In the end, those efforts failed, and Hoffa remained in prison (for a time with Bobby Baker) until President Nixon freed him on Christmas Eve, 1971.[138] The story behind Nixon's commutation is discussed in chapter 8; the complex pressure campaign of Garrison, Long, and Hoffa resurfaces in chapter 9.

Abraham was very likely the "New Orleans businessman rumored to be well connected with the Mafia" who Baker said "once sought me out to inquire whether President Lyndon Johnson might be willing to pardon Hoffa in exchange for one million dollars." Baker warned him not to try. "LBJ would be petrified at the possibility of discovery, and whoever made the offer would find his ass in jail."[139]

The FBI was aware of yet another potentially explosive Baker connection to New Orleans. In June 1964, Hoover's office sent an urgent message to six FBI field offices "to determine the extent of hoodlum financial interest and control" in a Louisiana vending machine company that was reportedly for sale. A "highly confidential source" in Philadelphia—an electronic bug on Mafia boss Angelo Bruno—"reported that the following hoodlums were interested in purchasing this vending machine company at one time and are possibly still interested: Carlos Marcello, New Orleans leading racketeer; Santo Trafficante, Florida representative of La Cosa Nostra; and Augustine Amato, a known associate of Angelo Bruno."[140] A deal involving three of the nation's biggest racketeers surely merited Hoover's interest, but the addition of Baker's name made it even more urgent. A Philadelphia businessman said he had teamed up with one of Bruno's closest business partners in the late summer of 1963 to pitch the sale of the vending machine company to Bobby Baker. All three men had joined Bruno to scope out business opportunities in the Dominican Republic earlier that summer. Baker reportedly said he was interested, named a price, and offered to split a 5 percent finder's fee between the two Bruno associates.[141] In a separate but evidently related deal that summer, Baker worked on arranging a Small Business Administration loan for Bruno's partner to purchase a bankrupt manufacturer of cigarette vending machines based in Long Island. (Its president, a good friend of mobster and former Havana casino operator Charles "The Blade" Tourine, went to prison for corporate fraud and illegally lending money to a Teamster official.)[142] Neither deal with Baker reached fruition, likely because of his legal difficulties in the fall of 1963. If they had, the Baker case might have blown even wider.

Endgame

Following Johnson's landslide election against Barry Goldwater in 1964, the Baker case faded to an ignominious end. The *Washington Post*, dissatisfied by the important issues left on the table, editorialized, "There is no greater danger to free government than the corruption of its legislative process. Congress has the most solemn obligation to get to the bottom of these alleged payments of money to influence its judgment. . . . Present indications are that the Senate Rules Committee is a long way indeed from having finished its job."[143] The committee's final report, issued in June 1965, condemned Baker's behavior and called for his indictment, while exonerating President Johnson. In its defense, the committee did hear from more than a hundred witnesses. It also proposed requiring senators and their employees to disclose major sources of outside income and to restrict Senate employees from engaging in outside activities that were "inconsistent" with their official duties. The full Senate, however, rejected even these modest reforms.[144]

As the investigation wound down, Baker kept silent, acting on advice of attorney Edward Bennett Williams. Silence brought him no immunity, however. On January 5, 1966, a federal grand jury indicted him on nine counts, including fraud and tax evasion. He was convicted the following year and finally sent to prison in 1971.[145] Just two days before his indictment, Baker's patron George Smathers suddenly announced his intention to retire from the Senate when his third term ended . . . three years hence. Smathers claimed he was suffering from a serious illness—an excuse he later conceded was false.[146]

Abe Fortas, Baker's first lawyer, saw his career soar and ultimately crash in the aftermath of the Baker investigation. In 1965, Johnson elevated his loyal adviser to the Supreme Court as an associate justice. Fortas continued to consult frequently with the president. In one instance, Justice Fortas served as a back channel for the FBI to feed derogatory information on Bobby Kennedy to President Johnson, regarding the illegal bugging of Baker's partner Fred Black—a case then pending before the Supreme Court.[147] The ethically challenged justice began his downfall when he signed a contract in 1966 with the family foundation of a former law client, Wall Street financier Louis Wolfson. The deal awarded him an annual lifetime retainer of $20,000—more than half his annual salary and a significant portion of the foundation's annual budget. Fortas returned the money months after Wolfson was indicted (and soon convicted) for fraud and perjury in the sale of shares of Merritt-Chapman & Scott. *Life* magazine exposed the unseemly (but not illegal) deal in May 1969, with help from Nixon's Justice Department, which saw an opening to remove the liberal justice from the bench. Fortas issued a contradictory and unconvincing response that won him no allies. Then, under threat of impeachment by House

Republicans, he stepped down from the bench, allowing President Nixon to appoint his successor.[148] As did Baker, Fortas had chosen to associate with a shady businessman connected in multiple ways with organized crime. Two of Wolfson's fellow shareholders in Merritt-Chapman & Scott were senior underworld colleagues of Meyer Lansky. One unindicted co-conspirator in Wolfson's case was Albert Parvin, the close business associate of Lansky and Levinson (chapter 4).[149] As early as 1950, Wolfson had attracted critical scrutiny from the Kefauver Committee for his collaboration with the Chicago Outfit in financing the 1948 election of a friendly governor in Florida (see "Nixon's Caribbean Milieu" online at rowman.com). In the mid-1950s, Drew Pearson learned that "the underworld is behind Florida financier Louis Wolfson's efforts to buy Montgomery Ward and that most of the money to buy Montgomery Ward proxies had come from Las Vegas or the Purple Gang in Detroit. Jim Hoffa, head of the Teamsters Union, is reported mixed up with the Purple Gang. He has bought two million dollars' worth of Montgomery Ward stock."[150] In 1963, a convicted swindler and gambler with extensive organized crime contacts told the FBI that Wolfson had established a large national betting organization with "numerous individuals who developed friendly relationships with coaches, players, trainers, etc. on many college and professional teams in various sports" who supplied information for betting purposes.[151]

Also faring poorly in the aftermath of the Baker case were some drivers of the broader federal war on organized crime. As Jimmy Hoffa declared with satisfaction immediately after the assassination of President Kennedy, "Bobby Kennedy is just another lawyer now." Although RFK stayed on as attorney general until September 1964, he lost much of his zeal and focus after the death of his brother. As an early sign that times had changed, the FBI quickly stopped sharing information on the Bobby Baker case with Justice Department organized crime prosecutors.[152] Soon after Johnson became president, moreover, Senator Cannon went to see him to condemn the FBI and IRS for their "Gestapo tactics" against Las Vegas casino owners. Johnson ordered the Justice Department and IRS to halt even legal bugging operations, crippling federal surveillance of the mob.[153] His order represented a marked break with his previous indifference to eavesdropping and his continuation of wiretaps against Martin Luther King.[154]

While civil libertarians applauded the new restraints on federal eavesdropping, crime investigators reacted to President Johnson's executive order with fury and suspicion. FBI special agent William Roemer, a celebrated nemesis of the Chicago Outfit, condemned the president's order as

a heinous slaughter, devastating to our coverage of the mob. . . . Now, all the intelligence that had been available as a result of our long, hard hours of installing and monitoring these devices was no longer on tap to us. . . .

When I received word of Johnson's executive order, I was flabbergasted. How could anyone put such a roadblock in the way of our efforts to track the mob? I could hardly believe it. When it was explained to me that the Washington field office had placed a bug on a Fred Black who was a friend of Bobby Baker, Johnson's chief aide when he was majority leader in the Senate—and that the device was picking up conversations involving Baker—I was given to understand that Johnson became alarmed. . . . There were those who even thought he might have been on the take, that the mob had gotten to him. I doubt that. However, if you judge a man by his acts, here was a man who did more to hinder the government agency fighting organized crime than any other president or leader in our history.[155]

Johnson was undeterred by critics. In his 1967 State of the Union address, he emphatically condemned the use of government wiretaps and bugs except in cases of national security—even though he relished reading the fruits of such techniques in the FBI's files on his political rivals.[156] The same year, Johnson's friend Tom Clark handed down a majority opinion of the Supreme Court overturning the conviction of a Chicago man who had bribed New York political authorities to win a liquor license for the Playboy Key Club. Clark argued that the conviction rested on the fruits of eavesdropping authorized by a New York law that lacked sufficient safeguards. "Few threats to liberty exist which are greater than that posed by the use of eavesdropping devices," declared the justice whose name was picked up by FBI bugs in connection with the Chicago Outfit parole scandal (chapter 2).[157]

The backlash against federal eavesdropping served Fred Black and Ed Levinson well. Black was convicted in 1964 of income tax evasion and lost his appeal in 1965. Then a new assistant attorney general appointed by President Johnson in early 1966 insisted on disclosing the government's illegal eavesdropping on Black's hotel suite, even though the bug produced none of the evidence used in the case. Extensive judicial hearings resulted in a new trial. This time Black was acquitted, dealing a tremendous blow to Justice Department morale.[158]

In addition, the government had to turn over all of its wiretap logs to Black's lawyer, Edward Bennett Williams. Armed with that information, Williams was able to leverage his lawsuit against the government for illegal surveillance of Levinson to force a settlement of the May 1967 federal indictment of Levinson and Ed Torres for income tax evasion. In March 1968, Levinson pleaded no contest, receiving a fine of just $5,000 from a Nevada judge despite having skimmed millions of dollars for the mob. Days later, Levinson dropped his lawsuit against the FBI for illegal bugging.[159] The government in turn dropped tax evasion charges against Levinson's fellow Fremont Hotel officer and Serv-U investor Ed Torres.[160] While prosecutors in the Justice Department were "shocked and demoralized" by the collapse of their case, Levinson and Torres were sitting pretty: They had sold their interests in the Fremont Hotel in 1966 for $16 million to Lansky's business associate Albert Parvin.[161]

LBJ left a mixed record on organized crime. Critics point out that the number of "man days" spent by personnel in the Organized Crime and Racketeering Section of the Justice Department collapsed almost in half from fiscal year 1964, Bobby Kennedy's last year as attorney general, to 1966. The number of man days spent by that section's staff before grand juries fell more than 72 percent, and the number of District Court briefs prepared or reviewed by the section plummeted 83 percent from 1963 to 1966.[162] William Hundley, assistant attorney general in charge of the criminal division, later declared, "The minute that bullet hit Jack Kennedy's head, it was all over. Right then. The organized program just stopped, and Hoover took control back."[163]

Yet that assessment is too harsh. President Johnson continued calling attention to organized crime as a significant national problem even after RFK left the Justice Department. More important, he fostered increased cooperation between the Justice Department and other agencies—the FBI excepted—in bringing federal resources to bear against organized crime. One result was the development of highly successful, geographically targeted "strike forces" to prosecute entrenched local criminal organizations.[164] In addition, the recommendations of a crime commission Johnson established led to legislation that enhanced federal investigative powers and sentencing standards against organized crime leaders.[165] As we will see in chapter 8, however, even as President Nixon expanded Johnson's war on crime, organized criminals with special political clout found ways to continue evading the law with impunity.

6

The Friends of LBJ—II

The Murchisons

I N THE COURSE OF ITS INVESTIGATION into Bobby Baker's business affairs, the Senate Rules Committee kept running into individuals and businesses connected to one of America's richest families, the Murchisons of Texas. Two senior Murchison representatives, based in Washington, D.C., and Dallas, provided the committee with tantalizing details about business deals involving Baker, Don Reynolds, Serv-U, and even the mysterious New Orleans businessman Nick Popich.[1] Their testimony provided a tiny but revealing glimpse into intersections between big business, political influence, and organized crime in the early 1960s. A wider view shows that the Murchisons financed and flattered every president from Roosevelt to Nixon. Their methods of operation were the very embodiment of deep politics in America.

Starting in the 1930s, the Murchisons built one of America's greatest fortunes.[2] The family patriarch, Clint Murchison Sr. (1895–1969), made his first millions in East Texas oil and gas. He and his sons shrewdly diversified into insurance, construction, transportation, publishing, ranching, professional sports, and racetracks. While building their empire, they also forged alliances with some of America's most powerful politicians and mobsters. To protect and augment the family's fortune in the Cold War years, the Murchisons and their retainers befriended J. Edgar Hoover and helped him promote the rise of anti-Communism. Masters of the political game, they "maintained a staff of attorneys, public relations men, and lobbyists in Washington second to none," in the words of crime reporter Ed Reid.[3] Bobby Baker became a key part of their political apparatus until his downfall in late 1963. Through the influence machines of Baker and the Murchisons, key organized crime figures were able to infiltrate Washington and make lucrative investments with political insiders.

Although relentlessly devoted to accumulating wealth, Clint Murchison Sr. never fit what author Bryan Burrough called "the stereotype of the raw, hard-living, bourbon-swilling, fistfighting, cash-tossing, damn-the-torpedoes Texas oil millionaire."[4] He sent his eldest son, John, to Yale, and the squat, bespectacled Clint Jr. to MIT for a master's degree in mathematics. The family enjoyed strong connections to Northeastern capital, including the Rockefellers' Chase Bank and the New York investment houses Allen & Co. and Goldman Sachs. In 1954 the senior Murchison, already one of the richest men in America, joined two financiers to take control of New York Central Railroad and Investors Diversified Services, the huge, Minneapolis-based mutual fund, from the Vanderbilt family. The deal also gave him a stake in William Zeckendorf's sprawling real estate empire, Webb & Knapp.[5] Disputes over corporate control would soon embroil the Murchison family in protracted proxy battles and legal fights, which established them as innovators in corporate secrecy. Reporter Leslie Waller noted that the Murchison brothers were "usually credited with first using Swiss banks to secretly buy up stock in companies they wanted to acquire. When the time came for a proxy fight, the Murchisons could unveil holdings the opposition never dreamed they had because the stock had been held in the name of a Swiss bank."[6]

The Murchisons and Organized Crime

The Murchisons went about making money with few self-imposed rules. If building their fortune meant doing deals with ex-criminals or reputed mobsters, what mattered most was the likely payoff.[7] The FBI's Dallas office contained nearly two dozen confidential files related (in the Bureau's words) to "business dealings that the Murchisons were involved with, many of them a little shady or tainted by connection to the mob."[8] According to veteran crime reporter Dan Moldea,

> the highly secretive [elder] Murchison was investigated by no fewer than nine federal agencies and two congressional committees during a ten-year period beginning in 1955. The Senate Commerce Committee wrote that Gerardo Catena of New Jersey, a top-ranking member of the Vito Genovese crime family, "allegedly owned almost 20% of all the production of Murchison Oil Lease [Company], Oklahoma" during the early 1950s.[9]

Catena was a formidable crime leader. In the 1920s and early 1930s, he ran up a string of convictions for robbery and jury tampering. After smuggling liquor during Prohibition with the famed New Jersey gangster and Lansky associate Abner Zwillman, Catena continued to forge alliances between Italian and Jewish gangsters in the fields of gambling, loan-sharking, and labor racketeering. In November 1957, he attended the infamous underworld convention in Apalachin, New York. Catena became an acting boss of New York's most powerful crime family when Vito Genovese went to prison in 1959 for selling heroin.[10]

The FBI soon determined that Catena was

the most prominent man in the New Jersey rackets and a member of the [National Crime] "Commission" with influence in gambling, labor unions, and various nationwide investments. The "Commission" has been identified by various highly placed informants as a committee of racketeers which sets policy for the United States in regard to gambling and other rackets. Catena reportedly served as strong-arm man for the late Abner "Longie" Zwillman, a deceased nationally notorious New Jersey gambling and racket leader, and since Zwillman's death has held a position of national prominence and leadership in the underworld.[11]

Catena owned stakes in a string of legitimate businesses, including music companies, vending machine operators, jukebox makers, and trucking firms, as well as oil and gas leases. He also owned hidden interests in Caribbean and Las Vegas gambling casinos with Santo Trafficante, Meyer Lansky, and other underworld gambling bosses. Indeed, the FBI learned from informants and electronic bugs that Catena's stake in Las Vegas casinos was second only to Lansky's. From the Flamingo, Fremont, Horseshoe Club, and Sands casinos, Catena "skimmed" an estimated $120,000 to $150,000 a month in the early 1960s. The secret distribution of untaxed casino cash to Catena was organized by Bobby Baker's business partners, Edward Levinson and Benjamin Sigelbaum.[12]

Clint Murchison Jr. (1923–1987), most famous as owner of the Dallas Cowboys, allegedly rubbed shoulders with other major mobsters as well. Moldea reported that he was "involved in business partnerships with numerous associates of Carlos Marcello" and "personally had real estate and banking ties with Marcello." Moldea also described the younger Murchison as a "close friend" of Dallas restaurant owner and sports gambler Joseph Campisi.[13] Various law enforcement files described Campisi as a prominent organized crime figure, even as the heir apparent to the head of Dallas's modest Italian American crime group. Campisi's phone records showed dozens of calls to members of the Marcello family. Asked about his ties to the Louisiana mob boss, Campisi told congressional investigators, "Every year I send sausage, 260 pounds of Italian sausage . . . for Christmas to give [to] the [Marcello] brothers and what friends I have there." Campisi was also involved in running gambling junkets from Dallas to the Flamingo hotel-casino in Las Vegas, which was partly owned by Lansky and Catena.[14]

Clint Jr. also had ties to the Chicago Outfit. In 1960, FBI bugs picked up conversations by a corrupt official of the International Laundry Workers Union with a senior associate of Outfit leaders. They discussed possible union loans to Murchison and his "crowd in Dallas" to finance one of his home-building companies, which had major industrial and residential projects in suburban Cook County.[15] In the mid-1970s, Clint Jr. financed the national franchise expansion of the popular barbecue restaurant chain founded by Chicago's Tony Roma. Years earlier, after a lackluster career in the restaurant industry, Roma had suddenly become manager of Chicago's Playboy Club and then operations manager of Playboy Clubs International after marrying a niece of the Chicago Outfit's top boss. IRS agents noted Roma's "associations with organized crime figures in Canada" and his suspected activities as a "trusted courier" for leading mobsters. Citing Murchison's connections with Roma and several alleged criminals, agents of the Treasury Department's Bureau of Alcohol, Tobacco, and Firearms reported, "It appears that Murchison is firmly entrenched with individuals who are proven national Mafia figures."[16]

The Murchisons, the Teamsters, and Irving Davidson

The Murchison family cultivated particularly close relations with union president Jimmy Hoffa and his mob allies to win loans from the Teamster Central States, Southeast and Southwest Areas Pension Fund. Hoffa and other Teamster leaders created the fund in 1955. Working with Allen Dorfman, the dapper stepson of a prominent Chicago labor racketeer, Hoffa turned it into a giant bank for investments in casinos, real estate, banks, and other ventures across the country. Through the late 1970s, when the Labor Department finally seized control, the fund lent more than half a billion dollars to parties connected to organized crime. The loans were often made at below-market interest rates, accompanied by generous "finders fees" and kickbacks, and allowed to go delinquent for years. Fully $300 million went to fund investments in Las Vegas, mostly hotels and casinos with secret underworld owners. Hoffa, Dorfman, and their colleagues also invested Teamster funds in Florida hotels, condos, and at least one financial institution—Miami National Bank—that would become a target of federal investigations into money laundering by Meyer Lanksy himself.[17]

Dorfman was murdered in a gangland hit in January 1983, just one month after a federal jury convicted him of conspiring to bribe Senator Cannon,

D-Nev., chair of the Senate Commerce Committee, to sidetrack legislation that would have deregulated trucking rates. Police found Clint Murchison Jr.'s contact information in Dorfman's private address book.[18] That should have come as no surprise. In 1959, Hoffa personally approved two Teamster pension fund loans totaling $6.7 million to finance a Murchison-backed development in Beverly Hills called Trousdale Estates.[19] The luxury subdivision became home to Groucho Marx, singer Dinah Shore, and former vice president Nixon. In 1961, Murchison's local development partner sold Nixon a prime lot for $35,000, far below the listed price of $104,000.[20]

The Trousdale Estate loans were arranged by the Murchisons' agent Irving Davidson. He began working for them in the mid-1950s as a business scout, public relations expert, and "fixer."[21] Davidson got to know Hoffa around 1959 through a syndicate-backed Teamster friend in Pittsburgh, Davidson's birthplace.[22] Davidson offered his Washington connections to aid Hoffa's influence campaign with both Richard Nixon and Lyndon Johnson. In return he gained access to the union's immense financial resources. An FBI memo from 1965 noted that Davidson "has been in contact with known hoodlums; is closely associated with James Hoffa . . . and through him has been able to obtain large loans for individuals and business concerns."[23] As a lobbyist for Nicaraguan dictator Anastasio Somoza and Haitian dictator François Duvalier, and a seller of arms to Batista's Cuba (chapter 4), Davidson was also in a good position to advise the Murchisons on their many investments in the Caribbean.[24]

With Davidson's help, the Murchisons invested in Florida real estate with close allies of Hoffa and the syndicate. In the early 1960s, for instance, the Murchisons teamed with Berlanti Construction Co. from New York to develop several islands off the coast of St. Petersburg. In 1963, the owner of Berlanti and his son disappeared just a few days after dining with Chicago Outfit boss Sam Giancana in a South Florida restaurant.[25] After the Berlantis came to a bad end, the Murchisons found another local development partner: World Wide Realty and Investing Corp.[26] Its owner, Arthur Desser, was a Beverly Hills attorney who became one of the nation's leading community developers.[27] In 1956, Desser made his first move into Florida, buying 3,200 acres of land north of Miami—for the development of Carol City—from a partnership with close ties to the Chicago Outfit and other racketeers.[28] He and his partner also purchased the southern portion of Key Biscayne, where Richard Nixon would establish his future Florida White House.[29] In 1958, Desser merged with Lefcourt Realty, a firm with New York roots. Lefcourt was owned by the vice chairman of the Bank of Miami Beach, which was founded in 1955 to deposit profits earned by the Lansky brothers and the Cleveland Syndicate from their Havana casinos.[30] Smaller investors in Lefcourt stock included the ubiquitous Irving Davidson, Bobby Baker, and Senator Smathers's administrative assistant Scott Peek.[31] Under Desser's leadership, Lefcourt received millions of dollars in loans from the Teamster-bankrolled Miami National Bank, which served as a money conduit for Lansky and his mob associates. Desser also joined the bank's board.[32] Lefcourt went bankrupt in the early 1960s owing to hurricane-related losses. It changed its name to World Wide Realty but its business remained much the same. Moving onto its board was the president of Miami National Bank, who would later be named in Senate testimony as a dealer in stolen securities with mob-connected swindlers in New York.[33] In 1965, World Wide Realty received a $5 million loan from the Teamster pension fund to finance a Florida development.[34] (Read more on the seamy world of Florida real estate in "Nixon's Caribbean Milieu" online at rowman.com.)

The Murchisons and Hoover

To protect and advance their business interests, the Murchisons systematically cultivated men of power. One of the most notable was J. Edgar Hoover. Clint Sr.'s friendship with the nation's chief lawman was cemented through personal favors and mutual devotion to anti-Communism. Hoover bet on horses at Murchison's Del Mar racetrack in Southern California. The FBI boss enjoyed all-expenses-paid vacations at Murchison's intimate Del Charro hotel in nearby La Jolla, a luxury inn that catered to conservative politicians (Vice President Nixon, Senators McCarthy and Smathers), movie stars (Clark Gable, Elizabeth Taylor), and mob associates (Ed Levinson, Stardust Hotel manager Johnny Drew). Hoover profited from Murchison's investment tips and gifts of stock. Murchison also arranged an "especially favorable contract" for the publication of Hoover's anti-Communist tract, *Masters of Deceit*. In return, Hoover ignored Murchison's connections to the Genovese crime family, the Chicago Outfit, Las Vegas gamblers, and the Teamsters. Hoover reportedly informed Murchison of upcoming decisions by regulatory agencies and the Supreme Court that could affect his business interests. Hoover allegedly even pressured his friend Al Hart—a Flamingo hotel-casino investor, Columbia Pictures director, and former beer runner for Al Capone—into selling the Del Mar racetrack lease to Murchison and fellow Texas oilman Sid Richardson in the early 1950s.[35]

In 1952, Murchison hired Hoover's administrative assistant, FBI special agent Thomas Webb, as his top political operative in Washington, D.C. Working with Irving Davidson, Webb also became Murchison's agent for negotiating Teamster loans.[36] Webb, in turn, introduced Davidson to Hoover.

"We used to have parties before the Redskin games, at Tom Webb's house or my house, and Hoover always came to them," Davidson boasted. "He was a darned good friend. I lived around the corner from him, three quarters of a block. I'd go over and say hello to him and [Hoover's longtime partner] Clyde Tolson. If Mr. Tolson was sick, I'd bring him a Cowboy jersey or some Polish Kielbasa."[37]

"Murchison owned a piece of Hoover," declared Bobby Baker. "Rich people always try to put their money with the sheriff, because they're looking for protection. . . . That's why men like Murchison made it their business to let everyone know Hoover was their friend. You can do a lot of illegal things if the head lawman is your buddy."[38]

The Murchisons and LBJ

The Murchisons' cozy relationship with Hoover was only a microcosm of their strategic investments in national politicians to protect and expand their business empire. Clint Sr. taught his sons to generously fund leaders of both political parties with campaign contributions and outright gifts. "Money is like manure," he used to say. "You gotta spread it around for things to grow."[39] In the early 1950s, Clint Sr. backed Sen. Joseph McCarthy and financed successful campaigns against his political critics.[40] A Murchison biographer notes that he "threw multi-thousand-dollar contributions the [Wisconsin] senator's way, and gave him the use of his fleet of airplanes. He also provided McCarthy with numerous stock market tips and financial advice—a service that Murchison gave other politicians as well."[41] A leading biographer of McCarthy adds, "By coincidence, perhaps, [he] voted with the oil interests on every piece of legislation of that era, including the 27.5 percent depletion allowance, the Tidelands Oil bill (which provided for state rather than federal control of submerged oil lands on the continental shelf), and the Kerr-Thomas Gas bill (which exempted the sale of natural gas from Federal Power Commission rate regulation)."[42] Unlike some Texas oilmen, however, Murchison began souring on McCarthy by 1953 and even urged him to issue a public apology to President Eisenhower.[43]

Like many Texans, Clint Sr.'s earliest political loyalties actually lay with the Democratic Party. He became a major contributor to the Democratic National Committee by 1935.[44] He and fellow oilman Sid Richardson befriended and even bankrolled President Franklin Roosevelt's hapless son Elliott; in return they got direct access to the White House to seek favorable tax treatment for the oil industry and possibly to settle a criminal case against one of Murchison's pipeline companies.[45]

Murchison and Richardson began financing the career of FDR's young Texas protégé, Congressman Lyndon Baines Johnson, by 1940.[46] They also helped bankroll his contested 1948 Senate primary victory, which Johnson won by a margin of eighty-seven stolen votes.[47] Through their attorney and lobbyist, Ed Clark, Murchison and the owners of Texas contractor Brown & Root passed stacks of $100 bills to Johnson, allowing the young congressman and then senator to build a political following in Washington. Throughout much of his career, even as vice president, LBJ continued to accept bundles of cash from oil lobbyists. According to biographer Robert Caro:

> For years, men had been handing him (or handing to his aides, for his use) checks or sometimes envelopes stuffed with cash—generally plain white letter-size envelopes containing hundred-dollar bills—for use in his own campaigns, or in the campaigns of others. . . .
>
> Lyndon Johnson's use of money in other politicians' campaigns had . . . been instrumental in his rise. It was money given to other candidates that, in 1940, had furnished him his first toehold on national political power. Obtaining an informal post with the moribund Democratic Congressional Campaign Committee, he had arranged for newly rich Texas contractors and independent oilmen, anxious to enlarge their political influence in Washington, to make contributions to the committee, with the stipulation that they be distributed at his discretion. . . .
>
> Tommy Corcoran handed him several cash-filled envelopes, filled with bills from the New York garment-center unions, and trusted couriers from Texas . . . handed him others. . . . Johnson was asking for contributions . . . on grounds of naked self-interest: political contributions should be given in return for past government help in acquiring wealth and upon the hope of future government protection of that wealth, and of government assistance in adding to it.
>
> Now, in the Senate, the cascade of cash continued. . . . Men familiar with this aspect of Texas politics agree that [among] his most important fund-raisers were Tommy Corcoran [and] . . . Ed Clark, courier for, among others, Clint Murchison, Brown & Root, and the Humble Oil Company.[48]

In return, Johnson wielded his influence to ensure generous tax subsidies to the oil and gas industry; hundreds of millions of dollars in civil and military contracts for Brown & Root; and favorable decisions by the Federal Communications Commission to benefit key radio station owners—including Johnson's wife, Lady Bird. On behalf of Murchison and other industry leaders, Johnson campaigned after World War II to overturn the regulation of natural gas prices by the Federal Power Commission. Standing in their way was a progressive member of the commission, Leland Olds. When President Truman nominated Olds for a third term in 1949, the newly minted Senator Johnson mounted a sneak smear campaign against the commissioner. Johnson cooked up the scheme with attorneys for Murchison and Brown & Root, as well as staff investigators at the House Un-American Activities Committee. They mined obscure and selective quotes from newspaper columns Olds had written in the 1920s to ambush the unsuspecting official during his confirmation hearings. While Johnson pretended to be neutral, he encouraged other members of the committee to charge that Olds supported Lenin, the "Marxist doctrine," and the "downfall of capitalism." As the hearings unfolded, a friendly headline in the *Houston Post* blared, "Leland Olds Labeled Crackpot and Traitor." Even LBJ's fundraiser and fixer Thomas Corcoran, about as amoral a man as Washington ever produced, said "it was the rottenest thing" Johnson had ever done. Truman's nominee went down to a crushing defeat. A year before Joe McCarthy began his own infamous red-baiting campaign, Johnson had cynically weaponized anti-Communism to destroy an enemy of his big business backers. Delighted by the outcome, Brown & Root flew Johnson back to Texas for a political tour, followed by a stay with Clint Murchison at a luxurious hunting lodge built by Sid Richardson.[49] Before long, Johnson began routinely attending breakfasts at Murchison's home to collect campaign cash for fellow Democrats from rich Texas oilmen. By the late 1950s, Murchison was plotting to put Johnson in the White House.[50]

Johnson's influence machine worked primarily through the Democratic Party, but not exclusively. His Senate aide Robert Baker delivered $5,000 in cash to the avaricious Sen. Styles Bridges at an "appreciation dinner" in New Hampshire sometime in the 1950s. Baker explained:

> Here was a case of LBJ putting his money to good use. Senator Bridges was the ranking Republican on the Senate Preparedness Committee, a unit serving the military-industrial complex which President Eisenhower warned against in his last days in office. In order to secure unanimous reports from that committee, and thus grease the skids for bills later to be acted on by the full Senate, or to assist Defense Department policies, Lyndon Johnson had long flattered him with shameless praise and had bribed him for his goodwill.[51]

As chairman of the Republican Policy Committee and ranking minority member of the Senate Appropriations Committee, Bridges supported Johnson and his business allies on a wide range of issues, including further deregulation of the natural gas industry. As Senate Majority Leader, Johnson led the battle to enact the Natural Gas Act of 1956, aided by his close ally, Florida Democrat George Smathers. At Johnson's direction, Ed Clark, the lawyer-lobbyist for Murchison and other rich gas producers, delivered tens of thousands of dollars in cash to Bridges in exchange for Republican votes. When the bill was unexpectedly held up by one senator's charges that an oil lobbyist had attempted to bribe him for a favorable vote, Johnson arranged for Bridges to be appointed to a special four-man Senate investigation. John-son next huddled with Vice President Nixon to give this bogus committee sole jurisdiction over the bribe inquiry. Its resulting whitewash backfired, however, as leading pundits denounced the cover-up of corrupt lobbying practices. Eventually President Eisenhower, normally a great friend of the oil industry, vetoed the gas bill.[52]

That act of political conscience was unusual. Murchison had backed Eisen-hower's run for the presidency in 1952 and helped finance his brother-in-law's farm in Virginia.[53] Eisenhower, in turn, supported continuation of oil depletion allowances and quotas on oil imports to boost prices for domestic oil. He appointed Robert B. Anderson, a leading Texas oil lobbyist and friend of Murchison, to be secretary of the navy and then Treasury.[54] Murchison's son, Clint Jr., became a golfing partner of Vice President Nixon and supplied the vice president with his favorite chili via J. Edgar Hoover.[55] The Murchison family helped finance Nixon's run for president in 1960—while hedging their bets by delivering $10,000 in cash to Robert Kennedy through Thomas Webb and Bobby Baker.[56]

In January 1963, the Murchisons' Dallas attorney and business partner, Bedford Wynne, chaired President Kennedy's second inaugural dinner, which raised nearly a million dollars to wipe out the Democratic Party's long-standing debt. The fundraising drive was anchored by a $1,000-a-plate din-ner attended by six hundred well-heeled supporters, many from the "Texas oil crowd," who were initiated into the "President's Club." The event was followed by an after-gala party at Vice President Johnson's home, featuring famous Hollywood stars.[57] Soon thereafter, "John Murchison, the Texas oil millionaire, had a 90-minute private talk with President Kennedy," reported Jack Anderson. "[H]e and other Texans are worried about the 27-1/2 per cent oil depletion allowance and have got nobody to defend their interests now that Sen. Bob Kerr of Oklahoma has passed away. Murchison's partner, Bedford Wynne, had masterminded the lavish $1,000-a-plate dinner . . . so he had no trouble getting Murchison in to see the President."[58] Anderson later reported, "Murchison returned to Texas smiling, and told fellow oilmen not to worry about tax reforms."[59] In tax proposals sent to Congress later that month, Kennedy opted not to fight the depletion allowance but did call for modest reforms in the oil and gas industry's tax treatment.[60]

Murchison and Bobby Baker

The Murchisons cultivated Bobby Baker as a conduit to Johnson and other powerful members of Congress. Baker could also be an incomparable source of intelligence on pending legislation and personal gossip about politicians whose support the family needed. The Senate aide recalled in his memoir that "Over the years I carried a lot of water for the Murchisons." Baker claimed he did so "at no great profit to myself, though I did accept their hospitality to parties in Washington, Dallas, and Miami."[61] Much later in his book, Baker acknowledged that in 1961, a senior Murchison partner gave him an insider stock tip, and then a loan when Baker wasn't liquid enough to profit from it, allowing him to clear more than $13,000.[62] Baker earned a $2,500 kickback for steering one of Murchison's companies, a federal contractor, to the law firm of the House Judiciary Committee chairman, possibly in order to win support for desired legislation.[63] Baker was also offered an opportunity to buy in cheaply to a Florida real estate venture financed by a Teamster pension fund loan that Webb had negotiated with Irving Davidson's help.[64] Webb's law firm also helped Baker's Serv-U Corp. win one of its important vending contracts in the Washington, D.C., area.[65] In 1962, a senior Murchison executive offered Baker $1.5 million to bail out a troubled motel investment. As details of the Murchisons' relations with Baker unfolded in Senate testimony, a *New York Times* reporter wrote, "it became plain that the affairs of the former protégé of President Johnson were a mystery wrapped in an enigma, wrapped in some wondrous bank loans."[66]

In the late 1950s, the Murchisons threw a three-day party at the opulent Fontainebleau Hotel in Miami Beach. Among the guests were Webb, Davidson, and a political operative of Hoffa's named Leonard Bursten. Bursten, a director of the infamous Miami National Bank, would later help Representative Multer organize a Bahamian bank suspected of handling hot money (chapter 5). At this time, however, Bursten was working with the Murchisons to promote a taxpayer-funded causeway from the Florida mainland to an undeveloped island just south of Miami Beach, which was mostly owned by an investment syndicate headed by Vice President Nixon's close friend Bebe Rebozo.[67] Also invited to the Murchisons' grand fête was Baker's friend Don Reynolds, the Maryland insurance agent whose subsequent testimony implicated Lyndon Johnson in a kickback. According to Reynolds, they brainstormed ways to get Baker to help a private mortgage insurance company compete with government insurance offered by the Federal Housing Administration. Returning to Washington, Reynolds, Webb, and Bursten enlisted Multer, a member of the banking committee, to promote the concept.[68]

Baker ended up backing a related venture called Mortgage Guaranty Insurance Corporation, or MGIC. MGIC was a Milwaukee company that helped make Baker's fortune. Many of its early stockholders were prominent Wisconsin Republicans.[69] In 1959, MGIC's president began offering Baker shares at insider prices, because the influential Johnson aide "knew a lot of people." Baker purchased many of the shares with sweetheart loans from First National Bank of Dallas, arranged without collateral by a top Murchison official, who later explained, "That's the way we do business in Texas."[70] A favorable IRS ruling in 1960, following heavy lobbying by a Wisconsin congressman who owned MGIC stock, sent its shares soaring. By 1964, Baker's holdings were worth $217,000.[71]

The Murchisons also gave Baker and his law partner commissions equal to 10 percent of profits from sales of meat from a packing plant they—and an "underworld character" from Brooklyn—owned in Haiti.[72] The Haitian company, HAMPCO, built Haiti's first modern slaughterhouse. After it passed inspection by the US Department of Agriculture in 1962, Irving Davidson lined up a buyer for the Murchisons' meat in Chicago. Baker helped swing a sales deal in Puerto Rico through his political connections with José A. Benítez, longtime chairman of that commonwealth's Democratic State Committee. Baker was investigated by the Justice Department for influencing the Agriculture Department's inspection but was never charged.[73] In 1963 alone, Baker cleared about $8,000 in commissions from both the buyers and the Murchisons, after he kicked some of his payments back to Thomas Webb.[74]

In return for such financial favors, the Murchisons entrusted Baker with sensitive political missions. In 1959 or early 1960, according to Baker, Webb gave him a briefcase stuffed with $25,000 in cash to pay off Sen. Estes Kefauver, the Tennessee Democrat famous for his anti-crime crusades. The Murchisons wanted—and got—Kefauver's help defeating a rival NFL team owner's efforts to take away their Dallas franchise, which became immensely valuable in subsequent years.[75] Less successfully, in May 1963, Baker accompanied Clint Jr. on a trip to California to persuade Gov. Edmund G. Brown to veto a state bill that required competitive bidding on the Del Mar Race Track lease, which the Murchisons owned through a charitable front. Brown ended up signing the bill, in order to give one of his major San Diego campaign contributors a shot at taking over the track.[76]

The Murchisons may also explain how Baker hooked up with two important partners of Carlos Marcello in New Orleans (chapter 5). Baker may have been referred by Irving Davidson, who had been a friend of Marcello since the early 1950s.[77] More likely, Baker was introduced through Webb, a friend and business partner of Marcello's crony Nick Popich.[78] Recall that the Murchison brothers were business partners of Marcello. They were also the largest landowners in the city of New Orleans. In 1959, the Murchisons, along with Dallas partner Toddie Wynne Jr., purchased a fifty-square-mile tract of land, then equal to a quarter of the city's entire area. The giant parcel was described by the *New York Times* as "the nation's largest metropolitan development area under single ownership." The swampy tract, known as New Orleans East, was sandwiched between Lake Pontchartrain and Lake Borgne.[79]

Two facts are of particular interest about New Orleans East. One is that the Murchisons' investment partners included LBJ's wife, Lady Bird. The other fact is that the value of New Orleans East received a substantial boost in 1961 when the National Aeronautics and Space Administration acquired a mothballed industrial site next to the Murchisons' land. NASA used the site to assemble the first-stage boosters for the Saturn I rocket, workhorse of the early manned space program overseen by Vice President Johnson. Within a few years, the plant employed more than 11,000 people.[80] New workers needed nearby homes in new subdivisions, which the Murchisons were eager to provide. In 1962, the *Chicago Tribune* reported that "The multimillionaire Murchison family of Texas has hit another financial jackpot, this time thru a New Orleans real estate investment that was turned into a potential bonanza by one of the government's biggest space projects." A year later, *Time* magazine was touting New Orleans East as one of the two most profitable developments in the Murchisons' national portfolio.[81]

These coincidences did not go entirely unnoticed. Democrats on the Senate Rules Committee blocked Nebraska Republican Carl Curtis from asking two relevant questions of Walter Jenkins, a top aide to President Johnson and former treasurer of Lady Bird Johnson's LBJ Company: "Have any of the companies in which you or the Johnsons were interested ever owned land in, on or near . . . the East New Orleans Michoud space center . . .?" and "Was the LBJ Company ever engaged in any joint ventures with any companies owned in whole or in part by the Murchisons?"[82] Bobby Baker himself refused to answer whether he was involved with Popich Marine Construction Co. in "any work on a space project near New Orleans, La., in which you had an interest."[83] The committee's counsel said there was no need to explore Baker's attempts to do business in New Orleans because it was "no different from what he did over the country."[84]

Chapter 7 examines another big business mogul with deep mob connections whose affairs overlapped more tenuously with Baker, but with even greater political ramifications during the last year of the Kennedy presidency.

7

Henry Crown, the Chicago Outfit, and the TFX Scandal

A ROUND 8:45 ON THE MORNING of November 22, 1963, a cheerful and optimistic President Kennedy emerged from his suite at Hotel Texas in Fort Worth with an entourage of politicians to greet the public. A few minutes later he joined the First Lady to address the city's chamber of commerce over breakfast. The chamber's president, Raymond Buck, was associate general counsel of Convair, the aircraft division of General Dynamics, one of the country's biggest military contractors. He had helped manage Lyndon Johnson's 1941 and 1948 campaigns for Senate and had actively supported LBJ's run for the presidential nomination in 1960.[1]

Kennedy knew his audience well. With a view to the 1964 election, he gave no hint that he might dump Johnson from the ticket. He made no mention of his recent nuclear test ban treaty with the Soviet Union, of any softening in his policies toward Castro, or of any consideration to withdrawing US troops from Vietnam. Instead, Kennedy boasted, "we have increased the defense budget of the United States by over 20 percent; . . . increased our Minuteman missile purchase program by more than 75 percent; doubled the number of strategic bombers and missiles on alert; . . . increased the tactical nuclear forces deployed in Western Europe by over 60 percent; added five combat ready divisions to the Army of the United States . . . and increased our special counter-insurgency forces which are engaged now in South Viet-Nam by 600 percent."

Kennedy reminded his audience that military procurement spending in Texas was the "fifth highest among all the States of the Union." He lauded Fort Worth's role in US national defense going back to the days of the Indian wars, followed by its history of building bombers for the army and air force. Coming soon, he promised, "a new Fort Worth product . . . the TFX Tactical Fighter Experimental . . . will serve the forces of freedom and will be the number one airplane in the world today. . . . So I am glad to . . . say that here in Fort Worth you people will be playing a major role in the maintenance of the security of the United States for the next 10 years."[2]

Production of the TFX fighter plane would soon ramp up at the local assembly lines of General Dynamics, despite a growing political scandal in Washington over alleged influence peddling in the awarding of the contract. But control of the company actually rested eight hundred miles northeast of Fort Worth. A 1959 merger put this huge military contractor in the hands of a supremely wealthy Chicago businessman, Henry Crown. His long-standing ties to the Chicago Outfit and other underworld figures played an important role in the deep politics of the Cold War era.

Henry Crown

Born Henry Krinsky to a Latvian (or Lithuanian) kitchen-match salesman (or sweatshop worker, depending on the story), Crown was a Jewish Horatio Alger who worked his way up to become one of America's richest businessmen. By the 1970s his net worth was estimated at $2 billion.[3] His fortune was founded on Chicago's biggest construction services company (Material Service), compounded by strategic investments in railroads, real estate, military contractors, and other sectors. A profile of the Crown family in the *New York Times* noted politely that it

> was no stranger to the political wars. When Henry Crown and his brother founded Material Service in 1919, he learned to play ball with the city's Democratic machine, which ran on generous political contributions. Says James O'Brien, chairman of a Material Service subsidiary, "Henry played by the rules, such as the rules were." In the process, he turned the company into a money machine that made him a millionaire within five years.[4]

By 1940, Henry and his brother Sol were already worth $10 million.[5] Crown insisted that he earned his fortune in the sand, gravel, and cement business through honest hard work.[6] Other authorities suggest that no one succeeded in the construction business in Chicago without coming to terms with labor racketeer Michael Carrozzo, boss of the Chicago laborers' union, who in turn reported to Al Capone's former bodyguard, Sam Nanini. According to Chicago crime historian Ovid Demaris, "Crown and Nanini were a powerful team: Crown with his political connections and Nanini with his contacts in

Syndicate-operated unions. Crown furnished materials and Nanini did the construction."[7]

Also crucial to Crown's success was the willingness of Chicago's Sanitary District to lease hundreds of acres of land to him without competitive bidding, at grossly submarket rents, so he could excavate gravel. Among the many politicians who got a cut from his business was the chairman of the state legislative committee that oversaw Illinois contractors and supply companies. In 1949, a Chicago newspaper exposed Crown's partnership with one of the city's most powerful insiders—Jacob M. Arvey, a nationally prominent Cook County Democratic boss and former political patron of the Chicago Outfit, in the hidden purchase of property alongside a major highway project.[8] In later years, Crown would also join Arvey as one of Chicago's most prominent donors to the state of Israel.[9] The *Chicago Tribune* called Arvey "as successful a political fixer as this town has known in many years" and noted that he had been "counsel for some of the toughest gamblers and gunmen this town has known."[10]

Crown also maintained close ties to the Republican Party through his attorney, Albert Jenner. Crown appointed this Illinois GOP activist to the board of General Dynamics. One of Crown's sons became a partner in Jenner's firm, specializing in criminal law, after clerking for Supreme Court justice Tom Clark.[11] Jenner and his firm had a long history of representing union clients with strong connections to the Chicago Outfit. The most notable of them was Teamster pension fund consultant Allen Dorfman. Dorfman, who was murdered in a gangland hit in 1983, was overheard by an FBI bug telling one mob associate, "You're better off coming to a firm like Jenner & Block. Let 'em take over the whole goddamn thing." In another conversation, he smugly told a group of co-conspirators, "The judges in our district are all Jenner appointees." During a bail hearing in 1982 following Dorfman's conviction with Chicago mobster Joseph "Joey the Clown" Lombardo in a major bribery case, Jenner vouched for his client as a "devoted family man" and "friend."[12]

In 1962, the Outfit's top representative on the Chicago Board of Aldermen was overheard by the FBI telling an associate, "Henry Crown, I've done him favors. . . . Everything they wanted, we broke our [expletive] for them. . . . They had a bad case in court, I told [Circuit Court Judge Pasquale] Sorrentino that if you got to lose the [expletive] election to see that it goes their way."[13] The alderman's boss in the Chicago Outfit, political fixer and master criminal strategist Murray Humphreys, was known by the FBI to be an intimate of the Crown family.[14]

Many of these relationships remained well buried, thanks to the power wielded by Crown and his political friends. The Chicago owner of the country's biggest racing wire, James Ragen, was murdered by members of the Chicago Outfit in 1946, apparently with the approval of Arvey's former secretary. The assassination allowed Capone's heirs to take over Ragen's business and greatly extend their national criminal reach. Shortly before his death, Ragen talked with the FBI about mob infiltration of his business. Drew Pearson learned from J. Edgar Hoover and other sources that Ragen pointed an accusing finger at several prominent mob associates who had "now reformed," including "the Hilton Hotel chain [and] Henry Crown, the big Jewish financier in Chicago."[15] The FBI's main files on Crown, however, were purged of such accusations. Instead, they characterized him simply as "a prominent businessman who is known to the Chicago office and who was a friend of the late Director Hoover."[16]

Ragen's mention of Hilton and Crown in the same breath was well informed. At the end of World War II, Crown gave business advice to Hilton and lined up financing for their joint purchase of the Stevens and Palmer House hotels in Chicago, two of the Windy City's biggest and most prestigious properties.[17] Crown became the third-largest shareholder of Hilton Hotels following its incorporation in 1946 and served for many years as its vice president and director. In 1949, Crown joined Conrad Hilton in a side deal to purchase the Waldorf Astoria in New York, one of the world's greatest hotels. Crown continued investing in real estate with the Hilton family for many years.[18]

Ragen was also well informed about the connection of Crown's friend to the Chicago Outfit. During World War II, Conrad Hilton purchased hotels in San Francisco and Los Angeles in partnership with a man described by the Chicago Crime Commission (perhaps too generously) as "the brains of all the Chicago rackets."[19] Soon thereafter, according to a trusted FBI informant, prominent "hoodlum interests" in Chicago became "deeply engrained in the Hilton chain." The source reported that Chicago Mafia boss Anthony Accardo and his Greek American lieutenant Gus Alex obtained "large blocks of stock in the Hilton Hotel chain" through Crown "in the days when Hilton was starting to acquire numerous hotels."[20] FBI informants also reported that New York mob bosses Frank Costello, Vincent Alo, and Anthony Salerno owned stakes in the hotel chain.[21] Such hidden ownership interests may help explain why John Rosselli's talent booking company won world production rights to entertainment at the Hilton chain in 1958. *Hollywood Reporter* called it "the biggest deal in club entertainment history."[22]

Crown and his family soon spread their wings far beyond Chicago. In 1949, Crown joined Al Hart, the former Capone man (chapter 6), on the board of directors of Columbia Pictures, whose cofounder Harry Cohn was a close friend of Rosselli. In 1950, Crown's son Lester created a huge new real estate alliance by marrying the daughter of New York hotel and theater mogul

J. Myer Schine.[23] Schine's fortune was estimated at more than $150 million by the mid-1960s, even after settling long-standing federal antitrust and criminal contempt charges dating back to 1949.[24] He owed at least some small part of that fortune to the mob. In 1947, his Roney Plaza hotel—the most celebrated property in Miami Beach at the time—leased its illegal bookie concession for $40,000 to New York mobster Frank Erickson, a partner of Costello and Lansky (chapter 3).[25] Meanwhile, over on the West Coast, the notorious gangster Mickey Cohen ran high-stakes crap games out of another luxury Schine property, the six-hundred-room Ambassador Hotel in Los Angeles. "At the time I was close to some people at the Ambassador Hotel who had to do with the operation of that establishment," Cohen reminisced. "I contacted these people and offered them a deal. . . . We had quite a run in the Ambassador."[26]

In 1953, Henry Crown joined the board of Madison Square Garden Corp., whose Roosevelt Raceway subsidiary put Frank Costello and Frank Erickson's son-in-law on its payroll after World War II.[27] The Garden's lead stockholders were wealthy Chicago investors James Norris and Arthur Wirtz, close business allies of Crown.[28] Among other prestige arenas, Norris and Wirtz also owned Chicago Stadium, site of the 1932, 1940, and 1944 Democratic National Conventions and the 1932 and 1944 Republican National Conventions. The two multimillionaires partnered with the vicious New York mob assassin Paolo "Frankie" Carbo in the International Boxing Club of New York and the International Boxing Club of Illinois. Together they had a lock on—and could fix—lucrative boxing matches at the Garden and other major venues.[29] Norris was a longtime friend of organized crime figures and, according to one federal witness, was a silent partner with Lansky in a Bahamian gambling casino in the early 1960s.[30] Wirtz was indisputably a trusted financial adviser to the Chicago Outfit.[31] He also owned a piece of Lefcourt Realty Corp., the mob-linked firm that developed sections of South Florida with the Murchisons.[32]

Crown and Hilton also dove into the treacherous waters of Havana gambling under the patronage of the General Batista. In 1954, following passage of a Cuban law that provided government financing and tax breaks for hotel construction, Hilton announced plans to build the largest hotel and casino in the country. By late 1957, plans were well under way to lease the casino to representatives of Santo Trafficante and Albert Anastasia, powerful Mafia bosses in South Florida and New York City, respectively. Then, in October 1957, Anastasia was gunned down while getting a shave in a New York hotel barbershop. After his death, shares in the lucrative Havana Hilton casino, which opened in 1958, were split among the Cuban culinary union's pension fund, Batista's ally Roberto Mendoza, and front men for several gangsters, including Trafficante.[33]

In 1962, Crown reportedly loaned $13 million to the Fontainebleau Hotel, situated at the head of Millionaire's Row in Miami Beach.[34] The glamorous hotel was featured in such Hollywood hits as *Goldfinger* and *Scarface*. It was also a favorite hangout for Chicago mobsters Sam Giancana and Joseph Fischetti and their friend Frank Sinatra. A Justice Department memo in 1965 cited reliable reports that the hotel's owner, Ben Novack, was a "front man . . . for notorious United States racketeers, including Sam Giancana, Thomas Lucchese (Three-Fingered Brown), Michael Coppola (Trigger Mike), Max Eder (Maxie Raymond), and Joseph Fischetti." It also claimed that he and former Havana gambler Charles Tourine lunched with Lucky Luciano in 1960, while on a trip to Italy.[35] In 1967, the *Miami Herald* charged that Lansky's friends in the old Jewish crime syndicate from Minneapolis, led by convicted bootleggers Isadore Blumenfeld and his brothers Yiddy and Harry Bloom, "openly owned the land on which the Fontainebleau stands."[36] The hotel's clients didn't seem to mind. The following year, the Fontainebleau served as headquarters of the Republican National Convention; Nixon's campaign took over the top three floors and penthouse.[37]

Crown also had property investments out West. In 1955, Meyer Lansky's former landlord at Havana's Hotel Nacional, Arnold Kirkeby,[38] bought 975 acres of Arizona ranchland at a hugely inflated price from Detroit Mafia bosses Joseph Zerilli and William Tocco. The transaction smacked of a payoff for some undisclosed deal.[39] Four years later, Henry Crown and the Phoenix-based developer Del Webb purchased the remainder of the ranch, giving the Zerilli group another windfall. Webb was one of the biggest forces in Las Vegas gambling, starting as a partner with Lansky and other mobsters in the Flamingo hotel-casino, which he built in the 1940s. Webb was also part-owner with Crown of the New York Yankees. As a friend of several presidents, and of J. Edgar Hoover, he wielded national political clout.[40]

Crown and the Empire State Building

Crown's most prestigious asset was the Empire State Building, New York City's iconic, 102-story art deco skyscraper. He began purchasing shares in its corporate holding company in 1951 and took control in 1954. Scandal-mongering journalists Jack Lait and Lee Mortimer were likely referring to Crown when they claimed that "at least one of the members of the syndicate which bought the Empire State Building . . . is a frontman [sic] who invests underworld millions in legitimate enterprises."[41] Crown put on its board his brother Irving and son Lester, both of whom were senior officers of Material

Service Corp., as well as Conrad Hilton and Hilton executive Joseph P. Binns.[42]

Also joining the board was Richard C. Patterson Jr., a former chairman of RKO Pictures and director of Consolidated Vultee Aircraft (Convair), a giant aircraft manufacturer with plants in Southern California and Texas. In all of these positions, Patterson represented the interests of Atlas Corp., an investment holding company founded by Floyd Odlum.[43] One of America's wealthiest men, Odlum "left an imprint on virtually every segment of corporate America," in the words of the *New York Times*. Once described as a "corpulent, slow-talking dude rancher with a taste for self-deprecating jokes, loud ties, and ill-matched western work shirts," this Methodist preacher's son was sometimes overshadowed by his second wife, Jacqueline Cochran, who became one of America's most accomplished aviators in the 1930s.[44] Starting as a young utilities lawyer with Simpson, Thacher & Bartlett in New York, Odlum turned savings of $40,000 in 1923 into an investment juggernaut valued at more than $121 million by 1940. Atlas Corp.—by then the biggest investment trust in the world—had major holdings in Hilton Hotels, Madison Square Garden, Hearst Publications, Schenley Industries, Pan Am, and United Fruit Co.[45] In 1933, along with his attorney and future LBJ adviser Ed Weisl, Odlum also purchased a major interest in Paramount Pictures (chapter 4).[46] Over the years, Odlum cultivated strong political ties to Presidents Roosevelt, Truman, Eisenhower, and Johnson.[47]

Crown, General Dynamics, and the Mob

Patterson's appointment to the board of Empire State Building Corp. reflected long-standing business connections between Crown and Odlum, going back to their joint investments in Hilton Hotels in the 1940s. In 1953, Atlas sold its controlling interest in Convair to General Dynamics, whose primary business was making submarines. In addition to $8.7 million in cash, Atlas received twenty thousand shares of General Dynamics and appointed Patterson to its board.[48] Six years later, in 1959, Crown merged his huge Material Service Corp. into General Dynamics in return for 20 percent of the military contractor's equity, making him its largest shareholder and Odlum's partner once again.[49]

When Crown took control of General Dynamics, there is no evidence that his friend J. Edgar Hoover warned anyone in Washington that one of the nation's leading military contractors was now in the hands of an ally of the Chicago Outfit. Crown installed as vice president of General Dynamics a crony named Patrick Hoy. Hoy personified the interface between big business and organized crime in Chicago, Southern California, and Las Vegas. Hoy had been president of the Sherman and Ambassador Hotels in Chicago, favorite mob hangouts.[50] Ovid Demaris notes that Hoy was a regular at nightclubs with Chicago mob superlawyer Sidney Korshak and Charles "Babe" Baron, "a close associate of [Jacob] Arvey and a Syndicate representative in Las Vegas."[51] According to one account, it was Henry Crown's protégé Patrick Hoy who introduced Korshak to Conrad Hilton's son and successor, Barron.[52] After 1966, following a shake-up in the ownership of General Dynamics, Hoy left to become vice chairman of the mob-linked Penn-Dixie Cement Co. He declared bankruptcy in 1967—owing the Crown family nearly $3.5 million—and pleaded guilty to a $2 million bank fraud in 1970.[53]

Writing in 1969, Demaris described Hoy's friend Korshak, a labor attorney with offices in Chicago and Beverly Hills, as "the Syndicate's topflight advance man on the West Coast." A 1978 report by the California Organized Crime Control Commission called Korshak "an attorney for Chicago organized crime figures and the key link between organized crime and big business."[54] US Justice Department officials called him a "senior adviser to organized crime groups in Chicago, California, Las Vegas, and New York."[55] An FBI report from 1963 claimed that Korshak "was considered the most powerful individual in the country—outside of the government."[56]

Korshak's influence over mob-connected unions was certainly legendary. A confidant of Jimmy Hoffa, Korshak helped select trustees of the Teamster pension fund.[57] "A nod from Korshak and the Teamsters change management," wrote famed Hollywood producer Robert Evans (*The Godfather, Chinatown*), who socialized with Korshak and employed his services. "A nod from Korshak, and Santa Anita [racetrack] closes. A nod from Korshak, and Madison Square Garden stays open. A nod from Korshak, and Vegas shuts down. A nod from Korshak, and the Dodgers suddenly can play night baseball."[58]

Convicted movie industry extortionist John Rosselli supposedly told a fellow gangster how Korshak acted as the legitimate face of organized crime: "One thing you've got to keep in mind with Korshak. He's made millions for Chicago and he's got plenty of clout in LA and Vegas. . . . Sid's really burrowed in. He's real big with the movie colony, lives in a big mansion in Bel Air, knows most of the big stars. . . . He calls himself a labor-relations expert but he's really a fixer. A union cooks up a strike and Sid arbitrates it. Instead of a payoff under the table, he gets a real big fee, pays taxes on it, and cuts it up. All nice and clean."[59]

Thanks no doubt to Crown, General Dynamics became one of Korshak's major corporate clients. Other clients included Paramount Pictures, Madison Square Garden, Schenley Industries, Del Mar Racetrack, the Desert Inn and Stardust hotel-casinos, and Hilton Hotels—a veritable road map of Chicago

Outfit investments.[60] If Hilton executives had any doubts about Korshak's clout, they were laid to rest in November 1964, when Korshak hosted a fundraising dinner for Loyola Medical School in Chicago at Conrad Hilton Hotel. The guest of honor was FBI director J. Edgar Hoover. "Korshak and the nation's top G-man were seated at the same table, despite the fact that Hoover's own agents had been gathering evidence on Korshak's activities on secret wiretaps for seven years," the *Los Angeles Times* reported years later, after Korshak was safely dead.[61]

General Dynamics Gets in Financial Trouble

The future aircraft division of General Dynamics had been a key supplier to the army's air force during World War II. Convair produced a staggering 33,000 military aircraft, including more than 18,000 B-24 Liberator bombers. Always remembering who signed its contracts, the company hired retired air force general Joseph McNarney, former head of the Air Materiel Command and a champion of Convair's problematic B-36 bomber, as CEO in 1952.[62] President Truman's air force secretary, Stuart Symington, was a good friend of Convair president Floyd Odlum, as was Defense Secretary Louis Johnson, a former director and Washington attorney for Convair.[63] A 1959 congressional investigation determined that Convair "employed one retired full General, one Lt. General, five Brigadier Generals, 13 Colonels, 13 Majors, a Vice Admiral, 19 Rear Admirals, 15 Navy Captains, 28 Commanders and 65 Lt. Commanders for a total of 186, the largest number of any defense contractor."[64] Upon taking over Convair in 1953, General Dynamics followed the same political path to success: It hired Frank Pace Jr., former director of the Bureau of the Budget and secretary of the army, as its executive vice president and then president.[65]

Under Pace's leadership, Convair began diversifying into civilian markets by building commercial passenger jets. Caught behind the more nimble Boeing and Douglas Aircraft, Convair developed a medium-range jet—the Model 880—under exclusive contract to Howard Hughes, owner of Trans World Airlines (TWA). Short of funds and unwilling to relinquish any control to potential lenders, Hughes dragged out his negotiations with Convair for delivery of the planes, putting the entire deal at risk. Hughes finally reached a last-minute refinancing agreement with his lenders at the very end of December 1960. The deal saved TWA from bankruptcy at the cost of Hughes having to put his shares in voting trust.[66] By that time, however, Convair's rivals had seized even more market share in the passenger jet industry. Weakened further by its failure to sell the follow-on Model 990 jet to American Airlines,

General Dynamics' Convair division suffered a loss of $425 million on its commercial aircraft programs, the biggest business loss in US history to that time. The debacle earned Convair's Model 880 the moniker "The Flying Edsel."[67] (By contrast, the Earth-bound Edsel cost Ford only about $200 million.) The specter of bankruptcy loomed large.

To raise cash for General Dynamics, Crown sold the Empire State Building Corporation in 1961 for an after-tax profit of $32 million.[68] The buyer was a general partnership organized by the renowned New York real estate investor Lawrence A. Wien. Wien had advised Conrad Hilton on tax-advantaged hotel deals. As it happened, he was also a trusted adviser to members of the old Cleveland crime syndicate, led by Moe Dalitz.[69] As crime reporter Ovid Demaris explained, "In 1959, Desert Inn Associates, another Wien syndication, purchased the Desert Inn in Las Vegas for $10 million and leased it back to its original owners until the year 2022. The Desert Inn boys were so happy with the tax-saving maneuver that they donated $50,000 to Wien's tax-exempt foundation."[70] The deal reduced the casino operators' *legal* tax obligations even as they continued cheating the IRS. Sally Denton and Roger Morris observed, "At the Desert Inn, ostensibly owned by Lawrence Wien's upstanding Manhattan investors and expanded with a Teamster loan, [FBI] microphones recorded an often shifting twelve-way split in 1961 and 1962, the skim divvied up between Dalitz, Giancana, Brooklyn's Joe Bonanno, Rosselli, Lansky, and others."[71]

Saving General Dynamics: The $7 Billion TFX Scandal

As General Dynamics continued its financial tailspin, laying off thousands of workers, it desperately looked for political salvation. As San Diego journalist John Lawrence recounted:

> On February 23, 1962, the San Diego City Council adopted an emergency resolution urging the federal government to award defense contracts to General Dynamics Convair to avert an economic setback in San Diego. . . . Governor [Edmund "Pat"] Brown designated a task force to study the situation. He said, "(The study of layoffs) will help us call attention to the federal government of how the best interests of the U.S. investment in the California aerospace industry can be promoted In Washington." . . . In April, Joseph S. Imrie, assistant secretary of the Air Force visited San Diego to review the defense contract situation.[72]

At the same time, Crown stepped in to force Pace to retire as CEO. (He went on to become the first chairman of the Corporation for Public

Broadcasting.) In February 1962, Crown turned control of the defense contractor over to Roger Lewis, former undersecretary of the air force. Under his leadership, the company bet everything on winning a $7 billion Pentagon contract for the next-generation air force/navy fighter plane, the Tactical Fighter (Experimental), or TFX, which entered service as the F-111. The TFX procurement broke all previous records for size. If General Dynamics failed to win the contract, *Fortune* magazine observed, "the company was down the road to receivership."[73]

Winning required something of a miracle. Four separate Pentagon evaluations, culminating in a unanimous decision of the Pentagon Selection Board in November 1962, gave the nod to an arguably better-performing and less-expensive design proposal from Boeing. Nonetheless, Defense Secretary Robert McNamara, Navy Secretary Fred Korth, and Air Force Secretary Eugene Zuckert overruled all the military panels and awarded the prototype contract that month to General Dynamics and its main partner, Long Island–based Grumman Corp. McNamara and several other civilians judged that Boeing's cost estimates were more open to question and that its design failed to incorporate enough interchangeable parts in navy and air force versions of the plane. That December, Vice President Lyndon Johnson celebrated the news to a cheering crowd of employees at the 607-acre General Dynamics plant in Fort Worth. The F-111 program resurrected Henry Crown's firm, along with its fifteen thousand subcontractors and suppliers.[74]

Rival contractors and clean-government proponents were quick to cry foul—just as Northrop did in 1949, when Secretary of Defense Louis Johnson awarded his law client Convair a contract for the hugely expensive B-36 bomber. Lending weight to their suspicion of a political fix was the publication of a story by a respected reporter with the *Fort Worth Press* on October 24, 1962—a month before the official announcement—citing "top Government sources" who confirmed that the award would go to General Dynamics.[75] If politics did swing the decision, which was never proven, Crown would have been well positioned to nudge the selection process in his favor. President Kennedy and Vice President Johnson owed their 1960 victory in part to the Democratic machines of Jacob Arvey in Illinois and Arvey's protégé Paul Ziffren in California, along with their hidden patrons in the Chicago Outfit, all of whom were tight with Crown.[76]

Prodded by Boeing's loyal senator, Washington Democrat Henry Jackson, the Senate Permanent Subcommittee on Investigations began holding hearings on the procurement decision in February 1963. The Pentagon and White House fought furiously to derail the inquiry. Drew Pearson reported that "Attorney General Bob Kennedy has been trying to persuade his old boss, Senate Rackets Chairman McClellan of Arkansas, to call off his probe of Secretary of Defense McNamara and the TFX." McClellan refused.[77] A parade of senior military officers testified that General Dynamics' design might even be unsuitable for landing on aircraft carriers. The committee obtained a memorandum by one of the Pentagon's top experts on the TFX, who declared, "There is no real, supportable case to be made" for the selection of General Dynamics "on the grounds of operations, technical management, or cost consideration." Unpersuaded by McNamara's defense, the *New York Times* editorial board declared, "Answers Needed on the TFX."[78]

The committee took a close look at US Navy secretary Fred Korth, a long-time friend and former assistant to Frank Pace, General Dynamics' CEO. Korth had been president of Continental National Bank of Fort Worth before joining the Pentagon. The hearings established that he had loaned $400,000 to the Convair Division in January 1962, before taking office but while the TFX competition was already under way. He continued to own a significant stake in the bank and to drum up new business for the institution while in office. Though Korth denied any conflict, he resigned his post in mid-October 1963, citing "long-standing personal reasons."[79] Speaking with McNamara on October 16, two days after Korth's resignation became public, President Kennedy expressed concern that some of the navy secretary's personal letters could cause "trouble" if "the committee" learned about them. McNamara replied, "We are cleaning out all his files. . . . We are going to stash it away as best we can. . . . [W]e are doing everything we can to limit the amount of material that will eventually come out." Kennedy agreed with the Pentagon chief that they should "avoid at least for a short run any indication that we forced him to resign" and have Korth "take the initiative" to insist that his problems were "completely unrelated to TFX."[80] Kennedy's subsequent public praise for Korth fooled no one; a senior *New York Times* columnist accused the administration of engaging in "deliberate concealment" and "a cover-up of the actual situation."[81]

Vice President Johnson was said to be "very concerned" about his fellow Texan and, without overtly intervening, prodded a friendly Justice Department official for information on its investigation of Korth.[82] Johnson's interest was understandable: The navy secretary had been Johnson's political manager in Fort Worth and owed his Pentagon job to the vice president.[83] On October 18, the Washington bureau chief of the *Chicago Tribune* commented that "One interesting sidelight to Korth's departure is that his going will leave Vice President Lyndon B. Johnson without a top man in the New Frontier," at the very time his former aide, Bobby Baker, was "under investigation for conflict of interest and influence peddling."[84] As he did for Baker, Johnson arranged for his adviser Abe Fortas to assist Korth in his time of travail. Johnson's diary shows that he spent much of the morning of October 18 on calls with President Kennedy, and with Fortas, discussing the "Fortas-Korth problem."[85]

The TFX investigation posed a special "problem" for Johnson. Besides his obvious interest in supporting a Texas defense plant, the vice president had a reputation for taking free flights from General Dynamics' partner, Grumman.[86] Grumman officials were also among the "biggest purchasers of $1,000 tickets" at the million-dollar Democratic fundraising extravaganza in January 1963, co-hosted by Johnson and chaired by Murchison's partner Bedford Wynne (chapter 6).[87] As Drew Pearson confided to his diary on June 1, 1963,

> Lyndon may be in for some trouble on the TFX contract. We have information that he met at the Carroll Arms Hotel with the chief executive of Grumman Aircraft and "Matty" Mathews, who runs the Senate Campaign Committee. Ross Gilpatric, the undersecretary of defense, was also present. . . . Lyndon practically runs the Defense Department, aside from McNamara. Korth, the secretary of the navy, is a Texan recommended by Lyndon . . . and the secretary of the air force, Gene Zuckert, is also close to Lyndon.[88]

By November, the TFX affair had become a major scandal, with potentially lethal political consequences for Johnson—at the very time the Bobby Baker investigation was heating to a boil. Investigators and reporters were beginning to link the two scandals. McClellan's committee leaked that it might interrogate Korth under oath about unconfirmed reports that Baker had tried to win vending contracts for Serv-U at the General Dynamics plant in Fort Worth.[89] McClellan said publicly that he "might have to take some testimony" about rumors that Baker had threatened to blow the lid on the TFX scandal if his friends in the Senate failed to support him in the Rules Committee investigation.[90] In an editorial, the *New York Times* cited the Baker and TFX scandals as major contributors to the loss of public confidence in government. It demanded full and fearless investigations, "no matter whose ox is gored."[91]

During public hearings on November 18 and 19, McClellan and two Republican members of his subcommittee accused Deputy Defense Secretary Roswell L. Gilpatric of understating his conflicts in the award of the TFX airplane contract. Investigators learned that General Dynamics CEOs Pace and Lewis were friendly with the Pentagon's number two man. Gilpatric was a former corporate attorney for both General Dynamics and Henry Crown; he attended board meetings, consulted on the company's acquisition of Material Service Corp., and even lobbied the air force to support Convair's B-58 program.[92] In public office, he continued to receive money from his law firm while the TFX award was being decided. When he returned to private practice in January 1964, after what his firm termed a mere "leave of absence," Gilpatric resumed his representation of General Dynamics.[93]

Such conflicts were deeply problematic at the time, not merely in hindsight. In a landmark ruling in 1961, based on a federal criminal statute (18 U.S.C. § 434) prohibiting government officials from rendering advice on matters in which they had a financial interest, the Supreme Court declared,

> The obvious purpose of the statute is to insure honesty in the Government's business dealings by preventing federal agents who have interests adverse to those of the Government from advancing their own interests at the expense of the public welfare. . . . The statute is thus directed not only at dishonor, but also at conduct that tempts dishonor. This broad proscription embodies a recognition of the fact that an impairment of impartial judgment can occur in even the most well-meaning men when their personal economic interests are affected by the business they transact on behalf of the Government. . . .
>
> The statute is directed at an evil which endangers the very fabric of a democratic society, for a democracy is effective only if the people have faith in those who govern, and that faith is bound to be shattered when high officials and their appointees engage in activities which arouse suspicions of malfeasance and corruption. The seriousness of this evil quite naturally led Congress to adopt a statute whose breadth would be sufficient to cope with the evil.[94]

On November 20, a member of the Senate investigations subcommittee strongly hinted that Vice President Johnson might have wielded his influence to steer the TFX award to his home-state contractor.[95] On November 22, Drew Pearson sent hundreds of client newspapers an explosive column by Jack Anderson for publication the next day, alleging that Johnson had intervened with Air Force Secretary Zuckert to swing the contract to General Dynamics. It also implicated Henry Crown and raised questions about links to Bobby Baker and his infamous Quorum Club, the reported site of sexual assignations between high-class prostitutes and politicians:

> It will be interesting to see whether Sen. John McClellan, D-Ark., really tries to find out how much Bobby Baker knows about the TFX controversy. The stern Senate investigations chairman has promised to look into published reports that Baker threatened to expose some TFX skullduggery if his own get-rich-quick activities are scrutinized too closely.
>
> McClellan's investigators will have quite a trail to follow. But if they follow it carefully it will take them through the Quorum Club which Bobby founded, and lead them in the direction of Vice President Lyndon Johnson. Long before the TFX contract was awarded to General Dynamics, the lobbyists and contractors had begun pulling and tugging on every possible political string to land this biggest military contract of the Kennedy Administration. . . .
>
> General Dynamics' board chairman, Henry Crown, slipped around Washington buttonholing politicians he knew. One was Lyndon Johnson. Crown, who contributed money to Eisenhower and Nixon in 1952 and 1956 when they were

certain to win, hedged his political bets in 1960 by putting money on both sides. He also took pains to put $1,000 behind LBJ's campaign for the Democratic nomination.

The Vice President had friends at General Dynamics' Ft. Worth plant and was anxious to have the contract go to Texas. Meanwhile, Jack Rettaliata, vice president of Grumman aircraft, a co-contractor with GD, was also slapping backs and buying drinks for men of influence. Some of the parties took place at Bobby's Quorum Club and Rettaliata picked up the tab for at least one private drinking party at the Q Club on Sept. 26, 1962.

This was two months before the TFX contract was signed. It was a joint proposal from General Dynamics and Grumman agreeing to work together on the TFX fighter plane that finally won the contract. In awarding it, the Pentagon's civilian chiefs overruled the military review boards which had unanimously recommended Boeing. Johnson's backstage role in the decision isn't known, except that he once spoke to Secretary of the Air Force Eugene Zuckert about the status of the contract. But inside the Pentagon, the TFX became known ironically as the LBJ. This may be unfair to the Vice President.

This much is known:

—Grumman's Rettaliata furnished the Vice President with a "demonstration plane" for at least one free flight to Texas. Johnson has flown frequently in Grumman Gulfstream executive planes, but Rettaliata insisted to this column that the arrangements were made with an air charter service.

—Rettaliata was in frequent touch with Vice President Johnson's office, specifically with his assistant Walter Jenkins, who claimed to this column that Rettaliata's visits and phone calls had dealt with the Gulfstream airplane, not the TFX contract.

—Matty Matthews, chief money raiser for the Senate Democratic Campaign Committee, formerly was on Grumman's payroll. Matthews was not only close to Bobby Baker, but so in love with Grumman that he mounted a picture of the Gulfstream above the bar at the Quorum Club. He also arranged for the Gulfstream to fly leading Democrats around the country, but swore to this column that the plane was always properly chartered.

—Rettaliata also was in close touch with Dick Maguire, who occupies the most secret office at the Democratic National Committee and arranges government favors for political contributors. Maguire's mail and phone calls are carefully screened by trusted aides.

—A reported $50,000 worth of tickets allegedly were purchased by Grumman officials and their friends for President Kennedy's $1,000-a-plate dinner last January. This took place two months after the award of the TFX contract. Rettaliata denied any knowledge of the dinner contributions, but a letter signed by him has now come to light urging Grumman subcontractors to buy advertisements in the Nassau County Democrats' Journal. This was distributed at a local $100-a-plate dinner.[96]

The column went out too late to appear in local papers during President Kennedy's visit to Fort Worth, where he lauded the TFX as the "number one airplane in the world today." Kennedy headed next for Dallas, where a *Dallas Morning News* headline read, "Nixon Predicts JFK May Drop Johnson." That prediction quickly became moot. As the presidential motorcade wound through the streets of Dallas en route to a luncheon speech at the Trade Mart, an assassin struck Kennedy down at 12:30. The TFX was suddenly blotted out of the nation's consciousness. Pearson canceled his column when news broke of the tragedy.[97] Also canceled, in Washington, were the follow-on TFX hearings planned by McClellan's subcommittee. Its investigation remained dormant through the rest of Johnson's presidency, resuming only in 1969.[98] Reflecting this power shift, General Dynamics stock jumped 6 percent on the first day of trading after the assassination and climbed about 30 percent over three months.[99]

The newly installed President Johnson spoke with Gilpatric just one month after the assassination, telling his Pentagon ally that no one had "caught more hell for . . . doing what other people wanted done than you have. So you just bear in mind if you got a brother, you haven't got one stronger than I am for you." Johnson added, "I've spent half of my waking hours courting [Senator] McClellan and some of the rest of them. . . . I've had him in here, and I've never mentioned you as the subject, but I'm trying to put a little money in the bank." After Gilpatric expressed his appreciation, Johnson went on, "I'm going to write a check on it, and you notice [the hearings have] slowed down considerably." Gilpatric replied, "That's right. I think we've seen the end of that."[100]

President Johnson wasn't actually so sure. As we saw in chapter 5, Johnson was still struggling to contain fallout from the Baker hearings in January and February 1964. On February 6, his good friend Frank Stanton, president of CBS, warned the president "there's some hurt, and there's an awful lot of loose talk about Bobby [Baker] and TFX and so forth. . . . I do think it's creating some doubts . . . this damned TFX talk is the thing that I think is, in some quarters, beginning to—I was at a bankers' meeting the other night in New York, a dinner, and some of the guys were talking about it then and saying—they weren't taking the position that it was true. They were just saying this troubled them." Johnson insisted there was nothing to the stories, that he had never abused his position in the White House to influence contracts.[101]

But even as Johnson was denying any involvement, Maryland insurance broker Don Reynolds was telling Senator Williams that Baker had shown him a bag stuffed with cash, allegedly to pay off the vice president for swinging the TFX contract to General Dynamics and Grumman.[102] Within days of Reynolds linking Johnson to the two great scandals, Drew Pearson published an inflammatory column accusing Baker's friend of improper and immoral conduct during his tenure in the State Department and air force in the late 1940s and early 1950s. Pearson's source was a memorandum prepared by a member of Air Force Secretary Eugene Zuckert's staff. Asked how the leak occurred, the air force refused to comment. White House press secretary Pierre Salinger made light of the issue, saying, "If we were going to be in a position of investigating every unauthorized leak to the press, it would require virtually a task force following reporters around town."[103]

Reynolds finally got an opportunity to air his allegations in secret testimony before the Rules Committee on December 1, 1964, after the presidential election and at the very tail end of the committee's investigation. Reynolds testified:

> I was in Bobby's office, and he said to me, "Did you see that man going out of the office?" and I said, "Yes." And he said, "that is Mr. [Roy] Evans," to the best of my recollection, the president of Grumman Aircraft.
>
> And he said, "Do you see this flight bag on my desk, this blue flight bag?" and I said, "Yes." He said, "Would you like to see what is in it?" I said, "Open it."
>
> And he opened it up and there were hundred-dollar bills that were bound in some brown paper or some sort of thing, and he says, "$100,000 for the TFX contract."

According to Reynolds, Baker told him that "the leader," Johnson, "had interceded to make sure that the TFX was awarded to General Dynamics Corporation."

The committee referred the matter to the FBI for investigation. McNamara "categorically" denied anyone at the White House interfered with his procurement decision. Grumman's senior vice president, Llewellyn J. Evans, told agents that he had met Baker only twice. In March 1961, he was introduced to Baker by the "Murchisons," but said only a few words to him. A year later, he met with Baker to furnish "a letter of contract to then Vice President Johnson setting forth the leasing terms under which Grumman would make available one of the company's Gulfstream aircraft for the use of the Vice President during the 1962 political campaign." (Why he dealt with Baker about Johnson's affairs was an important unanswered question.) Evans vigorously denied making any payoffs to Baker. So did Henry Crown. Baker denied receiving any bribes. Chairman Jordan declared that the FBI's report made it "obvious beyond a doubt that the testimony of Don B. Reynolds before this committee in executive session on Dec. 1, 1964 is unworthy of belief." Republicans dissented. *Time* magazine observed, "Unlike Reynolds, none of the persons interviewed by the FBI were under oath. The only part of Reynolds's testimony that has at any time been tested by a sworn statement from an adversary witness turned out to be true: that was Reynolds's claim that he had purchased advertising time on a Johnson-owned Austin TV station in return for selling insurance on Johnson's life."[104] But with no other witnesses to back him up, his sensational TFX bribery story died out.

The General Dynamics F-111 subsequently ran into numerous technical and production challenges, included grossly excessive weight and underpowered engines. Although the Boeing design might have fared no better, the F-111 was plagued by delays, soared in price, and was rejected by the navy as unsuitable.[105] When the Senate Permanent Subcommittee on Investigations finally did get around to issuing a report in December 1970, it produced no proof of a political fix. However, it called the F-111 procurement a "fiasco," blasted Gilpatric's "flagrant conflict of interest," accused Korth of improprieties, and condemned McNamara for permitting the fighter selection to be made "with no paper work, no documentation and no special staff studies."[106] By then General Dynamics' business—and Henry Crown's fortune—had been relaunched to new heights. It helped that Crown had a powerful friend in Richard Nixon. As vice president, Nixon sent Crown a personal letter of thanks for contributing generously to his 1960 campaign.[107] In the final days of his 1968 presidential campaign, candidate Nixon visited Fort Worth and declared, "The F-111 in a Nixon administration will be made into one of the foundations of our air supremacy."[108] A year later, President Nixon sat with Clint Murchison Jr. in plush seats provided by General Dynamics to watch a Washington Redskins–Dallas Cowboys game.[109] In January 1972, President Nixon approved the controversial $5.5 billion space shuttle development program, with General Dynamics as a prime subcontractor to North American Rockwell (successor to North American Aviation).[110] At about the same time, Henry Crown handed over a $25,000 contribution to the Committee to Re-Elect the President.[111]

Part III
RICHARD NIXON

8

President Nixon and the Mob, 1969–1974

There is one indisputable fact about Richard Nixon's career—his ascendancy to the pinnacle of American power has required twenty-five years of care and feeding by some very wealthy and very reactionary men, and an extraordinary number of them have maintained connections with the world of organized crime. During Nixon's years in office the underworld empire in the United States has prospered almost unrestricted by the Federal government. . . . The milieu in which he has traveled for three decades . . . throw[s] a long and permanent shadow over everything Richard Nixon the "public servant" has ever said, and over everything his political life has ever meant.

—investigative reporter Jeff Gerth, 1972[1]

John Dean: It'll cost money. It's dangerous. Nobody, nothing—people around here are not pros at this sort of thing. This is the sort of thing Mafia people can do: washing money, getting clean money, and things like that. . . . I would say these people are going to cost a million dollars over the next two years.

President Nixon: We could get that. . . . What I meant is, you could get a million dollars. And you could get it in cash. I know where it could be gotten. I mean, it's not easy, but it could be done.

—President Nixon and White House counsel John Dean, March 21, 1973[2]

THE SOUTHERN CALIFORNIA HOODLUM who said he helped launch Richard Nixon's political career in 1946 was never taken in by the candidate's subsequent claims to be a champion of law and order. After Nixon came back to win the 1968 presidential election on that platform, the long-retired Mickey Cohen wrote Jack Anderson: "In my wildest dreams (never) could I ever have visualized or imagined 17 or 18 years ago that the likes of Richard Nixon could possibly become the President of the United States. . . . Let's hope that he isn't the same guy that I knew: a rough hustler (and) a goddamn small-time ward politician. Let's hope this guy's thinking has changed, and let's hope it's for the betterment of our country."[3]

The next few years would demonstrate that Nixon's political style even in the White House remained very much that of a rough hustler. It was a style of conduct taught him by Murray Chotiner, the mob attorney and campaign strategist who allegedly introduced Cohen to Nixon and later joined the White House as special counsel to the president.[4] It was also a style of business characteristic of Nixon's close friends and investment partners in Florida, many of whom skirted close to organized crime. (See "Nixon's Caribbean Milieu" online at rowman.com.) It was a style that helped explain not only the Watergate scandal, but President Nixon's little-remembered record of favoring politically connected mobsters. That record is the focus of this chapter.

Letting Organized Crime Off the Hook

It should be acknowledged at the outset that President Nixon's Justice Department moved aggressively to indict several of the nation's leading mobsters, including Meyer Lansky, Chicago's Anthony Accardo, Philadelphia boss Angelo Bruno, and New York Mafia chiefs Carlo Gambino and Joseph Colombo. Nixon also supported and signed into law one of the toughest measures ever enacted against the mob: the Organized Crime Control Act of 1970.[5] Sponsored by the longtime crime fighter Sen. John McClellan, the act gave federal prosecutors added grand jury powers, the ability to protect witnesses, and harsh new civil and criminal penalties under a section known as the Racketeer Influenced and Corrupt Organization Act, or RICO. In the 1980s and 1990s, prosecutors would use RICO to put most of New York City's top Mafia bosses in prison.

Nixon supported such measures to strengthen executive power while, at the same time, using them selectively to reward or punish political enemies. Most of his Justice Department's organized crime targets, for example, were allies of big-city Democratic politicians.[6] And shortly after taking office, the new president fired one of the country's most effective organized crime prosecutors,

US Attorney for the Southern District of New York Robert Morgenthau. Replacing US attorneys is a president's political prerogative and common custom, but a Republican task force had recommended keeping Morgenthau on the job.[7] New York's Republican mayor, John Lindsay, lauded Morgenthau for serving "in the best tradition of non-partisan law enforcement."[8] The crusading US attorney was especially celebrated for his pathbreaking investigations into criminal use of Swiss and other secret foreign bank accounts to launder money, evade taxes, or defraud the government. Just before his firing, Morgenthau had directed a grand jury to investigate Cosmos Bank of Zurich, where Nixon was suspected of having a secret account (see "Nixon's Caribbean Milieu" online at rowman.com).[9] Morgenthau had also long been an enemy of Nixon's political ally Roy Cohn, who was facing trial on federal charges of conspiracy, mail fraud, bribery, extortion, and blackmail. As *Life* magazine told the story, one month before the 1968 election, Cohn brought together a dozen of his wealthy friends for lunch in Manhattan with Maurice Stans, Nixon's chief fundraiser, and Louis Nichols, a Nixon campaign adviser and close friend of Cohn who got to know both men from his days as assistant director of the FBI (chapter 3). The magazine continued:

> Cohn . . . was blunt about his interest in the campaign. He had been having a lot of legal troubles and court actions. What, he asked the visitors, would a Nixon administration do about his two chief tormentors, Chairman Manuel Cohen of the Securities and Exchange Commission, and Robert Morgenthau, U.S. Attorney for the southern district of New York? . . . Nichols guaranteed that Morgenthau would be replaced, and Stans gave assurance that a way could be found to force Cohen to resign. The luncheon group dispersed after signing checks and pledges to the Nixon-Agnew campaign totaling more than $40,000.[10]

The new administration forced Cohen out quickly. Given an ultimatum to resign or be fired, Morgenthau finally quit, effective January 15, 1970.

Nixon also fired US Attorney Ed Miller in San Diego, described by a local journalist as one of the city's "true battlers against entrenched corruption."[11] Miller had recently put a local racetrack operator, Russell Alessio, behind bars for interstate gambling in support of racketeering. Alessio's brother John was a millionaire banker, real estate investor, restaurateur, and former bookmaker, "described by federal authorities as having been close to Meyer Lansky." John Alessio got his start in business through San Diego's most prominent corporate titan, C. Arnholt Smith.[12] Smith, dubbed "Mr. San Diego" by the city's Rotary Club, owned the billion-dollar US National Bank, the San Diego Padres, and diverse interests in tuna canneries, real estate, silver mines, and the local Yellow Cab company. Unfortunately for Miller's career as a federal prosecutor, Smith also happened to be one of Nixon's closest personal associates and biggest campaign contributors—raising a million dollars, including a personal contribution of $250,000, for the 1968 election. Upon taking office, Nixon replaced Miller with a zealous Republican fundraiser and friend of Smith, Harry Steward.

Early in Nixon's presidency, a federal organized crime strike force began closing in on Smith for conspiring to violate federal tax laws and the Corrupt Practices Act by raising illegal political contributions and paying bribes through one of his companies. But when an IRS investigator handed the new US attorney a report on the illegal campaign contributions, Steward allegedly told him to "knock it off" and refused to issue a key grand jury subpoena.[13]

Reporters for *Life* magazine exposed the sordid story in March 1972. "The Nixon administration has seriously tampered with justice in the city of San Diego," they charged. "In an effort to protect certain of its most important friends there from criminal prosecution, the administration has in several instances taken steps to neutralize and frustrate its own law enforcement officials." They noted that Deputy Attorney General Richard Kleindienst had publicly come to Smith's defense. They also claimed that the administration called off a grand jury presentation against John Alessio and then "tried to get a federal agent who was involved in the investigations to circumvent his own agency's regulations so the White House could learn what he knew about Smith, Alessio and the U.S. attorney."[14]

In September 1973, with Watergate now a raging scandal, the *New York Times* reported that federal investigators were "increasingly interested in Mr. Smith's dealings with organized crime figures." Fighting a lawsuit brought by the Securities and Exchange Commission, Smith's business empire was defended by a former employee of La Costa developer and casino owner Moe Dalitz. A senior vice president of US National Bank, Lewis Lipton, had approved loans to "a coin-operated-machine company owned by the Mafia" and was reputed to be "well-connected in the Southern California underworld." Government investigators maintained that Russell Alessio's bookmaking operations "would not have survived without the cooperation of the underworld."[15]

White House interference slowed but ultimately failed to derail the wheels of justice. John Alessio and another of his brothers, Angelo, were convicted of criminal tax evasion. They served easy time at a federal facility for white-collar criminals, reportedly going hunting with guards and enjoying motel visits with a "movie starlet."[16] Then, in October 1973, Smith's US National Bank collapsed—the largest bank failure in US history to that time. The Nixon administration filed but then mysteriously dropped income tax fraud charges against Smith after a three-year investigation by IRS and FBI agents. In 1975, Smith pleaded no contest to bank fraud charges and received a modest fine and probation. Four years later, former US Attorney Miller, having won election as San Diego's district attorney, finally convicted Smith for grand theft and tax fraud. After years of appeals, Smith spent just eight months in a minimum-security "work furlough center."[17]

Will Wilson, the Lazy Prosecutor

To head the Justice Department's criminal division, overseeing the investigation and prosecution of organized crime, Nixon appointed Will Wilson, a former Texas state attorney general and conservative Democrat-turned-Nixon-Republican in the style of John Connally. Wilson expanded local "strike forces," multiagency teams of federal investigators and prosecutors, to wage war on mobsters across the country. He had support from the attorney general: "Never once while I was at Justice did I ever know John Mitchell to pull back from our sustained drive against organized crime," Wilson recalled later. The administration's first targets were Boston, New York, and Cleveland, all Democratic strongholds.[18]

Although Wilson promised associates that he would "wipe out organized crime in a year or two," critics complained that he instead targeted the likes of Harvard dropout Timothy Leary and an importer of erotic art from Europe. He "devoted much of his Washington time to private business dealings," according to one published profile. "Staff members conferring with him were often interrupted while he took telephone calls from his broker. He soon had the worst absentee record of any assistant attorney general."[19] Wilson's laziness—or worse—jeopardized federal cases against hundreds of organized crime figures. In violation of the law, Wilson directed subordinates to forge his signature on federal wiretap authorizations. A sharp-eyed defense attorney discovered the handwriting discrepancies and won a court ruling in March 1973 to suppress wiretap evidence that was critical to what the Justice Department billed as the biggest narcotics case in history. What's more, his folly put at risk criminal cases involving 1,400 convicts or defendants, mostly involved with organized crime and narcotics trafficking. (Two Supreme Court rulings handed down in 1974 condemned Wilson's violation but narrowed the scope of potential sanctions to cases involving some 626 defendants.)[20] All this may have been simple bad luck, or it may support unproven allegations that the Chicago Outfit had Wilson "in the bag" as far back as 1947, when he became district attorney of Dallas.[21] "Privately," wrote crime reporter Hank Messick, "a lot of people in official positions began to wonder" whether Nixon's Justice Department had implemented the defective wiretap procedures "as a safety valve, perhaps, to accommodate the persons controlling the developing cocaine business."[22]

As head of the Justice Department's criminal division, Wilson continued to deal with one of his former legal clients, Frank W. Sharp. Sharp was a Houston land developer and financier who headed a $100 million complex of banks and insurance companies. As a member of the Texas banking commission in the early 1960s, Wilson had voted to approve a charter for Sharp's state bank. When Sharp's empire collapsed in 1970, the SEC charged him with a scheme to "systematically loot" as many as a dozen companies and with exercising undue political influence in the state legislature and governor's office. The ensuing scandal decapitated the Texas Democratic Party. A state grand jury indicted the speaker of the state House of Representatives and several other prominent figures in connection with a bribe to pass two banking bills on Sharp's behalf. A Justice Department investigation of Sharp ended, curiously, with the banker pleading guilty to two minor charges and receiving a fine of only $5,000 and five years' probation. The feds—led by Deputy Attorney General Richard Kleindienst—gave him immunity from further prosecution. Rep. Henry Gonzalez, D-Tex., blasted the outcome, charging that "prosecution would have revealed the close and intimate relationship between this fabulous fraud and United States Assistant Attorney General Will Wilson. Will Wilson was right in the middle of the deals that built the Sharp empire."[23] Meanwhile, an affidavit by Sharp revealed that

> Wilson had shown him how to get around Texas banking regulations . . . that Wilson had received $297,000 worth of loans from Sharp; that one unsecured $30,000 loan had been made after Wilson had been appointed to his Justice Department post and while Sharp was under investigation by the S.E.C.; that Wilson's wealth had tripled, to $1.3 million, while he represented Sharp; and that Wilson had used his brokerage account to buy stock in the name of a Federal bank examiner who was supposed to be checking the accuracy of Sharp's books.[24]

Under political fire, Wilson finally resigned in October 1971, two years after taking office. Attorney General John Mitchell accepted his resignation "with regret," lauding the "experience, skill, and dedication" he brought to the war on organized crime.[25]

Dismantling the IRS

Another Nixon appointee proved even more devastating to the federal war on organized crime. In April 1973, the president named tax attorney Donald Alexander as commissioner of the Internal Revenue Service. Even before taking office, Alexander had tipped his hand by proposing that federal tax forms drop a question asking if the taxpayer had a foreign bank account—a question that could, for example, have exposed Nixon himself to perjury charges if he had undisclosed accounts in Switzerland or the Bahamas. Alexander finally got his way in the 1975 tax year.[26]

That proved to be only the opening salvo in Alexander's war to shut down the IRS Intelligence Division, which had a strong record of developing long-term cases against sophisticated criminal offenders. He took particular aim at Project Haven, a groundbreaking penetration of the secretive world of Caribbean banking to detect tax fraud by major corporations, celebrities, and mobsters. Alexander insisted the IRS had no place supporting Justice Department investigations of organized crime or narcotics trafficking, just as the rising cocaine trade was minting new billionaires. Leveraging the public's revulsion at Watergate-era revelations of government abuses, Alexander justified his wholesale dismantling of IRS investigative programs by falsely linking them to political spying.[27] Some reports suggest that the CIA, which had long-standing ties to money-laundering banks and politicians in the Caribbean, invoked claims of "national security" to back Alexander's termination of Project Haven, one of whose targets was Paul Helliwell's Castle Bank. Along the way, the IRS commissioner derailed 488 tax evasion cases, helping criminals to stash an estimated $50 billion in untaxed, offshore financial havens.[28] "The IRS investigation was shut down at the worst possible time," remarked criminologist Alan Block. "The IRS retreat from effective criminal law enforcement during the 1970s was of momentous significance, as this was the decade which experienced the related world-wide explosions in drug smuggling and money laundering."[29]

Easy on Crime

President Nixon made a great show of being tough on crime and demanding stiff minimum sentences, even for minor drug crimes. Yet in January 1972, top Justice Department officials approved a remarkable plea deal for mob-connected stock promoter S. Mort Zimmerman, who was once called "the nation's most investigated businessman." Zimmerman had been indicted the previous year on nineteen counts of mail and securities fraud for the looting of Miami-based State Fire & Casualty Co. He was subsequently indicted as well for attempting to pay an assistant US attorney $40,000 to have the first indictment dismissed. Prosecutors also knew that Zimmerman employed Detroit mobster Michael Polizzi as head of one of his company's subsidiaries, and that he engaged in apparently fraudulent securities deals with New Jersey mobster "Bayonne Joe" Zicarelli (chapter 4). Yet for all that, Zimmerman was allowed to plead guilty in return for a mere $30,000 fine and five years' probation. More stunning yet, he received immunity from all further pros- ecution. Shocked government investigators complained that "somebody in Washington pulled the string on us." The federal judge in the case declared, "our judicial system and society have been cheated." More than a few insid- ers speculated—but never proved—that the string-puller was Zimmerman's close business associate Fred LaRue, a top aide to John Mitchell, the attorney general who became director of Nixon's reelection campaign in 1972.[30]

Then, just before Christmas 1972, President Nixon pardoned New Jersey Mafia captain Angelo DeCarlo. DeCarlo was only a year into his twelve- year sentence for conspiracy to commit extortion and murder. A former legal client of Nixon adviser Murray Chotiner, DeCarlo was described by a federal prosecutor as "violent," "homicidal," and "a man who orders execu- tions." The FBI heard from a reliable informant that the pardon, approved by Attorney General Kleindienst in violation of normal procedures, followed secret contributions of $150,000 by singer Frank Sinatra. DeCarlo's close associates credited Sinatra's "close personal relationship with Vice President Spiro Agnew" with opening doors to the deal. An FBI inquiry found no proof and no charges were ever brought.[31] However, the main prosecution witness against DeCarlo complained in a Senate hearing that the US Marshal's Service had reneged on promises to protect him under a new identity.[32]

Nixon and the Teamsters

President Nixon's closest ties with the mob emerged from his long politi- cal alliance with the Teamsters Union. As with so many characters in this story, that alliance was founded on a combination of corruption and anti- Communism. Recall that the Teamsters had been prime allies of the Chicago Outfit, the International Alliance of Theatrical Stage Employees, and the Hollywood studios to crush a militant Congress of Industrial Organizations union and support the anti-Communist purge of the motion picture industry (chapter 3). In 1950, while running for the Senate, Nixon inserted into the *Congressional Record* a speech by the corrupt Teamster executive vice presi- dent, Dave Beck. Nixon lauded Beck as "one of the most outspoken and able opponents of communism in the labor movement. It is to his credit, particu- larly, that he saw the danger from communism, both to the labor movement and to our American system, long before others both in and out of labor unions recognized the seriousness of the problem."[33]

In 1956 the Teamsters, under then-president David Beck, gave Eisenhower and Nixon their largest union endorsement. Jimmy Hoffa succeeded Beck as president of the Teamsters in 1957, less than six months before Beck was convicted of embezzlement and tax evasion. The same year, Hoffa became the target of a relentless attack by the chief counsel for the Senate rackets committee, young Robert F. Kennedy. He also came under investigation by the Justice Department for involvement in a fraudulent Florida venture (Sun Valley) that sold boggy land to unsuspecting Teamster members as retirement property. In 1960, Hoffa reached out to Kennedy's opponent, Richard Nixon, through the ubiquitous Washington fixer Irving Davidson. Davidson arranged a meeting between the embattled Teamster boss and a political emissary from Vice President Nixon, former California Republican congressman Allan Oakley Hunter. Davidson described Hunter as "a very close personal friend of Vice President Nixon" and "a personal friend of the Murchisons." Hunter in turn was dazzled by Davidson's "amazing" range of contacts, including Caribbean dictators Somoza and Batista, Israeli defense minister Shimon Peres, "Jewish circles in the United States," Clint Murchison Jr., and Hoffa.[34] Hoffa, Hunter, and Davidson met in Miami Beach on December 13, 1959, during a Teamster convention, to discuss union support for Nixon in the 1960 campaign. The meeting began with everyone taking off their coats to show that no one was wearing a recording device. Hunter said his candidate had no prejudice against Hoffa and "appreciated the problems of working people and believed in the right of labor to organize and bargain collectively." Hoffa in turn complained to Oakley that he was "being made a scapegoat and a whipping boy" for problems that predated his presidency of the union. He wanted the Justice Department to back off of "nuisance suits" like the Sun Valley indictment, which he deemed "discriminatory and unfair." Shrewdly acknowledging that his outright endorsement would do Nixon no good, Hoffa proposed lining up local union officials to work on the candidate's behalf and using his union platform to attack Nixon's Democratic rivals. They agreed to continue their sub-rosa contacts through Davidson and Hunter.[35]

Without endorsing the Republican candidate, Hoffa got the union to condemn Kennedy as "a very real danger to our nation."[36] Nixon's former Justice Department official Will Wilson claimed that "Hoffa [gave] generously to Nixon's unsuccessful campaign against John Kennedy."[37] Weeks after Nixon lost that election by the narrowest of margins, columnist Drew Pearson reported that the vice president had intervened with Attorney General Rogers to "sit on" an indictment against Hoffa in the Sun Valley land fraud case through the election. (Two Justice Department prosecutors subsequently confirmed that pending cases against Hoffa were put on ice in 1960.)[38] In 1968, again according to Wilson, Teamster officials were "rumored" to have contributed $100,000 to Nixon's campaign, although the union formally endorsed Hubert Humphrey.[39] To win the editorial endorsement of the *Manchester Union Leader*, the largest newspaper in New Hampshire, and a recipient of Teamster pension fund loans, Nixon privately pledged to help Hoffa, who by then was serving time in prison.[40]

Nixon didn't forget his friends. Once ensconced in the Oval Office, President Nixon said of the Teamsters, "There is a great deal of gold there to be mined." He started developing that ore vein almost as soon as he took office. All of a sudden, "The key (federal) witness against Hoffa was indicted twice by the federal government and became the subject of an all-out investigation by several government agencies," according to former Justice Department investigator Walter Sheridan. "As the government kept applying pressure on this witness, Hoffa's agents continued to offer to alleviate his problem if he would agree to help Hoffa. Friends of Hoffa, both within and outside the Teamsters Union, found they now had an access, previously denied them, to both the Department of Justice and the White House."[41]

Murray Chotiner

One of the Teamsters' key political allies was Murray Chotiner, who left the White House in March 1971 to represent Hoffa while remaining an unofficial political adviser to the president. Chotiner had long been Nixon's backroom ambassador to the mob. From his days in the 1940s representing members of Mickey Cohen's gang, Chotiner took on even more notorious criminal clients during the Eisenhower years, while brazenly using his association with Vice President Nixon to peddle influence on behalf of special interests.[42] Eisenhower's Justice Department finally refused to have anything to do with him. "Chotiner was nothing but a two-bit crook," recalled Warren Olney, head of the department's criminal division:

> He was a very close associate of . . . those racketeers in Southern California, and had been right along. He was all mixed up in politics. He'd gotten on the Vice-President's train. . . . It was shortly after we took office that we heard that Murray Chotiner was running around making representations that he could square cases. [Attorney General] Bill Rogers put out a memorandum to every assistant in the department that Murray Chotiner was not to be allowed in the place, not to let him come into your office, or talk to him. That's the way he was regarded.[43]

One of Chotiner's clients in that era was Mickey Cohen's associate Ted Lewin. Drew Pearson described Lewin as a "notorious international gambler charged with fleecing American GI's in the Philippines."[44] Née Theodore Lieweraenowski, Lewin was an ex–heavyweight boxer and gambler from

New York. He moved in the 1930s to Southern California, where he was sus-pected of murdering a bookie and taking part in several bank robberies. He decamped to the Philippines, where he opened nightclubs, allegedly fronting for leading US mobsters. An exceptionally tough character, Lewin survived being captured by Japanese troops and forced to endure the Bataan Death March in World War II. After the war, Lewin partnered with right-wing Japanese godfather and narcotics trafficker Yoshio Kodama to open several popular nightclubs, brothels, and casinos in Tokyo before moving back to the Philippines. The CIA and FBI suspected Lewin of stock fraud, drug and arms trafficking, and counterfeiting US military scrip. He even set up an illegal gambling casino in Guatemala City after the CIA-backed coup in 1954.[45] The CIA learned in 1958 that this "known gambler and gangster" was arranging with Irving Davidson to sell Nicaraguan arms to an unknown client in the Far East.[46] Chotiner got involved when an air force investigation implicated Lewin in illegally exchanging more than $7 million worth of Philippines pesos into dollars, which he smuggled into a bank account in Reno. The State Department lifted Lewin's passport until Chotiner intervened with a friend of Nixon who ran the department's security office. Chotiner finally succeeded in getting the Justice Department to drop charges.[47]

Chotiner also represented two Atlantic City clothing contractors who were accused by the McClellan rackets subcommittee of defrauding the Defense Department of more than a million dollars and by the Internal Revenue Bureau of owing $2 million in back taxes and interest. During its investigation the subcommittee turned up the name of another former military uniform contractor whom Chotiner was also representing: Marco Reginelli. Senator McClellan's chief counsel, Robert Kennedy, described Reginelli as "the top hoodlum in the Philadelphia and New Jersey area."[48] He was head of the South Jersey numbers racket and a business partner of Philadelphia mobster Angelo Bruno (chapter 4). Reginelli had sixteen arrests and six convictions from 1917 to 1942, culminating in a dubious felony conviction under the Mann Act for transporting his girlfriend from New Jersey to Florida for immoral purposes (consensual sex). The latter conviction was cited by a New Jersey court to deny an application by the Italian-born Reginelli for natu-ralization in 1949. The Truman administration tried to deport him in 1952, but Reginelli appealed, winning a favorable ruling in Atlantic County Court. With Chotiner's help, the crime boss briefly became a US citizen. In early 1956, however, the Supreme Court of New Jersey judged Reginelli's testimony to have been "unworthy of belief" and "evasive . . . to a point of outright untruthfulness." In particular, the justices deemed his claims to have earned his living through betting on race horses "incredible, especially in view of his inability to recall the name of a single horse on which he had won a large sum of money." Reginelli died a few months later of natural causes—still in the United States.[49]

When Nixon finally became president, he brought Chotiner along for the ride, first as general counsel to the Office of the Special Representative for Trade Negotiations, then as special counsel to the president. "He was involved in White House crimes and misdeeds in numerous spheres," recounts Nixon biographer Anthony Summers. His many tasks included

> representing Nixon in contacts with an operative for billionaire Howard Hughes . . . overseeing the extortion of millions of dollars from the heads of the dairy industry . . . secretly threatening a troublesome Greek exile with deportation and likely imprisonment or even death should he reveal what he knew about Nixon's illegal acceptance of funds from the Greek military junta; directing the secret payouts to congressional candidates known as the Townhouse Operation; providing lists of political enemies for investigation by the IRS; spying on Democratic presidential candidate George McGovern . . . taking charge of a delivery of cash from renegade financier Robert Vesco . . . serving on a secret committee that arranged for construction union officials, including convicted criminals and one full-fledged Mafioso, to visit Nixon in the White House; intervening in the federal investigation of Teamsters Union leaders in a twelve-million-dollar building scam (those involved were dealt with more leniently); and playing a leading role in arranging the release of jailed Teamsters leader Jimmy Hoffa.[50]

In February 1970, after he became special counsel to the president, Chotiner was approached on Hoffa's behalf by Irving Davidson, who sought help releasing the union leader from prison. Chotiner and Davidson were friends and business associates. Both hailed from Pittsburgh's small Jewish community and made a living representing mobsters and businessmen seeking political favors. Davidson steered legal business his way and Chotiner reportedly interceded in a major federal prosecution of Davidson for a huge Teamster-backed land development fraud in Los Angeles County. Following Davidson's approach, an alarmed White House aide heard from a former Justice Department investigator that Chotiner was "handling" negotiations for Hoffa's parole "with the Las Vegas mob." Chotiner, however, later told federal investigators that he "declined to enter the Hoffa case in view of his White House position." He acknowledged working on Hoffa's release with Davidson and Hoffa's son the following year, when he was back in private practice. Chotiner pleaded Hoffa's case with Attorney General John Mitchell and reportedly with White House chief of staff H. R. Haldeman.[51]

Nixon could not afford politically to spring the convicted union boss from prison right away, but wheels were turning. In October 1969, William Loeb, publisher of the *Union Leader* in Manchester, New Hampshire, complained bitterly to a White House political aide that "you have not done a damn thing for me in connection with my request regarding Mr. Hoffa." Loeb was likely unaware that a senior legislative affairs official in the White House was already working to arrange a meeting between one of Hoffa's emissaries and top White House domestic affairs adviser John Ehrlichman to discuss Hoffa's parole "at the highest level."[52] By the spring of 1970, President Nixon had directed Haldeman to get Attorney General Mitchell and Labor Secretary George Shultz to work out a plan for Hoffa's release. That June, White House special counsel Charles Colson, who was in charge of political relations with organized labor, advised in a secret memo that "substantial sums of money, perhaps a quarter of a million dollars" could be raised "if we could arrange to have James Hoffa released from prison."[53] Colson made a practice of intervening with the Justice Department on behalf of union bosses who supported the administration.[54] On the matter of Hoffa's parole, however, Colson initially referred Teamster president Frank Fitzsimmons to Mitchell. Colson did arrange for Nixon to meet with Fitzsimmons in December 1970, for a session of "cordial back-patting."[55] Nixon told the union boss that he appreciated that his members were "stand-up guys," vernacular for people who would have his back in a fight. The following May, Haldeman mentioned plans developed with Colson to recruit Teamster "thugs" to beat up anti-war demonstrators. Nixon embraced the idea, saying "They've got guys who'll go in and knock their heads off." Haldeman responded, "Sure. Murderers. Guys that really, you know, that's what they really do . . . hope they really hurt 'em."[56]

The administration finally delivered for its Teamster supporters in 1971. First, Treasury Secretary John Connally approved an "unprecedented written agreement" to give Hoffa's predecessor Dave Beck a five-year moratorium on repaying $1.3 million in back taxes and penalties he still owed the IRS.[57] In October, Nixon appointed Hoffa's pliable successor, Fitzsimmons, to the administration's new Pay Board and Price Commission, set up to help control inflation and stabilize the economy.[58] By early November, following many discussions with Fitzsimmons, Nixon and Mitchell agreed to grant Hoffa executive clemency.[59] However, all agreed that Hoffa's freedom should be conditioned on him not engaging further in union politics. As Colson told the president on December 8, "Fitz wants to get Hoffa out because that's the only way that he can keep control of the pro-Hoffa forces within the Teamsters. . . . [But] if Hoffa gets out with no strings attached, he, Fitzsimmons, will undoubtedly, at some point, be in a power struggle and they lose. So he wants him out but he wants him out with strings."[60]

On December 23, 1971, Hoffa finally left prison a free man. But the terms of his commutation included a surprise restriction on Hoffa's ability to hold any union office until 1980, when his full sentence would have ended.[61] Failing at first to realize that he had been maneuvered out of his own union,

Hoffa told a TV interviewer, "President Nixon is the best qualified man at the present time for the Presidency of the United States in my own personal opinion." Frank Fitzsimmons, the biggest beneficiary of the deal to keep his rival at bay, applauded Nixon's "courage, vision, and experience" and derided Democratic challenger George McGovern as "no friend of American labor."

Fitzsimmons later denied claims by a union political activist who said he overheard the Teamster president planning the onerous conditions of Hoffa's release with Colson. Colson called charges of his involvement in the deal "just plain malarkey" and "all fantasy," even though on a secretly taped phone conversation he suggested to Nixon the possibility of revoking Hoffa's clemency "if at any time he went back into the labor movement." Colson also denied requesting money from any Teamster official while in the White House, though privately he admitted to federal prosecutors that he turned over "batches of checks" from Teamster officials to Nixon's campaign committee.[62] When Colson resigned from the White House in March 1973, a year before being indicted for Watergate-related offenses, the Teamsters put him on retainer for $100,000 a year.[63] In June 1974, President Nixon asserted executive privilege to block disclosure of documents relating to his clemency decision. The documents had been subpoenaed by Hoffa in a lawsuit contending that the ban on his participation in union activities was the result of a conspiracy between Nixon, Fitzsimmons, and Colson.[64]

The story of Hoffa's release took a wild turn in April 1973, when William Loeb's *Union Leader* published a front-page exposé charging that the White House, at Chotiner's direction, had raised a "secret campaign fund" of more than a million dollars "from certain gambling interests in Las Vegas" and from the Teamster pension fund. In return for this enormous payoff, the article claimed, the Justice Department barred Hoffa from running again for union office and dropped plans to indict top Teamster officials for taking kickbacks from Las Vegas gamblers who received pension fund loans. Adding further spice, the story asserted that two of the most notorious Watergate burglars, G. Gordon Liddy and E. Howard Hunt, had traveled to Las Vegas to pick up hundreds of thousands of dollars in cash. (Chotiner later sued for libel and the newspaper retracted its story.)[65] Other reporters heard—and in a few cases published—similar allegations about a Teamster/Las Vegas payoff.[66] The story was revived in 1976 by a protected government witness, deemed reliable by the head of the Justice Department's organized crime section, who told the FBI that he personally delivered $500,000 in cash to Colson at a Las Vegas restaurant in September 1971 "as a bribe to procure Hoffa's pardon." The money was allegedly raised by Anthony Provenzano, a convicted "capo" in the Genovese crime family and former president of New Jersey Teamster local 560, along with his enforcer, Salvatore Briguglio. A year later, however, the details changed significantly: *Time* magazine reported that a government informer said Provenzano and Briguglio delivered the cash, which represented the first half of a million-dollar payoff, to a "White House courier" in Las Vegas in January 1973. Colson denied knowing anything about the money, and federal investigators now questioned the informant's reliability. An attorney with the Watergate Special Prosecution Force concluded in 1977 that there was no "hard evidence of illegal Teamster contributions or quid pro quo payments to further the Teamster's or Hoffa's interests." He added, "The political activity, and level of contacts to influence the decisions of the Executive Branch concerning Hoffa was shown to be substantial, but evidence which would justify prosecution or further investigative efforts at this time is not indicated."[67] A General Accounting Office investigation determined only that Teamster officials had donated nearly $30,000 to Nixon campaign committees in November 1972.[68]

The Love Affair Continues

The administration's love affair with the Teamsters extended far beyond Hoffa's release. In 1972, Attorney General Kleindienst declined to prosecute an income tax case against Hoffa's attorney Morris Shenker, who was described by *Life* magazine in 1967 as the "foremost lawyer for the mob in the U.S." Shenker had represented more Mafia witnesses than any other attorney during the Kefauver Committee hearings in 1950–1951. By the early 1970s, he was the single-largest borrower of all time from the Teamster pension fund. Following Kleindienst's decision, Jim Drinkhall reported, "the entire file on the Shenker case disappeared from Justice Department files in St. Louis."[69] Only under later presidents was Shenker hit with a huge (and successful) lawsuit by the Labor Department for taking improper union loans and accused by the SEC of real estate loan fraud. He died in 1989 while under federal indictment for tax and bankruptcy fraud.[70]

Also in 1972, according to confidential admissions by Fitzsimmons himself to IRS investigators, the White House instructed Kleindienst to derail any Justice Department investigations against the Teamster president or his allies. The FBI soon learned from wiretaps and informants that Fitzsimmons had been meeting with members of the California Mafia in Palm Springs, and then with a Chicago crime boss and two notorious hit men, to negotiate criminal deals involving Teamster health and welfare funds.[71] The latter meeting took place at the Teamster-financed La Costa Country Club in Southern California, at the same time senior White House officials John Ehrlichman, Bob Haldeman, and John Dean were plotting their Watergate cover-up strategy in a room nearby. When his meetings were concluded, Fitzsimmons joined President Nixon for a flight back to Washington, D.C., aboard Air Force One. Alarmed federal agents began leaking details of these backroom deals. In April 1973, the *New York Times* reported that Kleindienst had pulled the plug on an FBI surveillance program that "had begun to help strip the cover from a Mafia plan to reap millions of dollars in payoffs from the welfare funds of the International Brotherhood of Teamsters." It added that the investigation "was reportedly producing disclosures potentially damaging and certainly embarrassing to Teamsters president Frank E. Fitzsimmons," who it described as "the Nixon administration's staunchest ally within the labor movement."[72] The *Los Angeles Times* reported a month later that the administration had declined to prosecute Fitzsimmons' son, owing to what a federal investigator called a "love affair" between Fitzsimmons and the White House. Said one FBI agent, "This whole thing of the Teamsters and the mob and the White House is one of the scariest things I've ever seen. It has demoralized the bureau. We don't know what to expect out of the Justice Department."[73]

In May 1973, the *Oakland Tribune* reported that Nixon's shadowy adviser Murray Chotiner had intervened in a federal investigation into a huge Teamster-financed real estate bankruptcy fraud in Los Angeles. One of the convicted participants was Leonard Bursten, the former associate of Hoffa and Murchison (chapter 6), who miraculously saw his prison sentence reduced from fifteen years to probation.[74] Similar magic assisted his partner Irving Davidson. Davidson pleaded guilty to concealing $500,000 in project assets from creditors, using a Panamanian shell company.[75] Remarkably, he received only a year of probation. Stunned reporters heard that the sentence reflected unspecified "intelligence work" that Davidson performed for the US government. "No useful purpose would be gained to impose any kind of sentence upon him which would destroy his usefulness to the international affairs of this country," said the judge.[76] That "usefulness" came as a surprise to the CIA, which considered Davidson a "con man and possible security risk" who "routinely exaggerates or distorts facts for own benefit, particularly as regards claiming close personal contacts and influence at highest levels."[77] But the master-fixer's good fortune didn't end there. "What happened after Davidson's guilty plea is not precisely clear," wrote the *Washington Post*'s Gordon Chaplin. "The record indicates his lawyers moved to have the plea expunged and vacated. The motion, in an unusual turn of events, was granted."[78]

In another alleged White House intervention on behalf of criminals with Teamster connections, the Senate Watergate Committee uncovered a secret $30,000 cash contribution to Nixon's 1972 campaign by Calvin Kovens, a Miami developer and recipient of Teamster loans who was convicted with

Hoffa of felony wire fraud in 1964. The contribution was arranged by Washington lobbyist and former Florida senator George Smathers. Smathers called Colson to say that he and Nixon's close friend Bebe Rebozo agreed that paroling Kovens early would help Nixon win the Jewish vote in southern Florida ("he's the most popular Jew in Dade County"). Colson passed the recommendation on to White House counsel John Dean, saying, "we had better attend to this and not let it slip." Colson added that the issue was "much too hot" for him and said the request "has to be handled with extreme care." Eight days after Smathers called, the parole board ruled in favor of Kovens. He was released from prison the same day as Hoffa.[79]

Kovens, as it happened, was a major shareholder, along with Frank Fitzsimmons, Teamster consultant Allen Dorfman, and Lansky's casino manager Dino Cellini, in Bally Manufacturing Co., a Teamster-financed gambling machine company whose first major investor was New Jersey Mafia boss Gerardo Catena.[80] Nixon's last attorney general, former Ohio senator William Saxbe, came under investigation by Nevada gaming authorities in 1974 for taking a gift of stock in Bally Manufacturing, though no legal action ensued. Shortly before Dorfman was murdered in a gangland hit in 1983, Saxbe was hired as special counsel to the Teamsters Central States Pension Fund, which Dorfman effectively controlled on behalf of the Chicago mob.[81]

Also representing the Teamsters in the post-Nixon years was Kleindienst. In 1974, the former attorney general pleaded guilty to lying at his Senate confirmation hearing but received only a suspended sentence. In 1975, Kleindienst became special counsel to the Central States Pension Fund. Three years later, federal prosecutors said he helped steer a $24 million union insurance contract to a swindler, who stole $5.5 million from the Teamsters and three other labor unions.[82] In 1979, Kleindienst, Irving Davidson, and Murchison agent Thomas Webb each paid $50,000 to the state of Arizona to settle a civil lawsuit charging them with "wanton, willful and malicious conduct" related to the case.[83] Kleindienst was acquitted in 1981 on criminal charges but was suspended by the Arizona Supreme Court from practicing law for lying about his legal work on the deal.[84]

Nixon's own ties to the Teamsters also outlasted his presidency. In 1975, the disgraced former chief executive made his first public appearance after resigning at a Teamster charity golf tournament. It was held just ten weeks after Hoffa's notorious disappearance. Among the players with Nixon were Fitzsimmons and Dorfman. Others included a New Jersey hoodlum and top suspect in the Hoffa killing who was convicted of murder three years later (Anthony Provenzano); a Chicago businessman indicted with Dorfman for misusing union pension funds (Jack Sheetz); a Las Vegas casino operator and convicted stock swindler (Allard Roen); and a front man for the Cleveland

Mafia who later died while under indictment for fraud (Jackie Presser). They played at La Costa Country Club in San Diego County, just thirty miles south of Nixon's "Western White House" in San Clemente. The Teamster-financed resort was developed by a partnership led by Morris "Moe" Dalitz, the former Cleveland Syndicate leader who became one of Las Vegas's most successful casino owners. As we saw, La Costa was also where Fitzsimmons allegedly discussed with a Chicago mob envoy splitting millions of dollars in kickbacks from prepaid Teamster health plans, before joining President Nixon for a flight back to Washington. The *New York Times* story on Nixon's first outing reported, "After he finished his round, Mr. Nixon spent about 45 minutes in a private meeting with a number of Teamster officials and others linked to the union, including Mr. Dorfman."[85]

Their chummy relationship mocked the very concept of "law and order" that Nixon had championed during his presidency. Two years after that charity event, a senior Justice Department attorney would write a memo describing what he called "pervasive Syndicate control of the Teamsters—a malignancy which rages and ravages as if the McClellan Committee's work of exactly twenty years ago had never existed."[86] Robert Kennedy's nemesis Jimmy Hoffa was dead, but the system of corruption he helped plant had sunk deeper roots than ever.

Nixon's long collaboration with the criminal underworld reflected his obsession to win at all costs, a compulsion that ultimately drove him and his close associates to engage in the many scandals collectively known as Watergate. There was no bright line dividing his relations with the mob from his cozy dealings with big oil and aerospace companies and even foreign dictatorships, which also made campaign contributions in return for favors.[87] Decades earlier, Franklin Roosevelt warned, "We now know that government by organized money is as dangerous as government by organized mob."[88] Richard Nixon's history suggests that few alliances are more dangerous than organized money *combined* with an organized mob.

9

Nixon, Howard Hughes, the CIA, and the Mob

The Road to Watergate

WATERGATE HAS BEEN CALLED by one US historian "perhaps the gravest political and constitutional crisis in our history."[1] Ironically, this mother of all modern political scandals began not with a bang but a whimper—or as President Nixon's press secretary called it dismissively, a "third-rate burglary attempt."[2] Shockingly, despite myriad government probes, lawsuits, news stories, and scholarly analyses, no one knows for sure what motivated the historic break-in at the Democratic National Committee (DNC) headquarters during the 1972 presidential campaign.[3] Another unresolved puzzle is why President Nixon, who was apparently ignorant of plans for the burglary, did not simply fire the culprits and cut his losses. What cost him the presidency was not the original crime, but his illegal attempt to cover it up. This chapter will argue that Nixon's downfall, although entirely his own responsibility, was set in motion by ripples from a deep political conspiracy originating as far back as the Eisenhower administration. It involved major players in organized crime, their lawyers and "protectors," the CIA, the FBI, and billionaire businessman Howard Hughes—in short, many of the key players already explored in this book.

Many congressional investigators, journalists, and historians believe the burglary was set in motion by White House insiders not to steal Democratic strategy documents, but to determine what dirty secrets the DNC's boss, Lawrence O'Brien, might have learned about Nixon while working as the Howard Hughes organization's top Washington political adviser after the 1968 election. In particular, did he know about the $100,000 in cash payoffs made by the reclusive, Las Vegas–based billionaire to Nixon via the president's close friend Bebe Rebozo in 1969 and 1970? (See "Nixon's Caribbean Milieu" online at rowman.com.) Public exposure of a huge "loan" to the Nixon family from Hughes in 1956 had helped cost Nixon the 1960 presidential election. The president's loyal supporters were determined to prevent another such career-ending exposé in 1972.[4]

However surprised Nixon may have been by the burglary, the arrest of its perpetrators quickly put him on the spot. The president was motivated to cover up White House involvement because two of its planners had engaged in a previous felony burglary set in motion by Nixon himself to acquire documents that might discredit Daniel Ellsberg, leaker of the top secret history of the Vietnam War known as the Pentagon Papers. The intruders were members of a secret "Special Investigations Unit," created at Nixon's behest to smear his enemies and protect his most sensitive secrets. Perhaps the most explosive of Nixon's own hidden misdeeds was his treasonous intervention with South Vietnam's leader during the 1968 campaign to sabotage President Johnson's proposed peace talks with North Vietnam, which might have swung the election to Vice President Hubert Humphrey.[5] (Nixon's agent for that intervention was Anna Chennault, widow of Maj. Gen. Claire Chennault, the China lobbyist.) In other words, Nixon could not allow the investigation of the Watergate burglary to run its course lest it expose his other crimes.[6]

Both the Watergate burglary and Nixon's cover-up, then, were broadly motivated by his fear of public exposure—and his determination to blackmail political opponents and investigators into remaining silent about what they knew. The deed that proved fatal to his career, the so-called "smoking gun," was a taped Oval Office conversation in which Nixon ordered his aides to get the CIA to tell the FBI that its Watergate probe was threatening to expose extremely sensitive intelligence secrets. To enlist the CIA's cooperation, Nixon proposed warning the agency that the FBI's investigation, left unchecked, could unravel the "whole Bay of Pigs thing," damaging both the CIA and American foreign policy. Just what the "Bay of Pigs" had to do with Watergate has been a matter of endless speculation and is the central focus of this chapter.

Nixon's cover-up strategy reflected his at least partial knowledge of deep political intrigues dating back to the late 1950s and early 1960s. Above all he aimed to exploit a secret the CIA would go to almost any lengths to protect: its involvement with notorious gangsters in plots to assassinate a foreign head of state, Fidel Castro, and its *possible* indirect responsibility for the murder of President Kennedy. Nixon's invocation of the "Bay of Pigs thing" capped a multiyear cover-up by powerful forces in the US intelligence community of secret crimes and abuses committed by senior CIA officials in the name of fighting Communism. Key players included CIA directors Allen Dulles and Richard Helms; mobsters Sam Giancana, Santo Trafficante, and John

Rosselli; Teamster boss and Syndicate ally Jimmy Hoffa; Howard Hughes; influential journalists Drew Pearson, Jack Anderson, and Hank Greenspun; and superlawyers Edward Bennett Williams and Edward P. Morgan. Their secret political pressure campaigns and institutional blackmail inspired Nixon's cover-up. However, their hidden alliances, forged years earlier, reemerged in the early 1970s to undercut Nixon's power base, first through leaks of the Hughes payoffs, and later by promoting a vigorous investigation of Nixon's role in Watergate.

Robert Maheu, Edward Bennett Williams, and the Interface of Crime and Intelligence

We begin this circuitous history by tracing the remarkable career of Robert Maheu. For a decade this low-key operator oversaw most of Howard Hughes's Nevada operations, including casinos, hotels, airports, ranches, and other businesses.[7] He also managed Hughes's political affairs, including the secret delivery of $100,000 in cash to Rebozo after the 1968 election. It was also Maheu who recruited Democratic Party boss Larry O'Brien as Hughes's top political adviser in Washington in 1968, giving Nixon reason to fear that O'Brien might destroy his 1972 reelection campaign by exposing the truth about those bribes.

Maheu was no ordinary business executive. Hughes didn't hire a bean counter or a manager to run his empire; in fact, Maheu had no particular business skills or financial acumen.[8] He was, instead, an expert in covert operations. In 1940, at the age of twenty-three, Maheu joined the FBI, where he was trained by the future Murchison agent, Thomas Webb. After hunting Nazi spies during World War II, he tried launching a small business, which failed miserably. Eventually he earned enough money from a private craps game to open his own investigative and public relations firm in 1954.[9] Maheu leveraged his relationship with other former federal agents to land his first regular client: the CIA's Office of Security. That branch handled many of the agency's most sensitive and illegal operations, including drug testing and mind-control experiments; domestic surveillance of antiwar activists; and even covert investigations of journalists such as Jack Anderson. Most controversially, as we will soon see, it also oversaw some plots to kill foreign leaders. One of the key Watergate burglars, James McCord, joined the Nixon campaign after a long career in the Office of Security.[10]

For a $500 monthly retainer, Maheu took "cutout" assignments from the CIA—"jobs in which the agency could not officially be involved," as he put it.[11] For his first such job, in 1954, Maheu helped foil a plot by Greek shipowner

Aristotle Onassis to get a lock on the Middle East oil market through an exclusive shipping contract with Saudi Arabia. Although Maheu's paying client was a rival shipowner, the CIA provided technical assistance and Maheu personally briefed Vice President Nixon and the National Security Council on his progress.[12] Maheu also procured prostitutes for the CIA, both to service and to compromise foreign officials. In 1957, at the CIA's behest, Maheu tried to smear the reputation of the nonaligned leader of Indonesia, President Sukarno, by producing a fake surveillance video that appeared to show him bedding a beautiful blond Soviet spy. Maheu also tried to arrange a tryst between Sukarno and an alluring female agent, to no avail.[13]

Maheu continued doing secret jobs for the CIA until about 1970.[14] But he earned much more by handling investigations for Washington "superlawyer" Edward Bennett Williams. Williams had been one of his closest friends from their days on the college debate team at College of the Holy Cross in Worcester, Massachusetts.[15] In one of their earliest cases together, Williams hired Maheu to investigate a politically charged murder case involving US intelligence agents and Communist partisans in World War II Italy, involving $100 million in lost Allied gold. The case, which had major political implications in Italy, interested the CIA deeply. Williams and Maheu managed to demonstrate the innocence of an accused American agent while blaming the Communists for absconding with the gold—a small but important victory in Cold War politics.[16]

Maheu had found the right ally in Williams. The lawyer had powerful connections everywhere in Washington. He was close to the CIA for his entire career.[17] He was one of the best sources for muckraking columnist Drew Pearson.[18] He would eventually become a key part of the Watergate story—representing both the Democratic National Committee and the *Washington Post*, two of Nixon's biggest enemies.

TABLE 9.1

Edward Bennett Williams's Law Clients

CIA	Mafia/Teamsters	Political
Aldo Icardi	Dave Beck	Sen. Joseph McCarthy
Richard Helms	Jimmy Hoffa	Bobby Baker
	Sam Giancana	Democratic National Committee
	Frank Costello	

In the 1950s, Williams made a name for himself by pulling off remarkable acquittals for New York Mafia don Frank Costello and corrupt Teamsters Union leader James Hoffa. Williams managed to spring Hoffa in a 1957 case involving the alleged bribery of a Senate staffer working for Robert Kennedy, chief counsel to the McClellan labor rackets committee.[19] At the suggestion of Williams, Hoffa hired Maheu in 1957 to "do electronics work," a euphemism for sweeping his office for electronic bugs.[20]

Last but not least, Williams referred the mega-industrialist Howard Hughes to Maheu in the mid-1950s. It was the start of a business marriage that would last through 1970 before exploding in an acrimonious divorce, mutual investigations, and lawsuits. Hughes first hired Maheu for surveillance jobs on Hollywood actress Ava Gardner and to discourage a couple of blackmailers.[21] In 1956, Hughes engaged Maheu to help Vice President Nixon thwart a Republican rival who wanted to replace him on Eisenhower's ticket.[22] In 1957, the increasingly elusive Hughes asked Maheu to become the public face of most of his business operations. To cement their relationship, Maheu moved his family from the Washington, D.C., suburbs to Los Angeles in 1961.[23]

Joining the Maheu family for Thanksgiving dinner that year was the dapper Italian-born mobster John Rosselli (sometimes spelled Roselli). Rosselli was the Chicago mob's trusted representative in its two biggest Western markets: Los Angeles and Las Vegas. His credentials included a prison record for labor racketeering and extortion of the movie industry, for which he was granted early parole along with leaders of the Outfit (chapters 2 and 3). When singer Frank Sinatra wanted to break into the movies with a leading role in the World War II blockbuster *From Here to Eternity*, Rosselli intervened with studio boss Harry Cohn to get him the part.[24] Rosselli also claimed to have helped make Marilyn Monroe a star.[25] In 1957 he helped pull together a consortium of major underworld investors from Chicago, New York, and Louisiana to build the luxurious Tropicana hotel and casino on the strip in Vegas. Rosselli also arranged Teamster financing for other mob casinos in Las Vegas and "dominated the booking of high-priced entertainment that the hotels used to attract gamblers," according to his biographers.[26]

The CIA, the Mob, and Maheu Plot to Kill Castro

Maheu and Rosselli were introduced to each other in Las Vegas in the late 1950s by Mafia lawyer Edward Bennett Williams. As their friendship blossomed, Maheu's children started calling the mobster "Uncle Johnny."[27] By 1961, Maheu and Rosselli were joined at the hip in what was perhaps the most sensitive operation in the CIA's history: the plot to assassinate Fidel Castro.

After Castro took power in 1959, Vice President Nixon chaired a high-level policy committee that reviewed and recommended covert operations against the new Cuban regime, which Nixon was certain had Communist leanings. Nixon later claimed to have been "the strongest and most persistent advocate for setting up and supporting" a CIA program to train Cuban exiles to over- throw Castro.[28] That program would be implemented by the new Kennedy administration in April 1961 with the disastrous invasion at the Bay of Pigs.

A key but hidden part of that plan was "the elimination of Fidel Castro," which the CIA's Western Hemisphere division chief first officially advocated in December 1959.[29] By April 1960, other advocates of political murder included Nixon's close friend and adviser William Pawley and the CIA's chief political action officer for the Cuba invasion, future Watergate burglar How- ard Hunt.[30] CIA director Allen Dulles almost certainly approved such a mis- sion—but never told President Eisenhower or President Kennedy.[31] Nor, for that matter, did Dulles even brief his successor as CIA director, John McCo- ne.[32] Some matters were simply too sensitive to share. Agency insiders gave their bosses in the White House "deniability," whether they wanted it or not.

After several ad hoc attempts to kill Castro failed, the CIA's covert opera- tions chief, Deputy Director for Plans Richard Bissell, asked the agency's Office of Security in August 1960 to recruit Mafia bosses with prior gambling interests in Cuba to carry out the job. An internal history of the operation years later speculated that the CIA was being steered by hidden hands, "pig- gybacking on the [national crime] syndicate and . . . supplying an aura of official sanction" to what was originally an underworld initiative.[33] Meyer Lansky, the king of Las Vegas and Cuban gambling, reputedly put out the first contract on Castro—for a million dollars—when the bearded rebel booted the mob out of Cuba.[34]

If ever an assignment called for using a private "cutout" to avoid impli- cating the government, this was it. The Office of Security knew just who could put them in contact with the appropriate Mafia bosses: their contract agent Robert Maheu.[35] Maheu called up his friend Rosselli to offer him an opportunity to serve his country. In early September 1960, over a meal in Beverly Hills, Maheu offered Rosselli $150,000 to assassinate Castro. Rosselli accepted the job but patriotically declined the cash. Maheu and Rosselli next met in New York with the chief of operational support in the CIA's Office of Security, a stunning breach of operational security.[36] Days later, all three flew to Miami. There, at a suite in the famed Fontainebleau Hotel, Rosselli introduced Maheu to two colleagues who would have to approve the Castro hit. One was Rosselli's powerful boss in Chicago, Sam Giancana, who was also a client of Edward Bennett Williams. The other was Santo Trafficante, the Mafia boss from Tampa who sometimes worked out of the Teamster Union office in Miami.[37] As a major owner of casinos in prerevolutionary Havana, Trafficante had dozens of Cuban exiles on his payroll, active in everything from *bolita* (numbers) rackets to narcotics trafficking. Many were being trained by the CIA in commando tactics in preparation for the Bay of Pigs invasion.[38]

On the downside, both Giancana and Trafficante had been subpoenaed along with Jimmy Hoffa by Robert Kennedy to testify before the Senate labor rackets committee in the late 1950s. After President Kennedy took office, the director of the CIA's Office of Security later noted, "Both were on the Attorney General's [list of] ten most-wanted men."[39] Through its choice of surrogates, the CIA was thus directly flouting the war on organized crime declared by the Kennedy brothers and belatedly pursued by J. Edgar Hoover. The agency's collaboration with mobsters sustained their hopes of "securing gambling, prostitution, and dope monopolies in Cuba in the event Castro is overthrown," to quote a memo by Hoover to CIA director Allen Dulles in December 1960.[40]

For all their wealth and power, however, these ruthless Mafia bosses proved unable to pierce Castro's security shield. They ruled out shooting the Cuban leader as too dangerous. Their repeated attempts to poison him fell victim to bad luck and logistical snafus. In all, Castro would survive more than a hundred assassination attempts by many enemies over more than two decades. It may also be, as some organized crime experts maintain, that Giancana and Trafficante simply strung the CIA along and never seriously mobilized their assets to kill Castro.[41]

But the dark secret of the CIA-Mafia plots was not safe. Rosselli and his Mafia partners quickly realized that Maheu was fronting for a CIA operation. Before long, so did Howard Hughes. Starting in the fall of 1960, Maheu shuttled frequently between his Los Angeles base and Miami, the launching pad for all CIA operations against Cuba.[42] He was gone so much that Hughes, Maheu's top client, demanded that he return. Rather than lose his business, Maheu sought—and amazingly received—permission from the CIA to tell Hughes that he was working on a top secret assignment that "included plans to dispose of Mr. Castro in connection with a pending invasion." As one account notes, "It was a piece of information that had not even been given to the president of the United States, John F. Kennedy."[43]

The incident strongly supports other evidence that Hughes already had an extensive covert relationship with the CIA.[44] The agency's Domestic Contacts Division (DCD) acknowledged in a secret 1974 memo that it "had close and continuing relationships with the Hughes Tool Company and the Hughes Aircraft Company since 1948. . . . In the case of Hughes Aircraft, DCD has contacted over 250 individuals in the company since the start of our association and about 100 in Hughes Tool over the same period. . . . In addition, there is some evidence in DCD files that both companies may have had contractual relationships with the Agency."[45] Over the years, that relationship would generate billions of dollars' worth of CIA contracts for Hughes Aircraft alone.[46]

Eventually J. Edgar Hoover got wind of the CIA's secret alliance with the mob. It leaked to the FBI when the jealous Chicago boss Giancana, much like Hughes a few years earlier, asked Maheu to spy on one of his lovers, the hit singer Phyllis McGuire. She was consorting with *Laugh-In* comedian Dan Rowan behind Giancana's back in Las Vegas. As a favor for Giancana's help in Cuba, Maheu agreed to "bug" Rowan's Las Vegas hotel room. Remarkably, the CIA gave him $1,000 to do the job.[47] The operation was worthy of the Keystone Kops—or the Watergate bunglers. Maheu farmed the job out to a Florida private eye, who left all his monitoring equipment in plain view in his hotel room. A maid spotted it and called hotel security. Wiretapping was a federal offense, so police called in the FBI. The detective gave up Maheu's name. Questioned by the feds, Maheu offered the implausible-sounding explanation that he had arranged to surveil the TV comedian "on behalf of the CIA relative to anti-Castro activities." The FBI didn't let the matter drop, and after more than a year of arm-twisting the head of the CIA's Office of Security finally gave Hoover a classified briefing about the assassination plots. The FBI director in turn informed Attorney General Robert Kennedy on May 22, 1961, that the CIA was now secretly working with Giancana on unspecified "anti-Castro activities."[48] On February 7, 1962, the CIA's director of security informed the FBI that the agency would "object to any prosecution" of Maheu or his colleagues "which would necessitate the use of CIA personnel or CIA information," adding that "introduction of evidence concerning the CIA operation would be embarrassing to the Government." The Justice Department had no objection and did not ask for further details.[49]

Adding tremendous spice to this already hot scenario was the FBI's discovery in early 1962 that Judith Campbell—a beautiful young divorcée from Los Angeles, friend of Rosselli, and "paramour" of Giancana—had made dozens of calls to the White House. One private investigator with mob connections described her to the FBI as "the girl who was 'shacking up with John Kennedy in the East.'" Sharing Giancana's lover was definitely ill-advised. The president broke off his affair after lunching privately with Hoover on March 22, 1962.[50]

Not until May 7, 1962, at the FBI's instigation, did top CIA officials, including Richard Helms, finally brief Bobby Kennedy about their plots with the Mafia.[51] After hearing the news, the attorney general lamented that his war on organized crime had been fatally subverted: "It would be very difficult to initiate any prosecution against Giancana, as Giancana could immediately bring out the fact that the U.S. Government had approached him to arrange for the assassination of Castro." One of his CIA briefers later recalled, "If you have seen Mr. Kennedy's eyes get steely and his jaw set and his voice get low and precise, you get a definite feeling of unhappiness."[52]

CIA officials reassured the attorney general that they had cut the Mafia loose and terminated their assassination plans. That claim was false; the directorate of plans was continuing to work with Rosselli and other gangsters without Kennedy's knowledge.[53] They plotted Castro's murder with other agents as well. Indeed, on November 22, 1963, even as President Kennedy was beginning his motorcade through the streets of Dallas, a senior CIA officer was holding a clandestine rendezvous in Paris with an apparently disloyal Cuban official. The CIA officer, masquerading as a personal emissary of Attorney General Kennedy, assured the Cuban that the White House was serious about overthrowing the Castro regime. He handed over a poison injector disguised as a simple pen and promised to smuggle into Cuba a sniper rifle with telescopic sight. But the only leader who got killed that day was President Kennedy. Historian Arthur Schlesinger Jr. observed, "The CIA was reviving the assassination plots at the very time President Kennedy was considering the possibility of normalization of relations with Cuba—an extraordinary action. If it was not total incompetence—which in the case of the CIA cannot be excluded—it was a studied attempt to subvert national policy."[54]

The Most Dangerous Question: Who Killed JFK?

The CIA could not have known in 1963—and likely still does not know today—whether its murder plots against Castro in some way rebounded against JFK in Dallas.[55] Some agency officials suspected that Castro had recruited Lee Harvey Oswald to retaliate against Kennedy, tit for tat. It was also conceivable that one or more of the CIA's own agents, who hated President Kennedy for failing to back the Bay of Pigs invasion with American air and naval power, had killed the president. (Within hours of the assassination, Bobby Kennedy reportedly told one anti-Castro Cuban leader, "One of your guys did it."[56]) Oswald, the reputed Dallas assassin, had enough murky relationships with the CIA, FBI, naval intelligence, pro-Castro, and anti-Castro Cuban exile organizations to fill dozens of subsequent conspiracy books. The man who silenced Oswald, Dallas nightclub owner Jack Ruby, maintained close ties to Giancana's Outfit as late as 1963, knew Rosselli, and likely met with Trafficante in Cuba in 1959.[57] Thorough investigation of any of these leads might expose some of the CIA's darkest secrets, including its dirty alliance with the Mafia. The agency, not surprisingly, went into full cover-up mode. It kept its own assassination schemes secret from the Warren Commission and offered few details to the FBI.[58]

The House Select Committee on Assassinations concluded in 1979 that Trafficante and his Louisiana ally, Carlos Marcello, "had the motive, means, and opportunity to assassinate President Kennedy" but admitted it had no proof of their involvement. Years later, Trafficante's attorney claimed that the mob boss admitted on his deathbed to being part of a conspiracy to kill Kennedy, apparently at the behest of Jimmy Hoffa. That alleged confession, like others in the case, is still highly controversial.[59] But a respected Cuban exile leader did testify before Congress about a chilling meeting with Trafficante one year before the JFK assassination to discuss a large Teamster pension fund loan. Trafficante was "very much upset" about "the way the President was getting into Hoffa" and predicted that Kennedy would not serve a second term. When the exile leader questioned his political prediction, Trafficante allegedly replied, "you don't understand me, he is going to be hit."[60]

Blowback and Blackmail

By its unwise choice of partners and projects, the CIA had left itself wide open to blackmail. If details of the anti-Castro plots became public, the agency could be destroyed. Unfortunately for the CIA, its co-conspirators thought nothing of breaking silence to gain leverage against the US government. They started turning the screws in 1966, when Giancana's lawyer, Edward Bennett Williams, reportedly invoked his client's history of government service to help spring the mob boss from jail.[61]

Robert Maheu likewise prevailed on the CIA to block an investigation by the Senate Judiciary Subcommittee on Administrative Practice and Procedure into his involvement in illegal wiretapping.[62] The subcommittee's chair, Sen. Edward Long of Missouri, was disturbed by recent revelations of extensive FBI electronic surveillance of the mob owners of Las Vegas casinos (chapter 5). The illegal wiretaps had been brought to light by Williams, attorney for several of those mobsters; his client Jimmy Hoffa suspected that he, too, had been a victim of illegal government eavesdropping.[63] FBI surveillance showed that Senator Long was a close friend and client of Jimmy Hoffa's attorney Morris Shenker, who paid Long tens of thousands of dollars for unexplained services, possibly to encourage his probe of illegal wiretaps as part of an effort to keep Hoffa out of jail.[64] Pressuring the federal government further on Hoffa's behalf, Shenker also told Long about Maheu's role in the illegal wiretapping of Greek shipowner Aristotle Onassis in 1954 and the bugging of Dan Rowen's Las Vegas hotel room on behalf of Sam Giancana. Learning of this leak, the director of the CIA's Office of Security warned CIA director Richard Helms that exposure of agency involvement with Giancana "could be most embarrassing." Fortunately for all concerned, Maheu's attorney, Edward P. Morgan, was a "very close friend" of Shenker. Through Shenker, Morgan convinced Senator Long in the summer of 1966 to drop his investigation of Maheu in the interests of national security.[65]

As it happens Morgan was also Teamster president Jimmy Hoffa's Washington attorney, handling his appeal from a 1964 conviction for labor racketeering.[66] Morgan, at the same time, was providing ammunition for Long's investigation by preparing a multimillion-dollar lawsuit on behalf of Bobby Baker's partner and Rosselli's friend Fred Black (chapter 5), charging that the FBI had bugged his suite.[67] Insiders were pulling strings on multiple levels that not even the CIA could fully fathom.

Morgan was a black-belt practitioner of deep politics, a ubiquitous insider who left little public trace and no published biography. He served as a special agent with the FBI from 1940 to 1947, overlapping with Maheu.[68] In 1951, he was recruited by the CIA's clandestine service branch and received a covert security clearance to handle legal work for a secret agency contract with Johns Hopkins University.[69] In private practice as an attorney, Morgan represented his close friend and fellow FBI alumnus Robert Maheu as soon as Maheu opened his private-eye office with CIA financial support.[70] Through Maheu, Morgan was one of the only non-agency individuals (aside from Howard Hughes) privy to the CIA-Mafia assassination plots from their earliest days.[71] He was also attorney to muckraking columnists Drew Pearson and Jack Anderson and their mutual friend, *Las Vegas Sun* publisher Hank Greenspun.[72] In the late 1960s, as noted, he represented Jimmy Hoffa, who was appealing his convictions. In 1973, Morgan would become Watergate counsel to the Democratic National Committee, replacing the law partner of another former Hoffa attorney, Edward Bennett Williams.

Morgan first met Rosselli in the 1950s through Greenspun, who handled publicity for the mob-owned Flamingo and Desert Inn casinos and ran guns to Israel before launching his career in newspaper publishing.[73] Morgan began representing Rosselli in various Las Vegas matters. In early 1967, Morgan worked with Rosselli, Greenspun, and Hoffa to persuade the owners of the Teamster-financed Desert Inn hotel-casino—who included Moe Dalitz and Sam Giancana—to sell out to Howard Hughes.[74] Morgan split $50,000 of his $150,000 finder's fee with Rosselli and $25,000 with Greenspun. Morgan, Rosselli, and Greenspun would reap hundreds of thousands of dollars in additional fees from Maheu by arranging several more deals for Hughes with mob casino owners in Las Vegas. Through Maheu, Morgan also received a $100,000 annual retainer to handle legal business for the Hughes empire.[75]

TABLE 9.2
Key Players in CIA–Mafia–Howard Hughes Intrigues Culminating in Watergate

Key Players	Pre-Watergate	Watergate
Robert Maheu	CIA contract agent Investigator for Jimmy Hoffa Helped Nixon in 1954–1956. Howard Hughes aide Managed CIA-Mafia assassination plots.	Leaked dirt on Hughes and Nixon in 1971–1972. Close ally and former employer of Larry O'Brien, chair of the Democratic National Committee.
Edward Bennett Williams	Represented Jimmy Hoffa and Sam Giancana. Introduced Maheu to Hughes and Rosselli.	Represented Democratic National Committee and the Washington Post.
Jack Anderson	Broke story of CIA-Mafia assassination plots.	Exposed Hughes payoffs to Nixon before 1972 election. Investigated by CIA. Target of assassination plot by White House "plumbers."
Hank Greenspun (publisher)	Friend of Hoffa, Maheu, Rosselli, Morgan, Anderson. Convicted with future Zicarelli associates of gun-running to Israel; pardoned by JFK. Fierce critic of Senator McCarthy.	Leaked story of Hughes payoff to Nixon. Target of attempted break-in by Hunt, Liddy, and Hughes security agent to recover Hughes memos that could damage White House.
Edward P. Morgan (attorney)	Friend of Greenspun from anti- McCarthy days. Represented Anderson, Giancana, Hoffa, Hughes, Rosselli. Pearson/Anderson source on CIA-Mafia plots.	Democratic National Committee attorney in 1973.

Life should have been good for Rosselli, but the FBI was following him around the clock by mid-1966. The Justice Department began threatening to deport him to Italy unless he became a federal informant. Not surprisingly, Rosselli began drinking heavily.[76] Rosselli called up his CIA contact in the Office of Security to complain about FBI harassment.[77] When his legal problems didn't go away, Rosselli saw to it that the CIA shared his pain.

Like Maheu, Rosselli knew the perfect agent to leverage his knowledge of national security secrets to ward off official investigators: Edward Morgan. In January 1967, on Rosselli's behalf, Morgan leaked to his close friends and clients Drew Pearson and Jack Anderson the explosive story about the Castro assassination plots.[78] Morgan knew that Pearson would in turn tell his close friend Chief Justice Earl Warren, who had led the presidential commission that investigated the JFK assassination in 1964.[79] Indeed, Pearson personally briefed President Johnson and Warren at length.[80]

Morgan distorted key details to maximize Rosselli's blackmail leverage. In his telling, it was the Kennedys, not the CIA, who spearheaded the plots, even though they had actually been hatched during the Eisenhower years. And to make the story even more incendiary, he maintained that JFK had been murdered by Castro in retaliation.[81] As Pearson's junior partner Jack Anderson informed their national readership on March 3, "President Johnson is sitting on a political H-bomb, an unconfirmed report that Sen. Robert Kennedy may have approved an assassination plot which then possibly backfired against his late brother." Citing a source's claim that "Bobby, eager to avenge the Bay of Pigs fiasco, played a key role in the planning," Anderson reported rumors that Castro became "aware of an American plot upon his life and decided to retaliate against President Kennedy."[82]

The column ran at a time of dramatically heightened public suspicion that Kennedy's assassination had been the work of a conspiracy. Several best sellers published in mid-1966 had cast serious doubts on the findings of the Warren Commission. By January 1967, nearly half of all Americans surveyed believed that Oswald did not act alone. The trend in domestic and world opinion had become of sufficient concern to officials in Washington that a senior CIA officer sent agency station chiefs a detailed dispatch on "Countering Criticism of the Warren Report." It noted, "Our organization itself is directly involved. . . . Conspiracy theories have frequently thrown suspicion on our organization, for example by falsely alleging that Lee Harvey Oswald worked for us. The aim of this dispatch is to provide material for countering and discrediting the claims of the conspiracy theories, so as to inhibit the circulation of such claims in other countries." It proposed using "propaganda assets to answer and refute the attacks of the critics" and planting suggestions that some conspiracy theories were being "deliberately generated by Communist propagandists." The CIA was fighting a losing battle, however. Just one month later, New Orleans District Attorney Jim Garrison blew the case open with a dramatic announcement that he planned to arrest conspirators who had used his city to plot the deed. He made further national publicity with his first arrest on March 1, undoubtedly fueling interest in the column Anderson ran two days later.[83]

Senior intelligence officials were under no illusion as to the source and purpose of the leak to Anderson about possible blowback from the CIA's own assassination conspiracies. A March 6 memo to assistant FBI director William Sullivan stated, "It appears Roselli [sic] is using his prior connections with the CIA to his best advantage. . . . The current Director of Security,

CIA, has advised through liaison channels that Roselli [sic] has CIA in an unusually vulnerable position and Roselli [sic] would have no qualms about embarrassing CIA to serve his own interests." The FBI in turn informed Sen. Robert Kennedy of these facts.[84]

President Johnson was deeply shaken by the news, even sleepless.[85] He had created the Warren Commission in 1964 to prevent just such a story from capturing the public's attention. As he told his close friend and commission member Sen. Richard Russell, "We've got to take [the assassination of President Kennedy] out of the arena where they're testifying that Khrushchev and Castro did this and did that and kicking us into a war that can kill forty million Americans in an hour."[86] Now, faced with renewed claims of Communist complicity in the murder of his predecessor, Johnson demanded a full intelligence briefing. CIA director Richard Helms ordered his inspector general to prepare a report on agency-sponsored assassination plots, including those against Castro. The "Secret Eyes Only" report, of which Helms destroyed all but one copy, flatly labeled as "not true" the claim advanced in the Anderson columns that "Robert Kennedy may have approved" the plots. The report also highlighted the danger of further damaging revelations, warning that none of the gangsters involved "would have compunctions about dragging in his CIA connection when he was being pushed by law enforcement agencies. . . . Roselli [sic] appears to be doing it in his conversations with Morgan."[87] The FBI's liaison to the CIA, Sam Papich, observed bleakly that Rosselli and Giancana now had the CIA "over a barrel" and couldn't be touched by the FBI.[88]

The Jimmy Hoffa Connection

Why did Morgan and Anderson falsely blame Robert Kennedy for the Castro assassination plots? One reason may be that Morgan was desperately fighting to overturn Hoffa's convictions in 1964, at the hands of Bobby Kennedy, for loan fraud and jury tampering. The "H-bomb" column appeared just two days after the Supreme Court refused to reconsider Hoffa's conviction for jury tampering.[89] We have seen that Morgan previously supplied ammunition to Senator Long's investigation of federal wiretapping to help Hoffa's case. Even before approaching Pearson, Morgan leaked portions of the assassination plot story to Hoffa's friend and Teamster pension-fund beneficiary Hank Greenspun, publisher of the *Las Vegas Sun*.[90] At about the same time, as we have also seen, Morgan was also teaming up with Hoffa, Greenspun, Maheu, and Rosselli to swing a hotel-casino deal for Hughes in Las Vegas.

The author of the assassination column, Jack Anderson, was hardly a disinterested reporter. Though no friend of Hoffa, he allegedly took generous gifts of cash from Hoffa's Washington fixer, I. Irving Davidson.[91] In 1968, Pearson invited Davidson and Allen Dorfman, the Chicago mob's chief contact for Teamster pension fund loans, to a private dinner at which Giancana's friend Frank Sinatra declared that Bobby Kennedy was not "qualified to be President of the United States."[92]

Even as Anderson's column was running in newspapers across the country in March 1967, Morgan, Rosselli, and Greenspun were meeting in Las Vegas with Jim Garrison, the controversial district attorney of New Orleans who had recently opened a major investigation into the JFK assassination. The CIA was naturally worried that it might become a subject of Garrison's probe.[93] In a phone conversation with Texas governor John Connally one day before Anderson's column ran, Connally relayed reports coming out of Garrison's camp suggesting that Castro had dispatched a team of assassins, including Oswald, in retaliation for CIA plots against his own life. President Johnson said he had already heard the same story. "One of Hoffa's lawyers went to one of our mutual friends and asked him to come and relay that to us," he told the governor, citing the approach by Drew Pearson on Morgan's behalf. Johnson added, "We've had that story on about three occasions, and the people here say there's no basis for it." He later revised that judgment after receiving briefings about the CIA's murder plots, however. In October 1968, Johnson privately confided to senior ABC reporter Howard K. Smith, "I'll tell you something [about John Kennedy's murder] that will rock you. Kennedy was trying to get to Castro, but Castro got to him first." Johnson refused to elaborate, hinting, "It will all come out one day."[94]

As LBJ guessed, Hoffa was deeply wrapped up in the case. In Las Vegas, Garrison's stay at the Sands hotel-casino was paid for by a trusted lieutenant of one of Hoffa's top underworld allies, Louisiana Mafia boss Carlos Marcello.[95] Just ten days after Anderson's column on the CIA plots ran in papers across the country, Hoffa's fixer Davidson—who had been working angles to win Hoffa a new trial on his 1964 conviction for jury tampering[96]—approached the FBI. Davidson cited Garrison's case to impeach the credibility of the government's chief witness against Hoffa, Louisiana Teamster official Edward Partin (chapter 5). Davidson claimed that Partin "will be subpoenaed by a grand jury in New Orleans, Louisiana, in the near future in connection with his possible involvement in [the Kennedy assassination]." Davidson said he had "heard there is a photograph available of Partin in the presence of Jack Ruby (deceased), convicted of killing Lee Harvey Oswald."[97] Garrison himself lent support to that claim, letting a Baton Rouge radio station know that he was investigating Partin's possible role in the JFK murder.[98]

Not by chance, these dark claims emerged after Hoffa's team failed to bribe Partin into recanting his testimony.[99] "Sensibly, Partin was scared," writes

Teamster expert Dan Moldea. "Not only was he being pressured by Jimmy Hoffa and Carlos Marcello; now he was being implicated in the Kennedy assassination. 'Soon after that, [Hoffa's attorney] Frank Ragano called me,' Partin says, 'and he said he could get Garrison off my back. In return, he wanted a signed affidavit saying that I lied in Hoffa's trial. Naturally I didn't sign. But later it came out that Ragano was in touch with both Trafficante and Marcello during that period.'"[100] Hoffa failed to win his appeals, but Morgan, Davidson, and other supporters pleaded his case at the White House and President Nixon commuted his sentence in 1971 (chapter 8).[101]

The Nixon White House Takes Note

Despite Morgan's pressure campaign on his behalf, Rosselli's legal troubles continued to mount. In July 1967, federal agents caught him cheating members of an exclusive private club in Los Angeles of $400,000 in a rigged gin rummy game. In a sinister development for the CIA's hierarchy, William Harvey, a celebrated former CIA officer and Maheu's successor as manager of the CIA's assassination project, came to the mobster's defense. Harvey told the FBI's Papich that Morgan had told Rosselli about the CIA's intervention to block Senator Long's investigation of Maheu. "Johnny [Rosselli] wondered why the 'Agency' could not do as much for him as it did for Bob Maheu," Harvey said pointedly. That December, Harvey warned Papich that if push came to shove, Rosselli's lawyers would subpoena top CIA officials. "Harvey feels the Agency must exert influence to have the indictment 'killed,'" Papich told the head of the CIA's Office of Security.[102]

The threat proved empty, at least for the time being. In May 1968 Rosselli was found guilty of immigration fraud, and that December he was convicted in the card-cheating case. Two years later, he lost a petition before the Supreme Court to block his deportation.[103] To aid his defense, Morgan referred Rosselli to a former partner of Edward Bennett Williams who had defended Sam Giancana and Edward Levinson.[104] Communicating with the CIA through Maheu, Rosselli's new lawyer threatened that "if someone did not intercede on [Rosselli]'s behalf, he would make a complete exposé of his activities with the Agency." CIA director Helms balked, so Rosselli and his new attorney went back to Jack Anderson to turn up the public heat.[105] At the same time—November 1970—Maheu lost his institutional loyalties when he was fired by Hughes in a dispute over management of his Nevada business empire. Maheu was now motivated to explode his own political bombshells.

After confirming some key details for the first time with Maheu, Anderson published two new columns on CIA assassination plots in January 1971.[106]

The first implicated the "dapper" and "ruggedly handsome gambler" Rosselli, along with Maheu and two senior CIA officers, in six attempts on Castro's life. Anderson's second, more explosive column, suggested (contrary to his 1967 exposé) that the CIA had operated behind President Kennedy's back. As he put it, the whole story could raise "some ugly questions that high officials would rather keep buried," including whether the plots "backfired against President Kennedy" in 1963.[107] Rosselli's ploy worked. The CIA intervened with the Immigration and Naturalization Service (INS) in order to prevent further disclosure of his past operational role with the CIA. The INS halted its deportation proceedings against the gangster, as government lawyers told a court that Rosselli had performed unspecified "valuable services to the national security."[108]

But Rosselli's blockbuster leak had unintended consequences. Anderson's first column caught the eye of President Nixon's chief of staff, H. R. Haldeman. He asked White House counsel John Dean to dig up any background on Maheu in the wake of his firing by Nixon's benefactor, Howard Hughes. The next day, with publication of Anderson's second column, Attorney General John Mitchell personally contacted Maheu. Nixon biographer Anthony Summers writes:

> At the time Maheu was under pressure to appear before a grand jury in connection with a Las Vegas gambling prosecution. He had so far denied knowledge of the Castro plot story but . . . thought things might "very easily get out of hand" with the grand jury and the press. Maheu came to Washington and, in private, told Mitchell "the entire Castro story." Mitchell, he remembered, was "shaking" by the time he finished. The attorney general forthwith offered him a deal: Instead of going before a grand jury on the Vegas matter, Maheu would merely be interviewed by senior Justice Department officials. In this formal session he did not expound on his work for the CIA. "I assured them," Maheu recalled, "I intend to keep my word and maintain the secrecy of the mission."
>
> Meanwhile, Assistant Attorney General Will Wilson was quickly assigned to review whatever the Justice Department might hold on the CIA-Mafia contacts. The Nixon White House, he would later tell Watergate investigators, was hoping to turn up proof that the Kennedy brothers had tried to kill Castro, news that could damage the surviving Kennedy brother, Edward, should he run for the presidency in 1972.[109]

After discussing "the political implications of the information" with his aide, Attorney General Mitchell showed Nixon the secret Justice Department file on the Castro plots, according to a Senate Watergate Committee staff memorandum first published in 2012.[110] Nixon knew that questions might be raised about his own involvement in the CIA plots. After all, as vice president, he had aggressively pushed the Eisenhower administration to overthrow

Castro. Nixon may or may not have known at that time about the assassination plots, but they were planned by officials under his general supervision.
As an investigator for White House counsel John Dean warned, any attempt
to publicize "Maheu's controversial activities . . . might well shake loose
Republican skeletons from the closet."[111]

Watergate: Maheu, Morgan, and the Hughes Connection

Among those skeletons was President Nixon's secret receipt of $100,000 in
cash from Howard Hughes in 1969–1970, in return for millions of dollars in
government favors. It was not the first time Nixon had taken money from
Hughes. Hughes's financial relationship with Nixon began with campaign
contributions in 1946 and became really serious in late 1956.[112] That year,
at Vice President Nixon's personal request, Hughes provided a loan of
$205,000—worth two million dollars today—on the flimsiest of collateral for
a failing drive-in hamburger restaurant in Los Angeles owned by Nixon's
brother Donald. Hughes didn't care about repayment, telling a top aide, "it's
a chance to cement a relationship." Just weeks later the Internal Revenue Service reversed its disapproval of a dubious tax shelter engineered by Hughes,
saving him millions of dollars.[113] Not long after, Hughes also received favorable rulings by the Civil Aeronautics Board and Justice Department on critical regulatory and antitrust matters worth millions of dollars more.[114]

Four years later, in the midst of the 1960 presidential race, John Kennedy's
campaign staff, led by Larry O'Brien, caught wind of this transaction. They
paid off one of Hughes's accountants to acquire incriminating documents,
which they leaked to Drew Pearson and Jack Anderson. The columnists'
exposé, which ran in dozens of newspapers and broadcast outlets, seriously
damaged Nixon's reputation. Some of Nixon's advisers blamed his extremely
narrow loss to Kennedy on the Hughes loan story.[115] The same scandal
haunted Nixon again in his 1962 gubernatorial campaign in California.[116] The
winner of that election, Edmund Brown, credited a timely magazine article
about the Hughes loan with helping him beat Nixon.[117]

That should have been the end of their relationship, but Nixon and Hughes
had an irresistible affinity for each other's power and money. In 1968, Hughes
told Maheu that he saw "a really valid possibility" of helping to engineer a
Republican victory "under our sponsorship and supervision every inch of
the way." Hughes made a disguised but legal donation of at least $50,000 to
the Nixon campaign. He also directed Maheu to see Nixon "as my special
confidential emissary."[118] Hughes added that he was "sure" Nixon knew "the
facts of life."[119] Rebozo soon began negotiating on Nixon's behalf in 1968 for

additional cash from Hughes. Maheu delegated the matter to Edward Morgan, who was then on a handsome retainer to the Hughes empire. As a condition for approving the payoff, Morgan insisted on giving the money directly to the candidate, ostensibly so he could assure Hughes that Nixon knew where the money came from.[120] Rebozo balked, knowing that Morgan also represented Nixon's nemesis Drew Pearson. Rebozo later testified during the Watergate inquiry that he could recall the 1960 Hughes loan controversy "vividly" and "just did not want to be responsible, in any way, for anything that might create embarrassment" by risking leaks to Pearson through Morgan.[121] So Hughes delayed his $100,000 in cash payments until 1969, when Maheu gave the job to Richard Danner, an old friend of Nixon and Rebozo who had just been hired by Maheu to run one of Hughes's casinos (see "Nixon's Caribbean Milieu" online at rowman.com).

Unfortunately for the president, however, Hughes fired Maheu in late 1970. The reclusive billionaire complained that Maheu had allowed his Las Vegas empire to lose millions of dollars, possibly at the hands of mob-connected executives whom Maheu allowed to stay on and run Hughes's casinos.[122] Embittered by his abrupt termination, Maheu suddenly became a danger to the White House as well as to Hughes and the CIA. In January 1971, President Nixon learned from Rebozo that Maheu had hired Democratic strategist Larry O'Brien after the 1968 campaign as a political adviser to the Hughes empire. The White House learned that the Democratic Party boss likely "knew a great deal" about Hughes's secret dealings with the Nixon administration.[123] John Dean further ascertained that Maheu was "the man who forwarded all Hughes' political contributions, personally, over the last ten years" and that "his tentacles touch many extremely sensitive areas of government, each one of which is fraught with potential for Jack Anderson type exposure." Dean's investigator recommended that before undertaking any political operation to discredit O'Brien, the White House should obtain "in-depth information" on Maheu's "covert activities from his Washington association with CIA in the early sixties to his Nevada involvement on behalf of Hughes."[124]

Just as the White House feared, Maheu began spilling some of the secrets he knew about Hughes to his friends Jack Anderson and Hank Greenspun. In August 1971, Anderson published a story alleging that Rebozo had received $100,000 from one of Hughes's casinos on Nixon's behalf.[125] It attracted no attention, but a month later, Greenspun set off panic in the White House by telling Nixon's press aide that what he knew about Hughes's contribution could "sink Nixon." (Nixon's personal attorney flew out to Las Vegas to deny the charge in person.)[126] On January 24, 1972, as Nixon's reelection campaign was heating up, Anderson published a new column repeating his allegation about the Rebozo cash.[127] "This time," notes Anderson biographer Mark Feldstein,

> Anderson's story produced immediate alarm in the White House, where Chief of Staff H. R. Haldeman closely guarded a file on Hughes that was marked "Top Secret—CONFIDENTIAL." Hours after Anderson's column was published, the President privately cursed "that goddamned Hughes thing." The next day, John Ehrlichman asked the White House counsel, John Dean, to "very discreetly" look into the matter.[128]

Dean learned with alarm that Jack Anderson was continuing to dig relentlessly into Hughes's connections to Nixon, along with other scandals that could hurt the administration.[129] Pounded by a steady stream of Anderson's embarrassing revelations in 1971 and 1972, White House officials contemplated extreme measures. Special Counsel Charles Colson reportedly ordered E. Howard Hunt and his partner G. Gordon Liddy to incapacitate or even murder the newsman. The two clandestine operatives met with a recently retired CIA physician who in 1960 had supplied botulin-laced cigars to assassinate Castro—the very plots that Anderson had exposed. They discussed various ways to poison the columnist but were told by superiors to stand down when their focus shifted to breaking into O'Brien's Watergate office.[130]

Meanwhile, others in the White House sought simply to discredit Anderson. They called in investigators from the FBI, the IRS, and even a high-powered private eye service, which at the same time was investigating Maheu on behalf of the Hughes organization.[131] The CIA's Office of Security assigned sixteen agents to surveil Anderson's every move, in blatant violation of the agency's charter.[132] James McCord—recently retired from the CIA's Office of Security to become the security director for the Nixon reelection campaign—assigned one of his own employees to infiltrate Anderson's office.[133] Among other things, McCord learned about Anderson's personal and business connections to Larry O'Brien, Hank Greenspun, Edward Morgan, and even to Irving Davidson, the Mafia-connected lobbyist for Jimmy Hoffa.[134] It was enough to prove that even a paranoid like Nixon really did have enemies.

As noted at the outset of this chapter, Nixon's fear that Maheu might have shared details of the Hughes-Nixon relationship with Larry O'Brien likely helped motivate the fateful break-in at the DNC chairman's offices on June 17, 1972. The ringleader of the burglary, G. Gordon Liddy, confirmed after years of silence that "The purpose of the . . . Watergate break-in was to find out what O'Brien had of derogatory nature about us."[135] His boss Jeb Magruder, deputy head of Nixon's reelection campaign, confirmed, "the primary purpose of the break-in was to deal with the information that has been referred to about Howard Hughes and Larry O'Brien and what that meant as far as the cash that had supposedly been given to Bebe Rebozo and spent later by the President possibly."[136]

Whatever the motive, the crime was radically self-defeating. It delivered the White House into the hands of an anti-Nixon network, starting with attorney Edward Bennett Williams. Besides all of his other associations, Williams represented both the DNC and the *Washington Post*. At 5 a.m. on Saturday, June 17, one of Williams's law partners was woken up with the news that five men had been arrested inside the DNC; he then quickly tipped off the managing editor at the *Washington Post*, a good friend, to cover the story. As the paper's hard-hitting coverage drew fierce counterattacks from the White House, Williams encouraged *Washington Post* executive editor Ben Bradlee—one of his closest friends—to continue reporting aggressively. A lawsuit filed by Williams's law firm on behalf of the DNC and O'Brien against the Republicans allowed the Democrats to depose senior administration officials and keep the case alive until Congress began its own investigations.[137] Williams was even godfather to a child of federal judge John Sirica, who tried the Watergate burglars and used the threat of lengthy sentences to force them to talk.[138] Not surprisingly, Williams ranked high on President Nixon's list of enemies. In a conversation with two top aides on September 15, 1972, Nixon said, "We're going after him. . . . I think we are going to fix the son of a bitch. Believe me. We are going to. We've got to, because he's a bad man." Haldeman chimed in, "That is a guy we've got to ruin."[139] Instead, of course, it was Nixon who was ruined, as Williams continued flying high.

Nixon's Cover-up and the "Bay of Pigs Thing"

Nixon didn't go down without a fight. Borrowing directly from the tactics of Rosselli, Williams, and Morgan, Nixon used the Watergate burglars' links to the still-secret Castro assassination plots to blackmail the CIA into promoting a cover-up of the break-in on national security grounds. He even got away with it—for a short time.

The Watergate burglars were no ordinary lot of ruffians. They included the suave Howard Hunt, a globetrotting CIA officer with World War II experience in China who helped engineer the overthrow of Guatemalan president Arbenz in 1954, and who was among the first agency officials to recommend assassinating Fidel Castro. His first Watergate recruit, Bernard Barker, was a former member of Batista's police who served as Hunt's right-hand man on the Bay of Pigs operation. Barker stayed on the CIA's payroll until 1966, when the agency dropped him for consorting with "gambling and criminal elements," a euphemism for Trafficante's organization.[140] Bay of Pigs veteran Rolando Martinez was still on the CIA's payroll when he broke into the Watergate offices of the DNC; just as sensitive, he took part in 1963 in a secret mob-backed raid on Cuba aimed at discrediting the Kennedy administration.[141] Then there was soldier of fortune Frank Sturgis, who took part in the same 1963 raid, as well as several plots to murder Castro.[142] Finally, James McCord, who was in charge of planting bugs in the DNC, had spent his career as a senior member of the CIA's Office of Security, where the CIA-Mafia plots were hatched. After the arrest of these most unusual burglars, Nixon's reelection committee arranged hush money payments to them through Hunt's close friend, the Cuban exile leader Manuel Artime. Captured during the Bay of Pigs invasion and later released, Artime continued reporting to the CIA while conspiring with a dissident Cuban official to assassinate Castro as late as 1965. A CIA memo released in 1993 acknowledged that "Artime and his group were supported by CIA, also was used by the Mafia in the Castro operation."[143]

Fully aware that Hunt and "this whole group of Cubans [was] tied to the Bay of Pigs," Nixon exploited their associations to coerce the CIA into participating in his cover-up.[144] Less than a week after the break-in, Haldeman told Nixon he thought the key to stopping the investigation was to play on the suspicion of FBI agents working the case that it was some kind of CIA operation. "The only way to do that is from White House instructions," Haldeman said. "And it's got to be to [CIA director Richard] Helms." Nixon then chimed in to suggest a script that his aides could use to persuade Helms to shut down the FBI: "Of course, this . . . Hunt . . . that will uncover a lot of things. You open that scab there's a hell of a lot of things and .-. . we just feel that it would be very detrimental to have this thing go any further." A little later the president elaborated, "When you . . . get these [CIA] people in, say: '. . . the President believes that it is going to open the whole Bay of Pigs thing up again. And . . . that they should call the FBI in and say that we wish for the country, don't go any further into this case, period!"[145] A few hours later, Nixon reiterated to Haldeman, "Tell them that if it gets out, it's going to make the CIA look bad, it's going to make Hunt look bad, and it's likely to blow the whole Bay of Pigs which we think would be very unfortunate for the CIA."[146]

When Haldeman relayed this message to Helms, the CIA director's reaction was striking. "Turmoil in the room," Haldeman recalled, "Helms gripping the arms of his chair, leaning forward and shouting, 'The Bay of Pigs had nothing to do with this. I have no concern about the Bay of Pigs.'" Yet the seemingly irrelevant historical reference did the job. For the next two weeks, Helms and his deputy asked the FBI to "desist from expanding this investigation" lest it "run afoul of [CIA] operations."[147]

Just what was the "Bay of Pigs thing" that so agitated Helms and prompted the CIA to impede the Watergate investigation? Haldeman later offered a most intriguing explanation: "When Nixon said 'It's likely to blow the whole Bay of Pigs thing' he might have been reminding Helms, not so gently, of the cover-up of the CIA assassination attempts on . . . Fidel Castro—a CIA operation that may have triggered the Kennedy tragedy and which Helms desperately wanted to hide."[148] That was the very hypothesis Anderson had planted in his 1971 columns, advancing the blackmail scheme hatched by Rosselli and his attorney Edward Morgan.

The brief cover-up instigated by the White House proved to be a Pyrrhic victory. Nixon lost a vigorous legal battle before the Supreme Court to keep his Oval Office conversations secret. When tapes of his June 23 meetings were made public on August 5, 1974, this so-called "smoking gun" proved that Nixon had directed a cover-up. Many of his remaining political supporters dropped him, making impeachment a foregone conclusion. President Nixon resigned four days later, on August 9.

Thus the scandal we call Watergate was not one single conspiracy by Nixon, nor a simple conspiracy by his opponents to run him from office. Rather, it was the culmination of many smaller plots and pressure campaigns mounted over the years by influential power brokers, drawing on their knowledge of the country's darkest political and national-security secrets. Watergate was like an eruption of pus from a sore on the body politic that had been festering for more than a decade.

Although Watergate investigators never pieced the whole story together, they had some glimmerings of how these covert networks played out in the Nixon scandals. Prosecutors secretly called in John Rosselli for questioning, a fact only disclosed years later. According to the mobster's attorney, prosecutors were checking out a theory that the White House ordered the break-in "because Nixon or somebody in the Republican Party suspected that . . . a document existed showing Nixon was involved with or knew what was going on with the CIA and the assassination of Castro. . . . They wanted to try to get this information that Nixon suspected [the Democrats] were going to try to use against him."[149] Evidence for this particular theory is thin at best.[150] But the fact that Watergate investigators took the time to interrogate Rosselli shows that his secrets still had power. A couple of years later, Rosselli would testify again before Congress, this time regarding the JFK assassination. For his troubles, the aging mobster ended up being assassinated himself—strangled, stuffed into a fifty-five-gallon drum, and dumped into waters off Florida. Many investigators suspect that the hit was ordered by Santo Trafficante.[151]

These political intrigues would have been impossible in a truly open society. They were enabled by what historian Arthur Schlesinger Jr. called "the secrecy system" that arose with the national security establishment during the Cold War to protect and promote executive power.[152] But that system protected a host of other deep political operators as well. The wielders of secret information and secret power—billionaires, CIA agents, mobsters, superlawyers, journalists, and lobbyists—were only rarely held accountable for their invisible deeds. Much the same is true today in the post-9/11 age. So long as powerful and corrupt interests continue to operate with little or no effective public scrutiny, America's political system will remain highly vulnerable to manipulation at great cost to our democracy.

Part IV
CONCLUSION

10

From Ronald Reagan to Donald Trump

The only real cure for the decay in our democracy is public interest, public understanding, and a public determination to demonstrate that "the people are the masters."

—Clark Mollenhoff, *Despoilers of Democracy* (1965)

I N LATE 1952, THE INFLUENTIAL SOCIOLOGIST C. Wright Mills commented at length on the salience of political corruption as an issue in the recent US presidential campaign. In an essay for the *New York Times Magazine*, he described the problem as a microcosm of broader moral failures in American society, ranging from cheating scandals in college sports to American "gangsters" operating "nation-wide businesses having syndicated connections with one another and with local authorities." Those failings reflected not the actions of a few corrupt individuals, but the loss of "older values and codes" that had kept people on the straight and narrow. Mills believed that public conduct had been degraded by the amorality of America's capitalist class, with its propensity to cut corners for profit. Corrupt politicians were simply following their lead. "From this point of view," he maintained, "the most important question about the [1952] Nixon [slush fund] affair is not whether Senator Nixon was or is morally insensitive, but whether or not any young man in American politics, who has come as far and as fast as Senator Nixon, could very well have done so today without possessing or acquiring a somewhat blunted moral sensitivity."[1]

Several years later, in his controversial (and now classic) volume *The Power Elite*, Mills offered less sanctimony and more insight into the systemic roots of corruption in American politics. Most important, he described how the Cold War was spurring the centralization of national economic and political power in the hands of largely unaccountable corporate executives, military elites, and executive branch officials—what President Eisenhower would later call the "military-industrial complex." One result of that centralization, Mills asserted, was "the decline of politics as genuine and public debate of alternative decisions." In the process, approachable government had been replaced by "the enlarged and military state." Politicians who once answered to the public now served mainly "the corporate chieftains." Mills declared bluntly, "American capitalism is now in considerable part a military capitalism, and the most important relation of the big corporation to the state rests on the coincidence of interests between military and corporate needs, as defined by warlords and corporate rich."[2]

Another important by-product of America's permanent war footing, Mills observed, was "the assumption that the security of the nation . . . rests upon great secrecy of plan and intent." Under the cloak of secrecy, he continued, "the power elite can mask their intentions, operations, and further consolidation." In such an environment of attenuated personal responsibility and public accountability, "the higher immorality is institutionalized. It is not merely a question of a corrupt administration in corporation, army, or state; it is a feature of the corporate rich . . ., deeply intertwined with the politics of the military state." At the same time, the capacity for abusing public office for private gain had increased enormously as "political institutions and economic opportunities" became ever more "concentrated and linked."[3]

Investigative reporter Drew Pearson, who did much to expose political corruption in his national columns and broadcasts, came to similar conclusions about the corrosive political effects of unending militarism throughout the Cold War. In the words of his partner, Jack Anderson:

A prolonged national war footing, [Pearson] believed, fostered a mentality intolerant of dissent and of individual rights; it exalted secrecy while making openness suspect; its celebrations of brutality favored the robed and unrobed vigilante; its dislocations and frustrations opened voids that invited the repressive demagogue; its grab bag of arms contracts and economic controls stimulated a plague of fixers and wire pullers; its necessities raised to power those Drew held as least fit to govern a democracy: authoritarians developed by the hierarchies of arms, acquisitiveness and industrial efficiency—namely, the generals, the Wall Street financiers, the production czars.[4]

Closely accompanying all of these trends was the rise of organized crime as a national force. The huge profits reaped by leading mobsters during Prohibition helped seed the extraordinary expansion of the US economy after the depressed 1930s. Gambling and other rackets generated cash that fueled stock market speculation and the rise of high-flying conglomerates well into the 1960s. Ignoring warnings by reformers about the dangers of mob "infiltration," many businesses welcomed underworld capital and employed gangster muscle to keep unions in check. At the same time, highly placed politicians and law enforcement officials tolerated, and sometimes even encouraged, organized crime so long as it did not threaten the power or ideological priorities of the growing national security state.

The Cold War encouraged such arrangements. In a society preoccupied by the threat of international Communism and fears of domestic radicalism, members of America's "power elite" welcomed stabilizing forces and institutions. As historian Albert Fried (among others) has noted, the FBI's director viewed syndicate members as

> pillars of the status quo. They at least had a vested interest in the health of the free enterprise system, in America's triumph over Communism and for that matter over Socialism and liberalism too—over anything that might remotely threaten their specific opportunities. Intelligent gangsters from Al Capone to Moe Dalitz and Meyer Lansky have always been fierce, voluble defenders of the capitalist faith, and to that extent they were and are J. Edgar Hoover's ideological kinsmen.[5]

Covert alliances between the underworld and upperworld allowed the savviest criminals to move with greater fluidity into more legitimate realms of business and politics. Former bootleggers and illegal casino operators became respected business leaders and philanthropists, just as eighteenth-century smugglers who financed the colonies' war for independence became respected statesmen.[6] Ironically, for all his shrewdness, Lansky never managed to convert his money into respectability. He grumbled that Prohibition-era partners like Samuel Bronfman and Lewis Rosenstiel became successful businessmen, while he remained a target of incessant investigations and harassment. To those respectable names one might add Moe Dalitz, winner of the Torch of Liberty Award from the Anti-Defamation League and the City of Peace Award from Israel; and former bootlegger Joe Linsey, friend of Presidents Truman and Kennedy, former chairman of Combined Jewish Philanthropies in Boston, and donor of the Joseph M. Linsey Sports Center at Brandeis University.[7] Such individuals, in the words of Gus Russo, "mastered the art of walking through life with one foot in the upperworld and one in the underworld."[8] Their transition from the criminal world into mainstream society affirmed the observation of sociologist Daniel Bell that many twentieth-century mobsters, like many ruthless nineteenth-century fortune-builders, "were seeking to become quasi-respectable and establish a place for themselves in American life. For the mobsters, by and large, had immigrant roots, and crime . . . was a route of social ascent and place in American life."[9]

Their personal successes often came at great cost to American democracy, however. Mob associates such as Roy Cohn, Lewis Rosenstiel, and Clint Murchison distracted attention from their criminal associations in part by fomenting McCarthyism. In so doing they poisoned US politics with accusations of disloyalty and treason, setting the stage for disasters such as America's military intervention in Vietnam. The secrecy that necessarily attended the mob's promotion of systematic corruption also fostered conspiratorial politics, whether by agents of Trujillo like Zicarelli, or by agents of the CIA like Rosselli, who leveraged his involvement in covert assassination plots to avoid prosecution and deportation. Many of these currents came together in the career of Richard Nixon. He made anti-Communism a signature issue, while making dirty compromises to advance his career. From Nixon's perspective, taking a few thousand dollars from Mickey Cohen was no worse than Franklin Roosevelt taking $100,000 from Joseph Kennedy, an alleged former bootlegger; it was just the way the game of politics was played.[10] As Nixon ascended to higher office, the favors he took and the favors he gave to criminals grew accordingly. In the end, however, he could not escape the deep forces he had helped create. The great political crisis that ended his public career reflected both the long-standing moral compromises of his corrupt milieu and the sub-rosa pressure campaigns that developed from them. Watergate was thus in part a culmination of forces that had been corrupting American politics and democratic ideals for many years.

From Ronald Reagan to Donald Trump

Richard Nixon was not the last president with ties to organized crime. Ronald Reagan might have remained a footnote to history without the promotional efforts of Music Corporation of America, which was founded by associates of the Capone mob in Chicago and represented by its lawyer Sidney Korshak. Such relationships followed him to the White House. Dan Moldea, who chronicled this history in *Dark Victory*, wrote, "As President, Reagan watched as his Justice Department quashed major federal investigations of the Mafia's penetration of both MCA and the entire motion picture industry, which were being conducted by the Los Angeles office of the U.S. Strike Force Against Organized Crime. Two highly respected Strike Force prosecutors

. . . lost their jobs because of their refusal to succumb to pressure from the Reagan Administration."[11] During the 1980 campaign, Reagan became cozy with Teamster vice president Jackie Presser, who took orders from Chicago and Cleveland Mafia bosses and whose father had been implicated in bribery, embezzlement, and other crimes.[12] Reagan's campaign chairman, Nevada senator Paul Laxalt, had appealed to President Nixon in 1971 to pardon Hoffa, based on his "extended discussion with Al Dorfman of the Teamsters, with whom I've worked closely for the past few years." According to Michael Newton, an authority on mob history,

[President Reagan's] first budget imposed an FBI hiring freeze coupled with dramatic staff reductions and a 33-percent cutback on investigations of organized crime. The White House also indicated that no further undercover operations against mobsters or white-collar criminals would be authorized in fiscal 1982. Congress blocked Reagan's attempt to abolish the Treasury Department's Bureau of Alcohol, Tobacco and Firearms—created to punish liquor violations, bombings, and federal weapons violations—but the president hamstrung investigations and enforcement by the IRS, the SEC, and the Justice Department's Organized Crime Strike Forces. Reagan also threw his weight behind a bill proposed by Senator Howard Cannon, seeking repeal of "wasteful and inefficient" federal taxes on legalized gambling. . . . In July 1983 he attended a convention of the Mob-infested International Longshoreman's Association, expelled from the AFL in 1953. . . . ILA boss Thomas Gleason, praised by Reagan for his "loyalty and integrity" in 1983, had been a servile tool of the Gambino Mafia family since 1963. . . . On June 1, 1982—ten days after [Teamster] president Roy Williams was indicted—Reagan addressed a Teamster convention in Vegas, telling the crowd, "I hope to be in team with the Teamsters." On June 12 Williams joined other union leaders at the White House for discussion of Reagan's tax-cut proposals. In May 1983 Reagan telephoned Jackie Presser to congratulate him on replacing Williams . . . Cleveland jurors convicted Presser's uncle, Allen Friedman, of embezzling $165,000 from the union, but October 1985 found Presser closeted in the West Wing for a ninety-minute conference with [Attorney General] Ed Meese.[13]

Since then, organized crime in America has evolved without disappearing. Aggressive prosecutors, armed with tough laws like the RICO statute, have sent thousands of gangsters to prison and decimated many traditional criminal enterprises. At the same time, some of those gangs remain surprisingly resilient. In 2016, federal prosecutors indicted forty-six alleged members and associates of four New York crime "families" on charges of fraud, extortion, gambling, and illegal sales of firearms and cigarettes. Although it was an impressive reminder that the American "Mafia" has not disappeared, many of these criminals, with street names like "Tony the Cripple," were not the tough and powerful mobsters of old. Former federal prosecutor Edward A. McDonald observed that these Mafia descendants no longer have the ability to earn vast profits and squeeze legitimate businesses by monopolizing vital markets like concrete and commercial waste disposal. "The Mafia is just not engaging in the significant criminal activities they were involved in the past," he said. "I'm not saying the war has been won, but it's pretty close."[14] Crime watcher Scott Burnstein observed that many remaining hoodlums are no longer "'greased in' to the high levels of political power . . . as in the Mafia's golden era of the 1950s, 60s, and 70s."[15]

Even as traditional criminal organizations have fallen on hard times, however, new ones have emerged, as noted in chapter 4. They include violent transnational gangs from Africa, the Balkans, Italy, the Middle East, East Asia, the former Soviet Union, and Latin America. President Donald Trump represents a unique bridge between the old and new worlds of organized crime. With a long history of business scams and tax violations, Trump has never been picky about his associates.[16] Indeed, crime and corruption were all but embedded in his DNA. Trump's grandfather made his money running a house of prostitution for gold miners in Canada's Yukon Territory. His father, real estate tycoon Fred Trump, partnered with a brick contractor who ran his business with members of New York's Genovese crime family. As Trump biographer David Cay Johnston remarked, "Donald got his showmanship from his dad, as well as his comfort with organized criminals."[17]

As a young real estate developer in the 1970s, Donald Trump hooked up with New York mob attorney Roy Cohn—described by Trump biographer Wayne Barrett as "a walking advertisement for every form of graft, the best-known fixer in New York"—to fight federal charges of discriminatory housing rentals. Cohn became a mentor to the up-and-coming property magnate. Both were attracted to the challenges of working political angles and underworld connections to defeat business competitors. To build his landmark Trump Tower and Trump Plaza in Manhattan, Trump hired demolition workers controlled by the Genovese crime family and purchased concrete from companies owned by bosses and associates of several New York Mafia families. Trump knew exactly what he was doing; one associate of Cohn recalled a meeting the attorney arranged between Trump and Genovese family underboss Anthony Salerno at his town house in 1983. In addition, Trump used Cohn to deal with John Cody, a convicted racketeer and Gambino family associate who headed Teamster Local 282, a mainstay of the building trades unions. As a goodwill gesture, Trump sold six prime units near the top of Trump Tower to a beautiful Austrian friend of Cody's and provided her with extraordinary assistance in making renovations. Such relationships helped Trump avoid potentially crippling work stoppages on his building projects.[18]

In Atlantic City, he employed similar business methods, buying land for his Trump Plaza casino at a highly inflated price from a hit man for the Philadelphia mob.[19] Australian authorities in the mid-1980s rejected a bid by the developer to build and operate a casino after police warned of his organized crime connections.[20] However, New Jersey gaming regulators overlooked Trump's record, allowing him to purchase the bankrupt Taj Mahal casino in Atlantic City from Resorts International (see "Nixon's Caribbean Milieu" online at rowman.com) in 1988. In 2016, *Politifact* recalled that within a couple of years of opening, the Taj Mahal was already embroiled in controversy:

> In 1992, a Senate subcommittee named Danny Leung, who was then the vice president for foreign marketing at Trump Taj Mahal, as an associate of the Hong Kong–based organized crime group 14K Triad.
>
> "Leung has also given complimentary tickets for hotel rooms and Asian shows to numerous members and associates of Asian organized crime," reads the report, which also identified three other triad-connected business associates or former employees of Trump's gambling empire.
>
> According to gaming regulators, Leung "flew in 16 Italian organized crime figures from Canada who stole more than $1 million from the casino in a credit scam," reported the *New York Daily News* in 1995. "The incident was never reported because Trump never filed charges."
>
> Leung, who had a separate contract to bring gamblers from Toronto to the casino, denied the affiliation to organized crime, and his casino and junket licenses were renewed. (The Trump Taj Mahal declared bankruptcy in 1991, and his other Atlantic City properties folded a decade later.)[21]

Trump shrewdly attempted to inoculate himself against legal fallout from such relationships by cultivating ties with the FBI, after learning that one of his mob-connected business partners was an FBI informant. The developer offered to "cooperate" with the bureau by harboring undercover agents in his first Atlantic City casino. Soon Trump was inviting his business partner's FBI handler to play golf, lunch with him at the 21 Club, attend a Michael Jackson concert, and more. Years later, the agent was generously understanding of Trump's associations with criminals. "New York was so totally corrupt and so controlled by the mob in the '80s that in order to be a successful businessman, you had to have some way to work that world," he told a reporter in 2016.[22] Trump himself proudly cited these associations as evidence of his business prowess. "I've known some tough cookies over the years," he told an interviewer during the 2016 campaign. "I've known the people that make the politicians you and I deal with every day look like little babies."[23]

As new centers of organized crime emerged beyond the traditional Mafia families, Trump followed the money. He eagerly rented or sold many of the most expensive units in his residential towers to racketeers, swindlers, and mob associates from around the globe. One such buyer was David Bogatin, a "high-level member of a Russian émigré crime family" who purchased five apartments in Trump Tower for $6 million in 1984 after meeting with Trump. After Bogatin fled the country to avoid prison and a $5 million fine for cheating the government out of gasoline taxes, the state of New York seized his apartments, declaring that he purchased them "to launder money, to shelter and hide assets."[24] Another Trump Tower apartment, directly below one owned by Donald, was raided in 2013 by federal agents who said they were breaking up "the world's largest sports book." The Justice Department alleged the ring was protected by a Russian mob boss who was then under indictment for bribing officials at the 2002 Winter Olympics in Salt Lake City. The same Russian showed up with an entourage at Trump's 2013 Miss Universe pageant in Moscow, reportedly as a VIP guest.[25]

Such transactions were typical, not extraordinary. Thanks to a loophole in money-laundering laws, writes reporter Craig Unger, "Trump began to sell condos in Trump Tower as an ideal vehicle through which criminals could put their dirty money into luxury condominiums while keeping their owner-ship anonymous." One investigator determined that, since the 1980s, Trump arranged more than a fifth of his condo sales in the United States through "secretive, all-cash transactions that enable buyers to avoid legal scrutiny by shielding their finances and identities." The suspect sales totaled $1.5 billion.[26] Trump's buyers and real estate partners have included corrupt "kleptocrats" from Azerbaijan, Republic of Congo, Haiti, Indonesia, Kazakhstan, the Phil-ippines, Saudi Arabia, and the former Soviet Union—in many cases creating conflicts of interest during his presidency.[27] The Trump Taj Mahal casino in Atlantic City also became a regular laundromat for washing Russian mob money. In 1998, the Treasury Department levied a $477,700 civil fine against the casino for "willful and repeated" violations of reporting requirements under the Bank Secrecy Act. That fine, the largest of its era, was dwarfed by a $10 million penalty assessed against the casino in 2015 for a continuing his-tory of such violations.[28]

Deals with Russian oligarchs and mobsters seem to have kept the Trump empire afloat as bankers grew shy of lending to it by the early 2000s.[29] After Trump's organization came up with tens of millions of dollars in cash to invest in golf courses, condominium projects, and other properties, his son Eric explained, "Well, we don't rely on American banks. We have all the fund-ing we need out of Russia."[30] One of Trump's major business partners in this period was Bayrock Group LLC, founded by a former Soviet official. Bayrock developed Trump-branded projects all over the world and helped to finance the Trump SoHo hotel in New York City. Its managing director had pleaded guilty to a $40 million stock-fraud and money-laundering conspiracy in the mid-1990s, and in 2015 worked with Trump's personal lawyer to promote a Trump Tower in Moscow. In 2010, a lawsuit filed by former employees accused Bayrock of being "covertly mob-owned and operated" and engaged in mail, wire, and bank fraud, tax evasion, money laundering, bribery, extortion, and embezzlement. The lawsuit cited alleged frauds relating to several Trump properties, but added in a footnote, "There is no evidence Trump took any part in, or knew of, their racketeering." The case was settled out of court in 2018.[31]

Mark Galeotti, an expert on the Russian mob, has cautioned against reading too much into these connections. He argued they may say more about Trump's reckless business style than his knowing collusion with Russian or other criminal organizations:

> I have seen no serious evidence of any explicit link between Trump and Russian mobsters. Rather, what I have seen is evidence of the extent to which the Trump Organization seems to have been willing to engage with dubious investors and buyers—some Russian, many not—whom more reputable corporations would not have touched. In the process, it is likely it laundered money from all kinds of questionable sources, but that is not the same as a direct link to gangsters. Above all, this is a story about corruption, framed in both legal and moral terms, and about a horrifying absence of ethics and transparency.[32]

The same story of corruption surrounds the Trump camp's dealings with Russian and East European businessmen during his presidency. Prominent among them is Dmitry Firtash, a Ukrainian oligarch who made his fortune transporting natural gas in partnership with Russia's state-owned Gazprom. In 2008, the US ambassador to Kiev stated in a cable that Firtash had "acknowledged ties to Russian organized crime figure Seymon Mogilevich, stating he needed Mogilevich's approval to get into business in the first place."[33] Mogilevich, a Ukrainian-born crime boss today living freely in Russia, was described by one of his convicted colleagues as "the most powerful mobster in the world." During Mogilevich's heyday, at least two of his lieutenants (including the above-mentioned David Bogatin) operated out of Trump Tower in Manhattan. When the FBI added Mogilevich to its "Ten Most Wanted Fugitives" list in 2009, it implicated him in "weapons trafficking, contract murders, extortion, drug trafficking and prostitution on an international scale" and said he used his vast wealth "to influence governments and their economies."[34] Firtash repeatedly denied having any business connections to Mogilevich, but the Department of Justice described Firtash as an "upper-echelon [associate] of Russian organized crime" in a court filing supporting his 2014 indictment for international bribery, racketeering, and money-laundering conspiracies.

In 2008, Trump's future campaign chairman, Paul Manafort, joined Firtash and a former real estate broker for Fred Trump to consider an $850 million deal to redevelop the Drake Hotel in New York City. The deal never went through, but the two men shared other interests. As NBC News reported:

> Firtash was a major backer of Ukraine's Party of Regions, the pro-Russian party for which Manafort worked for many years. . . . Manafort's firm made more than $17 million in gross revenue from the party in just two years, according to his recent Foreign Agent Registration Act filing. Another leaked [State Department] cable said that Manafort's job in 2006 was to give the Party of Regions an "extreme makeover" and "change its image from . . . a haven for mobsters into that of a legitimate political party."[35]

Firtash later blamed the Obama administration for orchestrating the ouster of Ukraine's pro-Russian government in 2014. He particularly disapproved of former vice president Joseph Biden, who pressed Ukraine's successor government to crack down on pervasive corruption in 2015.[36] While fighting Firtash's extradition to the United States, according to *Time* magazine, the oligarch's legal team helped orchestrate a political campaign against Biden, accusing him of arranging the firing of a Ukrainian prosecutor for investigating Biden's son Hunter:

> Firtash's lawyers have gathered documents that make controversial allegations against former special counsel Robert Mueller and former Vice President Joe Biden. Firtash's lawyers have passed these documents and other information to associates of Trump's personal lawyer Rudy Giuliani. In his frequent appearances on cable news, Giuliani has presented some of these documents to the American public as evidence for his claims of wrongdoing by Mueller and Biden. . . .
>
> Firtash has established close ties to the former mayor of New York City in part by recruiting several of Giuliani's associates. In July the oligarch hired two lawyers who have been helping Giuliani in his campaign to discredit Trump's critics: Victoria Toensing and Joseph DiGenova, a married couple Trump considered hiring in 2018 as part of his private legal team. Best known as diehard defenders of Trump on Fox News, the couple has combed through the oligarch's case files and used some of them in the effort to defend Trump on television and in the press.
>
> Toensing and DiGenova then hired another Giuliani associate, Lev Parnas, to serve as their interpreter in communications with Firtash in Vienna. . . . While on his way to Vienna on Oct. 9, Parnas was arrested at Dulles Airport in Washington and charged with violating campaign finance laws. The indictment against him alleges that Parnas and his business partners secretly channeled money from an unidentified Russian donor to various [Republican] political causes and candidates.[37]

In December 2019, US prosecutors accused Parnas, who had also worked with Giuliani on the campaign to impugn Joe Biden, of receiving $1 million from Firtash's Swiss attorney.[38] Although Giuliani said he had "nothing to do with Firtash," his frenetic meddling in Ukraine led President Trump to dismiss the respected US ambassador to Kiev and to hold up $400 million in US military aid pending the Ukrainian government's announcement of an investigation into the Biden family. A whistleblower complaint against some of these machinations prompted the House of Representatives to launch its impeachment investigation in September 2019.

This history may reflect a confluence of interests more than a political conspiracy between Trump's inner circle and transnational criminals. At minimum, however, it says a great deal about the way Trump turned the presidency into a vehicle for his personal aggrandizement and that of the billionaires who support him. His flouting of constitutional, legal, and ethical norms, and his blatant conflicts of interest in the White House, simply reflected his long-standing business associations and methods. At the very beginning of Trump's administration, FBI director and former organized crime prosecutor James Comey was alarmed to realize that the new president's incessant demands for loyalty, and attempts to draw senior officials into his political web, mirrored the Mafia's way of doing business: "The silent circle of assent. The boss in complete control. The loyalty oaths. The us-versus-them worldview. The lying about all things, large and small, in service to some warped code of loyalty."[39]

Journalist Masha Gessen, an expert on Russian corruption, commented at the height of the special prosecutor's investigation in early 2019:

> What we are observing is not most accurately described as the subversion of American democracy by a hostile power. Instead, it is an attempt at state capture by an international crime syndicate. What unites [the various players] is that they are all crooks and frauds. This is not a moral assessment, or an attempt to downplay their importance. It is an attempt to stop talking in terms of states and geopolitics and begin looking at Mafias and profits. . . .
>
> The Mafia state is efficient in its own way. It does not take over all state institutions, but absorbs only the ones necessary for extracting profit. . . . When we think about a normal state, [Hungarian sociologist Bálint] Magyar told me, "the assumption is that the state acts in the public interest, and if that doesn't happen, that's a deviation." That is true of how we think about democracies but also, to a large extent, of how we think about dictatorships as well: the dictator positions himself as the arbiter and sole representative of the national interest. A Mafia state, on the other hand, acts only in the personal profit-seeking interests of the clan. "That's not a deviation," Magyar said. "It's a substantive, structural characteristic of the state. The state itself, at the top, works as a criminal organization." . . .

The story is not that [Vladimir] Putin is masterminding a vast and brilliant attack on Western democracy. The story, it appears, is that the Russian Mafia state is cultivating profit-yielding relationships with the aspiring Mafia boss of the U.S. and his band of crooks, subverting democratic institutions in the process.[40]

Beyond the Mob

The murky line dividing the Russian "mafia" from many Russian "oligarchs" illustrates an important point: Organized crime today transcends traditional gangs. It is a form of big business. As the eye-opening leak of the "Panama Papers" revealed, unscrupulous law firms and offshore banks promote tax evasion and money laundering on a mammoth scale that would stun even Meyer Lansky.[41] Members of these dirty enterprises carry briefcases, not guns. They succeed because of lax enforcement, the protection of bank secrecy laws in the United States and other jurisdictions, and successful campaigns by corporate lobbyists to sabotage reforms.[42]

In recent years, authorities have implicated senior executives from such major banks as Bank of America, Bank of New York, Chase, Citibank, Deutsche Bank, HSBC, and Wachovia in laundering tens of billions of dollars for drug traffickers, tax evaders, and even terrorists.[43] Typically the institutions paid fines, but no executives went to jail, even after multiple criminal violations.[44] Law enforcement seems to have adopted a "too big to prosecute" doctrine. In 2009, the head of the United Nations Office on Drugs and Crime claimed that organized crime profits were critical to keeping many of the world's leading banks afloat after the 2008 financial crisis. If so, that may help account for the limited interest of both Democratic and Republican administrations in pursuing organized law-breaking by major financial institutions.[45]

I noted in the introduction the historical role of "protectors," usually respectable lawyers and lobbyists, in advancing the interests of organized criminals. That is no less true today. Commenting on American complicity in the looting of the former Soviet Union through the laundering of stolen assets, Franklin Foer notes that "Members of the [US] professional classes competed to sell their services to kleptocrats. In the course of that competition, they breezed past old ethical prohibitions, and the pressure rose to test the limits of the law."[46] Over the past two decades, the United States has become the world's preeminent tax haven, with states such as Delaware, Nevada, and South Dakota attracting armies of lawyers who specialize in creating anonymous corporate shells. As late as 2019, the American Bar Association reportedly continued to lobby against requirements to disclose the true owners of US corporations and limited liability companies to government authorities.

In late 2020, however, Congress finally passed the Corporate Transparency Act, requiring full disclosure of ownership to the Treasury.[47]

Focused on terrorism and other issues, the Justice Department devotes dwindling resources to economic crimes. The number of white-collar cases brought by federal prosecutors fell from ten thousand in 2011 to fewer than six thousand in 2018, despite official estimates that domestic financial crimes, *excluding* tax evasion, generate $300 billion a year. Meanwhile, systematic underreporting of income, overwhelmingly by the top 1 percent of earners, stands to cost the US Treasury *more than a trillion dollars* over the next decade. The IRS now audits less than 0.6 percent of tax returns, thanks to years of Republican-led budget cuts. The successful prosecution of Trump's 2016 campaign manager, Paul Manafort, and personal attorney Michael Cohen, on tax evasion and other charges came about only due to the investigation of the Trump campaign's suspected collusion with Russian election hackers.[48]

This blatant inattention to white-collar organized crime reflects the systematic corruption of American politics through the nearly unrestricted financing of campaigns.[49] In the mid-1970s, the culture of campaign corruption was boldly challenged by prosecutors, members of Congress, and dogged journalists who exposed the Watergate scandal and prompted the resignation of President Nixon. That trauma was followed by a cathartic wave of political reforms, including tougher federal restrictions on campaign funding to curb the influence of special-interest money in politics and expansion of the Freedom of Information Act to increase transparency in government. Those glory days have long passed. A revival of militarism in the post-9/11 era restored a cult of presidential power and executive secrecy that eroded democratic norms. A series of Supreme Court decisions has all but killed legal restrictions on campaign spending, giving billionaire donors such as the Koch brothers and casino mogul Sheldon Adelson outsized influence over party platforms and presidential priorities.[50] The toothless Federal Election Commission has even given the green light for so-called leadership political action committees to pay for politicians' foreign vacations, golf outings, and lavish restaurant meals—gifts that many would consider bribes. Court rulings have imposed highly restrictive definitions of political corruption, requiring proof of a quid pro quo that makes prosecuting politicians for bribery extremely difficult.[51] The Internal Revenue Service has almost entirely given up trying to police political expenditures by nonprofit groups.[52] Journalists can no longer follow political money in many cases, as "independent" campaign committees now cloak their contributors as tightly as Swiss banks did with their numbered accounts.[53] According to OpenSecrets, a watchdog group, "direct spending in U.S. federal elections by groups that do not disclose their donors has exceeded $1 billion" from 2006 to 2018. Some of that is almost certainly criminal foreign money.[54]

As a result, money now rules American politics. A *New York Times* investigation found that a mere 158 families and their companies contributed nearly half of all the early money to presidential candidates in the 2016 election, reflecting both the rapid rise in wealth of the top 0.1 percent and the dismantling of most campaign funding laws.[55] Another analysis determined that just seven Republican superdonors—collectively worth an estimated $142 billion—invested more than $350 million into federal and state campaigns in 2016.[56] (It remains to be seen whether the surge in contributions from smaller donors in 2020 will continue.) Meanwhile, lobbying firms on Washington, D.C.'s K Street are booming. Foreign governments and oligarchs have joined domestic interest groups to utilize their services as never before; a new tracking service revealed that foreign entities spent more than $500 million to influence American policy and public opinion in one eighteen-month period.[57] According to Associated Press, President Trump appointed more former lobbyists to cabinet-level positions in three years than his predecessors did in eight.[58] Based on the impact of all this concentrated money on national policy making, serious political scientists now argue the United States functions as an oligarchy, not a democracy.[59]

Traditional forms of organized crime could disappear, in other words, without diminishing the malign impact of deep politics in America. "Political insiders in Washington—politicians, lobbyists, political action committee directors, journalists, even government watchdogs—have become so accustomed to this cash economy of American politics that nobody bats an eye when, say, a congressman on the Armed Services Committee sends out fundraiser invitations to a host of defense contractors," observes OpenSecrets. "So who needs bribes? Who needs to take money under the table when it's so easy to take it above the table without breaking the law?"[60] No less an authority than Donald Trump said in 2015, "As a businessman and a very substantial donor to very important people, when you give, they do whatever the hell you want them to do. As a businessman, I need that."[61]

As economic and political power in America become ever more concentrated, millions of Americans are losing their trust in democracy.[62] In January 2016, the CEO of Gallup remarked that

A staggering 75% of the American public believe corruption is "widespread" in the U.S. government. . . . This sense of corruption probably contributes to much of the extreme anxiety and unrest we see today. . . . The perception . . . could be a symptom of citizen disengagement and anger. Or it could be a cause—we don't know. But it's very possible this is a big, dark cloud that hangs over this country's progress. And it might be fueling the rise of an unlikely, non-traditional leading Republican candidate for the presidency, Donald Trump.[63]

Trump confounded many political experts that year by audaciously running as a reformer of the very corruption he epitomized. His promises to "drain the swamp" were obviously disingenuous, but millions of voters ignored the ruse. Charles Homans, politics editor of the *New York Times Magazine*, offered an astute explanation:

> It's possible . . . to see Trump not as an exception but as the logical conclusion of a national fear of corruption that long ago curdled into a self-satisfied conviction that everything and everyone in politics already is corrupt. . . . He has always had a knack for channeling Americans' fundamental cynicism about politics, no doubt because he shares it. . . . If you believe all politicians are crooks, it no longer seems to matter much whether a particular one among them is: The answer to "*This* guy?" becomes "Why *not* this guy?" And in the end, you get the country you thought you had all along.[64]

No American who cares about the health and future of American democracy can remain complacent about the deeply corrosive effects of real and perceived corruption, and the self-defeating cynicism they can breed. Unfortunately, among the collateral victims of declining trust, aggravated by President Trump's sustained attacks on reporters and the "deep state," are the very institutions that protect us from corruption, including law enforcement organizations, the judiciary, and the media.[65] For this reason among others, Freedom House as of 2019 put American democracy "on a level with Greece, Croatia, and Mongolia," and on a declining trend.[66] Reversing this dangerous slide toward illiberalism will require a host of reforms, but they will not happen in a vacuum. Honest government must be supported and even driven from the bottom up, by people of courage and faith. America's great experiment with democracy will only survive if and when voters believe change is possible and channel their dissatisfaction by electing true advocates of reform to all levels of government.

Notes

Chapter 1

Key:

‡ This symbol indicates that additional notes may be found on the features tab at https://rowman.com/ISBN/9781538142493/Dark-Quadrant-Organized-Crime-Big-Business-and-the-Corruption-of-American-Democracy.

FOIA—files released under the Freedom of Information Act.

NARA—National Archives and Records Administration. When followed by a three-number grouping—such as "NARA 124-10328-10003"—the reference is to Record Identification Form numbers in the JFK assassination records at NARA.

1. Transparency International, "Corruption in the USA: The Difference a Year Makes," December 12, 2017, https://www.transparency.org/news/feature/corruption_in_the_usa_the_difference_a_year_makes.

2. "Kaiser Health Tracking Poll—Late Summer 2018," September 5, 2018, https://www.kff.org/health-costs/poll-finding/kaiser-health-tracking-poll-late-summer-2018-the-election-pre-existing-conditions-and-surprises-on-medical-bills/.

3. Transparency International, "Corruption Perceptions Index 2018," https://www.transparency.org/cpi2018.

4. Transparency International, "Corruption in the USA: The Difference a Year Makes," December 12, 2017, https://www.transparency.org/news/feature/corruption_in_the_usa_the_difference_a_year_makes. A large literature addresses how to define political corruption. I favor simple formulations like that of Transparency International ("abuse of entrusted power for private gain") and Michael Johnston ("the abuse of public roles or resources for private benefit"), bearing in mind that public roles can include nongovernmental positions in corporations and nonprofit institutions.

Michael Johnston, "Democracy without Politics? Hidden Costs of Corruption and Reform in America," in Michael Genovese and Victoria A. Farrar-Myers, eds., *Corruption and American Politics* (Amherst, NY: Cambria Press, 2010), 16.

5. Transparency International, "How Corruption Weakens Democracy," January 29, 2019, https://www.transparency.org/news/feature/cpi_2018_global_analysis.

6. Stephen M. Walt, "America's Corruption Is a National Security Threat," March 19, 2019, https://foreignpolicy.com/2019/03/19/americas-corruption-problem-is-a -national-security-threat/.

7. The literature on these issues is huge. See, for example, Zephyr Teachout, *Corruption in America* (Cambridge, MA: Harvard University Press, 2014) and chapter 10.

8. Isabel Sawhill, "Forget Collusion, the Problem Is Corruption and Complacency," March 28, 2019, https://www.brookings.edu/blog/up-front/2019/03/28/ forget-collusion-the-problem-is-corruption-and-complacency.

9. Gus Tyler, *Organized Crime in America* (Ann Arbor: University of Michigan Press, 1962), 18–19.

10. One prominent biographer of Sen. Joseph McCarthy shrugged off his many ethical violations: "It must be noted that politicians frequently receive compensation from the business lobbies. Inside tips, free vacations, the use of company planes, and secret contributions are all part of the game." David Oshinsky, *A Conspiracy So Immense: The World of Joe McCarthy* (New York: Oxford University Press, 2005), 64.

11. Alonzo L. Hamby, *Man of the People: A Life of Harry S. Truman* (New York: Oxford University Press, 1995), 584–93; Robert Ferrell, *Harry S. Truman: A Life* (Columbia: University of Missouri Press, 1984), 359; Andrew J. Dunar, *The Truman Scandals and the Politics of Morality* (Columbia: University of Missouri Press, 1984), 159. Several major collections of scholarly essays covering the Truman presidency offer no discussion at all of the scandals; see, for example, Michael J. Lacey, ed., *The Truman Presidency* (New York: Cambridge University Press, 1989), and Robert H. Bremner and Gary Reichard, *Reshaping America: Society and Institutions, 1945–1960* (Columbus: Ohio State University Press, 1982). For a short but critical treatment of the Truman scandals, see C. Vann Woodward, ed., *Responses of the Presidents to Charges of Misconduct* (New York: Dell, 1974), 275–95.

12. Arthur Schlesinger Jr., *A Thousand Days: John F. Kennedy in the White House* (Boston: Houghton Mifflin Co., 1965); Robert Caro, *The Passage of Power* (New York: Knopf, 2012); Robert Dallek, *Flawed Giant: Lyndon Johnson and His Times, 1961– 1973* (New York: Oxford University Press, 1998), 40–41. Richard Reeves devoted just two paragraphs to Baker and not a word to the fighter plane controversy in his eight-hundred-page history, *President Kennedy: Profile of Power* (New York: Simon & Schuster, 1993), 626–27. In contrast, Robert David Johnson, *All the Way with LBJ: The 1964 Presidential Election* (New York: Cambridge University Press, 2009), provides a serious discussion of the political threats to the new president posed by both scandals. Arthur Schlesinger Jr., *Robert Kennedy and His Times* (Boston: Houghton Mifflin Harcourt, 1978), also touches on both Bobby Baker and the TFX case.

13. Definitions of organized crime abound. A simple one, offered decades ago by two noted criminologists, is "illegal activities that organize the rackets and the vices." They cite, in particular, organized extortion, usury, the manufacture and distribu-

tion of illegal drugs, illegal gambling, and prostitution. I would add organized fraud to their list. Alan A. Block and William J. Chambliss, *Organizing Crime* (New York: Elsevier, 1981), 12, 63.

14. Lee Bernstein, *The Greatest Menace: Organized Crime in Cold War America* (Amherst: University of Massachusetts Press, 2002), 26.

15. James T. Patterson, *Grand Expectations: The United States, 1945–1974* (New York: Oxford University Press, 1996). Alonzo L. Hamby, *The Imperial Years: The U.S. Since 1939* (New York: Weybright and Talley, 1976), ignores organized crime altogether. Peter H. Schuck and James Q. Wilson, *Understanding America: The Anatomy of an Exceptional Nation* (New York: Public Affairs, 2008), claims to be a "comprehensive portrait" of modern United States by two dozen scholars, yet it offers not a word on the subject. Neither do James L. Sundquist, *Politics and Policy: The Eisenhower, Kennedy, and Johnson Years* (Washington, DC: Brookings Institution, 1968); Alan J. Levine, *"Bad Old Days:" The Myth of the 1950s* (New Brunswick, NJ: Transaction Publishers, 2008); or William H. Chafe, ed., *The Achievement of American Liberalism: The New Deal and Its Legacies* (New York: Columbia University Press, 2003). Robert Mason and Iwan W. Morgan, eds., *The Liberal Consensus Reconsidered: American Politics and Society in the Postwar Era* (Gainesville: University of Florida Press, 2007), has a single sentence on organized crime. Joseph Goulden, *The Best Years, 1945–1950* (New York: Athenium, 1976), mentions the Browne-Bioff Hollywood extortion case (293), without ever noting it was driven by the Chicago Outfit. Robert H. Bremner and Gary W Reichard, eds., *Reshaping America*, includes an essay by Eugene J. Watts, "Cops and Crooks: The War at Home," which remarks on the "sensational" attention paid to organized crime in the 1950s, while largely dismissing its significance (299). The volume also includes an essay on the American labor movement, which only briefly mentions investigations into corruption and racketeering in the Teamster union (John Barnard, "American Workers, the Labor Movement, and the Cold War, 1945–1960," 138). Exceptions to this scholarly neglect are largely confined to specialized histories of organized crime and urban politics.

16. Ferrell, *Harry S. Truman*; Hamby, *Man of the People*, 587. William Howard Moore rightly lamented that "virtually no studies of the [Truman] Administration have touched on the [Kefauver] Crime Committee"; *The Kefauver Committee and the Politics of Crime, 1950–1952* (Columbia: University of Missouri Press, 1974), 258. Gary W. Reichard, *Politics as Usual: The Age of Truman and Eisenhower* (Arlington Heights, IL: Harlan Davidson, 2004), provides one paragraph on the Kefauver hearings (73–74).

17. A major exception is Anthony Summers, *The Arrogance of Power: The Secret World of Richard Nixon* (New York: Viking, 2000). Summers is the controversial author of several best-selling biographies and popular works of modern history. Some of his more sensational claims—for instance, that J. Edgar Hoover was a cross-dresser—have been subjected to withering scorn by historians and other reviewers. In using his works selectively, I have generally followed the rule that strong claims require strong evidence. Critics who simply dismiss Summers's works outright are guilty of intellectual arrogance. His successful career as a journalist owes much to the deep research that informs most of his works, including hundreds of interviews and the use of many archives. In an often unflattering article about Summers and his

books, Steve Weinberg, former executive director of Investigative Reporters & Editors, wrote, "*The Arrogance of Power* demonstrates that the author spends long hours over many years traveling paper trails and people trails as he seeks to understand his subject. For all their flaws, Summers' books have value. Hooray for the publishers like Viking that pay authors enough in advance so that kind of research is possible to conduct. In many ways, *The Arrogance of Power* is the best one-volume, full-life biography of Nixon ever published" (Steve Weinberg, "The Nixon Sensationalism: A Failure of Accountability," *Baltimore Sun*, September 10, 2000). Nixon's former White House counsel John Dean was also skeptical about Summers but found him "a well-educated, savvy journalist who is witty and indefatigable—and certainly not a conspiracy nut. . . . Summers and his wife are careful, non-stop and exceedingly competent researchers. Observing them I detected no bias, agenda or preconceived notions, other than their interest in peeling Nixon like an onion. . . . My strongest criticism of the book is that the authors (who appear to relish scandal-mongering) have laced their narrative with occasional gratuitous sensationalism. . . . Suffice it to say, however, I found none of the authors' more breathtaking charges relating to Nixon to be baseless, or totally unbelievable. There are no equivalents to Hoover's dress. . . . None of the book's startling characterizations, like Nixon's ties to organized crime, can be simply disregarded. . . . [N]o one interested in history, politics, government or the American presidency should ignore it" (John Dean, "Nixon Revisited," *Chicago Tribune*, September 10, 2000).

18. Virgil Peterson, *The Mob: 200 Years of Organized Crime in New York* (Ottawa, IL: Green Hill Publishers, 1983), 10–23, 427.

19. William Chambliss, *On the Take: From Petty Crooks to Presidents* (2nd ed.) (Bloomington: Indiana University Press, 1988), 157. Unfortunately, this book is not a reliable guide to America organized crime in the post–World War II era.

20. Gus Russo, *The Outfit: The Role of Chicago's Underworld in the Shaping of Modern America* (New York: Bloomsbury, 2001), 7.

21. Albert Fried, *The Rise and Fall of the Jewish Gangster in America* (New York: Holt, Rinehart and Winston, 1980), 115–17; David Critchley, *The Origin of Organized Crime in America: The New York City Mafia, 1891–1931* (New York: Routledge, 2009), 140–42.

22. David Scott Witwer, *Shadow of the Racketeer: Scandal in Organized Labor* (Urbana and Chicago: University of Illinois Press, 2009), 56

23. John R. Commons, *Labor Unions and Trade Disputes* (Boston: Ginn, 1905), 42, 65; Andrew Wender Cohen, *The Racketeer's Progress: Chicago and the Struggle for the Modern American Economy, 1900–1940* (New York: Cambridge University Press, 2004), 10, 117; Robert Fitch, *Solidarity for Sale: How Corruption Destroyed the Labor Movement and Undermined America's Promise* (New York: PublicAffairs, 2006), 117–32.

24. Schlesinger, *Robert Kennedy and His Times*, 166.

25. Dan Moldea, *The Hoffa Wars: Teamsters, Rebels, Politicians and the Mob* (New York: Paddington Press, 1978), 37–38, 49–50.

26. Moldea, *The Hoffa Wars*, 123–24; Steve Brill, *The Teamsters* (New York: Simon & Schuster, 1978), 250–55; Gus Russo, *Supermob: How Sidney Korshak and His Criminal Associates Became America's Hidden Power Brokers* (New York: Bloomsbury, 2006), 166, 225.

27. The story of Beck's fall is told in Andrew Tully, *Treasury Agent: The Inside Story* (New York: Simon & Schuster, 1958), 219–26. The foreword to this book was written by Treasury Secretary Robert B. Anderson, who would plead guilty to tax fraud in 1987.

28. David Scott Witwer, *Corruption and Reform in the Teamsters Union* (Urbana and Chicago: University of Illinois Press, 2003), 82–86; Witwer, *Shadow of the Racketeer*, 46–52; Cohen, *The Racketeer's Progress*, 266; Gus Russo, *Supermob*, 30–31.

29. The Kefauver Committee reported that one of its "most shocking" discoveries was "the indisputable evidence . . . of cooperation with major hoodlums on the part of important segments of business enterprise. In Detroit, the committee found leading industrial concerns admitted cooperating with notorious hoodlums for the purpose of suppressing labor difficulties. . . . In New York, the same situation prevailed in connection with the Phelps-Dodge Co., which invited in hoodlums from the gang of Albert and Anthony Anastasia to help break a strike. Where business uses racketeers, there is a tendency for labor unions to use tactics of violence and vice versa. Finally, the committee found leading hoodlums holding valuable franchises in the liquor and automobile industries." US Congress, Senate, Special Committee to Investigate Organized Crime in Interstate Commerce, *The Kefauver Committee Report on Organized Crime* (New York: Didier, 1951), 152–53 (hereafter Kefauver Report). For more on Ford Motor Company, see Kefauver Report, 53–54, 156–57; Keith Sward, *The Legend of Henry Ford* (New York: Russell & Russell, 1968), 297–304, 329–32; Frank Browning and John Gerassi, *The American Way of Crime: From Salem to Watergate* (New York: Putnam, 1980), 393–405.

30. Not a single committee investigation into labor racketeering was launched due to complaints from management, he noted. Robert Kennedy, *The Enemy Within: The McClellan Committee's Crusade against Jimmy Hoffa and Corrupt Labor Unions* (New York: Harper & Brothers, 1960), 216–18. Such collaboration between the upperworld of capital and the underworld of crime persisted for decades, at least until deregulation and a conservative swing in national politics led by President Reagan began wiping out private-sector unions. In 1977, for example, reporter Jonathan Kwitny identified a long list of major corporations that arranged low-wage "sweetheart" contracts with the Teamsters union through Eugene R. Boffa Sr., "a convicted bank swindler from New Jersey who often deals with powerful racketeers in the Teamsters union." Jonathan Kwitny, "Big Firms Are Links to an Apparent Racket Involving Teamsters," *Wall Street Journal*, October 20, 1977; see also President's Commission on Organized Crime, *The Edge: Organized Crime, Business and Labor Unions* (Washington, DC: US Government Printing Office, 1986), 137.

31. Henry Luce, "The American Century," *Life*, February 17, 1941.

32. I deliberately avoid strong causal claims here. Jay Cost argues from a libertarian perspective that the "massive expansion in government" during the New Deal "produced a startling reinvigoration of corruption," and the continued expansion of government through the World War II period fostered the rise of "organized pressure groups" that "had a profoundly negative effect on the body politic, ultimately producing the rampant corruption of the current period." *A Republic No More: Big Government and the Rise of American Political Corruption* (New York: Encounter Books,

2015), 15. On the other hand, a study by two economists found "no empirical link between bigger government, or more regulation, and more corruption." Edward L. Glaeser and Raven E. Saks, "Corruption in America," *Journal of Public Economics* 90:6–7 (2006), 1053–72. It seems plausible, however, that rapid *growth* in the size of government may create opportunities for corruption by putting political institutions under stress.

33. Average federal spending jumped from 7.8 to 15.4 percent of GDP (calculated from St. Louis Federal Reserve Bank data at https://fred.stlouisfed.org/series/FYONGDA188S).

34. Doron Navot, "The Concept of Political Corruption: Lessons from a Lost Epoch," *Public Integrity* 16:4 (Fall 2014), 367.

35. The Kefauver Committee popularized the notion of "a nationwide crime syndicate known as the Mafia," which represented "a secret conspiracy against law and order" (Kefauver Report, 131). Many scholars have noted that the term "Mafia" exaggerates the role of Italian or Italian American criminals, ignoring the importance of criminals of Jewish, Irish, and other ethnicity. The FBI, after all but refusing to acknowledge the existence of organized crime, came up with the formal name "La Cosa Nostra," based on colloquial references by some mobsters to "our thing." "National crime syndicate," a term popularized by reporter Hank Messick, implies a greater degree of control and direction than actually existed in the crime community. Criminals who operated on a national scale usually knew each other and sometimes discussed operations or settled disputes, but they are better characterized as part of a national crime milieu. Good general histories of US organized crime include Stephen Fox, *Blood and Power: Organized Crime in Twentieth-Century America* (New York: William Morrow, 1989) and Thomas Reppetto, *American Mafia: A History of Its Rise to Power* (New York: Henry Holt, 2004).

36. Quoted in Hank Messick, *Syndicate Abroad* (Toronto: The Macmillan Co., 1969), 79.

37. Social critics have long noted that many of America's great eighteenth- and nineteenth-century business fortunes were built on corrupt and predatory behavior. As sociologist Edwin Sutherland documented in a famous study, business professionals routinely committed crimes such as embezzlement, fraud, conspiracy to divide markets, untruthful advertising, securities law violations, tax cheating, industrial spying, and safety violations. Many such crimes carried no great social stigma because ordinary people could not relate as victims. Edwin Sutherland, *White Collar Crime* (New York: Holt, Rinehart & Winston, 1949). For more recent treatments of corporate and white-collar crime, see Ferdinand Lundberg, *The Rich and the Super-Rich* (New York: Lyle Stuart, 1968), 106–31; Marshall Clinard, *Corporate Corruption* (New York: Praeger, 1990); Stephen Rosoff, Henry Pontell, and Robert Tillman, *Profit without Honor: White-Collar Crime and the Looting of America* (Upper Saddle River, NJ: Prentice Hall, 1998); and Jennifer Taub, *Big Dirty Money: The Shocking Injustice and Unseen Cost of White Collar Crime* (New York: Viking, 2020).

38. FBI report by Special Agent (SA) Frank H. Townsend, Los Angeles, March 1, 1962, "Crime Conditions in the Los Angeles Division," NARA 124-10328-10003. For similar assessments, see Wallace Turner, "Las Vegas: Gambling Creates New Force

in U.S.," *New York Times*, November 18, 1963, and Nicholas Pileggi, "The Lying, Thieving, Murdering, Upper-Middle-Class, Respectable Crook," *Esquire*, January 1966, 50–51.

39. Russo, *Supermob*, xv–xvi.

40. Block and Chambliss, *Organizing Crime*, 113–14; see also Jean-Louis Briquet and Gilles Favarel-Garrigues, *Organized Crime and States: The Hidden Face of Politics* (New York: Palgrave Macmillan, 2010).

41. Estes Kefauver, *Crime in America* (Garden City, NY: Doubleday, 1951), 56.

42. Kefauver Report, 175. For a history of the committee's investigation, see Moore, *The Kefauver Committee and the Politics of Crime*.

43. Ronald Goldfarb, *Villains, Imperfect Heroes: Robert F. Kennedy's War against Organized Crime* (New York: Random House, 1995), 41.

44. For an overview of the US context, see George C. S. Benson, *Political Corruption in America* (Lexington, MA: Lexington Books, 1978).

45. Lee Bernstein, in *The Greatest Menace*, argues that anti-crime rhetoric in the 1950s rivaled that directed against Communists. Much of this rhetoric, however, did not provoke real action until the Kennedy administration instilled new urgency in anti-racketeering efforts. Elsewhere I have written about the shifting focus of the Federal Bureau of Narcotics away from targeting Charles "Lucky" Luciano as enemy number one, to blaming Communist China for the worldwide heroin problem in the 1950s. Jonathan Marshall, "Cooking the Books: The Federal Bureau of Narcotics, the China Lobby and Cold War Propaganda, 1950–1962," *The Asia-Pacific Journal*, v. 11, Issue 37, No. 1, September 14, 2013.

46. From an interview with Al Capone by Cornelius Vanderbilt Jr., *Liberty Magazine*, August 27, 1931, republished at http://www.myalcaponemuseum.com/id234.htm.

47. Victor Navasky, *Kennedy Justice* (New York: Atheneum, 1977), 45–46. The most thorough treatment of the Kennedy administration's war on organized crime is Goldfarb, *Perfect Villains, Imperfect Heroes*.

48. James B. Jacobs, *Mobsters, Unions, and Feds: The Mafia and the American Labor Movement* (New York: New York University Press, 2006), 11.

49. See, for example, James D. Calder and William S. Lynch, "From Apalachin to the Buffalo Project: Obstacles on the Path to Effective Federal Responses to Organized Crime, 1957–1967," *Trends in Organized Crime* 11 (2008), 219–26, and the complaint of federal organized crime prosecutor Gerald Goettel, quoted in William Turner, *Hoover's FBI* (New York: Dell, 1971), 155. Turner, a former FBI agent, declared, "It ranks as one of the great derelictions of law enforcement history that Hoover, who had the manpower, prestige, and jurisdiction to crush organized crime in its formative stage, looked the other way" (170).

50. Oral history interview with William G. Hundley by James A. Oesterle, December 9, 1970, JFK Library. Hoover was not the only federal official during the Eisenhower years to dismiss organized crime as a major threat. Hundley said that when he was appointed to lead the Justice Department's prosecution of mobsters, "there was [sic] only a couple of guys in the OC section clipping newspapers. There was absolutely nothing going on in the Justice Department. . . . The Bureau certainly

wasn't doing anything. It came as quite a shock to me. I had come out of Internal Security, where you had agents coming out of your ears, and get over into Organized Crime and you couldn't find an agent." Ovid Demaris, *The Director* (New York: Harper's Magazine Press, 1975), 137–38. On the Eisenhower administration's lax efforts against organized crime, see Calder and Lynch, "From Apalachin to the Buffalo Project: Obstacles on the Path to Effective Federal Responses to Organized Crime, 1957–1967," 215–18.

51. Kenneth O'Reilly, *Hoover and the Un-Americans: The FBI, HUAC, and the Red Menace* (Philadelphia: Temple University Press, 1983), 194; Michael Newton, *The Mafia at Apalachin, 1957* (Jefferson, NC: McFarland, 2012), 116–21; Schlesinger Jr., *Robert Kennedy and His Times*, 264. Famed FBI agent William Roemer Jr. recalled that by late 1958, Hoover was already losing interest in the Top Hoodlum program: "Organized crime was no longer his priority." William Roemer Jr., *Man Against the Mob* (New York: Donald I. Fine, 1989), 47–48.

52. J. Edgar Hoover, *Masters of Deceit: The Story of Communism in America and How to Fight It* (New York: Henry Holt, 1958), vi.

53. Schlesinger, *Robert Kennedy and His Times*, 261.

54. Fox, *Blood and Power*, 181–220 (quote at 220).

55. Hank Messick, *John Edgar Hoover: A Critical Examination of the Director and of the Continuing Alliance between Crime, Business, and Politics* (New York: David McKay, 1972), 254.

56. Chicago Outfit boss Murray Humphreys, quoted in FBI report by SA William F. Roemer Jr., December 20, 1960, re "Gus Alex," NARA 124-10207-10147. In fairness, Humphreys also complained that FBI agents were "all over" him and his colleagues.

57. FBI airtel from SAC, Chicago, to Director, FBI, February 9, 1962, "Activities of Top Hoodlums in the Chicago Area," NARA 124-10202-10059.

58. G. L. Hostetter and T. Q. Beesley, "20th Century Crime," *The Political Quarterly* 14:3 (1933), reprinted in Tyler, ed., *Organized Crime in America*, 52–53.

59. President's Commission on Organized Crime, *The Impact: Organized Crime Today* (Washington, DC: US Government Printing Office, 1986), 29–31. See also Hans Nelen and Francien Lankhorst, "Facilitating Organized Crime: The Role of Lawyers and Notaries," in Dina Siegel and Hans Nelen, eds., *Organized Crime: Culture, Markets and Policies* (New York: Springer-Verlag, 2008), 127–42; David Middleton and Michael Levi, "The Role of Solicitors in Facilitating 'Organized Crime': Situational Crime Opportunities and Their Regulation," *Crime, Law and Social Change* 42:2–3 (2004), 123–61; David Middleton and Michael Levi, "Let Sleeping Lawyers Lie: Organized Crime, Lawyers and the Regulation of Legal Services," *The British Journal of Criminology* 55:4 (July 2015), 647–68.

60. "Lawyers and Lobbyists," *Fortune*, February 1952, 142.

61. FBI report by SA Andrew J. Shannon, September 30, 1958, "I. Irving Davidson," NARA 124-10221-10327; John H. Davis, *Mafia Kingfish: Carlos Marcello and the Assassination of John F. Kennedy* (New York: McGraw-Hill, 1989), 426. For general background on Davidson, see Gordon Chaplin, "The Fantastic Deals of I. Irving

Davidson," *Washington Post*, March 21, 1976, and Chaplin, "Behind the Schemes: Irv Davidson, D.C.'s Master Operator," *Washington Post*, April 2, 1980.

62. Gordon Chaplin, "Behind the Schemes," *Washington Post*, April 2, 1980.

63. Paul W. Williams, address to the New York University Law Alumni Association, cited in Tyler, ed., *Organized Crime in America*, 7.

64. For an excellent typology of "shadow government" theories, see David Chibo, "Political Science's 'Theory of Everything,'" November 30, 2016, at http://www.unz .com/article/political-sciences-theory-of-everything/. For a brief but useful discussion of the term "deep state," see Ryan Gingeras, "How the Deep State Came to America: A History," February 4, 2019, at https://warontherocks.com/2019/02/how-the-deep -state-came-to-america-a-history.

65. Mike Lofgren, *The Deep State: The Fall of the Constitution and the Rise of a Shadow Government* (New York: Viking, 2016); Michael J. Glennon, *National Security and Double Government* (New York: Oxford University Press, 2015); David Rohde, *In Deep: The FBI, the CIA, and the Truth about America's "Deep State"* (New York: W. W. Norton, 2020); Peter Dale Scott, *The American Deep State: Wall Street, Big Oil, and the Attack on U.S. Democracy* (London: Rowman & Littlefield, 2015).

66. Ryan Gingeras, *Heroin, Organized Crime, and the Making of Modern Turkey* (New York: Oxford University Press, 2014), 243–56.

67. US Congress, Senate, Special Committee to Investigate Organized Crime in Interstate Commerce, *Hearings before a Special Committee to Investigate Organized Crime in Interstate Commerce*, 81st Cong., 1st and 2nd sess. (Washington, DC: US Government Printing Office, 1950–1951), pt. 7, 621, 722–25, 1287–99, 1371–85 (hereafter Kefauver hearings); Peterson, *The Mob*, 234–36.

68. Peter Dale Scott, *Deep Politics and the Death of JFK* (Berkeley: University of California Press, 1996), 18–19, xii, 7, xi.

69. Donald R. Liddick, "Campaign Fund-raising Abuses and Money Laundering in Recent U.S. Elections: Criminal Networks in Action," *Crime, Law and Social Change* 34:2 (September 2000), 140.

70. For example, Messick grossly exaggerated Lansky's wealth and power, while Reid peddled myths about the history of the Italian Mafia, yet both provided much valuable reporting on organized crime in America. Although largely forgotten today, Drew Pearson was perhaps the most crusading (not the most objective or dispassionate) reporter of his time against political corruption and organized crime. He faced more than 275 libel suits but lost only 1. His client list of six hundred newspapers, including the *Washington Post*, spoke to his reputation. Although he made mistakes, Pearson "kept ahead of . . . competitors by his own audacity and the strength of his contributors." Oliver Pilat, *Drew Pearson: An Unauthorized Biography* (New York: Harper's Magazine Press, 1973), 240. Although I draw selectively from a variety of imperfect sources, I have avoided using some widely cited but dubiously self-serving accounts altogether, such as Sam and Chuck Giancana, *Double Cross: The Explosive, Inside Story of the Mobster Who Controlled America* (New York: Warner Books, 1992), and, with one exception, Martin Gosch and Richard Hammer, *The Last Testament of Lucky Luciano* (Boston: Little Brown, 1975), which purports to be a firsthand

account by Lucky Luciano. Serious questions have been raised by Peter Maas, among others, about the veracity of this latter tale. Unfortunately, such accounts continue to inform, or misinform, many popular and even scholarly histories of crime.

Chapter 2

1. Gosch and Hammer present an alleged account by Luciano of how the mob supported FDR at the Chicago convention in *The Last Testament of Lucky Luciano*, 159–64. As noted in chapter 1, this account is open to question, but it receives support from the memoir of New York crime boss Joseph Bonnano, *A Man of Honor: The Autobiography of Joseph Bonnano* (New York: Simon & Schuster, 1983), 307. Tammany bosses and New York gangsters such as Frank Costello apparently did share suites at the Drake Hotel in Chicago during the convention; Craig Thompson and Allen Raymond, *Gang Rule in New York: The Story of a Lawless Era* (New York: Dial Press, 1940), 244, 366–67. One of President Roosevelt's confidants in New York City was Bronx political boss Edward J. Flynn, who had hired the vicious gangster Dutch Schultz as deputy sheriff in 1925. Peterson, *The Mob*, 198, 152.

2. "Maurice M. Milligan Dies at 74," *New York Times*, June 17, 1959; Russo, *The Outfit*, 216. For friendly accounts of Truman's relations with the Pendergast machine, see David McCullough, *Truman* (New York: Simon & Schuster, 1992), 151–213 and Robert H. Ferrell, *Truman and Pendergast* (Columbia: University of Missouri Press, 1999).

3. McCullough, *Truman*, 198.

4. Russo, *The Outfit*, 214–16. Pendergast had brazenly appealed to Postmaster General James Farley to block the federal tax evasion case against Lazia. After some delay, the prosecution went forward. Lazia was assassinated while his case was on appeal. See Marc Mappen, *Prohibition Gangsters: The Rise and Fall of a Bad Generation* (New Brunswick, NJ: Rutgers University Press, 2013), 186–87; Rudolph Hartmann and Robert H. Ferrell, *The Kansas City Investigation: Pendergast's Downfall, 1938–1939* (Columbia: University of Missouri Press, 1999), 21–23; "Pendergast's Letter to Farley," *St. Louis Post-Dispatch*, December 1, 1934. Pendergast himself pleaded guilty to income tax evasion in 1939. For more on Lazia's career, see Frank R. Hayde, *The Mafia and the Machine: The Story of the Kansas City Mob* (Fort Lee, NJ: Barricade Books, 2007).

5. McCullough, *Truman*, 186. Russo relates a story that Truman, early in his career, personally collected bribes for the Pendergast machine. *The Outfit*, 218.

6. "Massacre Expose Now Election Issue," *New York Times*, November 5, 1934; McCullough, *Truman*, 201.

7. Russo, *The Outfit*, 218.

8. Robert H. Ferrell, *Choosing Truman: The Democratic Convention of 1944* (Columbia: University of Missouri Press, 1994), 10–14, 53–57; Sean Savage, *Truman and the Democratic Party* (Lexington: University of Kentucky Press, 1997), 25–26; Russo, *The Outfit*, 219–23; Fox, *Blood and Power*, 259–60; McCullough, *Truman*, 292–320.

9. Fletcher Knebel and Jack Wilson, "The Scandalous Years," *Look*, May 27, 1951.

10. The former US Attorney for the Western District of Missouri, Maurice M. Milligan, published his account in *Missouri Waltz: The Inside Story of the Pendergast Machine by the Man Who Smashed It* (New York: Charles Scribner's Sons, 1948).

11. Richard Lawrence Miller, *Truman: The Rise to Power* (New York: McGraw-Hill, 1986), 357–58.

12. Knebel and Wilson, "The Scandalous Years."

13. Many of these officials, it should be acknowledged, were Roosevelt-era appointees. McCullough, *Truman*, 870, 990; Woodward, ed., *Responses of the Presidents to Charges of Misconduct*, 284–88. One Pulitzer Prize–winning reporter declared, "The damage to the integrity of the nation's tax system was incalculable." Clark Mollenhoff, *Washington Cover-Up* (New York: Popular Library, 1963), 33.

14. Richard L. Williams, "The Hands in the Taxpayers' Pockets," *Life*, November 19, 1951, 146–60; Blair Bolles, *How to Get Rich in Washington* (New York: W. W. Norton, 1952), 4.

15. Peterson, *The Mob*, 250–51.

16. Alan Block, *East Side, West Side Organizing Crime in New York, 1930–1950* (New Brunswick, NJ: Transaction Publishers, 1983), 95–125; Burton Turkus and Sid Feder, *Murder, Inc.: The Inside Story of the Mob* (New York: Manor Books, 1951), 433–34; Leonard Katz, *Uncle Frank* (New York: Pocket Books, 1974), 187–89; Jay Maeder, "The Fugitive Mayor: William O'Dwyer's Abrupt Exit from City Hall," *New York Daily News*, September 6, 1998; Jules Abels, *The Truman Scandals* (Chicago: Henry Regnery, 1956), 34–36; George Walsh, *Public Enemies: The Mayor, the Mob, and the Crime That Was* (New York: W. W. Norton, 1980). On Deputy Fire Commissioner James J. Moran and O'Dwyer, see "The Bagmen," *Chicago Tribune*, March 8, 1952.

17. Peterson, *The Mob*, 256–57.

18. Kefauver Report, 105–25.

19. "O'Dwyer Denies Deal," *New York Times*, May 29, 1953.

20. Clark Mollenhoff, *Strike Force: Organized Crime and the Government* (Englewood Cliffs, NJ: Prentice-Hall, 1972), 54–77 (vote theft), 78–81 (Binaggio). Clark defended his conduct, and Hoover outlined restrictions on the FBI's investigation, in US Congress, Senate, Committee on the Judiciary, *Kansas City Vote Fraud, Hearings*, 80th Cong., 1st sess. (Washington, DC: US Government Printing Office, 1947).

21. Letter from Harry S. Truman to Bess W. Truman, August 8, 1946, Family, Business, and Personal Affairs Papers, Truman Library.

22. Testimony of M. H. Goldschein in Kefauver hearings, pt. 12, 4, 11; US Congress, House of Representatives, Committee on the Judiciary, Subcommittee to Investigate the Department of Justice, report, *Investigation of the Department of Justice*, 83rd Cong., 1st sess. (Washington, DC: US Government Printing Office, 1953), 92–94. The Washington *Evening Star* commented: "The whole affair is a sordid business, the worst thing that can happen in a democracy, and the President, having enlisted the support of Pendergast in the first instance, cannot escape some measure of connection with it" (quoted in Milligan, *Missouri Waltz*, 260).

23. Russell Porter, "U.S. Inquiry Asked in Binaggio Death," *New York Times*, April 9, 1950. Perhaps stung by the newspaper's attack, federal alcohol tax officials soon

seized a thousand cases of contraband liquor and arrested Kansas City mobster (and former Lazia bodyguard) Charles Carollo. "U.S. Arrests Felon Binaggio Deposed," *New York Times*, April 15, 1950.

24. Messick, *John Edgar Hoover*, 103–4; Mollenhoff, *Strike Force*, 55–57; US Congress, House of Representatives, Committee on Ways and Means, Subcommittee, *Internal Revenue Investigation, Hearings*, 82nd Cong., 1st sess. (Washington, DC: US Government Printing Office, 1951), 1643–50; US Department of Justice, "T. Lamar Caudle (1945–1947)," https://www.justice.gov/criminal/history/assistant-attorneys-general/theron-lamar-caudle; "T. Lamar Caudle Dead at 64," *New York Times*, April 2, 1969. For a sympathetic view of Caudle, see House Committee on the Judiciary, Subcommittee to Investigate the Department of Justice, *Investigation of the Department of Justice*, 88.

25. Abels, *The Truman Scandals*, 234–36, 242; House Committee on Ways and Means, Subcommittee, *Internal Revenue Investigation, Hearings*, 68–80, 126–53; Joel Seldin, "Alleged Pal of Costello in City Deal," *New York Herald Tribune*, July 1, 1958; Sen. John Williams (R-Del.), "Choice of Louis L. Pokrass as a Sponsor for Mid-Harlem Slum Clearance Project," *Congressional Record*, July 8, 1959, 12921–22.

26. Abels, *The Truman Scandals*, 257–58; Alexander Heard, *The Costs of Democracy* (Chapel Hill: University of North Carolina Press, 1960), 163n. For Erickson's New York rap sheet, see US Congress, Senate, Committee on the Judiciary, Subcommittee on Antitrust and Monopoly, *Professional Boxing, Hearings*, 86th Cong., 2nd sess. (Washington, DC: US Government Printing Office, 1961), 1224 (hereafter *Professional Boxing*).

27. For details on the RFC's dubious record in the Truman years, see Bolles, *How to Get Rich in Washington*, 30, 127–219.

28. Messick, *John Edgar Hoover*, 102.

29. Bolles, *How to Get Rich in Washington*, 175.

30. US Congress, Senate, Committee on Banking and Currency, *Study of Reconstruction Finance Corporation and Proposed Amendment of RFC Act, Report*, 82nd Cong., 1st sess. (Washington, DC: US Government Printing Office, 1951), 71, 85; Abels, *The Truman Scandals*, 79, 107; Bolles, *How to Get Rich in Washington*, 42.

31. Kefauver hearings, pt. 12, 29, 43; "Sax RFC Loan One of Many Shrewd Deals," *Chicago Tribune*, April 11, 1951; FBI report by SA William F. Roemer Jr., June 17, 1958, "Gus Alex," NARA 124-10201-10014; FBI report by SA John W. Roberts Jr., December 21, 1962, "The Criminal 'Commission,'" NARA 124-10216-10239 (slot machine king Eddie Vogel).

32. Gigi Mahon, *The Company That Bought the Boardwalk* (New York: Random House, 1980), 62–64; Alan A. Block, *Masters of Paradise: Organized Crime and the Internal Revenue Service in the Bahamas* (New Brunswick, NJ: Transaction Publishers, 1991), 44–46; "Jury Here Indicts 3 Leading Bookies," *New York Times*, October 1, 1964.

33. FBI report by SA M. B. Parker, "Nevada Gambling Industry," November 16, 1964, NARA 124-10342-10000. The Saxony employed Harry Blumin, the same accountant used by Meyer Lansky for his hotels in Florida and Cuba. US Congress, Senate, Committee on Banking and Currency, Subcommittee, *Study of Reconstruction*

Finance Corporation, Hearings (Washington, DC: US Government Printing Office, 1951), 1270, 1295; John Arnold, "Lansky's Ex-Auditor May Run MIA Hotel," *Miami Herald*, May 7, 1981. Blumin also did accounting for the Fontainebleau Hotel in Miami Beach and managed the mob-controlled Miami International Airport Hotel.

34. FBI airtel from SAC, Chicago, to Director, FBI, October 31, 1962, NARA 124-10196-10325; also airtel from SAC, Chicago, to Director, FBI, February 27, 1962, NARA 124-10202-10072. Teamster officials and pension fund consultants met frequently at the Saxony Hotel and deposited union funds, interest-free, in Sax's bank. US Congress, Senate, Select Committee on Improper Activities in the Labor or Management Field, *Investigation of Improper Activities in the Labor or Management Field, Hearings*, 86th Cong., 1st sess. (Washington, DC: US Government Printing Office, 1959), part 43, 16019–24, 16091, 16119 (hereafter McClellan hearings); Moldea, *The Hoffa Wars*, 98. George Sax was named Man of the Year by B'nai B'rith and the Israel Bonds organization (*Israel Honorarium*, 1968).

35. Senate Banking and Currency Committee, *Study of Reconstruction Finance Corporation*, 83–84; Abels, *The Truman Scandals*, 78; Bolles, *How to Get Rich in Washington*, 33–34.

36. John Dolen, "Racist, Corrupt—and Sheriff," *Fort Lauderdale*, December 1, 2017. See also "Nixon's Caribbean Milieu" online at rowman.com.

37. Warren Duffee, "RFC Records Show Contacts by Shaver," *South Haven* [Mich.] *Daily Tribune*, October 24, 1951; Messick, *John Edgar Hoover*, 102; Michael Newton, *Mr. Mob: The Life and Crimes of Moe Dalitz* (Jefferson, NC: McFarland, 2009), 133; Simon Frith and Andrew Goodwin, eds., *On Record: Rock, Pop and the Written Word* (New York: Routledge, 1990), 120 (Mercury Records).

38. Organized crime in Newport was finally run out of town by a reform sheriff, working with federal agents, in the early 1960s. Dr. Thomas Barker et al., *Wicked Newport: Kentucky's Sin City* (Charleston, SC: The History Press, 2008); memo from Theodore Vernier, Acting District Supervisor, to H. L. Giordano, Commissioner of Narcotics, November 26, 1965, "Organized Crime & Corruption in the Cincinnati, Ohio Area," container 52, records of the Drug Enforcement Administration, RG 170, NARA.

39. "Maragon Is Guilty of Lying to Senate," *New York Times*, April 27, 1950.

40. Abels, *The Truman Scandals*, 47–50; Dunar, *The Truman Scandals and the Politics of Morality*, 67–68; H. Walton Cloke, "Vaughan Says He Got $5,000 for Democratic Campaign," *New York Times*, August 31, 1949.

41. "Young Helis Relates Visit to Vaughan," *Washington Post*, September 2, 1949.

42. Costello and "Dandy Phil" Kastel teamed up in the 1930s with Governor Huey Long to install thousands of slot machines in Louisiana. FBI memo from SAC, Newark, to Director, FBI, March 30, 1956, in FBI FOIA releases on Abner Zwillman; Drew Pearson, "Vaughan Helped Tanforan Track," *Washington Post*, August 5, 1949; Tyler Abell, ed., *Drew Pearson Diaries 1949–1959* (London: Jonathan Cape, 1974), July 18, 1949, 66; Hank Messick, *Secret File* (New York: G. P. Putnam's Sons, 1969), 286. In the late 1930s, Helis, Costello, and Kastel were partners in Alliance Distributors, a liquor wholesaler. Drew Pearson, "Liquor Racketeers Change Line," *Washington Post*, January 14, 1950; Kefauver Report, 97–98.

43. Michele Pantaleone, *Mafia e droga* (Turin: Einaudi, 1966), 112–17 (Sorge); Scott, *Deep Politics and the Death of JFK*, 1993, 202–3 (Rimrock Tidelands); Ovid Demaris, *The Director: An Oral Biography of J. Edgar Hoover* (New York: Harper's Magazine Press, 1975), 23.

44. John C. O'Brien, "Vaughan Says FBI Exonerated Him in Tax Bribery Inquiry," *Philadelphia Inquirer*, September 1, 1949. Maragon later told Drew Pearson that Helis actually raised about $27,500 for Truman's 1948 campaign. Abell, *Drew Pearson Diaries*, March 28, 1951, 156.

45. "Vaughan Asked Tax Inquiry Intervention, Pearson Says," *Austin Statesman*, September 1, 1949.

46. The security approval was granted in 1955. CIA memo from Jim Kesler to John Greaney, March 21, 1968, NARA 104-10104-10348.

47. James Doherty, "Parole Scandal Reveals Capone Gang's Crime Empire," *Chicago Tribune*, May 13, 1948; Alston J. Smith, *Syndicate City: The Chicago Crime Cartel and What to Do about It* (Chicago: Henry Regnery, 1954), 163; "Clark, Truman, and the Gangsters," *Chicago Tribune*, May 15, 1948; Ruby Cooper, "How Tom Clark Sprung Capone," *Daily Worker*, August 10, 1949.

48. "Impeachment Next," *Chicago Tribune*, July 2, 1948; "High Court Post to Clark," *Chicago Tribune*, July 29, 1949.

49. The apparently forgetful Truman biographer Robert Farrell declared that "everything at [J]ustice had run fair well" under Clark. Farrell, *Harry S. Truman*, 365.

50. "2 Gangster Aids Step into Case from Politics," *Chicago Tribune*, September 27, 1947; US Congress, House of Representatives, Committee on Expenditures in the Executive Departments, Subcommittee, *Investigation as to the Manner in which the United States Board of Parole Is Operating and as to Whether There Is a Necessity for a Change in Either the Procedure or Basic Law, Hearings*, 80th Cong., 2nd sess. (Washington, DC: US Government Printing Office, 1948), 170–72 (hereafter Parole Hearings).

51. Letter from Joseph W. Sanford to Mr. Loveland, July 21, 1945, in Parole Hearings, 95. The warden later asserted that he was referring to payments to attorneys, not bribes.

52. Russo, *The Outfit*, 226. Rosselli was transferred the following year to a prison in Indiana. FBI report on Louis Campagna et al., October 3, 1947, file 58-2000-131, FBI FOIA release on John Rosselli.

53. FBI memo, September 18, 1947, re Paul De Lucia, and Chicago FBI report on Louis Campagna et al., October 3, 1947, in file 58-2000, FBI FOIA release on John Rosselli; William F. Roemer Jr., *Accardo: The Genuine Godfather* (New York: Donald I. Fine, 1995), 100.

54. "Politician Got $10,000 'Fee' to Get Parole, Gangster Says," *Washington Post*, February 18, 1948; Parole Hearings, 72–73. In the late 1930s, Bernstein was twice indicted for vote fraud in Jacob Arvey's Democratic 24th ward but beat the charges both times on technicalities. James Doherty, "Link Paroles to Vote Deal," *Chicago Tribune*, October 1, 1947; James Doherty, "Disputes Arvey Testimony to U.S. Parole Quiz," *Chicago Tribune*, March 17, 1948. A former tax expert for the Capone organization, Abraham Teitelbaum, retained Bernstein as his own tax counsel, calling him "a very

capable man." House Committee on Ways and Means, Subcommittee, *Internal Revenue Investigation*, 1316.

55. Parole Hearings, 336–37, 358, 494–95, 501–9; Mary Spargo, "$25,000 Paid in Freeing 4 Gangsters," *Washington Post*, March 3, 1948. Dallas-based Maury Hughes was the leading defense attorney for mobsters in his city, including Joseph Civello, who went to prison on narcotics charges, and Benjamin Binion, who took over gambling rackets in Civello's wake. (One criminal active in Dallas said Hughes handled all "payoffs and collections" for the local syndicate.) Hughes also had ties to the Chicago Outfit; he represented Mike Potson, manager of Colosimo's Café in Chicago, an Outfit front, on income tax evasion charges. FBI memo by Tobias E. Matthews, Mexico City, re James Weinberg, August 6, 1946, NARA 124-10303-10147; FBI report by Harold Edgerton, Dallas, re Joseph Francis Civello, May 17, 1968, NARA 124-10290-10440; Parole Hearings, 360 (Dallas), 337, 495 (Potson).

56. Parole Hearings, 366 (Clark); see also supporting testimony of Boris Kostelanetz, former special assistant to the attorney general, at 542–44.

57. James Doherty, "Parole Scandal Reveals Capone Gang's Crime Empire"; Parole Hearings, 591, 608.

58. FBI report from Kansas City office, October 1, 1947, re Louis Campagna et al., in file 58-2000-16, FBI FOIA release on John Rosselli. Gioe denied the allegation in an interview in the Chicago FBI office on October 3, 1947. However, Gioe's release was facilitated by the agreement of Harry Ash, superintendent of crime prevention for the state of Illinois, to become Gioe's parole adviser, at the request of the Chicago Outfit's attorney Sidney Korshak. Ash testified that he had known Gioe since 1915 (Parole Hearings, 4–6). Ash was also Korshak's former law partner (Russo, *The Outfit*, 230).

59. Parole Hearings, 348–53; James Doherty, "Link Paroles to Vote Deal," *Chicago Tribune*, October 1, 1947; Doherty, "Parole Scandal Reveals Capone Gang's Crime Empire," *Chicago Tribune*, May 13, 1948.

60. Savage, *Truman and the Democratic Party*, 45.

61. Quoted in Russo, *The Outfit*, 241.

62. "Group Asks Recommittal of Capone Pals," *Washington Post*, June 17, 1948; "The Capone Paroles," *Chicago Tribune*, November 14, 1949; "Ricca Turned Loose," *Chicago Tribune*, December 11, 1949; James Doherty, "Deny Rehearing to 2 Caponeites in Parole Fight," *Chicago Tribune*, December 18, 1949; "Gangster at Liberty," *Chicago Tribune*, February 14, 1950; James Doherty, "Highest Court Stalls Parole of 2 Hoodlums," *Chicago Tribune*, November 14, 1950; "FBI to Probe 3 Gangsters' 1947 Paroles," *Washington Post*, November 30, 1952. Justice Clark recused himself from voting on these cases.

63. "FBI to Probe 3 Gangsters' 1947 Paroles," *Washington Post*, November 30, 1952. McGranery also later testified about the way in which Tom Clark bypassed him on several important criminal cases, including the 1946 Kansas City vote fraud case and a huge mail fraud indictment against a Kansas City bond dealer. "You cannot dismiss matters under these circumstances without leaving real suspicion and a cause . . . for that suspicion," he declared. "Bypassed by Clark, McGranery States," *New York Times*, May 16, 1953.

64. Warren Olney III, "Law Enforcement and Judicial Administration in the Earl Warren Era," an oral history conducted 1970 through 1977 by Miriam F. Stein and Amelia R. Fry, Regional Oral History Office, The Bancroft Library, University of California, Berkeley, 1981.

65. "Dillon Gets 15 Month Term," *Chicago Tribune*, March 23, 1954.

66. For D'Andrea's hard-luck story, see report by Chicago FBI office, October 2, 1947, re Louis Campagna et al., file 58-2000-171, FBI FOIA release on Rosselli.

67. "Gioe, Extortionist, Slain," *Chicago Tribune*, August 19, 1954.

68. "Capone Gangster Dead in Florida," *New York Times*, May 31, 1955.

69. "Paul Ricca Dead," *New York Times*, October 12, 1972.

70. For a lengthy account of Rosselli and the parole scandal, see Lee Server, *Handsome Johnny: The Life and Death of Johnny Rosselli; Gentleman Gangster, Hollywood Producer, CIA Assassin* (New York: St. Martin's Press, 2018), 217–27, 246–50.

71. Witwer, *Shadow of the Racketeer*, 252.

72. Quoted in Roemer, *Accardo*, 104–5.

73. Humphreys had fond memories of the attorneys who got the job done. Paul Dillon in particular "was a hell of a guy. They were dyed-in-the-wool guys. Dyed-in-the-wool." FBI airtel from SAC, Chicago, to Director, FBI, "Murray L. Humphreys," October 21, 1964, NARA 124-10285-10194. Humphreys confused some details of the case, including the name of Dallas attorney Maury Hughes. On Clark and the 1946 investigations, see Russo, *The Outfit*, 210, 235.

74. Alexander Charns, *Cloak and Gavel: FBI Wiretaps, Bugs, Informers, and the Supreme Court* (Chicago: University of Illinois Press, 1992), 50. Clark also backed Hoover in promoting federal loyalty investigations. Athan Theoharis, *Seeds of Repression: Harry S. Truman and the Origins of McCarthyism* (Chicago: Quadrangle Books, 1971), 104–5, 126–30; Robert Justin Goldstein, "Prelude to McCarthyism: The Making of a Blacklist," *Prologue Magazine* 38, no. 3 (Fall 2006), https://www.archives.gov/publications/prologue/2006/fall/agloso.html.

75. Senate Committee on Banking and Currency, Subcommittee, *Study of Reconstruction Finance Corporation, Hearing* (Fulbright); US Congress, Senate, Committee on Expenditures in the Executive Departments, *Influence in Government Procurement, Hearing*, 82nd Cong., 1st sess. (Washington, DC: US Government Printing Office, 1951) (McClellan and Nixon). On Nixon's role in the Truman investigations, see Irwin F. Gellman, *The Contender: Richard Nixon, the Congress Years, 1946–1952* (New York: The Free Press, 1999), 376–88. I use the term "relatively" honest in view of Bobby Baker's claim that Kefauver took a bribe from Clint Murchison Jr. to help bring the Dallas Cowboys into the National Football League. Some authors also claim that he was blackmailed into limiting his committee's investigation of organized crime.

76. Roger Morris, *Richard Milhous Nixon: The Rise of an American Politician* (New York: Henry Holt, 1990), 308–10 (supporters); 361 (legislation), 309 (quote).

77. At Chotiner's funeral, President Nixon called him an "ally in political battles, a valued counsellor and a trusted colleague. But above all, Murray Chotiner was my friend." "President Mourns Chotiner," *Palo Alto Times*, February 4, 1974.

78. Drew Pearson and Jack Anderson, *U.S.A.—Second-Class Power?* (New York: Simon & Schuster, 1958), 281; Drew Pearson, "Mickey Cohen Talks about Nixon," *Toledo Blade*, October 31, 1968.

79. Sources on Cohen include Mickey Cohen, *Mickey Cohen: In My Own Words* (Englewood Cliffs, NJ: Prentice-Hall, 1975); Tere Tereba, *Mickey Cohen: The Life and Crimes of L.A.'s Notorious Mobster* (Toronto: ECW Press, 2012); John Buntin, *L.A. Noir: The Struggle for the Soul of America's Most Seductive City* (New York: Harmony Books, 2009); Brad Lewis, *Hollywood's Celebrity Gangster: The Incredible Life and Times of Mickey Cohen* (New York: Enigma Books, 2007); Ed Reid, *Mickey Cohen: Mobster* (New York: Pinnacle Books, 1973).

80. Drew Pearson and Jack Anderson, "Nixon's Relations with Gamblers, Underworld Warrant Scrutiny," *Atlanta Constitution*, October 31, 1968; Cohen, *Mickey Cohen*, 232–33; Summers, *Arrogance of Power*, 55.

81. "Gallery Interview: Mickey Cohen," *Gallery*, January 1976, 129.

82. Summers, *Arrogance of Power*, 57.

83. Drew Pearson and Jack Anderson, "Nixon's Relations with Gamblers, Underworld Warrant Scrutiny," *Atlanta Constitution*, October 31, 1968; Tereba, *Mickey Cohen*, 270–71. In his memoir, Cohen inflated the size of the group contribution to $75,000; Cohen, *Mickey Cohen*, 233; the same figure is quoted by Buntin, *L.A. Noir*.

84. Summers, *The Arrogance of Power*, 56–57; letter from Chotiner to WTOP and other radio stations, May 23, 1958, in "1956, May 4–Feb 1974" file, "Chotiner, Murray" folder, Vice Presidential Collection, Nixon papers, Nixon Library. Chotiner won a public apology from *Behind the Scenes* magazine for its March 1956 story, "Nixon's Secret Link to the Underworld," but that story did not relate to Cohen's contributions.

85. Richard Donovan, "Birth of a Salesman," *Reporter*, October 14, 1952, 31–32. Drew Pearson privately estimated that Nixon's campaign cost a total of $1.6 million. That seemingly outsized figure has some support; Abell, *Drew Pearson Diaries*, 238, 229; Morris, *Richard Milhous Nixon*, 616. Names of donors, generally without dollar amounts, may be found in "List of Contributors" folder, box 5, Campaign—1950—Nixon files, Nixon Library.

86. Morris notes that "When [Nixon's] 1950 Senate campaign reported its finances in Sacramento after the primary and general election, the Brewster-Grunewald 'advance,' like so much else, never appeared." Morris, *Richard Milhous Nixon*, 576.

87. Edward Ryan, "'Mystery Man' of Tax Fraud Inquiry: Henry W. Grunewald, Expert Wire-Puller, Actually Knows Many High Officials; Got Start as Spy Chaser," *St. Louis Post-Dispatch*, March 10, 1952; "Dinty Moore Raid Crowds Broadway," *New York Times*, November 29, 1922; "Kessler on Trial as Liquor Plotter," *New York Times*, November 14, 1923.

88. Thomas Corcoran with Philip Kopper, *Rendezvous with Democracy: The Memoirs of 'Tommy the Cork,'* unpublished autobiography, chapter X, 10, in Thomas Corcoran papers, box 586, Library of Congress; and unsigned, undated document by Corcoran in Grunewald file, box 134, Corcoran papers; also David McKean, *Tommy the Cork: Washington's Ultimate Insider from Roosevelt to Reagan* (South Royalton, VT: Steerforth Press, 2004), 237–38.

89. Ryan, "'Mystery Man' of Tax Fraud Inquiry," *St. Louis Post-Dispatch*, March 10, 1952.

90. Tris Coffin and Douglass Cater, "About Pace: The Story of Senator Brewster," *Reporter*, June 10, 1952, 15–16; House Committee on Ways and Means, Subcommittee, *Internal Revenue Investigation*, 2922–43 (Brewster).

91. Abell, *Drew Pearson Diaries*, 331.

92. Abels, *The Truman Scandals*, 176. Grunewald also gave lavish gifts to Assistant Internal Revenue Commissioner Daniel Bolich, who was a friend of New York mobster Frank Costello.

93. Abels, *The Truman Scandals*, 179–83; Abell, *Drew Pearson Diaries*, 42, 336; Messick, *Secret File*, 206 (Flamingo); House Committee on Ways and Means, Subcommittee, *Internal Revenue Investigation*, 2914 (gambling winnings); 2993–3003 (American Distilling).

94. "Grunewald Dies in Capital at 65," *New York Times*, September 26, 1958; "U.S. Court Denies Grunewald Plea," *New York Times*, April 11, 1956; "Grunewald, Silent Witness, Cited by House for Contempt, 332 to 0," *New York Times*, April 10, 1952; Department of Justice news release on the indictment of Grunewald on ten counts of perjury, July 22, 1954, and Department of Justice news release on the indictment of Grunewald on five counts of perjury, September 21, 1954, in DOJ files on Grunewald, FOIA release to author. The Supreme Court overturned his conviction due to the statute of limitations (Robert Walsh, "Grunewald Conviction Is Reversed," *Washington Star*, June 3, 1957). On the FBI's wiretapping of Grunewald for political purposes, see Athan Theoharis, *Chasing Spies: How the FBI Failed in Counterintelligence but Promoted the Politics of McCarthyism in the Cold War Years* (Chicago: Ivan R. Dee, 2002), 230–34.

95. "The Truman Administration during 1949: A Chronology," Truman Library, at https://www.trumanlibrary.org/chron/49chron2.htm (quote).

96. Jack Anderson and Ronald May, *McCarthy: The Man, the Senator, the Ism* (Boston: Beacon Press, 1952), 252–54; Richard Rovere, *Senator Joe McCarthy* (London: Methuen, 1960), 121.

97. US Congress, Senate, Committee on Rules and Administration, Subcommittee on Privileges and Elections, report, *Investigations of Senators Joseph R. McCarthy and William Benton Pursuant to S. Res. 187 and S. Res. 304*, 82nd Cong., 2nd sess. (Washington, DC: US Government Printing Office, 1953), 38–39; Anderson and May, *McCarthy*, 128–37; Abels, *The Truman Scandals*, 46–48.

98. "Six Riddles: The Strange Story of McCarthy's Complex Financial Transactions and Tax Troubles," *The Progressive*, April 1954, 15–16.

99. Senate Committee on Rules and Administration, Subcommittee on Privileges and Elections, *Investigations of Senators Joseph R. McCarthy and William Benton*; Louis and Yazijian, *The Cola Wars*, 83–84.

100. "Transcript of Senate Resolution 301: Censure of Senator Joseph McCarthy (1954)," at https://www.ourdocuments.gov/doc.php?flash=true&doc=86&page=transcript.

101. Senate Subcommittee on Privileges and Elections, *Investigation of Senators Joseph R. McCarthy and William Benton*, 13, 15–19; "Six Riddles," *The Progressive*,

April 1954, 12–14; Anderson and May, *McCarthy*, 152–56; Jack Anderson with James Boyd, *Confessions of a Muckraker: The Inside Story of Life in Washington during the Truman, Eisenhower, Kennedy and Johnson Years* (New York: Random House, 1979), 248–49. The story of Lustron and the RFC, minus any mention of McCarthy, is told in Abels, *The Truman Scandals*, 97–104 and Bolles, *How to Get Rich in Washington*, 185–95.

102. "May 29, 1952: Truman Announces He Will Not Run Again," https://almost chosenpeople.wordpress.com/2017/01/02/march-29-1952-truman-announces-he -will-not-run-again/.

103. "Republican Party Platform of 1952," The American Presidency Project, http://www.presidency.ucsb.edu/ws/index.php?pid=25837; Mollenhoff, *Washington Cover-Up*, 34.

104. "Hoodlum Politics," *Life*, October 20, 1952.

105. Mollenhoff, *Washington Cover-Up*, 34. Political scientist David Frier confirms that the landslide Republican victory "was attributable in no small measure to [their] campaign promise to rid the nation of conflict of interest scandals such as had occurred during the Truman administration." David A. Frier, *Conflict of Interest in the Eisenhower Administration* (Baltimore: Pelican Books, 1970), 6.

Chapter 3

1. Stephen M. Walt, "America Is Wide Open for Foreign Influence," April 8, 2019, https://foreignpolicy.com/2019/04/08/america-is-wide-open-for-foreign-influence/.

2. Regin Schmidt, *Red Scare: FBI and the Origins of Anticommunism in the United States, 1919–1943* (Copenhagen: Museum Tusculanum Press, 2000); Murray B. Levin, *Political Hysteria in America: The Democratic Capacity for Repression* (New York: Basic Books, 1971), 28–90; Alfred McCoy, *Policing America's Empire: The United States, the Philippines, and the Rise of the Surveillance State* (Madison: University of Wisconsin Press, 2009), 293–348.

3. "Churchill Delivers Iron Curtain Speech," https://www.history.com/this-day -in-history/churchill-delivers-iron-curtain-speech.

4. Athan Theoharis, *Seeds of Repression: Harry S. Truman and the Origins of Mc-Carthyism* (Chicago: Quadrangle Books, 1971); Robert Justin Goldstein, "Prelude to McCarthyism: The Making of a Blacklist," *Prologue* 38 (Fall 2006). Administration officials too often stoked public fears in a manner later adopted by Senator McCarthy. In 1949, for example, Attorney General J. Howard McGrath warned, "There are today many Communists in America. They are everywhere—in factories, offices, butcher stores, on street corners, in private businesses. And each carries in himself the germ of death for society." Athan Theoharis and John Stuart Cox, *The Boss: J. Edgar Hoover and the Great American Inquisition* (Philadelphia: Temple University Press, 1988), 221–22.

5. Robert K. Carr, *The House Committee on Un-American Activities, 1945–1950* (Ithaca: Cornell University Press, 1952), 455–56.

6. Neal Gabler, *An Empire of Their Own: How the Jews Invented Hollywood* (New York: Crown, 1988), 351–65.

7. The underworld associates of Mayer and Warner are noted in Charles Rappleye and Ed Becker, *All American Mafioso: The Johnny Rosselli Story* (New York: Doubleday, 1991), 60–61.

8. Rappleye and Becker, *All American Mafioso*, 64–69; Rosselli testimony, Kefauver hearings, part 5, 396.

9. Russo, *The Outfit*, 142–64; Server, *Handsome Johnny*, 117–52, 175–217; Smith, *Syndicate City*, 137–63; Witwer, *Shadow of the Racketeer*, 59–74, 83–102, 108–16. Rosselli testified that he ordered Bioff to call off a strike against his friend Harry Cohn's Columbia Pictures; Kefauver hearings, part 5, 394–95.

10. Dan Moldea, *Dark Victory: Ronald Reagan, MCA, and the Mob* (New York: Viking, 1986), 27. An attorney for Paramount Pictures estimated that the studio paid mobsters roughly 5 percent of payroll in exchange for heading off union demands for pay increases of 25 to 30 percent. Loew's and RKO saved an estimated $3 million in labor costs. Witwer, *Shadow of the Racketeer*, 92–93.

11. Rappleye and Becker, *All American Mafioso*, 88–90; Gerald Horne, *Class Struggle in Hollywood, 1930–1950: Moguls, Mobsters, Stars, Reds, and Trade Unionists* (Austin: University of Texas Press, 2001), 49–50.

12. Cecilia Rasmussen, "Police Scandal Is Worst Since 1930s," *Los Angeles Times*, September 17, 1999; Buntin, *L.A. Noir*, 72–75.

13. Horne, *Class Struggle in Hollywood*, 48.

14. Gary Baum and Daniel Miller, "The Hollywood Reporter, after 65 Years, Addresses Role in Blacklist," *The Hollywood Reporter*, November 30, 2012.

15. US Congress, House of Representatives, Committee on Education and Labor, Special Subcommittee, *Jurisdictional Disputes in the Motion-Picture Industry*, hearings, 80th Cong., 1st sess. (Washington, DC: US Government Printing Office, 1948), 2029–30 (hereafter Hollywood extortion hearings); Russo, *The Outfit*, 142–64; Connie Bruck, *When Hollywood Had a King* (New York: Random House, 2003), 93; Horne, *Class Struggle in Hollywood*, 55.

16. Bruck, *When Hollywood Had a King*, 58–59.

17. IATSE continued to be represented by the same lawyer who defended Bioff at his extortion trial (Bruck, *When Hollywood Had a King*, 103).

18. Russo, *The Outfit*, 171, 243.

19. "J. M. Schenck Pardoned," *New York Times*, January 4, 1947. FDR's son James intervened with Treasury Secretary Henry Morgenthau Jr. in 1939 to go easy on Schenck in his tax prosecution, only to be upbraided by his father. Ronald Kessler, *The Sins of the Father: Joseph P. Kennedy and the Dynasty He Founded* (New York: Warner Books, 1996), 104–5.

20. Horne, *Class Struggle in Hollywood*, 22, quoting the CSU *Bulletin*.

21. Horne, *Class Struggle in Hollywood*, 184; Donald Critchlow, *When Hollywood Was Right: How Movie Stars, Studio Moguls, and Big Business Remade American Politics* (New York: Cambridge University Press, 2013), 81–82; John Sbardellati, *J. Edgar Hoover Goes to the Movies: The FBI and the Origins of Hollywood's Cold War* (Ithaca: Cornell University Press, 2012), 109; "Nailed: Hollywood's Most Vicious Lie

of the Year," *Hollywood Sun*, April 3, 1946, reprinted in Hollywood extortion hearings, 2025.

22. Joseph Tuohy testimony in Hollywood extortion hearings, 1285–86, 1293 (Tobin); 1283, 1288, 1294 (Tuohy and Twentieth Century-Fox). On Tobin's record, see Witwer, *Corruption and Reform in the Teamsters Union*, 107–17.

23. Bruck, *When Hollywood Had a King*, 92–106

24. Horne, *Class Struggle in Hollywood*, 48–49.

25. Critchlow, *When Hollywood Was Right*, 54, 82–83; Bruck, *When Hollywood Had a King*, 96–97, 109. MPA's main publicist until May 1947 was novelist and screenwriter Ayn Rand.

26. Bruck, *When Hollywood Had a King*, 105, 111; Critchlow, *When Hollywood Was Right*, 84.

27. Testimony of Jack L. Warner, https://www.thompsonschools.org/cms/lib/CO01900772/Centricity/Domain/3627/HUAC%20Testimony.pdf.

28. Critchlow, *When Hollywood Was Right*, 94, 109. Nixon's papers provide ample evidence of the political and financial support he enjoyed from top studio executives and producers such as Jack Warner, Samuel Goldwyn, Cecil B. DeMille, Walt Disney, Louis Mayer, and Young Frank Freeman of Paramount Pictures.

29. Jerry W. Sanders, *Peddlers of Crisis: The Committee on the Present Danger* (Boston: South End Press, 1983), 51, 86; Curt Cardwell, *NSC 68 and the Political Economy of the Early Cold War* (New York: Cambridge University Press, 2011), 200.

30. Sanders, *Peddlers of Crisis*, 61–62, 91.

31. Samuel Goldwyn to CPD Vice Chairman Tracy Voorhees, December 27, 1951, and membership lists, in "Committee on the Present Danger—Correspondence (2)" file, Floyd Odlum papers, Dwight Eisenhower Library.

32. Ovid Demaris, *Captive City: Chicago in Chains* (New York: Lyle Stuart, 1969), 223–24; Moldea, *Dark Victory*, 135–36; Russo, *Supermob*, 99 (Store Properties), 39–42 (Greenberg).

33. Tim Adler, *Hollywood and the Mob* (London: Bloomsbury, 2007), 50; Ovid Demaris, *The Last Mafioso* (New York: Times Books, 1981), 109. One of Goldwyn's earliest partners in the movie business, Archibald Selwyn, had been financed by the notorious Jewish gangster Arnold Rothstein.

34. Carr, *The House Committee on Un-American Activities*, 47.

35. Gary Wills, *Nixon Agonistes: The Crisis of the Self-Made Man* (Boston: Houghton Mifflin, 1970), 26–27.

36. Morris, *Richard Milhous Nixon*, 265–66, 326, 351–52.

37. Wills, *Nixon Agonistes*, 28.

38. Richard Nixon, *Six Crises* (New York: Doubleday, 1962), 4.

39. Carr, *The House Committee on Un-American Activities*, 279n.

40. Nixon confided to two former FBI agents that "he had worked very close (sic) with the Bureau and with [Louis] Nichols during the past year on [the Hiss-Chambers] matter"; Theoharis and Cox, *The Boss*, 252.

41. O'Reilly, *Hoover and the Un-Americans*, 5–8, 76–129.

42. "Hall against Thomas Bid to Return to Congress," *New York Times*, February 8, 1954.

43. Robert J. Donovan, *Conflict and Crisis: The Presidency of Harry S. Truman, 1945–1948* (Columbia: University of Missouri Press, 1977), 414.

44. Carr, *The House Committee on Un-American Activities*, 100.

45. Mazo and Hess, *President Nixon*, 72. Douglas punched below the belt as well, accusing Nixon of following the direction of left-wing Rep. Vito Marcantonio.

46. Marquis Childs, "The Hiss Case and the American Intellectual," *Reporter*, September 26, 1950, 27.

47. Anderson and May, *McCarthy*, ch. 26; Robert Goldston, *The American Nightmare* (New York: Bobbs-Merrill, 1973), 69–71.

48. Roy Cohn, *McCarthy* (New York: New American Library, 1968), 8–9; "The Numbers Game," *The Progressive*, April 1954, 22.

49. Quoted in Schlesinger Jr., *Robert Kennedy and His Times*, 247n.

50. Members of this group passed to Senator McCarthy a secret and potentially explosive FBI report on Soviet espionage activities in the United States they received from a source in military intelligence. Messick, *John Edgar Hoover*, 117–20.

51. Messick, *John Edgar Hoover*, 112–17. The American Jewish League Against Communism was founded in March 1948. Its first executive director was Benjamin Schultz, a Yonkers rabbi who drew praise mainly from right-wing anti-Semites; Gabler, *An Empire of Their Own*, 379–81. In 1955, Cohn was chairman of its executive committee and Sokolsky was president.‡

52. Gabler, *An Empire of Their Own*, 385.

53. Anthony Summers, *Official and Confidential: The Secret Life of J. Edgar Hoover* (New York: G. P. Putnam's Sons, 1993), 250–52; Burton Hersh, *Bobby and J. Edgar* (New York: Basic Books, 2008), 48–49; Messick, *John Edgar Hoover*, 112–16. Although his support of the league endeared Rosenstiel to many Republicans, earlier he hedged his bets by contributing heavily to the Democratic Party in 1948, putting the Truman administration in his debt. Truman's chief fundraiser, Louis Johnson, intervened to help Rosenstiel and his vice president, John Leban, in a tax case; Abels, *The Truman Scandals*, 133–34.

54. Demaris, *The Director*, 95–101; Messick, *John Edgar Hoover*, 224–28.

55. The Forand Bill delayed the imposition of excise taxes on stockpiled whiskey, saving Schenley as much as $50 million. Nichols retired from Schenley in 1968 but remained president of the J. Edgar Hoover Foundation; Michael Dorman, *Pay-Off: The Role of Organized Crime in American Politics* (New York: Berkley Medallion, 1973), 215–23; Summers, *Official and Confidential*, 251–53; Messick, *John Edgar Hoover*, 167–68; Nicholas Gage, "Rosenstiel Link to Crime Denied," *New York Times*, March 12, 1971; William Lambert, "The Hot Shot One-Man Roy Cohn Lobby," *Life*, September 5, 1969, 29.

56. Susan Rosenstiel testimony before the New York State Joint Legislative Committee on Crime, Its Causes, Control, and Effect on Society, executive session, February 9, 1970, 14 (Hotel Nacional and Lansky), 35–37 (Zicarelli and Vincent Alo), 40 (Fontainebleau Hotel), 203 (Bruno); also Tom Renner, "Legislature Probing Link between Mob and Mighty," *Newsday*, January 28, 1971.

57. Nicholas Gage, "Rosenstiel Link to Crime Denied," *New York Times*, May 12, 1971. In 1971 her credibility took a hit after she pleaded guilty to perjury in an unre-

lated pretrial deposition in a civil suit (Juan Vasquez, "Mrs. Rosenstiel Accused in a Suit," *New York Times*, February 9, 1971). In 1974, a member of the Watergate Special Prosecution Force, who listened to her accuse Nixon, Lansky, and her ex-husband of various crimes, judged that she was "unbalanced and shows signs of paranoia. She is clearly out to get her husband who seems to figure in most every unsupported allegation." Memo for the files by Phil Bakes, "Interview with Mrs. S. Rosenstiel," September 19, 1974, "Rosenstiel Allegations" file, Watergate Special Prosecution Force papers, NARA. Her later claims to have witnessed J. Edgar Hoover in drag with her husband and Roy Cohn, recounted in Summers's biography of Hoover, did nothing to boost her credibility (*Official and Confidential*, 253–56).

58. Cohn, *McCarthy*, 47.

59. Rovere, *Senator Joe McCarthy*, 194–95; Robert Griffith, *The Politics of Fear: Joseph R. McCarthy and the Senate* (Amherst: University of Massachusetts Press, 1970), 256, 249.

60. See correspondence in FBI files on Schine released at https://vault.fbi.gov/gerard-david-schine/Gerard%20David%20Schine%20Part%2001%20of%2001/.

61. "Chicago Indictment Accuses Western Union of Plot to Operate a Racing News Service," *New York Times*, April 27, 1940; "Government Loses Race Betting Case," *New York Times*, December 20, 1941; "Race News Figure Tells of Telegraph Holdings," *Los Angeles Times*, June 14, 1950; "Racing News Chief Denies Bookie Tie," *New York Times*, June 14, 1950; William Moore, "Tells Attempt to Run St. Louis Police Board," *Chicago Tribune*, July 20, 1950; "Democrats Named Gamblers' Lawyer," *New York Times*, September 12, 1950; Harold Hinton, "Gov. Smith Denies Favor to Binaggio," *New York Times*, September 30, 1950; "Social & Personal," *Jerusalem Post*, May 29, 1960 (Israel Bonds); Claudia Maclachlan and Roy Malone, "Molasky Empire Beset by Turmoil," *St. Louis Post Dispatch*, September 20, 1981. Molasky was represented in the Kefauver hearings by St. Louis mob attorney Morris Shenker, who became Jimmy Hoffa's attorney and one of the biggest borrowers in history from the Teamster pension fund. US Congress, Senate, Special Committee to Investigate Organized Crime in Interstate Commerce, *Second Interim Report Pursuant to S. Res. 202, Report no. 141*, 82nd Cong., 1st sess. (Washington, DC: US Government Printing Office, 1951), 8.

62. Hersh, *Bobby and J. Edgar*, 390–93; Nicholas von Hoffman, *Citizen Cohn: The Life and Times of Roy Cohn* (New York: Doubleday, 1988), 416 (Mafia), 282–83 (Hoover), 459–60 (Rosenstiel); Robert Friedman, "The Strange Career of Roy Cohn," *Juris Doctor*, April 1977, 17–27. Lansky was no fan of Cohn, declaring to one friend that the attorney was guilty of "a (obscenity) stock swindle" with Lionel Corp. (FBI telegram from SAC, New York, to Director, FBI, June 11, 1962, NARA 124-10334-10194). For details on a ten-count federal indictment handed down in 1963, linking Cohn to figures involved in the fraudulent manipulation of United Dye & Chemical Corp. stock, see Keith Wheeler and William Lambert, "Is He a Liar under Oath?" *Life*, October 4, 1963. Cohn was represented on a separate charge of distributing pornography, stemming from his work for Garfinkle's Union News Company, by New Jersey lawyer and congressman Cornelius Gallagher, who was a close ally of mobster "Bayonne Joe" Zicarelli (chapter 4). See von Hoffman, *Citizen Cohn*, 260, 334–42;

"Charge Roy Cohn Conspired to Sell Indecent Literature," *Daily Worker*, June 27, 1957. Susan Rosenstiel testified that Cohn paid off Rep. Cornelius Gallagher in 1961 (executive session testimony before the New York State Joint Legislative Committee on Crime, Its Causes, Control, and Effect on Society, February 9, 1970, Alan Block papers). Cohn and his associates also provided a $100,000 unsecured loan to Sen. Edward Long, D-Missouri, "to finance a chain of high-interest lenders in Missouri." (Hersh, *Bobby and J. Edgar*, 463).

63. "Roy Cohn Disbarred," *San Francisco Chronicle*, June 24, 1986; "The 4 Cases Cited in the Cohn Ruling," *New York Times*, June 24, 1986.

64. Albin Krebs, "Roy Cohn, Aide to McCarthy and Fiery Lawyer, Dies at 59," *New York Times*, August 3, 1986; Arnold Lubasch, "U.S. Is Suing Cohn for $7 Million in Taxes and Fees Dating to 1959," *New York Times*, April 4, 1986.

65. Joseph Keeley, *The China Lobby Man* (New Rochelle, NY: Arlington House, 1969), 248–51; Anderson and May, *McCarthy*, 192–94.

66. Felix Greene, *A Curtain of Ignorance: How the American Public Has Been Misinformed about China* (Garden City, NY: Doubleday, 1964), 43.

67. Alva Johnston, "White House Tommy," *Saturday Evening Post*, July 31, 1937.

68. Barbara Tuchman, *Stilwell and the American Experience in China, 1911–45* (New York: Macmillan, 1971), 477; Graham Peck, *Two Kinds of Time* (Boston: Houghton Mifflin, 1950), 474, 636; Paul Frillmann, *China: The Remembered Life* (Boston: Houghton Mifflin, 1968), 152; Israel Epstein, *The Unfinished Revolution in China* (Boston: Little, Brown, 1947), 338; Gilbert Stuart autobiography in Stuart papers, box 1, Hoover Institution, citing investigations by Col. Harry Cooper of the army's Criminal Investigation Division.

69. Abell, *Drew Pearson Diaries*, 60. According to a Truman White House memo, "the Treasury finally decided that since he had made this money in China, while he was a non-resident of the United States, it was not taxable." "Confidential Memo on the China Lobby," June 12, 1951, in "China Lobby, General" file, President's Secretary's File, Truman papers, Truman Library.

70. Letter from Willauer to his wife, Louise, March 15, 1946, box 1, Willauer papers, Princeton University. Willauer was the former roommate of Corcoran's brother Howie at Exeter, Princeton, and Harvard Law School.

71. David McKean, *Tommy the Cork*, 211–13; William Leary, *Perilous Missions: Civil Air Transport, the Chinese Civil War, and CIA Covert Operations in East Asia, 1946–1955* (Tuscaloosa: University of Alabama Press, 1984), 38–72, 82; Christopher Robbins, *Air America: The Story of the CIA's Secret Airlines* (New York: G. P. Putnam's Sons, 1979), 48, 55–57. Corcoran signed a formal service agreement with the CIA in 1948.

72. Nancy Bernkopf Tucker, *Patterns in the Dust: Chinese-American Relations and the Recognition Controversy, 1949–1950* (New York: Columbia University Press, 1983), 91.

73. William Leary, *Perilous Missions*, 94–98; Marilyn Bender and Selig Altschul, *The Chosen Instrument: Pan Am, Juan Trippe, The Rise and Fall of an American Entrepreneur* (New York: Simon & Schuster, 1982), 477–84.

74. Leary, *Perilous Missions*, 100 et seq.

75. See, for example, Ken Hughes, *Chasing Shadows: The Nixon Tapes, the Chennault Affair, and the Origins of Watergate* (Charlottesville: University of Virginia Press, 2014).

76. The executive chairman of Aid Refugee Chinese Intellectuals (ARCI), Christopher Emmet, lauded its role in "making Americans more aware of the Chinese anti-Communist cause. . . . The reason is that the humanitarian appeal for relief incidentally permits giving all the political facts about persecution, etc. . . . It does not invite argument and attack as in the case of direct political propaganda." Jonathan Marshall, "Chinagate," *Libertarian Review*, June 1978, 35–38; see also Ross Koen, *The China Lobby in American Politics* (New York: Harper & Row, 1974), 53–54.

77. Charles Wertenbaker, "The China Lobby," *Reporter*, April 15, 1952, 17–18; Charles Wertenbaker, "China Lobby—II," *Reporter*, April 29, 1952, 8; "China Bills, Laws and Policies," *CQ Almanac 1949*; *Washington Post*, September 18, 1949.

78. Edward A. Harris, "The Men behind McCarthy," *The New Republic*, April 24, 1950.

79. Draft memo for W. A. Harriman from J. S. Lanigan, re "China Lobby," October 4, 1951, in "China Lobby, General" file, President's Secretary's File, Truman papers, Truman Library.

80. Wertenbaker, "The China Lobby," 21; Jack Lait and Lee Mortimer, *Washington Confidential* (New York: Crown, 1951), 165; Jesse Abramson, "Charnay Starts Boxing Firm as Rival to Garden," *New York Herald Tribune*, June 29, 1949.

81. Abell, *Drew Pearson Diaries*, 280, 345 (Las Vegas and Detroit mob); *Reporter*, April 21, 1955; "Wolfson Claims Backing of a Million Shares in Fight for Control of Ward," *Wall Street Journal*, March 23, 1955 (Charnay and Wolfson); William Moore, "Beck Union to Spend Million in Own Defense," *Chicago Tribune*, April 13, 1957 (Teamsters). On Charnay's indictment and acquittal on stock manipulation charges in a case related to Wolfson's Merritt-Chapman and Scott, see Richard Phalon, "U.S. Indicts Charnay," *New York Herald Tribune*, June 22, 1962; "3 Truck Officials Acquitted of Fraud," *New York Times*, June 9, 1965.‡

82. *Reporter*, April 29, 1952.

83. Wallace Turner, *Gambler's Money: The New Force in American Life* (Boston: Houghton Mifflin, 1965), 10. An exception is the biography by journalist Michael Y. Ybarra, *Washington Gone Crazy: Senator Pat McCarran and the Great American Communist Hunt* (Hanover, NH: Steerforth Press, 2004).

84. Richard Donovan and Douglass Cater, "Of Gamblers, a Senator, and a Sun That Wouldn't Set," *Reporter*, June 9, 1953, 29. McCarran also managed to exempt roulette, 21, and craps from a 10 percent tax imposed on gambling devices. William S. Fairfield, "Las Vegas: The Sucker and the Almost-Even Break," *Reporter*, June 9, 1953, 21. On his intervention with the IRB in a huge mail fraud case, see Abels, *The Truman Scandals*, 164.

85. Sally Denton and Roger Morris, *The Money and the Power: The Making of Las Vegas and Its Hold on America* (New York: Alfred A. Knopf, 2001), 54, 46–47; Ybarra, *Washington Gone Crazy*, 664–67. A highly confidential source told the FBI that McCarran had taken a bribe to influence the Civilian Production Administration to cancel its "freeze order" on the construction of the Flamingo (FBI memo

from A. Rosen to E. A. Tamm, August 1, 1946, re "Benjamin 'Bugsy' Siegel"). FBI headquarters approved an investigation but asked that the Los Angeles office handle the McCarran inquiry "in a most discreet manner." FBI memo to Assistant Director A. Rosen, August 8, 1946, re "Benjamin Siegel"; telegram from Hoover to Special Agent in Charge of the Los Angeles field office, A. E. Ostholthoff, August 7, 1946. FBI Vault, "Bugsy Siegel," part 1, 86, 99–101, https://vault.fbi.gov/Bugsy%20Siegel%20. FBI eavesdropping on Siegel turned up information that "he was not concerned with Senator McCarran because he was already cooperative. . . . [redacted] suggested to Siegel that when he next saw McCarran he should caution Senator McCarran 'to play cozy' in the event Senator McCarran was questioned by the FBI concerning their activities." (FBI memo to A. Rosen, August 21[?], 1946, re "Benjamin 'Bugsy' Siegel," FBI Vault, "Bugsy Siegel," part 2, 81).

86. Ed Reid and Ovid Demaris, *The Green Felt Jungle* (New York: Trident Press, 1963), 150-52; Russo, *The Outfit*, 269; Moore, *The Kefauver Committee and the Politics of Crime*, 51–52, 159–60; Jerome Edwards, *Pat McCarran, Political Boss of Nevada* (Reno: University of Nevada Press, 1982), 151–55.

87. "Pat Geary," https://godfather.fandom.com/wiki/Patrick_Geary.

88. Jonathan Marshall, "The Institute of Pacific Relations: Politics and Polemics," *Bulletin of Concerned Asian Scholars*, VIII (April–June 1976), 36; Alfred Steinberg, "McCarran, Lone Wolf of the Senate," *Harper's*, November 1950, 87.

89. Theoharis, *Chasing Spies*, 210–12.

90. William W. Stueck Jr., *The Road to Confrontation: American Policy toward China and Korea* (Chapel Hill: University of North Carolina Press, 1981), 116; "Ambassador from Nevada," *Reporter*, September 13, 1949, 25.

91. "China Bills, Laws and Policies," *CQ Almanac 1949*, 5th ed. (Washington, DC: Congressional Quarterly, 1950).

92. Drew Pearson, *Washington Merry-Go-Round: The Drew Pearson Diaries, 1960–1969* (Washington, DC: Potomac Books, 2015), 155 (January 13, 1963). Pearson learned, for example, that Phillips Petroleum bought Bridges's vote on a natural gas bill with a large bribe. Abell, *Drew Pearson Diaries*, 526. Bridges also took $35,000 a year from John L. Lewis and managed to be out of town on the day when the Taft-Hartley Act came up for a vote. Robert S. Allen and William V. Shannon, *Truman Merry-Go-Round* (New York: Vanguard Press, 1950), 288.

93. Kenneth S. Chern, "Politics of American China Policy, 1945: Roots of the Cold War in Asia," *Political Science Quarterly* 91:4 (1976), 634–35.

94. Wertenbaker, "The China Lobby," 19. A White House memo alleged that Clark's trip was subsidized by the Nationalist government, as was the public relations man (Eddie Lockett) who wrote Clark's report. "Confidential Memo on the China Lobby," June 12, 1951, in "China Lobby, General" file, President's Secretary's File, Truman papers, Truman Library.

95. Pearson, *Washington Merry-Go-Round*, 41–42 (October 13, 1960).

96. Wertenbaker, "The China Lobby," 17; Abell, *Drew Pearson Diaries*, 326.

97. Abels, *The Truman Scandals*, 177–78.

98. *Time*, April 7, 1952, 24; Abels, *The Truman Scandals*, 171, 195–201. Bridges defended his conduct in testimony before the House Committee on Ways and Means, Subcommittee, *Internal Revenue Investigation*, 3189–3216.

99. "China Bills, Laws and Policies," *CQ Almanac 1949*.

100. "China Bills, Laws and Policies," *CQ Almanac 1949*.

101. Abels, *The Truman Scandals*, 26; McFarland and Roll, *Louis Johnson and the Arming of America*, 127–28; *Fortune*, September 1949. For more on Johnson's various conflicts, improprieties, and political connections, see Allen and Shannon, *Truman Merry-Go-Round*, 446, 464; Abels, *The Truman Scandals*, 305, 128, 156; and I. F. Stone series on Crowley, Emanuel, Johnson, the Alien Property Custodian and General Dyestuffs in *PM*, January 1945, reprinted in US Congress, Senate, Committee on the Judiciary, Subcommittee to Investigate the Administration of the Internal Security Act and Other Internal Security Laws, *Morgenthau Diary (Germany)*, 90th Cong., 1st sess. (Washington, DC: US Government Printing Office, 1967), 921–30.[‡]

102. Anthony R. Carrozza, *William D. Pawley* (Washington, DC: Potomac Books, 2012), 165.

103. "The Angels of the Truman Campaign," *Time*, June 6, 1949; McFarland and Roll, *Louis Johnson*, 137–39; Virgil Peterson, *Barbarians in Our Midst* (Boston: Little, Brown, 1952), 299–301 (Helis and organized crime); David McCullough, *Truman*, 679 (Odlum). Helis was a director of Rimrock Tidelands, connected to the Sicilian Mafia through Santo Sorge (Scott, *Deep Politics and the Death of JFK* (1993), 202). Hosiery manufacturer Abraham Feinberg, an ardent Zionist and Haganah agent, told an aide to President Truman in the fall of 1948 that he could deliver $100,000 to finance the campaign. Feinberg recalled, "I had already got the commitments for the $100,000 from people around the country, all of whom understood that without Truman, Israel would have had very difficult days and times trying to even come into existence. As that train went into towns where there were Jewish communities, I arranged that a Jewish delegation would ask to see the president and be received on the train and that, in as many cases as possible, they would bring him donations above these original commitments. So, the trip was a triumphant trip from his point of view as a politician. . . . He often said, 'If not for my friend Abe, I couldn't have made the trip and I wouldn't have been elected.'" Oral history interview with Abraham Feinberg, New York City, August 23, 1973, Truman Library; also John B. Judis, *Genesis: Truman, American Jews, and the Origins of the Arab/Israeli Conflict* (New York: Farrar Straus and Giroux, 2014), 338.

104. Johnson had previously intervened with the Internal Revenue Bureau on behalf of Schenley Industries. McFarland and Roll, *Louis Johnson*, 143.

105. Lait and Mortimer, *Washington Confidential*, 327. Their allegations are consistent with more scrupulous accounts in Demaris, *Captive City*, 222–23 and Russo, *Supermob*, 109–14. On Arvey's ties to the Chicago Outfit, see chapters 2 and 7.

106. Oral history interview with George E. Allen, May 15, 1969, Truman Library; oral history interview with Felix E. Larkin, former general counsel, Department of Defense, September 18 and October 23, 1972, Truman Library.

107. McFarland and Roll, *Louis Johnson and the Arming of America*, 185–86; Drew Pearson, "Politics Ensnares B-36 Probe," *Washington Post*, May 31, 1949; Larkin in-

terview, op cit.; Fred Cook, *The Warfare State* (New York: Macmillan, 1962), 189–90; Walter Millis, *Arms and the State* (New York, 1958), 242; Paul Hammond, "Super Carriers and B-36 Bombers," in Harold Stein, ed., *American Civil-Military Decisions* (Tuscaloosa: University of Alabama Press, 1963). The B-36 affair became an object lesson in the revolving doors when air force general Joseph T. McNarney, one of the bomber's staunchest defenders, landed a job as Convair's president almost immediately after retiring from the Pentagon in 1952.

108. McFarland and Roll, *Louis Johnson*, 254.

109. *Time*, January 9, 1950, 5; January 25, 1951, 18; September 25, 1950, 9. Johnson was also suspected of feeding anti-Acheson material to Senator Bridges; Alfred Steinberg, *The Man from Missouri* (New York: G. P. Putnam's Sons, 1962), 354.

110. Tucker, *Patterns in the Dust*, 77; Bruce Cumings, *The Origins of the Korean War: The Roaring of the Cataract, 1947–1950* (Princeton, NJ: Princeton University Press, 1990), 159–60.

111. McFarland and Roll, *Louis Johnson*, 258.

112. Drew Pearson, "China Lobby Aims at U.S. Policy," *Washington Post*, June 18, 1951, and "Johnson Law Firm Penalized," *Washington Post*, July 2, 1951; Abell, *Drew Pearson Diaries*, 212.

113. "Confidential Memo on the China Lobby," June 12, 1951, in "China Lobby, General" file, President's Secretary's File, Truman papers, Truman Library. The memo is not signed.

114. Drew Pearson noted, "Johnson was close to Gen. Julius Klein, a Chicago newspaperman who now heads Pan American Airways' public relations lobby and who has also been active in the 'get Acheson' drive. Klein has been working with Senators Brewster, Wherry and Taft in the drive to boot MacArthur and fire Acheson. The White House received information that Johnson had been playing hand-in-glove with Brewster and Klein in regard to Formosa and other matters." Drew Pearson, untitled column, *Asbury Park Evening Press*, September 20, 1950.

115. McFarland and Roll, *Louis Johnson*, 356. Johnson's law firm received lobbying fees of $18,000 from Pan Am in both 1948 and 1949. Drew Pearson, "Pan American Decision Reviewed," *Washington Post*, July 14, 1950. Also representing Pan Am was the family law firm of Florida senator George Smathers (*Newsday*, October 11, 1971).

116. Bender and Altschul, *The Chosen Instrument*, 437.

117. Drew Pearson, "O'Connell Resigns Post in Protest of 'Shabby Treatment,'" *Lubbock Evening Journal*, July 14, 1950; Marilyn Bender, "Pan Am's Summer of Struggle," *New York Times*, July 18, 1982.

118. *Pearson Diary*, 376; Drew Pearson, "Causes of Rebuke to Military," *Washington Post*, August 31, 1950; William Shannon and Douglas Cater, "How They Put Over the Franco Loan," *Reporter*, August 29, 1950, 16.

119. Oral history interview with Bobby Baker by Donald Ritchie, Senate Historical Office, June 1, 2009, 185, at https://www.documentcloud.org/documents/836424-baker-text.html#document/.

120. McFarland and Roll, *Louis Johnson*, 259–62; Johnson testimony, *Military Situation in the Far East*, 2577–78.

121. Tai-Hsun Tsuan, "An Explanation of the Change in United States Policy Towards China in 1950," PhD dissertation, University of Pennsylvania, 1969, 17–18.

122. *New York Times*, January 11, 1950, 3; Acheson testimony in *Military Situation in the Far East*, III, 1820–21.

123. United Press dispatch, January 5, 1950, in box 17, Charles Cooke papers, Hoover Library.

124. Tucker, *Patterns in the Dust*, 91.

125. Charles Cooke, "Our Policies and Prospects in the Far East," speech to Detroit Economic Club, September 26, 1949, in *Vital Speeches of the Day*, 16 (December 15, 1949), 133–36.

126. Charles Cooke, "United States Relations with the Republic of China, 1945–1955," September 17, 1959, box 17, Cooke papers, Hoover Library.

127. Pawley to Secretary of State, November 7, 1949, in Cooke papers, box 17; undated memo in Cooke papers, box 17; James Webb to Pawley, December 15, 1949, in US Congress, Senate, Committee on the Judiciary, Subcommittee to Investigate the Administration of the Internal Security Act and Other Internal Security Laws, *Communist Threat to the United States Through the Caribbean, Hearings*, 86th Cong., 2nd sess. (Washington, DC: US Government Printing Office, 1960), 730.

128. Cooke letter to Sen. William Knowland, R-Calif., April 10, 1950, box 17, Cooke papers, Hoover Library; Cooke testimony in US Congress, Senate, Committee on the Judiciary, Subcommittee to Investigate the Administration of the Internal Security Act and Other Internal Security Laws, *Internal Security Report for 1956*, 85th Cong., 1st sess. (Washington, DC: US Government Printing Office, 1957), 197–201; Cooke testimony, US Congress, Senate, Committee on the Judiciary, Subcommittee to Investigate the Administration of the Internal Security Act and Other Internal Security Laws, *Institute of Pacific Relations, Hearings*, 82nd Cong., 1st sess. (Washington, DC: US Government Printing Office, 1950), 1507–8.

129. "Probable Violations of Law in Connection with Procurement Activities of Agents of the Chinese Government in the United States," December 7, 1951, sent as enclosure to Mr. Murphy by Jim Lanigan, December 8, 1951, in "China Lobby: Data" file; and "Watch List Summary of Commerce International Corporation and Affiliates," memo by R. L. Pritchard, September 13, 1951, in "China Lobby: Commerce Department" file, President's Secretary's File, Truman papers, Truman Library; Cumings, *The Origins of the Korean War*, 511.‡

130. General Kiang letters to James Gray, CIC, April 6 and 10, 1950, Cooke papers, box 17; Cooke, "Seminar on East Asia," box 17, Cooke papers. CIC was paid a fee of up to 1.5 percent of expenses. Cooke was originally paid an annual salary of $30,000, later reduced to $24,000. A. E. Cates Jr. letter to Cooke, December 6, 1954, box 15, Cooke papers.

131. Memo to Chiang from Omar Pfeiffer, deputy to Charles Cooke, June 19, 1950, box 18, Cooke papers. In early 1950, Fassoulis provided $500,000, from sources unknown, "for a public relations campaign on Taiwan's behalf" (Cumings, *The Origins of the Korean War*, 512); see also Alfred Friendly, "'Squeeze'—Four Agencies Probe Acts of Chiang's United States Contractor," *Washington Post*, September 9, 1951.

132. Hsiao-ting Lin, *Accidental State: Chiang Kai-shek, the United States, and the Making of Taiwan* (Cambridge: Harvard University Press, 2016), 165–69; Hsiao-tin Lin, "Taiwan's Secret Ally," *Hoover Digest*, April 6, 2012.

133. "Probable Violations of Law in Connection With Procurement Activities of Agents of the Chinese Government in the United States," December 7, 1951, sent as enclosure to Mr. Murphy by Jim Lanigan, December 8, 1951, in "China Lobby: Data" file, President's Secretary's File, Truman papers, Truman Library; Anthony Leviero, "Senate Unit Helps to Hunt Grafting in China Nationalist Agency Here," *New York Times*, September 10, 1951; Burton Crane, "China Plane Graft Denied by Agency," *New York Times*, September 11, 1951; "China Aide Widens Charges of Graft," *New York Times*, September 12, 1951; "The Case of the Chinese Officers," *Nation*, September 29, 1951. Quote is from Anthony Leviero, "Ouster of General Revives Scrutiny of Graft in China," *New York Times*, August 31, 1951.

134. "Promoter Seized in $350,000 Fraud," *New York Times*, December 31, 1955.

135. John Tompkins, "Bon Ami Urging SEC to Ease Order That Suspended Trading," *New York Times*, February 14, 1959.

136. "Man, 47, Convicted in Bank Loan Fraud," *New York Times*, June 23, 1970; "U.S. Jury Indicts 4 in Bank Loans," *New York Times*, September 4, 1969; quote in "Tulsa Insurer Chief Admits Fraud Guilt," *New York Times*, June 9, 1970.

137. US Congress, Senate, Committee on Government Operations, Permanent Subcommittee on Investigations, *Organized Crime: Stolen Securities, Hearings*, 92nd Cong., 1st sess. (Washington, DC: US Government Printing Office, 1971), 850.

138. Oral history interview with Bobby Baker by Donald Ritchie, 101.

139. Memorandum from Col. C. B. Hansen to CIA director Walter Bedell Smith, March 19, 1952, at https://www.cia.gov/library/readingroom/document/cia-rdp80r01731r001300130010-7.pdf. The source for this allegation may have been a "Dr. Kan," an associate of the Nationalist general and political leader Li Tsung-jen (Li Zongren). A White House investigator opined that "Dr. Kan has a rather unsavory reputation and we are skeptical as to his motives and his veracity." He added, however, that "CIA has information regarding the surreptitious transfer of funds by Chinese officials from Formosa to Europe and the United States." Memo from James S. Lanigan to Theodore Tannenwald Jr., October 9, 1951, in "U.S. Chambers of Commerce in China" file, President's Secretary's File, Truman papers, Truman Library.

140. Russell Warren Howe and Sarah Hays Trott, *The Power Peddlers: A Revealing Account of Foreign Lobbying in Washington* (Garden City, NY: Doubleday, 1977), 34; Greene, *A Curtain of Ignorance*, 55; "China Bills, Laws and Policies," *CQ Almanac 1949*, 5th ed.

141. Anthony Leviero, "Lobbying Inquiry Sought by Morse," *New York Times*, June 6, 1951.

142. Wertenbaker, "The China Lobby," 21; William Costello, *The Facts about Nixon* (New York: Viking, 1960), 71–72; *Time*, November 13, 1950; Drew Pearson, "Change in China Policy," *Gadsden Times*, September 4, 1958; Drew Pearson, "Nixon's on a Slow Boat to Quemoy because of China Lobby Funds," *St. Petersburg Times*, October 17, 1960; Jack Anderson, "Chiang Bitter toward Nixon," *Ukiah Daily Journal*,

January 31, 1972; Morris, *Richard Milhous Nixon*, 590. Louis Kung also invested in oil ventures with President Eisenhower's golfing partner and financial benefactor George E. Allen. Drew Pearson, "Oil Helped China Lobby's Friends," *Washington Post*, October 19, 1960; Drew Pearson and Jack Anderson, *The Case Against Congress* (New York: Simon & Schuster, 1968), 438; Ovid Demaris, *Dirty Business: The Corporate-Political-Money-Power Game* (New York: Harper's Magazine Press, 1974), 188 et seq.

143. Irwin Gellman, *The Contender: Richard Nixon, the Congress Years, 1946–1952* (New York: The Free Press, 1999), 394 (Alfred Kohlberg).

144. Koen, *The China Lobby in American Politics*, 8; Wertenbaker, "The China Lobby," 24; Jacques Despuech, *Le trafic des piastres* (Paris: Deux Rives, 1953).

145. Drew Pearson, "Johnson's Law Firm Penalized," *Washington Post*, July 2, 1951.

146. Wertenbaker, "The China Lobby," 11; William S. Fairfield, "How Speculators Increase Our Food Bill," *Reporter*, March 20, 1951, 10–11.

147. Anthony Leviero, "Lobbying Inquiry Sought by Morse," *New York Times*, June 6, 1951; I. F. Stone, *Hidden History of the Korean War* (New York: Monthly Review Press, 1969), 350–52; also *New York Times*, August 8, 11, and 23, 1950.

148. Drew Pearson, "Chiang's Kin Big Cleanup Bared," *Washington Post*, July 16, 1951. For an account of apparently corrupt dealings by T. L. Soong's representative in Shanghai after World War II, see Bolles, *How to Get Rich in Washington*.

149. *Time*, March 20, 1950, 10; *Time*, July 17, 1950, 9; Rovere, *Senator Joe McCarthy*, 35–56; Abell, *Drew Pearson Diaries*, 250. A Senate subcommittee's investigation of McCarthy's finances raised the unanswered question of whether he had "confidential information with respect to the trend of the soybean futures markets." "Six Riddles," *The Progressive*, April 1954, 18. Highly profitable soybean deals were also conducted by World Commerce Corporation, formed after World War II by leading Anglo American intelligence officials, including OSS director William Donovan. "Big Profit Charged in U.S. Crop 'Deal,'" *New York Times*, May 23, 1950; "Anglo-U.S. Group Called 'Little ECA,'" *New York Times*, January 2, 1949. For more on soybean speculation in 1950, see Cumings, *The Origins of the Korean War*, 152–55.

150. Elting Arnold, "Memorandum for the Files: Treasury Activity Regarding Investigation of 'China Lobby,'" April 11, 1952, in "Treasury Dept—China Lobby, Internal Rev Investigation, 1951–52" file, Edward H. Foley Jr. papers, Truman Library. See also Truman's memo to the attorney general and secretary of the Treasury, June 11, 1951, in "China Lobby, General" file, President's Secretary's File, Truman papers, Truman Library.

151. "Lead to Be Followed by Justice, Treasury, Federal Reserve Bank and CIA," memo in "China Lobby: Central Intelligence Agency" file, President's Secretary's File, Truman papers, Truman Library.

152. James S. Lanigan memo to Theodore Tannenwald Jr., October 9, 1951, in "U.S. Chambers of Commerce in China" file, President's Secretary's File, Truman papers, Truman Library. Lanigan and Tannenwald were staff seconded by W. Averell Harriman from the Mutual Security Administration.

153. Koen, *The China Lobby in American Politics*, ix, discussed in Jonathan Marshall, "Cooking the Books: The Federal Bureau of Narcotics, the China Lobby and Cold War Propaganda, 1950–1962," *The Asia-Pacific Journal*, v. 11, issue 37, no. 1, September 14, 2013, https://apjjf.org/2013/11/37/Jonathan-Marshall/3997/article.html.

154. Jonathan Marshall, "Opium and the Politics of Gangsterism in Nationalist China, 1927–1949," *Bulletin of Concerned Asian Scholars* VIII (July–September 1976), 36 (air force), 41–42 (Tai Li and opium); also William O. Walker III, *Opium and Foreign Policy: The Anglo-American Search for Order in Asia, 1912–1954* (Chapel Hill: University of North Carolina Press, 1991), 150–51. On Tai Li, opium, and Maj. (later Lt. Col.) Hsiao Hsin-ju (Xiao Bo), assistant military attaché in the Chinese embassy, see P. L. Thyraud de Vosjoli, *Lamia* (Boston: Little, Brown, 1970), 86. Hsiao was a close friend of US Navy Lt. Commander Milton Miles, who became the head of OSS China and the official US liaison to Gen. Tai Li [Dai Li], head of Chiang's secret police. Carolle J. Carter, *Mission to Yenan: American Liaison with the Chinese Communists, 1944–1947* (Lexington: University of Kentucky Press, 1997), 157–58; Maochun Yu, *OSS in China: Prelude to Cold War* (Annapolis: Naval Institute Press, 1996); Maochun Yu, *The Dragon's War: Allied Operations and the Fate of China, 1937–1947* (Annapolis: Naval Institute Press, 2006). Frederic E. Wakeman, *Spymaster: Dai Li and the Chinese Secret Service* (Berkeley: University of California Press, 2003), 328, writes that Miles was "aware, and even appreciative, of Dai Li's smuggling empire, which was by VJ Day constructed upon a unique foundation of prewar narcotics traffic and wartime U.S. supply and transportation sources." In 1951, reporter Michael Straight noted that one of the KMT's major political tools, the People's Political Council, was "rigged by an adventurist named C. C. Huang, who narrowly escaped conviction while he was Consul General in San Francisco on charges of smuggling narcotics in the US." "Corruption and Chiang Kai-shek," *The New Republic*, October 8, 1951, 12.

155. Wakeman, *Spymaster*, 324–28; Walker, *Opium and Foreign Policy*, 151.

156. Marshall, "Cooking the Books."

157. Bertil Lintner, *Burma in Revolt: Opium and Insurgency since 1948* (Chiangmai: Silkworm Books, 1999), n50.

158. Marshall, "Cooking the Books"; Daniel Fineman, *A Special Relationship: The United States and Military Government in Thailand, 1947–1958* (Honolulu: University of Hawaii Press, 1997), 131–46; Peter Dale Scott, *The American War Machine* (Lanham, MD: Rowman & Littlefield, 2010), 71–95; Robbins, *Air America*, 84–87.

159. Alfred W. McCoy, *The Politics of Heroin: CIA Complicity in the Global Drug Trade* (Brooklyn: Lawrence Hill Books, 1991), 191.

160. Lintner, *Burma in Revolt*, 191.

161. Fineman, *A Special Relationship*, 144.

162. McCoy, *The Politics of Heroin*, 184–85.

163. Fineman, *A Special Relationship*, 151.

164. Correspondence on the Thai highway deal, which involved Phao's Bangkok confidant Willis Bird, is in the "Helliwell, Paul" file, box 140, Corcoran papers. Corcoran took credit for helping the company win its first big federal contract in Texas, which all but guaranteed "Lyndon's financial future in politics." See his draft autobi-

ography, *Rendezvous with Destiny,* "My Friendship with Lyndon," chapters 4–6, box 586, Corcoran papers.

165. Jim Drinkhall, "IRS vs. CIA," *Wall Street Journal,* April 18, 1980; Scott, *American War Machine,* 71–80; Block, *Masters of Paradise,* 169–70; Leary, *Perilous Missions,* 70–73; Joan Nielsen, "Republican Has Order of White Elephant," *Miami News,* October 1, 1954. The CIA's security staff noted that Helliwell had been employed by the agency as an "intermittent consultant" since July 27, 1949 (Letter from Ermal Geiss, Chief, Personnel Security Branch, CIA, to Christopher Callan, FBI, October 26, 1949, https://www.cia.gov/library/readingroom/docs/DOC_0005252018.pdf). Helliwell led the statewide campaign for Eisenhower-Nixon in 1952 while helping a Miami city commission investigate the *bolita* racket. "Helliwell Appointed by Givens," *Miami News,* August 23, 1952. Helliwell recruited former OSS chief William Donovan to speak on Eisenhower's behalf during the GOP primary. Charles Hesser, "People Want Ike, Says Donovan Here," *Miami News,* June 16, 1952.

166. Fineman, *A Special Relationship,* 205–7, 215–20 (Thai lobby); 144–49, 252 (Phao and opium). Helliwell hosted Phao in Miami, then joined him in Washington in late 1954. "Thailand General on Visit Here," *Miami News,* November 15, 1954; "Socially Yours," *Miami News,* November 28, 1954; letter from Helliwell to Phao, December 16, 1954, Helliwell file, Corcoran papers, Library of Congress.

167. Peter Dale Scott, *Drugs, Oil, and War* (Lanham, MD: Rowman & Littlefield, 2003), 197–98; cf. 60–62.

168. Letter from Helliwell to Corcoran, August 3, 1959, Helliwell file, Corcoran papers, Library of Congress.

169. Of twenty-two Foreign Service officers with responsibility for China, twenty "were either marginalized or dismissed" from 1950 to 1953. Hannah Gurman, *The Dissent Papers: The Voices of Diplomats in the Cold War and Beyond* (New York: Columbia University Press, 2012), 72–73.

170. Ellen Schrecker, *Many Are the Crimes: McCarthyism in America* (Princeton, NJ: Princeton University Press, 1998), 372.

171. James Deakin, *The Lobbyists* (Washington, DC: Public Affairs Press, 1966), 158; William Shannon, "The Franco Lobby," *Reporter,* June 20, 1950, 19–22; William Shannon and Douglas Cater, "How They Put Over the Franco Loan," *Reporter,* August 29, 1950, 14–16; Theodore Draper, "The Pentagon's Castles in Spain," *Reporter,* November 11, 1952, 33–34; Theodore Lowi, "Bases in Spain," in Harold Stein, ed., *American Civil-Military Decisions,* 681–95; Pearson and Anderson, *The Case against Congress,* 356–60.

172. The history of the CIA coup in Guatemala is documented in Richard H. Immerman, *The CIA in Guatemala: The Foreign Policy of Intervention* (Austin: University of Texas Press, 1982); Stephen Schlesinger and Stephen Kinzer, *Bitter Fruit: The Story of the American Coup in Guatemala* (Cambridge: Harvard University Press, 2005); Piero Gleijeses, *Shattered Hope: The Guatemalan Revolution and the United States, 1944–1954* (Princeton, NJ: Princeton University Press, 1991); and Nicholas Cullather, *Operation PBSUCCESS: The United States and Guatemala, 1952–1954* (Central Intelligence Agency, Center for the Study of Intelligence, History Staff, 1994). The important role of Corcoran is also noted in James Lockhart, "The Dulles

Supremacy: Allen Dulles, the Clandestine Service, and PBFortune," in Christopher Moran et al., eds., *Spy Chiefs: Volume 1: Intelligence Leaders in the United States and United Kingdom* (Washington, DC: Georgetown University Press, 2018), 101–2, and Thomas C. Mann, memorandum of conversation with Corcoran, May 15, 1950, in "Ambassador to Guatemala, 1948–51, Crisis" file, Patterson papers, Truman Library. On the CIA's recruitment of pilots from Civil Air Transport, see Immerman, *The CIA in Guatemala*, 140.

173. Joseph Morgan, *The Vietnam Lobby: The American Friends of Vietnam, 1955–1975* (Chapel Hill: University of North Carolina Press, 1997), 4–6, 21–25; Stanley D. Bachrack, *The Committee of One Million: "China Lobby" Politics, 1953–1971* (New York: Columbia University Press, 1976), 60–62; Marvin Liebman, *Coming Out Conservative* (San Francisco: Chronicle Books, 1992), 157–58.

174. David Halberstam, *The Best and the Brightest* (New York: Modern Library, 2001), xxvi.

175. Telephone conversation between President Johnson and the president's special assistant for national security affairs (William Bundy) Washington, May 27, 1964, 11:24 a.m., in US, Department of State, *Foreign Relations of the United States, 1964–68*, Volume XXVII, *Mainland Southeast Asia: Regional Affairs* (Washington, DC: USGPO, 2000) document 53.

176. Brian VanDeMark, *Into the Quagmire: Lyndon Johnson and the Escalation of the Vietnam War* (New York: Oxford University Press, 1995), 25; LBJ phone conversation with publisher John Knight, February 3, 1964, transcript at https://prde.upress.virginia.edu/conversations/9040021/notes_open.

177. From an unpublished essay on Watergate, ca. 1974.

Chapter 4

1. Peter Dale Scott and Jonathan Marshall, *Cocaine Politics: Drugs, Armies, and the CIA in Central America* (Berkeley: University of California Press, 1991), 52–53; Scott, *Deep Politics and the Death of JFK* (1993), 97–103.

2. Juan Alberto Cedillo, *La Cosa Nostra en México* (Barcelona: Grijalbo, 2011); Luis Astorga, "Organized Crime and the Organization of Crime," in *Organized Crime and Democratic Governability: Mexico and the US-Mexican Borderlands*, edited by John J. Bailey and Roy Godson (Pittsburgh: University of Pittsburgh Press, 2000), 62–73; Scott, *The American War Machine*, 46–54.

3. Eduardo Sáenz Rovner, *The Cuban Connection: Drug Trafficking, Smuggling, and Gambling in Cuba from the 1920s to the Revolution* (Chapel Hill: University of North Carolina Press, 2008); Jack Colhoun, *Gangsterismo: The United States, Cuba and the Mafia, 1933 to 1966* (New York: OR Books, 2013); Enrique Cirules, *The Mafia in Havana: A Caribbean Mob Story* (Melbourne, Vic.: Ocean Press, 2004); T. J. English, *Havana Nocturne: How the Mob Owned Cuba . . . and Then Lost It to the Revolution* (New York: William Morrow, 2008); Peter Moruzzi, *Havana before Castro: When Cuba Was a Tropical Playground* (Salt Lake City: Gibbs Smith, 2008); Rosalie

Schwartz, *Pleasure Island: Tourism and Temptation in Cuba* (Lincoln: University of Nebraska Press, 1999).

4. An early example of the literature on this phenomenon was Claire Sterling, *Thieves' World: The Threat of the New Global Network of Organized Crime* (New York: Simon & Schuster, 1994). The United Nations General Assembly adopted a Convention against Transnational Organized Crime in 2000.

5. McCoy, *The Politics of Heroin*, 53–63.

6. McCoy, *The Politics of Heroin*, 162–92 (1950s Southeast Asia), 436–60 (Afghanistan). For the CIA's relations with Central American drug traffickers, see Scott and Marshall, *Cocaine Politics*.

7. For the bombing of Orlando Letelier's car, see Scott and Marshall, *Cocaine Politics*, 32–33. For the murder of Henry Liu, see David E. Kaplan and Alec Dubro, *Yakuza: Japan's Criminal Underworld* (Berkeley: University of California Press, 2012), 260–61; and Ko-Lin Chin, *Heijin: Organized Crime, Business, and Politics in Taiwan* (Armonk, NY: M. E. Sharpe, 2003), 6, 36, 211–12.

8. Jack Anderson, "Medals and Junkets Aid in Saving Trujillo Sugar," *The Bulletin* (Bend, Ore.), September 7, 1960.

9. Germán E. Ornes, *Trujillo: Little Caesar of the Caribbean* (New York: Thomas Nelson & Sons, 1958), 35–39; Albert C. Hicks, *Blood in the Streets: The Life and Rule of Trujillo* (New York: Creative Age Press, 1946), 27–28.

10. R. Michael Malek, "Rafael Leonidas Trujillo Molina: The Rise of a Caribbean Dictator," (PhD dissertation, University of California, Santa Barbara, 1971), 176.

11. Ornes, *Trujillo*, 56–57; Malek, "Rafael Leonidas Trujillo Molina," 172–76, 183–87; Robert D. Crassweller, *Trujillo: The Life and Times of a Caribbean Dictator* (New York: Macmillan, 1966), 34, 71.

12. Fred Goff and Michael Locker, "The Violence of Domination: US Power and the Dominican Republic," in *Latin American Radicalism: A Documentary Report on Left and Nationalist Movements*, eds. Irving Louis Horowitz et al. (New York: Random House, 1969), 253.

13. Crassweller, *Trujillo*, 138, 206–7, 212; Ornes, *Trujillo*, 142, 225–26, 255.

14. Ornes, *Trujillo*, 225.

15. Crassweller, *Trujillo*, 126–28, 207–8, 279; Edward de Graff, "The Strange Legacy of 'El Benefactor,'" *The Reporter*, July 6, 1961, 30–31; John Bartlow Martin, *Overtaken by Events: The Dominican Crisis from the Fall of Trujillo to the Civil War* (Garden City, NY: Doubleday, 1966), 39.

16. Malek, *Rafael Leonidas Trujillo Molina*, 196; Eric Roorda, *The Dictator Next Door: The Good Neighbor Policy and the Trujillo Regime in the Dominican Republic, 1930–1945* (Durham: Duke University Press, 1998), 111, 114; Hicks, *Blood in the Streets*, 128–31; Charles Ameringer, *Caribbean Legion: Patriots, Politicians, Soldiers of Fortune, 1946–1950* (University Park: Pennsylvania State University Press, 1996), 19.

17. Ameringer, *Caribbean Legion*, 11–15, 19–20.

18. Michael R. Hall, *Sugar and Power in the Dominican Republic: Eisenhower, Kennedy and the Trujillos* (Westport, CT: Greenwood Press, 2000), 50–51; see also Stephen G. Rabe, *Eisenhower and Latin America: The Foreign Policy of Anti-Communism* (Chapel Hill: University of North Carolina Press, 1988), 154, and G. Pope Atkins, *The*

Dominican Republic and the United States: From Imperialism to Transnationalism (Athens: University of Georgia Press, 1998), 104–5.

19. Bernard Diederich, *Trujillo: The Death of a Dictator* (Princeton, NJ: Markus Wiener, 2000), 7.

20. Stuart A. McKeever, *The Galíndez Case* (Bloomington, IN: AuthorHouse, 2013), Kindle location 1697.

21. Tad Szulc, "Secret Trujillo Papers Disclose Intense Sugar Lobbying in U.S.," *New York Times*, July 3, 1962; Hall, *Sugar and Power in the Dominican Republic*, 60–73; Atkins, *The Dominican Republic and the United States*, 110; see also Daniel M. Berman and Robert A. Heineman, "Lobbying by Foreign Governments on the Sugar Act Amendments of 1962," *Law and Contemporary Problems*, v.28, no. 2 (1963), 416–27.

22. Howe and Trott, *The Power Peddlers*, 141. President Kennedy told reporters, "I think it's an unfortunate situation where men are paid large fees by foreign governments to secure quotas and where, in some cases, there are contingency fees." "Transcript of President's News Conference," *New York Times*, July 6, 1962.

23. The quote is from a document, evidently prepared by Francis Rosenbaum in 1957, found in the office of the Dominican attorney general by the FBI in 1963. FBI report by Special Agent Heinrich von Eckardt, Santo Domingo, April 25, 1963, and FBI report by Special Agent Charles E. Lennon, February 7, 1964, re "Francis Newman Rosenbaum," in Alan Block papers. See also McKeever, *The Galíndez Case*, Kindle locations 3712–14.

24. Association for Diplomatic Studies and Training, oral history of Ambassador Joseph S. Farland, January 31, 2000, at www.adst.org/OH%20TOCs/Farland,%20 Joseph%20S.toc.pdf. Hereafter "Farland oral history." Farland recalled that Dominican ambassador Manuel de Moya "had a love nest just outside of the city that you entered by a maze of hedges so no car could be observed. It was totally wired. There were two-way mirrors. There was a supply of whatever one wanted in the way of your desire. A number of our congressmen made use of that and were photographed and taped." Farland said he transferred back to Washington his deputy chief of mission, who patronized that "love house," accepted gifts, and "was definitely in the pocket of Trujillo." See also Martin, *Overtaken by Events*, 35; Goff and Locker, "The Violence of Domination," 256. On the alleged bribery of Farland's aide, see also memo from J. Edgar Hoover to Attorney General Kennedy, August 13, 1962, NARA 124-10183-10253.

25. Gen. Arturo Espaillat, *Trujillo: The Last Caesar* (Chicago: Henry Regnery Co., 1963), 75–81. A Dominican military attaché, Ernesto Vega Pagan, told the FBI of delivering $1 million to Washington in the company of Trujillo's lawyer and political agent Francis Rosenbaum in 1957. He said that Rosenbaum claimed to have made at least two other such trips. FBI report by Steve D. Evans, San Juan, November 19, 1962, re "Francis Newman Rosenbaum," in Alan Block papers.

26. Memo from J. Edgar Hoover to Attorney General Kennedy, August 13, 1962, re bribery and conflicts of interest in Dominican sugar lobbying, NARA 124-10183-10253; *Congressional Record*, August 24, 1960. See also *Reporter*, September 15, 1960, 8, 10; Pearson and Anderson, *The Case against Congress*, 409–10.

27. Hall, *Sugar and Power in the Dominican Republic*, 98; Espaillat, *Trujillo*, 86; Pearson and Anderson, *The Case against Congress*, 160–61; see also memo from J. Edgar Hoover to Attorney General Kennedy, August 13, 1962, re bribery and conflicts of interest in Dominican sugar lobbying, NARA 124-10183-10253.

28. McKeever, *The Galíndez Case*, 231, 313; Alan A. Block, "The National Intelligence Service—Murder and Mayhem: A Historical Account," *Crime, Law & Social Change* 38 (2002), 105.

29. Hall, *Sugar and Power in the Dominican Republic*, 53.

30. Francis Rosenbaum document cited in FBI report by Special Agent Heinrich von Eckardt, Santo Domingo, April 25, 1963, in Alan Block papers. On Johnston, see also memo from J. Edgar Hoover to Attorney General Kennedy, August 13, 1962, NARA 124-10183-10253.

31. Pearson and Anderson, *The Case against Congress*, 408.

32. Drew Pearson, "Congress Group Trujillo's Guests," *Washington Post*, June 7, 1957; Jack Anderson, "Medals and Junkets Aid in Saving Trujillo Sugar," *The Bulletin* (Bend, Ore.), September 7, 1960; "Support for Trujillo Hurts United States," *Free Lance-Star* (Fredericksburg, Va.), March 6, 1961. Cooley denied ever personally taking money from Trujillo (Tad Szulc, "Secret Trujillo Papers Disclose Intense Sugar Lobbying in U.S.," *New York Times*, July 3, 1962).

33. McKeever, *The Galíndez Case*, 313; see also memos from J. Edgar Hoover to Attorney General Kennedy, October 30, 1961, and August 13, 1962, NARA 124-10183-10253. McCormack was later exposed for giving free run of his office to political fixer Nathan Voloshen. Voloshen's mob clients included Salvatore Granello, who figures later in this chapter. William Lambert, "The Murky Men from the Speaker's Office," *Life*, October 31, 1969, 52+.

34. Drew Pearson, "Kin of Officials Close to Trujillo," *Washington Post*, June 5, 1957. Moore allegedly also took money from Trujillo to join a Dominican shipyard venture; "Too Shy on Mamie Kin," *Spokesman Review*, March 17, 1958.

35. McKeever, *The Galíndez Case*, 163 (Nixon), 41–42 (Frank); see also Miguel Cruz Tejada, "Trujillo aportó US$25 mil a la campaña de Richard Nixon," *Diario Libre*, May 30, 2007.

36. Stephen Ambrose, *Nixon: The Education of a Politician, 1913–1962* (New York: Simon & Schuster, 1987), 366–67; see also Hall, *Sugar and Power*, 53–54.

37. Pearson and Anderson, *The Case against Congress*, 408; Espaillat, *Trujillo*, 78.

38. Peter Maas, "Boswell of the Jet Set," *Saturday Evening Post*, January 19, 1963; "Igor Cassini Indicted in Trujillo Quiz," *Toledo Blade*, February 8, 1963; "Igor Cassini Gets $10,000 Fine for Failing to Register as Agent," *New York Times*, January 11, 1964; "Igor Cassini, Hearst Columnist, Dies at 86," *New York Times*, January 9, 2002; Peter Maas, "Unregistered Foreign Agents Used to Be Indicted, Not Wrist-slapped," *Washington Post*, August 31, 1980; William Stadiem, *Jet Set: The People, the Planes, the Glamour, and the Romance in Aviation's Glory Years* (New York: Random House, 2014), 172–74, 196–202, 235; Randall Bennett Woods, *Fulbright: A Biography* (New York: Cambridge University Press, 1994), 305–8; Schlesinger, *Robert Kennedy and His Times*, 387–88. For Cassini's side of the story, see Igor Cassini with Jeanne Molli, *I'd Do It All Over Again* (New York: G. P. Putnam's Sons, 1977), 209–39.

39. Wenzell Brown, "Dictator on Our Doorstep," *The Saturday Review*, June 1, 1946, 16.
40. Howe and Trott, *The Power Peddlers*, 507–8.
41. Theodore Draper, "Trujillo's Dynasty," *The Reporter*, November 27, 1951, 24; Hall, *Sugar and Power in the Dominican Republic*, 53.
42. Douglass Cater and Walter Pincus, "The Foreign Legion of U.S. Public Relations," *The Reporter*, December 22, 1960, 15–18; Atkins, *The Dominican Republic and the United States*, 90; "Mystery Man for Trujillo Gets New Term—8 to 24 Mo.," *Chicago Tribune*, November 3, 1960; Espaillat, *Trujillo*, 83–85; Jeremy Scott, *The Irresistible Mr. Wrong: The Six Mistresses of Misfortune* (London: Robson Press, 2012), ch. 19.‡
43. Espaillat, *Trujillo*, 181; Goff and Locker, "The Violence of Domination," 255–59. On Olmsted, who invested in Dominican forestry products and promoted Dominican tourism, see Christopher Hitchens, *Blood, Class and Empire: The Enduring Anglo-American Relationship* (New York: Nation Books, 1990), 290; *Reports of Overseas Private Investment Corporation Determinations*, Volume 1, eds. Mark Kantor et al. (New York: Oxford University Press, 2011), 61; Crassweller, *Trujillo*, 323. Olmsted quote from http://www.olmstedfoundation.org/who-we-are/general-olmsted.

Olmsted was in charge of clandestine operations (G-5) for the US Army in the China-Burma-India theater in World War II. He later headed the US military assistance program in the Dominican Republic. Nixon mentioned Olmsted's strong support for Senator Goldwater's foreign policy positions and his generous contributions to Republican candidates in a letter to Rep. Gerald Ford, March 11, 1965, in "Olmsted, George" folder, Wilderness Years: Series I: Correspondence: Series A, box 29, Nixon papers, Nixon Library. Olmsted and Anna Chennault raised nearly a quarter million dollars for Nixon's 1968 campaign; Anna Chennault letter to Herbert Kalmbach, October 4, 1968, "Chennault, Anna" file, Nixon papers, Nixon Library.

Berle's first job out of college was as a military intelligence officer assigned to settling land titles of US sugar companies in the Dominican Republic. During World War II he was the State Department's intelligence coordinator (Mark Stout, "The Pond: Running Agents for State, War, and the CIA," CIA Historical Document, April 14, 2007, at https://www.cia.gov/library/center-for-the-study-of-intelligence/csi-publications/csi-studies/studies/vol48no3/article07.html). He also sat on the board of various CIA front organizations; Eric Thomas Chester, *Covert Network: Progressives, the International Rescue Committee and the CIA* (New York: Routledge, 2015); Jim Schachter, "Adolf Berle, Late Professor of Law, a Founder of 50's CIA Drug Test Front," *Columbia Daily Spectator*, October 31, 1977.

The J. M. Kaplan Fund was identified as a CIA financial conduit in Neil Sheehan, "Order by Johnson Reported Ending CIA Student Aid," *New York Times*, February 15, 1967.

44. Carrozza, *William D. Pawley*; Max Holland, "Private Sources of U.S. Foreign Policy: William Pawley and the 1954 Coup d'État in Guatemala," *Journal of Cold War Studies* 7 (Fall 2005), 36–73. On Trujillo's funding of the overthrow of Arbenz ($60,000), see Crassweller, *Trujillo*, 335. A copy of the top secret "Report on the

Covert Activities of the Central Intelligence Agency," sent to President Eisenhower on September 30, 1954, is available at https://www.cia.gov/library/readingroom/docs/CIA-RDP86B00269R000100040001-5.pdf.

45. Carrozza, *William D. Pawley*, 271–72, 275–76.

46. Memorandum from the Officer in Charge of Dominican Republic Affairs (Fromer) to the Acting Assistant Secretary of State for Inter-American Affairs (Rubottom), Washington, February 15, 1957, re "Re-evaluation of Overall U.S. Policy Towards Dominican Republic in the Light of the Murphy Case Developments," in Office of the Historian, Bureau of Public Affairs, US Department of State, *Foreign Relations of the United States, 1955–1957, VI, American Republics: Multilateral; Mexico; Caribbean*, document 318 (hereafter "FRUS").

47. Carrozza, *William D. Pawley*, 272–75; report of SAC Miami, November 29, 1956, "Patriotic Club of July 26, Miami Cuban-Dominican Political Matters," NARA 124-10296-10196; report by SA George E. Davis Jr., Miami, July 23, 1958, re "Carlos Prío Socarrás," NARA 124-10296-10176; FBI Legal Attaché, Havana, to Director, FBI, November 2, 1957, re "Norberto Felipe Martinez Garcia," NARA 124-10284-10178.

48. The Association for Diplomatic Studies and Training, oral history of Henry Dearborn, April 24, 1991, at www.adst.org/OH%20TOCs/Dearborn,%20Henry.toc .pdf (hereafter "Dearborn oral history").

49. On Frank, see McKeever, *The Galíndez Case*, chapter 4; Block, "The National Intelligence Service," 99–100.

50. Sandy Smith, "Mobsters in the Marketplace," *Life*, September 8, 1967, 101; George Lardner Jr., "Last Hurrah Night at the Polish-American Club," *St. Petersburg Times*, August 19, 1968; Alan A. Block, "Violence, Corruption, and Clientelism: The Assassination of Jesús de Galíndez, 1956," *Social Justice* 36 (Summer 1989), 84.

51. FBI report by Special Agent John Patrick Devlin, June 27, 1963, NARA 124-10300-10046 (gambling); report by Special Agent Joseph L. Tangel, September 14, 1959, NARA 124-90103-10093, and special agent in charge, New York, to director, FBI, March 24, 1964, NARA 124-10348-10023 (Cotroni and narcotics). For an overview of the Cotroni syndicate, see Peter Edwards, *Northern Connection: Inside Canada's Deadliest Mafia Family* (Montreal: Optimum, 2006). The Federal Bureau of Narcotics described Giuseppe Cotroni as the "head of the largest and most notorious narcotic syndicate on the North American Continent." US Congress, Senate, Committee on Government Operations, Permanent Subcommittee on Investigations, *Organized Crime and Illicit Traffic in Narcotics, Hearings*, 88th Cong., 2nd sess. (Washington, DC: US Government Printing Office, 1964), 1003.

52. Alan A. Block and Marcia J. Block, "Fascism, Organized Crime and Foreign Policy: An Inquiry Based on the Assassination of Carlo Tresca," *Research in Law, Deviance and Social Control* 4 (1982), 53–84; Nunzio Pernicone, *Carlo Tresca: Portrait of a Rebel* (Oakland, CA: AK Press, 2010), 277–302. Galante was arrested in 1959 and later convicted on narcotics conspiracy charges. FBI memo, "La Cosa Nostra: Montreal, Quebec, Canada," January 26, 1965, NARA 124-10223-10378.

53. Peter Weiss, "Gallagher Aided CIA's Dominican Activities," *Bergen Record*, June 21, 1973.

54. FBI report by Special Agent Lincoln Stokes, March 16, 1959, NARA 124-90110-10031; CIA deputy director, Plans, to Director, FBI, June 19, 1961, NARA 124-90138-10090.

55. Sandy Smith, "The Fix," *Life*, September 1, 1967, 44–45; "In Response to the Attorney General," *Life*, August 30, 1968, 13; Thomas Reppetto, *Bringing Down the Mob: The War against the American Mafia* (New York: Henry Holt, 2006), 131; Peter Weiss, "Gallagher Aided CIA's Dominican Activities," *Bergen Record*, June 21, 1973. Gallagher was briefly considered as a possible running mate with President Johnson in 1964 until the FBI informed Johnson of his links to the underworld (Fred Graham, "FBI Data in 1960 Cited Gallagher," *New York Times*, August 25, 1968). Zicarelli was convicted in 1971 and sentenced to ten years in prison for bribing politicians to protect his gambling operations. Gallagher pleaded guilty in 1972 to tax evasion and perjury. In later years, Gallagher was also close to mob lawyer and former Trujillo lobbyist Francis Rosenbaum (Jack Anderson, "Greek Dealer's Arms Intrigues Girdled Globe," *Washington Post*, August 11, 1984).

56. Wenzell Brown, "Dictator on Our Doorstep," *The Saturday Review*, June 1, 1946, 16; Hicks, *Blood in the Streets*, 55–56; Crassweller, *Trujillo*, 311–12; Daniel James, "Murders Charged to Trujillo," *Spokesman-Review*, March 23, 1957; Silvio Torres-Saillant and Ramona Hernández, *The Dominican Americans* (Westport, CT: Greenwood Press, 1998), 110. On Zicarelli's role, see Ralph Salerno and John Tompkins, *The Crime Confederation: Cosa Nostra and Allied Operations in Organized Crime* (Garden City, NY: Doubleday, 1969), 388; Block, "The National Intelligence Service," 96.

57. See, for example, memorandum of conversation, Department of State, Washington, April 26, 1956, "Disappearance of Dr. Jesus de Galindez, Spanish Republican Exile," in *FRUS, 1955–1957, Volume VI, American Republics*, document 308.‡

58. Memorandum from the Officer in Charge of Dominican Republic Affairs (Fromer) to the Acting Assistant Secretary of State for Inter-American Affairs (Rubottom), "Re-evaluation of Overall U.S. Policy Towards Dominican Republic in the Light of the Murphy Case Developments," *FRUS, 1955–1957, VI, American Republics*, document 318; memorandum for the files by Spencer M. King, February 20, 1957, re "Interest of Other Agencies in State of U.S. Relations with the Dominican Republic," ibid., doc. 320.

59. As a special agent for the FBI from 1942–1944, Joseph Farland did top secret work on security for the atomic bomb. His mission in the Dominican Republic was known only to John Foster and Allen Dulles and J. Edgar Hoover (and, presumably, President Eisenhower). See Farland oral history.

60. The two men also took frequent trips to the Dominican Republic to introduce investors to the country in return for a percentage of their business (McKeever, *The Galíndez Case*, 203–4). Among the investors, as noted below, were mob-connected gamblers from Las Vegas. They also represented Louis Wolfson's mob-connected construction firm, Merritt, Chapman and Scott, in the Dominican Republic (FBI report by Steve D. Evans, San Juan, November 19, 1962, re "Francis Newman Rosenbaum," in Alan Block papers). For seamy details of their careers, see Bolles, *How to Get Rich in Washington*, 178–203; Leslie Waller, *The Swiss Bank Connection* (New

York: New American Library, 1972), 174–75; Neil Sheehan, "More Americans Cheating with Swiss Bank Accounts," *New York Times*, November 30, 1969; "Lawyer Accused of Perjury," *New York Times*, December 4, 1969; "Four Sentenced for Fraud Involving Federal Contracts," *New York Times*, February 11, 1970; "Swiss Court Ruling," *New York Times*, March 3, 1970; "Penn Central Funds Raided for $4 Million," *New York Times*, April 9, 1972.

61. Block, "The National Intelligence Service," 103; Douglass Cater and Walter Pincus, "The Foreign Legion of U.S. Public Relations," *The Reporter*, December 22, 1960, 18.

62. According to a document apparently written by Francis Rosenbaum in 1957, Rep. Thomas S. Gordon, D-IL and chairman of the House Foreign Affairs Committee, received $15,000 to undermine Representative Porter's push for an investigation. In all, members of the House Foreign Affairs Committee received $75,000. Rep. B. Carroll Reece, R-Tenn. and former chairman of the Republican National Committee, received $15,000. FBI report by Special Agent Heinrich von Eckardt, Santo Domingo, April 25, 1963, in Alan Block papers. These were just initial payments. As noted above, Rosenbaum reportedly helped Ernesto Vega Pagan, an aide to Trujillo, deliver $1 million to Manuel de Moya, the Dominican ambassador in Washington, D.C., for political bribes in 1957. General Espaillat told the FBI that he considered Rosenbaum to be part of de Moya's "payoff team." FBI report by Steve D. Evans, San Juan, November 19, 1962, re "Francis Newman Rosenbaum," in Alan Block papers. Block provides the names of other politicians in "The National Intelligence Service," 105–6.

63. Frank's conviction was overturned; on retrial, he received a trivial penalty of $500 for each count of the indictment. Department of Justice officials explained privately that despite evidence implicating Frank, they were unable to "prepare a sufficiently watertight case that would support indictments for conspiracy to kidnap." See State Department circular, November 22, 1957, in *FRUS, 1955–1957, VI, American Republics*.

64. David Talbot, *The Devil's Chessboard: Allen Dulles, the CIA, and the Rise of America's Secret Government* (New York: Harper, 2015), 323–29.

65. US Congress, Senate, Committee on the Judiciary, *Organized Crime in America, Hearings*, part 1, 98th Cong., 1st sess. (Washington, DC: US Government Printing Office, 1983), 266–67.

66. Crassweller, *Trujillo*, 329–41 (Abbes, Guatemala, and Honduras), 353 (Haiti).

67. Dick Russell, *The Man Who Knew Too Much* (New York: Carroll & Graf, 1992), 460 (Herminio Díaz García, head of security at the Hotel Havana Riviera's casino).

68. Besides Gallagher, Trujillo's supporters in Congress included Reps. Victor Anfuso (D-NY), Abraham Multer (D-NY), and Daniel Flood (D-PA). See Espaillat, *Trujillo*, 171, and Crassweller, *Trujillo*, 324–26. On Anfuso's ties to New York crime boss Frank Costello, see Ezio Costanzo, *The Mafia and the Allies: Sicily 1943 and the Return of the Mafia* (New York: Enigma Books, 2007), 81. On Multer, see Pearson and Anderson, *The Case against Congress*, 191–92. On Flood, see William Kashatus, *Dapper Dan Flood: The Controversial Life of a Congressional Power Broker* (University Park: Pennsylvania State University Press, 2010), 95, 133, 253.

69. For example, Lexington, Kentucky, betting pioneer Edward W. Curd, a some-time bookmaker for New York Mafia boss Frank Costello, fled to the Dominican Republic in the mid-1950s to avoid a criminal indictment for income tax evasion. Ornes, *Trujillo*, 257; Arne K. Lang, *Sports Betting and Bookmaking: An American History* (Lanham, MD: Rowman & Littlefield, 2016), 267; "Curd, Bookmaker Credited with Creating 'Juice,' Dies," *Las Vegas Sun*, May 16, 2002.

70. Leslie Velie, "Suckers in Paradise," *Saturday Evening Post*, March 28 1953, 32–33.

71. Justice Department memorandum, "Sequence of Events in Dominican Republic," US Congress, House of Representatives, Committee on the Judiciary, *Nomination of Gerald R. Ford to be Vice President of the United States, Hearings*, 93rd Cong., 1st sess. (Washington, DC: US Government Printing Office, 1973), 792; SAC, Miami, to Director, FBI, June 25, 1968, "Criminal Influence in Miami Hotels, Motels, and Night Clubs," NARA 124-10291-10389. Lansburgh operated the Flamingo hotel-casino in Las Vegas. In 1973, he pleaded guilty to defrauding the IRS by concealing Lansky's interest in the property. David G. Schwartz, *Suburban Xanadu: The Casino Resort on the Las Vegas Strip and Beyond* (London: Routledge, 2003), 143; "Morris Lansburgh Is Dead at 58," *New York Times*, February 11, 1977.

72. Ornes, *Trujillo*, 255.

73. Besides Johnny Meyer, the invitees were Wilbur Clark, Morris Kleinman, Allard Roen, and Eli Boyer. See FBI report of George M. Kirk Jr., Los Angeles, February 5, 1964, re "Eli Boyer," NARA 124-10278-10304.

74. Espaillat, *Trujillo*, 50–51.

75. "Trujillo Lets Columbus Have Scant Publicity in Island He Found," *St. Petersburg Times*, March 27, 1959; Martin, *Overtaken by Events*, 18.

76. Jim Barry, "Not for Nuthin," *Philadelphia City Paper*, July 5–12, 2001.

77. FBI report by SA J. Robert Pearce, Philadelphia, June 28, 1961, re Angelo Bruno, NARA 124-10205-10469. Other owners of the Monte Carlo casino included Joseph Stassi, a partner of Trafficante at the Sans Souci nightclub; Carlo Ippolito, a hoodlum from Trenton; Miami gangster Charles "the Blade" Tourine; and George Levine, operator of the Oriental Park Racetrack outside Havana.

78. FBI summary of interview with Bernard Allen, May 25, 1961, NARA 124-10205-10469; see also Joseph L. Tangel report, October 1, 1959, re "Activities of Top Hoodlums in the United States," NARA 124-10290-10313. The memo indicated that Bruno was close to former Miami consul Augusto Ferrando, discussed below.

79. Ornes, *Trujillo*, 6–7; Crasweller, *Trujillo*, 293–99; "Dominican Event All Set to Roll," *Billboard*, December 17, 1955, 71. On Nixon, see William Turner, *The Cuban Connection: Nixon, Castro, and the Mob* (Amherst, NY: Prometheus Books, 2013), Kindle locations 1736–56.

80. FBI report by J. Robert Pearce, Philadelphia, June 28, 1961, re Angelo Bruno, NARA 124-10205-10469; FBI report by J. Robert Pearce, Philadelphia, September 28, 1961, re Angelo Bruno, NARA 124-10197-10473; FBI report by J. Robert Pearce, January 16, 1959, re Angelo Bruno, NARA 124-10203-10263.

81. Tad Szulc, "Johnston Sought Dominican Help for a Gambler," *New York Times*, December 18, 1963.

82. Joseph A. Verica report to Director, FBI, re Angelo Bruno, July 28, 1962, NARA 124-10222-10224.

83. James Deakin, "Two Senators Trying to Save Gangster from Being Deported," *St. Louis Post-Dispatch*, June 5, 1955; Jack Williams, "As Block to Impastato," *Kansas City Times*, June 24, 1955; William Ouseley, *Open City: True Story of the KC Crime Family 1900–1950* (Kansas City: The Covington Group, 2008), 197–99. Nicolo Impastato moved French heroin via Havana and Tampa to Midwest markets. Jack Anderson, *Washington Exposé* (Washington, DC: Public Affairs Press, 1967), 453.

84. Crassweller, *Trujillo*, 346–48; Background Paper Prepared by the Officer in Charge of U.S. OAS Delegation Matters (Redington), "Situation in the Caribbean," August 7, 1959, *FRUS, 1958–1960, V, American Republics*, document 90.‡

85. FBI memorandum, May 21, 1959, "Anti–Fidel Castro Activities," NARA 124-10292-10156. Former ambassador Farland said, "Trujillo had the largest espionage system in the Caribbean." Joseph S. Farland, recorded interview by Larry Hackman, July 24, 1968, John F. Kennedy Library Oral History Program.

86. Memorandum from E. Tomlin Bailey, Director, State Department Office of Security, to FBI director John Edgar Hoover, May 1, 1959, re Anti–Fidel Castro Activities, NARA 124-90136-10054.

87. CIA cable from Havana to Director, March 31, 1959, NARA 104-10177-10433; see also David Grann, "The Yankee Commandante," *New Yorker*, May 28, 2012.

88. Espaillat, *Trujillo*, 146–48; Fabian Escalante, *The Secret War: CIA Covert Operations against Cuba 1959–62* (Ocean Press, 1995), ch. 2; Turner, *The Cuban Connection*, Kindle Edition), Kindle locations 1520–33.

89. Espaillat, *Trujillo*, 148–49; Crassweller, *Trujillo*, 349–50.

90. Colhoun, *Gangsterismo*, Kindle edition, locations 1266–78.

91. Espaillat, *Trujillo*, 144.

92. Aran Shetterly, *The Americano: Fighting with Castro for Cuba's Freedom* (Chapel Hill: Algonquin Books, 2007), 182.

93. Carrozza, *William D. Pawley*, 231–33. On Trujillo's efforts to unify anti-Castro exiles in Miami, Mexico, and the Dominican Republic, see SAC, Miami, to Director, FBI, May 15, 1959, file 105-1742-220, FBI Cuba 109-12-210—Volume 6—Serials 292–450, at http://maryferrell.org/showDoc.html?docId=146612#relPageId=7.

94. FBI memo from A. H. Belmont to Hoover, May 1, 1959, NARA 124-10294-10047.

95. Espaillat, *Trujillo*, 60–61.

96. Memorandum from E. Tomlin Bailey, Director, State Department Office of Security, to FBI Director Hoover, May 1, 1959, re Anti–Fidel Castro Activities, NARA 124-90136-10054 (Roberto "Chili" Mendoza).

97. The senior police official was Orlando Piedra; the Trafficante associate was Norman Rothman. See report by legal attaché in Havana to Director, FBI, June 25, 1958, re "American Gambling Activities in Cuba," NARA 124-90068-10101; FBI report by SA Thomas H. Errion, September 30, 1950, re Orlando Eleno Piedra, NARA 124-10280-10171; memorandum from E. Tomlin Bailey, Director, State Department Office of Security, to FBI Director John Edgar Hoover, May 1, 1959, re Anti–Fidel

Castro Activities, NARA 124-90136-10054; Colhoun, *Gangsterismo*, Kindle locations 1278–1312; Espaillat, *Trujillo*, 152.

98. Escalante, *The Secret War*, ch. 2. On joint counterrevolutionary operations by Trujillo and Jiménez in the Caribbean, see Aaron Coy Moulton, "Building Their Own Cold War in Their Own Backyard: The Transnational, International Conflicts in the Greater Caribbean Basin, 1944–1954," *Cold War History* 15 (2015), 135–54.

99. Shetterly, *The Americano*, 176–77 (FBI); Paul Bethel to Noel, June 30, 1959, NARA 124-90136-10241 (CIA). See also Ambassador Phillip Bonsal, Havana, to Secretary of State, August 6, 1959, NARA 124-90136-10104; FBI legal attaché, Havana, July 6, 1959, re "William Alexander Morgan," NARA 124-90136-10071.

100. FBI memo, January 8, 1959, re William Alexander Morgan, NARA 124-90136-10036; memo from CIA Deputy Director of Plans to Director, FBI, May 15, 1960, re William Alexander Morgan, NARA 124-90136-10174. Morgan worked for a Dayton company called Mus-ad that was said by Toledo police to be "hoodlum" controlled (FBI report by Leman Stafford Jr., Miami, March 9, 1960, re William Alexander Morgan, NARA 124-90136-10159). Two minor underworld associates of the firm were Joseph Yoppolo and Irving Shapiro (Shetterly, *The Americano*, 115).

101. McClellan Hearings, part 54, 19089.

102. FBI report by Leman Stafford Jr., Miami, March 9, 1960, re William Alexander Morgan, NARA 124-90136-10159; also Shetterly, *The Americano*, 162–64.

103. FBI report, Leman L. Stafford Jr., Miami, February 26, 1960, re Dominick Edward Bartone, NARA 124-10218-10123; FBI report by Michael H. Farrin, Cleveland, December 21, 1959, re Dominick Edward Bartone, NARA 124-10283-10237; FBI report by SA Michael Farrin, Cleveland, February 25, 1960, re Dominick Edward Bartone, NARA 124-10218-10127. On Triscaro's Mafia ties, see Greg Stricharchuk, "Jackie Presser: Media Muscle Man," *Cleveland Magazine*, October 1980; Peter Vaira and Douglas Roller, "Report on Organized Crime and the Labor Unions," Department of Justice, 1978, available at http://www.laborers.org/VAIRA_MEMO.html.

104. Moldea, *The Hoffa Wars*, 49.‡

105. William Patrick Dean, *Ultra-Large Aircraft, 1940–1970: The Development of Guppy and Expanded Fuselage Transports* (Jefferson, NC: McFarland, 2018), 49–58; Turner, *The Cuban Connection*, Kindle locations 1520–33.

106. Interview with Fredesvindo Bosque Cueto, April 7, 1960, by SA Leman Stafford Jr., Miami, NARA 124-90071-10043.‡

107. Report by SA Leman L. Stafford Jr., Miami, October 14, 1959, re "Dominick E. Bartone," NARA 124-10283-10227; report by SA Michael H. Farrin, Cleveland, December 21, 1959, re "Dominick Edward Bartone," NARA 124-10283-10237; report by SA Michael Farrin, Cleveland, February 25, 1960, re "Dominick Edward Bartone," NARA 124-10218-10127; FBI report, Leman L. Stafford Jr., Miami, February 26, 1960, re "Dominick Edward Bartone," NARA 124-10218-10123; report of SA Leman Stafford Jr., Miami, May 10, 1960, re "Dominick Edward Bartone," NARA 124-10221-10095; "Three from City 'Star' in Plane Deal Quiz," *Cleveland Plain Dealer*, July 1, 1959; "Two Plead Guilty to Arms Charges," *Miami News*, December 11, 1959; McClellan Hearings, 19042–105.

108. Report by SA Leman Stafford Jr., Miami, March 9, 1960, re William Alexander Morgan, NARA 124-90136-10159; interview with Alexander Rourke in FBI report, New York, January 18, 1960, re "Foreign Political Matters—Cuba Anti-Fidel Castro Activities," NARA 124-90071-10066.

109. FBI memo, Miami, December 14, 1961, re "Augusto Maria Ferrando," NARA 124-90136-10263; SAC, New York, to Director, FBI, December 7, 1960, re "Dominican Republic," NARA 124-90136-10214.

110. Report by SA Leman L. Stafford Jr., Miami, October 14, 1959, re Dominick E. Bartone, NARA 124-10283-10227; Espaillat, *Trujillo*, 148–49. In all, Morgan said he received $400,000 from the Dominicans; Espaillat said he received $500,000 in cash, plus another $100,000 for expenses.

111. FBI legal attaché, Havana (James Haverty), to Director, FBI, July 29, 1959, NARA 124-90136-10075.

112. CIA report, August 7, 1959, "Counter-Revolutionary Activities of William Alexander Morgan," NARA 124-90136-10089.

113. Cable from James Haverty, Legat, Havana, to Director, FBI, August 3, 1959, NARA 124-10283-10222.

114. US Department of State, *Foreign Relations of the United States, 1958–1960, Volume VI: Cuba* (Washington, DC: USGPO, 1991), 579.

115. Report of SA Leman Stafford Jr., Miami, October 14, 1959, re Dominick Bartone, NARA 124-10283-10227; R. Hart Phillips, "Castro Lionized for Tricking Foe," *New York Times*, August 16, 1959; Crassweller, *Trujillo*, 350–51; Shetterly, *The Americano*, 199–202; Espaillat, *Trujillo*, 158–60.[‡]

116. Colhoun, *Gangsterismo*, Kindle locations 1349–1381; report of SA Robert James Dwyer, Miami, September 14, 1959, re Anti–Fidel Castro Activities, NARA 124-90076-10166; Shetterly, *The Americano*, 196; *FRUS, 1958–1960, VI: Cuba*, 579.

117. Shetterly, *The Americano*, 208.

118. State Department dispatch, September 10, 1959, re "Local Reaction to Announcement of Loss of Citizenship of William Alexander Morgan," NARA 124-90136-10128.

119. Report by SAC, Cleveland, to Director, FBI, October 23, 1959, re Dominick Bartone, NARA 124-10283-10227; report of SA Leman Stafford Jr., Miami, August 17, 1959, re William Alexander Morgan, NARA 124-90136-10159; see also report of SA Leman L. Stafford Jr., Miami, October 14, 1959, re Dominick E. Bartone.

120. FBI report by Michael Farrin, Cleveland, May 7, 1961, re "Dominick Edward Bartone," NARA 124-10215-10343.

121. FBI report by SA Thomas Errion, Miami, November 17, 1959, re Rolando Arcadio Masferrer Rojas, NARA 124-90089-10230.

122. Turner, *The Cuban Connection*, Kindle locations 1598–1637.

123. Report by SA Thomas Errion, Miami, November 17, 1959, re Rolando Arcadio Masferrer Rojas, NARA 124-90089-10230; report by SA John Lenihan, New York, January 4, 1960, re Bernard J. Ezhaya, NARA 124-10280-10177.

124. CIA interview with Rothman, June 29, 1961, NARA 1994.04.11.11:57:40:820005.

125. SAC, Miami, to Director, FBI, September 8, 1959, NARA 124-90100-10267. "FBI reports indicate that Rothman supplied dynamite to an unnamed Cuban exile

group to blow up Cuban aircraft at the Miami International Airport in August 1959. He sold more than 100 pounds of dynamite to another Cuban exile group 'to blow up the Revolución newspaper' in Havana. Rothman also assembled a private air force to carry out bombing missions in Cuba. North American mercenary pilots flying small airplanes set sugar-cane fields ablaze with incendiary bombs, and destroyed sugar mills with iron bombs in a campaign to destabilize the Cuban economy. . . . FBI records also disclose that Rothman, Stretch Rubin, and Mafia arms dealer Joseph Merola purchased a B-26 aircraft for bombing missions in Cuba." Colhoun, *Gangster-ismo*, Kindle locations 1382–1415.

126. FBI report by Allan Trankley, Miami, January 31, 1969, re Norman Rothman, NARA 124-10226-10305; report by SA James D. Hayes, Miami, February 16, 1960, re Alberto Juan Ardura Moya, NARA 124-10300-10063; report by SA Stephen J. Labadie, Tampa, June 14, 1961, re Santo Trafficante Jr., NARA 124-10199-10343; report of John Lenihan, Miami, April 29, 1963, re Charles W. Bray, Felix Alderisio, Santo Trafficante, Pan American Bank of Miami (Victim), NARA 124-10195-10472; SAC Miami to Director, FBI, July 17, 1959, re Fulgencio Batista y Zaldivar, NARA 124-10213-10448.[‡]

127. FBI report of SA Richard Gordon Douce, Cleveland, July 31, 1959, re "Stuart Sutor," NARA 124-90100-10230; report by Edward Kinzer, Chicago, May 10, 1959, re "Bernard J. Ezhaya," NARA 124-10280-10185; SAC, Miami, to Director, FBI, August 21, 1961, re Edward Browder Jr., NARA 124-10206-10434; "Mannarino, Canada Crime Chief Linked," *Pittsburgh Press*, February 24, 1962; "Mannarino Prosecution Ends Case," *Pittsburgh Press*, March 1, 1962.

128. CIA memorandum, July 10, 1961, re Norman Rothman, NARA 1994.04.11.11:57:40:820005. Rothman was a partner in the El Morocco club in Cuba with two of Cotroni's associates from the Canadian end of the "French Connection": Lucien Rivard and Paul Mondoloni. A 1958 FBN report said that Mondoloni was selling Rothman and various Italian American criminals up to 150 kilograms a month of heroin (Valentine, *The Strength of the Wolf*, 187).

129. Federal Bureau of Narcotics report, "Joseph ZICARELLI," April 1961, in Douglas Valentine papers, National Security Archive, George Washington University.

130. "Defendant Cleared in Bond Theft Case," *New York Times*, March 3, 1962; "Mannarino Acquitted in Bond Theft," *Pittsburgh Post-Gazette*, March 14, 1962. In November 1971, however, Rothman was found guilty in federal court of interstate transportation of stolen securities in a separate case. FBI memorandum from SAC, Miami, to Director, FBI, re Norman Rothman, February 24, 1972, NARA 124-10226-10309.

131. Report by SA George E. Davis, Cleveland, March 30, 1959, re "Ohio National Guard Armory Theft," NARA 124-90100-10137; report by Richard Gordon Douce, Pittsburgh, April 20, 1959, re "Ohio National Guard Armory Theft," NARA 124-90100-10162; CIA, "Memorandum for the Record," April 25, 1975, re "Rothman, Norman," NARA 1993.07.23.08:09:01:840410; FBI memo from Special Agent in Charge, Miami, to Director, FBI, June 27, 1961, NARA 124-10289-10371; "6 Convicted of Gun-Running," *New York Times*, February 5, 1960; Colhoun, *Gangsterismo*,

Kindle locations 3124–39; Paul Meskil, "How U.S. Made Unholy Alliance with the Mafia," *New York Daily News*, April 23, 1975.

132. SAC, Miami, to FBI Director, April 29, 1960, re "Anti–Fidel Castro Activities," NARA 124-10221-10094.‡

133. Key sources include US Congress, Senate, Select Committee to Study Governmental Operations with Respect to Intelligence Activities, *Alleged Assassination Plots Involving Foreign Leaders: An Interim Report of the Select Committee to Study Government Relations with Respect to Intelligence Activities, United States Senate* (Washington, DC: US Government Printing Office, 1975), hereafter "*Alleged Assassination Plots*," and US Congress, House of Representatives, Select Committee on Assassinations, *Investigation of the Assassination of President John F. Kennedy of the US House of Representatives, Ninety-Fifth Congress, Second Session: Appendix to Hearings,* Vol. X, *Anti-Castro Activities and Organizations, Lee Harvey Oswald in New Orleans, CIA Plots against Castro, Rose Cheramie* (Washington, DC: US Government Printing Office, 1979).

134. Government informant Carl Noll implicated Guatemalan interior minister Eduardo Rodriguez Genis and his law partner, Antonio Valladares, in the heroin trade, along with Marcello, Sam Mannarino, and Norman Rothman. See interview with Carl Irving Noll by George C. Corcoran Jr., narcotic agent, December 18, 1959, Misc. Narcotic Files 0660 Foreign Reports Germany thru Hawaii, box 157, Records of the Bureau of Narcotics and Dangerous Drugs, RG 170; report by Special Agent Regis Kennedy, February 8, 1960, NARA 124-10214-10022; report by Special Agent Furman G. Boggan, September 10, 1960, NARA 124-10216-10166. Valladares, who was described in one CIA memo as "anti commie Guat lawyer in Mexico City," appears to have contributed to plots to overthrow the Arbenz government in 1954. See CIA memo from Lincoln to director, CIA, January 21, 1954, https://www.cia.gov/library/readingroom/docs/DOC_0000914100.pdf.

135. FBI memos from special agent in charge, Milwaukee, to Director, FBI, March 24, 1962, NARA 124-10206-10310 and April 6, 1962, NARA 124-10206-10305; memo from special agent in charge, Washington Field Office, to director, FBI, May 1, 1962, NARA 124-10206-10297; David E. Kaiser, *The Road to Dallas: The Assassination of John F. Kennedy* (Cambridge: Harvard University Press, 2008), 138. According to former Justice Department prosecutor G. Robert Blakey, wiretaps revealed that Marcello flew into Miami aboard a Dominican Air Force jet. G. Robert Blakey and Richard Billings, *The Plot to Kill the President* (New York: Times Books, 1981), 243.

136. SNIE, "Threats to the Stability of the U.S. Military Facilities Position in the Caribbean Area and Brazil," March 10, 1959, in *FRUS, 1958–1960, V, American Republics*, document 111.

137. Espaillat, *Trujillo*, 152–56; background paper prepared by the Officer in Charge of US OAS Delegation Matters (Redington), "Situation in the Caribbean," August 7, 1959, *FRUS, 1958–1960, V, American Republics*, document 90. Trujillo's son Ramfis led the operation to crush the abortive invasion in June 1959, including the cold-blooded murder of captives. Crassweller, *Trujillo*, 365–66.

138. Crassweller, *Trujillo*, 357–59, 371–72; Special National Intelligence Estimate, SNIE 80/1-59, December 29, 1950, "The Situation in the Caribbean through 1960," *FRUS, 1958–1960, V, American Republics*, document 126.

139. Crassweller, *Trujillo*, 382–84; "The Next in Line," *The Reporter*, February 18, 1960, 2–4.

140. *Alleged Assassination Plots*, 192 (citing Special Group Minutes, February 10, 1960).

141. McKeever, *The Galíndez Case*, Kindle locations 4998 and 4623 (alleged Trujillo payoffs to Smathers); Pearson and Anderson, *The Case against Congress*, 410 (law firm); Robert Sherrill, *Gothic Politics in the Deep South: Stars of the New Confederacy* (New York: Grossman, 1968), 181 ("good friend"). A friendly biographer insists that Smathers was "far from being an ally of the dictator" and that "there is no evidence to suggest any 'payola.'" Brian Lewis Crispell, *Testing the Limits: George Armistead Smathers and Cold War America* (Athens: University of Georgia Press, 1999), 160–61.

142. Carrozza, *William D. Pawley*, 279; Hall, *Sugar and Power*, 93–94; Dearborn oral history.‡

143. Memorandum of a Conversation, Department of State, Washington, March 18, 1960, in *FRUS, 1958–1960, VI, Cuba*, document 487. The same month, Smathers wrote his friend and presidential candidate Sen. John Kennedy, "I hold no brief for any dictatorship . . . [but] we can only be honest in saying that it is better to deal with one which is well disposed towards the United States than one which is violently anti-American." Crispell, *Testing the Limits*, 161.

144. Carrozza, *William D. Pawley*, 236; JDH memo to Vice President Nixon, May 11, 1960, in "Pawley, William Douglas" folder, box 582, Nixon papers, Nixon Library.

145. Ambassador Joseph S. Farland, US Embassy in Ciudad Trujillo, to Richard Rubottom Jr., Assistant Secretary of State for Inter-American Affairs, March 22, 1960, Rusk exhibit #1, NARA 157-10005-10249.

146. "Editorial Note," *FRUS, 1958–1960, V, American Republics*, document 305; *Alleged Assassination Plots*, 192; Hall, *Sugar and Power*, 94–95.‡

147. Memorandum of discussion at the 453d meeting of the National Security Council, July 25, 1960, *FRUS, 1958–1960, VI, Cuba*, document 565.

148. Crassweller, *Trujillo*, 414–19.‡

149. Frank Chavez Jr., secretary-treasurer of Teamsters Local 901 in San Juan, was considered by the FBI to be "armed and dangerous." He was investigated for violating the Foreign Agents Registration Act because of his ties to Trujillo's former intelligence chief Arturo Espaillat. After the assassination of Trujillo, Chavez allegedly conspired with the dictator's brothers Héctor and José Arizmendi to stage a coup against Balaguer and was further implicated in killing two pro-democracy activists. FBI report by SA John A. Norris Jr., San Juan, February 20, 1962, re "Frank Chavez, Jr.," NARA 124-10201-10432; SAC New York to Director, FBI, April 15, 1963, re "Criminal Informant," NARA 124-90066-10211. Chavez himself was murdered in 1967. "Hoffa Backer Killed in San Juan Office," *Chicago Tribune*, August 17, 1967.

150. Memorandum for the Record, "Record and Related Policy Decisions on Passing Arms to Dominican Dissidents," June 7, 1961, Rusk exhibit #4, NARA 157-10005-10249.

151. *Alleged Assassination Plots*, 193–94.

152. "Editorial Note," *FRUS, 1958–1960, V, American Republics*, document 305; *Alleged Assassination Plots*, 195.

153. *Alleged Assassination Plots*, 196–205; Memorandum for the Record, "Record and Related Policy Decisions on Passing Arms to Dominican Dissidents," June 7, 1961, Rusk exhibit #4, NARA 157-10005-10249; telegram from the consulate general in the Dominican Republic to the Department of State, January 4, 1961, *FRUS, 1961–1963, XII, American Republics*, document 300.

154. Airgram from the consulate general in the Dominican Republic to the Department of State, March 22, 1961, *FRUS, 1961–1963, XII, American Republics*, document 304.

155. Christian Herter memorandum to President Kennedy, "Possible Action to Prevent Castroist Takeover of Dominican Republic," April 14, 1961, Rusk exhibit #2, NARA 157-10005-10249.

156. Memorandum from J. Edgar Hoover to Robert Kennedy, August 10, 1961, "Dominican Lobbying Activities in the United States," NARA 124-10183-10253.

157. Memorandum of Conversation, February 14, 1961, re "Sugar," in *FRUS, 1961–63, IX, Foreign Economic Policy*, document 337.

158. At its peak, the FBI's probe included twelve telephone taps, three electronic bugs, and physical surveillance on eleven individuals. FBI memo from W. R. Wannall to William Sullivan, "Dominican Lobbying Activities in the United States," December 22, 1966, NARA 124-10187-10079.

159. Weiner, *Enemies*, 224, 485n.

160. Cassini sounded the alarm on the basis of reports passed to him by his society friend and Dominican diplomat, Porfirio Rubirosa. Cassini, *I'd Do It All Over Again*, 200–201.

161. Hall, *Sugar and Power*, 114; on Murphy's career and politics, see "Robert D. Murphy, Diplomat, Dies at 83," *New York Times*, January 11, 1978.

162. Murphy's April 16 letter to Joseph Kennedy is available from the Kennedy Library's digital collection, identifier JFKPOF-115a-006-p0003, and online at https://www.jfklibrary.org/asset-viewer/archives/JFKPOF/115a/JFKPOF-115a-006.

163. Memorandum from the President's Special Assistant for National Security Affairs (Bundy) to President Kennedy, May 2, 1961, *FRUS, 1961–1963, XII, American Republics*, document 306.

164. Hall, *Sugar and Power*, 115.

165. National Security Council action May 5, 1961, approved by President Kennedy May 16, 1961, in *Alleged Assassination Plots*, 209.

166. Memorandum of conversation with Adolf Berle, May 3, 1961, Rusk exhibit #11, NARA 157-10005-10249; *Alleged Assassination Plots*, 208.

167. Turner, *The Cuban Connection*, Kindle locations 1816–17. Senator Smathers spoke with President Kennedy about the possibility of assassinating Trujillo and recalled that JFK "was not as outraged about that as I was." See testimony of Sen. George Smathers before the Committee to Study Governmental Operations with Respect to Intelligence Activities, July 23, 1975, executive session, NARA 157-10005-10252.

168. *Alleged Assassination Plots*, 205, 213.

169. *Alleged Assassination Plots*, 200–201.

170. *Alleged Assassination Plots*, 214.

171. Testimony of Dean Rusk before the Committee to Study Governmental Operations with Respect to Intelligence Activities, executive session, July 10, 1975, NARA 157-10005-10249.

172. Telegram from the Department of State to the Consulate General in the Dominican Republic, June 1, 1961, *FRUS, 1961–1963, XII, American Republics*, document 309.

173. Telegram from the Consulate General in the Dominican Republic to the Department of State, February 24, 1961, *FRUS, 1961–1963, XII, American Republics*, document 303.

174. Howard J. Wiarda, *The Aftermath of the Trujillo Dictatorship: The Emergence of a Pluralist Political System in the Dominican Republic* (PhD dissertation, University of Florida, 1965), 64; memorandum from the President's Special Assistant (Richard Goodwin) to the President's Special Assistant for National Security Affairs (William Bundy), June 8, 1961, *FRUS, 1961–1963, XII, American Republics*, document 312; Special National Intelligence Estimate, "The Dominican Situation," July 25, 1961, *FRUS, 1961–1963, XII, American Republics*, document 317.

175. Carrozza, *William D. Pawley*, 289.

176. State Department paper, "Course of Action in the Dominican Republic," July 17, 1961, *FRUS, 1961–1963, XII, American Republics*, document 315.

177. Wiarda, *The Aftermath*, 69.

178. Abraham Lowenthal, *The Dominican Intervention* (Cambridge: Harvard University Press, 1972), 13; Martin, *Overtaken by Events*, 204 (graft) and 84–340 on his role as ambassador in 1962.

179. Goff and Locker, "The Violence of Domination," 263.

180. Lowenthal, *The Dominican Intervention*, 14, 27–28.

181. Theodore Draper, "The Roots of the Dominican Crisis," *The New Leader*, May 24, 1965; Eric Thomas Chester, *Rag-Tags, Scum, Riff-Raff, and Commies: The U.S. Intervention in the Dominican Republic, 1965–1966* (New York: Monthly Review Press, 2001), 30–33.

182. Martin, *Overtaken by Events*, 361.‡

183. "Sequence of Events in Dominican Republic," Gerald Ford nomination hearings, Appendix 7, 631–32.

184. FBI report by SA Eugene J. Hindes, New York, December 28, 1962, re "Salvatore Granello," NARA 124-90066-10170; report by Eugene J. Hindes, New York, June 27, 1962, re "Salvatore Granello," NARA 124-90066-10093; report by Eugene Hindes, New York, July 30, 1963, re "Salvatore Granello," NARA 124-90066-10189.

185. The two associates were veteran gamblers Joseph Nesline of Washington, D.C., and Charles "the Blade" Tourine of Florida. FBI report by SA John R. Buckley, Washington Field Office, June 12, 1963, re "Joseph Francis Nesline," NARA 124-90096-10144; SAC Miami to Director, FBI, July 10, 1963, re "Interview Program: Criminal Intelligence Matters," NARA 124-10207-10079.‡

186. Giancana's chief agent on this mission was Chicago gambler Leslie Kruse. Memo from SAC Chicago to FBI, June 19, 1963, NARA 124-10196-10107; SAC,

Chicago, to FBI, June 28, 1963, re "Samuel M. Giancana," NARA 124-10198-10004; SA Marshall E. Rutland, Chicago, to FBI, August 5, 1963, re "Samuel M. Giancana," NARA 124-10354-10120; report by Chicago SA Elliott W. Anderson, September 19, 1963, re "Leslie Earl Kruse," NARA 124-90086-10265; report by James P. Flynn, January 29, 1964, re "La Cosa Nostra," NARA 124-10206-10406; Reid and Demaris, *Green Felt Jungle*, 73 (Licavoli and Desert Inn). Ed Reid notes that Giancana's search for gambling opportunities in the Dominican Republic and Jamaica started in 1962. Ed Reid, *The Grim Reapers: The Anatomy of Organized Crime in America* (Chicago: Henry Regnery, 1969), 129.

187. FBI teletype from SAC, New York, to Director, FBI, August 26, 1963, NARA 124-90024-10042.

188. FBI memo, May 7, 1964, "Proposed Business Activity in the Dominican Republic by Angelo Bruno and Others," NARA 124-10211-10363 and 124-10211-10373.

189. *Miami Herald*, September 18, 1949.‡

190. Testimony of José Alemán before US Congress, House of Representatives, Select Committee on Assassinations, *Investigation of the Assassination of President John F. Kennedy, Hearings,* 95th Cong., 2nd sess. Washington, DC: US Government Printing Office, 1979, V, 303–304; testimony of Santo Trafficante, ibid., 374–75. Hereafter HSCA hearings.

191. FBI memo, May 7, 1964, "Proposed Business Activity in the Dominican Republic by Angelo Bruno and Others," NARA 124-10211-10363 and 124-10211-10373; report by SA Stephen J. Labadie, Tampa, December 11, 1963, re "Santo Trafficante, Jr.," NARA 124-10211-10211.

192. FBI report by SA Robert W. Holmes, July 15, 1963, "Angelo Bruno," NARA 124-10283-10475.

193. Tad Szulc, "Johnston Sought Dominican Help for a Gambler," *New York Times*, December 18, 1963; Ovid Demaris, *Dirty Business: The Corporate-Political-Money-Power Game* (New York: Harper's Magazine Press, 1974), 312.

194. "Baker Loans Put at $2.5 Million," *New York Times*, March 4, 1964; "Bosch's Own Woes Called Spur to Crisis," *Chicago Tribune*, May 8, 1963; G. R. Schreiber, *The Bobby Baker Affair* (Chicago: Henry Regnery Company, 1964), 135–36 (Baker and Levinson); FBI report by SA Robert W. Holmes, July 15, 1963, "Angelo Bruno," NARA 124-10283-10475.

195. Martin, *Overtaken by Events*, 364; Hoover memo to Attorney General Katzenbach, "Dominican Situation Internal Security," June 3, 1965, NARA 124-10186-10055.

196. Memos by Hoover to RFK re "Dominican Lobbying Activities in the United States," May 25 and 31; June 2, 8, 14, 19, and 23; July 3, 11, 13, 14, 17, and 24; August 10, 25, and 30; September 15; October 16; and November 2, 1961; January 4 and 30, 1962, NARA 124-10183-10253.

197. Trujillo may have been an investor as well. FBI memorandum, February 23, 1961, re "Foreign Political Matters—Dominican Republic," in Alan Block papers; for more on International Airport Hotel System, see Reid, *Grim Reapers*, 190–96.

198. On bananas, see Irwin Alpert, "Mr. New Haven," *Sunday Herald* (New Haven, CT), May 11, 1958; "Banana Injunction Granted in Miami," *St. Petersburg*

Times, May 1, 1947; FBI report of Eugene J. Hindes, November 14, 1962, re Salvatore Granello, NARA 124-90066-10202. On fighter plane deal: FBI report of Edward J. Devins, February 26, 1960, re "Enrique A. Garcia, Jr.," NARA 124-90076-10039; FBI report by Thomas G. Forsyth III, September 24, 1962, re "Samuel Mannarino," NARA 124-10286-10008; Schreiber, *The Bobby Baker Affair*, 137. Cooper's conviction was upheld on appeal in 1964 (*Wall Street Journal*, June 1, 1981).‡

199. FBI report by Eugene J. Hindes, New York, 12/28/62, re Salvatore Granello, NARA 124-90066-10170 (front man); "Fast Road to Fortune Poses Riddles," *Milwaukee Journal*, February 28, 1964. Testimony by Cooper's lawyer, George Simon, suggests that Cooper also played a role with Morris Lansburgh in operating the Jaragua Hotel (Bobby Baker hearings, 1018).

200. Demaris, *Dirty Business*, 309.

201. The Parvin Foundation's most famous director was US Supreme Court Justice William Douglas. He also attended Bosch's inauguration and advised him on writing a new constitution. US Congress, House of Representatives, Committee on the Judiciary, Special Subcommittee on H. Res. 920, final report, *Associate Justice William O. Douglas*, 91st Cong., 2nd sess. (Washington, DC: US Government Printing Office, 1970), 413–16, 756–58; "Sequence of Events in Dominican Republic," Gerald Ford nomination hearings, Appendix 7, 630–31; Demaris, *Dirty Business*, 311–12; Chester, *Rag-Tags, Scum, Riff-Raff, and Commies*, 20–24, 29–30, 35; Martin, *Overtaken by Events*, 309–10, 374–75; "Kaplan Fund, Cited as C.I.A. 'Conduit,' Lists Unexplained $395,000 Grant," *New York Times*, September 3, 1964; "Thomas Defends CIA-Aided Work," *New York Times*, February 22, 1967; "Douglas Reported to Have Had Strange Ties with Red Once Active in 'Uprisings,'" *Gettysburg Times*, December 16, 1970.

202. Keith Wheeler, "Scandal Grows and Grows in Washington," *Life*, November 22, 1963; Bobby Baker, *Wheeling and Dealing: Confessions of a Capitol Hill Operator* (New York: W. W. Norton, 1978), 211.

203. Robert Lacey, *Little Man: Meyer Lansky and the Gangster Life* (New York: Little Brown, 1991), 229 (Lansky and Hotel Nacional lease); Hank Messick, *The Silent Syndicate* (New York: Macmillan, 1967), 274 (Cleveland Syndicate).

204. Wallace Turner, "Baker Assisted Nevada Gambler in Business Deal," *New York Times*, November 7, 1963; Reid, *Grim Reapers*, 131.

205. Testimony of John Gates, chairman of Intercontinental Hotels, in Bobby Baker hearings, 1389.

206. Reid, *Grim Reapers*, 125–27; Fred Black testimony in Bobby Baker hearings, 442; Gene Blake, "U.S. Sifts Baker Link to Gamblers in S&L," *Washington Post*, January 18, 1964.

207. Demaris, *Dirty Business*, 312; Reid, *Grim Reapers*, 135; Baker, *Wheeling and Dealing*, 168.

208. FBI report by SA Edward Hegarty, December 24, 1964, "Angelo Bruno," NARA 124-10218-10146.

209. Draper, "The Roots of the Dominican Crisis"; Chester, *Rag-Tags, Scum, Riff-Raff, and Commies*, 38–41. For indications that the military coup was financed by US business interests in the country, see remarks of Sen. Wayne Morse, *Congressional Record*, 1963, 18483.

210. Ronald Hilton, "Report on Santo Domingo," *New York Times*, October 1, 1963.

211. Lowenthal, *The Dominican Intervention*, 42–43; Chester, *Rag-Tags, Scum, Riff-Raff, and Commies*, 42.

212. Teletype from FBI, Miami, April 24, 1964, re "Angelo Bruno," NARA 124-10211-10350; report by SA Edward D. Hegarty, Philadelphia, August 20, 1964, re "Angelo Bruno," NARA 124-10225-10302.

213. Report from SA Stephen J. Labadie, Tampa, to FBI, August 7, 1964, re Santo Trafficante, NARA 124-10215-10002 and 124-10215-10002; FBI report, June 15, 1965, re "Santo Trafficante, Jr.," NARA 124-10306-10012; FBI memo, May 7, 1964, "Proposed Business Activity in the Dominican Republic by Angelo Bruno and Others," NARA 124-10211-10363 and 124-10211-10373; SAC Miami to Director, FBI, April 29, 1965, re "Michael Julius McLaney," NARA 124-90154-10178.

214. Airtel from SAC, Philadelphia, to FBI Director, May 28, 1964, re "Angelo Bruno," NARA 124-10225-10236.

215. In 1964, Hoffa's attorney Morris Shenker visited the Dominican Republic to consider buying the Hispañola Hotel with associates in the Kansas City Mafia but was discouraged by the country's political turmoil (Denny Walsh, "A Two-Faced Crime Fight in St. Louis," *Life*, May 29, 1970, 31). At the time, Shenker was Missouri coordinator for the Johnson-Humphrey campaign.

216. Theodore Draper, "A Case of Defamation: U.S. Intelligence Versus Juan Bosch," *New Republic*, February 19, 1966, and February 26, 1966; Weiner, *Enemies*, 253–63.

217. This was the first US invasion of a Latin America nation in nearly forty years, and the third in the history of the Dominican Republic (1905 and 1916). For accounts, see Lowenthal, *The Dominican Intervention*, and Chester, *Rag-Tags, Scum, Riff-Raff, and Commies.*[‡]

218. Fred Goff and Michael Locker, "The Nationalist Pivot," in Horowitz, ed., *Latin American Radicalism*, 280–82; "2 Eisenhower Aides Given Democratic Campaign Jobs," *New York Times*, September 21, 1964 (Rabb).

219. FBI memo from SAC, New York, to Director, FBI, July 12, 1965, NARA 124-10301-10038; FBI memo from W. R. Wannall to William Sullivan, May 18, 1965, re "I. Irving Davidson," NARA 124-10301-10046; CIA memo from M. Forsythe to JMWAVE, August 23, 1967, NARA 104-10216-10064.

220. Abe Fortas, memorandum for the record, May 15, 1965, re "Contact with Dr. Joaquin Balaguer," *FRUS, 1964–1968, XXXII, Dominican Republic, Cuba, Haiti, Guyana*, doc. 70. The State Department's Historical Office mistakenly conflates Irving Davidson with "C. J. Davidson," a pseudonym used by Fortas for security. Fortas gained another personal connection to the Dominican Republic and the mob in 1966, when his wife, Carol Agger, began working for the Parvin Foundation.

221. See, for example, CIA memorandum from Deputy Director for Plans to Director of Central Intelligence (Richard Helms), December 8, 1966, NARA 104-10234-10259; CIA Intelligence Information Cable, July 22, 1965, NARA 124-10301-10034; FBI memorandum from SAC, New York, to Director, FBI, July 12, 1965, NARA 124-10301-10038.[‡]

222. In late 1965, CIA director Richard Helms told his covert operations chief that President Johnson had told him several times that "he expected the Agency to devote the necessary personnel and material resources in the Dominican Republic required to win the presidential election for the candidate favored by the United States Government. The President's statements were unequivocal. He wants to win the election, and he expects the Agency to arrange for this to happen." See Memorandum from Acting Director of Central Intelligence Helms to the Deputy Director for Plans of the Central Intelligence Agency (Fitzgerald), December 29, 1965, in *FRUS, 1964–1968, XXXII, Dominican Republic, Cuba, Haiti, Guyana,* doc. 151. Chester adds, "Balaguer's campaign benefitted from the covert aid and advice given by CIA experts in political and psychological warfare, while Bosch's base of support was eroded by successive waves of terror as semi-official death squads exacted their vengeance on rebel fighters and PRD militants. . . . In the end, only massive fraud could ensure Balaguer's victory." Chester, *Rag-Tags, Scum, Riff-Raff, and Commies,* 9; see also Weiner, *Enemies,* 263, and Norman Gall, "The Strange Dominican Election," *The New Leader,* June 20, 1966, 3–7.

223. Peter Weiss, "Gallagher Aided CIA's Dominican Activities," *Bergen Record,* June 21, 1973; memorandum from Vice President Humphrey to President Johnson, July 5, 1966, re "Visit to the Dominican Republic for the Inauguration of President Balaguer, June 30–July 2, 1966," Johnson Library, declassified June 10, 1994.

224. Walter Pincus, "Dominican Has D.C. Lobbyist," *The Evening Star* (Washington, DC), June 9, 1965; FBI memorandum from SAC, New York, to Director, FBI, July 12, 1965, NARA 124-10301-10038; FBI report on Irving Davidson, correlation summary, July 30, 1969, NARA 124-10302-10106 (Davidson); Russell Sackett, Sandy Smith, and William Lambert, "The Congressman and the Hoodlum," *Life,* August 9, 1968, 24 (Hoffman and Zicarelli). An associate of Zicarelli recalled seeing the mobster in Hoffman's office with Balaguer in 1963 (FBI report by SA Paul Durkin, Newark, August 16, 1965, re "Harold Konigsberg," NARA 124-10348-10067).

225. McKeever, *The Galíndez Case,* Kindle location 5196; Chester, *Rag-Tags, Scum, Riff-Raff, and Commies,* 272–74.

226. On Weisl's early support for Johnson, see Robert Dallek, *Lone Star Rising: Lyndon Johnson and His Times, 1908–1960* (New York: Oxford University Press, 1991), 162–63. Dallek notes that during the critical 1948 Senate election, Weisl "arranged contributions from wealthy New York attorneys and movie people like George Skouras of Twentieth Century-Fox and Howard Hughes of RKO" (308). As Paramount's corporate attorney, Weisl also lined up support for Johnson among managers of Texas movie theaters controlled by Paramount. Weisl sat on the board of Lehman Brothers, which managed Johnson's investments. He also helped secure advertisers for Johnson's radio and TV stations (Michael Janeway, *The Fall of the House of Roosevelt: Brokers of Ideas and Power from FDR to LBJ* (New York: Columbia University Press, 2004), 41, 160. Lew Wasserman, the powerful head of Music Corporation of America (MCA), recalled, "I first got in the LBJ orbit indirectly when he ran for Congress. Edwin Weisl, who was a dear friend of the president's and at that point in time was attorney and an old friend of mine. He was our attorney corporately and my personal attorney in the East. . . . And he came along and said

he wanted contributions for some fellows running for Congress and, subsequently, contributions for some fellows running for the Senate." Lew Wasserman, oral history interview, December 21, 1973, by Joe B. Frantz, LBJ Library. Harry McPherson, who worked closely with Johnson in the Senate and White House, recalled the role of attorney Gerald Siegel as a liaison between Johnson and the Jewish community: "Gerry Siegel was in contact with a man, and I remember the name of Barney Balaban, who was, I think, the head of Paramount Pictures and very active as a friend of Israel. Johnson's connection and Gerry Siegel's connection in 1957, in the early part of that, with Paramount was through Edwin Weisl Sr., who was later to come down and be the counsel of the space investigation when the Russians put up Sputnik. Weisl and Eliot Janeway and others had produced a lot of Jewish money for Johnson way back. And my understanding is . . . that it started when Johnson first ran, that he got some money from Jewish contributors in New York." Harry McPherson oral history interview, September 19, 1985, by Michael Gillette, LBJ Library. Connie Bruck characterizes Weisl as Johnson's "Wall Street mentor" and notes that he was one of the first advisers Johnson called after the assassination of President Kennedy. Bruck, *When Hollywood Had a King*, 217–18.

227. Vance first worked closely with Johnson in the late 1950s, when he joined Weisl to staff special hearings chaired by Johnson on the Soviet Union's launch of the *Sputnik* satellite. In 1960, Vance followed Weisl to the Democratic convention in Los Angeles to promote Johnson as a presidential candidate. Cyrus Vance oral history interview, November 3, 1969, by Paige E. Mulhollan, LBJ Library.

228. Goff and Locker, "The Nationalist Pivot," 287; Donald Bartlett and James Steele, *Howard Hughes: His Life and Madness* (New York: W. W. Norton, 1979), 414–22; Lewis H. Diuguid, "The New Imperialism? Gulf & Western Cuts Cane and Red Tape in Caribbean," *Washington Post*, June 7, 1970.

229. Chester, *Rag-Tags, Scum, Riff-Raff, and Commies*, 273; Alan Riding, "The Caribbean Role of G&W," *New York Times*, June 24, 1975; Pamela Hollie, "G&W to Sell Dominican Holdings," *New York Times*, June 13, 1984. In 1966, before G&W moved in, Bobby Baker's associate José Antonio Benítez, head of the Democratic Party in Puerto Rico, had tried to purchase the Hotel Hispaniola after conferring with Irving Davidson (FBI correlation summary, July 30, 1969, "I. Irving Davidson," NARA 124-10302-10106).

230. One author describes the company as "synonymous with the evils associated with foreign control. Gulf & Western, through such activities as union-busting and bribery, managed to antagonize both the left and the right. . . . Sometimes referred to as a 'state within a state,' its annual sales exceeded the nation's GNP. . . . The company also held a major share of the tourist industry, with its own multi-million dollar resort complexes (Casa del Campo and Altos de Chavon) in La Romana, as well as control of luxury hotels in Santo Domingo. In 1969, Gulf & Western set up an industrial free zone (in which goods are manufactured using cheap Dominican labor) near La Romana—the first company to do so—under a 30-yr. government contract." Harry S. Pariser, *Adventure Guide to the Dominican Republic*, 2nd ed. (Edison, NJ: Hunter Publishing, 1995), 42. Other critical accounts include "Gulf & Western in the Dominican Republic," *The Sisyphus Papers*, V (September 1976), 1–26; Fred Goff, "The Gulf

& Westernization of the Dominican Republic," *NACLA Latin America and Empire Report*, April 1975; and Penny Lernoux, *Cry of the People* (New York: Penguin Books, 1982), 236–42. Gulf & Western noted in its own defense that it paid workers better than state-run sugar operations in the country, and it reinvested millions of dollars to create new jobs. Diuguid, "The New Imperialism," *Washington Post*, June 7, 1970.

231. Seymour Hersh, "U.S. Probe of G&W Centers on Allegedly Hidden Finances," *International Herald Tribune*, July 27, 1977; Jeff Gerth, "Overstating of Profits Laid to Gulf & Western," *New York Times*, August 17, 1979; Jeff Gerth, "Prolonged Court Fight Looms as G&W Halts SEC Talks," *New York Times*, August 21, 1979; Larry Kramer, "G&W Accused of Securities Violations," *Washington Post*, November 27, 1979.

232. Dennis McDougal, *The Last Mogul: Lew Wasserman, MCA, and the Hidden History of Hollywood* (New York: Crown, 1998), 367, 232, 319; Russo, *Supermob*, 42–43, 320–21, and *passim* on Korshak; Bruck, *When Hollywood Had a King*, 46, 217, and *passim* on Stein, Korshak, and the mob. Weisl joined the board of Gulf & Western following the Paramount acquisition ("2 Directors Named by Gulf & Western," *New York Times*, October 22, 1966).

233. Russo, *Supermob*, 362–69.

234. "Hotel Purchase Linked to Mafia," *New York Times*, January 17, 1970; "2 Alleged Leaders in Mafia Indicted," *New York Times*, April 29, 1970; "Reputed Leader in Mob Is Killed in Philadelphia," *New York Times*, March 22, 1980.

235. Juanita Darling, "Colombian Cartels Find New Drug Paths," *Los Angeles Times*, November 17, 1997; Larry Rohter and Clifford Krauss, "Dominicans Allow Drugs Easy Sailing," *New York Times*, May 10, 1998; "Mexican Cartels, Russian Mob Operating in D.R., Gov't Says," *EFE*, July 17, 2012, at http://latino.foxnews.com/latino/news/2012/07/17/mexican-cartels-russian-mob-operating-in-dr-govt-says; "Dominican Republic Emerges as Drug Trafficking Center of the Caribbean," *Huffington Post*, January 23, 2013, at https://www.huffingtonpost.com/2013/01/23/dominican-republic-emerge_n_2533210.html.

Chapter 5

1. Robert Caro, *The Passage of Power* (New York: Alfred Knopf, 2012), xiii. *Life* eventually did publish an account of LBJ's finances: Keith Wheeler and William Lambert, "How L.B.J.'s Family Amassed Its Fortune," *Life*, August 21, 1964, 62–72.

2. April 23, 1964, call between Johnson and O'Brien, https://allthewaywithlbj.files .wordpress.com/2008/06/lbj_obrien_23apr_afraid_of_corruption_issue.mp3.

3. Abe Fortas Oral History Interview, August 14, 1969, by Joe B. Frantz, LBJ Library. Fortas represented LBJ in 1948 over the disputed vote count in the Texas Senate primary.

4. Robert Donovan, "Scandals Worry Capital," *Boston Globe*, November 12, 1963.

5. Keith Wheeler, "Scandal Grows and Grows in Washington," *Life*, November 22, 1963, 40.

6. Cabell Phillips, "Major Political Scandal Looming in the Bobby Baker Case," *New York Times*, January 26, 1964.

7. James Reston, "Damaging Consequences of the Baker Case," *New York Times*, March 25, 1964.

8. Their rivalry, grounded both in political competition and social snobbery, has been widely discussed. See Jeff Shesol, *Mutual Contempt: Lyndon Johnson, Robert Kennedy, and the Feud that Defined a Decade* (New York: W. W. Norton, 1997), and Baker, *Wheeling and Dealing*, 116–30, 136–39, 145–47, etc.

9. Baker interview, quoted in Burton Hersh, *Bobby and J. Edgar*, 404.

10. Lawrence F. O'Brien Oral History Interview III, October 30, 1985, by Michael L. Gillette, LBJ Library; Lawrence F. O'Brien Oral History Interview VI, February 11, 1986, by Michael L. Gillette, LBJ Library; Harry McPherson Oral History Interview I, December 5, 1968, by T. H. Baker, LBJ Library; Baker, *Wheeling and Dealing*, 51, 54; Robert Caro, *Master of the Senate* (New York: Knopf, 2002), 390–97.

11. Keith Wheeler, "Scandal Grows and Grows in Washington," *Life*, November 22, 1963, 40.

12. Baker, *Wheeling and Dealing*, 132; William Lambert, "The Strange Help-Hoffa Campaign of the U.S. Senator from Missouri," *Life*, May 26, 1967, 28.

13. From *Chicago Daily News*, 1962, quoted in Schreiber, *The Bobby Baker Affair*, 32.

14. Baker, *Wheeling and Dealing*, 53; Larry Hancock, *Someone Would Have Talked* (Southlake, TX: JFK Lancer Productions, 2006), 245.

15. Robert Caro, *The Passage of Power*, 276–80; Alfred Steinberg, *Sam Johnson's Boy: A Close-Up of the President from Texas* (New York: Macmillan, 1968), 598; Baker, *Wheeling and Dealing*, 175–76, 182–83.

16. Hancock, *Someone Would Have Talked*, 319–21.

17. Frederic Collins, "Senator Williams—The Public Eye," *New York Times*, February 9, 1964; Carol Hoffecker, *Honest John Williams: U.S. Senator from Delaware* (Newark: University of Delaware Press, 2000), 90–109 (Truman tax scandals) and 175–204 (Bobby Baker).

18. Pearson, *Washington Merry-Go-Round*, entry for November 8, 1963, 203. Pearson's source was the Washington lawyer Edward P. Morgan, who got the information from Baker's lawyer, Edward Bennett Williams. For more on both men, see chapter 9.

19. Baker later said of them, "Smathers, his assistant Scotty Peek, and I shared a high appreciation for the good life. We all had a little high roller in us; we'd reveled together a bit by the time Senator Smathers offered me stock in the Winn-Dixie [grocery] company . . . [and] permitted me to buy into a land deal near Orlando." Baker noted that Smathers's friendship was useful to Lyndon Johnson, since his Interstate and Foreign Commerce Committee "had jurisdiction, among other things, over radio and television legislation." Baker, *Wheeling and Dealing*, 56, 65.

20. Jonathan Marshall, "Sex Scandals and Sexual Blackmail in America's Deep Politics," *Lobster* 73 (Summer 2017), at https://www.lobster-magazine.co.uk/free/lobster73/lob73-scandals-blackmail.pdf; Bobby Baker oral history interview by Donald Ritchie, 11, 111; Baker, *Wheeling and Dealing*, 80; Schreiber, *The Bobby Baker Affair*, 104, 110; Seymour Hersh, *The Dark Side of Camelot* (Boston: Little, Brown, 1997),

398–410; Evan Thomas, *Robert Kennedy: His Life* (New York: Simon & Schuster, 2000), 255–56, 265–68, 448; Summers, *Official and Confidential*, 310–12; Scott, *Deep Politics and the Death of JFK* (1993), 230–32; Johnson, *All the Way with LBJ*, 28 (RFK briefing), 48 (Hoover and Dirksen quote). In his 2009 interview, Baker alleged that Congressman Gerald Ford had an assignation with Rometsch in the hotel suite of defense lobbyist Fred Black Jr., which the FBI had bugged. *Life* magazine ran its first photo of "the Germany call girl" on November 8, 1963, in a story titled, "That High-Living Baker Boy Scandalizes the Capital," 32.

21. Reeves, *President Kennedy: Profile of Power*, 288.

22. Telephone conversation between Lyndon B. Johnson and George Smathers, January 10 or 11, 1964, Tape WH6401.11, #1312, https://millercenter.org/the-presidency/secret-white-house-tapes/conversation-george-smathers-january-11-1964.

23. Steinberg, *Sam Johnson's Boy*, 596–97; Caro, *The Passage of Power*, 286.

24. Robert Pack, "One Deal Too Many," *Washingtonian*, February 1986, 102; Clark Mollenhoff, *Despoilers of Democracy* (Garden City, NY: Doubleday, 1965), 268.

25. Steinberg, *Sam Johnson's Boy*, 597–98.

26. Baker, *Wheeling and Dealing*, 170–71.

27. Vice President Lyndon B. Johnson's daily diary, LBJ Library, http://www.lbjlibrary.net/collections/daily-diary.html.

28. Vice President Lyndon B. Johnson's daily diary, February 26–28, 1963; Reid, *The Grim Reapers*, 140; FBI report from SA Robert Holmes et al., July 15, 1963, NARA 124-10283-10475.

29. Vice President Lyndon B. Johnson's daily diary, August 21, 1963.

30. Baker, *Wheeling and Dealing*, 169–70.

31. Mollenhoff, *Strike Force*, 104–5; see also Norman Mailer, *Of a Fire on the Moon* (New York: Random House, 2014), 171; Robert Pack, "One Deal Too Many," *Washingtonian*, February 1986, 102–3; Drew Pearson and Jack Anderson, "Space Plant Deals Bared by Hotel 'Bug,'" *Washington Post*, December 26, 1967. For Webb's claims of innocence, see James E. Webb oral history interview, April 29, 1969, by T. H. Baker, LBJ Library. Baker discusses his many debts to Senator Kerr in his memoir, *Wheeling and Dealing*.

32. "Lyndon B. Johnson and Clark M. Clifford on 23 December 1966," Conversation WH6612-09-11194-11195-11196, *Presidential Recordings Digital Edition* [*Lyndon B. Johnson and Civil Rights*, Vol. 2, ed. Kent B. Germany] (Charlottesville: University of Virginia Press, 2014–), http://prde.upress.virginia.edu/conversations/4005314; Shesol, *Mutual Contempt*, 147–49.

33. Theoharis and Cox, *The Boss*, 351. For the attorney general's denials, see Drew Pearson and Jack Anderson, "RFK Denies Initiating Baker Probe," *Washington Post*, January 22, 1968, and John Delane Williams and Debra Conway, "The Don Reynolds Testimony and LBJ," *Kennedy Assassination Chronicles* 7 (Spring 2001), 16–17. The former chief counsel to the Republican minority on the Rules Committee later claimed that Kennedy did leak damaging documents to Senator Williams "to get rid of Johnson." Hersh, *The Dark Side of Camelot*, 407.

34. Baker, *Wheeling and Dealing*, 267–68. An FBI report on Johnson's visit to Baker's Carousel motel linked the property to "hoodlum interests" and immoral activities. Theoharis and Cox, *The Boss*, 345–46. One person who did not abandon Baker was Jimmy Hoffa. The convicted Teamster president made sure that Johnson's former aide was protected and well-treated in federal prison. Baker, *Wheeling and Dealing*, 17–20.

35. Baker, *Wheeling and Dealing*, 179.

36. Edwin Lahey, "Casinos of Vegas 'Home' to the FBI," *Boston Globe*, September 30, 1962.

37. Gene Blake, "Investment of Teamster Funds Eyed," *Los Angeles Times*, April 21, 1963; Gene Blake and Jack Tobin, "Hotel Financing by Union Hidden," *Los Angeles Times*, August 27, 1962.

38. "Las Vegas Casino Heads Upheld on Quiz Refusal," *Los Angeles Times*, July 12, 1963.

39. Reid and Demaris, *The Green Felt Jungle*, 91; see also Reid, *The Grim Reapers*, 123–24.

40. Wallace Turner, "Baker Assisted Nevada Gambler in Business Deal," *New York Times*, November 7, 1963; "Baker and Korth," *New York Times*, November 10, 1963. Turner's story was preceded by David Kraslow, "Baker Gaming Interests in Caribbean Probed," *Los Angeles Times*, November 6, 1963, and Jack Landau, "Baker Set Up Casino Meeting, Owner Says," *Washington Post*, November 6, 1963.

41. FBI transcript of Bruno conversation with Ben Golob, January 31, 1964, NARA 124-10340-10025.

42. Wallace Turner, "Las Vegas: Gambling Creates New Force in U.S.," *New York Times*, November 18, 1963.

43. "Crime Hearings Told of 'Cosa Nostra' Syndicate," *CQ Almanac*, v. 19, 1963. On the staging of the Valachi hearings by the Justice Department, and conflicts with Hoover, see Schlesinger Jr., *Robert Kennedy and His Times*, 268–69. On problems with Valachi's credibility, see Gordon Hawkins, "God and the Mafia," reprinted in John E. Conklin, *The Crime Establishment: Organized Crime and American Society* (Englewood Cliffs, NJ: Prentice-Hall, 1973), 54–67.

44. "The Valachi Hippodrome," (editorial), *New York Times*, October 3, 1963; see also Jack Gould, "TV: Valachi Testifies before Senate Subcommittee," *New York Times*, September 28, 1963.

45. Mollenhoff, *Strike Force*, 104–5.

46. Robert Pack, "One Deal Too Many," *Washingtonian*, February 1986, 101–2; oral history interview with Harry Easley, Webb City, Missouri, August 24, 1967, Truman Library, https://www.trumanlibrary.org/oralhist/easleyh.htm#67. Black testified to knowing Las Vegas attorney, politician, and mob-connected casino investor Cliff Jones since 1933. Jones in turn introduced Black to Levinson in early 1961. Bobby Baker hearings, 430–32.

47. Reid and Demaris, *The Green Felt Jungle*, 132–47; Hancock, *Someone Would Have Talked*, 246. James Gladstone, *The Man Who Seduced Hollywood: The Life and Loves of Greg Bautzer* (Chicago: Chicago Review Press, 2013), 88 (Siegel); Wallace

Turner, "Baker Assisted Nevada Gambler in Business Deal," *New York Times*, November 7, 1963; Reid, *The Grim Reapers*, 136.

48. FBI report, "American Gambling Activities in Cuba," January 14, 1958, NARA 124-90068-10038; Black testimony, Bobby Baker hearings, 430–32.

49. Erin Neff, "Political, Business Leader Jones Dies at 89," *Las Vegas Sun*, November 19, 2001.

50. Donald Craig Mitchell, *Wampum: How Indian Tribes, the Mafia, and an Inattentive Congress Invented Indian Gaming and Created a $28 Billion Gambling Empire* (New York: Overlook Press, 2016), 49. Bobby Baker said Black was a gambling addict who "owed quite a bit of money to the casinos in las Vegas." Oral history interview with Bobby Baker by Donald Ritchie, 112.

51. On the life of Dalitz, see Newton, *Mr. Mob*.

52. Wallace Turner, "Las Vegas: Casinos' Hoodlums Face a Cleanup," *New York Times*, November 20, 1963. On the Cleveland group's stake in the Hotel Nacional's casino, see FBI legal attaché, Havana, to Director, FBI, June 25, 1958, "American Gambling Activities in Cuba," NARA 124-90068-10101.

53. Rappleye and Becker, *All American Mafioso*, 168–69.

54. Rappleye and Becker, *All American Mafioso*, 301, 310.

55. Hersh, *Bobby and J. Edgar*, 402.

56. Fred Black testimony, Bobby Baker hearings, 430–31.

57. Russo, *The Outfit*, 310; Roemer, *Roemer: Man against the Mob*, 129. In April 1960, Stardust shareholder Wilbur Clark arranged Johnson's highly publicized presidential campaign rally in Las Vegas. Sarah McLendon, "Campaigning Johnson Applauded in Las Vegas," *Austin Statesman*, April 25, 1960; Senator Lyndon B. Johnson's Daily Diary, April 24, 1960.

58. Schreiber, *The Bobby Baker Affair*, 27–28.

59. Report by FBI special agent John Edward Shedd, February 14, 1963, re "Edward Levinson," NARA 124-10342-10129. At the January 18, 1963, Democratic Dinner and Gala at the International Inn, LBJ and Lady Bird partied with Bedford Wynne—Clint Murchison Jr.'s partner in the Dallas Cowboys—and his wife. Vice President Lyndon Johnson's daily diary, January 18, 1963. (See chapter 6 for more on the Murchisons.) The dinner, chaired by Wynne, raised nearly a million dollars and erased the Democratic Party's debt (Edward Folliard, "$1 Million Salute Given to JFK," *Boston Globe*, January 19, 1963). Levinson's favored architect did win the contract but denied making any contributions or even discussing the matter with Levinson (Richard Hardwood, "U.S. Releases Text of 'Bugs' on Baker," *Washington Post*, November16, 1966).

60. FBI report, "American Gambling Activities in Cuba," January 14, 1958, NARA 124-90068-10038; Wikipedia, "Hotel Habana Riviera," https://en.wikipedia.org/wiki/Hotel_Habana_Riviera; T. J. English, *Havana Nocturne*, 168, 188; Reid, *Grim Reapers*, 125. For general background on Levinson, see Turner, *Gambler's Money*, 78–88, and Montgomery County Police Department, Vice-Intelligence Division report OCR 76-32, "CARRAFA, Eugene Michael," August 3, 1976, NARA 180-10117-10032.

61. Reid and Demaris, *Green Felt Jungle*, 89–93. Sydney Wyman of St. Louis, who was also involved with Hoffa's attorney Morris Shenker at the Dunes, was another part owner.

62. Newton, *Mr. Mob*, 69 (Levinson); Messick, *John Edgar Hoover*, 146; Corey Levitan, "J. Edgar's La Jolla: Remembering the Hotel Del Charro," *La Jolla Light*, June 6, 2018.

63. Wallace Turner, "Las Vegas: Gamblers' Venture in the Stock Market Backfired," *New York Times*, November 21, 1963; report by FBI special agent John Edward Shedd, February 14, 1963, re "Edward Levinson," NARA 124-10342-10129 (Levinson, Garfield, and Catena); "Texas Gulf Sulphur Holders Seek to Unite 2 Suits Claiming Firm Concealed Ore Data," *Wall Street Journal*, January 23, 1963; *United States of America, Appellee, v. Virgil D. Dardi, Robert B. Gravis, Charles Rosenthal and Charles Berman, Defendants-appellants*, 330 F.2d 316 (2d Cir. 1964) (Garfield, Murchison, and Franklin County Coal Corp.).

64. FBI memorandum for Marvin Watson, Special Assistant to the President, August 5, 1966, at https://archive.org/stream/EdwardBennettWilliams/1363814-0; FBI report by SA M. B. Parker, Las Vegas, November 16, 1964, "Nevada Gambling Industry," NARA 124-10342-10000; FBI report by James Flynn, New York, July 1, 1963, "La Cosa Nostra," NARA 124-10337-10014; Messick, *Syndicate Abroad*, 85–97.

65. Teletype from FBI headquarters to field offices in Cleveland and Detroit, June 26, 1964, NARA 124-10342-10126.

66. Torres testimony, Bobby Baker hearings, 1416–24.

67. John Gilbertson, "Plane Politics: Lyndon Johnson, Howard Cannon, and Nevada's 1964 Senatorial Election," *Nevada Historical Society Quarterly* 46:4 (Winter 2003), 262–63.

68. FBI memo, "Howard Walter Cannon," March 23, 1987, in FBI FOIA release on Cannon.

69. Bobby Baker hearings, 2068, 2089, 2220.

70. Sandy Smith, "Mobsters in the Marketplace," *Life*, September 8, 1967, 98–100.

71. Smith, "Mobsters in the Marketplace"; FBI report by SA M. B. Parker, Las Vegas, November 16, 1964, "Nevada Gambling Industry," NARA 124-10342-10000.

72. Lacey, *Little Man*, 289.

73. Neil Sheehan, "Crooked Deals in Swiss Accounts Aided by Inaction of Banks," *New York Times*, December 1, 1969; Waller, *The Swiss Bank Connection*, 128–30. For a list of shareholders in the Bank of World Commerce, see Reid, *The Grim Reapers*, 125–27. The FBI learned in the summer of 1963 through wiretaps that Miami National Bank owner Lou Poller had approached Sigelbaum to purchase 50 percent of the stock in a Swiss bank in Zurich. Sigelbaum said he was "definitely interested." Based on other information in the report, it is clear that the bank was Exchange and Investment Bank, which was registered in Zurich until moving to Geneva in 1965. See FBI memo from C. A. Evans to Belmont, August 22, 1963, NARA 124-10207-10109; Nicholas Faith, *Safety in Numbers: The Mysterious World of Swiss Banking* (New York: Viking, 1982), 220; Stanley Penn, "Man Who Feds Think Handles Mob Money Is Caught in Canada," *Wall Street Journal*, December 9, 1975. For a January 22, 1963,

transcript of one of Sigelbaum's conversations on money laundering, with mentions of Poller, see NARA 124-10339-10041.

74. See, for example, FBI report by Don W. Walters, July 22, 1964, NARA 124-10208-10414; FBI report by James P. Flynn, July 1, 1963, NARA 124-10337-10014; report by SA John R. Kinsinger, May 31, 1963, NARA 124-10200-10429; SAC Miami to Director, FBI, June 25, 1968, NARA 124-10291-10389.

75. Hank Messick, *Lansky* (New York: Putnam, 1971), 266–67. The FBI first learned of this leak in 1963 (FBI telegram from SAC Miami to Director, FBI, August 22, 1963, NARA 124-10339-10055).

76. Mitchell, *Wampum*; FBI report by SA M. B. Parker, Las Vegas, November 16, 1964, NARA 124-10342-10000 (Flamingo).‡

77. Report by FBI special agent John Edward Shedd, February 14, 1962, re "Edward Levinson," NARA 124-10342-10129; cf. Gene Blake and Jack Tobin, "Teamsters Funds Quiz May Widen," *Los Angeles Times*, August 28, 1962.

78. Messick, *Syndicate Abroad*, 67. Rabb was also a director of Seven Arts Productions, Ltd., which invested in the early 1960s in a Bahamian casino in partnership with Meyer Lansky.

79. Ronald Kessler, "A Nixon 'Friend' Investigated," *Washington Post*, February 24, 1970 (Harry Garfinkle).

80. FBI report by SA Eugene J. Hindes, New York, December 28, 1962, re "Salvatore Granello," NARA 124-90066-10170. An informant cited in the same report doubted this boast, saying that Smathers had a "reputation for honesty and integrity" at least equal to that of his peers.

81. Bobby Baker hearings, 1008–15 (George Simon testimony); 396–400 (Black testimony).

82. Fred Black testimony, Bobby Baker hearings, 416; Pearson and Anderson, *The Case against Congress*, 193 (investors in District of Columbia National Bank); Schreiber, *The Bobby Baker Affair*, 139–40 (Farmers and Merchants State Bank/D.C. National Bank); *New York Times*, February 21, 1964 (home loan).

83. S. Oliver Goodman, "New Bank for District Authorized," *Washington Post*, March 2, 1962.‡

84. "Abraham Multer, Ex-Congressman," *New York Times*, November 7, 1986. For a less-polite review of his many ethically challenged deals, see Jack Anderson, "House Speaker Resists Ethics Move," *Washington Post*, June 4, 1966.

85. Sheridan, *The Fall and Rise of Jimmy Hoffa*, 151; Espaillat, *Trujillo: The Last Caesar*, 171; Estelle Brand, "Washington Report," *The Wisconsin Jewish Chronicle*, August 24, 1951; Messick, *John Edgar Hoover*, 112–15.

86. Interview of Leonard Bursten by FBI agents William Wightman and George Davis Jr., February 15, 1960, NARA 124-10296-10108; FBI airtel from SAC, Washington Field Office, to Director, FBI, May 11, 1961, NARA 124-10214-10444; Jack Anderson, "Congressman Starts Foreign Bank," *Washington Post*, August 23, 1961.‡

87. Miami National Bank advertisement in *Miami News*, November 8, 1956. "The Miami National Bank pumped millions of dollars a year of syndicate capital into the Swiss bank [Exchange & Investment Bank] and got it back through various New York and Bahamian banks." Messick, *Lansky*, 269; also Waller, *The Swiss Bank Connection*,

129; Moldea, *Hoffa Wars*, 106; Messick, *Syndicate Abroad*, 137; FBI report by SA Fred Doerner Jr., Miami, March 19, 1963, NARA 124-90031-10015.

88. *Wall Street Journal*, March 26, 1971. One of those convicted in the case, Samuel Cohen, had taken control of Miami National Bank with Poller in 1960 with help from a $4 million Teamster pension fund loan. He bought out the Teamster investment in 1964.

89. Memo from Robert D. Peloquin and Edward F. Harrington to William G. Hundley, chief, Organized Crime and Racketeering Section, Department of Justice, January 12, 1965, Alan Block papers; portions quoted in Messick, *Syndicate Abroad*, 85. Several weeks later, the *New York Times* reported that the movement of "untaxed profit from underworld activities" in the United States to offshore banks in the Bahamas and Switzerland "has become a major concern for law enforcement in the United States." Wallace Turner, "Hidden Money: Bahamas Called Way Station to Swiss Banks," *New York Times*, February 17, 1965.

90. Intelligence report by IRS special agent Richard E. Jaffe to chief, Intelligence Division, Jacksonville District, IRS, January 10, 1963, Alan Block papers.

91. Hank Messick, *The Private Lives of Public Enemies* (New York: P. H. Wyden, 1973), 232–33; Messick, *Syndicate Abroad*, 86–97, Reid, *Grim Reapers*, 125–27; Jacques Derogy, *Israel Connection: La Mafia en Israel* (Paris: Plon, 1980), 70–72; Clyde Farnsworth, "A Global Bank Tangle and Its Lost Millions," *New York Times*, April 9, 1975; FBI report by Frank H. Townsend, March 1, 1962, "Crime Conditions in the Los Angeles Division," NARA 124-10328-10003.

92. Depositors at the Bank of World Commerce included Meyer Lansky and Joseph Stacher, who moved to Israel to avoid the reach of US law enforcement; and Morris Dalitz, who was honored for his financial contributions to Israel (Newton, *Mr. Mob*, 209). On Hoffa's support for Israel, see Robert I. Friedman, "Fastest Pen in the West," *Washington Journalism Review*, April 1984; Brian Greenspun, "Brian Greenspun Joins Tributes to Worthy Men," *Las Vegas Sun*, February 17, 2008; Pearson diary, 385 (May 27, 1958); Ralph and Estelle James, *Hoffa and the Teamsters: A Study of Union Power* (Princeton, NJ: D. Van Nostrand Co., 1965), 235; FBI memo from SAC, Las Vegas, to Acting Director, FBI, April 17, 1973, FBI files on Hank Greenspun.

93. Memo from SAC, Washington Field Office, to Director, FBI, May 10, 1961, re "I. Irving Davidson—Registration Act—Nicaragua—Israel," NARA 124-10214-10443. On Davidson's own account at the Swiss-Israel Trade Bank, see FBI memo by SA Gerard C. Carroll, Washington Field Office, June 14, 1961, re "I. Irving Davidson," NARA 124-10214-10420. On Davidson's friendship with Israeli military intelligence directors Generals Aharon Yariv and Elie Zeira, see Davidson letter to Acting FBI director L. Patrick Gray, July 25, 1972, NARA 124-10302-10123. Multer was a member of the American Friends of Hebrew University, a life member of the Zionist Organization of America, and one of the "top leaders in Jewish National Fund circles in America." "Multer to Address Jewish Fund Dinner," *Poughkeepsie Journal*, January 7, 1957.

94. Ofer Aderet, "Yehuda Assia Banker to the Mossad, Dies at 99," *Ha'aretz*, September 3, 2016. Some of the complex machinations of the Swiss-Israel Trade Bank and its offshoot, American Bank & Trust, are reported in Richard Karp, "Sleeping

Watchdogs: How the American Bank & Trust Co. Went Bankrupt," *Barron's*, December 20, 1976, and Richard Karp, "Hands across the Sea: Millions Were Looted from the American Bank & Trust," *Barron's*, December 27, 1976. Prominent Democratic Party fundraiser Abraham Feinberg, who served as chairman of American Bank & Trust, apparently organized covert US donor funding of Israel's nuclear weapons program. Avner Cohen, *Israel and the Bomb* (New York: Columbia University Press, 1998), 70; Eric Pace, "Abraham Feinberg, 90, Philanthropist for Israel," *New York Times*, December 7, 1998; Seymour Hersh, *The Samson Option: Israel's Nuclear Arsenal and American Foreign Policy* (New York: Random House, 1991).

The immensely resourceful Assia was a close friend (from World War II days) of Thailand's "Mr. Opium," Gen. Phao Sriyanonda (chapter 3). Phao spent his final years in exile in Geneva, living for part of 1957 in Assia's apartment, and no doubt banking with him as well. By that time, Phao was reputedly "one of the richest men in the world." Details of Phao's long history with Assia may be found in the report by Paul Helliwell's OSS and banking partner, Edward Philip Barry, "Report of Trip with General Phao, July 22 thru August 11th," August 1959, in Helliwell file, Corcoran papers, Library of Congress. On Phao see Lintner, *Burma in Revolt*, 192 (richest). On Barry's intelligence and banking background, see Alan A. Block and Constance A. Weaver, *All Is Clouded by Desire: Global Banking, Money Laundering, and International Organized Crime* (Westport, CT: Praeger, 2004), 36–37.

95. Jonathan Nitzan and Shimshon Bichler, *The Global Political Economy of Israel: From War Profits to Peace Dividends* (London: Pluto Press, 2002), 116. San Souci had supported a Teamster pension fund loan to Dominick Bartone, the trafficker in arms and aircraft to Cuba and the Dominican Republic in the late 1950s (Sheridan, *The Fall and Rise of Jimmy Hoffa*, 76–79, 111–12, 199–200). Irving Davidson told the FBI that he knew the "wheeler and dealer" San Souci "quite well," let Souci use his office on K Street, and even gave him an Israeli Uzi submachine gun (FBI memo, SAC Washington Metropolitan Field Office to Director, May 11, 1961, re "I. Irving Davidson Registration Act-Nicaragua-Israel," NARA 124-10214-10444; FBI report by SA Gerard Carroll, June 14, 1961, "I. Irving Davidson," NARA 124-10214-10420). After his death, San Souci was replaced on the board of Bank of World Commerce by former Los Angeles Teamster official Mike Singer, who invested with Bobby Baker in the Waikiki Savings & Loan Assn. FBI report by Frank H. Townsend, March 1, 1962, "Crime Conditions in the Los Angeles Division," NARA 124-10328-10003.

96. FBI memo, SAC Washington Metropolitan Field Office to Director, May 11, 1961, re "I. Irving Davidson Registration Act-Nicaragua-Israel," NARA 124-10214-10444.

97. Drew Pearson, "Bogus Bonds Linked to Hoffa Aide," *Washington Post*, June 28, 1961.‡

98. Pearson and Anderson, *The Case against Congress*, 191–92.

99. E. W. Kenworthy, "Baker Question Raises Large Questions," *New York Times*, November 17, 1963.

100. Robert Caro, *The Passage of Power*, 295; Baker, *Wheeling and Dealing*, 271; Evelyn Lincoln, *Kennedy and Johnson* (New York: Holt, Rinehart and Winston, 1968), 205.

101. Steinberg, *Sam Johnson's Boy*, 668.

102. Cabell Phillips, "Baker Withholds Subpoenaed Data," *New York Times*, February 20, 1964; William B. Collins, "Baker Philosophy: Silence Is Golden," *Philadelphia Inquirer*, February 23, 1964; Cabel Phillips, "Senators Study Baker Ties to Gambling Interest," *New York Times*, February 28, 1964. The illegal wiretapping was subject of a long article by Richard Harwood, "Wiretapping Caper Backfires on the FBI," *Philadelphia Inquirer*, June 26, 1964.

103. Lacey, *Little Man*, 298; Mollenhoff, *Strike Force*, 187; FBI telegram from SAC Miami to Director, FBI, August 22, 1963, NARA 124-10339-10055.

104. Steinberg, *Sam Johnson's Boy*, 670–72 (Don Reynolds, Sen. John Williams).

105. Jordan called Johnson just three hours after telling distrustful reporters that he had not spoken with the president since he took office. "Lyndon Johnson and B. Everett Jordan (President Johnson joined by Walter Jenkins) on 6 December 1963," Tape K6312.04, PNO 28, http://prde.upress.virginia.edu/conversations/9020083.

106. "Lyndon Johnson and George Smathers on 10 January 1964," Tape WH6401.11, Citation #1312, http://prde.upress.virginia.edu/conversations/9030116.

107. Ben Franklin, "Smathers Linked to a Baker Deal in Florida Land," *New York Times*, January 14, 1964; Sherrill, *Gothic Politics*, 174–75.

108. LBJ telephone call with George Smathers, January 29, 1964, 6:20 p.m., Tape WH6401.25, conversation #1642, LBJ recordings, https://www.discoverlbj.org/item/tel-01642.

109. "Republicans Attack Conduct of Baker Investigation," *CQ Almanac*, v. 20, 1964.

110. Lyndon Johnson telephone call with Cartha "Deke" DeLoach, March 12, 1964, 2:15 p.m., conversation #2489, https://www.discoverlbj.org/item/tel-02489.

111. *Lyndon B. Johnson, The Presidential Recordings, Toward the Great Society, March 9, 1964–April 13, 1964*, v. 5, eds. David Shreve and Robert David Johnson, 206–8.

112. Cabell Phillips, "Baker Panel Rejects Plea to Hear More Witnesses," *New York Times*, March 24, 1964.

113. Telephone conversation between LBJ and Hubert Humphrey, May 13, 1964, 5:30 p.m., conversation #3445, https://www.discoverlbj.org/item/tel-03445.

114. Johnson, *All the Way with LBJ*, 126.

115. Telephone conversation between LBJ and Abe Fortas, September 10, 1964, 11:26 a.m., conversation #5565, LBJ Recordings, https://www.discoverlbj.org/item/tel-05565.

116. Johnson, *All the Way with LBJ*, 304.

117. "Senators Told of Trip by Baker to New Orleans with 2 Women," *New York Times*, December 5, 1964; "Tie Baker, Banker to Girls and Party," *Newsday*, December 4, 1964; Dom Bonafede, "Senators Probing Baker Case Hear Intriguing Story . . . of Guys and Dolls," *Boston Globe*, December 5, 1964.

118. Bobby Baker hearings, 1150–54, 2138–44, 2155–56.

119. Bobby Baker hearings, 1475, 1353, 1347.

120. Bobby Baker hearings, 2156–58.

121. FBI report by SA Furman G. Boggan, May 5, 1961, "Carlos Marcello," NARA 124-10210-10317 (restaurant); FBI report, "Alleged Plans to Ship Guns from Louisiana to Honduras," March 1, 1961, NARA 124-10288-10385; FBI memo from SAC, New Orleans, to Director, FBI, April 11, 1961, re "William Wayne Dalzell," NARA 124-10288-10385 (Honduras); Marcello testimony before House Select Committee on Assassinations, January 11, 1978, NARA 180-10131-10312; FBI report by SA Jack Louis Marshall, May 28, 1964, "Charles Tourine," NARA 124-90096-10028 (Tourine).

122. HSCA briefing memo, "Marcello, Carlos, Background," January 11, 1978, NARA 180-10118-10067. The Lake Pontchartrain training camp site was subsequently acquired by Sam Marcello.

123. President's Commission on the Assassination of President Kennedy, *Hearings*, X (Washington, DC: US Government Printing Office, 1964), 35, 44–45 (testimony of Carlos Bringuier, April 7–8, 1964).

124. The full inventory of weapons and explosive seized on July 31, 1963, is detailed in FBI report of SA Warren C. Debrueys, August 14, 1963, re Victor Dominador Espinosa Hernandez, NARA 124-10217-10019. The link between the training camp and the arms depot is noted in FBI report by SA Warren deBrueys, October 3, 1963, "Anti–Fidel Castro Activities," NARA 124-10203-10314; CIA memorandum for chief, LEOB/SRS, December 28, 1967, re "Highlights on the Cast of Characters Involved in Garrison's Investigation," NARA 1993.07.20.15:30:56:680280.

125. Warren Hinckle and William Turner, *The Fish Is Red: The Story of the Secret War against Castro* (New York: Harper & Row, 1981), 162–63, 198–200 (Michael McLaney and Sam Benton). At the time of the FBI raid, Sam Benton was a protected customs informant (FBI report by William Mayo Drew Jr., August 8, 1963, NARA 124-10204-10283). Benton was indicted in 1971 for his alleged role in the $50 million Picture Island Computer stock swindle, along with alleged Mafia associates John Lombardozzi and Leslie Zacharias. *New York Times*, July 17, 1971; "Six Go on Trial Today on Alleged Promotion of Worthless Company," *Wall Street Journal*, May 2, 1972.

126. George Lardner Jr., "U.S. vs. Marcello," *Washington Post*, February 19, 1980.

127. The most complete account of Marcello's life is Davis, *Mafia Kingfish*.

128. Kefauver report, 63–64.

129. Bill Davidson, "New Orleans: Cosa Nostra's Wall Street," *Saturday Evening Post*, February 29, 1964, 15–21.

130. HSCA hearings appendix, volume IX, 70.

131. HSCA briefing memo, "Marcello, Carlos, Background," January 11, 1978, NARA 180-10118-10067.

132. Dorman, *Pay-off*, 157. Halfen continued to claim business ties with Marcello as late as 1969, saying that the mob boss was "indebted" to him "for some past favor." See FBI report by SA John C. McCurnin, April 9, 1969, NARA 124-10203-10293.

133. Michael Dorman, "LBJ and the Racketeers," *Ramparts*, May 1968, 34.

134. For further details on the Halfen case, besides Dorman's works, see Gus Russo, *Live by the Sword: The Secret War against Castro and the Death of JFK* (Baltimore: Bancroft Press, 1988), 283–84, 414–15. For coverage of Halfen's 1954 trial and conviction, see Bill Joines, "Slot Machine Tax Case Already Has 16 Witnesses," *Austin Statesman*, June 22, 1954, and "Joe Steele and Big Fix Halfen Receive Sentences and Fines," *Austin Statesman*, July 9, 1954.

135. Davis, *Mafia Kingfish*, 273.

136. FBI report by SA August Kempff, May 11, 1964, re Joseph Y. Stein and Leonard B. Stallman, NARA 124-90086-10125; FBI report by SA Gregg Van de Loo, March 29, 1971, re "Tom Connally Moore," NARA 124-90025-10015. Abraham reportedly met with members of the Marcello family in January 1969 to discuss a major real estate deal (FBI report by SA John C. McCurnin, April 9, 1969, NARA 124-10203-10293). On Abraham's reputation as a "close associate of the then Governor Jimmie Davis" and as "one of the largest bettors on football games in Louisiana," see FBI file summary, July 21, 1967, NARA 124-10286-10282.

137. Sheridan, *The Fall and Rise of Jimmy Hoffa*, 380–81; Mollenhoff, *Strike Force*, 106. Hoffa's lawyer, Frank Ragano, recalled the Teamster boss saying of President Johnson in late 1963, "I gave him $100,000 in cash contributions over the years and he knows [Bobby's] on my ass." Ragano also notes, however, that LBJ kept Robert Kennedy on as attorney general until the Justice Department succeeded in convicting Hoffa in two major cases. Frank Ragano and Selwyn Raab, *Mob Lawyer* (New York: Charles Scribner's Sons, 1994), 150, 184.

138. Sheridan, *The Fall and Rise of Jimmy Hoffa*, 424–32. In 1969, Marcello allegedly used Abraham as a driver for Ragano (FBI report by SA John C. McCurnin, April 9, 1969, NARA 124-10203-10293).

139. Baker, *Wheeling and Dealing*, 17.

140. FBI airtel from Director, FBI, to Philadelphia, Miami, New Orleans, New York, Tampa, and Washington field offices, June 12, 1964, NARA 124-10211-10403; see also airtel from SAC, Philadelphia, to Director, FBI, May 28, 1964, "Angelo Bruno," NARA 124-10225-10236; FBI report by SA Edward Hegarty, August 20, 1964, "Angelo Bruno," NARA 124-10225-10302; report by SA Regis Kennedy, July 24, 1964, "La Cosa Nostra," NARA 124-10223-10428.

141. FBI report by SAs Edward Hegarty and Joseph Verica, interview with Benjamin Abramson, June 2, 1964, NARA 124-10225-10302. The close Bruno partner was Ben Golob.

142. Urgent teletype from SAC, Philadelphia, to Director, FBI, August 26, 1963, NARA 124-10225-10418; airtel from Director, FBI, to SAC, Philadelphia, September 3, 1963, NARA 124-10225-10418; teletype from SAC, Philadelphia, to Director, FBI, June 1, 1964, NARA 124-10211-10385 (Ben Golob, Baker, and Continental Vending Machine); Nicholas Gage, "Kerkorian Is Named at Crime Hearing," *New York Times*, September 28, 1971 (Harold Roth and Tourine); *United States of America v. Harold Roth and Herbert S. Sternberg*, 333 F.2d 450 (2d Cir. 1964) (violation of Labor Management Relations Act of 1947); Securities and Exchange Commission, *News Digest*, October 11, 1968 (stock fraud). The FBI believed that New Jersey Mafia boss Gerardo Catena was a major hidden owner in Continental Vending Machine ("Miami Brief for

Attorney General's Criminal Intelligence Conference," October 10–11, 1962, NARA 124-10194-10182).

143. "Corruption on the Hill," *Washington Post*, December 6, 1964.

144. Cabell Phillips, "Report Denouncing Baker Closes Inquiry by Senators," *New York Times*, July 1, 1965; "Republicans Attack Conduct of Baker Investigation," *CQ Almanac*, v. 20, 1964.

145. Fred Graham, "Baker Indicted for Fraud and Evading Income Tax," *New York Times*, January 6, 1966; Neil Genzlinger, "Bobby Baker, String-Puller Snared in Senate Scandal, Dies at 89," *New York Times*, November 17, 2017.

146. Martin Waldron, "Smathers to Quit as Senator in '69," *New York Times*, January 4, 1966; "George A. Smathers, United States Senator, 1951–1969," Oral History Interviews, Senate Historical Office, Washington, D.C., October 17, 1989, https://www.senate.gov/artandhistory/history/resources/pdf/OralHistory_SmathersGeorge.pdf ("Really, I didn't have a health problem").

147. Laura Kalman, *Abe Fortas: A Biography* (New Haven: Yale University Press, 1990), 312–17.

148. Kalman, *Abe Fortas*, 360–78; Curt Gentry, *Edgar Hoover: The Man and the Secrets* (New York: W. W. Norton, 1991), 628–29; Mollenhoff, *Strike Force*, 117–18; Theoharis, *The Boss*, 403–4; Charns, *Cloak and Gavel*, 100–105; Michael Bobelian, *Battle for the Marble Palace: Abe Fortas, Earl Warren, Lyndon Johnson, Richard Nixon and the Forging of the Modern Supreme Court* (Tucson: Schaffner Press, 2019), 284–96; Wolfgang Saxon, "Louis Wolfson, Central to the Fall of a Justice, Is Dead at 95," *New York Times*, January 2, 2008.

149. Messick, *The Private Lives of Public Enemies*, 203 (Yiddie Bloom and Joseph Linsey); Demaris, *Dirty Business*, 316 (Parvin). Fortas's wife, Carolyn Agger, was counsel to the Albert Parvin Foundation; also on its payroll, as noted in chapter 4, was Supreme Court justice William Douglas, a mentor and colleague of Fortas.

150. Abell, *Drew Pearson Diaries*, March 4, 1955, 345.

151. FBI report by SAs Frederick Roderick and Ambrose Law, April 10, 1963, interview with Harry Hall, NARA 124-90026-10187.

152. Turner, *Hoover's FBI*, 168–69; Mollenhoff, *Strike Force*, 5.

153. Mollenhoff, *Strike Force*, 188–89. Senator Cannon was later the target of a bribe attempt that led to the conviction of Teamster Union president Roy Williams, Teamster pension fund consultant Allen Dorfman, and Chicago mobster Joseph Lombardo in December 1982. Although Cannon was not indicted, taped phone calls and testimony introduced at the trial implicated him in a deal to impede federal legislation to deregulate trucking in exchange for an opportunity to purchase union-owned land in Las Vegas at well below its market value. Cannon was defeated for reelection in November 1982, and Dorfman was murdered in a gangland hit in January 1983. See James Neff, *Mobbed Up: Jackie Presser's High-Wire Life in the Teamsters, the Mafia, and the F.B.I.* (New York: Atlantic Monthly Press, 1989), 284–90, 293–97, 301, 367; Ben Franklin, "Jury Hears Talk on Tape about a Teamster Pledge of Property," *New York Times*, November 18, 1982; Douglas Frantz, "Court Hears Taped Bribe Bid at Trial," *Chicago Tribune*, November 18, 1982; Douglas Frantz, "Teamster Bribe Jurors Hear Sen. Cannon on Tape," *Chicago Tribune*, November 24, 1982; William Rempel,

"Teamsters Chief, 4 Others Convicted in Bribery Fraud," *Newsday*, December 16, 1982; Douglas Frantz, "Double Life of Allen Dorfman," *Chicago Tribune*, January 21, 1983; Allen Friedman and Ted Schwarz, *Power and Greed: Inside the Teamsters Empire of Corruption* (New York: Franklin Watts, 1989), 260–61. Various other allegations of Cannon's friendliness toward mobsters are raised in FBI memo, "Howard Walter Cannon," March 23, 1987, in FBI FOIA release on Cannon.

154. "The ban on all forms of listening devices and practices represented an important contradiction. . . . LBJ, after all, had not previously criticized bugs and taps in the course of his extensive legislative career. He had not openly decried their effectiveness under the few circumstances of surveillance for which he had intimate knowledge. Moreover, upon becoming president he continued the taps on Martin Luther King, Jr., thereby condoning the thinly defended 'national security' rationale. Also, he ordered the installation of a secret taping system in the Oval Office. . . . Not only was Johnson an avid consumer of massive amounts of information about the lives and peccadilloes of people in his political circles, as Vice President he had been privy to a significant amount of national security intelligence derived from bugs and taps. From his autobiography, however, the impression is given that his only views of bugs and taps were that they were dangerously intrusive of privacy and they were a lazy substitute for good police work." Calder and Lynch, "From Apalachin to the Buffalo Project: Obstacles on the Path to Effective Federal Responses to Organized Crime, 1957–1967," 244.

155. Roemer, *Man against the Mob*, 227–28. Indications that LBJ may have had close ties to Hoffa and Marcello fed suspicions about his motives. See, for example, "Hoffa Asks Union to Back Johnson," *New York Times*, October 18, 1964; Sheridan, *The Fall and Rise of Jimmy Hoffa*, 155, 300, 380–81 (Hoffa); Dorman, *Pay-Off*, 151–76 (Halfen); Russo, *The Outfit*, 464–65 (LBJ's faltering war on organized crime).

156. Mollenhoff, *Strike Force*, 107; Shesol, *Mutual Contempt*, 353.

157. Mollenhoff, *Strike Force*, 108. Note that Clark's personal interest in the issue of eavesdropping does not discredit the Court's defense of Fourth Amendment rights.

158. Mollenhoff, *Strike Force*, 109–13. The FBI's unauthorized bugging of Black created an enormous rift between Hoover and Attorney General Nicholas Katzenbach. For this story, see Theoharis, *The Boss*, 380–93, and Alexander Charns, *Cloak and Gavel*, 39–40, 56–63. Black went to prison years later for conspiracy to distribute drugs and tax evasion.

159. Schreiber, *The Bobby Baker Affair*, 142–43; Peter Kann, "Grand Jury Will Hear Tax-Evasion Charges against Some Casino Owners in Las Vegas," *Wall Street Journal*, November 23, 1966; Wallace Turner, "7 Nevada Gaming Figures Indicted on Tax Charges," *New York Times*, May 12, 1967; "Parvin Dohrmann Story," *Los Angeles Times West Magazine*, November 15, 1970; David Kraslow, "Accusations over Electronic Spying Place FBI in Awkward Position," *Washington Post*, December 20, 1968; Robert Pack, "One Deal Too Many," *Washingtonian*, February 1986, 150; Messick, *Secret File*, 363–64.

160. "Levinson, U.S. Close Vegas Tilt," *Washington Post*, March 29, 1968.

161. Mollenhoff, *Strike Force*, 116–17 (quote from *Los Angeles Times*); Demaris, *Dirty Business*, 313 (sale).

162. Victor Navasky, *Kennedy Justice* (New York: Atheneum, 1977), 49n.

163. Summers, *Official and Confidential*, 332; also Goldfarb, *Perfect Villains, Imperfect Heroes*, 256.

164. Calder and Lynch, "From Apalachin to the Buffalo Project: Obstacles on the Path to Effective Federal Responses to Organized Crime, 1957–1967," 250–64.

165. Patrick J. Ryan, *Organized Crime: A Reference Handbook* (Santa Barbara: ABC-CLIO, 1995), 73–74.

Chapter 6

1. Remarkably, however, there is no mention of the Murchisons in Caro, *The Passage of Power*.

2. Jane Wolfe, *The Murchisons: The Rise and Fall of a Texas Dynasty* (New York: St. Martin's Press, 1989), 219–20.

3. Reid, *The Grim Reapers*, 138.

4. Bryan Burrough, *The Big Rich: The Rise and Fall of the Greatest Texas Oil Fortunes* (New York: Penguin Press, 2009), 167.

5. William D. Cohan, *Money and Power: How Goldman Sachs Came to Rule the World* (New York: Random House, 2011),115–17; Burrough, *The Big Rich*, 286–92; John Brooks, "The Great Proxy Fight," *New Yorker*, July 3, 1954, 28–47. Clint Murchison's biography includes a lengthy appreciation from John J. McCloy, chairman of the Chase Bank; Ernestine Orrick Van Buren, *Clint: Clinton William Murchison, A Biography* (Austin: Eakin Press, 1986), xiv.

6. Wolfe, *The Murchisons*, 259–70; Robert E. Bedingfield, "New Efforts to Achieve Peace Fail in Alleghany Proxy Fight," *New York Times*, April 5, 1961; Waller, *The Swiss Bank Connection*, 176.

7. This story is largely untold by Murchison family biographers, who ignore the role of Thomas Webb, the family's Washington, D.C., representative.

8. FBI memo from Marie Fagnant to Laura Denk and Kevin Tiernan, re "Summary of Clint Murchison Jr. and Sr. C-References," July 18, 1997, https://www.maryferrell.org/showDoc.html?docId=202871#relPageId=2. According to the FBI's Freedom of Information office, these files have been destroyed (letter to author, April 30, 2019).

9. Dan Moldea, *Interference: How Organized Crime Influences Professional Football* (New York: William Morrow, 1989), 104–5.

10. Richard Linnett, *In the Godfather Garden: The Long Life and Times of Richie "the Boot" Boiardo* (New Brunswick, NJ: Rutgers University Press, 2013), 67–74.

11. FBI report by SA Kenneth Hackman, December 21, 1962, "Criminal Influence of International Brotherhood of Teamsters (IBT), Local 575 . . .," NARA 124-10291-10347.

12. Linnett, *In the Godfather Garden*, 78–80; FBI report by SA M. B. Parker, November 16, 1964, "Nevada Gambling Industry," NARA 124-10342-10000; FBI report by SA John Kinsinger, May 31, 1963, "La Causa [sic] Nostra—Las Vegas Division," NARA 124-10200-10429.‡

13. Moldea, *Interference*, 104–5, 295–96.‡

14. Blakey and Billings, *The Plot to Kill the President*, 291, 313–14; FBI report by SA Alan E. Drayton, June 29, 1973, "Joseph Campisi," NARA 124-90021-10067; FBI report by SA Forrest F. John, January 17, 1969, "Joseph Campisi," NARA 124-90021-10022; FBI report by SA John J. Landers, July 20, 1970, "Joseph Campisi," NARA 124-90021-10033; Airtel from SAC, Dallas, to Director, FBI, May 20, 1970, "Joseph Campisi" [Campisi made eighteen calls to Vincent Marcello from August to December 1969]; FBI report by SA John J. Landers, March 25, 1974, "Joseph Campisi," NARA 124-90021-10071; FBI report by SA Forrest F. John, March 25, 1968, "Joseph Campisi," NARA 124-90021-10023; FBI report by SA Forrest F. John, February 28, 1967, "Joseph Campisi," NARA 124-90021-10008.

15. FBI report by SA Ralph Hill, May 26, 1960, re "Anthony Joseph Accardo," NARA 124-10203-10000 and 124-90079-10014. On Centex's projects in Cook County, see Joseph Ator, "Murchison Building Wasteland into New Orleans Subdivision," *Chicago Tribune*, November 5, 1961.

16. Demaris, *Captive City*, 87–92; Russo, *Supermob*, 251; Moldea, *Interference*, 294–95. London police objected to granting a liquor license to Roma on grounds of his alleged associations with organized crime figures such as convicted murderer and former Teamster official Anthony Provenzano. *Private Eye*, November 16, 1984.

17. Moldea, *Hoffa Wars*, 123–24; Brill, *The Teamsters*, 250–55; Russo, *Supermob*, 166, 225; Gene Blake, "It's Not Hard to [sic] Jimmy Hoffa's Piggy Bank," *Washington Post*, April 4, 1963. On connections to Lansky and other mobsters, see also "Teamsters Invest Millions in Florida," *Miami Herald*, August 25, 1975.

18. John O'Briend and Ronald Koziol, "Black Book Reveals Dorfman Associates," *Chicago Tribune*, January 22, 1983.

19. Gene Blake and Jack Tobin, "Local Teamster Loans Detailed," *Los Angeles Times*, May 17, 1962; Russo, *Supermob*, 261.

20. Trousdale Estates was founded on the former estate of the late oilman Edward L. Doheny, whose $100,000 payoff to Interior Secretary Albert Fall in 1921 triggered the Teapot Dome scandal. Summers, *Arrogance of Power*, 221; "Nixon Buys Lot in Beverly Hills as Site of New Home," *Chicago Tribune*, April 2, 1961; "Moving Day for the Nixons," *Newsweek*, June 26, 1961, 27; "Nixon Defends His Actions in All Previous Campaigns," *Los Angeles Times*, May 30, 1962.[‡]

21. Murchison's Washington representative Thomas Webb Jr. testified that he had associated with Irving Davidson in a Murchison investment vehicle called the Burbank Corp., "since about 1954 or 1955." US Congress, Senate, Committee on Governmental Affairs, Permanent Subcommittee on Investigations, *Labor Union Insurance, Hearings, Part 2*, 95th Cong., 1st sess. (Washington, DC: US Government Printing Office, 1978), 1002.[‡]

22. FBI memo, SAC Washington Metropolitan Field Office to Director, FBI, May 11, 1964, re "I. Irving Davidson Registration Act-Nicaragua-Israel," NARA 124-10214-10444; Sheridan, *The Fall and Rise of Jimmy Hoffa*, 140 (Pittsburgh).[‡]

23. FBI memo from W. R. Wannall to William Sullivan, May 18, 1965, re "I. Irving Davidson," NARA 124-10301-10046.[‡]

24. FBI Memo from A. H. Belmont to Director, FBI, May 1, 1959, NARA 124-10294-10047.‡

25. On Murchison, Tierra Verde, and the Berlanti family, see "Murchisons Reported Buying Tierra Verde," *St. Petersburg Times*, May 29, 1959. The Berlantis seem to have acquired it in 1959 with backing from the Murchisons; see "Conservationists Defeat Tierra Verde Bay," *St. Petersburg Times*, June 21, 1967; Robert Stiff, "Voice from the Past," *The Evening Independent* (St. Petersburg), September 18, 1974; Debra DiGiacomandrea, "Tierra Verde: From Rattlesnake Haven to Homes," *The Evening Independent*, January 29, 1985. On the mysterious death of Louis and Fred Berlanti, see Jack Alexander, "Ever Alert Watch Discourages Mafia in Pinello County," *The Evening Independent*, January 3, 1968. Berlanti's Miami attorney said Louis Berlanti was broke and "had been in Miami trying to arrange an $18-million foreign loan to bail him out of financial difficulties." Robert Stiff, "Voice from the Past," *The Evening Independent*, September 18, 1974.

26. "Tierra Verde Promoter of the '50s Convicted," *St. Petersburg Times*, March 28, 1970.

27. David Steinberg, "New Lefcourt Co. Head Is Community Builder," *New York Herald Tribune*, May 10, 1959; "15,000-Home Town Planned in Charles," *Baltimore Sun*, May 3, 1959; "Desser, Garfield, Map Golf Links, Hotel for RM," *Desert Sun*, April 15, 1960.

28. Carol City today has more than sixty thousand inhabitants. The sellers included John D. MacArthur, whose Bankers Life and Casualty of Chicago financed the development; wealthy investor Ralph Stolkin, a close friend and business partner of Sidney Korshak, the Chicago mob's superlawyer; Stanford Clinton, attorney for Chicago Mafia boss Anthony Accardo and general counsel to the Teamster pension fund; and Julius Gaines, a business partner of South Florida racketeer and Havana casino operator Charles "The Blade" Tourine. Receiving a commission on the deal was James Gottlieb, a Las Vegas casino investor and close associate of Jimmy Hoffa. Nancy Kriplen, *The Eccentric Billionaire: John D. MacArthur—Empire Builder, Reluctant Philanthropist, Relentless Adversary* (New York: AMACOM, 2008), 96–98 (MacArthur and Coral City); "Step by Step Growth of Carol City Traced," *Miami News*, November 9, 1958; FBI report by SA John J. Flynn Jr., Los Angeles, June 29, 1962, NARA 124-90044-10005 (Desser purchase); FBI report by SA William Roemer, October 29, 1959, NARA 124-10202-10020; Russo, *Supermob*, 128–30, 402 (Stolkin); FBI report, "Charles Tourine," July 28, 1961, NARA 124-90096-10178 (Gaines and Tourine).

29. "Lefcourt Realty Proposes Stock Offering" *SEC News Digest*, January 30, 1959; Larry Solloway, "Old Cape Florida Light to Be Beacon for Miami Luxury Development," *New York Times*, February 14, 1960. In 1966, World Wide Realty sold one hundred waterfront lots on Key Biscayne to a consortium led by Bebe Rebozo. Nixon in turn purchased two of those lots in 1967. Gerth, "Nixon and the Mafia," *Sundance*, November/December 1972, 42, 64.

30. "Boca Raton Realty Deal Announced," *Fort Lauderdale News*, May 7, 1958; "2 Firms with Big Holdings in Florida Effect Merger," *Miami News*, October 16, 1958; *Miami Herald*, December 2 and 7, 1965, and *Miami News*, September 2, 1965.‡

31. Bobby Baker hearings, 1118 (Peek and Baker); FBI report by SA Gerard C. Carroll, June 14, 1961, NARA 124-10214-10420 (Davidson's purchase of two thousand shares of Lefcourt in February 1960).

32. Moldea, *Hoffa Wars*, 106; http://surfsidekidnapping.org/site/.

33. *Miami Herald*, June 6, 1965; US Congress, Senate, Committee on Government Operations, Permanent Subcommittee on Investigations, *Organized Crime: Stolen Securities, Hearings*, 92nd Cong., 1st sess. (Washington, DC: US Government Printing Office, 1971), part 3, 856 (testimony of Edward Wuensche re Vance Foster). One of Foster's colleagues in stolen securities deals was Satiris Fassoulis (chapter 3).

34. *Miami Herald*, June 6, 1965. Former Miami National Bank owner George Horvath testified that World Wide Realty also received financing indirectly from the notorious Swiss mob money-laundering conduit, Exchange and Investment Bank. Donald M. Rothberg and Dick Barnes, "Conflict of Interest, Kickbacks Common," *Palo Alto Times*, September 1, 1975.

35. Sources for these stories include former senior FBI and Justice Department officials. Gentry, *J. Edgar Hoover*, 383; Summers, *Official and Confidential*, 184–90, 232–35; Hank Messick, *John Edgar Hoover* (New York: David McKay Co., 1972), 144–48; Scott, *Deep Politics* (1993), 207; Russo, *Supermob*, 37–38; Theoharis and Cox, *The Boss*, 296; Matt Potter, "Oil and Politics in La Jolla," *San Diego Reader*, January 5 and 12, 2011; Van Buren, *Clint*, 297; Turner, *Hoover's FBI*, 70–71.

36. Webb was an employee of the Murchisons' Dallas-based construction firm, Tecon Corp. On his role in negotiating Teamster loans for Trousdale Estates and Wertco, a residential real estate company in Florida whose directors included Bobby Baker's friend Don Reynolds, see Gene Blake, "Baker Link to Teamster Fund Sought," *Los Angeles Times*, October 31, 1963. On Hoover and the mob, see Summers, *Official and Confidential*, 232; Messick, *John Edgar Hoover*; and Newton, *Mr. Mob*, 69–70.

37. Summers, *Official and Confidential*, 233–34. Davidson's claims should be treated with care, as he had a penchant for self-aggrandizement.

38. Summers, *Official and Confidential*, 232–34; also E. W. Kenworthy, "Baker Convicted on 7 of 9 Counts," *New York Times*, January 30, 1967.

39. Summers, *Official and Confidential*, 180; Baker, *Wheeling and Dealing*, 50; Burrough, *The Big Rich*, 159–60. Murchison was speaking about business investments, but his observation applied also to politics.

40. At McCarthy's request, Murchison donated $10,000 to defeat the reelection of Maryland senator Joseph Tydings, who had investigated (and condemned) McCarthy's charges against the State Department in 1950. "There's nobody in this country that's doing the job McCarthy's done," Murchison said. "And I tell you there's nobody better than Joe to do it." Alvin Davis, "Joe Is Doing the Job, Says Texas Angel," *New York Post*, July 7, 1953; Wolfe, *The Murchisons*, 189–96.

41. Wolfe, *The Murchisons*, 194.

42. Oshinsky, *A Conspiracy So Immense*, 303.

43. Van Buren, *Clint*, 306, 350; Wolfe, *The Murchisons*, 199–201.

44. Alan Peppard, "How FDR's Island Visit Helped Birth an Era of Texas Power," *Dallas News*, December 4, 2014.

45. Burrough, *The Big Rich*, 139–44.

46. Clint Murchison and his business partner Toddie Wynne each contributed $5,000 to the Democratic National Committee in October 1940 through Johnson. Robert A. Caro, *The Path to Power* (New York: Alfred A. Knopf, 1982), 649.

47. Robert Caro tells this story in *Means of Ascent* (New York: Knopf, 1990).

48. Caro, *Master of the Senate*, 404-7. Caro also discusses Johnson's lavish fundraising in *Means of Ascent* and *The Path to Power*.

49. Caro, *Master of the Senate*, 247–305; see also Rowland Evans and Robert Novak, *Lyndon B. Johnson: The Exercise of Power* (New York: New American Library, 1966), 35–39; Robert Dallek, *Lone Star Rising: Lyndon Johnson and His Times, 1908-1960* (New York: Oxford University Press, 1991), 375–78. In 1951, gas producers finally received a favorable vote from the Federal Power Commission after Sen. Robert Kerr, an Oklahoma Democrat and oil millionaire, called in political chits with President Truman. Bolles, *How to Get Rich in Washington*, 19–20.

50. Van Buren, *Clint*, 286, 312–17; Wolfe, *The Murchisons*, 315. Clint Sr. soured on LBJ after he joined Kennedy's ticket in 1960, but Clint Jr. remained friendly enough to be a guest of President Johnson at the White House (Wolfe, *The Murchisons*, 345). Clint Jr. also hired LBJ's confidant Abe Fortas as general counsel to his Dallas insurance holding company, Greatamerica Corp. Baker, *Wheeling and Dealing*, 50.

51. Baker, *Wheeling and Dealing*, 86–87.

52. Caro, *Master of the Senate*, 664–76.

53. Van Buren, *Clint*, 302–3; Wolfe, *The Murchisons*, 197–98; Burrough, *The Big Rich*, 219–21.[‡]

54. Sherrill, *Gothic Politics in the Deep South* (Submerged Land Act of 1953); Robert Sherrill, *The Accidental President* (New York: Grossman, 1967), 144–45 (Anderson).[‡]

55. Clint Murchison Jr. letters to Nixon, July 12, 1957, and August 18, 1959; Nixon letter to Clint Murchison Jr., August 28, 1959; Rose Mary Woods memo, February 26, 1957, in "Murchison, Clint," folder, box 539, Series 320, Nixon papers, Nixon Library.

56. Baker, *Wheeling and Dealing*, 50.

57. Edward Folliard, "$1 Million Salute Given to JFK," *Boston Globe*, January 19, 1963; Betty Beale, "Stars Wow, Are Wowed at Private Party at LBJ's," *Boston Globe*, January 27, 1963; Drew Pearson, "Grumman, Democrats, and Money," *Washington Post*, May 23, 1963 (Texas oil crowd). On the prominent role of Grumman Aircraft at this fundraiser, during the TFX fighter plane competition, see chapter 7.

58. Drew Pearson, "What Morse Told Longshoremen," *Washington Post*, January 29, 1963. Pearson commented, "the Murchison family has been recent backers of both Johnson and Kennedy, nor have they subscribed recently to the hate campaigns of other Texas oil millionaires. They have even sponsored some liberal causes." "Johnson's Early Booster," *Tuscaloosa News*, December 1, 1963.

59. Jack Anderson, "Oilman Wynne Pays Cordial Call," *Washington Post*, August 20, 1963.

60. Edward Cowan, "Oil and Gas Men Face Tax Change," *New York Times*, January 25, 1963; "Reform and the Oil Lobby," *New York Times*, February 1, 1963.

61. Baker, *Wheeling and Dealing*, 50. Baker also enjoyed hospitality at Murchison's Spanish Cay in the Bahamas (testimony by Robert Thompson and Webb, Bobby

Baker hearings, 107, 284). Baker brought one of his call girls to a business-social dinner with Webb and Wynne, who was a nonresident member of the Quorum Club. Wheeler, "Scandal Grows and Grows in Washington," *Life*, 40B, 92A, 92B.

62. Robert Thompson testimony, Bobby Baker hearings, 992–93, 1000; Baker, *Wheeling and Dealing*, 169. The shares were of Investors Diversified Services, a takeover target of the Murchisons.

63. Pearson and Anderson, *The Case against Congress*, 120–21; Cabell Phillips, "Celler Split a Fee with Baker's Firm," *New York Times*, January 27, 1965; Cabell Phillips, "Celler and Law Partner Defend Payment of Fee to Baker Firm," *New York Times*, January 28, 1965.

64. Webb testimony, Bobby Baker hearings, 267–69, 281–83; Keith Wheeler, "Scandal Grows and Grows in Washington," *Life*, November 22, 1963, 94; FBI memo from G. H. Scatterday to A. Rosen, November 29, 1961, re "Isadore Irving Davidson," NARA 124-10301-10072; FBI memo from W. R. Wannall to William Sullivan, May 18, 1965, re "I. Irving Davidson," NARA 124-10301-10046; FBI report on Irving Davidson, correlation summary, July 30, 1969, NARA 124-10302-10106 (Webb and Davidson); "Republicans Attack Conduct of Baker Investigation," *CQ Almanac*, v. 20, 1964; Gene Blake, "Baker Link to Teamster Fund Sought," *Los Angeles Times*, October 31, 1963; Baker, *Wheeling and Dealing*, 179.

65. Bobby Baker hearings, 241 (Law testimony regarding Melpar).

66. E. W. Kenworthy, "Murchison Official Aided Baker in Purchase of Stock," *New York Times*, January 29, 1964.

67. Webb testimony in Bobby Baker hearings, 275–76; Jeff Gerth, "Nixon and the Miami Connection," in Steve Weissman, ed., *Big Brother and the Holding Company: The World behind Watergate* (Palo Alto: Ramparts Press, 1974), 270–71.‡

68. Gordon Chaplin, "The Fantastic Deals of I. Irving Davidson," *Potomac*, March 21, 1976, 39; "Republicans Attack Conduct of Baker Investigation," *CQ Almanac*, v. 20, 1964.

69. "Stock Details Given," *New York Times*, November 13, 1963.

70. Robert F. Thompson testimony, Bobby Baker hearings, 986–90.

71. Schreiber, *The Bobby Baker Affair*, 171; Baker, *Wheeling and Dealing*, 156–59; Edward Nellor, *Washington's Wheeler Dealers: Broads, Booze & Bobby Baker!* (New York: Bee-Line Books, 1967), 31–32. Baker's friend Scott Peek, the former aide to Senator Smathers, also profited from MGIC stock. Multer gave MGIC a favorable hearing before his committee (*New York Times*, January 22, 1964).

72. Schreiber, *The Bobby Baker Affair*, ch. 8; Reid, *The Grim Reapers*, 137–39; Webb testimony in Bobby Baker hearings, 270–71, 288–89; Benítez testimony, Bobby Baker hearings, 1030–33. The alleged "underworld character" was Samuel Ferber, who introduced Irving Davidson to Haiti. Sen. Hugh Scott, Bobby Baker hearings, 2217; *New York Times*, November 14, 1963; Airtel from SAC, Washington Field Office, to Director, FBI, January 29, 1964, NARA 124-10301-10051; "Outside Contact Report," November 2, 1978, re I. Irving Davidson, at http://jfk.hood.edu/Collection/Weisberg%20Subject%20Index%20Files/D%20Disk/Davidson%20I%20Irving/Item%2008.pdf. An early rap sheet for Sam Ferber is available at https://dc.lib.jjay .cuny.edu/index.php/Detail/Object/Show/object_id/242.

73. On this complicated deal, see Schreiber, *The Bobby Baker Affair*, 114–29; E. W. Kenworthy, "Baker Is Linked to Import Deal," *New York Times*, November 13, 1963; Ben Franklin, "Inquiry May Call the Murchisons," *New York Times*, November 16, 1963; Jerry Landauer, "Hearing Discloses Baker Was Also Involved in Meat Exports, Earning 'Finder's Fees,'" *Wall Street Journal*, February 5, 1964.

74. Cabell Phillips, "Baker Made $8,000 in Fees in Haitian Meat Deal," *New York Times*, February 5, 1964.

75. Baker, *Wheeling and Dealing*, 48–49.

76. Schreiber, *The Bobby Baker Affair*, 171–72; Matt Potter, "The Big Rich, Part Two," *San Diego Reader*, January 12, 2011 (Brown and John Alessio).

77. Jim Amoss and Fen Montaigne, "Brilab Defendant: FBI Offered Deal," *New Orleans Times-Picayune*, July 9, 1981; transcript of Davidson's call with Jim Draykol, July 17, 1979, from FBI Brilab surveillance, https://www.maryferrell.org/showDoc.html?docId=145551. During the course of this conversation, Davidson explained that he was trying to persuade Clint Murchison Jr. to buy Marcello's extensive landholdings.

78. Bobby Baker hearings, 278, 284.

79. Arnold Lubasch, "City-within-a-City Rising in the South," *New York Times*, June 4, 1961.‡

80. "History of MAF," https://mafspace.msfc.nasa.gov/become-maf-tenant__trashed/history-maf/; Ned Hémard, "Happy Folly," http://www.neworleansbar.org/uploads/files/ENews080625NostalgiaHappyFolly.pdf.

81. "Space Is Good for Murchisons," *Chicago Tribune*, June 10, 1962; "High Finance: Gladder to Get Out Than Sorry to Lose Out," *Time*, April 19, 1963. As early as 1961, a writer cited the NASA Michoud plant as "the basis of the current civic activity [in New Orleans] for Murchison's real estate." Joseph Ator, "Murchison Building Wasteland into New Orleans Subdivision," *Chicago Tribune*, November 5, 1961.

82. William Moore, "Block Attempt to Sift Johnson Financial Setup," *Chicago Tribune*, February 27, 1965.

83. Question by Sen. Hugh Scott in Bobby Baker hearings, 1347.

84. McLendon, Bobby Baker hearings, 2142.

Chapter 7

1. Oral history transcript, Raymond E. Buck, interview 1, May 27, 1969, by David G. McComb, LBJ Library Oral Histories, LBJ Presidential Library. In his interview, Buck noted that Johnson "was influential in keeping the government from closing down the Consolidated Vultee Plant in Fort Worth after World War II and from cancelling the contract for the B-36, which would have put twenty thousand people out of work in this community."

2. Text of Kennedy's speech at https://www.presidency.ucsb.edu/documents/remarks-the-breakfast-the-fort-worth-chamber-commerce. A sound recording is available from the Kennedy Library at https://www.jfklibrary.org/asset-viewer/archives/JFKWHA/1963/JFKWHA-244-003/JFKWHA-244-003.

3. Conrad Hilton, *Be My Guest* (New York: Simon & Schuster, 1957). 208–13; *Forbes*, December 8, 1980; *Business Week*, March 31, 1986; Drew Pearson, "General Dynamics' Stockholder," *Washington Post*, June 14, 1950; Richard Griffin, "Taking Account of Henry Crown," *New York Times*, December 12, 1976; Joan Cook, "Henry Crown, Industrialist, Dies," *New York Times*, August 16, 1990.

4. "The Ordeal of Lester Crown," *New York Times*, December 7, 1986.

5. Richard Griffin, "Taking Account of Henry Crown," *New York Times*, December 12, 1976.

6. Charles Gotthart, "Crown, Starting on $20,000, Hits Business Peak," *Chicago Tribune*, December 14, 1949.

7. Demaris, *Captive City*, 218. Nanini, president of Rock Road Construction Company, supported Chicago mobster Louis Campagna's application for parole in 1947 (Parole Hearings, 74). Nanini later became a successful developer in Tucson, Arizona. Kimberly Matas, "Bill Nanini, Builder of Tucson National, Philanthropist, Dies," *Arizona Daily Star*, September 22, 2009.

8. Demaris, *Captive City*, 117, 169, 214–26; "Accused Labor Chief Dies," *New York Times*, August 5, 1940; *United States v. Carrozzo* (N.D. Ill. 1941) 37 F. Supp. 191; Russo, *Supermob*, 21; *Fortune*, April 1956, 176, 179, 182; "Chicago Realty Deal Defended by Arvey," *Washington Post*, December 14, 1949. The latter story notes that a third partner on the real estate deal was former Chicago trucking operator John Gottlieb, a friend of Hoffa who later became an investor in the Dunes hotel-casino in Las Vegas. On Arvey, see also Peterson, *Barbarians in Our Midst*, 209, 212. Gus Russo added, "With the political influence of his pal Arvey, Crown obtained lucrative city contracts in Chicago such as the award to furnish all the pencils and paper for the city's school system. He also supplied the coal for over four hundred schools, earning an additional $1 million per year." (Russo, *Supermob*, 19).‡

9. Jacob M. Arvey, "Chicagoans Have Made Great Contributions toward the Growth and Development of Israel," *Chicago Tribune*, April 26, 1971; "Arvey Honored as 2,000 Buy Israeli Bonds," *Chicago Tribune*, November 7, 1954.

10. "Mr. Arvey in Search of a Candidate," *Chicago Tribune*, November 19, 1946. In 1950, Arvey's machine backed Marshall Korshak, brother of mob lawyer Sidney Korshak, for state senator against an African American union leader and reform candidate, who complained that mob money was financing several leading Democratic candidates. Robert Howard, "Arvey Forces Fight to Last Ditch in Area," *Chicago Tribune*, April 9, 1950. For profiles of Arvey's career, including his shifting alliances with racketeers and legitimate politicians, see Joe Kraus, *The Kosher Capones: A History of Chicago's Jewish Gangsters* (Ithaca, NY: Cornell University Press, 2019), 14, 69, 89–99, and Savage, *Truman and the Democratic Party*, 41–48.

11. For an early mention of Jenner's Republican activism, see "GOP County Chief Seeking Coy Aspirants," *Chicago Tribune*, November 4, 1949. On Crown's son John, see Kevin Heise, "Ex-Cook County Circuit Judge John J. Crown," *Chicago Tribune*, March 6, 1977.

12. In 1953, Jenner represented a union associate of Dorfman, Frank Darling, before a special subcommittee of the House Committee on Education and Labor, which was investigating union welfare funds and racketeering. On Dorfman's re-

corded advice, see "Underworld Plug," *Wall Street Journal*, March 8, 1983. In 1974, while serving as minority (Republican) counsel to the House Judiciary Committee's impeachment inquiry, Jenner also represented two of Dorfman's mob codefendants in a $1.4 million Teamster pension fraud case (Denny Walsh, "Ex-Teamster Aide Enjoys a Vacation before Arrest," *New York Times*, March 1, 1974). Jenner later defended Dorfman against federal claims, sustained at trial, that he conspired with Teamster president Roy Williams and others to bribe Nevada senator Howard Cannon (William Crawford Jr. and Ronald Koziol, "Dorfman Is Called Mob's Conduit to Teamster Funds," *Chicago Tribune*, July 1, 1981). On Jenner's praise of Dorfman, see Douglas Frantz, "Dorfman Freed on Firm's Stock, $1 Million Bond," *Chicago Tribune*, December 18, 1982.

13. FBI telegram from SAC, Chicago, to FBI headquarters, November 8, 1962, "Activities of Top Hoodlums, Chicago Division," NARA 124-10196-10332 (John D'Arco). Judge Sorrentino was investigated for but never convicted of corruption (Aamer Madhani, "Judge Pasquale A. 'Buck' Sorrentino, 84," *Chicago Tribune*, October 19, 2001).

14. FBI telegram from SAC, Chicago, to Director, FBI, January 7, 1960, "Murray Llewelyn Humphreys," Humphreys file, FBI FOIA. The document notes that Crown's son Lester was involved with Humphreys in renting the penthouse of a Miami hotel.

15. Abell, *Drew Pearson Diaries*, 470. This story is consistent with the recollection of *Chicago Tribune* reporter James Doherty, who heard from Hoover himself "how powerful this mob has grown in Chicago, how much money they have, how many of the big hotels they own in Chicago." Parole Hearings, 360. Kraus cites evidence that Arvey's former secretary and close political colleague, Arthur X. Elrod, approved Ragen's murder (*The Kosher Capones*, 95–96, 118–19). The Kefauver Committee commented, "To the extent that the Capone crime syndicate controls the wire service, it is in that proportionate measure a partner of every bookmaker of any consequence in the country." US Congress, Senate, Special Committee to Investigate Organized Crime in Interstate Commerce, *Second Interim Report . . . Pursuant to S. Res. 202*, Report no. 141, 82nd Cong., 1st sess. (Washington, DC: US Government Printing Office, 1951), 11.

16. FBI airtel from SAC, Chicago, to Director, FBI, re Henry Crown, August 24, 1973, FBI FOIA release on Henry Crown. The only derogatory information in the bureau's files pertained to Crown's alleged membership in the American League Against War and Fascism in 1936, information supplied by the House Un-American Activities Committee to the Office of Naval Investigations during a background check of Crown after his takeover of General Dynamics. The Chicago FBI office recommended that no action be taken against Crown in view of the age of the issue and the fact that he was "one of the outstanding financiers of this country." FBI memo from SAC, Chicago, to Director, FBI, re Henry Crown, September 1, 1960, in FBI case file 100-HQ-433865, Records of the Federal Bureau of Investigation, Record Group 65, NARA.

17. Busch, "Hilton the Host," *Life*, November 28, 1949, 98; Hilton, *Be My Guest*, 238–40.

18. Noel F. Busch, "Hilton the Host," *Life*, November 28, 1949, 98; Hilton, *Be My Guest*, 238–40; Charles Gotthart, "Crown, Starting on $20,000, Hits Business Peak," *Chicago Tribune*, December 14, 1949; "Connie Hilton's Hotel Empire," *Fortune*, 1953, at http://fortune.com/2013/12/13/connie-hiltons-hotel-empire-fortune-1953/; Hilton Hotels Corporation, *1954 Annual Report*, 2.‡

19. Russo, *Supermob*, 93, 95.

20. FBI report by SA Robert A. Cook, Chicago, March 10, 1961, "Gus Alex," NARA 124-10199-10112; FBI report, Los Angeles office, "Sidney R. Korshak," August 13, 1963 (FOIA release); Russo, *Supermob*, 95. Another silent owner was said to be Frank Ferraro, who was described by Robert Kennedy as "the most vicious and ruthless of all members of the Chicago underworld."

21. Report by SA Joseph L. Tangel, New York, September 14, 1959, "Activities of Top Hoodlums in the New York Field Division," NARA 124-90103-10093 (Costello and Alo); FBI Correlation Summary on Anthony Salerno, September 14, 1964, Salerno files, FBI FOIA release.

22. Rappleye and Becker, *All American Mafioso*, 169.‡

23. "Miss Renee Schine Becomes a Bride," *New York Times*, December 29, 1950. The extravagantly expensive wedding was held at the Waldorf Astoria hotel in New York, recently purchased by Crown and Hilton.‡

24. "J. Myer Schine, 78, Hotel Man, Dead," *New York Times*, May 10, 1971. "Schine Served on Contempt Charges," *Motion Picture Daily*, April 2, 1954.

25. Kefauver hearings, pt. 1, 97, 348–49, 352; Arthur Jay Harris, "He Did a Job on the Mob," *Miami New Times*, April 23, 1998.‡

26. Reid, *Mickey Cohen*, 125–26; Tereba, *Mickey Cohen*. For a copy of Cohen's rap sheet, see *Professional Boxing*, 1209.

27. Kefauver hearings, pt. 7, 772–805.

28. In 1972, Wirtz joined Crown to buy control of the Chicago Bulls. Norris sat with Crown on the board of the Chicago, Rock Island and Pacific Railroad Co. (in which Moe Dalitz also owned shares), and of West Indies Sugar Company, which had large landholdings in the Dominican Republic. Norris also sat on the board of First National Bank of Chicago, one of Crown's main financial backers. On Norris, see D'Arcy Jenish, *The NHL: A Centennial History* (AnchorCanada, 2016), 71. Rafael Trujillo purchased the Dominican holdings of West Indies Sugar in 1957 (Louis and Yazijian, *The Cola Wars*, 300).

29. W. K. Stratton, *Floyd Patterson: The Fighting Life of Boxing's Invisible Champion* (New York: Houghton Mifflin Harcourt, 2012), 38–39, 235n13; Nick Tosches, *The Devil and Sonny Liston* (Boston: Little Brown, 2000), 73–79, 106; Russell Porter, "Executive Shift Made by Garden," *New York Times*, June 9, 1955; "2 New Executives Take Over Garden," *New York Times*, June 10, 1955; Joseph Nichols, "2 Boxing Promoters Told to End Links to Madison Square Garden," *New York Times*, June 25, 1957; *Professional Boxing*, 120, 270, 401–3, 433, 590 et seq., 886 et seq.

30. Peterson, *The Mob*, 328–30; Allen Witwer, "Crime Text Opens $2 Million Door for Intertel," *Las Vegas Sun*, March 24, 1971. Witwer handled public relations for the Grand Bahama Development Co. and managed the Del Charro Hotel in La Jolla, owned by Clint Murchison. (Another key PR man for Lucayan Beach Hotel,

which housed Lansky's casino, was Roy Cohn's friend and future Nixon speechwriter William Safire.) Witwer identified two prominent bookies as fronts for Norris in the casino operation (Allen Witwer, "Bahamas Game Same, Whatever Name," *Las Vegas Sun*, March 27, 1971). Norris allowed the radio on his yacht "to be used to relay credit information back and forth" between the US mainland and the Monte Carlo Casino on Grand Bahama Island (Richard Oulahan and William Lambert, "The Scandal in the Bahamas," *Life*, February 3, 1967). On New York bookmaker Max Courtney (Morris Schmertzler), who hooked up with Norris and Wirtz at the St. Louis Stadium Corp. before joining Lansky in the Bahamas, see *Professional Boxing*, 342–43, 582; Messick and Nellis, *The Private Lives of Public Enemies*, 211.

31. On May 17, 1960, Chicago Outfit boss Murray Humphreys told a colleague that when the Golden Nugget casino was for sale several years earlier, "I had Wirtz look over their statement and everything. . . . You take a guy like Wirtz, and he knows his figures, he's the guy with the figures. . . . We had both figures, the underneath and the over. They had 750 stockholders, and then they had the under the table stockholders, and we went over everything." FBI report by SA Marshall Rutland, July 29, 1960, re "Anthony Joseph Accardo," NARA 124-10203-10000.

32. *Miami News*, October 16, 1958; Eileen Connelly, "They Built New York: Abraham Lefcourt," *The Real Deal*, October 28, 2015. Wirtz controlled First National Bank of South Miami (https://en.wikipedia.org/wiki/Wirtz_Corporation). Wall Street stockbroker David Baird, who also owned shares in Lefcourt, became a director of Madison Square Garden in 1962. Baird had previously been replaced on Lefcourt's board by Wirtz but was appointed a financial adviser to the real estate firm ("Lefcourt Corp. Affirms Deal," *Miami News*, February 3, 1959).

33. English, *Havana Nocturne*, 133, 188, 227–29; FBI report on Cuban gambling by FBI legal attaché, Havana, May 9, 1958, NARA 124-90068-10093.

34. FBI report, "Miami Brief for Attorney General's Criminal Intelligence Conference, Washington, D.C., October 10–11, 1962," NARA 124-10194-10182.

35. Messick, *Syndicate Abroad*, 214–15.

36. Clarence Jones and James Savage, "Mob Money: Silent Host in Beach Hotels," *Miami Herald*, January 29, 1967; "Fontainebleau: Mob Money's Beach Prize," *Miami Herald*, January 30, 1967.‡

37. J. Anthony Lukas, "Report from Convention City," *New York Times*, July 9, 1972.

38. Kirkeby owned such landmark properties as the Beverly Wilshire Hotel in Los Angeles; the Gotham and Warwick hotels in New York; the Blackstone and Drake hotels in Chicago; and the Kenilworth in Miami Beach. With the Chicago-Tampa Development Company, he built a new suburb on Santo Trafficante's turf in the late 1920s. In 1940, Kirkeby became president of the National Cuba Hotel Corporation, which leased the Hotel Nacional in Havana to Lansky. The FBI identified him as a close associate of such mobsters as Benjamin Siegel, Abner Zwillman, Rocco and Charles Fischetti, and Meyer Lansky. He was also close to the Chicago syndicate's superlawyer, Sidney Korshak. FBI report, June 25, 1968, re "Criminal Influence in Miami Area Hotels, Motels and Night Clubs," NARA 124-10291-10389; Michael

Gross, *Unreal Estate: Money, Ambition, and the Lust for Land in Los Angeles* (New York: Broadway Books, 2011), 158–66; Russo, *Supermob*, 97–98.

39. Investigative Reporters and Editors, "Del Webb's Other Side: Hidden Ties to Mobsters," *Newsday*, March 19, 1977.‡

40. Investigative Reporters and Editors, "Del Webb's Other Side: Hidden Ties to Mobsters," *Newsday*, March 19, 1977; Michael F. Wendland, *The Arizona Project* (Kansas City: Sheed, Andrew and McMeel, 1977), 90–91; State of New Jersey, Department of Law and Public Safety, Division of Gaming Enforcement, *Report to the Casino Control Commission with Regard to the Application of Del. E. Webb Corporation of New Jersey and Del E. Webb Corporation for a Casino License* (Trenton, 1981), 82–86; Jane Ammeson, "The Busy Life of Billionaire Lester Crown," *Chicago Life*, February 7, 2008 (Crown and Yankees). The Investigative Reporters and Editors story states that Webb "was a personal friend of Franklin D. Roosevelt, Dwight D. Eisenhower and J. Edgar Hoover." A senior Justice Department prosecutor recalled, "No [FBI] bugs went in on Webb's places. . . . Hoover gave Webb a pass. He was his buddy." Summers, *Official and Confidential*, 231. For details on Webb's legitimate associations in the casino business, see Tom Alexander, "What Del Webb Is Up to in Nevada," *Fortune*, May 1965, 132, 185–86.

41. Lait and Mortimer, *U.S.A. Confidential*, 309.

42. "Join Empire State Company's Board," *New York Times*, November 11, 1954; Richard Griffin, "Taking Account of Henry Crown," *New York Times*, December 12, 1976. Binns was also a director of Seven Arts, which developed the Bahamian casino tied to Lansky, Norris, and other mobsters.‡

43. Atlas received more than 100,000 common shares and more than 50,000 preferred shares in the new Hilton Hotels Corp. in 1946. It sold most of its shares in 1948 and 1949 for a profit of more than $1.6 million. Atlas Corporation, *Silver Anniversary Report—Review of the Past Quarter Century—Report for the Year Ended December 31, 1954*.

44. Roger Franklin, *The Defender: The Story of General Dynamics* (New York: Harper and Row, 1986), 127–28 (quote); Rhonda Smith-Daugherty, *Jacqueline Cochrane: Biography of a Pioneer Aviator* (Jefferson, NC: McFarland, 2012).

45. Ferdinand Lundberg, *America's 60 Families* (New York: Halcyon House, 1938), 32; "Atlas into Hearst," *Time*, March 10, 1941; "Odlum's Activity Wide," *New York Times*, September 5, 1941; "Atlas Corporation," May 2, 1952, in "The Atlas Story (1)" file, Floyd Odlum papers, Dwight Eisenhower Library; report on Atlas Corp. holdings as of December 31, 1942, in "Atlas—Miscellaneous Reports, 1942–1955 (1)" file, Odlum papers.‡

46. Richard B. Jewell, *RKO Radio Pictures: A Titan Is Born* (Berkeley: University of California Press, 2012); "Atlas Corporation," May 2, 1952, "The Atlas Story" (1) file, Odlum papers; Atlas Corporation, *Silver Anniversary Report—Review of the Past Quarter Century—Report for the Year Ended December 31, 1954*; FBI report by SA R. T. Pugh, September 29, 1941, re Edwin L. Weisl, file no. 77-434, FBI FOIA release on Weisl.

47. Odlum took senior posts in the Roosevelt administration at the Office of Production Management and War Production Board, for which President Truman

awarded him the Presidential Certificate of Merit in 1947. (Letter from D. Lawrence Groner, Medal for Merit Board, to Floyd Odlum, July 16, 1947, in "Correspondence, 1947–48," file, box 1, Odlum papers, Eisenhower Library.) As we have seen (chapter 3), he was one of the biggest contributors to Truman's 1948 campaign, through his friend Louis Johnson, who would soon become secretary of defense. In 1952, Odlum switched sides and, with his famous wife, staged a huge rally at Madison Square Garden to convince Dwight Eisenhower to run for president. Years later, Eisenhower worked on his memoirs at Odlum's ranch in Indio, California. Lyndon Johnson was also a devoted friend, not least because Odlum's wife saved his political career—and his life—during the 1948 Senate race by flying the Texas congressman to the Mayo Clinic in Minnesota to have kidney stones removed (Jacqueline Cochran, oral history interview I, April 7, 1974, by Joe B. Frantz, LBJ Library). Johnson won that primary by just a few votes, almost certainly thanks to a fraudulent count, for which he earned the nickname "Landslide Lyndon." In 1954, after Johnson racked up a huge victory in the Senate primary, Odlum and Weisl sent LBJ a congratulatory telegram, saying they were "very happy to know there was really a landslide." Johnson replied, "One of the high points of that election was the telegram of congratulations from you and Eddie Weisl. Victory is always sweet but it is even sweeter when a man has friends like you and Eddie who share the enjoyment. Thank you very much—not just for the telegram but for the years of close friendship and good counsel." Lyndon Johnson letter to Odlum, August 2, 1954, in "J, 1953–54" file, Odlum papers, Eisenhower Library. In his waning days as president, Johnson spoke at a dinner honoring Odlum, calling the investor his "dear old friend of many years." Lyndon B. Johnson: "Remarks at a Dinner Honoring Floyd B. Odlum, Founder and Chairman of the Arthritis Foundation," May 20, 1968," at http://www.presidency.ucsb.edu/ws/?pid=28874.

48. "General Dynamics Buys Into 'Convair,'" *New York Times*, March 31, 1953; Franklin, *The Defender*, 144; memo, "Convair," December 31, 1953, in "A-C-GD Merger, 1953–54 (2)" file, Odlum papers, Eisenhower Library.

49. "Directors of General Dynamics, Material Service Vote Merger," *New York Times*, June 27, 1959.[‡]

50. "Hoy Elected President of 2 Hotel Firms," *Chicago Tribune*, April 22, 1955; "Hoy Elected Gen. Dynamics Vice President," *Chicago Tribune*, May 6, 1960; "Patrick H. Hoy, 59, of Penn Dixie Dies," *New York Times*, August 22, 1973.[‡]

51. Demaris, *Captive City*, 230. Demaris also notes Hoy's close association with Ralph Stolkin, the mob-linked Florida land investor (chapter 6) who tried to purchase RKO from Howard Hughes in 1952. Hoy was also a good friend of John D'Arco, alderman of Chicago's First Ward, who reported secretly to Sam Giancana and other mobsters (FBI telegram from SAC, Chicago, to FBI headquarters, November 8, 1962, "Activities of Top Hoodlums, Chicago Division," NARA 124-10196-10332 and telegram from SAC, Chicago, to FBI headquarters, March 5, 1963, NARA 124-10210-10024).

52. Moldea, *Dark Victory*, 339.

53. "Patrick Hoy Declared Bankrupt," *Chicago Tribune*, November 29, 1967 (total debts of $8.5 million); "Ledgers Show Hoy Did Not Repay Crowns," *Chicago Tribune*, September 30, 1970; "Indictment Links Hoy to Bank Frauds," *Chicago Tribune*, June

27, 1969; "I'm Guilty of Fraud, Hoy Says," *Chicago Tribune*, October 8, 1970; "Industrialist Pleads Guilty to $2 Million Bank Fraud," *New York Times*, October 8, 1970; "Sentence for Fraud," *New York Times*, November 18, 1970.

54. "Hilton Casino OK Held Up," *The Record* [Bergen County], January 30, 1985.

55. Harvey Fisher, "Hilton Loses Bid for Casino License," *The Record*, March 1, 1985.

56. FBI Correlation Summary on Sidney R. Korshak, August 12, 1968, Korshak files, FBI FOIA release.

57. Russo, *Supermob*, 166–67.

58. Henry Weinstein, "Sidney Korshak, Alleged Mafia Liaison to Hollywood, Dies at 88," *Los Angeles Times*, January 22, 1996.[‡]

59. Demaris, *The Last Mafioso*, 272.

60. Russo, *Supermob*, 324–25.

61. Weinstein, "Sidney Korshak," *Los Angeles Times*, January 22, 1996; cf. "Mrs. Lewis Gives Million to Loyola U," *Chicago Tribune*, November 25, 1964.[‡]

62. John Lawrence, "General Dynamics, Once a San Diego Mainstay, Now Dearly Departed," *San Diego Free Press*, 1969 (republished July 16, 2016), at https://sandiegofreepress.org/2016/07/general-dynamics-san-diego/; Fred Cook, *The Warfare State*, 189–90.

63. Elliott V. Converse III, *Rearming for the Cold War, 1945–1960* (Washington, DC: Historical Office, Office of the Secretary of Defense, 2012), 295. Symington helped arrange Odlum's hiring of General McNarney at Convair in 1952. Jack Raymond, *Power at the Pentagon* (New York: Harper & Row, 1964), 209–10.

64. Lawrence, "General Dynamics."

65. Richard Pearson, "Frank Pace, Ex-Secretary of Army, Dies," *Washington Post*, January 10, 1988.

66. Hughes hated to lose control of the company. That was a factor behind his decision several years later to sell the airline and reinvest the proceeds in Nevada gambling casinos, most of which were owned by mobsters.

67. John Lee, "Company Thrived on Defense Work, but General Dynamics Lost Way in Commercial Field," *New York Times*, January 26, 1962; "The Convair Division of General Dynamics," http://www.456fis.org/CONVAIR_DIVISION_GENERAL _DYNAMICS.htm.

68. "General Dynamics' Ordeal," *Time*, January 5, 1962; Richard Griffin, "Taking Account of Henry Crown," *New York Times*, December 12, 1976.

69. Turner, *Gamblers' Money*, 193–94; Patman report, ix. For general background on Wien, see Alfonso Narvaez, "Lawrence A. Wien, 83, Is Dead; Lawyer Gave Millions to Charity," *New York Times*, December 12, 1988; "Jewish Charities Elect President," *New York Times*, April 5, 1960.[‡]

70. Demaris, *Captive City*, 226.

71. Denton and Morris, *The Money and the Power*, 242.

72. Lawrence, "General Dynamics."

73. Richard Austin Smith, "The $7-Billion Contract That Changed the Rules," *Fortune*, March 1963.

74. Franklin, *The Defender*, 172–73, 196–97; John King Jr., "Boom of TFX Is Heard through Texas," *New York Times*, April 15, 1963. For McNamara's defense, see "McNamara on TFX," *Flight International*, April 18, 1963, 565.

75. Seth Kantor's story, "TFX Contract Is Reported in Bag for General Dynamics," was the subject of extensive testimony. United States Congress, Senate Committee on Government Operations, Permanent Subcommittee on Investigations, *TFX Contract Investigation, Hearings*, 88th Cong., 1st sess. (Washington, DC: US Government Printing Office, 1963–1964), 1251–90.

76. Russo, *The Outfit*, 402–3; Russo, *Supermob*, 241. Ziffren, a chair of the California Democratic Party, brought the 1960 Democratic convention to Los Angeles. Arvey supervised the 1952 and 1956 Democratic conventions, held in Chicago, and helped ensure that Illinois went for Kennedy/Johnson in 1960. The head of the FBI's Los Angeles field office wrote Hoover in 1960, "Ziffren, hoodlum-founded though he is, is probably the shrewdest, most cunning, far-sighted, behind-the-scenes political manipulator ever encountered in California—where kingmakers have historically ruled politicians" (Russo, *Supermob*, 244).

Seymour Hersh suggested that even dirtier forces of blackmail were at play. Based on evidence from FBI files, he speculated that the head of security for General Dynamics, I. B. Hale, sponsored a break-in at the apartment of President Kennedy's mistress Judith Campbell in August 1962. Hersh, *The Dark Side of Camelot*, 317–21; FBI memo from C.A. Evans to Belmont, August 17, 1962, "John Rosselli," NARA 124-10226-10086.

77. Drew Pearson, "Washington Merry-Go-Round," *La Habra Star*, April 12, 1963.

78. Mollenhoff, *Despoilers of Democracy*, 175–83; S. M. Amadae, *Rationalizing Capitalist Democracy: The Cold War Origins of Rational Choice Liberalism* (Chicago: University of Chicago Press, 2003), 66; "Answers Needed on the TFX," *New York Times*, June 11, 1963.

79. Fred Korth testimony, *TFX Contract Investigation, Hearings*, 1882–83; Franklin, *The Defender*, 201, 207; Mollenhoff, *Despoilers of Democracy*, 211–25; Tom Wicker, "Korth Reported Asked to Resign for 'Indiscretion,'" *New York Times*, October 19, 1963; "Korth Declares His Resignation Was Not Forced," *New York Times*, October 20, 1963; "Senators to Investigate Bank's Present to Korth," *New York Times*, November 9, 1963. One news story attributed Korth's resignation to a dispute with McNamara over plans for a nuclear-powered aircraft carrier; Robert E. Thompson, "Navy Sec'y Korth Quits after Row with McNamara," *Boston Globe*, October 15, 1963.[‡]

80. President Kennedy conversation #2 with Robert S. McNamara, October 16, 1963, 5:00 p.m., Dictabelt 27D, https://www.jfklibrary.org/asset-viewer/archives/JFK POF/TPH/JFKPOF-TPH-27D/JFKPOF-TPH-27D.

81. Arthur Krock, "The Korth Case," *New York Times*, November 3, 1963.

82. Ramsey Clark, oral history interviews by Larry J. Hackman, July 7 and July 20, 1970, Robert F. Kennedy Library Oral History Program.[‡]

83. Kalman, *Abe Fortas*, 209.

84. Walter Trohan, "Report from Washington," *Chicago Tribune*, October 19, 1963. Johnson protested against Korth's ouster; Schlesinger Jr., *Robert Kennedy and His Times*, 384.

85. Fred Korth, recorded interview by Joseph E. O'Connor, January 27, 1966, John F. Kennedy Library Oral History Program; Vice President Lyndon B. Johnson Daily Diary, October 18, 1963, at http://www.lbjlibrary.net/collections/daily-diary .html.

86. Benjamin C. Bradlee, *Conversations with Kennedy* (New York: W.W. Norton, 1975), 216. As noted above, LBJ's 1941 and 1948 campaigns had been co-managed by Raymond Buck, associate general counsel of Convair.

87. Drew Pearson, "Grumman, Democrats, and Money," *Washington Post*, May 23, 1963.

88. Pearson, *Washington Merry-Go-Round*, 186. Zuckert said LBJ made only one casual reference to him about the TFX at a cocktail party in 1962 (Drew Pearson, "Yankees Learn Talkathon Secret," *Atlanta Journal*, July 14, 1963).

89. Thomas Collins, "TFX Probers Hunt Korth-Baker Link," *Newsday*, October 23, 1963.

90. David Kraslow, "Baker Reported Set to 'Tell All' in TFX Probe," *Philadelphia Inquirer*, November 14, 1963.

91. "Baker and Korth," *New York Times*, November 10, 1963.

92. "Statement of Mr. Gilpatric's Prior Associations with Boeing and General Dynamics," in *TFX Contract Investigation, Hearings*, 419–20; testimony of Roswell Gilpatric in ibid., 2544 et seq; Jack Raymond, "Possibility of a Johnson Role in TFX Contract Raised," *New York Times*, November 20, 1963; Jack Raymond, "Gilpatric Called in Plane Inquiry," *New York Times*, March 21, 1963; Jack Raymond, "Gilpatric's Role in TFX Questioned," *New York Times*, November 19, 1963; "Brains behind the Muscle," *Time*, April 7, 1961; Franklin, *The Defender*, 205–6.

93. Mollenhoff, *Despoilers of Democracy*, 194–210.

94. *United States v. Mississippi Valley Generating Co.*, 364 U.S. 520 (1961).

95. Jack Raymond, "Senators to Renew TFX Study with Testimony from Gilpatric," *New York Times*, November 10, 1963; Jack Raymond, "Possibility of a Johnson Role in TFX Contract Raised," *New York Times*, November 20, 1963; Hanson Baldwin, "Johnson and Pentagon," *New York Times*, November 28, 1963. It is at least plausible that Johnson influenced the secretary of defense. McNamara's deputy, Roswell Gilpatric, recalled that President Kennedy "seemed to me to have a real respect for Johnson's political savviness. He was always telling McNamara, 'Now you go talk to Lyndon about this,' or 'Talk to the vice president about this.'" Roswell L. Gilpatric Oral History Interview—JFK#3, June 30, 1970, by Dennis J. O'Brien, Kennedy Library.

Korth recalled that Johnson was not the only prominent politician lobbying behind the scenes for General Dynamics: "I remember contacts that were made to me by Senator [Robert S.] Kerr who strongly urged upon me a decision for General Dynamics of Fort Worth, because in this instance, the Douglas plant at Tulsa, it was indicated, would have some of the subcontracting work. . . . Kerr indicated to me at a party given out at the then–Vice President's home that he was going to talk with [Air Force] Secretary [Eugene] Zuckert to try to influence him to the same decision for the same reason. Now, I accept Secretary Zuckert's statement that he did not have undue influence." (Kerr, the powerful and unscrupulous Oklahoma Democrat, was Bobby Baker's main patron after Johnson.) Fred Korth, recorded interview by Joseph E. O'Connor, January 27, 1966, John F. Kennedy Library Oral History Program.

96. Jack Anderson, "Bobby Baker Knows Where TFX Skeletons Are Buried," *Garden City Telegram*, November 23, 1963; for a previous column addressing some of these issues, see Jack Anderson, "New Leads for TFX Case Inquiry," *Los Angeles Times*, July 3, 1963. Pearson later came to suspect that LBJ "had nothing to do with the whole matter." Instead, the journalist speculated privately, President Kennedy may have dictated McNamara's decision in order to promote employment by Grumman in Massachusetts, "where Teddy Kennedy was running for election." Pearson, *Washington Merry-Go-Round*, 369–70.

97. Pearson, *Washington Merry-Go-Round*, 369.

98. Scott, *Deep Politics and the Death of JFK* (1993), 220–21; Mollenhoff, *Despoilers of Democracy*, 295–99; Demaris, *Captive City*, 226–27; Laurence Barrett, "Senate Probe of TFX Quietly Shuffled Aside—Inquiry into Texas Contractor Has Greater Connotations with Johnson as President," *Los Angeles Times*, December 9, 1963; Jack Raymond, "TFX Inquiry Seems Ended as McClellan Delays Hearings Indefinitely," *New York Times*, December 15, 1963; "Senate to Resume TFX Award Inquiry," *New York Times*, December 23, 1964; "Senate to Reopen TFX Plane Inquiry," *New York Times*, August 17, 1966.

99. Jonathan Marshall, "How Kennedy Assassination Affected Some Stock Prices," *San Francisco Chronicle*, November 18, 1996; William Brown Jr., "Friends in High Places: The Wealth Effects of JFK's Assassination on the Assets of LBJ's Supporters," *Public Choice* 86:3 (March 1996), 247–56.

100. President Johnson telephone call with Roswell Gilpatric, December 23, 1963, 11:45 a.m., starting about 4:40, LBJ Library, https://discoverlbj.org/item/tel-00647.

101. President Johnson telephone call with Frank Stanton, February 6, 1964, LBJ Library, https://discoverlbj.org/item/tel-01907.

102. Drawing on the papers of the chief Rules Committee investigator, Robert David Johnson writes that Don Reynolds "claimed that Baker had shown him a sack containing $200,000 in cash," allegedly a payoff to LBJ from General Dynamics and Grumman. "The Rules Committee, citing inaccuracies in Reynolds's account, refused to investigate. [Senator] Williams, desperate, contended that even if Reynolds himself were 'inaccurate or confused,' the awarding of the TFX contract was 'so irregular' that a payoff must have occurred. That line of thinking unsurprisingly failed to persuade committee Democrats." Johnson, *All the Way with LBJ*, 47–48. A memo by Williams dated Reynolds's allegations to February 9, 1964. Steinberg asserts that Reynolds first made the allegations in closed-door testimony on November 22, 1963, but he may be mistaken. Steinberg, *Sam Johnson's Boy*, 611.

103. David Kraslow, "Air Force Won't Talk on Baker Probe Report," *Los Angeles Times*, February 12, 1964.

104. E. W. Kenworthy, "FBI Discredits Payoff Charges by Baker Witness," *New York Times*, March 3, 1965; "Investigations: The FBI Report," *Time*, March, 12, 1965; FBI memo, "Henry Crown," April 2, 1971, in FBI case file 100-HQ-433865, Record Group 65, Records of the Federal Bureau of Investigation, NARA. President Johnson discussed Reynolds's charges with Secretary of Defense Robert McNamara on December 9, 1964, 11:50 a.m. Conversation WH6412-01-6606-6607, http://prde.upress.virginia.edu/conversations/4002648.

105. "Weight Problem Besets Navy TFX," *New York Times*, May 10, 1965; "Navy Concedes TFX Will Be in Use Late," *New York Times*, October 18, 1967; Franklin, *The Defender*, 211–17. One major study concluded that "the F-111 program was a symbol for the failures" of defense management. "The Navy never procured or deployed its version of the aircraft as the Navy version was cancelled in 1968. . . . The Air Force ultimately procured only one-third as many F-111s as originally planned and did so at twice the originally expected costs." Robert Coulam, *Illusions of Choice: The F-111 and the Problems of Weapons Acquisition Reform* (Princeton, NJ: Princeton University Press, 1977), 4. Another summary of the program notes that the plane eventually became "a highly effective all-weather interdiction aircraft" for the air force but the program's many shortcomings made it "the major aeronautical fiasco of the 1960s." Federation of American Scientists, "F-111," at https://fas.org/man/dod-101/sys/ac/f-111.htm. For an unsparing critique, see Commander Gerald L. Talbot Jr. and Colonel Kirk L. Lewis, "The TFX Decision: The Joint Canard," National War College, December 18, 1992.

106. Mollenhoff, *Game Plan for Disaster* (New York: W. W. Norton, 1976), 164–65. Even some previous administration insiders were sheepish. President Kennedy's national security adviser, McGeorge Bundy, said in a confidential oral history interview in 1964, "I would suppose that when you finally get to the bottom of the TFX that it was not an entirely technical decision. . . . And not entirely [McNamara's]. And I would suppose that no one will ever be able to know that," McGeorge Bundy, recorded interview by Richard Neustadt, March 1964, John F. Kennedy Library Oral History Program.

107. Crown letter to Nixon, October 17, 1961, "Crown, Henry" folder, box 194, Series 320, Nixon papers, Nixon Library.

108. I. F. Stone, "Nixon and the Arms Race: The Bomber Boondoggle," *New York Review of Books*, January 2, 1969.

109. Moldea, *Interference*, 457n4. Crown was invited to dine at the Nixon White House on April 8, 1971. Listed just ahead of him on the alphabetical guest list was Nixon's political crony Murray Chotiner. "Clement Stone Dinner," in "Chotiner, Murray (1 of 4)" folder, White House Central File, Nixon papers, Nixon Library.

110. Carol Ritch, "Nixon OK's $5 Billion Space Shuttle Project," *San Diego Union*, January 6, 1972.

111. Memo from Henry S. Ruth Jr., Deputy Special Prosecutor, Watergate Special Prosecution Force, to Clarence Kelley, Director, FBI, August 20, 1973, in FBI case file 63-HQ-16121, RG 65, NARA. Crown refused to answer questions about his contribution.

Chapter 8

1. Jeff Gerth, "Nixon and the Mafia," *Sundance*, November–December 1972, 68; reprinted with some changes in "Nixon and the Miami Connection," in Steve Weissman, ed., *Big Brother and the Holding Company*.

2. Miller Center, University of Virginia, "You Could Get a Million Dollars," https://millercenter.org/the-presidency/educational-resources/you-could-get-a-million-dollars.

3. Mark Feldstein, *Poisoning the Press* (New York: Farrar, Straus and Giroux, 2010), 100.

4. Chotiner was appointed special counsel on January 13, 1970. He resigned in March 1971 to represent Jimmy Hoffa and other private clients. However, he continued to advise the president and worked on Nixon's 1972 reelection campaign. Some of Chotiner's political memos may be found in the White House Central File, Alphabetical Name Files, Chotiner, Murray, Nixon papers, Nixon Library.

5. Richard Nixon, "Remarks on Signing the Organized Crime Control Act of 1970," October 15, 1970, at http://www.presidency.ucsb.edu/ws/index.php?pid=2720.

6. Mollenhoff, *Strike Force*, 6–7.

7. Hinckle and Turner, *The Fish Is Red*, 287.

8. Edward Ranzal, "Morgenthau Resigns Post, Citing Nixon 'Ultimatum,'" *New York Times*, December 23, 1969.

9. "Transatlantic Ripples from the Cosmos Bank," *Business Week*, September 14, 1974, 38; Summers, *The Arrogance of Power*, 258.

10. William Lambert, "The Hot-Shot Roy Cohn Lobby," *Life*, September 5, 1969, 26.

11. Don Bauder, "In Miller Obit, U-T Misses Historic Sleaze Story," *San Diego Reader*, March 4, 2013.

12. Kenneth Gilpin, "John Alessio, 87, Businessman and California Political Force," *New York Times*, April 5, 1998; Martin Tolchin, "U.S. Aide Helped 3 Visit a Prisoner," *New York Times*, November 22, 1972 (Lansky).

13. Don Bauder, "Sleaze Saga," *San Diego Reader*, September 4, 2003.

14. Denny Walsh and Tom Flaherty, "Tampering with Justice in San Diego," *Life*, March 24, 1972.

15. Denny Walsh, "Banker Friend of Nixon Is Target of U.S. Inquiry," *New York Times*, September 10, 1973. On Lipton, see Lowell Bergman and Maxwell Robach, "Nixon's Lucky City: C. Arnholt Smith and the San Diego Connection," *Ramparts*, October 1973; *Berkeley Barb*, November 2, 1973; Ovid Demaris, *Poso del Mundo* (Boston: Little Brown, 1970), 147–49; Alfred Wright, "Johnny Is in Agua Hot," *Sports Illustrated*, August 3, 1970.

16. Bergman and Robach, "Nixon's Lucky City: C. Arnholt Smith and the San Diego Connection," *Ramparts*, October 1973. When federal authorities caught on to the scandalously lenient conditions at Lompoc, John Alessio was moved to a less hospitable prison at McNeil Island in Washington.

17. Kenneth Gilpin, "John Alessio, 87, Businessman and California Political Force," *New York Times*, April 5, 1998; Everett Holles, "Arnholt Smith Case Dropped by IRS," *New York Times*, June 26, 1974; "Arnholt Smith Guilty of Evading Taxes," *Washington Post*, May 4, 1979; Associated Press, "Ex-Financier C. Arnholt Smith Released from Custody," July 21, 1985.

18. Will R. Wilson Sr., *A Fool for a Client* (Austin: Eakin Press, 2000), 31–32.

19. Donald Jackson, "The Promoter and the Crime Buster," *Life*, September 24, 1971, 59–62.

20. William Chapman, "Alleged Wiretapping Errors Imperil Federal Prosecutions," *Washington Post*, October 3, 1973; *United States v. Giordano*, 416 U.S. 505 (1974); Charles Pulaski Jr., "Authorizing Wiretap Applications under Title III: Another Dissent to Giordano and Chavez," *University of Pennsylvania Law Review* 123 (1975), 750–821.

21. This claim was made to the Dallas Police detective George Butler by convicted murderer, drug trafficker, and Chicago mobster Paul Roland Jones. HSCA hearings, IX, 611; Scott, *Deep Politics and the Death of JFK* (1993), 161. As state attorney general, Wilson did help drive the Maceo brothers, notorious gamblers and former bootleggers, out of Galveston in 1957.

22. Hank Messick, *Of Grass and Snow: The Secret Criminal Elite* (Englewood Cliffs, NJ: Prentice-Hall, 1979), 38. Messick notes that one of the key defendants in the so-called Operation Eagle case, Juan Restoy, was killed in a shootout with federal agents after he threatened to expose a friend of President Nixon (6).

23. Martin Waldran, "The Frank Sharp Affairs: Vast Scandal Stuns Democrats in Texas," *New York Times*, August 1, 1971; Waldran, "Stock Fraud Scandal Having a Long Run in Texas," *New York Times*, March 8, 1973. Regarding White House discussions of the political impact of the Sharp scandals on the Texas Democratic Party, as well as on Wilson and Treasury Secretary John Connally, see Brian McCall, *The Power of the Texas Governor: Connally to Bush* (Austin: University of Texas Press, 2009), 37–40.

24. Dorman, *Pay-Off*, 297; see also Jack Anderson, *The Anderson Papers* (New York: Ballantine Books, 1974), 167, and Sam Kinch Jr. and Ben Proctor, *Texas under a Cloud: Story of the Texas Stock Fraud Scandal* (New York: Jenkins Publishing, 1972), 129–31.

25. Dorman, *Pay-Off*, 298.

26. Block, *Masters of Paradise*, 225.

27. Block, *Masters of Paradise*, 226–38. For Alexander's side of the story, and much background, see US Congress, House of Representatives, Committee on Government Operations, *Oversight Hearings into the Operations of the IRS, Hearings*, 94th Cong., 1st sess. (Washington, DC: US Government Printing Office, 1976).

28. Jim Drinkhall, "IRS vs. CIA," *Wall Street Journal*, April 18, 1980; "IRS Fears $50 Billion Is Hidden in Foreign Banks," *San Francisco Chronicle*, April 12, 1980.

29. Block, *Masters of Paradise*, 13–14.

30. Jonathan Kwitny, "As Feds Closed In, Promoter Closed Deal with Top Nixon Aide," *Wall Street Journal*, April 24, 1974; see also Michael Dorman, *Vesco: The Infernal Money Making Machine* (New York: Berkley Publishing, 1975), 41–45.

31. FBI memorandum by J. Keith to Mr. Cleveland, May 24, 1973, re "Frank Sinatra," in FBI files on Sinatra at https://archive.org/stream/SinatraFBI/sinatr4c#page/n55; "DeCarlo of Mafia Dead of Cancer," *New York Times*, October 21, 1973; Chris Rojek, *Frank Sinatra* (Malden, MA: Polity Press, 2004), 93–94; Newton, *Mr. Mob*, 241; Moldea, *Hoffa Wars*, 316; Demaris, *Dirty Business*, 329. Another source, said to

be a former gangster, claims that DeCarlo's pardon "was orchestrated by [New Jersey Mafia boss Gerardo] Catena." Myron Sugerman, *The Chronicles of the Last Jewish Gangster* (Myron Sugarman publisher, 2017), ix. White House press secretary Ronald Ziegler insisted the commutation of DeCarlo's sentence was based strictly on compassionate grounds, without intervention by Sinatra or Agnew. Oval Office conversation between President Nixon and Ziegler, January 26, 1973, Conversation 843-4, http://www.easynixon.org/tapes/843-004.

32. David Scheim, *Contract on America: The Mafia Murders of John and Robert Kennedy* (Silver Spring, MD: Argyle Press, 1983), 305–6.

33. *Congressional Record*, v. 96, part 17, A6707 (September 18, 1950).

34. On Davidson's ties to Nixon's office, see "Davidson, I. Irving" folder, Series 320, Nixon papers, Nixon Library. (Four letters and memos were withdrawn from the folder at the donor's request.) Hunter described Davidson's background in letters to Nixon, January 14, 1958, and December 21, 1959, in "Hunter, Oakley," folder, Series 320, Nixon papers, Nixon Library.‡

In a letter to Luis Somoza on July 7, 1960, Davidson boasted that during the 1960 election campaign he offered both Johnson and Nixon camps the "invaluable" services of "12,000 militant workers" in the Teamsters Union. See US Congress, Senate, Foreign Relations Committee, *Nondiplomatic Activities of Representatives of Foreign Governments, Hearings*, 87th Cong., 2nd sess. (Washington, DC: US Government Printing Office, 1962), 1527–31, 1587.

35. Hunter letters to Nixon, December 21, 1959, and January 5, 1960, in "Hunter, Oakley," folder, box 363, Series 320, Nixon papers, Nixon Library; Drew Pearson, "Nixon-Hoffa 'Alliance' Described," *Washington Post*, January 5, 1961; Sheridan, *The Fall and Rise of Jimmy Hoffa*, 141–42, 156–57. Davidson continued to show his support for Nixon. Justice Department records show that he made $1,000 contributions to Nixon in 1968, 1969, 1970, and 1972.

36. Lamar Waldron, *Watergate: The Hidden History* (Berkeley: Counterpoint, 2012), 121.

37. Wilson, *A Fool for a Client*, 33. According to an indicted Hoffa aide turned government informant, the union leader visited New Orleans in 1960 to arrange a $500,000 cash contribution for Nixon from Louisiana Mafia boss Carlos Marcello (supposedly witnessed by Marcello's friend Irving Davidson). Another $500,000 was earmarked to come from Mafia bosses in New Jersey and Florida (presumably Trafficante). Moldea, *The Hoffa Wars*, 108–9, 260; Sheridan, *The Fall and Rise of Jimmy Hoffa*, 5, 158–69, 165–66; Schlesinger, *Robert Kennedy and His Times*, 280. The informant, Edward Grady Partin, was a government witness against Hoffa, but his credibility is questionable. James DiEugenio, "A Strange New Watergate Book," September 2, 2012, https://consortiumnews.com/2012/09/02/a-strange-new-watergate-book; Moldea, *The Hoffa Wars*, 160.

38. Drew Pearson, "Nixon Figured in Hoffa Delay," *Washington Post*, January 4, 1961; James Neff, *Vendetta: Bobby Kennedy Versus Jimmy Hoffa* (New York: Little, Brown, 2015), 187–88. Moldea writes that "according to one of Hoffa's closest associates, the Teamster leadership was well aware of the fact that in 1960 Vice President Nixon had intervened on Hoffa's behalf to quash the Sun Valley indictment" (*The*

Hoffa Wars, 259). After Nixon's defeat in the 1960 election, Rogers reinstated the indictment, causing Nixon some embarrassment with Hoffa; however, the indictment was dismissed because the Justice Department failed to empanel the grand jury properly.

39. Wilson, *A Fool for a Client*, 33. The union officially endorsed Hubert Humphrey for president in 1968.

40. Sheridan, *The Fall and Rise of Jimmy Hoffa*, 454.

41. Sheridan, *The Fall and Rise of Jimmy Hoffa*, 8, 437.

42. Pearson and Anderson, *U.S.A.—Second-Class Power?*, 281–82; also C. P. Trussell, "Nixon's Aide in '52 Denies Trying to Sway Contracts," *New York Times*, May 4, 1956; Philip Potter, "McClellan Told U.S. Aides Were 'Cautioned' on Chotiner," *The Sun* (Baltimore), May 4, 1956; "Unit Says Chotiner Wrote to President," *New York Times*, June 7, 1956; Jay Walz, "Schwartz Cites Adams Letters on Airline Case," *New York Times*, February 18, 1958 (CAB). Numerous letters and memos to and from Chotiner were withdrawn by Nixon from the files donated to the Nixon Library, as indicated in a withdrawal sheet in the "Chotiner, Murray (1957–1958)" folder, Vice Presidential files, Nixon Library. Memos by Nixon aides relating to political damage control may be found in "1956, May 4–Feb 1974" file, Chotiner, Murray folder, Vice Presidential Collection, Nixon papers, Nixon Library.

43. Warren Olney III, "Law Enforcement and Judicial Administration in the Earl Warren Era," an oral history conducted 1970 through 1977 by Miriam F. Stein and Amelia R. Fry, Regional Oral History Office, The Bancroft Library, University of California, Berkeley, 1981.

44. Drew Pearson, "Washington Merry-Go-Round," *Lowell Sun*, November 3, 1962.

45. "The Plug-Ugly American," *Time*, December 21, 1959; Wilson Whyte, "Baseball Expert Lines Up New Book on Mobsters in Japan," *Japan Times*, August 1, 2009; Robert Whiting, *Tokyo Underworld: The Fast Times and Hard Life of an American Gangster in Japan* (New York: Pantheon, 1999), 43–45, 84–86; Sterling Seagrave, *The Marcos Dynasty* (New York: Harper and Row, 1988); Wayland Speer letter to Harry Anslinger, March 6, 1953, Personal and Confidential, Wayland L. Speer's Foreign Assignment file, 0660-A-3 Correspondence File, box 165, BNDD archives, RG 170, NARA; American Embassy in Guatemala to Department of State, July 19, 1957, 814.45/7-1957, Record Group 59, Records of the Department of State, NARA; Rappleye and Becker, *All American Mafioso*, 149–51 (Guatemala). Lewin also negotiated with Somoza lobbyist and mob fixer Irving Davidson to buy thirty thousand assault rifles from Nicaragua for resale in the Far East; telegram from CIA Director, "Information on Irving I. Davidson," June 20, 1956, NARA 104-10073-10049; Air Intelligence Information Report, June 4, 1958, NARA 104-10234-10283.

46. Report by Walter E. A. Wolf, Air Intelligence, June 4, 1958, "Possible Weapons Purchase of Israel from Nicaragua," NARA 104-10234-10283; CIA report from Director, June 6, 1958, NARA 104-10216-10079.

47. Drew Pearson "Ex-Nixon Manager Represented Racketeers, Obtained Leniency," *Standard-Examiner* (Ogden, UT), June 4, 1960.

48. Russell Baker, "Senate Restudies Work of Chotiner," *New York Times*, May 14, 1956; C. P. Trussell, "Senators Score Uniform Makers," *New York Times*, September 6, 1957; "$1,968,772 Tax Claimed," *New York Times*, November 7, 1956; "Nixon Silent on '52 Aide," *New York Times*, May 8, 1956; C. P. Trussell, "Nixon's 1952 Manager Involved in Inquiry on Buying of Uniforms," *New York Times*, April 25, 1956; C. P. Trussell, "Nixon's Aide in '52 Denies Trying to Sway Contracts," *New York Times*, May 4, 1956; Drew Pearson, "More of Chotiner Activities Related," *Washington Post*, May 11, 1956; United States Senate Committee on Government Operations, Permanent Subcommittee on Investigations, *Textile Procurement in the Military Services, Hearings*, 84th Cong., 1st sess. (Washington, DC: US Government Printing Office, 1955), 1589–1602, 1616.

49. Drew Pearson, "Mickey Cohen's Relations with Nixon and Chotiner," November 1, 1968, Digital Research Archive, at https://auislandora.wrlc.org/islandora/object/pearson%253A26854#page/1/mode/1up; Moldea, *The Hoffa Wars*, 105; Costello, *The Facts about Nixon*, 215; Summers, *Arrogance of Power*, 52 (Chotiner); David Langum, *Crossing over the Line: Legislating Morality and the Mann Act* (Chicago: University of Chicago Press, 1994), 3, 253 (Reginelli and Mann Act); *In the Matter of the Petition of Marco Reginelli, No. 2186-P-9291, for Naturalization*, Supreme Court of New Jersey, 20 N.J. 266 (1956) (Reginelli verdict); FBI report by J. Robert Pearce, Philadelphia, June 28, 1961, NARA 124-10205-10469; FBI report by J. Robert Pearce, Philadelphia, April 30, 1962, NARA 124-10203-10367 (Reginelli and Bruno).

50. Summers, *Arrogance of Power*, 53–54; see also J. Anthony Lukas, *Nightmare: The Underside of the Nixon Years* (New York: Viking, 1976), 117, 161. Some of Chotiner's activities and alleged campaign violations are documented in the "Chotiner, Murray" file of the Watergate Special Prosecutor's Campaign Contributions Task Force, WSPF files, NARA.

51. FBI interview with Chotiner, June 1, 1973, in CCTF #803 file 1, WSPF papers, NARA; interview with Irving Davidson by Mike Ewing and Ralph Salerno, November 2, 1978, at http://jfk.hood.edu/Collection/Weisberg%20Subject%20Index%20Files/D%20Disk/Davidson%20I%20Irving/Item%2008.pdf; Feldstein, *Poisoning the Press*, 106; Moldea, *The Hoffa Wars*, 261 (Mollenhoff and Las Vegas mob); *Oakland Tribune*, May 4, 1973 (land fraud case). On Chotiner's intervention with Haldeman in November 1971, see Jack Anderson, "Haldeman Arranged Hoffa's Release," *Washington Post*, May 3, 1973.

52. Letter from William Loeb, President, Union Leader Corporation, to Harry Dent, White House, October 29, 1969, Nixon Library, at https://www.nixonlibrary.gov/sites/default/files/virtuallibrary/documents/jan10/021.pdf; Bill Timmons memo to John Ehrlichman, August 13, 1969, in Ehrlichman 1969–1970 folder, box 278, White House Central Files, Nixon papers, Richard Nixon Library.

53. Haldeman diary, April 3, 1970, at https://www.nixonlibrary.gov/sites/default/files/virtuallibrary/documents/haldeman-diaries/37-hrhd-journal-vol04-19700403.pdf; Charles Colson memo to Egil Krogh, June 16, 1970, in Watergate Special Prosecutor's Campaign Contributions Task Force #803 file 1, WSPF papers, NARA. This memo, released in full to the author in 2019, indicates that offer of funds in return for Hoffa's release came from Colson's friend Charles Botsford, who had been ap-

proached by a retired Washington, D.C., attorney named Thomas Farrell. On Colson's wide-ranging efforts to obstruct justice in labor-related racketeering cases, see James Neff, *Mobbed Up: Jackie Presser's High-Wire Life in the Teamsters, the Mafia, and the F.B.I.* (New York: Atlantic Monthly Press, 1989), 164–65; Ronald Kessler, "Colson Agreed to Aid Suspect," *Washington Post*, December 2, 1973.

54. Neff, *Mobbed Up*, 164–65. In December 1973, for example, Colson intervened to prevent the imminent indictment of Daniel F. Gagliardi, a New York union official and mob associate, on charges relating to Teamsters Union extortion activity in Westchester County. A Justice Department investigation revealed that Gagliardi had helped force road construction contractors to purchase fuel from a favored contractor at a price premium of 15 to 25 cents per gallon. In response to Gagliardi's plea for help, Colson wrote one his aides, "Watch for this. Do all possible." The case was subsequently dropped. Justice Department prosecutors denied they had received political pressure and the Watergate Special Prosecution Force declined to pursue the matter. Ronald Kessler, "Colson Agreed to Aid Suspect," *Washington Post*, December 2, 1973; FBI memo, "Samuel Tritto, Daniel Gagliardi, et al.," August 2, 1974; memo from Richard J. Davis to Thomas McBride, August 21, 1974, "Daniel Gagliardi—Peter Brennan Allegation"; memo by Henry S. Ruth Jr., August 29, 1974, re "Samuel Tritto; Daniel Gagliardi, et al." in SP Memos file 1, WSPF papers, NARA.

55. Memo from Colson to John Dean, July 7, 1971 (with attached transcript of Colson's conversation with Fitzsimmons on July 6), Hoffa file, WSPF papers, NARA; memo from John Galus, "Office Interview of Charles Colson," August 12, 1974, Watergate Special Prosecutor's Campaign Contributions Task Force #803, file 1, WSPF papers, NARA.

56. Neff, *Mobbed Up*, 174; Seymour Hersh, "1971 Tape Links Nixon to Plan to Use 'Thugs,'" *New York Times*, September 24, 1981.

57. "Teamsters and the White House," *San Francisco Chronicle*, May 31, 1973; Demaris, *Dirty Business*, 331.

58. Phlip Shabecoff, "White House Appoints 22 to Pay and Price Boards," *New York Times*, October 23, 1971.

59. Haldeman diary, November 1, 3, and 9, 1971, NARA, Online Public Access Catalog Identifier: 7787364; White House conversation 301-25D, November 3, 1971; 613-12, November 4, 1971; 307-27, December 8, 1971; Haldeman notes of a meeting with Mitchell, December 8, 1971, at https://www.nixonlibrary.gov/sites/default/files/virtuallibrary/documents/jan10/072.pdf.

60. Nixon telephone call with Colson, December 8, 1971, White House conversation 016-053, http://www.easynixon.org/tapes/016-053; see also Nixon conversation with Mitchell, December 8, 1971, White House conversation 307-027, http://www.easynixon.org/tapes/307-027. As early as November 1, Colson suggested to Nixon the possibility of revoking Hoffa's clemency "if at any time he went back into the labor movement." Nixon telephone call with Colson, November 1, 1971, White House conversation 013-060, http://www.easynixon.org/tapes/013-60. Mitchell raised the same possibility in an Oval Office discussion with the president that day. White House conversation 610-001, http://www.easynixon.org/tapes/610-001. These White House tapes are preserved by NARA.

61. Fred Graham, "Nixon Commutes Hoffa Sentence, Curbs Union Role," *New York Times*, December 24, 1971. On the last-minute legal work on this commutation restriction by John Dean, see Jack Goldsmith, *In Hoffa's Shadow: A Stepfather, a Disappearance in Detroit, and My Search for the Truth* (New York: Farrar, Straus and Giroux, 2019), 167–69.

62. ABC News, "Hoffa," November 30, 1974, produced by Stephen Fleischman; oral history interview with Charles W. Colson, September 21, 1988, Nixon Library; John Galus memo, "Office Interview of Charles Colson," August 12, 1974, CCTF #803 file 1, WSPF papers, NARA.

63. Seymour Hersh, "Colson Is Accused of Improper Use of His Influence," *New York Times*, July 1, 1973.

64. "Nixon Won't Yield Hoffa Documents," *San Francisco Chronicle*, June 1, 1974; "Judge Backs Nixon on Claim by Hoffa for Data on Case," *New York Times*, June 4, 1974.

65. Arthur Egan Jr., "Teamsters Aided Watergate," *Manchester Union Leader*, April 27, 1973. Chotiner sued the newspaper for defamation. Robert L. Palmer memo, "Telephone Conversation with John Milne," December 10, 1973, in CCTF #803 file 1, WSPF papers, NARA; Moldea, *The Hoffa Wars*, 319.

66. Jack Anderson, "Haldeman Arranged Hoffa's Release," *Washington Post*, May 1, 1973; James L. Quarles III memo to Thomas F. McBride, "Summary of Information re James R. Hoffa," August 30, 1973; Larry Hammond memo, "Office Interview of Mr. Clark Mollenhoff," April 16, 1974, in CCTF #803 file 1, WSPF papers, NARA; FBI interviews in CCTF #803 file 2, WSPF papers, NARA; John Galus memo to Thomas McBride and Charles Ruff, August 12, 1974, "The Hoffa Release: Bribery Allegations," CCTF files, Special Prosecutor memos, WSPF papers, NARA; Philip Shabecoff, "Teamster Chief Denies Charges," *New York Times*, July 6, 1973.[‡]

67. Memo from William S. Lynch, chief, Organized Crime and Racketeering Section, Department of Justice, to Charles Ruff, Special Prosecutor, August 9, 1976, re "Hoffa Pardon—Possible Bribery," in SP files—Hoffa, WSPF papers, NARA; "Teamsters' Watergate Connection," *Time*, August 8, 1977; Jo Thomas, "Teamster Informant Drawing Skepticism," *New York Times*, August 3, 1977 (Ralph Picardo); Alan L. Adlestein, "Closing Memorandum, File No. 803—Teamsters," January 13, 1977. In 2019, Jack Goldsmith resurrected the payoff story, citing claims by his stepfather, Chuckie O'Brien, to have carried a briefcase containing $1 million from Fitzsimmons to a contact at the Madison Hotel in Washington, D.C. (Goldsmith, *In Hoffa's Shadow*, 172–75). There are many problems with this story. O'Brien's own lawyer called him "an absolute stranger to the truth" (230). He could not identify the person to whom he handed the money. It is doubtful that Fitzsimmons would entrust such a sensitive job to a man whose talents he held in such low esteem. Last but not least, it is not clear why anyone needed to bribe Nixon to do something he saw as being in his own political interest.

68. Memo by Clarence Kelley, Director, FBI, "International Brotherhood of Teamsters—Campaign Contributions," July 26, 1974, in Unions file, WSPF papers, NARA.

69. Jim Drinkhall, "Trustees of the Central States Pension Fund Loan $1.4 Million to Organized Crime Figures," *Overdrive*, July 1973.[‡]

70. "Morris Shenker, 82, Lawyer in St. Louis and Hoffa Defender," *New York Times*, August 11, 1989; Wallace Turner, "Las Vegas Casino Owner Thriving in a High-Risk, High-Stakes Setting," *New York Times*, February 21, 1984; "Loan Fraud Is Laid to Dunes Operator," *New York Times*, October 14, 1977.

71. Demaris, *Dirty Business*, 333.

72. Denny Walsh, "U.S. Said to Bar Bugging on Teamsters-Mafia Link," *New York Times*, April 29, 1973; Neff, *Mobbed Up*, 180–81.

73. "Teamsters' Ties to Mafia—and to White House," *Los Angeles Times*, May 31, 1973. See also "House Panel Said to Weigh Report of a Justice Department Deal with Fitzsimmons," *New York Times*, July 20, 1973. Francis R. Fitzsimmons was finally indicted in 1979 by a federal grand jury on charges of accepting more than $100,000 in bribes from a Detroit trucking company. See "Union Chief's Son and 2 Officials of Trucking Concern Are Indicted," *New York Times*, August 3, 1979.

74. *Oakland Tribune*, May 4, 1973.

75. "Probation Ordered in Beverly Ridge Fraud," *Los Angeles Times*, December 9, 1972; Gene Blake, "Former Beverly Ridge Official Pleads Guilty," *Los Angeles Times*, October 17, 1972; *New York Times*, August 13, 1972.

76. "Bankruptcy Useful," *The Dispatch* (Lexington, NC), December 11, 1972.

77. Memo from CIA Director, December 11, 1972, re "Isadore Irving Davidson," NARA 104-10216-10052. Davidson described himself to prosecutors as having been "a top notch informant to the FBI and CIA," but the CIA found no evidence that it ever used Davidson in an operational capacity or as an informant. CIA memorandum from Director, Domestic Contact Service to Deputy Director for Personnel Security, April 9, 1971, re Isadore Irving Davidson, NARA 104-10234-10276; CIA Assistant General Counsel John K. Greaney Memorandum for the Record, July 16, 1971, re "Isadore Irving Davidson," NARA 1994.05.16.14:31:36:280005. As noted in chapter 4, Davidson did act as an intermediary between the State Department and former Dominican Republic president Joaquín Balaguer in 1965. He also produced a letter of support from a senior Israeli intelligence official.

78. Gordon Chaplin, "Power Player," *Washington Post*, April 2, 1980.

79. Senate Watergate Report, 147, 278; "eyes only" memorandum from Colson to Dean, December 30, 1971, in CCTF #803 file, WSPF papers, NARA; William Amlong, "Smathers Acted as a Lawyer to Free Kovens from Prison," *Miami Herald*, July 2, 1973; Demaris, *Dirty Business*, 337–38; Moldea, *The Hoffa Wars*, 293. Hoffa's confidant Chuckie O'Brien claimed that Kovens handed over millions of dollars in cash to Hoffa after their release, money he had kept for the union leader from illicit deals over the years. Goldsmith, *In Hoffa's Shadow*, 92, 188.‡

80. Sal Recchi, "Gaming Giant Has Checkered Past, Local Ties," *Boca Raton News*, July 15, 1979; Kwitny, *Vicious Circles*, 168–69; Jim Drinkhall, "Bally Manufacturing Corporation," *Overdrive*, June 1974.

81. *Palo Alto Times*, February 16, 1974; *Wall Street Journal*, July 23, 1975; Kwitny, *Vicious Circles*, 168–69; "FBI Said to Check a Saxbe Associate," *New York Times*, November 7, 1973; William Farrell, "Saxbe's Route to Capital Began on Ohio Campus," *New York Times*, November 21, 1973.

82. Robert Lindsey, "4 Indicted in Alleged $5 Million Theft of Union Funds," *New York Times*, June 16, 1978.

83. Kleindienst's law firm partners, including Richard Danner's friend and Hoffa's former attorney Edward P. Morgan, settled for $66,000. Al Senia, "Kleindienst and 2 Others Agree to Pay in Lawsuit," *Washington Post*, June 6, 1979; John Crewdson, "Kleindienst Says He's Innocent of Perjury in Teamsters' Fund Case," *New York Times*, April 29, 1981; US Congress, Senate, Committee on Governmental Affairs, *Labor Union Insurance Activities of Joseph Hauser and His Associates, Report 96-426*, 96th Cong., 1st sess. (Washington, DC: US Government Printing Office, 1979), 26, 159. The crooked mastermind of this insurance kickback case, Joseph Hauser, turned federal informant and implicated Davidson and Louisiana Mafia boss Carlos Marcello in crimes. A federal jury convicted Marcello but acquitted Davidson; "BRILAB Jury Convicts Carlos Marcello and Former Louisiana Official," *New York Times*, August 4, 1981.

84. Bart Barnes, "Richard Kleindienst, Attorney General during Watergate, Dies," *Washington Post*, February 4, 2000; Ted Rushton, "Kleindienst Suspended for Year in Arizona," *Washington Post*, April 24, 1982; cf. *State Bar of Arizona, Brief in the Matter of a Member of the State Bar of Arizona, Richard Kleindienst*, 79-1-S19.‡

85. "Nixon, in a Rare Appearance, Plays Golf with Fitzsimmons," *New York Times*, October 18, 1975.

86. Goldsmith, *In Hoffa's Shadow*, 249.

87. For examples of illegal contributions, see Summers, *Arrogance of Power*, 284–86, 395–97.

88. Quote from Jacob Hacker and Nathaniel Lowentheil, "How Big Money Corrupts the Economy," *Democracy Journal*, Winter 2013, at http://www.democracyjournal.org/27/how-big-money-corrupts-the-economy.php.

Chapter 9

1. UC San Diego historian Michael Parrish, in *San Diego Union Tribune*, quoted at http://books.wwnorton.com/books/The-Wars-of-Watergate/, accessed September 3, 2018.

2. Quoted in Karlyn Barker and Walter Pincus, "Watergate Revisited; 20 Years after the Break-in, the Story Continues to Unfold," *Washington Post*, June 14, 1992.

3. Police arrested the burglars on June 17, 1972, but there was at least one prior attempted break-in. Numerous theories are noted in Edward Epstein and John Berendt, "Did There Come a Point in Time When There Were 43 Different Theories of How Watergate Happened?" *Esquire*, November 1973.

4. For an early argument along these lines, see J. Anthony Lukas, *Nightmare: The Underside of the Nixon Years* (New York: Viking, 1976).

5. For a good treatment of this story, see Hughes, *Chasing Shadows*. For more recent revelations, see John A. Farrell, *Richard Nixon: The Life* (New York: Doubleday, 2017), 342–44.

6. John Dean, *The Nixon Defense: What He Knew and When He Knew It* (New York: Viking, 2014), 2–4, 9, 37–38, 87; Hughes, *Chasing Shadows*, 153–54; Richard Nixon, *The Memoirs of Richard Nixon* (New York: Grosset & Dunlap, 1978), 637. Presidential aide Bob Haldeman said the "most important" reason Nixon supported a cover-up was "to avoid exposure of the 'other things' (as he always called them), the actions ranging from the Ellsberg break-in to Chuck Colson's projects," H. R. Haldeman with Joseph DiMona, *The Ends of Power* (New York: Times Books, 1978), 217. Jeb Magruder, a senior campaign official, said, "My understanding of why we had to keep it [the Watergate burglary] under wraps was because these same burglars and their leaders, Liddy and Hunt, were the same people who had broken into Daniel Ellsberg's psychiatrist's office. So then we got into this elaborate cover-up that eventually led to the destruction of the Nixon Presidency." See his remarks in *Watergate and Afterward: The Legacy of Richard M. Nixon*, eds. Leon Friedman and William F. Levantrosser (Westport, CT: Greenwood Press, 1992), 45.

7. Robert Maheu and Richard Hack, *Next to Hughes: Behind the Power and Tragic Downfall of Howard Hughes by His Closest Adviser* (New York: HarperCollins, 1992), 3.

8. Donald L. Barlett and James B. Steele, *Empire: The Life, Legend, and Madness of Howard Hughes* (New York: W. W. Norton, 1979), 435–36.

9. Maheu and Hack, *Next to Hughes*, 22–40; Senate Watergate Committee memo, "Notes on Thomas Doughterty Webb Jr.," January 2, 1974, in "Webb, Thomas" file, WSPF papers, NARA. Nixon similarly got his first professional stake from poker winnings in World War II.

10. Maheu and Hack, *Next to Hughes*, 71; CIA document, "Summary of Agency Employment: James McCord, Jr.," 1993.07.21.10:29:32:250620, JFK Assassination records, NARA. From 1948 to 1951, McCord was a special agent of the FBI.

11. CIA memo for Director of Central Intelligence, January 1, 1975, re "Robert A. Maheu," NARA 104-10122-10141. Maheu was recruited by Robert H. Cunningham, chief, Special Security Division, who had known Maheu in the FBI. On Maheu's recruitment and earliest days with the CIA, see also Maheu's testimony before the Senate Select Committee to Study Governmental Operations with Respect to Intelligence Activities (Church Committee), July 30, 1975, NARA 157-10011-10048; Matt Schudel, "Robert Maheu, 90," *Washington Post*, August 6, 2008; "Confidant and Aide to Howard Hughes," *Los Angeles Times*, August 6, 2008; "Former Howard Hughes Confidant Dies at 90," *Las Vegas Sun*, August 5, 1998.

12. Maheu's testimony before the Church Committee, July 30, 1975, NARA 157-10011-10048; Maheu and Hack, *Next to Hughes*, 42–53; Peter Evans, *Ari: The Life and Times of Aristotle Socrates Onassis* (New York: Summit Books, 1986), 124–38; Jim Hougan, *Spooks: The Haunting of America—The Private Use of Secret Agents* (New York: William Morrow, 1978), 287–306; Summers, *Arrogance of Power*, 153–54, 195–96; Robert Pack, *Edward Bennett Williams for the Defense* (New York: Harper & Row, 1983), 173–79; Charles Babcock, "Maheu Admits '54 Anti-Onassis Drive," *Washington Post*, August 2, 1978. For confirmation of the CIA role, see J. S. Earman, CIA Inspector General, "Report on Plots to Assassinate Fidel Castro," May 23, 1967, pp. 14, 72, NARA 1994.04.15.10:12:09:030005 (hereafter "IG Report").

13. CIA memo for Director of Central Intelligence, January 1, 1975, re "Robert A. Maheu," NARA 104-10122-10141, suggests that procuring women was a major role for Maheu during the 1950s. On Sukarno, see also Maheu and Hack, *Next to Hughes*, 71–75; Joseph Burkholder Smith, *Portrait of a Cold Warrior* (New York: G. P. Putnam's Sons, 1976), 238–40, 248; "Intelligence Agencies Held Unchecked," *New York Times*, January 26, 1976.

14. Memo from Robert W. Gambino, Director of Security, for CIA General Counsel, August 27, 1976, re "Robert Maheu," NARA 1993.07.21.08:58:07:430620.

15. Maheu and Hack, *Next to Hughes*, 19; Dan Moldea, *The Hoffa Wars*, 129.

16. Hinckle and Turner, *The Fish Is Red*, 273; Evan Thomas, *The Man to See: Edward Bennett Williams* (New York: Simon & Schuster, 1991), 86–91; Pack, *Edward Bennett Williams for the Defense*, 183–200.

17. Williams defended CIA director Richard Helms for lying to Congress about CIA efforts to sabotage the Chilean elections. He was offered the job of CIA director by both Presidents Ford and Reagan. He also sat on the President's Foreign Intelligence Advisory Board during the Ford and Reagan administrations. Thomas, *The Man to See*, 340, 334, 472; Pack, *Edward Bennett Williams for the Defense*, 29–39; *San Francisco Examiner*, August 14, 1988; *New York Times*, February 27, 1987.

18. Thomas, *The Man to See*, 86. In the early 1950s, Williams and Pearson were on the opposite sides of at least two libel suits, but they soon became friends, no doubt for mutual career benefits.

19. Pack, *Edward Bennett Williams for the Defense*, 203–41.

20. Rappleye and Becker, *All American Mafioso*, 184.

21. Hughes also hired Maheu to surveil a man who was dating the actress Hughes would later marry, Jean Peters. Elaine Davenport and Paul Eddy with Mark Hurwitz, *The Hughes Papers* (London: Sphere Books, 1977), 45; *Los Angeles Times*, May 11, 1974.

22. Summers, *Arrogance of Power*, 154.

23. Maheu and Hack, *Next to Hughes*, 55–67, 89, 135; Davenport and Eddy, *The Hughes Papers*, 56.

24. Russo, *The Outfit*, 282. Sinatra was a client of lawyer Williams (Pack, *Edward Bennett Williams for the Defense*, viii).

25. Maureen Hughes, *The Countess and the Mob* (Bloomington, IN: iUniverse, 2010), 49.

26. Rappleye and Becker, *All American Mafioso*, 163, 169. The Teamster Central States Pension Fund—whose trustees answered to Hoffa—was the largest source of financing for casino operators in Las Vegas in the late 1950s and 1960s. See Reid and Demaris, *The Green Felt Jungle*, 83, 91; Gene Blake and Jack Tobin, "Gamblers Given Teamster Loans," *Los Angeles Times*, May 11, 1962; "Teamster Funds Help Spur Vegas," *Los Angeles Times*, May 13, 1962.

27. Maheu and Hack, *Next to Hughes*, 109–11; Moldea, *The Hoffa Wars*, 129; Rappleye and Becker, *All American Mafioso*, 184–85; memo by FBI SA Edward J. Dunn Jr., Miami, March 22, 1977, re "Roskil" [Rosselli killing], NARA 124-10289-10035. Maheu told the FBI he met Rosselli in 1958 or 1959 at the El Rancho Vegas Hotel through an introduction from Williams.

28. Lamar Waldron, *Watergate: The Hidden History* (Berkeley: Counterpoint, 2012), 76–77, 83–84, 90–96; Richard Nixon, "Cuba, Castro, and John F. Kennedy," *Reader's Digest*, November 1964, 288. As Waldron points out, the CIA radically ramped up the scale of its invasion plan after the 1960 election; President Kennedy was unaware that the plan presented to him was not the one Eisenhower had approved. Nor was he aware that CIA advisers had told members of the exile army to go ahead and invade Cuba even if Kennedy got cold feet and called the mission off—on the assumption that Kennedy would be forced to come to their rescue.

29. Memo for DCI from J. C. King, December 11, 1959, cited in US Central Intelligence Agency, *Official History of the Bay of Pigs Operation*. Volume III: *Evolution of CIA's Anti-Castro Policies, 1959–January 1961* (1979, released 1998), 29.

30. Newman, *Countdown to Darkness*, Kindle location 2441 (Pawley); E. Howard Hunt, with Greg Aunapu, *American Spy: My Secret History in the CIA, Watergate & Beyond* (Hoboken, NJ: John Wiley & Sons, 2007), 117. Hunt relates that his April 1960 memorandum to Richard Bissell declared, "first and foremost, all efforts should be made to assassinate Castro before or coincident with the invasion. . . . Without Castro to inspire them the Rebel Army and militia would collapse in leaderless confusion." His memorandum has not surfaced in CIA files.

31. *Alleged Assassination Plots*, 91–99, 110–15, 117–25. President Eisenhower had rejected the idea of assassinating Castro out of concern that his brother Raul was "worse"; Waldron, *Watergate*, 105. For a critical analysis of claims that the Kennedy brothers were early backers of the assassination plots, see J. Alan Wolske, "Jack, Judy, Sam, Bobby, Johnny, Frank . . .: An Investigation into the Alternate History of the CIA-Mafia Collaboration to Assassinate Fidel Castro, 1960–1997," *Intelligence and National Security* 15:4 (Winter 2000), 104–30.

32. *Alleged Assassination Plots*, 92, 99–105.

33. IG Report, 14; 1977 CIA Task Force Report quoted at House of Representatives, Select Committee on Assassinations, staff report, *The Evolution and Implications of the CIA-Sponsored Assassination Conspiracies against Fidel Castro*, March 1979 (hereafter "HSCA Staff Report"), in HSCA Hearings, v. 10, 157, 172 (piggybacking); Rappleye and Becker, *All American Mafioso*, 180; Moldea, *Hoffa Wars*, 126; Scott Breckenridge, *The CIA and the Cold War: A Memoir* (Westport, CT: Praeger, 1973), 113.

34. James Cockayne, *Hidden Power: The Strategic Logic of Organized Crime* (New York: Oxford University Press, 2016), 231–32.

35. IG Report, 15. Actually, the Office of Security first considered using Guy Banister, an ex-FBI chief of Chicago who became a private investigator in New Orleans, but Banister was assigned instead to another Cuban operation. Banister had been an office mate of Maheu and Carmine Bellino in 1954. He later became a key figure in the JFK assassination story. Waldron, *Watergate*, 104. Maheu later told his friend Pierre Salinger, Kennedy's former Hoffa investigator and press secretary, "that the CIA had been in touch with Nixon, who had asked them to go forward with this project. . . . It was Nixon who had [Maheu] do a deal with the Mafia in Florida to kill Castro." However, this claim remains unproven (Summers, *Arrogance of Power*, 196–97).

36. Maheu and Rosselli met with the senior CIA official, James O'Connell, at the Hilton Plaza Hotel in New York City on September 14, 1960. O'Connell was Rosselli's CIA contact until May 1962, when he was replaced by William Harvey (CIA memo, "The Johnny Roselli [sic] Matter," NARA 1993.07.26.17:44:39:000590). Maheu had previously introduced Rosselli to several top CIA and air force intelligence officers at a party at his home in Virginia, in total violation of good security procedures (Maheu and Hack, *Next to Hughes*, 114).

37. Moldea, *The Hoffa Wars*, 124.

38. This group's main contact for arranging Castro's assassination was the Lansky-funded Cuban politician Manuel Antonio de Varona, whose CIA paymaster was future Watergate burglar E. Howard Hunt. However, Hunt testified that he was unaware of Varona's involvement in the assassination plots (IG Report, 29–30, 64; Summers, *Arrogance of Power*, 194; Rappleye and Becker, *All American Mafioso*, 192–93).

39. Howard Osborn, Director of Security, memorandum for Director of Central Intelligence, re "Roselli, [sic] Johnny," November 19, 1970, NARA 1993.07.26.17:44:39:000590.

40. December 21, 1960, FBI memorandum, re "Manuel Antonio Varona," NARA 124-90055-10230; also summarized in IG Report, 29–30.

41. See, for example, Roemer, *Roemer: Man against the Mob*, 157–58. Roemer was the top FBI agent tasked with investigating Giancana and the Chicago Outfit during this period.

42. Maheu also found time before the 1960 election to convince a reporter from the *St. Louis Post-Dispatch* to kill a negative breaking story on the 1956 Hughes "loan" to Donald Nixon. Maheu succeeded—but Drew Pearson and Jack Anderson then went public with the full, damaging account. Summers, *Arrogance of Power*, 215–16.

43. Barlett and Steele, *Empire*, 284.

44. Hughes allowed the CIA to use a Bahamian island that he leased, Cay Sal, for intelligence operations and raids against Cuba, including the Bay of Pigs invasion. See Hinckle and Turner, *The Fish Is Red*, 279–80; Dick Russell, "An Ex-CIA Man's Stunning Revelations on 'The Company,' JFK's Murder, and the Plot to Kill Richard Nixon," *Argosy*, April 1976; "Oz Moody: A Florida Treasure Looks Back," *Florida Monthly*, December 2001, 36–38. Edward Morgan testified to the Church Committee that Hank Greenspun "knew that Hughes was extremely close to the CIA." See testimony of Edward P. Morgan, March 19, 1975, 34, NARA 157-10011-10040.

45. CIA memorandum by Carroll Delaney, executive officer, Domestic Collection Division, for Inspector General, April 24, 1974, re "DCD Response to the Agency-Watergate File Review," NARA 104-10062-10072.

46. One published estimate put the value of CIA contracts at $6 billion from the mid-1960s to the mid-1970s; "The Hughes Legacy: Scramble for Billions," *Time*, April 19, 1976, 23. In 1966, Albert D. Wheelon resigned as deputy director of the CIA in charge of its science and technology division—including development of spy satellites—to become president of Hughes Aircraft Co., where he built its satellite-manufacturing business into the largest in the world. See Stephen Miller, "Rocket Scientist Albert Wheelon Led CIA Spy-Satellite Program," *Wall Street Journal*, October 1, 2013. Hughes biographers Bartlett and Steele note, "The Hughes payroll was

studded with former intelligence operatives, government agents, and retired army, navy, and air force officers. The Hughes Aircraft Company was deeply involved in the intelligence community's spy-satellite program." In addition, the CIA chose Hughes Tool Company as its contractor and cover in 1970 for Project Jennifer, a quarter-billion-dollar scheme to raise a sunken Soviet submarine from the floor of the Pacific Ocean. Barlett and Steele, *Empire*, 458. They also note that the CIA signed at least thirty-two contracts totaling $6.6 billion from June 1968 to March 1975, not including the vessel used in Project Jennifer, or many other classified contracts (Donald Barlett and James Steele, "CIA Has 'Many Contracts' with Hughes Organizations," *Philadelphia Inquirer*, December 14, 1975). Maheu recalled one phone conversation with Hughes in early 1969 where the billionaire "suggested that I try to work out some kind of arrangement with the CIA whereby either he or the Hughes Tool Company become a front for this intelligence agency. I told Mr. Hughes that I could not understand why he would have such a desire and he pointed out to me that if he ever became involved in any problem with the government, either with a regulatory body or with an investigative arm of the government, that he thought it would be very beneficial to him [if we were] a front of some sort through one of his businesses for the CIA." Davenport and Eddy, *The Hughes Papers*, 244–45.

47. IG Report, 57–58; Sheffield Edwards (CIA's Office of Security), memorandum for the record, May 14, 1962, re "Arthur James Balletti et al—Unauthorized Publication or Use of Communications," and Howard Osborn, CIA Office of Security, memorandum for Director of Central Intelligence, June 24, 1966, re "Johnny Roselli, [sic]" NARA 1993.07.21.08:58:07:430620. The timing was either late 1961 or very early 1962. For intimations of a more complicated backstory, including CIA suspicions that Giancana was talking to associates about the assassination plots, see *Alleged Assassination Plots*, 78–79, and HSCA Staff Report, 174–75.

48. IG Report, 59–62; Rappleye and Becker, *All American Mafioso*, 213–14; Barlett and Steele, *Empire*, 283–84; Maheu and Hack, *Next to Hughes*, 121–22; memorandum from Director, FBI, to Attorney General, May 22, 1961, "Arthur James Balletti, et al.," NARA 124-10216-10045. An attachment to the latter memo indicates that Richard Bissell, the CIA's deputy director of plans, had recently "told the Attorney General that some of the CIA's associated planning included the use of Giancana and the underworld against Castro."

49. *Alleged Assassination Plots*, 130–31.

50. FBI memorandum from C. A. Evans to Belmont, March 15, 1962, "Judith E. Campbell," NARA 124-10225-10038; *Alleged Assassination Plots*, 129–30.

51. IG Report, 62a; HSCA Staff Report, 153; Rappleye and Becker, *All American Mafioso*, 216–17.

52. *Alleged Assassination Plots*, 131–34; IG Report, 62a. Bobby Kennedy may have blocked Giancana's arrest at one point because he knew too much; Russo, *The Outfit*, 446–47.

53. *Alleged Assassination Plots*, 133–34; IG Report, 64–65. In 1963, following publication of an article in the *Chicago Sun-Times* revealing that Giancana had worked for the CIA, Richard Helms told CIA director John McCone that the plots had ended in May 1962. See Waldron, *Watergate*, 247–48. I suspect that the article was an FBI leak.

Articles suggesting a CIA link to Giancana appeared in the *Chicago Sun-Times* on August 16, 1963 ("CIA Sought Giancana Help for Cuba Spying") and *Chicago Daily News* on August 20, 1963 ("The Truth about Cosa Nostra Chief and the CIA"). See Howard Osborn, CIA Office of Security, memorandum for Director of Central Intelligence, June 24, 1966, re "Johnny Roselli, [sic]" NARA 1993.07.21.08:58:07:430620; IG Report, 67–69.

54. Quoted in Anthony Summers, *Conspiracy* (New York: McGraw-Hill, 1980), 426.

55. In 2012, a former CIA analyst published a volume arguing that Fidel Castro had advance knowledge of Lee Harvey Oswald's intention to kill President Kennedy but did nothing to stop him, having been a target himself of many US-sponsored assassination attempts. Brian Latell, *Castro's Secrets: The CIA and Cuba's Intelligence Machine* (New York: St. Martin's Press, 2012).

56. David Talbot, *Brothers: The Hidden History of the Kennedy Years* (New York: The Free Press, 2007), 10.

57. Scheim, *Contract on America*, 103–6; Blakey and Billings, *The Plot to Kill the President*, 282–307.

58. The cover-up took place within the CIA as well. Immediately after the assassination, CIA director Richard Helms appointed John Whitten, the agency's covert operations chief for Mexico and Central America, to head an internal investigation. Within two days, he produced an initial report, which Helms shared with President Johnson, concluding that Oswald was the assassin and likely acted alone, not as a Soviet or Cuban agent. In time Whitten received reports from the FBI that led him to believe that his initial findings were premature and that important information about Oswald had been withheld from him. When Whitten raised his concerns, Helms handed the investigation over to the CIA's counterintelligence chief, James Angleton, whose highly secretive operations in the Soviet Union and Mexico likely involved Oswald. Whitten later testified, "The way things developed, a lot of things happened that I did not know or I did not find out." He added, "I did not know anything about the assassination plans of the CIA against Castro. . . . Had I known that, my investigation would have been entirely different." When asked whether "Helms was acting properly when he failed to tell the Warren Commission about the assassination plots," Whitten replied, "No. I think that was a morally highly reprehensible act, which he cannot possibly justify under his oath of office, or any other standard of professional public service. . . . I think that Helms withheld the information because he realized it would have cost him his job and would have precipitated a crisis for the Agency, which could have had very adverse effects on the Agency." House Select Committee on Assassination, classified testimony of "John Scelso" [John Whitten], May 16, 1978, 111–16, 124, 137, 153–54, NARA 180-10131-10330.

59. Ragano and Raab, *Mob Lawyer*, 144–45, 348. G. Robert Blakey, who was chief counsel to the House Select Committee on Assassinations, said of Ragano's claim, "This is the most plausible, most coherent (assassination) theory." See Jeffrey Hart, "Yes, the Mob Killed Jack Kennedy," *Herald-Journal* (Spartanburg, South Carolina), January 25, 1992. Serious questions about Ragano's account were raised in Anthony and Robyn Summers, "The Ghosts of November," *Vanity Fair*, November 2001.

Moldea defends Ragano in "Did Jimmy Hoffa, Carlos Marcello, and Santo Trafficante Kill President John Kennedy?" (presentation to the Mob Museum, October 24, 2017) at https://www.moldea.com/MobMuseum10242017.pdf. For a discussion of alleged confessions by Trafficante, Rosselli, Ragano, and Marcello, see Waldron, *Watergate*, 206–9.

60. HSCA, hearings, V, 306. Aleman's meeting with Trafficante was first recounted in George Crile, "The Mafia, the CIA, and Castro," *Washington Post*, May 16, 1976.

61. Waldron, *Watergate*, 351. For a contemporary report on the mystery of Giancana's release, see Philip Warden, "Celler to Ask Report on Giancana from Katzenbach," *Chicago Tribune*, June 7, 1966. For accounts questioning whether Giancana and Williams actually played the CIA card, see Thomas, *The Man to See*, 198; Goldfarb, *Perfect Villains, Imperfect Heroes*, 276; and Nicholas Gage, "2 Mafiosi Linked to CIA Treated Leniently by U.S.," *New York Times*, April 13, 1976.

62. IG Report, 72–74; Waldron, *Watergate*, 352–53.

63. Thomas, *The Man to See*, 200–202.

64. Gentry, *J. Edgar Hoover*, 586–88; William Lambert, "Strange Help—Hoffa Campaign of the U.S. Senator from Missouri," *Life*, May 26, 1967, 28; Sheridan, *Fall and Rise of Jimmy Hoffa*, 414–16. Long referred clients to Shenker, including Bobby Baker's business partner, the indicted income tax evader Fred Black. Black attended a fundraising dinner for Long at Baker's suggestion in early 1963. The FBI learned details through a bugged conversation between Black and Las Vegas gambler Ed Levinson. Drew Pearson and Jack Anderson, "FBI Bug Gets Tidbit on Bugging Foe," *Washington Post*, December 30, 1967.

65. Memorandum in Edward P. Morgan's CIA file re "Inquiry by the Senate Administrative Practices Subcommittee," no date; Howard Osborn, director of Security, memo to Director of Central Intelligence, re "Pros and Cons of the Robert Maheu Case," June 30, 1966; James P. O'Connell, Assistant Deputy Director of Security, Memorandum for Director of Security, May 31, 1966, re "Maheu, Robert A.," NARA 1993.07.26.17:44:39:000590. In the latter memo, O'Connell wrote, "In considering the Sam [Giancana] incident, I feel it is imperative that it not be raised in this or any other Hearing."

66. Barlett and Steele, *Empire*, 286, 301, 323; Davenport and Eddy, *The Hughes Papers*, 63–64; Hinckle and Turner, *The Fish Is Red*, 267; FBI memo from Bishop to M. A. Jones, May 13, 1971, re "Edward Pierpont Morgan," NARA 124-90133-10235.

67. FBI memo from Bishop to M. A. Jones, May 13, 1971, re "Edward Pierpont Morgan," NARA 124-90133-10235; Mahoney, *Sons and Brothers*, 333–34. Mahoney writes: "Senator Edward Long of Missouri, a Hoffa loyalist, seized on the government's brief in the Black appeal and called for an investigation. . . . On December 10, Hoover let loose, charging that Kennedy had directly approved the electronic surveillance. . . . The charges and countercharges between Hoover and Kennedy went on for weeks in the press." (334)

68. FBI memo from Callahan to H. N. Bassett, July 3, 1972, re "Edward P. Morgan," NARA 124-90133-10251. In 1950, after handling a congressional investigation of Pearl Harbor, Morgan became counsel to a special Senate committee investigating charges by Sen. Joseph McCarthy against the State Department. The following year he

became director of enforcement in Office of Price Stabilization, where he aroused the ire of J. Edgar Hoover by trying to recruit FBI agents for his team.

69. Sidney H. Beman, Acting Chief, WE-4, to Office of Security, "Request for Operational Clearance for Edward P. Morgan, November 21, 1950," NARA 104-10071-10301. The security clearance was granted by Robert H. Cunningham, an officer in the CIA's Office of Security, who also arranged Maheu's employment by the CIA starting in 1953. James P. O'Connell, Assistant Deputy Director of Security, Memorandum for Director of Security, May 31, 1966, re "Maheu, Robert A.," NARA 1993.07.26.17:44:39:000590.

70. See Edward P. Morgan's closed session testimony to Church Committee, March 19, 1976, NARA 157-10011-10040. Maheu testified that he hired Morgan to represent him in 1964, to prepare a will, but acknowledged being a friend of Morgan since about 1940 (Maheu testimony, September 23, 1975, NARA 157-10011-10049).

71. CIA memo, April 1967, "Robert H. Maheu," NARA 1993.07.26.17:44:39:000590; Rappleye and Becker, *All American Mafioso*, 220.

72. Morgan said he got to know Pearson well over many years as a result of his role as counsel to several high-profile congressional investigations. He also said Greenspun was "like a member of my own family." See Edward P. Morgan's closed session testimony to the Church Committee, March 19, 1976, NARA 157-10011-10040. Greenspun told an FBI agent that he had known Morgan since 1954 and had used his legal services several times; FBI Special Agent in Charge, Las Vegas, to Director, FBI, February 17, 1961, NARA 124-10279-10181. Among other matters, Morgan defended Greenspun against charges of inciting the murder of Sen. Joseph McCarthy (FBI memo from Callahan to H. N. Bassett, July 3, 1972, re Edward P. Morgan, NARA 124-90133-10251). Greenspun bailed Rosselli out of jail after an arrest in Las Vegas on December 29, 1966, for not registering as a felon (Waldron, *Watergate*, 363). Greenspun was also friendly with Hoffa, who financed one of his investments and shared a passion for Israel, and with Maheu, who bought one of his properties at a handsome price with Hughes's money.

73. CIA memo, April 1967, "Robert H. Maheu," NARA 1993.07.26.17:44:39:000590.

74. Barlett and Steele, *Empire*, 286–87, 291–95; Davenport and Eddy, *The Hughes Papers*, 67; memo by FBI SA Edward J. Dunn Jr., Miami, March 22, 1977, re "Roskil" [Rosselli killing], NARA 124-10289-10035; FBI SAC Las Vegas, February 14, 1961; Senate Watergate Committee interview with Rosselli, February 20, 1974, in "Rosselli, John" file, WSPF papers, NARA. Before the purchase of the Desert Inn hotel and casino from the owners of record, including former Cleveland gambler and bootlegger Morris Dalitz, Hughes had moved into the hotel's upper floor. Dalitz had opposed the move, until Jimmy Hoffa put the arm on him. Maheu reached Hoffa through Edward Bennett Williams. See Maheu and Hack, *Next to Hughes*, 159.

75. CIA memo, April 1967, "Robert H. Maheu," NARA 1993.07.26.17:44:39:000590; memorandum of interview with Edward Morgan, December 7, 1971, in "Morgan, Edward P." file, WSPF papers, NARA; Rappleye and Becker, *All American Mafioso*, 220. As part of his legal representation, Morgan supported Maheu's and Danner's campaign to get the Justice Department to drop an antitrust investigation into Hughes's purchase of hotels and casinos in Las Vegas. See Senate Watergate Report, 986–87.

This issue was flagged by the Senate Watergate Committee as one possible motivation for the $100,000 in cash payoffs arranged by Maheu from Hughes to Nixon via Bebe Rebozo. The good times for Morgan ended when Hughes fired Maheu in late 1970, declaring that his longtime manager "stole me blind." Eddy and Davenport, *The Hughes Papers*, 208.

76. *Alleged Assassination Plots*, 85n4; Rosselli testimony before Church Committee, June 24, 1975, NARA 157-10014-10001, 66–71; memorandum from Samuel Papich to Director, FBI, May 18, 1966, "Report of Meeting Between Colonel Sheffield Edwards and 'Johnny' Roselli, [sic] NARA 104-10133-10090; CIA memo, April 1967, "Robert H. Maheu," NARA 1993.07.26.17:44:39:000590, citing Maheu's reports on Rosselli's erratic behavior.

77. In December 1966, the CIA resisted a request from the FBI to have Sheffield Edwards testify before a grand jury on his contacts with Rosselli. Waldron, *Watergate*, 362–63.

78. A detailed study of this episode by the CIA's inspector general in 1967 concluded that "Roselli [sic] is the source, Morgan the channel, and [Jack] Anderson and Pearson the recipients" of leaks about the CIA-Mafia assassination plots against Castro (IG Report, 126). Maheu was also a source for Anderson. Based on Anderson's help in handling a hostile Senate hearing, the columnist wrote, "Hughes was a friend who owed me a favor. Intermediaries persuaded Maheu to confide in me. He confirmed that the CIA had asked him to sound out the Mafia, strictly off the record, about a contract to hit Fidel Castro." Jack Anderson with Daryl Gibson, *Peace, War, and Politics: An Eyewitness Account* (New York: Tom Doherty Associates, 1999), 119 (Morgan's approach to Anderson in 1967), 269 (Anderson's introduction of Morgan to Greenspun), 268 (Brewster hearing), 108 (Maheu confirmation).

79. Closed session testimony by Edward P. Morgan to the Church Committee, March 19, 1976, NARA 157-10011-10040. Rosselli first leaked a version of the story to Hank Greenspun—another client of Morgan's—at the *Las Vegas Sun*. Greenspun's story caught the attention of both the FBI and CIA. Jack Anderson already knew Maheu by this point, having been introduced by their mutual friends Greenspun and Morgan.

80. Michael Beschloss, *Taking Charge: The Johnson White House Tapes, 1963–1964* (New York: Simon & Schuster, 1997), 562; Waldron, *Watergate*, 367.

81. Perhaps it was mere coincidence, but Morgan's story served the political interests of President Johnson, who was facing possible competition from RFK in the 1968 primary. In later Senate testimony, Morgan was unable to identify who told him that Robert Kennedy was behind the plots: "All I know is what I was told." He named Maheu and Rosselli as sources of the Castro retaliation theory but admitted he had no evidence and added, "No one that I recall told me specifically that Castro had hired Oswald to kill Kennedy . . . but in my honest judgment, there is no question but that that's the answer of how Kennedy happened to be assassinated." See Edward P. Morgan's closed session testimony to the Church Committee, March 19, 1976, NARA 157-10011-10040, 21, 27, 30–31, 66.

82. Jack Anderson, "RFK-Castro Link Rumors Persistent," *Asbury Park Evening Press*, March 3, 1967. The *Washington Post* waited until March 7 to publish a heavily

edited version of the column, toning down the Robert Kennedy references. Pearson had some doubts about the story of Castro using Oswald to retaliate. He wrote in his diary for March 13, 1967, "I am not sure whether there is a clear-cut connection between Castro and Oswald." And on March 20 he wrote, "While I was away, Jack wrote part of the story. It was a poor story and violated a confidence. Finally, it reflected on Bobby Kennedy without actually pinning the goods on him. The *Washington Post* and the *New York Post* did not run it. I think they were right." Pearson, *Washington Merry-Go-Round*, 457–58, 470.

83. Dispatch from Chief, WO/VIEW, to Chiefs, Certain Stations and Bases, January 4, 1967, NARA 104-10009-10022; "New Oswald Clue Reported Found," *New York Times*, February 19, 1967; "Garrison Arrests an Ex-Major in 'Conspiracy' to Kill Kennedy," *New York Times*, March 2, 1967. Adding to the CIA's misery, Garrison soon picked up and publicized a report in a left-wing Italian newspaper alleging that his chief suspect, New Orleans businessman Clay Shaw, had worked for a commercial front in Italy used by the CIA as a cover for "illegal political-espionage activities." Shaw was acquitted of all charges. Max Holland, "The Lie That Linked CIA to the Kennedy Assassination," *Studies in Intelligence*, Vol. 45, no. 5, May 8, 2007, at https://www.cia.gov/library/center-for-the-study-of-intelligence/kent-csi/vol45no5/html/v45i5a02p.htm.

84. FBI memorandum from W. R. Wannall to W. C. Sullivan, "Central Intelligence Agency's Intentions to Send Hoodlums to Cuba to Assassinate Castro," March 6, 1967, NARA 124-10278-10289.

85. Gentry, *J. Edgar Hoover*, 597.

86. Lamar Waldron with Thom Hartmann, *Ultimate Sacrifice* (New York: Carroll & Graf, 2005), 772.

87. IG Report, 118, 129. Rosselli later admitted to Senate investigators that he had no information implicating Castro and just made "a wild guess" that the Cuban leader might be involved in Kennedy's death. See testimony of John Rosselli before the Senate Select Committee on Intelligence, April 23, 1976, NARA 157-10014-10000.

88. HSCA Report, 178.

89. Gentry, *J. Edgar Hoover*, 597; Mahoney, *Sons and Brothers*, 334.

90. Anderson with Gibson, *Peace, War, and Politics*, 108; Davis, *Mafia Kingfish*, 330. Greenspun received a loan of several million dollars from the Teamster pension fund to build his Paradise Valley Estates and Golf Course in Nevada, at a below-market interest rate; Ralph and Estelle James, *Hoffa and the Teamsters: A Study of Union Power* (Princeton, NJ: D. Van Nostrand Co., 1965), 235. An FBI informant explained that Hoffa's support for Israel "is what brought [Hoffa lobbyist Irving] Davidson, Greenspun, and Hoffa together" (FBI report from Robert B. Herrington, to Director, FBI, May 8, 1964, NARA 124-10289-10384). Drew Pearson noted in his diary that Greenspun was championing Hoffa's cause, explaining that "Hank met Hoffa when he flew to Israel last fall, and was impressed by him." (Diary entry of May 27, 1958, in Abell, ed., *Drew Pearson Diaries*, 385.)

91. Feldstein, *Poisoning the Press*, 78.

92. Sheridan, *The Fall and Rise of Jimmy Hoffa*, 443.

93. IG Report, 120, 127.

94. Max Holland, "The Assassination Tapes," *Atlantic*, June 2004.

95. Sandy Smith, "Carlos Marcello, King Thug of Louisiana," *Life*, September 8, 1967, 94–95.

96. Sheridan, *The Fall and Rise of Jimmy Hoffa*, 190, 404; Gordon Chaplin, "Behind the Schemes," *Washington Post*, August 2, 1980.

97. FBI memo, March 13, 1967, "Assassination of John Fitzgerald Kennedy, November 22, 1963," FBI 62-109060 JFK HQ file, section 19.

98. Partin did know something of potential relevance to the JFK assassination: He had passed a lie detector test supporting his claims that Hoffa had shown interest in obtaining plastic explosives to kill Attorney General Kennedy (FBI memo from A. Rosen to Mr. DeLoach, March 15, 1967, FBI 62-109060 JFK HQ file, section 120). The Justice Department took Partin's assassination story seriously enough to be concerned about a trip to Washington on March 1, 1967, by Hoffa's enforcer, Puerto Rican Teamster boss Frank Chavez (Gentry, *J. Edgar Hoover*, 597).

99. Sandy Smith, "The Fix," *Life*, September 1, 1967, 22.

100. Moldea, *The Hoffa Wars*, 180; cf. Sheridan, *The Fall and Rise of Jimmy Hoffa*, 423.

101. Morgan approached White House special counsel Charles Colson in 1970 with incriminating documents relating to Partin in order to cast doubt on Hoffa's conviction. Colson passed Morgan and other supplicants on to John Dean. John Galus memo to file 803, August 12, 1974, "Office Interview of Charles Colson," box 153 of Campaign Contributions Task Force papers, Special Prosecutor memos file, WSPF papers, NARA.

102. Howard Osborne, Director of Security, memorandum for the record, re "Meeting Between William K. Harvey and Mr. Sam Papich, FBI Liaison," November 8, 1967; Osborne memorandum for the record, "Meetings Between William K. Harvey and John Roselli [sic]," December 11, 1967, NARA 1993.07.26.17:44:39:000590. Harvey replaced Maheu as Rosselli's case officer in April 1962.

103. The decision was rendered on November 9, 1970, weeks before Maheu was fired by Hughes. Rosselli was also facing sentencing for his involvement in the Friars Club case.

104. Thomas Wadden had extensive experience with mob clients. He served as witness for the severance contract of $2.1 million received by bookmakers Frank Ritter, Max Courtney, and Charles Brudner from the Monte Carlo Casino in the Bahamas in 1967 (Pack, *Edward Bennett Williams for the Defense*, 343). He also represented Teamster president Roy Williams in the Senator Cannon bribery case, and his fees from the Teamsters union and Central States pension fund apparently exceeded $2 million (James Warren, "Lawyers Subpoenaed in Mob Inquiry," *Chicago Tribune*, April 15, 1985).

105. Howard Osborn, Director of Security, memorandum for Director of Central Intelligence, re "Roselli [sic], Johnny," November 19, 1970, NARA

1993.07.26.17:44:39:000590; cf. Rappleye and Becker, *All American Mafioso*, 296; Anderson with Gibson, *Peace, War and Politics*, 107; Demaris, *Captive City*, 14.

106. Maheu insisted that he was not the source for Anderson's 1971 stories, and Anderson told James O'Connell of the CIA's Office of Security that his sources were in the Justice Department. See James P. O'Connell memorandum for the record, January 19, 1971, re "Robert A. Maheu," and O'Connell memorandum for the record, January 18, 1971, re "Johnny Roselli" [sic], NARA 1993.07.21.08:58:07:430620. However, Anderson writes that Maheu "confirmed that the CIA had asked him to sound out the Mafia, strictly off the record, about a contract to hit Fidel Castro." See Anderson with Gibson, *Peace, War and Politics*, 108. Other sources were a retired detective with long-standing organized crime associations, Joseph Shimon, and William Harvey, a senior CIA officer who began directing the assassination program in 1962 (HSCA Report, 169, 182).

107. Jack Anderson, "Castro Death Plot Charged to CIA," *New Orleans States-Item*, January 18, 1971; Jack Anderson, "Castro Plot Raises Ugly Questions," *Washington Post*, January 19, 1971. For the record, the House Select Committee on Assassinations "found no evidence that these operations provoked Premier Castro to assassinate President Kennedy in retaliation." See HSCA Report, 181.

108. Howard Osborn, Director of Security, memorandum for CIA Executive Director-Comptroller, February 15, 1972, Doc ID 1451843, CIA "Family Jewels" release, June 25, 2007; James P. O'Connell, Deputy Director of Security, Memorandum for the Record, March 1, 1971, re "John Roselli [sic]," NARA 1993.07.21.08:58:07:430620; James O'Connell memorandum for the record, January 31, 1972, re "John Roselli [sic]," NARA 1993.07.21.08:58:07:430620; Waldron, *Watergate*, 468; Hinckle and Turner, *The Fish Is Red*, 286. The latter source incorrectly dates the intervention to 1969.

109. Summers, *Arrogance of Power*, 197; cf. Maheu and Hack, *Next to Hughes*, 126–27. The gambling case involved hidden ownership at the Frontier hotel and casino, where Rosselli had the gift shop lease under Richard Danner's management. Prior to the sale to Hughes, Rosselli had facilitated a secret ownership interest by Anthony Zerilli, a leading Detroit mobster.

110. Memorandum by Terry Lenzner and Marc Lackritz to Senator Ervin, re "Relevant to S. Res. 60 of John Rosselli's testimony about his CIA activities," no date, Miscellaneous Records of the Church Committee, NARA 157-10014-10242; also in "Rosselli, John" file, WSPF papers, NARA.

111. Caulfield to Dean, February 1, 1972, in US Congress, Senate, Select Committee on Presidential Campaign Activities, *Executive Session Hearings*, 93rd Cong., 2nd sess. (Washington, DC: US Government Printing Office, 1974), Book 21, 9755 et seq. Hereafter Senate Watergate hearings. I do not share the view of John Davis (*Mafia Kingfish*, 366) and other authors that Nixon feared public exposure of his own involvement in the assassination plots, which has never been demonstrated. In particular, Nixon did not support paying hush money to E. Howard Hunt for that reason. Hunt had to be silenced because of his role in the illegal burglary of the office of Daniel Ellsberg's psychiatrist in September 1971.

112. Summers, *Arrogance of Power*, 153.

113. This coincidence was noted in a memorandum from John Dean to John Ehrlichman on February 3, 1972, regarding the Hughes loan, reprinted in Bruce Oudes, ed., *From the President: Richard Nixon's Secret Files* (New York: Harper & Row, 1989), 364–65. See also Barlett and Steele, *Empire*, 199–204.

114. Oudes, *From the President*, xxvii; Summers, *Arrogance of Power*, 155; Noah Dietrich and Bob Thomas, *Howard: The Amazing Mr. Hughes* (New York: Fawcett, 1972), 281–85. Some of the benefits Hughes received after his loan included "approval of previously denied St. Louis–Miami route for TWA, government reversal of a ten-year-old decision against letting Hughes lend TWA $5 million from HAC coffers, recomputation of mail transport credits to TWA generating a multimillion-dollar refund out of what had been a TWA debt, SEC approval of a TWA stock transfer that it had turned down four times previously, reversal of an unfavorable IRS judgment against Hughes's Medical Institute in Miami, and the dropping of a Justice Department antitrust action against Toolco." Carl Oglesby, *The Yankee and Cowboy War: Conspiracies from Dallas to Watergate* (Kansas City: Sheed Andrews and McMeel, 1976), 186. According to George Washington University professor Mark Feldstein, "Later evidence would show that the vice president had personally phoned Hughes to ask for the money, which was used to help Nixon pay for an elegant, 9,000-square-foot Tudor house in Washington with eight bedrooms, six bathrooms, a library, a butler's pantry and a solarium." Mark Feldstein, "JFK's Own Dirty Trick," *Washington Post*, January 14, 2011.

115. Mark Feldstein, "JFK's Own Dirty Trick," *Washington Post*, January 14, 2011; cf. Feldstein, *Poisoning the Press*, 61–74; Anderson and Boyd, *Confessions of a Muckraker*, 326–33; Summers, *Arrogance of Power*, 157. The loan to Don Nixon was secured by a lot worth only about $13,000. See Clayton Fritchey, "Henry Ruth Strikes Out," *Washington Post*, October 28, 1975.

116. During the campaign, a Democratic trickster slipped a Chinese-language sign reading "What about the Hughes loan?" into a Nixon appearance in Los Angeles's Chinatown. Bruce Felknor, *Political Mischief: Smear, Sabotage, and Reform in U.S. Elections* (New York: Praeger, 1992), 142.

117. "James R. Phelan, 85, Is Dead," *New York Times*, September 12, 1997; also Haldeman with DiMona, *Ends of Power*, 20.

118. Michael Drosnin, *Citizen Hughes: In His Own Words—How Howard Hughes Tried to Buy America* (New York: Holt, Rinehart & Winston, 1985), 300.

119. Summers, *Arrogance of Power*, 279. But the obligations flowed both ways. Maheu said that after Danner's visit to Mitchell, he told the Hughes executive in charge of political contributions that "certain political obligations had to be met" and that $50,000 should be made "available to Mr. Danner." See Lukas, *Nightmare*, 115.

120. Lukas, *Nightmare*, 114.

121. Senate Watergate hearings, Book 21, 9942–43, 9986; Book 24, 11418–20; SWR, 935–36. Rebozo's political instincts were sound. Remarkably, Morgan would become counsel to the Democratic National Committee in March 1973 for its lawsuit against the Nixon team stemming from Watergate. Waldron, *Watergate*, 678.

122. Drosnin, *Citizen Hughes*, 393–94 (mysterious losses), 473–74 (ongoing mob control of Hughes's casinos); Demaris, *The Last Mafioso*, 203.

123. John Dean III, *Blind Ambition* (New York: Simon & Schuster, 1976), 66–70.

124. John Caulfield to John Dean, "Hughes Retainer to Larry O'Brien and Related Matters," January 25, 1971; John Dean to H. R. Haldeman, January 26, 1971; Caulfield to Dean, "Hughes' Retainer of Larry O'Brien," February 1, 1971, "Hughes Retainer to Larry O'Brien," Senate Watergate hearings, Book 21, 9749, 9751–53, 9755; Dean, *Blind Ambition*, 391. In his January 25 memo, Caulfield noted, "Mayhew [sic] was a close associate of rogue FBI agent John Frank, generally believed to have engineered the assassination of Jesus de Galindez in New York City on March 12, 1956 on behalf of the assassinated Rafael Trujillo."

125. Through Maheu, Anderson had access to Hughes's private papers, which were still under court seal. Jack Anderson, "Howard Hughes: Hidden Kingmaker," *Washington Post*, August 6, 1971; Anderson with Gibson, *Peace, War, and Politics*, 272. To protect his source, Anderson included a quote from Maheu, refusing to comment.

126. Drosnin, *Citizen Hughes*, 419–20.

127. Jack Anderson, "Two Ghosts Haunt Nixon's Campaign," *Washington Post*, January 24, 1972.

128. Feldstein, *Poisoning the Press*, 222–23.

129. In 1969, Pearson and Anderson had broken a story about Bebe Rebozo and Herbert Klein, Nixon's communications director, visiting Nevada "to smooth the feathers of Howard Hughes, the biggest owner of Nevada real estate, who has protested vigorously against previous underground nuclear tests." "ABM Effect Tested in Nevada," *Los Angeles Times*, June 26, 1969. In late January 1972, Dean learned that Anderson was once again snooping around the 1956 Hughes loan, including new information, which suggested that Hughes had received a hugely favorable IRS ruling shortly after Nixon received the loan. See Bruce Kehrli to Haldeman re Howard Hughes, January 18, 1972; John Dean to Haldeman and Ehrlichman re Hughes Loan to Don Nixon, January 31, 1972; and John Dean to Haldeman, February 3, 1972, reprinted in Bruce Oudes, ed., *From the President*, 357, 360, 364–65. Anderson was also anathema to the administration because of his coverage of the ITT scandal.

130. Feldstein, *Poisoning the Press*, 281–86; G. Gordon Liddy, *Will* (New York: St. Martin's Press, 1980), 286–95; Bob Woodward, "Hunt Told Associates of Orders to Kill Jack Anderson," *Washington Post*, September 21, 1975; Anderson with Gibson, *Peace, War, and Politics*, 228–30; IG Report, 21–22 (Dr. Edward Gunn, Chief, Operations Division, Office of Medical Services). Hunt considered using Frank Sturgis to help kill Anderson, but he turned out to be a friend of Anderson. Hunt later claimed that Colson ordered him only to incapacitate Anderson. See "Hunt Tells of Plot to Drug Columnist," *San Francisco Chronicle*, September 29, 1975.

131. Feldstein, *Poisoning the Press*, 278–79; Jack Anderson, "Watergate Scandal Like an ITT Rerun," *Sumter Daily Item*, March 1, 1973; Anderson with Gibson, *Peace, War, and Politics*, 230–33. For general background on Intertel, see Jim Hougan, *Spooks*; Tom Zito, "Peloquin of Intertel: Intelligence Security, 'Targets of Opportunity,'" *Washington Post*, February 20, 1977.

132. Jim Hougan, *Secret Agenda: Watergate, Deep Throat, and the CIA* (New York: Random House, 1984), 85–95; Anderson with Gibson, *Peace, War, and Politics*, 233–41.

133. Feldstein, *Poisoning the Press*, 280.

134. James McCord, "Counter-Espionage Agent for the Republicans: The True Story of the Watergate Case," in US Congress, House of Representatives, Committee on Armed Services, Special Subcommittee on Intelligence, *Inquiry into the Alleged Involvement of the Central Intelligence Agency in the Watergate and Ellsberg Matters*, hearings, 94th Cong., 1st sess. (Washington, DC: US Government Printing Office, 1975), 838–43.

135. Liddy, *Will*, 324–25; cf. E. Howard Hunt, *Undercover* (London: W. H. Allen, 1974), 232. There is ample evidence of the Nixon camp's obsession with O'Brien. Even Bobby Baker got dragged into their efforts to neutralize the Democratic Party chief, reporting in his memoir that Rebozo and Nixon's attorney and fundraiser Herbert Kalmbach were "almost desperate to uncover dirt involving Larry O'Brien." Baker, *Wheeling and Dealing*, 252–54.

136. J. Anthony Lukas, "Why the Watergate Break-in?" *New York Times*, November 30, 1987.

137. Thomas, *The Man to See*, 58, 233–34, 275. On Joseph Califano's tip to Howard Simons at the *Post*, see also Ben Bradlee, *A Good Life: Newspapering and Other Adventures* (New York: Simon & Schuster, 1995), 324–25. In March 1973, Califano had to drop the DNC as a client when Judge Richey ruled he had a conflict of interest with his representation of the *Washington Post*. His replacement as counsel to the DNC lawsuit was Edward Morgan. Waldron, *Watergate*, 678.

138. Thomas, *The Man to See*, 68, 277. Thomas does not claim that Williams influenced Sirica's approach to the Watergate trial, but Williams did get Sirica to go easy on Woodward and Bernstein after they improperly approached grand jurors on the case.

139. Transcript of Nixon conversation with H. R. Haldeman and John Dean, September 15, 1972, at http://nixon.archives.gov/forresearchers/find/tapes/watergate/wspf/779-002.pdf. Nixon added the intriguing comment, "He misbehaved very badly in the Hoffa matter. Our—some pretty bad conduct there, too, but go ahead." Later, Nixon targeted Williams for tax audits. See Nixon conversation with Charles Colson, January 1, 1973, in Stanley Kutler, *Abuse of Power: The New Nixon Tapes* (New York: The Free Press, 1997), 192. For whatever reason, the IRS audited Williams for three consecutive years during the Nixon administration. Stanley I. Kutler, *The Wars of Watergate: The Last Crisis of Richard Nixon* (New York: W. W. Norton, 1992), 105.

140. Waldron, *Watergate*, 86, 111.

141. David Kaiser, *The Road to Dallas: The Assassination of John F. Kennedy* (Cambridge: Harvard University Press, 2008), 160–65; Carrozza, *William D. Pawley*, 255–65.

142. Waldron, *Watergate*, 473.

143. Lukas, *Nightmare*, 278–79 (hush money); FBI interview with Artime, June 23, 1972, NARA 124-10289-10440 (Artime and Watergate defendants); IG Report, 110–20 (Artime and AMLASH plot); S. D. Breckinridge memo to DDCI, October 5, 1976, NARA 1993.08.04.14:48:42:280064 (Artime and Mafia plots).

144. Haldeman, *The Ends of Power*, 25 (recalling June 20 conversation with Nixon); Richard Nixon, *RN: The Memoirs of Richard Nixon* (New York: Grosset and Dunlap, 1978), 641.

145. White House conversation with H. R. Haldeman, June 23, 1973, at http://watergate.info/1972/06/23/the-smoking-gun-tape.html.

146. White House conversation with H. R. Haldeman, June 23, 1973, at http://nixon.archives.gov/forresearchers/find/tapes/watergate/wspf/741-010.pdf; Haldeman with DiMona, *The Ends of Power*, 33.

147. Memorandum from CIA director Helms to Deputy Director Vernon Walters, June 28, 1972, re "Watergate Affair," in US Congress, House of Representatives, Committee on the Judiciary, *Statement of Information, Hearings*, 93rd Cong., 2nd sess. (Washington, DC: US Government Printing Office, 1974), Book II ("Events Following the Watergate Break-In"), 459; Fred Emery, *Watergate* (New York: Touchstone, 1994), 193. In particular, Deputy CIA Vernon Walters told FBI director L. Patrick Gray that the bureau's efforts to trace the Watergate burglars' cash through Mexican banks "could trespass" onto some of the agency's covert projects. L. Patrick Gray, *In Nixon's Web: A Year in the Crosshairs of Watergate* (New York: Times Books, 2008), 72.

148. Haldeman with DiMona, *The Ends of Power*, 35, 38–40. It is important to emphasize that Nixon was manipulating the CIA's sensitivity over the assassination issue, not his own.

149. Rappleye and Becker, *All American Mafioso*, 307.

150. There is little credible evidence implicating Nixon in the plots to murder Castro. See Evan Thomas, "Whose Obsession Is It, Anyway? Oliver Stone Can't Resist Linking Nixon to JFK's Assassination, but He's Wrong," *Newsweek*, December 11, 1995; Christopher Matthews, "New Tapes Debunk Oliver Stone's 'Nixon,'" *San Francisco Examiner*, January 1, 1998. For a contrary view, see Summers, *Arrogance of Power*, 177 et seq.

151. Nicholas Gage, "Rosselli Called a Victim of Mafia Because of His Senate Testimony," *New York Times*, February 25, 1977. Sam Giancana was also the victim of a mob hit.

152. Arthur Schlesinger Jr., *The Imperial Presidency* (Boston: Houghton Mifflin, 1973), 331.

Chapter 10

1. C. Wright Mills, "A Diagnosis of Our Moral Uneasiness," *New York Times Magazine*, November 23, 1952.

2. C. Wright Mills, *The Power Elite* (New York: Oxford University Press, 1957), 274–76.

3. Mills, *The Power Elite*, 293–94, 343–46.

4. Anderson with Boyd, *Confessions of a Muckraker*, 102.

5. Fried, *The Rise and Fall of the Jewish Gangster in America*, 257.

6. Peter Andreas, *Smuggler Nation: How Illicit Trade Made America* (New York: Oxford University Press, 2013); see also Gustavus Myers, *The History of the Great American Fortunes* (Chicago: C. H. Kerr, 1910).

7. *Las Vegas Sun*, September 17, 1982 (Dalitz and ADL); Michael Newton, *Mr. Mob*, 245 (City of Peace award); "Linsey to Head Ball Patrons," *Jewish Advocate*, January 3, 1963 (Combined Jewish Philanthropies); "Brandeis Will Dedicate Linsey Center Sunday," *Jewish Advocate*, September 7, 1967.

8. Gus Russo, *The Outfit*, 168.

9. Daniel Bell, "Crime as an American Way of Life: A Queer Ladder of Social Mobility," in *The End of Ideology* (Cambridge, MA: Harvard University Press, 1960), 138, 148.

10. Fox, *Blood and Power*, 61.

11. Moldea, *Dark Victory*; quote from Dan Moldea, "The Corruption of Ronald Reagan," July 15, 1999, at http://www.moldea.com/ReaganRedux.html.

12. Neff, *Mobbed Up*.

13. Newton, *Mr. Mob*, 269–71. Another expert observes, "there is another, strikingly different side to the Reagan record on organized crime. During his terms as president, federal prosecutors have brought more than one thousand largely successful indictments against Mafia figures throughout the nation. . . . But the debts—his friendship with Laxalt, his appointments of Presser, Donovan and [Roy] Brewer, and his nonchalant support of Donovan as two witnesses against the labor secretary were murdered and Senate probers were threatened—cannot be ignored." Scheim, *Contract on America*, 317, 319.

14. Eli Rosenberg, "46 Charged in Mafia Racketeering Conspiracy," *New York Times*, August 4, 2016. See also Selwyn Rabb, *Five Families: The Rise, Decline, and Resurgence of America's Most Powerful Mafia Empires* (New York: St. Martin's, 2016), xiv. For an earlier assessment, see Peter Reuter, "The Decline of the American Mafia," *The Public Interest* 120 (Summer 1995), 89–99.

15. Quoted in Seth Ferranti, "What Happened to the American Mafia," July 12, 2015, https://www.vice.com/en_us/article/kwxbpa/what-happened-to-the-american-mafia-712. See also Alex Norcia, "The American Mafia Has Become an Unhinged Reality Show," March 19, 2019, at https://www.vice.com/en_us/article/8xy7wx/the-american-mob-has-become-an-unhinged-maga-qanon-reality-show.

16. For a sampling of Trump's record, see Paul Waldman, "Trump's History of Corruption Is Mind-Boggling," *Washington Post*, September 5, 2016; John Feffer, "Trump's Dirty Money," July 25, 2018, https://lobelog.com/trumps-dirty-money; David Barstow, Susanne Craig, and Russ Buettner, "Trump Engaged in Suspect Tax Schemes as He Reaped Riches from His Father," *New York Times*, October 2, 2018; Adam Davidson, "Is Fraud Part of the Trump Organization's Business Model?" October 17, 2018, https://www.newyorker.com/news/swamp-chronicles/is-fraud-part-of-the-trump-organizations-business-model. On his corrupt record as president, see David Leonhardt, "Trump's Corruption: The Definitive List," *New York Times*, October 28, 2018; Fred Hiatt, "It's Not News That Trump Is Corrupt. What's New Is How He Is Succeeding in Corrupting Our Government," *Washington Post*, October 6, 2019; Nicholas Confessore et al., "The Swamp That Trump Built," *New York Times*,

October 10, 2020; and Dan Alexander, *White House, Inc. How Donald Trump Turned the Presidency Into a Business* (New York: Portfolio/Penguin, 2020).

17. Wayne Barrett, *Trump: The Deals and the Downfall* (New York: HarperCollins, 1992), 51–52; Chauncy Devega, "Pulitzer-winning Reporter David Cay Johnston: 'The Evidence Suggests Trump Is a Traitor,'" August 23, 2018, https://www.salon.com/2018/04/23/pulitzer-winning-reporter-david-cay-johnston-the-evidence-suggests-trump-is-a-traitor/.

18. Barrett, *Trump*, 131, 195–201; Craig Unger, *House of Trump, House of Putin: The Untold Story of Donald Trump and the Russian Mafia* (New York: Dutton, 2018), 24–25; Robert O'Harrow Jr., "Trump Swam in Mob-infested Waters in Early Years as an NYC Developer," *Washington Post*, October 16, 2015; David Cay Johnston, "Just What Were Donald Trump's Ties to the Mob?" May 22, 2016, http://www.politico.com/magazine/story/2016/05/donald-trump-2016-mob-organized-crime-213910; Linda Qiu, "Yes, Donald Trump Has Been Linked to the Mob," March 2, 2016, https://www.politifact.com/truth-o-meter/statements/2016/mar/02/ted-cruz/yes-donald-trump-has-been-linked-mob/; Jeff Stein, "Donald Trump's Mafia Connections: Decades Later, Is He Still Linked to the Mob?" January 10, 2019, https://www.newsweek.com/2019/01/18/donald-trump-mafia-connections-decades-later-linked-mob-1285771.html.

19. Barrett, *Trump*, 241–42; see also other transactions discussed at 216–18, 229. Salvatore Testa was himself killed in a mob hit in 1984.

20. Christopher Knaus, "Trump's Bid for Sydney Casino 30 years Ago Rejected Due to 'Mafia Connections,'" *The Guardian*, August 15, 2017.

21. Linda Qiu, "Yes, Donald Trump Has Been Linked to the Mob," March 2, 2016, https://www.politifact.com/truth-o-meter/statements/2016/mar/02/ted-cruz/yes-donald-trump-has-been-linked-mob/; see also Molly Gordy, "Trump Supports Casino Suspect," *New York Daily News*, September 25, 1995.

22. Robert O'Harrow Jr., "Trump's Ties to an Informant and FBI Agent Reveal His Mode of Operation," *Washington Post*, September 17, 2016. Peter Dale Scott has observed that organized crime enforcement "turns informants into double agents with status within the police as well as the mob. The protection of informants and their crimes encourages favors, payoffs, and eventually systemic corruption. The phenomenon of 'organized crime' arises: entire criminal structures that come to be tolerated by the police because of their usefulness in informing on lesser criminals." Scott, *Deep Politics* (1996), xii.

23. Tom Robbins, "Trump and the Mob," April 27, 2016, https://www.themarshallproject.org/2016/04/27/trump-and-the-mob. In a 2013 interview with David Letterman, Trump said of New York's Mafia leaders, "I have met on occasion a few of those people. They happen to be very nice people." But he offered some sage advice: "You just don't want to owe them money. Don't owe them money." Quoted in Ed Pilkington, "'Very Nice People,' Trump Said of the Mafia. 'Just Don't Owe Them Money,'" *Guardian*, October 2, 2019.

24. Barrett, *Trump*, 202–5.

25. David Corn and Hannah Levintova, "How Did an Alleged Russian Mobster End Up on Trump's Red Carpet?" September 14, 2016, https://www.mother

jones.com/politics/2016/09/trump-russian-mobster-tokhtakhounov-miss-universe
-moscow/; Michael Weiss and Casey Michel, "The Alleged Russian Mobsters in
Trump World's Orbit: A Dirty Dozen," November 16, 2019, https://www.thedaily-
beast.com/the-alleged-russian-mobsters-in-trump-worlds-orbit-a-dirty-dozen.

26. Unger, *House of Trump, House of Putin*, 13, 142; Thomas Frank, "Secret
Money: How Trump Made Millions Selling Condos to Unknown Buyers," January
12, 2018, https://www.buzzfeednews.com/article/thomasfrank/secret-money-how
-trump-made-millions-selling-condos-to; see also David Leonhardt, "The Urgent
Question of Trump and Money Laundering," *New York Times*, September 9, 2018.

27. Casey Michel, "The Trump Organization's Problem with Possible Money
Laundering," May 8, 2019, https://thinkprogress.org/here-are-the-kleptocrats-and-
crooked-foreign-politicians-whove-invested-in-trump-properties-460093120e48/;
David A. Fahrenthold and Jonathan O'Connell, "'I Like Them Very Much': Trump
Has Long-standing Business Ties with Saudis, Who Have Boosted His Hotels Since
He Took Office," *Washington Post*, October 11, 2018; Tom Burgis, "Tower of Secrets:
The Russian Money behind a Donald Trump Skyscraper," *Financial Times*, July 11,
2018; "Soviet-born Mobster Accused of Trying to Launder Cash Through Trump
Projects," *Times of Israel*, March 26, 2019. On Trump's questionable deals in Panama
City, see Heather Vogell et al., "Pump and Trump," October 17, 2018, https://features
.propublica.org/trump-inc-podcast/trump-family-business-panama-city-khafif/.

28. Unger, *House of Trump, House of Putin*, 121–22; Financial Crimes Enforcement Network, "FinCEN Fines Trump Taj Mahal Casino Resort $10 Million for
Significant and Long Standing Anti–Money Laundering Violations," press release,
March 6, 2015, https://www.fincen.gov/news/news-releases/fincen-fines-trump-taj
-mahal-casino-resort-10-million-significant-and-long. Trump had only a minority
share in the casino's operating company after 2009.

29. Some of the less-reputable individuals are described in Michael Weiss and
Casey Michel, "The Alleged Russian Mobsters in Trump World's Orbit: A Dirty
Dozen," November 16, 2019, https://www.thedailybeast.com/the-alleged-russian
-mobsters-in-trump-worlds-orbit-a-dirty-dozen.

30. Unger, *House of Trump, House of Putin*, 207; Frank, "Secret Money"; Russ
Baker, C. Collins, and Jonathan Larsen, "Why FBI Can't Tell All on Trump, Russia," March 27, 2017, at http://whowhatwhy.org/2017/03/27/fbi-cant-tell-trump-
russia; James Henry, "The Curious World of Donald Trump's Private Russian
Connections," *The American Interest*, December 19, 2016, http://www.the-american
-interest.com/2016/12/19/the-curious-world-of-donald-trumps-private-russian
-connections/; Diana Pilipenko, "Cracking the Shell: Trump and the Corrupting Potential of Furtive Russian Money," February 13, 2018, https://www.americanprogress
.org/issues/democracy/reports/2018/02/13/446576/cracking-the-shell/.

31. Unger, *House of Trump, House of Putin*, 132–34, 139–42, 159–61; Grant Stern,
"A Russian Mobster Built Trump SoHo into Putin's Money Laundering Racket," July
8, 2017, https://thesternfacts.com/russian-mobster-built-trump-soho-into-putins-
money-laundering-racket-652cf639e8f0. A copy of the lawsuit is available at https://
www.documentcloud.org/documents/4345746-Kriss-Lawsuit-Bayrock-Verified
-Complaint-6-20.html. The parties settled the lawsuit in 2018; Chris Dolmetsch and

David Voreacos, "Trump-Linked Real Estate Firm Settles Suit by Ex-Employee," February 22, 2018, https://www.bloomberg.com/news/articles/2018-02-22/trump -linked-real-estate-firm-settles-suit-by-former-executive.

32. Quoted in Seth Feranti, "How Putin's Russia Became Mafia Heaven," May 29, 2018, https://www.vice.com/en_us/article/gykvey/why-is-the-russian-mafia-vor-v -zakone-so-powerful-putin-trump. For a critical assessment of Trump's ties to corrupt Russian actors, see Seth Hettena, *Trump/Russa: A Definitive History* (Brooklyn: Melville House, 2018).

33. US embassy cable, "Ukraine: Firtash Makes His Case to the USG," December 10, 2008, http://www.guardian.co.uk/world/us-embassy-cables-documents/182121. For more on Firtash, see Catherine Belton, *Putin's People: How the KGB Took Back Russia and Then Took on the West* (New York: Farrar, Straus and Giroux, 2020), 335–40.

34. Robert I. Friedman, "The Most Dangerous Mobster in the World," *Village Voice*, May 26, 1998; Robert I. Friedman, *Red Mafiya: How the Russian Mob Has Invaded America* (New York: Little Brown, 2000); Brian Frydenborg, "The 1995 Gangster Meeting in Israel That Blows Opens the Trump-Russia Saga," August 30, 2017, https://www.linkedin.com/pulse/1995-gangster-meeting-israel-blows-opens-trump -russia-frydenborg/ (Bogotin, Ivankov, and Trump Tower); Federal Bureau of Investigation, "FBI Ten Most Wanted Fugitive: Semion Mogilevich," October 21, 2009, https://archives.fbi.gov/archives/news/stories/2009/october/mogilevich_102109; Michael Weiss and Casey Michel, "The Alleged Russian Mobsters in Trump World's Orbit: A Dirty Dozen," November 16, 2019, https://www.thedailybeast.com/the -alleged-russian-mobsters-in-trump-worlds-orbit-a-dirty-dozen.

35. Tom Winter, "DOJ: Ex-Manafort Associate Firtash Is Top-Tier Comrade of Russian Mobsters," July 26, 2017, https://www.nbcnews.com/news/us-news/doj-ex -manafort-associate-firtash-top-tier-comrade-russian-mobsters-n786806; also Tom Winter and Ken Dilanian, "Donald Trump Aide Paul Manafort Scrutinized for Russian Business Ties," August 18, 2016, https://www.nbcnews.com/news/us-news/ donald-trump-aide-paul-manafort-scrutinized-russian-business-ties-n631241; Andrew Kramer, "Ukrainian Gas Broker Faces Scrutiny," *New York Times*, April 20, 2014; Kyle Mackie, "US: Ukrainian Oligarch and His Associate Are Tied to Russian Organized Crime," July 27, 2019, https://www.occrp.org/en/27-ccwatch/cc-watch -briefs/6775-us-ukrainian-oligarch-and-his-associate-are-tied-to-russian-organized -crime; Michael Weiss and Casey Michel, "The Alleged Russian Mobsters in Trump World's Orbit: A Dirty Dozen," November 16, 2019, https://www.thedailybeast.com/ the-alleged-russian-mobsters-in-trump-worlds-orbit-a-dirty-dozen. On a possible connection between Manafort and Mogilevich, see Betsy Swan, "Mueller Reveals New Manafort Link to Organized Crime," November 2, 2017, https://www.thedailybeast .com/mueller-reveals-new-manafort-link-to-organized-crime.

36. Betsy Swan, "Indicted Oligarch Dmytro Firtash Praises Paul Manafort," March 20, 2019, https://www.thedailybeast.com/indicted-oligarch-dmytro-firtash-praises -paul-manafort-says-trump-has-third-grade-smarts.

37. Simon Shuster, "How a Ukrainian Oligarch Wanted by U.S. Authorities Helped Giuliani Attack Biden," October 15, 2019, https://time.com/5699201/exclusive-how

-a-ukrainian-oligarch-wanted-by-u-s-authorities-helped-giuliani-attack-biden/; see also Jo Becker et al., "Why Giuliani Singled Out 2 Ukrainian Oligarchs to Help Look for Dirt," *New York Times*, November 25, 2019; Ken Dilanian, Dan De Luce, and Tom Winter, "Ukrainian Oligarch Firtash Linked to Giuliani Pals' Gas Deals and Biden Dirt Digging," October 16, 2019, https://www.nbcnews.com/politics/ trump-impeachment-inquiry/ukrainian-oligarch-firtash-linked-giuliani-pals-gas -deals-biden-dirt-n1067516; Robert Mackey, "Is a Ukrainian Oligarch Helping Trump Smear Biden to Evade U.S. Corruption Charges?" October 17, 2019, https:// theintercept.com/2019/10/17/ukrainian-oligarch-helping-trump-smear-biden -evade-u-s-corruption-charges/; Stephanie Baker and Irina Reznik, "To Win Giuliani's Help, Oligarch's Allies Pursued Biden Dirt," October 18, 2019, https://www.bloom berg.com/news/articles/2019-10-18/to-win-giuliani-s-help-oligarch-s-allies-pursued -biden-dirt. On the alleged mob connections of Parnas's partner Igor Fruman, see Aubrey Belford and Veronika Melkozerova, "Meet the Florida Duo Helping Giuliani Investi- gate for Trump in Ukraine," July 22, 2019, https://www.occrp.org/en/investigations/ meet-the-florida-duo-helping-giuliani-dig-dirt-for-trump-in-ukraine.

38. Brendan Pierson and Karen Freifeld, "Giuliani Associate Paid $1 Million by Indicted Ukrainian Oligarch's Lawyer: Prosecutor," December 17, 2019, https://www .reuters.com/article/us-usa-trump-giuliani-parnas-oligarch-idUSKBN1YL26B.

39. James Comey, *A Higher Loyalty: Truth, Lies, and Leadership* (New York: Flat- iron Books, 2018), 221, 7.

40. Masha Gessen, "The Trump-Russia Investigation and the Mafia State," Janu- ary 31, 2019, https://www.newyorker.com/news/our-columnists/the-trump-russia -investigation-and-the-mafia-state.

41. The leak of more than eleven million files from the Panamanian law firm of Mossack Fonseca exposed "the offshore holdings of world political leaders, links to global scandals, and details of the hidden financial dealings of fraudsters, drug traffickers, billionaires, celebrities, sports stars and more." See International Con- sortium of Investigative Journalists, "About the Investigation," https://www.icij.org/ investigations/panama-papers/pages/panama-papers-about-the-investigation/. See also the more recent leak of FinCEN files; International Consortium of Investigative Journalists, "Global Banks Defy US Crackdowns by Serving Oligarchs, Criminals and Terrorists," September 20, 2020, at https://www.icij.org/investigations/fincen-files/ global-banks-defy-u-s-crackdowns-by-serving-oligarchs-criminals-and-terrorists.

42. Franklin Foer, "How Kleptocracy Came to America," *The Atlantic*, March 2019.

43. The literature on this subject is huge. See, for example, Jeffrey Robinson, *The Laundrymen: Inside Money Laundering* (New York: Arcade Publishing, 1996); Block and Weaver, *All Is Clouded by Desire*; US Congress, Senate, Committee on Govern- mental Affairs, Permanent Subcommittee on Investigations, Minority Staff, report, *Correspondent Banking: A Gateway for Money Laundering*, 107th Cong., 1st sess. (Washington, DC: US Government Printing Office, 2001); US Congress, Senate, Com- mittee on Homeland Security and Governmental Affairs, Permanent Subcommittee on Investigations, Majority and Minority Staff, report, *Keeping Foreign Corruption Out of the United States: Four Case Histories* (Washington, DC: 2010); US Congress,

Senate, Committee on Homeland Security and Governmental Affairs, Permanent Subcommittee on Investigations, Majority and Minority Staff, report, *U.S. Vulnerabilities to Money Laundering, Drugs, and Terrorist Financing: HSBC Case History* (Washington, DC, 2012); Ed Vulliamy, "How a Big US Bank Laundered Billions from Mexico's Murderous Drug Gangs," *The Observer*, April 2, 2011; Ed Caesar, "Deutsche Bank's $10-Billion Scandal," *New Yorker*, August 29, 2016; Max de Haldevang, "The Top 50 Global Banks Allegedly Involved in a $21 Billion Russian Money-Laundering Scheme," March 21, 2017, https://qz.com/938504/the-top-50-global-banks-allegedly-involved-in-the-20-8-billion-russian-laundromat-money-laundering-scheme/; Oliver Bullough, *Moneyland: The Inside Story of the Crooks and Kleptocrats Who Rule the World* (New York: St. Martin's, 2019). On the notorious older case of Bank of Commerce and Credit International, see James Ring Adams and Douglas Frantz, *A Full Service Bank: How BCCI Stole Billions around the World* (New York: Pocket Books, 1992); Peter Truell and Larry Gurwin, *False Profits: Inside Story of BCCI, the World's Most Corrupt Financial Empire* (Boston: Houghton Mifflin, 1992).

44. Matt Taibbi, "Outrageous HSBC Settlement Proves the Drug War Is a Joke," *RollingStone*, December 13, 2012; Patrick Radden Keefe, "Why Corrupt Bankers Avoid Jail," July 31, 2017, https://www.newyorker.com/magazine/2017/07/31/why-corrupt-bankers-avoid-jail; Alan Puke, "Drug Warrior Jeff Sessions Lets a Megabank Skate on Laundering Money into Mexico," May 25, 2017, https://thinkprogress.org/jeff-sessions-soft-on-banks-tough-on-minor-offenses-7380295efc0.

45. Rajeev Syal, "Drug Money Saved Banks in Global Crisis, Claims UN Adviser," *The Guardian*, December 12, 2009.

46. Franklin Foer, "Russian-Style Kleptocracy Is Infiltrating America," *The Atlantic*, March 2019, https://www.theatlantic.com/magazine/archive/2019/03/how-kleptocracy-came-to-america/580471/.

47. Max de Haldevang, "The American Bar Association Is Fighting Washington's Efforts to Tackle Money Laundering," July 1, 2019, https://qz.com/1646365/the-american-bar-association-is-fighting-congresss-efforts-to-tackle-money-laundering/; Heather Vogell, "Why Aren't Hedge Funds Required to Fight Money Laundering?" January 23, 2019, https://www.propublica.org/article/why-arent-hedge-funds-required-to-fight-money-laundering.

48. US Department of Treasury, *National Money Laundering Risk Assessment, 2018*, https://home.treasury.gov/system/files/136/2018NMLRA_12-18.pdf; Damian Paletta, Robert O'Harrow Jr., and Michelle Ye Hee Lee, "Manafort, Cohen Cases Reveal Weaknesses in Enforcement of Tax and Election Laws," *Washington Post*, August 25, 2018; Jesse Eisinger, "Why Manafort and Cohen Thought They'd Get Away with It," *New York Times*, August 24, 2018; Jesse Eisinger and Paul Kiel, "IRS Fraud Cases Plummet after Budget Cuts," *New York Times*, October 1, 2018; Richard Cebula and Edgar Feige, "America's Unreported Economy: Measuring the Size, Growth, and Determinants of Income Tax Evasion in the U.S.," *Crime, Law and Social Change* 57, no. 3 (April 2012), 265–85; Ishaan Tharoor, "The 'Paradise Papers' Expose Trump's Fake Populism," *Washington Post*, November 8, 2017; Natasha Sarin and Lawrence Summers, "Shrinking the Tax Gap: Approaches Ad Revenue Potential," November 18, 2018, https://www.taxnotes.com/special-reports/compliance/shrinking-tax

-gap-approaches-and-revenue-potential/2019/11/15/2b47g. The Justice Department's criminal complaint, to which Manafort pleaded guilty, stated he "funneled millions of dollars in payments into foreign nominee companies and bank accounts," "laundered more than $30 million to buy property, goods, and services in the United States," and "cheated the United States out of over $15 million in taxes." "Superseding Criminal Information," *United States of America v. Paul J. Manafort, Jr., District Court for the District of Columbia*, document 419, filed September 14, 2018, at https://www.justice .gov/file/1094141/download.

49. For an explicit likening of campaign funding to organized crime, see Donald R. Liddick, "Campaign Fund-raising Abuses and Money Laundering in Recent U.S. Elections: Criminal Networks in Action," *Crime, Law and Social Change* 34, no. 2 (September 1, 2000), 111–57.

50. For a sampling of the literature, see Jane Mayer, *Dark Money: The Hidden History of the Billionaires behind the Rise of the Radical Right* (New York: Doubleday, 2016); Timothy Kuhner, *Capitalism v. Democracy: Money in Politics and the Free Market Constitution* (Stanford: Stanford University Press, 2014); Richard Hasen, *Plutocrats United: Campaign Money, the Supreme Court, and the Distortion of American Elections* (New Haven: Yale University Press, 2016); Heath Brown, *Pay-to-Play Politics: How Money Defines the American Democracy* (Santa Barbara: ABC-CLIO, 2016); Wendell Potter and Nick Penniman, *Nation on the Take: How Big Money Corrupts Our Democracy and What We Can Do about It* (New York: Bloomsbury, 2016); Thomas Edsall, "After Citizens United, a Vicious Cycle of Corruption," *New York Times*, December 6, 2018; Eli Clifton, "U.S. News Media Can't Talk about Adelson Foreign Policy," June 19, 2018, at https://lobelog.com/u-s-news-media-cant-talk -about-adelson-foreign-policy/.

51. Eleanor Clift, "Campaign Slush Funds Send Pols to Disney, Beach, Golfing," September 10, 2018, https://www.thedailybeast.com/campaign-slush-funds-send -pols-to-disney-beach-golfing; Peter J. Henning, "It's Getting Harder to Prosecute Politicians for Corruption," February 16, 2018, http://theconversation.com/its -getting-harder-to-prosecute-politicians-for-corruption-91609.

52. Maya Miller, "How the IRS Gave Up Fighting Political Dark Money Groups," April 18, 2019, https://www.propublica.org/article/irs-political-dark-money-groups -501c4-tax-regulation.

53. "U.S. Treasury Moves to Protect Identities of 'Dark Money' Political Donors," Reuters, July 16, 2018.

54. Anna Massoglia and Karl Evers-Hillstrom, "Lawmakers Make Bipartisan Push to Crack Down on Money Laundering and 'Dark Money' Shell Companies," June 19, 2019, https://www.opensecrets.org/news/2019/06/bipartisan-push-to-crack-down -on-money-laundering-and-dark-money-shell-companies/.

55. Nicholas Confessore, Sarah Cohen, and Karen Yourish, "Just 158 Families Have Provided Nearly Half of the Early Money for Efforts to Capture the White House," *New York Times*, October 11, 2015.

56. Ed Pilkington and John Swaine, "The Seven Republican Super-Donors Who Keep Money in Tax Havens," *The Guardian*, November 7, 2017.

57. Anna Massoglia and Geoff West, "Foreign Interests Have Spent Over $530 Million Influencing US Policy, Public Opinion Since 2017," August 14, 2018, https://truthout.org/articles/foreign-interests-have-spent-over-530-million-influencing-us-policy-since-2017/. For a brief commentary by a political scientist, see Stephen M. Walt, "America Is Wide Open for Foreign Influence," April 8, 2019, https://foreign policy.com/2019/04/08/america-is-wide-open-for-foreign-influence/. President Trump's connections to foreign lobbyists are too numerous to list, but his personal attorney, Rudolph Giuliani, ran a firm that represents a variety of foreign clients, including ones in Ukraine and the Iranian anti-regime group MEK. "Giuliani works for foreign clients while serving as Trump's attorney," *Washington Post*, July 10, 2018.

58. "Trump Outpaces Obama, Bush in Naming Ex-Lobbyists to Cabinet," September 17, 2019, https://apnews.com/08dce0f5f9c24a6aa355cd0aab3747d9.

59. Martin Gilens and Benjamin I. Page, "Testing Theories of American Politics: Elites, Interest Groups, and Average Citizens," *Perspectives on Politics*, v 12, no. 3 (September 2014), 564–81.

60. "They Don't Have to Be Crooks, Just Human," https://www.opensecrets.org/resources/dollarocracy/10.php.

61. Peter Nicholas, "Donald Trump Walks Back His Past Praise of Hillary Clinton," *Wall Street Journal*, July 29, 2015.

62. Pew Research Center, "Public Trust in Government: 1958–2019," https://www.people-press.org/2019/04/11/public-trust-in-government-1958-2019/.

63. Jim Clifton, "Explaining Trump: Widespread Government Corruption," January 6, 2016, https://news.gallup.com/opinion/chairman/188000/explaining-trump-widespread-government-corruption.aspx. See also David Cole, "How Corrupt Are Our Politics?" *New York Review of Books*, September 25, 2014.

64. Charles Homans, "Americans Think 'Corruption' Is Everywhere. Is That Why We Vote for It?" *New York Times*, July 10, 2018.

65. Mike Abramowitz, "The Struggle Comes Home: Attacks on Democracy in the United States," in Freedom House, *Freedom in the World 2019*, https://freedomhouse.org/sites/default/files/Feb2019_FH_FITW_2019_Report_ForWeb-compressed.pdf.

66. Freedom House press release, "Freedom in the World 2019, Featuring Special Release on United States," February 4, 2019, https://freedomhouse.org/article/new-report-freedom-world-2019-featuring-special-release-united-states.

Selected Bibliography

See https://rowman.com/ISBN/9781538142493/Dark-Quadrant-Organized-Crime-Big
-Business-and-the-Corruption-of-American-Democracy for complete bibliography.

Archives and Unpublished Documents

Association for Diplomatic Studies and Training

Oral History Interviews

Ambassador Joseph S. Farland, January 31, 2000
Henry Dearborn, April 24, 1991

CIA Reading Room, at https://www.cia.gov/library/readingroom/home/

Dwight Eisenhower Library

Papers

Robert Anderson
Jacqueline Cochran
Floyd Odlum
William Rogers

Federal Bureau of Investigation Files

Sen. Howard W. Cannon

Louis Chesler
Roy Cohn
Henry Crown
Morris Dalitz
Abraham Feinberg
Hank Greenspun
Henry Grunewald
Murray Humphreys
Sydney Korshak
Meyer Lansky
Charles Rebozo
John Rosselli
Anthony Salerno
G. David Schine
Benjamin "Bugsy" Siegel
Al Schwimmer
Frank Sinatra
George Sokolsky
Abner Zwillman

Harry S. Truman Library

Oral History Interviews

George E. Allen, May 15, 1969
Eben A. Ayers, April 19, 1967
John M. Cabot, July 18, 1973
Thomas D. Cabot, June 6, 1975
Harry Easley, August 24, 1967
Abraham Feinberg, August 23, 1973
Felix E. Larkin, September 18 and October 23, 1972
David H. Stowe, July 27, 1963

Papers

Dean Acheson
Edward H. Foley Jr.
Richard C. Patterson Jr.
President's Secretary's Files

Hoover Institution

Papers

Charles Cooke
Stanley Hornbeck
Gilbert Stuart

John F. Kennedy Library

JFK White House Telephone Records

Oral History Interviews

Harold Brown, May 14, 1964
John E. Byrne, September 16, 1969
McGeorge Bundy, March 1964
Ramsey Clark, July 7 and 20, 1970
Joseph Farland, July 24, 1969
William G. Hundley, December 9, 1970
Laura Bergquist Knebel, December 8, 1965
Fred Korth, January 27, 1966
Norbert Schlei, February 20–21, 1968
Walter Sheridan, June 12, 1970
George A. Smathers, March 31, 1964

Library of Congress

Papers

Thomas Corcoran

Los Angeles Police Department Intelligence Reports, 1955–1960

Lyndon Baines Johnson Library

Senator and Vice President Lyndon B. Johnson's Daily Diary

LBJ Recordings, November 1963–January 1969

Oral History Interviews

Raymond Buck, May 27, 1969
Jacqueline Cochran, April 7, 1974
Abe Fortas, August 14, 1969
Harry McPherson, December 5, 1968, and September 19, 1985
Lawrence F. O'Brien, October 30, 1985, and February 11, 1986
Cyrus R. Vance, November 3, 1969
Lew Wasserman, December 21, 1973
James E. Webb, April 29, 1969

National Archives and Records Administration

Records of the Department of State, Record Group 59
Records of the Drug Enforcement Administration, Record Group 170

Records of the Federal Bureau of Investigation, Record Group 65
Records of the Watergate Special Prosecution Force, Record Group 460
JFK Assassination Records Collection

Richard Nixon Library

H. R. Haldeman Diary

Nixon Papers

Laguna Nigel Series 320
President's Personal File
White House Central File
Wilderness Years
1950 Senate Campaign

Oral History Interviews

Charles W. Colson, September 21, 1988

White House Recordings

Princeton University

Papers

Whiting Willauer

Rutgers University, Center for Law and Justice

Papers

Alan A. Block

Teamster Central States, Southeast and Southwest Areas Pension Fund—Meeting Minutes

United States Senate, Historical Office

Oral History Interviews

Robert "Bobby" Baker, 2009
Sen. George Smathers, 1989

University of South Florida, Tampa Library

Oral History Interview

Manuel Garcia, October 12, 1982

Court Cases

Benjamin Cohen v. United States, 363 F.2d 321 (1966)

Calvin Kovens and Leon Cohen v. United States, 338 F.2d 611 (5th Cir. 1965)

Estate of Burton W. Kanter, De v. CIR, 11-1310 (7th Cir. 2011)

Hyman-Michaels Company v. Commissioner, United States Tax Court, 22 T.C.M. 1135 (1963)

In the Matter of the Petition of Marco Reginelli, No. 2186-P-9291, For Naturalization, Supreme Court of New Jersey, 20 N.J. 266 (1956)

John Schlick v. Penn-Dixie Cement Corporation et al., 507 F.2d 374 (2d Cir. 1974)

Joshua S. Kanter, Estate of Burton W. Kanter, and Estate of Naomi R. Kanter v. Commissioner of Internal Revenue, United States Court of Appeals, Seventh Circuit, 590 F.3d 410, 414 (7th Cir. 2009)

Securities and Exchange Commission v. Gerson Blatt, Barton S. Udell, and John Pullman, 583 F.2d 1325 (5th Cir. 1978)

State Bar of Arizona, Answering Brief, *In the Matter of a Member of the State Bar of Arizona, Richard G. Kleindienst, Respondent*, Arizona Supreme Court No. SB-60-2, 1981

State Bar of Arizona, *Brief in the Matter of a Member of the State Bar of Arizona, Richard Kleindeinst*, 79-1-S19, 1980.

Surowitz v. Hilton Hotels Corp., 383 U.S. 363 (1966)

Susan L. Rosenstiel v. Lewis S. Rosenstiel, No. 67 Civ. 1883, 368 F. Supp. 51 (1973)

United States v. Carrozzo, 37 F. Supp. 191 (N.D. Ill. 1941)

United States v. Dardi, 330 F.2d 316 (2d Cir. 1964)

United States v. Giordano, 416 U.S. 505 (1974)

United States v. Harold Roth and Herbert S. Sternberg, 333 F.2d 450 (2d Cir. 1964)

United States v. Ingemar Johansson, Roy Cohn and Thomas Bolan et al., 447 F.2d 702 (5th Cir. 1971).

United States v. James R. Hoffa, Benjamin Dranow, Zachary A. Strate, Jr., S. George Burris, Abe I. Weinblatt, Calvin Kovens, and Samuel Hyman, United States Court of Appeals, 367 F.2d 698 (7th Cir. 1966)

United States v. Salvatore Granello, A/K/A Sally Burns, and Hyman Levine, A/K/A George Levine, 365 F.2d 990 (1966)

United States, Appellee, v. Virgil D. Dardi, Robert B. Gravis, Charles Rosenthal and Charles Berman, 330 F.2d 316 (2d Cir. 1964)

Government Documents

California State Legislature, Assembly, Interim Committee on Judiciary, Subcommittee on Rackets. Organized Crime in California. Sacramento: Legislature of the State of California, 1959.

Central Intelligence Agency, *Official History of the Bay of Pigs Operation.* Volume III: *Evolution of CIA's Anti-Castro Policies, 1959–January 1961.* 1979, released 1998.

Central Intelligence Agency, Report by J. S. Earman, CIA Inspector General, "Report on Plots to Assassinate Fidel Castro," May 23, 1967.

Central Intelligence Agency, Report by Nicholas Cullather, "Operation PB Success: The United States and Guatemala, 1952–1954." Washington, DC, 1994.

Federal Trade Commission, *Annual Report of the Federal Trade Commission, 1971.* Washington, DC: US Government Printing Office, 1971.

President's Commission on Organized Crime, *The Impact: Organized Crime Today.* Washington, DC: US Government Printing Office, 1986.

Public Papers of the Presidents of the United States, Harry S. Truman, 1945–1953. Washington, DC: US Government Printing Office, 1961–1966.

State of New Jersey, Department of Law and Public Safety, Division of Gaming Enforcement, *Report to the Casino Control Commission with Regard to the Application of Del. E. Webb Corporation of New Jersey and Del E. Webb Corporation for a Casino License.* Trenton, 1981.

State of New Jersey, Department of Law and Public Safety, Division of Gaming Enforcement, *Report to the Casino Control Commission with Reference to the Casino License Application of Resorts International Hotel, Inc.* Trenton, 1978.

State of New York, Joint Legislative Committee on Crime, Its Causes, Control, and Effect on Society, Executive Session Hearings with Susan Rosenstiel, February 9, 1970.

US Congress, House of Representatives, Committee on Appropriations, *Treasury Department Appropriation Bill for 1946, Hearings.* 79th Cong., 1st sess. Washington, DC: US Government Printing Office, 1945.

US Congress, House of Representatives, Committee on Armed Services, Special Subcommittee on Intelligence, *Inquiry into the Alleged Involvement of the Central Intelligence Agency in the Watergate and Ellsberg Matters, Hearings.* 94th Cong., 1st sess. Washington, DC: US Government Printing Office, 1975.

US Congress, House of Representatives, Committee on Education and Labor, Special Subcommittee, *Jurisdictional Disputes in the Motion-Picture Industry, Hearings.* 80th Cong., 1st sess. Washington, DC: US Government Printing Office, 1948.

US Congress, House of Representatives, Committee on Expenditures in the Executive Departments, Subcommittee, *Investigation as to the Manner in Which the United States Board of Parole Is Operating and as to Whether There Is a Necessity for a Change in Either the Procedure or Basic Law, Hearings.* 80th Cong., 2nd sess. Washington, DC: US Government Printing Office, 1948.

US Congress, House of Representatives, Committee on Government *Operations, Oversight Hearings into the Operations of the IRS, Hearings.* 94th Cong., 1st sess. Washington, DC: US Government Printing Office, 1976.

US Congress, House of Representatives, Committee on Interstate and Foreign Commerce, Subcommittee, *Investigation of Regulatory Commissions and Agencies, Hearings.* 85th Cong., 2nd sess. Washington, DC: US Government Printing Office, 1958.

US Congress, House of Representatives, Committee on the Judiciary, *Nomination of Gerald R. Ford to be Vice President of the United States, Hearings.* 93rd Cong., 1st sess. Washington, DC: US Government Printing Office, 1973.

US Congress, House of Representatives, Committee on the Judiciary, Special Subcommittee on H. Res. 920, *Associate Justice William O. Douglas, Report.* 91st Cong., 2nd sess. Washington, DC: US Government Printing Office, 1970.

US Congress, House of Representatives, Committee on the Judiciary, *Statement of Information, Hearings.* 93rd Cong., 2nd sess. Washington, DC: US Government Printing Office, 1974.

US Congress, House of Representatives, Committee on the Judiciary, Subcommittee on Antitrust, *Investigation of Conglomerate Corporations, Hearings.* 91st Cong., 2nd sess. Washington, DC: US Government Printing Office, 1970.

US Congress, House of Representatives, Committee on the Judiciary, Subcommittee to Investigate the Department of Justice, *Investigation of the Department of Justice, Report.* 83rd Cong., 1st sess. Washington, DC: US Government Printing Office, 1953.

US Congress, House of Representatives, Committee on Ways and Means, Subcommittee, *Internal Revenue Investigation, Hearings.* 82nd Cong., 1st sess. Washington, DC: US Government Printing Office, 1951.

US Congress, House of Representatives, Select Committee on Assassinations, *Investigation of the Assassination of President John F. Kennedy, Hearings and Appendix.* 95th Cong., 2nd sess. Washington, DC: US Government Printing Office, 1979.

US Congress, House of Representatives, Select Committee on Small Business, Subcommittee No. 1 on Foundations, *Tax Exempt Foundations: Their Impact on Small Business, Hearings.* 88th Cong., 2nd sess. Washington, DC: US Government Printing Office, 1964.

US Congress, Senate, Committee on Armed Services, *Military Situation in the Far East, Hearings.* 82nd Cong., 1st sess. Washington, DC: US Government Printing Office, 1951.

US Congress, Senate, Committee on Banking and Currency, Subcommittee, *Study of Reconstruction Finance Corporation, Hearings.* 82nd Cong., 1st sess. Washington, DC: US Government Printing Office, 1951.

US Congress, Senate, Committee on Banking and Currency, *Study of Reconstruction Finance Corporation and Proposed Amendment of RFC Act, Report.* 82nd Cong., 1st sess. Washington, DC: US Government Printing Office, 1951.

US Congress, Senate, Committee on Expenditures in the Executive Departments, *Influence in Government Procurement, Hearings.* 82nd Cong., 1st sess. Washington, DC: US Government Printing Office, 1951.

US Congress, Senate, Committee on Foreign Relations, *Nondiplomatic Activities of Representatives of Foreign Governments, Hearings.* 87th Cong., 2nd sess. Washington, DC: US Government Printing Office, 1962.

US Congress, Senate, Committee on Governmental Affairs, Permanent Subcommittee on Investigations, Minority Staff, *Correspondent Banking: A Gateway for Money Laundering, Report.* 107th Cong., 1st sess. Washington, DC: US Government Printing Office, 2001.

US Congress, Senate, Committee on Government Operations, Permanent Subcommittee on Investigations, *Oversight of Labor Department's Investigation of Teamster Central States Pension Fund, Hearings.* Washington, DC: US Government Printing Office, 1981.

US Congress, Senate, Committee on Government Operations, Permanent Subcommittee on Investigations, *Organized Crime: Securities, Theft and Frauds, Hearings.* 2nd series, 93rd Cong., 1st sess. Washington, DC: US Government Printing Office, 1973.

US Congress, Senate, Committee on Government Operations, Permanent Subcommittee on Investigations, *Organized Crime and Illicit Traffic in Narcotics, Hearings.* 88th Cong., 2nd sess. Washington, DC: US Government Printing Office, 1964.

US Congress, Senate, Committee on Government Operations, Permanent Subcommittee on Investigations, *Organized Crime: Stolen Securities, Hearings.* 92nd Cong., 1st sess. Washington, DC: US Government Printing Office, 1971.

US Congress, Senate, Committee on Government Operations, Permanent Subcommittee on Investigations, *Textile Procurement in the Military Services, Hearings.* 84th Cong., 1st sess. Washington, DC: US Government Printing Office, 1955.

US Congress, Senate, Committee on Government Operations, Permanent Subcommittee on Investigations, *TFX Contract Investigation, Hearings.* 88th Cong., 1st sess. Washington, DC: US Government Printing Office, 1963–1964.

US Congress, Senate, Committee on Governmental Affairs, *Labor Union Insurance Activities of Joseph Hauser and His Associates, Report 96-426.* 96th Cong., 1st sess. Washington, DC: US Government Printing Office, 1979.

US Congress, Senate, Committee on Homeland Security and Governmental Affairs, Permanent Subcommittee on Investigations, Majority and Minority Staff, report, *Keeping Foreign Corruption Out of the United States: Four Case Histories.* 111th Cong., 2nd sess. Washington, DC: US Government Printing Office, 2010.

US Congress, Senate, Committee on Homeland Security and Governmental Affairs, Permanent Subcommittee on Investigations, Majority and Minority Staff, report, *U.S. Vulnerabilities to Money Laundering, Drugs, and Terrorist Financing: HSBC Case History.* 112th Cong., 2nd sess. Washington, DC: US Government Printing Office, 2012.

US Congress, Senate, Committee on Governmental Affairs, Permanent Subommittee on Investigations, *Labor Union Insurance, Hearings, Part 2.* 95th Cong., 1st sess. Washington, DC: US Government Printing Office, 1978.

US Congress, Senate, Committee on the Judiciary, *Kansas City Vote Fraud, Hearings.* 80th Cong., 1st sess. Washington, DC: US Government Printing Office, 1947.

US Congress, Senate, Committee on the Judiciary, *Organized Crime in America, Hearings.* 98th Cong., 1st sess. Washington, DC: US Government Printing Office, 1983.

US Congress, Senate, Committee on the Judiciary, Subcommittee on Antitrust and Monopoly, *Professional Boxing, Hearings.* 86th Cong., 2nd sess. Washington, DC: US Government Printing Office, 1961.

US Congress, Senate, Committee on the Judiciary, Subcommittee to Investigate the Administration of the Internal Security Act and Other Internal Security Laws, *Communist Threat to the United States Through the Caribbean, Hearings.* 86th Cong., 2nd sess. Washington, DC: US Government Printing Office, 1960.

US Congress, Senate, Committee on the Judiciary, Subcommittee to Investigate the Administration of the Internal Security Act and Other Internal Security Laws, *Institute of Pacific Relations, Hearings.* 82nd Cong., 1st sess. Washington, DC: US Government Printing Office, 1950.

US Congress, Senate, Committee on the Judiciary, Subcommittee to Investigate the Administration of the Internal Security Act and Other Internal Security Laws, *Internal Security Report for 1956.* 85th Cong., 1st sess. Washington, DC: US Government Printing Office, 1957.

US Congress, Senate, Committee on the Judiciary, Subcommittee to Investigate the Administration of the Internal Security Act and Other Internal Security Laws, *Morgenthau Diary (Germany).* 90th Cong., 1st sess. Washington, DC: US Government Printing Office, 1967.

US Congress, Senate, Committee on Rules and Administration, *Financial or Business Interests of Officers or Employees of the Senate, Hearings.* 88th Cong., 2nd sess. Washington, DC: US Government Printing Office, 1964.

US Congress, Senate, Committee on Rules and Administration, Subcommittee on Privileges and Elections, *Investigations of Senators Joseph R. McCarthy and William Benton Pursuant to S. Res. 187 and S. Res. 304, Report.* 82nd Cong., 2nd sess. Washington, DC: US Government Printing Office, 1953.

US Congress, Senate, Select Committee on Improper Activities in the Labor or Management Field, *Investigation of Improper Activities in the Labor or Management Field, Hearings.* 85th Cong., 2nd sess. Washington, DC: US Government Printing Office, 1958–59.

US Congress, Senate, Select Committee on Presidential Campaign Activities, *Final Report.* 93rd Cong., 2nd sess. Washington, DC: US Government Printing Office, 1974.

US Congress, Senate, Select Committee on Presidential Campaign Activities, *Presidential Campaign Activities of 1972, Watergate and Related Activities, The Hughes-Rebozo Investigation and Related Matters, Hearings.* Washington, DC: US Government Printing Office, 1973.

US Congress, Senate, Select Committee on Presidential Campaign Activities, *Executive Session Hearings.* 93rd Cong., 2nd sess. Washington, DC: US Government Printing Office, 1974.

US Congress, Senate, Select Committee to Study Governmental Operations with Respect to Intelligence Activities, *Alleged Assassination Plots Involving Foreign Leaders: An Interim Report of the Select Committee to Study Government Relations with Respect to Intelligence Activities; Interim Report.* 94th Cong., 1st sess. Washington, DC: US Government Printing Office, 1975.

US Congress, Senate, Special Committee to Investigate Organized Crime in Interstate Commerce, *Hearings before a Special Committee to Investigate Organized Crime in Interstate Commerce*. 81st Cong., 2nd sess. Washington, DC: US Government Printing Office, 1950–1951.

US Congress, Senate, Special Committee to Investigate Organized Crime in Interstate Commerce, *The Kefauver Committee Report on Organized Crime*. New York: Didier, 1951.

US Congress, Senate, Special Committee to Investigate Organized Crime in Interstate Commerce, *Second Interim Report Pursuant to S. Res. 202, Report no. 141*. 82nd Cong., 1st sess. Washington, DC: US Government Printing Office, 1951.

US Congress, Senate, Special Committee to Investigate the Munitions Industry, *Munitions Industry*. 74th Cong., 1st sess. Washington, DC: US Government Printing Office, 1935.

US Department of State, Office of the Historian, Bureau of Public Affairs, *Foreign Relations of the United States*, various volumes, 1947–1968.

Selected Books

Abell, Tyler, ed. *Drew Pearson Diaries 1949–1959*. London: Jonathan Cape, 1974.

Abels, Jules. *The Truman Scandals*. Chicago: Henry Regnery, 1956.

Adler, Tim. *Hollywood and the Mob: Movies, Mafia, Sex and Death*. London: Bloomsbury, 2007.

Alexander, Dan. *White House, Inc. How Donald Trump Turned the Presidency Into a Business*. New York: Portfolio/Penguin, 2020.

Allen, Robert S., and William V. Shannon. *Truman Merry-Go-Round*. New York: Vanguard Press, 1950.

Ambrose, Stephen. *Nixon: The Education of a Politician, 1913–1962*. New York: Simon & Schuster, 1987.

Ameringer, Charles. *Caribbean Legion: Patriots, Politicians, Soldiers of Fortune, 1946–1950*. University Park: Pennsylvania State University Press, 1996.

Anderson, Jack. *The Anderson Papers*. New York: Ballantine Books, 1974.

Anderson, Jack. *Washington Exposé*. Washington, DC: Public Affairs Press, 1967.

Anderson, Jack, and Ronald May. *McCarthy: The Man, the Senator, the Ism*. Boston: Beacon Press, 1952.

Anderson, Jack, with Daryl Gibson. *Peace, War, and Politics: An Eyewitness Account*. New York: Tom Doherty Associates, 1999.

Anderson, Jack, with James Boyd. *Confessions of a Muckraker: The Inside Story of Life in Washington during the Truman, Eisenhower, Kennedy and Johnson Years*. New York: Random House, 1979.

Atkins, G. Pope. *The Dominican Republic and the United States: From Imperialism to Transnationalism*. Athens: University of Georgia Press, 1998.

Bachrack, Stanley D. *The Committee of One Million: "China Lobby" Politics, 1953–1971*. New York: Columbia University Press, 1976.

Bailey, John J., and Roy Godson, eds. *Organized Crime and Democratic Governability: Mexico and the US-Mexican Borderlands.* Pittsburgh: University of Pittsburgh Press, 2000.

Baker, Bobby. *Wheeling and Dealing: Confessions of a Capitol Hill Operator.* New York: W. W. Norton, 1978.

Barlett, Donald L., and James B. Steele. *Empire: The Life, Legend, and Madness of Howard Hughes.* New York: W. W. Norton, 1979.

Barrett, Wayne. *Trump: The Deals and the Downfall.* New York: HarperCollins, 1992.

Bell, Daniel. *The End of Ideology.* Cambridge, MA: Harvard University Press, 1960.

Belton, Catherine. *Putin's People: How the KGB Took Back Russia and Then Took on the West.* New York: Farrar, Straus and Giroux, 2020.

Ben-Veniste, Richard. *The Emperor's New Clothes: Exposing the Truth from Watergate to 9/11.* New York: St. Martin's Press, 2009.

Bender, Marilyn, and Selig Altschul. *The Chosen Instrument: Pan Am, Juan Trippe, The Rise and Fall of an American Entrepreneur.* New York: Simon & Schuster, 1982.

Bernstein, Lee. *The Greatest Menace: Organized Crime in Cold War America.* Amherst: University of Massachusetts Press, 2002.

Blakey, G. Robert, and Richard Billings. *The Plot to Kill the President.* New York: Times Books, 1981.

Block, Alan. *East Side, West Side: Organizing Crime in New York, 1930–1950.* New Brunswick, NJ: Transaction Publishers, 1983.

Block, Alan A. *Masters of Paradise: Organized Crime and the Internal Revenue Service in the Bahamas.* New Brunswick, NJ: Transaction Publishers, 1991.

Block, Alan A., and Constance Weaver. *All Is Clouded by Desire: Global Banking, Money Laundering, and International Organized Crime.* Westport, CT: Praeger, 2004.

Block, Alan A., and William J. Chambliss. *Organizing Crime.* New York: Elsevier, 1981.

Bobelian, Michael. *Battle for the Marble Palace: Abe Fortas, Earl Warren, Lyndon Johnson, Richard Nixon and the Forging of the Modern Supreme Court.* Tucson: Schaffner Press, 2019.

Bolles, Blair. *How to Get Rich in Washington.* New York: W. W. Norton, 1952.

Bradlee, Ben. *A Good Life: Newspapering and Other Adventures.* New York: Simon & Schuster, 1995.

Bremner, Robert H., and Gary Reichard, eds. *Reshaping America: Society and Institutions, 1945–1960.* Columbus: Ohio State University Press, 1982.

Brill, Steve. *The Teamsters.* New York: Simon & Schuster, 1978.

Brown, Heath. *Pay-to-Play Politics: How Money Defines the American Democracy.* Santa Barbara: ABC-CLIO, 2016.

Browning, Frank, and John Gerassi. *The American Way of Crime: From Salem to Watergate.* New York: Putnam, 1980.

Bruck, Connie. *When Hollywood Had a King: The Reign of Lew Wasserman, Who Leveraged Talent into Power and Influence.* New York: Random House, 2003.

Bullough, Oliver. *Moneyland: The Inside Story of the Crooks and Kleptocrats Who Rule the World.* New York: St. Martin's, 2019.

Buntin, John. L.A. *Noir: The Struggle for the Soul of America's Most Seductive City.* New York: Harmony Books, 2009.

Burbank, Jeff. *Las Vegas Babylon: The True Tales of Glitter, Glamour, and Greed.* London: Robson Books, 2005.

Burrough, Bryan. *The Big Rich: The Rise and Fall of the Greatest Texas Fortunes.* New York: Penguin, 2009.

Caro, Robert. *Master of the Senate.* New York: Knopf, 2002.

Caro, Robert. *Means of Ascent.* New York: Knopf, 1990.

Caro, Robert. *The Passage of Power.* New York: Knopf, 2012.

Caro, Robert. *The Path to Power.* New York: Knopf, 1982.

Carr, Robert K. *The House Committee on Un-American Activities, 1945–1950.* Ithaca: Cornell University Press, 1952.

Carrozza, Anthony R. *William D. Pawley: The Extraordinary Life of the Adventurer, Entrepreneur, and Diplomat Who Co-Founded the Flying Tigers.* Washington, DC: Potomac Books, 2012.

Carter, Carolle J. *Mission to Yenan: American Liaison with the Chinese Communists, 1944–1947.* Lexington: University of Kentucky Press, 1997.

Cassini, Igor, with Jeanne Molli. *I'd Do It All Over Again.* New York: G. P. Putnam's Sons, 1977.

Chafe, William H., ed. *The Achievement of American Liberalism: The New Deal and Its Legacies.* New York: Columbia University Press, 2003.

Chambliss, William. *On the Take: From Petty Crooks to Presidents.* 2nd ed. Bloomington: Indiana University Press, 1988.

Charns, Alexander. *Cloak and Gavel: FBI Wiretaps, Bugs, Informers, and the Supreme Court.* Chicago: University of Illinois Press, 1992.

Chester, Eric Thomas. *Covert Network: Progressives, the International Rescue Committee and the CIA.* New York: Routledge, 2015.

Chester, Eric Thomas. *Rag-Tags, Scum, Riff-Raff, and Commies: The U.S. Intervention in the Dominican Republic, 1965–1966.* New York: Monthly Review Press, 2001.

Chester, Lewis, Godfrey Hodgson, and Bruce Page. *An American Melodrama: The Presidential Campaign of 1968.* New York: Viking, 1969.

Chin, Ko-Lin. *Heijin: Organized Crime, Business, and Politics in Taiwan.* Armonk, NY: M. E. Sharpe, 2003.

Cirules, Enrique. *The Mafia in Havana: A Caribbean Mob Story.* Melbourne, Vic.: Ocean Press, 2004.

Clinard, Marshall. *Corporate Corruption.* New York: Praeger, 1990.

Cockayne, James. *Hidden Power: The Strategic Logic of Organized Crime.* New York: Oxford University Press, 2016.

Cohan, William D. *Money and Power: How Goldman Sachs Came to Rule the World.* New York: Random House, 2011.

Cohen, Andrew Wender. *The Racketeer's Progress: Chicago and the Struggle for the Modern American Economy, 1900–1940.* New York: Cambridge University Press, 2004.

Cohen, Avner. *Israel and the Bomb.* New York: Columbia University Press, 1998.

Cohen, Mickey. *Mickey Cohen: In My Own Words.* Englewood Cliffs, NJ: Prentice-Hall, 1975.

Cohen, Warren. *The Chinese Connection: Roger S. Greene, Thomas W. Lamont, George E. Sokolsky and American–East Asian Relations.* New York: Columbia University Press, 1978.

Cohn, Roy. *McCarthy.* New York: New American Library, 1968.

Colhoun, Jack. *Gangsterismo: The United States, Cuba and the Mafia, 1933 to 1966.* New York: OR Books, 2013.

Comey, James. *A Higher Loyalty: Truth, Lies, and Leadership.* New York: Flatiron Books, 2018.

Converse, Elliott V. III. *Rearming for the Cold War, 1945–1960.* Washington, DC: Historical Office, Office of the Secretary of Defense, 2012.

Cook, Fred. *The Warfare State.* New York: Macmillan, 1962.

Cost, Jay. *A Republic No More: Big Government and the Rise of American Political Corruption.* New York: Encounter Books, 2015.

Costanzo, Ezio. *The Mafia and the Allies: Sicily 1943 and the Return of the Mafia.* New York: Enigma Books, 2007.

Costello, William. *The Facts about Nixon.* New York: Viking, 1960.

Crassweller, Robert D. *Trujillo: The Life and Times of a Caribbean Dictator.* New York: Macmillan, 1966.

Crispell, Brian Lewis. *Testing the Limits: George Armistead Smathers and Cold War America.* Athens: University of Georgia Press, 1999.

Critchley, David. *The Origin of Organized Crime in America: The New York City Mafia, 1891–1931.* New York: Routledge, 2009.

Critchlow, Donald. *When Hollywood Was Right: How Movie Stars, Studio Moguls, and Big Business Remade American Politics.* New York: Cambridge University Press, 2013.

Croft, Roger. *Swindle! A Decade of Canadian Stock Frauds.* Toronto: Gage Publishing, 1975.

Cullather, Nicholas. *Operation PBSUCCESS: The United States and Guatemala, 1952–1954.* Central Intelligence Agency, Center for the Study of Intelligence, History Staff, 1994.

Cumings, Bruce. *The Origins of the Korean War: The Roaring of the Cataract, 1947–1950.* Princeton, NJ: Princeton University Press, 1990.

Curtis, Michael, and Susan Aurelia Gitelson, eds. *Israel in the Third World.* New Brunswick, NJ: Transaction Publishers, 1976.

Dallek, Robert. *Flawed Giant: Lyndon Johnson and His Times, 1961–1973.* New York: Oxford University Press, 1998.

Dallek, Robert. *Lone Star Rising: Lyndon Johnson and His Times, 1908–1960.* New York: Oxford University Press, 1991.

Davenport, Elaine, and Paul Eddy, with Mark Hurwitz. *The Hughes Papers.* London: Sphere Books, 1977.

Davis, John H. *Mafia Kingfish: Carlos Marcello and the Assassination of John F. Kennedy.* New York: McGraw-Hill, 1989.

Deakin, James. *The Lobbyists.* Washington, DC: Public Affairs Press, 1966.

Deitche, Scott M. *Cigar City Mafia: The Complete History of the Tampa Underworld.* Fort Lee, NJ: Barricade Books, 2004.

Deitche, Scott M. *The Silent Don: The Criminal Underworld of Santo Trafficante, Jr.* Fort Lee, NJ: Barricade Books, 2009.

Demaris, Ovid. *Captive City: Chicago in Chains.* New York: Lyle Stuart, 1969.

Demaris, Ovid. *The Director: An Oral Biography of J. Edgar Hoover.* New York: Harper's Magazine Press, 1975.

Demaris, Ovid. *Dirty Business: The Corporate-Political-Money-Power Game.* New York: Harper's Magazine Press, 1974.

Demaris, Ovid. *The Last Mafioso.* New York: Times Books, 1981.

Demaris, Ovid. *Poso del Mundo.* Boston: Little Brown, 1970.

Denton, Sally, and Roger Morris. *The Money and the Power: The Making of Las Vegas and Its Hold on America.* New York: Alfred A. Knopf, 2001.

Derogy, Jacques. *Israel Connection: La Mafia en Israel.* Paris: Plon, 1980.

Diederich, Bernard. *Trujillo: The Death of a Dictator.* Princeton, NJ: Markus Wiener, 2000.

Donovan, Robert J. *Conflict and Crisis: The Presidency of Harry S. Truman, 1945–1948.* Columbia: University of Missouri Press, 1977.

Dorman, Michael. *Pay-Off: The Role of Organized Crime in American Politics.* New York: Berkley Medallion, 1973.

Dorman, Michael. *Vesco: The Infernal Money Making Machine.* New York: Berkley Publishing, 1975.

Dunar, Andrew J. *The Truman Scandals and the Politics of Morality.* Columbia: University of Missouri Press, 1984.

Edwards, Jerome. *Pat McCarran, Political Boss of Nevada.* Reno: University of Nevada Press, 1982.

Eisenberg, Dennis, Uri Dan, and Eli Landau. *Meyer Lansky: Mogul of the Mob.* New York: Paddington Press, 1979.

Emery, Fred. *Watergate.* New York: Touchstone, 1994.

English, T. J. *Havana Nocturne: How the Mob Owned Cuba . . . and Then Lost It to the Revolution.* New York: William Morrow, 2008.

Escalante, Fabian. *The Secret War: CIA Covert Operations Against Cuba 1959–62.* Melbourne: Ocean Press, 1995.

Evans, Les, and Allen Myers. *Watergate and the Myth of American Democracy.* New York: Pathfinder Press, 1974.

Evans, Peter. *Ari: The Life and Times of Aristotle Socrates Onassis.* New York: Summit Books, 1986.

Evans, Rowland, and Robert Novak. *Lyndon B. Johnson: The Exercise of Power.* New York: New American Library, 1966.

Faith, Nicholas. *Safety in Numbers: The Mysterious World of Swiss Banking.* New York: Viking, 1982.

Farrell, John A. *Richard Nixon: The Life.* New York: Doubleday, 2017.

Farrell, Ronald, and Carole Case. *The Black Book and the Mob: The Untold Story of the Control of Nevada's Casinos.* Madison: University of Wisconsin Press, 1995.

Feldstein, Mark. *Poisoning the Press: Richard Nixon, Jack Anderson, and the Rise of Washington's Scandal Culture.* New York: Farrar, Straus and Giroux, 2010.

Ferrell, Robert H. *Choosing Truman: The Democratic Convention of 1944.* Columbia: University of Missouri Press, 1994.

Ferrell, Robert H. *Truman and Pendergast.* Columbia: University of Missouri Press, 1999.

Fineman, Daniel. *A Special Relationship: The United States and Military Government in Thailand, 1947–1958.* Honolulu: University of Hawaii Press, 1997.

Fitch, Robert. *Solidarity for Sale: How Corruption Destroyed the Labor Movement and Undermined America's Promise.* New York: PublicAffairs, 2006.

Fox, Stephen. *Blood and Power: Organized Crime in Twentieth-Century America.* New York: William Morrow, 1989.

Franklin, Roger. *The Defender: The Story of General Dynamics.* New York: Harper and Row, 1986.

Fried, Albert. *The Rise and Fall of the Jewish Gangster in America.* New York: Holt, Rinehart and Winston, 1980.

Friedman, Allen, and Ted Schwarz. *Power and Greed: Inside the Teamsters Empire of Corruption.* New York: Franklin Watts, 1989.

Friedman, Robert I. *Red Mafiya: How the Russian Mob Has Invaded America.* New York: Little Brown, 2000.

Frier, David A. *Conflict of Interest in the Eisenhower Administration.* Baltimore: Pelican Books, 1970.

Gabler, Neal. *An Empire of Their Own: How the Jews Invented Hollywood.* New York: Crown, 1988.

Gellman, Irwin F. *The Contender: Richard Nixon, the Congress Years, 1946–1952.* New York: The Free Press, 1999.

Genovese, Michael, and Victoria A. Farrar-Myers, eds. *Corruption and American Politics.* Amherst, NY: Cambria Press, 2010.

Gentry, Curt. *J. Edgar Hoover: The Man and the Secrets.* New York: W. W. Norton, 1991.

Gingeras, Ryan. *Heroin, Organized Crime, and the Making of Modern Turkey.* New York: Oxford University Press, 2014.

Glatt, John. *The Prince of Paradise: The True Story of a Hotel Heir, His Seductive Wife, and a Ruthless Murder.* New York: St. Martin's Press, 2013.

Gleijeses, Piero. *Shattered Hope: The Guatemalan Revolution and the United States, 1944–1954.* Princeton, NJ: Princeton University Press, 1991.

Glennon, Michael J. *National Security and Double Government.* New York: Oxford University Press, 2015.

Glenny, Misha. *McMafia: A Journey through the Global Criminal Underworld.* New York: Random House, 2008.

Goldfarb, Ronald. *Perfect Villains, Imperfect Heroes: Robert F. Kennedy's War against Organized Crime.* New York: Random House, 1995.

Goldsmith, Jack. *In Hoffa's Shadow: A Stepfather, a Disappearance in Detroit, and My Search for the Truth.* New York: Farrar, Straus and Giroux, 2019.

Goldston, Robert. *The American Nightmare.* New York: Bobbs-Merrill, 1973.

Goulden, Joseph. *The Best Years, 1945–1950.* New York: Athenium, 1976.

Gray, L. Patrick. *In Nixon's Web: A Year in the Crosshairs of Watergate.* New York: Times Books, 2008.

Greene, Felix. *A Curtain of Ignorance: How the American Public Has Been Misinformed about China.* Garden City, NY: Doubleday, 1964.

Griffin, Joe. *Mob Nemesis: How the FBI Crippled Organized Crime.* New York: Prometheus Books, 2002.

Griffith, Robert. *The Politics of Fear: Joseph R. McCarthy and the Senate.* Amherst: University of Massachusetts Press, 1970.

Gross, Michael. *Unreal Estate: Money, Ambition, and the Lust for Land in Los Angeles.* New York: Broadway Books, 2011.

Halberstam, David. *The Best and the Brightest.* New York: Modern Library, 2001.

Haldeman, H. R., with Joseph DiMona. *The Ends of Power.* New York: Times Books, 1978.

Hall, Michael R. *Sugar and Power in the Dominican Republic: Eisenhower, Kennedy and the Trujillos.* Westport, CT: Greenwood Press, 2000.

Hamby, Alonzo L. *Man of the People: A Life of Harry S. Truman.* New York: Oxford University Press, 1995.

Hamby, Alonzo L. *The Imperial Years: The U.S. Since 1939.* New York: Weybright and Talley, 1976.

Hammer, Richard. *The Last Testament of Lucky Luciano: The Mafia Story in His Own Words.* Boston: Little Brown, 1975.

Hancock, Larry. *Someone Would Have Talked.* Southlake, TX: JFK Lancer Productions, 2006.

Hanna, David. *Virginia Hill: Queen of the Underworld.* New York: Belmont Tower Books, 1975.

Hartmann, Rudolph, and Robert H. Ferrell. *The Kansas City Investigation: Pendergast's Downfall, 1938–1939.* Columbia: University of Missouri Press, 1999.

Hasen, Richard. *Plutocrats United: Campaign Money, the Supreme Court, and the Distortion of American Elections.* New Haven: Yale University Press, 2016.

Hayde, Frank R. *The Mafia and the Machine: The Story of the Kansas City Mob.* Fort Lee, NJ: Barricade Books, 2007.

Heard, Alexander. *The Costs of Democracy.* Chapel Hill: University of North Carolina Press, 1960.

Hellerman, Michael. *Wall Street Swindler.* Garden City, NY: Doubleday, 1977.

Hersh, Burton. *Bobby and J. Edgar: The Historic Face-off Between the Kennedys and J. Edgar Hoover Transformed America.* New York: Basic Books, 2008.

Hersh, Seymour. *The Dark Side of Camelot.* Boston: Little Brown, 1997.

Hersh, Seymour. *The Samson Option: Israel's Nuclear Arsenal and American Foreign Policy.* New York: Random House, 1991.

Hettena, Seth. *Trump/Russa: A Definitive History.* Brooklyn: Melville House, 2018.

Hicks, Albert C. *Blood in the Streets: The Life and Rule of Trujillo.* New York: Creative Age Press, 1946.

Hilton, Conrad. *Be My Guest.* New York: Simon & Schuster, 1957.

Hinckle, Warren, and William Turner. *The Fish Is Red: The Story of the Secret War against Castro.* New York: Harper & Row, 1981.

Hoffecker, Carol. *Honest John Williams: U.S. Senator from Delaware.* Newark: University of Delaware Press, 2000.

Hoover, J. Edgar. *Masters of Deceit: The Story of Communism in America and How to Fight It.* New York: Henry Holt and Co., 1958.

Horne, Gerald. *Class Struggle in Hollywood, 1930–1950: Moguls, Mobsters, Stars, Reds, and Trade Unionists.* Austin: University of Texas Press, 2001.

Horowitz, Irving Louis et al., eds. *Latin American Radicalism: A Documentary Report on Left and Nationalist Movements.* New York: Random House, 1969.

Hougan, Jim. *Secret Agenda: Watergate, Deep Throat, and the CIA.* New York: Random House, 1984.

Hougan, Jim. *Spooks: The Haunting of America—The Private Use of Secret Agents.* New York: William Morrow, 1978.

Howe, Russell Warren, and Sarah Hays Trott. *The Power Peddlers: A Revealing Account of Foreign Lobbying in Washington.* Garden City, NY: Doubleday, 1977.

Hughes, Ken. *Chasing Shadows: The Nixon Tapes, the Chennault Affair, and the Origins of Watergate.* Charlottesville: University of Virginia Press, 2014.

Hughes, Maureen. *The Countess and the Mob.* Bloomington, IN: iUniverse, 2010.

Hunt, E. Howard. *Undercover.* London: W. H. Allen, 1974.

Immerman, Richard H. *The CIA in Guatemala: The Foreign Policy of Intervention.* Austin: University of Texas Press, 1982.

Jacobs, James B. *Mobsters, Unions, and Feds: The Mafia and the American Labor Movement.* New York: New York University Press, 2006.

James, Ralph, and Estelle James. *Hoffa and the Teamsters: A Study of Union Power.* Princeton, NJ: D. Van Nostrand Co., 1965.

Janeway, Michael. *The Fall of the House of Roosevelt: Brokers of Ideas and Power from FDR to LBJ.* New York: Columbia University Press, 2004.

Johnson, Robert David. *All the Way with LBJ: The 1964 Presidential Election.* New York: Cambridge University Press, 2009.

Kaiser, David E. *The Road to Dallas: The Assassination of John F. Kennedy.* Cambridge: Harvard University Press, 2008.

Kalman, Laura. *Abe Fortas: A Biography.* New Haven, CT: Yale University Press, 1990.

Kaplan, David E., and Alec Dubro. *Yakuza: Japan's Criminal Underworld.* Berkeley: University of California Press, 2012.

Kashatus, William. *Dapper Dan Flood: The Controversial Life of a Congressional Power Broker.* University Park: Pennsylvania State University Press, 2010.

Katz, Leonard. *Uncle Frank.* New York: Pocket Books, 1974.

Kaufman, Edy et al. *Israel–Latin American Relations.* New Brunswick, NJ: Transaction Books, 1979.

Keeley, Joseph. *The China Lobby Man.* New Rochelle, NY: Arlington House, 1969.

Kennedy, Robert. *The Enemy Within: The McClellan Committee's Crusade against Jimmy Hoffa and Corrupt Labor Unions.* New York: Harper & Brothers, 1960.

Kinch. Sam Jr., and Ben Proctor. *Texas under a Cloud: Story of the Texas Stock Fraud Scandal.* New York: Jenkins Publishing, 1972.

Kobler, John. *Capone: The Life and World of Al Capone.* New York: G. P. Putnam's Sons, 1971.

Koen, Ross. *The China Lobby in American Politics.* New York: Harper & Row, 1974.

Kraus, Joe. *The Kosher Capones: A History of Chicago's Jewish Gangsters.* Ithaca: Cornell University Press, 2019.

Kriplen, Nancy. *The Eccentric Billionaire: John D. MacArthur—Empire Builder, Reluctant Philanthropist, Relentless Adversary.* New York: AMACOM, 2008.

Kuhner, Timothy. *Capitalism v. Democracy: Money in Politics and the Free Market Constitution.* Stanford: Stanford University Press, 2014.

Kutler, Stanley. *Abuse of Power: The New Nixon Tapes.* New York: The Free Press, 1997.

Kutler, Stanley. *The Wars of Watergate: The Last Crisis of Richard Nixon.* New York: W. W. Norton, 1992.

Kwitny, Jonathan. *The Fountain Pen Conspiracy.* New York: Alfred A. Knopf, 1973.

Kwitny, Jonathan. *Vicious Circles: The Mafia in the Marketplace.* New York: W. W. Norton, 1979.

Lacey, Michael J., ed. *The Truman Presidency.* New York: Cambridge University Press, 1989.

Lacey, Robert. *Little Man: Meyer Lansky and the Gangster Life.* New York: Little Brown, 1991.

Lait, Jack, and Lee Mortimer. *U.S.A. Confidential.* New York: Crown, 1952.

Lait, Jack, and Lee Mortimer. *Washington Confidential.* New York: Crown, 1951.

Lang, Arne K. *Sports Betting and Bookmaking: An American History.* Lanham, MD: Rowman & Littlefield, 2016.

Langum, David. *Crossing over the Line: Legislating Morality and the Mann Act.* Chicago: University of Chicago Press, 1994.

Latell, Brian. *Castro's Secrets: The CIA and Cuba's Intelligence Machine.* New York: St. Martin's Press, 2012.

Leamer, Laurence. *The Kennedy Men, 1901–1963.* New York: William Morrow, 2001.

Leary, William. *Perilous Missions: Civil Air Transport, the Chinese Civil War, and CIA Covert Operations in East Asia, 1946–1955.* Tuscaloosa: University of Alabama Press, 1984.

Lee, R. Alton. *Eisenhower and Landrum-Griffin: A Study in Labor-Management Politics.* Lexington: University Press of Kentucky, 1990.

Lernoux, Penny. *Cry of the People.* New York: Penguin Books, 1982.

Levine, Alan J. *"Bad Old Days": The Myth of the 1950s.* New Brunswick, NJ: Transaction Publishers, 2008.

Lewis, Brad. *Hollywood's Celebrity Gangster: The Incredible Life and Times of Mickey Cohen.* New York: Enigma Books, 2007.

Liddy, G. Gordon. *Will.* New York: St. Martin's Press, 1980.

Liebman, Marvin. *Coming Out Conservative.* San Francisco: Chronicle Books, 1992.

Liman, Arthur, and Peter Israel. *Lawyer: A Life of Counsel and Controversy.* New York: Public Affairs, 1998.

Lincoln, Evelyn. *Kennedy and Johnson.* New York: Holt, Rinehart and Winston, 1968.

Linnett, Richard. *In the Godfather Garden: The Long Life and Times of Richie "the Boot" Boiardo.* New Brunswick, NJ: Rutgers University Press, 2013.

Lintner, Bertil. *Burma in Revolt: Opium and Insurgency Since 1948.* Chiangmai: Silkworm Books, 1999.

Lofgren, Mike. *The Deep State: The Fall of the Constitution and the Rise of a Shadow Government.* New York: Viking, 2016.

Louis, J. C., and Harvey Z. Yazijian. *The Cola Wars: The Story of the Global Corporate Battle Between the Coca-Cola Company and PepsiCo, Inc.* New York: Everest House, 1980.

Lowenthal, Abraham. *The Dominican Intervention.* Cambridge: Harvard University Press, 1972.

Lukas, J. Anthony. *Nightmare: The Underside of the Nixon Years.* New York: Viking, 1976.

Lundberg, Ferdinand. *America's 60 Families.* New York: Halcyon House, 1938.

Lundberg, Ferdinand. *The Rich and the Super-Rich.* New York: Lyle Stuart, 1968.

Maheu, Robert, and Richard Hack. *Next to Hughes: Behind the Power and Tragic Downfall of Howard Hughes by His Closest Adviser.* New York: HarperCollins, 1992.

Mahon, Gigi. *The Company That Bought the Boardwalk.* New York: Random House, 1980.

Mahoney, Richard. *Sons & Brothers: The Days of Jack and Bobby Kennedy.* New York: Arcade Publishing, 1999.

Mappen, Marc. *Prohibition Gangsters: The Rise and Fall of a Bad Generation.* New Brunswick, NJ: Rutgers University Press, 2013.

Martin, John Bartlow. *Overtaken by Events: The Dominican Crisis from the Fall of Trujillo to the Civil War.* Garden City, NY: Doubleday, 1966.

Mason, Robert, and Iwan W. Morgan, eds. *The Liberal Consensus Reconsidered: American Politics and Society in the Postwar Era.* Gainesville: University of Florida Press, 2007.

Mayer, Jane. *Dark Money: The Hidden History of the Billionaires behind the Rise of the Radical Right.* New York: Doubleday, 2016.

Mazo, Earl, and Stephen Hess. *President Nixon.* New York: Harper & Row, 1968.

McCall, Brian. *The Power of the Texas Governor: Connally to Bush.* Austin: University of Texas Press, 2009.

McClintick, David. *Indecent Exposure: A True Story of Hollywood and Wall Street.* New York: William Morrow, 1982.

McCoy, Alfred W. *The Politics of Heroin: CIA Complicity in the Global Drug Trade.* Brooklyn: Lawrence Hill Books, 1991.

McDougal, Dennis. *The Last Mogul: Lew Wasserman, MCA, and the Hidden History of Hollywood.* New York: Crown, 1998.

McFarland, Keith D., and David L. Roll. *Louis Johnson and the Arming of America.* Bloomington: Indiana University Press, 2005.

McKean, David. *Tommy the Cork: Washington's Ultimate Insider from Roosevelt to Reagan.* South Royalton, VT: Steerforth Press, 2004.

McKeever, Stuart A. *The Galíndez Case.* Bloomington, IN: AuthorHouse, 2013.

Mellen, Joan. *Our Man in Haiti: George de Mohrenschildt and the CIA in the Nightmare Republic.* Waterville, OR: Trine Day, 2012.

Mellen, Joan. *The Great Game in Cuba: CIA and the Cuban Revolution.* New York: Skyhorse Publishing, 2016.

Messick, Hank. *The Beauties and the Beasts: The Mob in Show Business.* New York: David McKay, 1973.

Messick, Hank. *John Edgar Hoover: A Critical Examination of the Director and of the Continuing Alliance between Crime, Business, and Politics.* New York: David McKay, 1972.

Messick, Hank. *Lansky.* New York: Putnam, 1971.

Messick, Hank. *Of Grass and Snow: The Secret Criminal Elite.* Englewood Cliffs, NJ: Prentice-Hall, 1979.

Messick, Hank. *The Private Lives of Public Enemies.* New York: P. H. Wyden, 1973.

Messick, Hank. *Secret File.* New York: G. P. Putnam's Sons, 1969.

Messick, Hank. *The Silent Syndicate.* New York: Macmillan, 1967.

Messick, Hank. *Syndicate Abroad.* Toronto: The Macmillan Co., 1969.

Miller, Aragorn Storm. *Precarious Paths to Freedom: The United States, Venezuela, and the Latin American Cold War.* Albuquerque: University of New Mexico Press, 2016.

Miller, Richard Lawrence. *Truman: The Rise to Power.* New York: McGraw-Hill, 1986.

Milligan, Maurice M. *Missouri Waltz: The Inside Story of the Pendergast Machine by the Man Who Smashed It.* New York: Charles Scribner's Sons, 1948.

Millis, Walter. *Arms and the State.* New York: Twentieth Century Fund, 1958.

Mills, C. Wright. *The Power Elite.* New York: Oxford University Press, 1957.

Mitchell, Donald Craig. *Wampum: How Indian Tribes, the Mafia, and an Inattentive Congress Invented Indian Gaming and Created a $28 Billion Gambling Empire.* New York: Overlook Press, 2016.

Moldea, Dan. *Dark Victory: Ronald Reagan, MCA, and the Mob.* New York: Viking, 1986.

Moldea, Dan. *The Hoffa Wars: Teamsters, Rebels, Politicians and the Mob.* New York: Paddington Press, 1978.

Moldea, Dan. *Interference: How Organized Crime Influences Professional Football.* New York: William Morrow, 1989.

Mollenhoff, Clark. *Despoilers of Democracy.* Garden City, NY: Doubleday, 1965.

Mollenhoff, Clark. *Game Plan for Disaster.* New York: W. W. Norton, 1976.

Mollenhoff, Clark. *Strike Force: Organized Crime and the Government.* Englewood Cliffs, NJ: Prentice-Hall, 1972.

Mollenhoff, Clark. *Washington Cover-Up.* New York: Popular Library, 1963.

Morgan, Joseph. *The Vietnam Lobby: The American Friends of Vietnam, 1955–1975.* Chapel Hill: University of North Carolina Press, 1997.

Morris, Roger. *Richard Milhouse Nixon: The Rise of an American Politician.* New York: Henry Holt, 1990.

Moruzzi, Peter. *Havana before Castro: When Cuba Was a Tropical Playground.* Salt Lake City: Gibbs Smith, 2008.

Murray, George. *The Legacy of Al Capone.* New York: G. P. Putnam's Sons, 1975.

Myers, Gustavus. *The History of the Great American Fortunes.* Chicago: C. H. Kerr, 1910.

Naím, Moisés. *Illicit: How Smugglers, Traffickers, and Copycats Are Hijacking the Global Economy.* New York: Anchor Books, 2005.

Neff, James. *Mobbed Up: Jackie Presser's High-Wire Life in the Teamsters, the Mafia, and the F.B.I.* New York: Atlantic Monthly Press, 1989.

Neff, James. *Vendetta: Bobby Kennedy Versus Jimmy Hoffa.* New York: Little, Brown, 2015.

Nellor, Edward. *Washington's Wheeler Dealers: Broads, Booze & Bobby Baker!* New York: Bee-Line Books, 1967.

Newton, Michael. *Mr. Mob: The Life and Crimes of Moe Dalitz.* Jefferson, NC: McFarland, 2009.

Newton, Michael. *The Mafia at Apalachin, 1957.* Jefferson, NC: McFarland, 2012.

Nitzan, Jonathan, and Shimshon Bichler. *The Global Political Economy of Israel: From War Profits to Peace Dividends.* London: Pluto Press, 2002.

Nixon, Richard. *RN: The Memoirs of Richard Nixon.* New York: Grosset and Dunlap, 1978.

Nixon, Richard. *Six Crises.* New York: Doubleday, 1962.

O'Reilly, Kenneth. *Hoover and the Un-Americans: The FBI, HUAC, and the Red Menace.* Philadelphia: Temple University Press, 1983.

Ornes, Germán E. *Trujillo: Little Caesar of the Caribbean.* New York: Thomas Nelson & Sons, 1958.

Oshinsky, David. *A Conspiracy So Immense: The World of Joe McCarthy.* New York: Oxford University Press, 2005.

Ottenberg, Miriam. *The Federal Investigators.* Englewood Cliffs, NJ: Prentice-Hall, 1962.

Oudes, Bruce, ed. *From the President: Richard Nixon's Secret Files.* New York: Harper & Row, 1989.

Pack, Robert. *Edward Bennett Williams for the Defense.* New York: Harper & Row, 1983.

Patterson, James T. *Grand Expectations: The United States, 1945–1974.* New York: Oxford University Press, 1996.

Pearson, Drew, and Jack Anderson. *The Case against Congress.* New York: Simon & Schuster, 1968.

Pearson, Drew, and Jack Anderson. *U.S.A.—Second-Class Power?* New York: Simon & Schuster, 1958.

Pearson, Drew. *Washington Merry-Go-Round: The Drew Pearson Diaries, 1960–1969.* Washington, DC: Potomac Books, 2015.

Penslar, Derek. *Jews and the Military: A History.* Princeton, NJ: Princeton University Press, 2013.

Pernicone, Nunzio. *Carlo Tresca: Portrait of a Rebel.* Oakland, CA: AK Press, 2010.

Peterson, Virgil. *Barbarians in Our Midst.* Boston: Little, Brown, 1952.

Pilat, Oliver. *Drew Pearson: An Unauthorized Biography.* New York: Harper's Magazine Press, 1973.

Pizzo, Stephen, Mary Fricker, and Paul Muolo. *Inside Job: The Looting of America's Savings and Loans.* New York: McGraw-Hill, 1989.

Plummer, Brenda Gayle. *Haiti and the United States: The Psychological Moment.* Athens: University of Georgia Press, 1992.

Potter, Wendell, and Nick Penniman. *Nation on the Take: How Big Money Corrupts Our Democracy and What We Can Do about It.* New York: Bloomsbury, 2016.

Rabb, Selwyn. *Five Families: The Rise, Decline, and Resurgence of America's Most Powerful Mafia Empires.* New York: St. Martin's, 2016.

Rabe, Stephen G. *Eisenhower and Latin America: The Foreign Policy of Anti-Communism.* Chapel Hill: University of North Carolina Press, 1988.

Ragano, Frank, and Selwyn Raab. *Mob Lawyer.* New York: Charles Scribner's Sons, 1994.

Rappleye, Charles, and Ed Becker. *All American Mafioso: The John Rosselli Story.* New York: Doubleday, 1991.

Raymond, Jack. *Power at the Pentagon.* New York: Harper & Row, 1964.

Reeves, Richard. *President Kennedy: Profile of Power.* New York: Simon & Schuster, 1993.

Reichard, Gary W. *Politics as Usual: The Age of Truman and Eisenhower.* Arlington Heights, IL: Harlan Davidson, 2004.

Reid, Ed, and Ovid Demaris. *The Green Felt Jungle.* New York: Trident Press, 1963.

Reid, Ed. *Mickey Cohen: Mobster.* New York: Pinnacle Books, 1973.

Reid, Ed. *The Grim Reapers: The Anatomy of Organized Crime in America.* Chicago: Henry Regnery, 1969.

Reppetto, Thomas. *American Mafia: A History of Its Rise to Power.* New York: Henry Holt, 2004.

Reppetto, Thomas. *Bringing Down the Mob: The War against the American Mafia.* New York: Henry Holt, 2006.

Reynolds, Robert Grey Jr. *Tampa, Florida: Italian and Cuban Mafia Gambling and Political Corruption.* Los Gatos, CA: Smashwords, 2015.

Robinson, Jeffrey. *The Laundrymen: Inside Money Laundering.* New York: Arcade Publishing, 1996.

Roemer, William F. Jr. *Accardo: The Genuine Godfather.* New York: Donald I. Fine, 1995.

Roemer, William F. Jr. *Man against the Mob.* New York: Donald I. Fine, 1989.

Rojek, Chris. *Frank Sinatra.* Malden, MA: Polity Press, 2004.

Roorda, Eric. *The Dictator Next Door: The Good Neighbor Policy and the Trujillo Regime in the Dominican Republic, 1930–1945.* Durham, NC: Duke University Press, 1998.

Rosoff, Stephen, Henry Pontell, and Robert Tillman. *Profit without Honor: White-Collar Crime and the Looting of America.* Upper Saddle River, NJ: Prentice Hall, 1998.

Rovere, Richard. *Senator Joe McCarthy.* London: Methuen, 1960.

Rovner, Eduardo Sáenz. *The Cuban Connection: Drug Trafficking, Smuggling, and Gambling in Cuba from the 1920s to the Revolution.* Chapel Hill: University of North Carolina Press, 2008.

Russell, Dick. *The Man Who Knew Too Much.* New York: Carroll & Graf, 1992.

Russo, Gus. *Live by the Sword: The Secret War against Castro and the Death of JFK.* Baltimore: Bancroft Press, 1999.

Russo, Gus. *The Outfit: The Role of Chicago's Underworld in the Shaping of Modern America.* New York: Bloomsbury, 2001.

Russo, Gus. *Supermob: How Sidney Korshak and His Criminal Associates Became America's Hidden Power Brokers.* New York: Bloomsbury, 2006.

Salerno, Ralph, and John Tompkins. *The Crime Confederation: Cosa Nostra and Allied Operations in Organized Crime.* Garden City, NY: Doubleday, 1969.

Sanders, Jerry W. *Peddlers of Crisis: The Committee on the Present Danger.* Boston: South End Press, 1983.

Savage, Sean. *Truman and the Democratic Party.* Lexington: University of Kentucky Press, 1997.

Sbardellati, John. *J. Edgar Hoover Goes to the Movies: The FBI and the Origins of Hollywood's Cold War.* Ithaca: Cornell University Press, 2012.

Scheim, David E. *Contract on America: The Mafia Murders of John and Robert Kennedy.* Silver Spring, MD: Argyle Press, 1983.

Schlesinger, Arthur Jr. *A Thousand Days: John F. Kennedy in the White House.* Boston: Houghton Mifflin Co., 1965.

Schlesinger, Arthur Jr. *Robert Kennedy and His Times.* Boston: Houghton Mifflin Harcourt, 1978.

Schmidt, Regin. *Red Scare: FBI and the Origins of Anticommunism in the United States, 1919–1943.* Copenhagen: Museum Tusculanum Press, 2000.

Schoultz, Lars. *That Infernal Little Cuban Republic: The United States and the Cuban Revolution.* Chapel Hill: University of North Carolina Press, 2011.

Schrecker, Ellen. *Many Are the Crimes: McCarthyism in America.* Princeton, NJ: Princeton University Press, 1998.

Schreiber, G. R. *The Bobby Baker Affair.* Chicago: Henry Regnery Company, 1964.

Schuck, Peter H., and James Q. Wilson. *Understanding America: The Anatomy of an Exceptional Nation.* New York: Public Affairs, 2008.

Schulte-Bockholt, Alfredo. *The Politics of Organized Crime and the Organized Crime of Politics.* Lanham, MD: Lexington Books, 2006.

Schwartz, David G. *Suburban Xanadu: The Casino Resort on the Las Vegas Strip and Beyond.* London: Routledge, 2003.

Schwartz, Rosalie. *Pleasure Island: Tourism and Temptation in Cuba.* Lincoln: University of Nebraska Press, 1999.

Scott, Jeremy. *The Irresistible Mr. Wrong: The Six Mistresses of Misfortune.* London: Robson Press, 2012.

Scott, Peter Dale. *The American Deep State: Wall Street, Big Oil, and the Attack on U.S. Democracy.* London: Rowman & Littlefield, 2015.

Scott, Peter Dale. *The American War Machine.* Lanham, MD: Rowman & Littlefield, 2010.

Scott, Peter Dale. *Crime and Cover-up: The CIA, the Mafia, and the Dallas-Watergate Connection.* Santa Barbara: Open Archive Press, 1993.

Scott, Peter Dale. *Deep Politics and the Death of JFK.* Berkeley: University of California Press, 1963, and rev. ed., 1996.

Scott, Peter Dale. *Drugs, Oil, and War.* Lanham, MD: Rowman & Littlefield, 2003.

Scott, Peter Dale, and Jonathan Marshall. *Cocaine Politics: Drugs, Armies, and the CIA in Central America.* Berkeley: University of California Press, 1991.

Seagrave, Sterling. *The Marcos Dynasty.* New York: Harper and Row, 1988.

Server, Lee. *Handsome Johnny: The Life and Death of Johnny Rosselli; Gentleman Gangster, Hollywood Producer, CIA Assassin.* New York: St. Martin's Press, 2018.

Sheridan, Walter. *The Fall and Rise of Jimmy Hoffa.* New York: Saturday Review Press, 1972.

Sherrill, Robert. *The Accidental President.* New York: Grossman, 1967.

Sherrill, Robert. *Gothic Politics in the Deep South: Stars of the New Confederacy.* New York: Grossman, 1968.

Shesol, Jeff. *Mutual Contempt: Lyndon Johnson, Robert Kennedy, and the Feud that Defined a Decade.* New York: W. W. Norton, 1997.

Shetterly, Aran. *The Americano: Fighting with Castro for Cuba's Freedom.* Chapel Hill, NC: Algonquin Books, 2007.

Shields, Jerry. *The Invisible Billionaire: Daniel Ludwig.* Boston: Houghton Mifflin, 1986.

Siegel, Dina, and Hans Nelen, eds. *Organized Crime: Culture, Markets and Policies.* New York: Springer-Verlag, 2008.

Slater, Leonard. *The Pledge.* New York: Pocket Books, 1971.

Sloane, Arthur A. *Hoffa.* Cambridge, MA: MIT Press, 1991.

Smith, Joseph Burkholder. *Portrait of a Cold Warrior.* New York: G. P. Putnam's Sons, 1976.

Stein, Harold, ed. *American Civil-Military Decisions.* Tuscaloosa: University of Alabama Press, 1963.

Steinberg, Alfred. *The Man from Missouri.* New York: G. P. Putnam's Sons, 1962.

Steinberg, Alfred. *Sam Johnson's Boy: A Close-Up of the President from Texas.* New York: Macmillan, 1968.

Sterling, Claire. *Thieves' World: The Threat of the New Global Network of Organized Crime.* New York: Simon & Schuster, 1994.

Stone, I. F. *Hidden History of the Korean War.* New York: Monthly Review Press, 1969.

Stratton, W. K. *Floyd Patterson: The Fighting Life of Boxing's Invisible Champion.* New York: Houghton Mifflin Harcourt, 2012.

Summers, Anthony. *The Arrogance of Power: The Secret World of Richard Nixon.* New York: Viking, 2000.

Summers, Anthony. *Official and Confidential: The Secret Life of J. Edgar Hoover.* New York: G. P. Putnam's Sons, 1993.

Sundquist, James L. *Politics and Policy: The Eisenhower, Kennedy, and Johnson Years.* Washington, DC: Brookings Institution, 1968.

Sutherland, Edwin. *White Collar Crime.* New York: Holt, Rinehart & Winston, 1949.

Sward, Keith. *The Legend of Henry Ford.* New York: Russell & Russell, 1968.

Talbot, David. *Brothers: The Hidden History of the Kennedy Years.* New York: The Free Press, 2007.

Talbot, David. *The Devil's Chessboard: Allen Dulles, the CIA, and the Rise of America's Secret Government.* New York: Harper, 2015.

Teachout, Zephyr. *Corruption in America.* Cambridge, MA: Harvard University Press, 2014.

Tereba, Tere. *Mickey Cohen: The Life and Crimes of L.A.'s Notorious Mobster.* Toronto: ECW Press, 2012.

Theoharis, Athan, ed. *Beyond the Hiss Case: The FBI, Congress, and the Cold War.* Philadelphia: Temple University Press, 1982.

Theoharis, Athan. *Chasing Spies: How the FBI Failed in Counterintelligence but Promoted the Politics of McCarthyism in the Cold War Years.* Chicago: Ivan R. Dee, 2002.

Theoharis, Athan. *Seeds of Repression: Harry S. Truman and the Origins of McCarthyism.* Chicago: Quadrangle Books, 1971.

Theoharis, Athan, and John Stuart Cox. *The Boss: J. Edgar Hoover and the Great American Inquisition.* Philadelphia: Temple University Press, 1988.

Thomas, Dana. *Lords of the Land: The Triumphs & Scandals of America's Real Estate Barons from Early Times to the Present.* New York: G. P. Putnam's Sons, 1977.

Thomas, Evan. *The Man to See: Edward Bennett Williams.* New York: Simon & Schuster, 1991.

Thomas, Evan. *Robert Kennedy: His Life.* New York: Simon & Schuster, 2000.

Thompson, Douglas. *Mafialand: How the Mob Invaded Britain.* Edinburgh: Mainstream Publishing, 2014.

Tinnin, David B. *Just about Everybody vs. Howard Hughes: The Inside Story of the TWA–Howard Hughes Trial.* Garden City, NY: Doubleday, 1973.

Tosches, Nick. *The Devil and Sonny Liston.* Boston: Little Brown, 2000.

Tuchman, Barbara. *Stilwell and the American Experience in China, 1911–45.* New York: Macmillan, 1971.

Tully, Andrew. *Treasury Agent: The Inside Story.* New York: Simon & Schuster, 1958.

Turkus, Burton, and Sid Feder. *Murder, Inc.: The Inside Story of the Mob.* New York: Manor Books, 1951.

Turner, Wallace. *Gambler's Money: The New Force in American Life.* Boston: Houghton Mifflin, 1965.

Turner, William. *The Cuban Connection: Nixon, Castro, and the Mob.* Amherst, NY: Prometheus Books, 2013, Kindle Edition.

Turner, William. *Hoover's FBI.* New York: Dell, 1971.

Tyler, Gus. *Organized Crime in America.* Ann Arbor: University of Michigan Press, 1962.

Unger, Craig. *House of Trump, House of Putin: The Untold Story of Donald Trump and the Russian Mafia.* New York: Dutton, 2018.

Valentine, Douglas. *The Strength of the Wolf: The Secret History of America's War on Drugs.* New York: Verso, 2004.

Van Buren, Ernestine Orrick. *Clint: Clinton William Murchison, A Biography.* Austin: Eakin Press, 1986.

VanDeMark, Brian. *Into the Quagmire: Lyndon Johnson and the Escalation of the Vietnam War.* New York: Oxford University Press, 1995.

Von Hoffman, Nicholas. *Citizen Cohn: The Life and Times of Roy Cohn.* New York: Doubleday, 1988.

Von Tunzelmann, Alex. *Red Heat: Conspiracy, Murder, and the Cold War in the Caribbean.* New York: Henry Holt, 2011.

Vosjoli, P. L. Thyraud de. *Lamia.* Boston: Little, Brown, 1970.

Wakeman, Frederic E. *Spymaster: Dai Li and the Chinese Secret Service.* Berkeley: University of California Press, 2003.

Waldron, Lamar. *Watergate: The Hidden History.* Berkeley: Counterpoint, 2012.

Walker, William O. III. *Opium and Foreign Policy: The Anglo-American Search for Order in Asia, 1912–1954.* Chapel Hill: University of North Carolina Press, 1991.

Waller, Leslie. *The Swiss Bank Connection.* New York: New American Library, 1972.

Walsh, George. *Public Enemies: The Mayor, the Mob, and the Crime That Was.* New York: W. W. Norton, 1980.

Weiner, Tim. *Enemies: A History of the FBI.* New York: Random House, 2012.

Weissman, Steve, ed. *Big Brother and the Holding Company: The World behind Watergate.* Palo Alto: Ramparts Press, 1974.

Wendland, Michael F. *The Arizona Project.* Kansas City: Sheed, Andrew and McMeel, 1977.

White, Theodore H. *Making of the President, 1968.* London: Jonathan Cape, 1969.

Whiting, Robert. *Tokyo Underworld: The Fast Times and Hard Life of an American Gangster in Japan.* New York: Pantheon, 1999.

Wills, Gary. *Nixon Agonistes: The Crisis of the Self-Made Man.* Boston: Houghton Mifflin, 1970.

Wilson, Will R. Sr. *A Fool for a Client.* Austin: Eakin Press, 2000.

Winter-Berger, Robert. *The Washington Pay-Off: An Insider's View of Corruption.* Seacaucus, NJ: Lyle Stuart, 1972.

Wise, David. *The Politics of Lying: Government Deception, Secrecy, and Power.* New York: Random House, 1973.

Wise, T. A. *The Insiders.* Garden City, NY: Doubleday, 1962.

Witwer, David Scott. *Corruption and Reform in the Teamsters Union.* Urbana and Chicago: University of Illinois Press, 2003.

Witwer, David Scott. *Shadow of the Racketeer: Scandal in Organized Labor.* Urbana and Chicago: University of Illinois Press, 2009.

Wolfe, Jane. *The Murchisons: The Rise and Fall of a Texas Dynasty.* New York: St. Martin's Press, 1989.

Woodiwiss, Michael. *Organized Crime and American Power.* Toronto: University of Toronto Press, 2001.

Woods, Randall Bennett. *Fulbright: A Biography.* New York: Cambridge University Press, 1994.

Woodward, C. Vann, ed. *Responses of the Presidents to Charges of Misconduct.* New York: Dell, 1974.

Ybarra, Michael Y. *Washington Gone Crazy: Senator Pat McCarran and the Great American Communist Hunt.* Hanover, NH: Steerforth Press, 2004.

Yu, Maochun. *OSS in China: Prelude to Cold War.* Annapolis: Naval Institute Press, 1996.

Yu, Maochun. *The Dragon's War: Allied Operations and the Fate of China, 1937–1947.* Annapolis: Naval Institute Press, 2006.

Index

WAR AND PEACE LIBRARY
Series Editor: Mark Selden